The
Golden Age
Is In Us

VERSO
London · New York

The
Golden Age
Is In Us

JOURNEYS & ENCOUNTERS

1987–1994

Alexander Cockburn

VERSO

London · New York

Copyright © 1995 Alexander Cockburn
All rights reserved.

Verso
UK: 6 Meard Street, London W1V 3HR
USA: 180 Varick Street, New York, NY 10014

Verso is the imprint of New Left Books

ISBN: 0-86091-434-8

British Library Cataloguing-in-Publication Data
A catalogue record for this book is available from the British Library.

Library of Congress Cataloging in Publication Data
A catalog record for this book is available from the Library of Congress.

Jacket and book design by Deborah Thomas
Typeset in Bodoni by NorthStar, San Francisco, California
Manufactured in the USA by The Courier Companies

*Enthusiastic partisans of the idea of progress
are in danger of failing to recognize – because they
set so little store by them – the immense riches accumulated
by the human race on either side of the narrow furrow on which
they keep their eyes fixed; by underrating the achievements of the past,
they devalue all those which still remain to be accomplished. If men have
always been concerned with only one task – how to create a society fit to
live in – the forces which inspired our distant ancestors are also
present in us. Nothing is settled; everything can still be altered.
What was done, but turned out wrong, can be done again.
'The Golden Age, which blind superstition had
placed behind (or ahead of) us, is in us.'*

Claude Lévi-Strauss, Tristes Tropiques

Foreword

➤

The Golden Age was first, a time that cherished
Of its own will, justice and right; no law,
No punishment, was called for; fearfulness
Was quite unknown, and the bronze tablets held
No legal threatening ...

Ovid, Metamorphoses

GOLDEN AGE? *In* us? Everyone has their vision of the Golden Age. My friend
and neighbor, Joe Paff, thinks we're in the Golden Age of Cooking right now,
and that all the greatest cooks in world history are alive today. (I don't hold
with this, but that's another story.)

In antiquity, the Golden Age was fairly specific in outline, particularly in the
matter of death. There, as opposed to the successor ages of silver, bronze and
iron, death came as a pleasant sleep, followed by easy release into a spirit form
which continues to inhabit the earth, attending its own funeral, dispensing
wealth to its favorites. So death in the Golden Age was always incorporated into
life as a sensate pleasure, followed immediately by an improved life, the way
most folks would like it.

Listings for the Golden Age in dictionaries of mythology are rare. But turn
to 'Saturnalia' and you'll find it. These days, Saturnalia spells 'drunken sex
spree', which has its element of truth, but the rest of the older meaning involved
subversion of the social order.

In this pre-spring festival, senators and slave owners put aside their stately togas and kindred marks of rank and donned shapeless garments, known as *syntheses*. The prime metaphor of the Saturnalia was freedom from all bondage – the bondage of poverty, of wealth, of the laws and above all, of time. Slaves set up a mock king and were served delicious fare by their masters. Such delicacies, given to the powerless by the powerful, were called 'second tables', because the tables were temporarily turned. Each household became a mimic republic, in which the slaves held first rank. The law courts were closed. The image of Saturn, whose ankle was bound with a woolen fetter the rest of the year, was freed. Gifts were exchanged. The Lord of Misrule reigned.

There was always something dangerous about jovial Saturn, an element of the hooved and horned, and later he became transformed into the witch-pleasing devil of the Middle Ages. The debauched aspects of the Saturnalia became emphasized, and the revolutionary aspects began to fade away.

So the Golden Age is subversive and it's fun, which means that for us on the left, it should be our goal and our sales pitch. People love utopias that make sense. These days most utopias are drafted by the sort of people who drew up the plans for Pelican Bay Prison, grandchild of Quaker-inspired lock-ups of the early nineteenth century.

There are plenty of Golden Ages in my book alluring to some, though not always to me. There are the dreams of Robespierre, of Doug Lummis's 'public happiness'. There are the Golden Ages evoked by Hawaiians and by California Indians. There are Golden Ages nourished by Eastern European nationalists. There's the Golden Age of childhood innocence, frantically protected by the Satan-hunters. Sex is part of the Golden Age, and there's much in my book about the fears of those who try to keep the woolen handcuff on Saturn's leg all year round.

These days we're shy imaginers of Utopias on hold. We know we live in the age of iron, lamented by Hesiod and Ovid. All the more reason not to lose heart. There is abundance, if we arrange things differently. The world can be turned upside down; that is, the right way up. The Golden Age is *in us*, if we know where to look, and what to think.

1987

➤

The Argument

IN WHICH I am discovered in Key West considering funerals. Observations of Key West and its inhabitants; a history of imperial addictions; the wreck of the *Atocha*; Arise, Sir Vladimir! A British plan to knight Lenin; the tale of Speck and Lady; fishing on the flats, a meeting of hammerhead and tarpon; the stock market crash; a tour cross country; why David Horowitz missed Doris Day; what Harold Washington found when he took over Chicago; a saga of Vietnam vets in Metalline Falls; my mother's illness in Ireland. Of intimations of mortality I sing.

AUGUST 20   *Key West, Florida*

THERE WAS A FUNERAL in the graveyard across the street this morning; an old-fashioned black one, with a drummer out in front of the coffin. Thump thump thump. I find myself sketching out the music for my own funeral: the aria at the start of *Cosi Fan Tutte*, sung by the flirty girls.

Leftists' funerals can be a trial: too much sententious linking of the expired human with the forward, though mostly thwarted, march of history. Self-scripted weddings are a kindred problem, in that the effort of not going by the book lends an uncertain timbre to the proceedings. I remember one where the couple announced in a sort of descant how much they desired one another, while the guests all looked down at their shoes.

Leftists tend to like cremations, which couch the phoenix theme in the secular context of efficient resource management, though there's the old problem about what to do with the ashes.

➤

AUGUST 22   *Key West*

I GOT STUCK BEHIND a trolley car this morning, moving slowly along Duval Street with a fellow making spacious motions, like a medieval peasant broadcasting seed. A young trolley car driver had just died and they were distributing his ashes around the town. 'We're just dropping off one of our drivers', they shouted drolly by way of explanation.

People are worried about getting AIDS from mosquitoes. I've not heard of any authoritative conclusion either way. Watching the possibly lethal bugs buzz about makes one realize how people felt about mosquito noises in the heyday of yellow fever. I read somewhere recently that between 1819 and 1836 the British army had a death rate of 483 per thousand men on station in Sierra Leone.

AUGUST 25   *Key West*

'THIS IS A TOWN where it is normal to be crazy', Tanju Mishara, a Turkish-born psychologist who lives here, said to me today. 'You can be a lawyer in this town, mess yourself over with drugs and alcohol, be out at night chasing after fifteen-year-old girls, not be married, not have a little house with a picket fence, not have two and a half children and two and a half cars, not wear a suit and tie – and still be perfectly respectable.' Tanju spends much of her time listening, in a professional capacity, to Key Westers and some of her time 'evaluating' them in accordance with the demands of the justice system of Monroe County. 'Why do crazy people end up on the Keys? Because it's hot, because it's south, or 'west of the tropics', as one writer put it. Whether you're a paranoid schizophrenic or a normal everyday crazy person, there's more tolerance here.'

The way a lot of people have crossed the law on the Keys is by smuggling drugs. There are plenty of amiable graduates of Raiford and Elgin state prisons around. Ten years ago marijuana was a mainspring of Key West's economy. Around the mangrove inlets on the Gulf side of the Keys, one can still find smugglers' stop-off points of yesteryear.

With the Reagan administration came increased vigilance by coast-guardsmen and customs officials. Entrepreneurs turned to cocaine – smaller in bulk, higher in value – and the smuggling moved mostly up the Keys to Miami. But like most other places these days, Key West is a cocaine town and suffers from the change. A marijuana culture is at least tranquil, if a shade moronic. Cocaine culture is megalomaniacal, paranoid, corrupting.

➤➤

SEPTEMBER 4   *Key West*

STANDING ON THE DOCK at the old Navy base in the Truman Annex one can see, 2,000 feet above Cudjoe Key, Fat Albert, a blimp laden with surveillance gear for detecting smugglers' planes and boats crossing the Florida Straits. To one's left are hydrofoils and frigates, ready to join such task forces as an invasion of Central America might require. Beyond the ships are the ruins of Fort Zachary Taylor, built at enormous expense in the nineteenth century to guard against invaders who never came. Sixty miles westward over the horizon in the Tortugas is the vaster obsession of Fort Jefferson, a sixteen-million-brick monument to military paranoia begun in 1846 and finally abandoned by the Navy in 1909 without a gun ever having been fired in anger. Closer at hand are silver coins and crates of 350-year-old silver bars from the Spanish treasure ship found on July 20, 1985. The *Atocha* went down off the Marquesas Keys in a hurricane on September 5, 1622, dumping its cargo of silver, gold and emeralds on the sandy bottom. Mel Fisher and his Treasure Salvors searched the area

for sixteen years; then at last a diver named Greg Warcham found himself
looking at 'a reef of silver'. As far as the Spanish empire was concerned, that
silver was a drug far more deadly than the cocaine against which Fat Albert is
guarding. The treasure shipments from the New World rotted out the imperial
economy with unproductive wealth and ultimately destroyed it. In Fisher's
museum at the end of Greene Street, you can see the gold bars, the silver ingots,
the emerald cross intended to glow on a Castilian breast.

➤➤

SEPTEMBER 5   *Key West*
APROPOS CHANGE in the Soviet Union, and cautionary cries from our leaders
that 'nothing has really changed', Patrick tells me a story about the British
Foreign Office in the wake of the Russian Revolution of 1917. Britain's imperial
strategists feared the possibility of a separate Soviet truce with Germany and
the withdrawal of Russia from the war. Finally an elderly diplomat spoke up.
After years of working with Czarist Russia he had noticed, he said, that
Russians had a great love of decorations and medals. The shrewd course
therefore would be to offer Lenin a substantial decoration and knighthood,
with some lesser honor for his associate Trotsky.

The point my brother makes with the story is that every now and then axioms
and rules that are useful, indeed highly plausible, 98 percent of the time turn
out to have no relevance at all. History has simply gone in another direction.

➤➤

SEPTEMBER 12   *Key West*
MOURN SPECK AND LADY, canine victims of the imperial presidency. Shortly
after noon on Sunday, September 6, Air Force One was heading toward Forbes
Field, the airport serving Topeka, Kansas. In the plane President Reagan was
reviewing his impending speech in Topeka on the occasion of Alf Landon's
100th birthday.

At approximately 12:15 p.m., as the imaginative eyes of the MTAA officers
anticipated the arrival of Mr. and Mrs. Reagan, their physical eyes observed
two large dogs – one black, one gray – copulating at the intersection of two
taxiways.

A witness then saw two MTAA security officers approach the dogs. The action
was somewhat obscured by the long grass, but in the words of this witness,
speaking anonymously to the Topeka *Capitol-Journal*, 'I saw the uniformed
officer, with the full force of a large man, strike these dogs about five or six
times.' The MTAA officers retreated. At about 2 p.m. the same officers returned. 'The next thing I see', the witness reported, 'is a rifle coming out and

firing downward at where the animals were. All I heard was one shot.' The dogs were then loaded into plastic bags, thrown onto a flatbed truck and driven to the southern end of the airfield.

So much for the newsclips from the *Capitol-Journal*. J. spoke with the individual who first alerted the press, and reviewed the episode with Hancock, the White House, the Secret Service, the Sheriff's Department, the Kansas Department of Wildlife and Parks.

In fact, the incident began one full hour before Air Force One landed, at 1:17 p.m. as scheduled. The dogs were then mating fifty to one hundred feet from Taxiway C, in the tall grass not far from the fuel storage area. While the dogs were at it, the press plane was taxiing nearby, on its way to a parking area. The spot where the dogs were was no less than 2,000 feet from Runway 31, where the President was scheduled to land. Even if the dogs had continued their relations for the next hour, it would have been a long run for them to reach the President, and would have been impossible for the President and Nancy to have seen them, given the distance and the tall grass. White House press spokesman Charles Bacarisse told us, 'Maybe if the dogs were in the line of sight, if they were in camera view, they would have to have been moved.' So the dogs were slaughtered in case someone in the press plane managed to photograph them in the same frame as Air Force One.

➤→

OCTOBER 11   *Key West*

THE CHANGES KEY WEST wreaks on those who settle there – or those who spend more than a brief sojourn – are subtle but marked in the speed of their advance. All over town you see Crusoes at various stages in their removal from the mainland of life: here a recent castaway from the north, still trim but in the process of shedding long pants, pressed shirts and the hoops of the superego; there a twenty-year native, scruffy in cotton singlet and shorts, head tied with a bandanna, ears pierced, eyes agleam with mysterious purpose.

The hinder part of Key West is Stock Island, a southern tundra of trailer parks, body shops, deserted shrimp docks, mysterious marinas and a spectacular car dump simmering under the unrelenting sky. Here is where the last revelers go each night. Bars in the city close at 4 a.m., at which point the long-distance drinkers head for the laxer climes across the bridge, where bars can stay open twenty-four hours.

Caught in the sleepless valley between a late night party and an early date to go flats fishing, I sat outside the Boca Chica Lounge watching the revels in their terminal stages.

A couple came out. He outlined his personal plans. She said they were fine, but first she'd like some breakfast at Wag's. Screw Wag's, he said, swaying slightly. Past them as they argued edged a magnificent black transvestite, leading a Navy boy by the hand. Screw Wag's and screw you, the girl said, and went off in a cab. The guy bounced into his pickup, roared up the highway toward Miami, did a rapid U-turn across the median, picked up speed and smashed boldly into a stop sign, reversed, and ran over it again.

➤

October 12   *Key West*
JEFFREY CARDENAS, who's doing well as a guide, which he seems to prefer to photography, took me out yesterday. We headed toward the Marquesas Keys for about an hour as the sun came up. There were great white herons on the flats spearing pinfish: roseate spoonbills, frigate birds, pelican rookeries. We got to the flats and Jeffrey turned off the motor.

He told me about a prehistoric sight he had witnessed the other day. The tarpon, a migratory fish, swims up through the Marquesas every spring, then heads into the Gulf and around the Panhandle. Tarpon shoals come along 'trails', or channels, which every good guide will know, glistening as they roll along from side to side. These prehistoric fish have air bags, which they must regularly replenish in order to maintain equilibrium. Jeffrey and his anglers had been waiting excitedly for a school of 300 tarpon to get near enough for them to pole forward and try some casts. Then, still a quarter of a mile away, the shoal had started to zig-zag wildly. Off the far side, the people in the boat could see another large shoal approaching. Suddenly the two met and the sea erupted.

The tarpon's natural predator is another prehistoric animal, the hammer-head shark, which trails the tarpon shoal throughout its migration. Tarpon weigh up to 150 pounds, hammerheads up to 1,500 pounds. That morning, no doubt as always, the hammerheads hit the tarpon with tremendous force. As fish, berserk with panic, soared into the air the sharks pursued them, their eyes swiveling independently at either end of their six-foot-wide hammerheads. For a full ninety seconds the water boiled, working up a four-foot ground swell, and then the tarpon were gone, heading into the Gulf with the sharks unrelentingly in pursuit.

➤

October 18   *Washington, D.C.*
DAVID HOROWITZ AND PETER COLLIER, the Reagan era's farcical echo of the age of Whittaker Chambers, have organized what they call a Second Thoughts Conference. H. persuaded me to drop in on the final session. Both Horowitz and Collier face the dilemma of all renegades living on their memories: that

sooner or later their stories will grow whiskers too, and fresh renegades will jostle them aside.

Horowitz recalled the upbringing of his sister and himself in a Communist family, where, as so often happened, the children observed and resented the long hours their parents spent away from them, doing 'party work'. 'My sister will never forgive them', he cried to the audience of some 200; then depicted his own deprivation. *He had never been allowed to go to Doris Day and Rock Hudson movies*, but rather was forced to sit through uplifting Soviet features. Here, at last, one could see the rebel with his cause.

➡

OCTOBER 19   *Lewisburg, Pennsylvania*
AT BUCKNELL TODAY TO give a talk, I sat in the office of a member of the political science faculty. On the bookshelf was a portrait of Mao and out the window I could see in the distance the outlines of Lewisburg Federal Penitentiary. At the start of the meeting, a student rushed in to announce that there was incredible news on the television. The stock market had dropped 508 points and it looked as though capitalism was kaput. There was a bellow of applause from the lefty crowd.

➡

OCTOBER 23   *New York*
BY NIGHTFALL ON 'BLACK MONDAY', October 19, the mullahs were out on the streets, shouting 'Repent', 'The binge stops here', 'The party's over' and similar intimations of Closing Time in the West. But while the mullahs were keening, the guardians of capital were manfully plugging the dike. The Dow Jones index closed Monday night at an official drop of 508 points, even though the volume of trading had the index lagging by two hours. By Tuesday morning the Federal Reserve, major banks and Dow-listed companies had rallied the bulls. Two banks lowered their interest rate, and blue chips rose as the big corporations bought up their own stock by the sackful. Other large indexes were still in decline, but the Dow, symbolically all-important, edged up and the panic began to subside.

As the bulls fought back, progressives and liberal Democrats joined a chorus alternately panic-stricken and gleeful, urging joint Congressional and presidential action to curb the deficit, balance the budget, raise taxes – in short, do everything humanly possible to ensure the onset of a major depression. This call – I.F. Stone in *The Nation*, for example – for belt-tightening austerity as a corrective to 'profligate' ways is economic nonsense, as Roosevelt discovered when he abandoned his balanced-budget pledges of 1932; political nonsense, as

Fritz Mondale discovered in 1984; blindness, since most of the country has enjoyed no party in the past decade and can therefore scarcely be asked to leave one now.

Today offers an opportunity for the left to challenge the Belt Tighteners' Chorus and make a compelling case for its economic vision and program. Even if the financial markets are overheated, the overall economy is in precisely the opposite condition. The amount of US plant put to productive use is lower than it was when Ronald Reagan took over. The age-adjusted unemployment rate is higher. Unemployed people and resources cannot generate the revenues, hence the taxes, that would assist in paying off the deficit. Real wages, median incomes and medan household spending have never, even during the present 'party', recovered to the level of the early 1970s. Corporate investment and GNP growth rates have also slowed over the past three years.

For most Americans, borrowing is not a 'binge' – I.F. Stone's silly word – but the only way of staying above water. When Reagan said plaintively in the midst of 'Black Monday' that the economic indicators were unchanged, he was right. But people haven't been looking at those indicators properly. In 1982 the stock market boom commenced its rise from a very low level. It was preceded by a severe decline beginning in the late 1960s. In real values, the peak of the Reagan stock boom, on August 25 of this year, was lower than the average in 1965, the peak of the postwar boom, by more than 10 percent. In other words, there has been a long-term economic decline, best expressed in the falling rate of profit, which has produced weak stock values and thus the takeover frenzy at the corporate level. This is not an overblown economy but a sluggish one, sustained chiefly by military spending.

So there is nothing irrational about Monday's panic. The bulls are winning skirmishes, just as they did in the days and months after 'Black Tuesday' 1929, but recession is inevitable, its severity depending on the madness of plans hatched in Congress to balance the budget, curb the deficit and shackle demand with further taxes.

The call now should be not for an onslaught on the deficit but for a restructuring of the deficit so that more spending is done by the public sector under properly public control; not for a decrease in investment but for lowered real interest rates and investment guided by humane public criteria; for democratic allocation of the surplus value.

At this stage of the game there is no policy solution designed to improve one condition that will not in turn make something else worse. There is a logic to cutting the deficit, and that logic is premised on stabilizing the financial markets. It produces disaster in jobs and spending. The logic of economic growth and low real interest rates demands continued heavy borrowing, and that undermines the financial system. There's a logic to raising interest rates to defend the dollar, but that similarly implies an assault on jobs and spending.

Growth requries redistribution of income. There is no solution alluring to all sides, and these days, it goes without saying, the financial markets win every time.

➤

NOVEMBER 16   *Boulder, Colorado*
BELOW THE FIRST SCARP of the Rockies; home to 80,000 people of whom about 1,000 are lawyers. This is the crossroads of the nation's cocaine traffic. First stop on my book tour for *Corruptions*.

There's been an early snowfall. It was swirling over the wreck of a Continental jet at the airport when I landed and as we drove down to Denver this morning the Rockies gleamed in sharp outline. At KOA for a call-in show, I spoke with Gary Tessler, who punched the buttons with increasing moodiness as friendly calls poured in. 'I wish we could get some right-wingers to denounce you', he sighed. 'Gary', I said on the air, 'I've just returned from the Soviet Union, charged by the Central Committee of the Soviet Communist Party to award you with this pin, the order of Lenin, Second Class, in recognition of your organizing work among the masses.' I ceremonially pinned a little enamel head of Lenin, which I had bought in Moscow, on Tessler's jacket and he laughed bravely. Later Tessler told me that this is the station for which Alan Bird was working when he was murdered by the anti-Semitic Nazi group, the Order.

➤

NOVEMBER 18   *Boulder*
TERRIBLE NEWS FROM IRELAND. Mama has been diagnosed with cancer of the stomach. She's in the Mercy Hospital in Cork for treatment. I've agreed that Andrew will go over, and then – unless there's an emergency – I will be there in December when he goes off to Thailand.

➤

NOVEMBER 19   *Chicago*
DISTRAUGHT, I IMAGINE, over the crash, Continental is running its flights abominably late, so I miss a session at Great Expectations Bookstore in Evanston. I've liked this place ever since I went there last spring and heard Jeff Rice, one of the partners running the place and a former SDS organizer, say firmly down the phone, 'No, we do not stock Alan Bloom.' Since Great Expectations is exceptionally well-stocked I asked why, and Rice said he didn't see why they should have to disseminate such actively pernicious drivel as *The Closing of the American Mind*.

I headed toward the Loop to do a radio show with Mort Downey. He'd had Philip Agee on his Channel Five show in New York not long before, and as Agee waited for the chat to begin Downey strode toward him, holding Agee's book *On the Run* aloft. This book, Downey thundered to the audience, is the most disgusting piece of un-American trash I have ever read, and hurled it to the floor, where it slithered in among the feet of the technicians. The audience roared. Afterward, as Agee was walking across the parking lot, one of the show's technicians walked up and said he thought Downey was a madman but he had to make a living, and would Agee please sign this book. He produced the copy Downey had hurled aside.

I was eager to meet the great man, but he is too busy with his new career in a New York TV studio and merely boomed at me from there via satellite. Near the end of the show Downey says something like, 'Now your father, Claud, was he a radical, Alex?' 'He was a Communist, Mort', I answered. 'And you, Alex, are you a Marxist?' 'Yes, Mort.' 'And I've heard that all Marxists are atheists. Are you an atheist, Alex?' 'Yes, Mort.'

The night of my arrival I'd had a delicate time with Milt Rosenberg weaving through differences about Jesse Jackson and about Israel. To my surprise Rosenberg had spoken up for a Palestinian state on the West Bank. Rosenberg's station is clear channel, with its sound beaming all the way down to the southern states, and suddenly the airwaves filled with the articulate anger of an elderly, very radical coal miner, retired in Arkansas and describing the pitiable little shantytowns of homeless people just down the road from where he lives. The next caller was a young businessman asking what precisely I mean by the word 'wealthy'. 'I don't feel wealthy, Mr. Cockburn, and I earn $125,000 a year, and I imagine you must earn twice that.'

➡

NOVEMBER 20   *Madison, Wisconsin*

ROGER HOROWITZ MET ME at the airport and we hastened to the Peoples Bookstore, run by Gillam Kerley. Kerley has just been released from Leavenworth Federal Prison Camp, where he had enjoyed the distinction of being the only American in prison for draft resistance, having drawn a three-year term for refusing to register for the draft – the harshest sentence given a nonregistrant since the Vietnam War.

Last year a Madison police officer was suspended after being caught defacing a statue of a black woman and child in a public park. He was also charged with spray-painting 'Niggers Suck' on a black-owned building. He later resigned. Out of 43,368 students at the University of Wisconsin in the fall of 1987 only 2,400 more from minorities. Of the 6,921 faculty there was a minority representation of 142. In the opening of 1987 the Phi Gamma Delta fraternity, known as Fiji, was suspended for having held a blackface party called Fiji Island. Outside their premises members had set up a figure of a black man with a bone through his nose.

In the spring of 1986 members of another fraternity held a party where they had a 'Harlem room'. Members had their faces painted black and served watermelon punch and fried chicken. The black minority has reacted vigorously, the administration nerves itself for action and the racists shout about free speech.

➤

NOVEMBER 21   *Chicago*
THIS EVENING IN SAUER'S restaurant I looked at a stage on which stood more than a dozen veterans of the Abraham Lincoln Brigade and their wives. We – hundreds of people – were all there to honor the fiftieth anniversary of the Brigade, and in particular Oliver Law. A proclamation was read out: 'Whereas over 200 Chicagoans joined this international movement to stop the spread of fascism, and whereas Oliver Law, a leader of movements for the relief of the poor and for political rights for blacks and working people in Chicago in the early 1930s was a commander in the Abraham Lincoln Brigade, thus becoming the first black American to lead an integrated military force in the history of the United States, ... Now, therefore, I, Harold Washington, Mayor of the City of Chicago, do hereby proclaim Oliver Law and Abraham Lincoln Brigade Day in Chicago.'

I gave a reminiscence of my father's days in the Spanish militia, when his life was saved because the string holding his oversize militia pants broke, causing pants to descend, and him to fall to the ground, evading the machine-gun bullets slicing through the air at brain level.

When Washington took over Jane Byrne's office he found that virtually all the crucial administrative files were missing, along with television, typewriters, an Oriental rug and a video camera setup. All that remained in the former mayor's desk drawer was a paper clip.

➤

NOVEMBER 22   *Seattle*
THE AIR AND THE RAIN in the Pacific Northwest remind me of Ireland. I sit in a Japanese restaurant with Kate Dwyer and her friends Rick and Lisa Wood. Rick makes his money in about three months every year, as captain of a fishing trawler working below Alaska. He talks of seas breaking over the boats in air so cold that the water freezes on impact and the men walk around the boat with baseball bats bashing the ice to break it off. When the water freezes on the superstructure quicker than the men can break it off, the weight pulls the boat

over. 'Then', he says matter of factly, 'you drown.' I remember a song Hugh
O'Reilly sings sometimes in O'Reilly's bar, in Ardmore, back in Ireland.

> Methinks I see a host of craft
> Spreading their sails a-lee,
> As down the Humber they do glide,
> All bound for the far North Sea.
> Methinks I see on each small craft
> Many a heart so brave,
> Going out to earn his daily bread
> Upon the restless wave.
>
> October night was such a sight,
> T'was never seen before,
> There were masts and yards and broken spars
> All washed upon that shore.
> There was many a heart of sorrow,
> Aye and many a heart so brave,
> There was many a fine and hearty lad
> To find a watery grave.
>
> *Chorus*
> And it's three score and ten
> Boys and men were lost from Grimsby town.
> From Yarmouth out to Scarborough
> Many hundreds more were drowned.
> Our herring crafts, our trawlers,
> Our fishing smacks as well,
> They longed to fight that bitter night
> And battle with the swell.

➨

NOVEMBER 26   *Seattle*

HAROLD WASHINGTON IS DEAD of a heart attack at the age of sixty-five, the
average life expectancy of black males in the United States.

NOVEMBER 27   *Spokane, Washington*

THANKSGIVING JUST BEYOND SPOKANE at the house of Sue and Tom Schmidt.
Outside, the pine trees stand stark against the stars, and facing southeast you

can feel the tilt east of the high plains. A Vietnam vet named Sean Daly tells an interesting story.

Some sixty miles north of Spokane in eastern Washington is the town of Colville. The country round about is rugged, cut through with glacial valleys sheltering fertile farms. Over to the east across the mountains is neo-Nazi terrain, near Metaline Falls and Coeur d'Aleine. The economy of the region is depressed: mines closed up, lumber run down. The Colville region is Vietnam vet counry: rural, remote and, best of all, cheap.

About four years ago some Vietnam vets going to the Mental Health Center in Colville for individual counseling organized a group, meeting once a week in a collective session. After eighteen months they went public, debuting as Vets for Peace with a booth at the Colville County Fair. This initiative did not pass unnoticed by the local Veterans of Foreign Wars service office, which exerted itself to organize a countergroup of vets. A bureaucrat from the health and social services department called Lloyd Humphries urged Vets for Peace to merge with the new group for their weekly sessions and finally a joint gathering was convened. The Vets for Peace were not delighted by the consequences. They have a rule for such meetings: no weapons, no booze. One of the vets in the countergroup was half stewed and others carried knives.

Vets for Peace said it would boycott the Mental Health Center and did so for the following eighteen months. The bureaucracy, Feds twined octopus-like with the Washington Department of Health and Human Services, then announced that they were withdrawing recognition from the group, though each of its members could return for individual counseling. The group jacked up its collective social and political presence in the community, organizing community vigils, leafletting lines for *Platoon*, and so forth.

Early last year Dan Rather came to Colville. With him he brought CBS producer Paul Fine and a production unit and began to make a documentary about Colville area vets. Vets for Peace made sure the CBS people knew about their existence and waited eagerly for the opportunity to try to counter the mad-dog image of a bunch of Rambo crazies in the hills: the so-called 'bush-vet', beloved by journalists chirping about post-traumatic stress disorder and avoiding politics in any form.

The chance never came. Rather and his crew spent their time talking to the state-sanctioned vet group and flew off into the sunrise. Still smarting from this experience Vets for Peace were then approached by the *Spokesman-Review*. The reporter talked sympathetically with them by the hour. The photographer arrived and they stood proudly under their Vets for Peace banner as he clicked away. One more shot, he asked, just them and no banner against a mountain backdrop. Innocently they complied. In the published story they got two paragraphs, buried in blather about the countergroup. And the photograph: men without a banner, socially atomized against bush vet backdrop.

NOVEMBER 28 *Spokane*

FIRST TO THE LOCAL listener-subscribed radio station for an interview. Then in the evening I give a talk. Sue, a karate adept of high degree, musters herself and others in case one of the local Nazis makes a rush for the speaker, but all goes well.

➳

NOVEMBER 29 *Spokane*

WE DROVE ACROSS the plain to visit Morton Alexander on the famed Tolstoy Commune, active relic of the sixties. Here, just south of Spokane, is the site of a famous Indian victory. The ambushed soldiers broke and ran, here where now stands the gas station, there round the motel, there through the wood, hunted to earth. We found Morton's house in the canyon and swigged deeply on his plum and elderberry wine. Tom Schmidt had once owned the mimeograph machine that had been the property of the man – hero actually, mercilessly hounded by the FBI – running the Fair Play for Cuba Committee. It was therefore the machine that had produced the leaflets that eventually reached Lee Harvey Oswald and were handed out by him in Dallas in 1963. Tom had trundled himself, his worldly goods and the machine down to Tuskeegee, Alabama, where he sufficiently annoyed the watchdogs of the state that they burned his house down, destroying the machine in the process. Morton recalled a fabled local episode, the great Tolstoy Farm dope bust of 1972. Tom told me something I'd not known, that Elvis Presley said back in the late fifties, when asked about his views on a certain situation: 'I've only two uses for niggers – they can buy my records and they can shine my shoes.' Tom was driving through the South at the time and found a lot of black people without much use for Presley.

➳

DECEMBER 6 *San Francisco Bay Area*

LISTENER-SUBSCRIBED RADIO is the amniotic fluid for any progressive community. TV – outside the informality of public access cable – rigidifies, schmaltzes, ceremonializes, destroys vitality, creates the anomie of the spectacle and the atomized spectator. Radio is a web that implicates rather than excludes. With Fred Gardner I meet up with Kayo Hallinan. They'd worked together for the defendants in the Presidio Mutiny. Another defending lawyer had been Brendan Sullivan, more recently counsel to Oliver North. I'd met Kayo and his brother Ringo even earlier, when we had all gone on our first march together, from Aldermaston to London in the Easter CND march of 1959.

Fred's current breadwinning job is managing editor of *Synapse*, weekly paper of the UCSF medical school. He shows me a story in it about trachoma in the Egyptian hamlet of Gamileya. Trachoma is a chlamydial infection of the conjunctiva that causes the inner surface of the eyelids to become chronically inflamed. In Gamileya, Western standards of blindness do not apply. Only those with no light perception are considered blind. People there who would be considered legally blind in the US ride motorcyles: 'In Gamileya people do not require normal vision to conduct their daily activities', Sandy Lane had written. 'Most visually impaired adults are illiterate, so they do not need signs to read. There are no street signs or house numbers to read in the hamlet. The structure of the village changes very slowly. If a new house is built every five years the visually impaired can learn to find their way around it... Plowing, sowing seed and harvesting ripe produce do not require much vision. If there is some small task they are unable to do, their extended family does it for them. Thus, they do not perceive themselves as disabled.

➤

DECEMBER 7   *Bay Area*
ANOTHER MEETING ABOUT the mainstream media, which is duly attacked. A Trotskyist gets up and says that this sort of thing is all very well, but only when *The Nation* and KPFA are themselves perceived as being enemies of socialist advance and are ruthlessly destroyed will ... etc., etc. Some groups on the left really have to give up this creaking argot of 'ruthlessly denouncing' this, or 'mercilessly exposing' that. Exposing and denouncing aren't necessarily bad activities, but the language has to be something people recognize as part and parcel of their own lives. 'Striking hard blows' at the enemy. No one does that, at least in English. The end of all this jargon is the old Comintern directive my father once came across at the *Daily Worker:* 'The lower organs of the Party must make even greater efforts to penetrate the more backward parts of the proletariat.' My father said this would be construed by the masses as a dirty joke. The comrades looked at him askance.

➤

DECEMBER 9   *Ann Arbor/Detroit*
AFTER A FUND-RAISER for *Against the Current*, I talk to Peter Werbe, who runs a popular late-night talk show and who is part of the collective that puts out the anarchist magazine *The Fifth Estate*. He hands me its fall issue, which contains a long essay by George Bradford on deep ecology and the organization Earth First! and a couple of its moving spirits, Edward Abbey and Dave Foreman. Both enunciate a neo-Malthusian view of population growth that is cruel in its particulars: 'The best thing would be to just let nature seek its own balance, to

let the people here [in Ethiopia] just starve', says Foreman – and racist in general, as Abbey makes clear in declaring that 'the immigration issue really is a matter of "we" versus "they",' that the great threat to US culture, a 'product of northern European civilization', is Latinization.

Some defectors from Earth First! in Olympia, Washington, recently started up a newsletter called *Alien-Nation,* which had a kick at the Foreman strain in Earth First! in its first issue: 'A dominant point of view and a distinct image had been cultivated and maintained within the organizational journal that comes out of Tucson, Arizona. This image of a rough and ready, red-necked, alcoholic, kick-ass hombre out to protect the wilderness reeks of sexism, racism, and the worst kind of wild west imagery... It has become the opinion of our group that his image and point of view is real within the upper echelons of EF! and is extremely right wing, if not decidedly fascist in its orientation.' Foreman himself was fairly upfront in a letter last year to Bradford: 'My honest feeling is that the vast majority of those who consider themselves Earth First!ers agree with my position. I am all for cooperation with other groups where it fits, but we have a particular point of view which we are trying to articulate. Call it fascist if you like, but I am more intrested in bears, rain forests, and whales than in people.'

➤

DECEMBER 10   *Washington, D.C.*

IT'S GORBY'S LAST DAY in town, and the Hammer and Sickle hangs proudly along Pennsylvania Avenue. He's capitalism's favorite Communist, the first lawyer ever to be in charge of the S.U. as Lynn Turgeon never tires of pointing out to me. I'm not sure this is a confidence-inspiring credential. He certainly is eager to please. He's no Khrushchev, though. Hard to imagine him bashing away at his UN desk with a shoe, like K. in his moment of greatness that made the Central Committee back in Moscow think that he had most definitely gone too far.

The trouble is with all my fellows here who think that just because Gorby is popular, and presentable, somehow everything is going to be okay, lion will couch with lamb, etc. What do they think the cold war has been about?

➤

DECEMBER 25   *Ardmore, Co. Waterford*

MINOR DISAPPOINTMENT. Kitty gives me a nice toy train and my nephew Alexander a pen. Just when I was playing happily with the train, it was surmised that there had been a mix-up and my train was torn away.

1988

➤

The Argument

IN WHICH I am discovered in Ireland, where my mother is ill. The death of Sean McBride; my sister's views on Sally Bowles; my removal from Florida to California; the Adobe Motel, Santa Cruz and Watsonville; Reagan's emergence as a Leninist; introduction to the narrative of the *Anderson Valley Advertiser*; an exchange over Earth First!; the Harvard Class of '63 explains itself; a gay pastor's tale; transvestism and astrology explored; Gorbachev attacked; a journey to Atlanta, thence to New Orleans; meditation on Reagan and Fort Wacky; invocation of masque and carnival, Comus and Rex; the man who exposed My Lai; explorations on the trail of the French Revolution; visions of Robespierre and Saint-Just; my sister and her pipe. Of Reagan's end, of worlds upside down, of worlds false and real, I sing.

JANUARY 2   *Ardmore, Co. Waterford*
THE ANNOYING THING about Ireland is that you can spend half your life telling
people to disabuse themselves of caricatures of the country and then you go
home to find the old place busily caricaturing itself.

A friend of mine went to visit someone who had not managed natural motions
of any sort in over a week and found him sitting in bed, swollen in form and a
retainer swabbing his face with gin. 'Why are you doing that?' the friend cried
to the retainer, who said it's what he did to himself when he felt off color and
went off to replenish the swab. 'It's as much as I can do to stop him using the
vodka', croaked the stricken patient from his bed.

I read the local paper, *The Dungarvan Observer*. Mayor Daley of Chicago
came from Dungarvan, and had family close by in Kiley's Cross. In a review of
1987 *The Dungarvan Observer* had the following entry under November: 'Elsie
Power celebrated her one hundredth birthday at St. Joseph's Hospital, Dungarvan. Nazi war criminal Pieter Menten died in his native Holland. He hid for
over 30 years and owned Cameragh House near Mentonbridge. An increase for
water charges was passed by the town council by 5 votes to 4.'

➡

JANUARY 19   *Ardmore*
To ANDREW COCKBURN
guest ORIENTAL HOTEL, BANGKOK, THAILAND
MAMA HAD A QUALITATIVE IMPROVEMENT about ten days ago. Docs — to Mama
directly and in passing to me – say they are encouraged. Hart even seems to
have mooted the vague possibility that she might be able to go back to Rock
House at some unspecified point between chemotherapy treatments. As of
Monday she began a new course of chemo, which means she had a dose of the
potion then and will have another in eight days. This makes her throw up a lot
and feel miserable, though I found her in good heart last night. Tony Bernard
the wigman is making her a wig. At the moment she has a crest of hair and I tell

her she looks like those splendid Indian chiefs done I think by McKinney and Hall in the early nineteenth century, before Hollywood iconography made them all into copperskinned Bedouins with feathers on their heads. The big call today is for what used to be called boudoir caps, as worn by Mrs. Tiggywinkle in the Potter cycle. To be frank I haven't been pestering the docs every few days because it's apparent to me as much as to them that she is better, or at least moving in that direction.

She lives the life of Louis Fourteenth, though her schedule would have killed the Sun King dead in a week. A typical day about a week ago brought an Ardmore delegation in the mid morning, Nancy Minchin at lunchtime, Sally Keane in early afternoon, Donal Musgrave in mid afternoon, self at five and Richard Wood at six. The only pause in this relentless round was over the weekend when the people of Ireland went off to Dublin for the removal and interment of Sean McBride.

I visit Molly Keane off and on, who sits in bed scribbling away. I've been keeping clear of O'Reilly's, having found that things only seem to warm up there about four in the morning though for general joie de vivre it's unsurpassed. Old Henry O'Reilly suddenly shouted, 'Let d'ere be THURMOIL.'

Only irking thing is lack of fish, owing to stormy conditions. Mick Fitzgerald has come up with one cod, so far; mostly it's been boiling bacon, which is all right by me, though Ella, a dear little dog I must say, shouts for entrecôte. I never knew that tending to the physical and spiritual needs of one cat and one dog could be so demanding on one's time.

➤

JANUARY 20   *Ardmore*
'HE, TOO, HAS BEEN changed in his turn. / Transformed utterly: / A terrible beauty is born.' Yeats wrote those lines in *Easter, 1916* about John McBride. On January 15 his son Sean, one of Ireland's greatest citizens, died at the age of eighty-three.

Sean McBride's mother was Maud Gonne. When Sean was born in Paris in 1904, both Yeats and Ezra Pound were on hand to cluck down into the infant's cradle. He was taken to Dublin to be baptized but, citing the revolutionary disposition of the parents, the parish priest refused to officiate.

His father was a Fenian, whose nationalist and anti-British sentiments had caused him to form an Irish brigade to fight with the Boers in the Transvaal war. In the spring of 1916 he was on his way to work in Dublin when he saw John Connally and 'some of the boys' digging trenches. There and then he joined the Easter rising, and along with his companions in the Post Office, was condemned to die by the British. He was offered a blindfold at his execution but spurned it, exclaiming, 'Nonsense, I have been gazing down rifle barrels at the British all my life.' Sean returned to Ireland from Paris in 1918, fought in the war of independence and attracted the eye of Michael Collins, whose aide and bodyguard he became during the treaty negotiations with the British.

The Irish organized themselves badly in these talks in London. They drank too much and were flattered by high society. Communications with De Valera back in Dublin were a logistical nightmare. Churchill called Collins in one day, spun the globe, which was well splattered with British territories colored red, and said, 'Why don't you come in with us and help me run the world.' As he signed the treaty Collins muttered, 'I'm signing my death warrant', and he was right. De Valera, Sean McBride and the Republicans refused to recognize the treaty, its oath of allegiance to the Crown and the lack of a unified Ireland. Collins was soon dead in an ambush, killed not far from where I write these lines. McBride was soon in Mountjoy prison, watching his companions being led out. None of them knew they were being taken to the execution yard. McBride's cellmate was Rory O'Connor, sentenced to die by Free Staters including Kevin O'Higgins, whose best man he had been a year before. Outside Ireland few remember the bitterness of that civil war.

McBride was in and out of prison for the next fifteen years, working as a journalist under an assumed name, organizing the IRA underground. In 1936 he became that body's chief of staff, but he was out of it a year later, opposed to the planned bombing campaign in England (which put Brendan Behan behind bars for the first time). McBride also regarded De Valera's proposed constitution, removing the oath of allegiance and affirming Irish unity, as meaning that from then on the struggle could be pursued by constitutional means, and he held to that position to the end of his life.

The British always hated him. As his coffin was being lowered into his mother's grave yesterday, the *Times* of London ran a furious editorial calling him the 'cosmopolitan high priest' of the 'cult of violence' and saying that so far as reconciliation in the north was concerned, 'the absence of Sean McBride will only help'.

McBride said near the end of his life that 'within twenty years, perhaps ten, Britain will have left the Six Counties, certainly will withdraw its army, there will be unity, in whatever form. Three reasons: the paramilitaries of both sides are exhausted, people in Britain generally don't know or care very much about it, British governments are becoming increasingly unwilling to meet the costs. All of this will produce a political solution.'

McBride, as the abuse echoing around his coffin testifies, was hated by all the right people. Of the use of violence he said in the end, 'The degree of oppression must be so acute as to endanger your own survival, that of your country, your family, and it must involve methods in excess of what is required to deal with the situation.'

I met him in the early fifties at a Christmas party at Luggala, home of

Oonagh Oranmore in the Wicklow Mountains. There was an old Victorian party game in which one contestant would think of a word and then be asked by the others to do certain things 'in the manner of the word'. Then the group would try to guess what the word was. McBride was asked to hang his shoes on the chandelier and then take them down in the manner of the word. His word, it turned out, was 'lovingly'. He took down the shoes, stroking them with profound affection.

➤

JANUARY 23   *Ardmore*

BRUCE ANDERSON SENDS me an interesting interview with Earth First!'s David Foreman. Foreman argued that the worst thing James Watt ever did for the environmental movement was to double the Sierra Club membership with his conduct as Secretary of the Interior. Suddenly the Sierra Club had a lot of 'soft' members, liable to be offended by its magazine, which had to become tamer. And, since the soft new members were less likely to renew their subscriptions, the group was forced to do more direct mail to keep getting new subscribers because it had got habituated to the bigger cash flow from the bigger membership base. The direct mail experts sank their teeth in, and soon the Sierra Club was spending its days sending out garbage mail to raise the money to send out more garbage mail.

➤

FEBRUARY 1   *Ardmore*

RE-READ CHRISTOPHER ISHERWOOD'S *Lions and Shadows*. Jean Ross and my father Claud met in Berlin in the early 1930s, in the era portrayed by Isherwood in *Goodbye to Berlin* and other pieces. Jean has always been described, by Isherwood among others, as a model for the character Sally Bowles.

My half-sister Sarah, daughter of Claud and Jean, disputed this publicly a couple of years ago. The occasion was a revival of *Cabaret*, itself derived from the Isherwood story. There was also an insinuation, remotely inspired by Isherwood's schoolboyish speculation in *Christopher and His Kind*, that Jean had performed louchely on the stage of the Berlin Opera.

Her mother Jean, wrote Sarah, 'never liked *Goodbye to Berlin*, nor felt any sense of identity with the character of Sally Bowles, which in many respects she thought more closely modeled on one of Isherwood's male friends. (His homosexuality could not at that time be openly admitted.)' Sarah then argued that the significant differences between Sally and her supposed model are attributable to Isherwood's preference for convention over reality: 'The convention does not permit an attractive young woman to have much in the way of intellectual accomplishments, and Isherwood follows it loyally. There is nothing in his portrait of Sally to suggest that she might have had any genuine ability as an actress, still less as a writer. My mother, on the other hand, was at least talented enough as an actress to be cast as Anitra in Max Reinhardt's production of *Pier Gynt* and competent enough as a writer to earn her living, not long afterwards, as a scenario-writer and journalist ... Above all, the convention requires that a woman must be either virtuous (in the sexual sense) or a tart. So Sally, who is plainly not virtuous, must be a tart ... To depend for a living on providing sexual pleasure, whether or not in the context of marriage, seemed to [Jean] the ultimate denial of freedom and emancipation. The idea so deeply repelled her that she simply could not, I think, have been attracted to a man who was rich, or allied herself permanently to anyone less incorrigibly impecunious than my father. She did not see the question as one of personal morality, but as a political one.'

➤→

FEBRUARY 5   *Aptos, California*

DAISY INSTALLED at UC Santa Cruz. I am a few miles down the road in Aptos. Here beside the Pacific my motel is reasonably well known to the local sheriff's department whose police cars regularly cruise the premises, breaking up domestic altercations, monitoring the drug trade and otherwise sifting through the small change of American life. The motel houses people who work, often in the crevices of the California construction boom, and people who don't work and who spend their lives waiting for modest disbursements from social welfare agencies of one sort or another.

No flop house, the place is in face 'ordinary', as that word might apply to the tier below petty bourgeois respectability. Drugs are an integral part of this ordinariness, ranging from the free-basing habits of a veteran of the Delta force – the rapid deployment commandos mustered during Carter's presidency – who was finally evicted after supposedly twice trying to kill the motel manager, to the cocaine usage maintained by at least a third of our community of some fifty souls, to the 'ecstasy' (a mild psychotropic) administered by the motel's hippie sector to themselves, their dog and their plentiful pet rats, to the marijuana used as a simple stand-by, to the drink which claims some half-dozen full-time alcoholics and a considerable number of medium-intensity boozers. Television is a constant in the rooms, flickering behind the curtains that the American residents tend to keep tightly drawn even at noon.

Political opinion in the motel is probably best represented by a carpenter with a robustly populist view of the world, fortified and nourished by right-wing magazines such as *Soldier of Fortune* and the left-conspiratorialism of the Christic Institute.

North up the coast from the motel, across the far-from-grandiose roofs of the $700,000 homes of doctors and other professionals, is Santa Cruz. This town is now a political and cultural outcrop, or chapter continued, of the 1960s. When the sheriff recently attempted to close some massage parlors on the grounds that they were in fact brothels, the local women's groups reacted angrily, denouncing this affront to the right of women to control their own bodies. A recent mayor was a socialist. Above the town is the exceptionally beautiful campus of the University of California at Santa Cruz, founded in the early 1960s. On the far side of the Santa Cruz Mountains lies the Santa Clara valley, the town of San Jose and Silicon Valley. A quarter of a century ago the valley was lush with meadows and, in the spring, yellow with mustard blossom. Today the city is larger than San Francisco, polluted, balkanized by freeways and so inhospitable that the county is now experiencing net out-migration.

To the south of my motel is the agricultural zone. The pickers and cutters, centered in Watsonville, are Mexican, mostly from the province of Michoacan and commuting between the two places on a regular basis. Watsonville has been convulsed by fierce labor struggles. From south of the border, in Mexico itself, or further south, from Chile, have come imports of vegetables and fruits picked by seasonal workers (paid only a few cents a day, many of them on the vast plantations instituted in the Pinochet era in obedience to the IMF's urgings to expand the agro-export sector).

Undercut by these imports, the packing houses in Watsonville cut wages and demanded concessions. Finally the workers at one such plant struck. They held out for over a year. The bank foreclosed on the adamant owner. With spinach rotting in the fields, the new owner partially gave way. There had barely been a strike-breaker in fourteen months. On their knees women from the packaging house moved from the plant to one of the local churches to give thanks to God.

➤

MARCH 1   *Aptos*
REAGAN'S EMERGENCE AS a Leninist has caused some surprise and irritation in the capital. Lou Cannon was interviewing him for *The Washington Post* last week and asked whether Gorbachev was really and truly different from all the others. Ron said yes, he'd met most of the Soviet leaders (not true, of course) and what separated Mikhail Sergeyevich from the pack was that he wanted 'to do what Lenin was teaching' and extract the Bolshevik kernel from Stalin's perversions. Lenin, the President explained, had favored auguries of *glasnost* and *perestroika* and 'had programs that he called the New Economics and things of that kind'. Ron had evidently noted the rehabilitation of Bukharin and figured it was finally safe to come out for the NEP.

MARCH 5   *Aptos*
GREAT NEWS from Ireland. Mama is back home and doesn't need any more
chemo.

≕→

MARCH 9   *Aptos*
THE NEW AGERS are counterattacking. 'Contrary to your understanding, it is
only a change in consciousness that can lead to a change in action. Consciousness is not changed by social action, no matter how lofty the goal or how
necessary the change. Consciousness is changed by a process totally unknown
to you, which is why you cannot understand the New Age. The New Age is
nothing less than a different state of consciousness than the one that you have;
and your mind cannot understand it because it is not something that can be
understood in the mind. My hope and prayer is that you are able, sometime, to
still your mind enough to let your real self, your higher self, fill full to
overflowing within you the peace that cannot be understood in the mind. The
greatest lack of morality occurs when any of us dare to judge another of our
fellow beings.'

≕→

MARCH 10   *Aptos*
THE ANDERSON VALLEY ADVERTISER is pusblished weekly out of Boonville, a
small town in Northern California, and edited by a friend of mine, a large man
called Bruce Anderson. Bruce offers the real Prairie Home Companion. He's
Garrison Keillor for people with brains.

The *Advertiser* is everything a local paper should be. It covers the school
district and the police blotter. It harasses the lumber companies, broad-rumped
bureaucrats, Nike-shod liberals and other enemies of the human spirit. It also
runs a column by me.

One of the many people the *Advertiser* does not care for is young Rep. Bosco,
now in his third term as representative from the Redwood Empire. What
agitates many of Rep. Bosco's constituents is that he is fence-straddling on one
of the hottest issues facing Northern California today, namely off-shore drilling.
The possibility that oil rigs may one day soon rise from the ocean floor off
Mendocino and Humboldt Counties is one that tempts many locals in the
direction of armed struggle.

Rep. Bosco failed to show Feb. 1 for the hearings in Eureka, and Bruce just
ran a purported interview between Rep. Bosco and one 'David Yesson' of the
Des Moines Register. Bruce had Bosco describe his constituents as 'know-noth-
ing malcontents' who care only 'where their next joint is coming from'. Bellows
of fury from Bosco and David Yepsen of the *Register*.

Dear Mr. Cockburn,

... I'd like to take you to task for your comments about Earth First! in the February issue of *Z* magazine. Now, I'm not going to defend Edward Abbey's screeds against impending 'Latinization' of America. I enjoy Abbey's writing and agree with him much of the time, but he's really been known to be a bit of a jackass at times. This time, I'd say he's really distinguished himself (one might note that the patterns of corruption and autocracy which he ascribes to Latin American culture could be found in all their glory in the Irish and Italian metropolis of Chicago in 1928). That aside, what I believe people in the Earth First! movement are saying about immigration is that we don't want to see America any more overrun by humans than it already is. Any humans, from anywhere. Including here. And even so, we're not exactly standing at the borders in our bedsheets beating off the wogs with axe-handles.

Immigration is a minor footnote to Earth First!'s platform. Our major concern is with preserving nature. Period. What just plain confounds many mainstream radicals is that yes, we really do believe that nature is more important than human beings. To someone like yourself, steeped in the rationalism (and anthropocentrism) of the Western intellectual tradition, this may seem to be an absolutely outlandish viewpoint. In fact, many of Earth First!'s critics on the left apparently decided it is so outlandish that it must be a facade concealing some more sinister agenda. Racism. Sexism. Elitism. Fascism.

In fact, with Earth First! what you see is what you get. We mean what we say. If I were asked to choose between a future world of happy humans and no rainforests and a world with happy rainforests and no humans, I'd pick the latter, without any hesitation. I wouldn't pick it because I hate humans, I'd pick it because I don't think humans have the right to destroy the natural world to fulfill their own selfish ends. In my view, that's just putting the importance of the human race in perspective. Sure, we have a right to eat, reproduce and be happy, just like all the rest of the planet's plants and critters. But cut down 150-year-old pine trees to make disposable chopsticks? I'm not so sure about that. Maybe we ought to wash our chopsticks and save them for later.

I also think the recent attacks on Earth First! raise a very disturbing issue – the left's unwillingness to tolerate cultural diversity. I can't speak for Earth First! as a whole. I'm a pretty mild-mannered guy who lives in Rhode Island, reads their newsletter, and makes it out to the great West as often as I can afford to. I am not, as *Alien-Nation* would have it, 'a rough and ready, red-necked, kick-ass hombre'. But I do like a beer or two now and then, I enjoy country music, I like cars (and so do you). Does all this mean that I must be racist, sexist, reactionary slime?

The real opportunity of the left in the 1990s is that a huge majority of the people in America agree with many of our deepest beliefs. Most people in

America aren't exactly cheerleaders for racism, sexism and pollution at this point.

If the left is not about learning to understand and respect each other and our differences, if it's really about picking the one right way to be a human being and refusing to tolerate any deviation, then the left might as well be Pat Robertson. Or to hit below the belt, the Khmer Rouge. 'If I can't dance, I don't want to join your revolution.'

Mark McDonough
Providence, Rhode Island

I was reading Foreman's arguments for true wilderness and his praise of the hunter-gatherers when someone called to say that Raymond Williams was dead. I started looking through his *The Country and the City*. 'As we perceive a total environment', Williams wrote, 'and as we register the consequence of so many abstracted and separated activities, we begin to see that all the real decisions are about modes of social interest and control. We begin to see, in fact, that the active powers of ... capital, in all its possible forms, are our most active enemies and they will have to be not just persuaded – but defeated and superceded ... The different social consciousness of the dispossessed labourers and of the urban workers, born in protest and despair, has to come through in new ways as a collectively responsible society ... It is still in so many places a beautiful country, and many of us can work in different ways to keep it and enhance it. I have had the luck to thin a wood and watch the cowslips and bluebells and foxgloves come back; to repair and rebuild old drystone walls; to hedge the ditch after long neglect, and to see from skilled men how the jobs should be done. And if we look up from the idea of the city, we find in and through the extraordinary pressures a good deal of caring and intelligent work to make the cities cleaner and finer, to bring out their best qualities ... I am convinced that resistance to capitalism is the decisive form of the necessary human defense.'

➤

APRIL 28   *Aptos*
FRED GARDNER GAVE me his copy of the first Harvard and Radcliffe 25th Anniversary Report. The 1,312-page volume is dispatched free of charge to the 1,444 classmates, of whom 275 out of 306 attending Radcliffe sent in reports of their Stories-So-Far, thus establishing a record 90 percent participation, as against the 80 percent participation of the 1,138 Harvard classmates responding. The sixties did self-confession a good turn.

Having graduated from Oxford in 1963, I've spent more or less exactly the same amount of time on earth as the respondents. Like me, they were at college at the time of the Cuban missile crisis, had just graduated when Kennedy was assassinated, were in their mid-to-late twenties at the time of Tet and the May-June events in Paris, spent their thirties during the growth of the women's movement, and entered their forties as Ronald Reagan entered the Oval Office.

The strange thing seems is how little ruling this particular swath of the ruling class seems to be doing. If you searched through the people I was at Oxford with, no doubt you would probably find the due percentage working their way toward the top of the significant bureaucracies and financial institutions, even Parliament. Such respondents whose stories I have studied in the Harvard/Radcliffe book don't seem to have their hands on the levers of power, even if they are as authentically ruling-class as David Rockefeller Jr. ('I am not ashamed to report several ways in which continuity has triumphed over turbulence in my own life'). On the evidence of this group, most thickly clustered in Massachusetts, California and New York (in that order), the ruling-class function is most frequently expressed in the reduplication of the system's values, in teaching.

But more than anything, this sample of the ruling class imagines itself to be happy. Entry after entry glows with satisfaction at a life thus far well-lived. The class of '63 seems to have escaped mortal injury in Southeast Asia or indeed any other battleground of empire, with only one exception in the person of Arthur Stillman, who died in an ambush by Pathet Lao near Vientiane in 1969 while working as deputy chief of International Voluntary Services, and whose daughter I met in Thailand.

The satisfaction comes in varying brands. Somewhat traditional in idiom is the happiness of Terry Bartolet, an orthopedic surgeon: 'My family is my greatest source of joy and inspiration. Ginny has sacrificed many personal aspects of her life for my occupation and pursuit of happiness ... Twenty years after Harvard I still marvel at a beautiful set of legs, still wonder if I ever could have played professional baseball, still wonder why Ford stopped manufacturing two-seater Thunderbirds, still have never smoked grass, still enjoy rock 'n roll, and still am madly in love with my ninth-grade sweetheart, Ginny. Life goes on and in the words of Lee Treviño, "The older I get, the better I used to be."'

'My wife looks down her long nose from her high horse and goes fox hunting', reports emergency physician Roger Branson from Connecticut. 'As near as I can figure, the fox hunt is the pre-internal combustion equivalent of a motorcycle gang. Prosperity is lots of fun.' In more modish idiom Eleanor Wahl Murray reports that 'in 1982 my husband Bruce (Harvard, MBA '66) did "our mid-life crisis." We sold our dream house, cars, furniture and moved aboard our 40-foot sailboat. We spent the next three years following the sun between Maine and the Bahamas. This nomadic existence was idyllic: new vistas, interesting people, great exercise and no boredom. Learning to live with another person (even after twenty years of marriage) was a challenge. Having met the challenge, we came ashore in 1985 and are currently working together at our MicroAge Computer Store in Daytona Beach.'

Divorce, which has happened to a large number of classmates, particularly in the early 1970s, is mostly not represented here as traumatic. 'As I write this', Eric Birch reports, 'the divorce is almost final. I've just passed the three-year mark as a vice-president with Nashua Corporation and am waiting more or less patiently for legal permission to marry the lady I live with ... The children are well, reflecting a caring mother and a generally friendly divorce procedure ...'

≫→

APRIL 29   *Aptos*

THE TUG OF WAR in President Reagan's mind continues. He's said that Gorbachev 'actually is advocating some of the things that Lenin talked about that were not as restrictive and single-minded as Stalin was.'

≫→

APRIL 30   *Aptos*

I'VE FOUND RAYMOND SOKOLOV in the Harvard book. I visited Devil's Island with him in the mid seventies, before going up the Marouini River in a pirogue along with Monsieur Oiseau, who boasted of his enormous penis and the Indians tried to catch him with no trousers on, to see if it was true. I now see Ray editing *The Wall Street Journal*'s Arts Page whenever I fight my way through that newspaper's virtually impenetrable security systems to hand in my own column. Sokolov reports with sarcasm that 'after twenty-five years of postgraduate toil and thirty-four student years of children's private school tuition, I am completely satisfied.' And here is Carter Burden – indisputably ruling class – who owned *The Village Voice* when I first came to New York. He says he is happy, at least strongly implies it. Here's Fred Gardner, franker than most in reporting bruising encounters with drugs as well as the 'organized left' at the time he set up the first GI coffeehouse in 1967.

≫→

MAY 5   *Aptos*

FINISHED THE YEARBOOK: a spell-binding entry by Edward Thomas Hougen:

'The past twenty five years have been for me a rich adventure in the Christian faith. Following my graduation from Harvard, I attended seminary where I met my wife, who was also studying the Christian ministry.

'After getting married, and as a consequence, having some firsthand sexual experience to reflect upon, I came to the conclusion that what the church had taught me concerning the nature and meaning of sexuality was false. I wrote my

B.D. thesis on "An Evaluation of the Contemporary Christian Sex Ethic". In it I argued that the fundamental themes of the Christian faith and scripture neither require nor support a sexual ethic based upon exclusivity and possessiveness.

'Upon completing seminary I was ordained in the United Church of Christ (UCC) and became the associate pastor of the First Congregational Church in South Hadley, Massachusetts. When I attempted to share my thesis with several adult leaders within the congregation in an effort to begin a dialogue on sexual ethics, I learned to my dismay that there was great resistance within the institutional church not only to embracing my ideas but even to examining them. I decided to keep quiet rather than jeopardize my job, which I both enjoyed and in all other areas was rather good.

'Four years later I became the pastor of Central Congregational Church in Orange, Mass. It was in Orange that I joined my wife's example and took a lover. My greater inhibition in putting my sexual ethic into practice I attributed to the fact that my primary sexual preference was homosexual, and I had to unlearn a great deal of internalized homophobia before I was willing to establish an open gay liaison. After several years of practicing in secret what at the time was referred to as an open marriage, I concluded that it was wrong of me to keep silent about my beliefs simply out of fear of professional and social reprisal. In 1975 my wife and I came out publicly concerning our views and practices. We had anticipated that my homosexuality would be the most explosive issue, but we discovered that it was our redefinition of Christian marriage that most shocked and outraged people.

'My wife and I, along with our daughter, five, and our son, three, moved to Boston where I became the pastor of the Metropolitan Community Church (MCC), which was part of a denomination with a special outreach and ministry to the gay community. The first few months were difficult: We were stoned out of the house we rented in Jamaica Plain because of the neighborhood's objection to our values and lifestyle; we were tried by a specially convened ecclesiastical council and dismissed from ministerial standing in the UCC; we lost our middle-class income in the change from a traditional pastorate into MCC. Furthermore, many within the gay community, of which I was now an ostensible leader, looked askance at my choosing to remain married while at the same time openly enjoying a relationship with a male lover. Nevertheless, this was an exhilarating period of growth in my life and faith as I discovered the world of gay activism.

'After years of pastoring MCC Boston, I decided that paying clergy was a mistake that squandered a church's limited resources and focused most of the congregation's energy upon maintaining its own institutional life rather than addressing the needs of the world outside. I served as a part-time volunteer pastor for six months, but when a sizable minority of the congregation continued to oppose this new arrangement, I resigned. My wife and lover and I began to meet regularly as a house church.

'The next three years I worked at various secretarial jobs while applying to law schools. Despite my having scored in the 99 percent on the LSAT, no law school would admit me. I felt very dead-ended. When an openly gay candidate was running for the Boston City Council, my wife persuaded me to quit my job as a data entry operator and become a full-time volunteer in the campaign. I did, and he was narrowly elected.

'While working on the campaign, one of my co-workers asked me if I wanted to take over his gay bar magazine which he had been planning to fold. I bought it for $1, and for the past four years have been publishing a monthly magazine called *The Guide to the Gay Northeast*. During this period the magazine has more than quadrupled its size and circulation; it is currently distributed throughout New England, New York, Philadelphia and eastern Canada. This past year I've begun to clear my modest salary.

'What I have discovered over these years is that it doesn't matter whether one's forum is the pulpit of a traditional church or the pages of a gay bar magazine. In advancing the Christian themes of truth, justice, love, and liberation, one's life is guaranteed to be rich in surprises, blessings and rewards, in my case not the least of which have been my extraordinary wife, children and lover.'

➣→

MAY 9   *Aptos*
BIG FUSS OVER the Reagans' love of astrology. Much of the clucking is being done by people who themselves turn zealously to their favored horoscope. The United States retains, unusually for an advanced industrial society, about the same per capita level of religious superstition as Bangladesh.

At least some astrology is surely just a strategy of female credentialing, alluring to men precisely because it borrows from the myth of the instinctual Eve. It is the twinkling penumbra of Reagan's incandescent belief in the motions of the 'free market'. Submission to the 'laws' of this same utterly imaginary force permits him and his fellow believers to argue that intervention in the market's mysterious workings, to subsidize the needy or house the homeless, is to tinker with an inspired mechanism and court disaster.

➣→

MAY 12   *Aptos*
WHEN A PORTRAIT of the late Mayor Harold Washington dressed in female un-derwear was hung in the School of the Art Institute of Chicago, a delegation of

nine city councilors ripped it from the wall. The painting, called 'Mirth and Girth', was by a student named David Nelson. Marshall Field V, onetime publisher of the *Chicago Sun Times* and the *Chicago Daily News*, now president of the Institute, declared, 'We do not condone the use of the First Amendment to disparage the memory of a great leader like Harold Washington.'

People get very charged up about men wearing women's clothes. I once suggested that *The New Yorker*'s editor, Robert Gottlieb, lighten up by slipping into a cute little nurse's uniform every now and again. Letters poured in from excited readers and my advice was quoted all over the place. At the beginning of *Corruptions* I recalled a phase in my own psychosexual development – I was twelve or so – when I would come down to dinner in a long dress and carefully applied makeup, to the muted disquiet of my parents.

In the latest issue of *Zeta*, Lydia Sargent throws down what she clearly regards as an un-pick-up-able gauntlet by writing, 'I won't wear a dress until I can see Dave Dellinger at a civil disobedience in ... panty hose ... Well, maybe not Dave. Perhaps Alex Cockburn. In that slinky number with very high heels and the sexy underwear.'

Why not? J. took some photographs of me in her slip and some of her clothes. We'll see how they come out.

⇥

MAY 13   *Aptos*
A FELLOW HAS written me an interesting letter about stars and history. It seems that on the evening before Reagan's appearance at Bitburg cemetery there was a concurrence of a full moon while at its perigree with the earth, along with a total eclipse of the moon. Elsewhere in the heavens Saturn, Uranus, Neptune and Pluto appeared to move retrograde. The same four planets appeared retrograde a year later when Reagan bombed Libya. Aleister Crowley fans will be excited to learn that the Defense Logistics Agency Commodity Assignment number for meteorological instruments is 6660.

⇥

MAY 15   *Aptos*
PHILBY DIED IN Moscow on May 11. I suppose there'll be another eruption of spy-mania.

Philby was once asked about the Cambridge spy 'ring' and answered briskly: 'There was no Cambridge ring. It's a load of nonsense invented by journalists and spy writers. I was not recuited at Cambridge. Burgess was not recruited at Cambridge. Blunt was not recruited at Cambridge. Maclean I don't know about, but I doubt it. As to how it all began, when I was a nineteen-year-old undergraduate trying to form my views on life, I had a good look around and I reached a simple conclusion – the rich had had it too damn good for too long and the poor had had it too damn bad and it was time that it was all changed.' Having reached this analysis Philby joined the Cambridge Socialist Society and campaigned for the Labour Party in the 1931 election with a stump speech beginning, 'My friends, the heart of England does not beat in stately homes and castles. It beats in the factories and on the farms.' The betrayal of Labour by Ramsey MacDonald with his coalition 'National Government' sent Philby abroad to see how the left was faring in other countries and when on his return to Britain in the spring of 1934 he was asked if he would like to join the Russian intelligence service, he 'did not hesitate'.

Philby's father St John finally settled in Saudi Arabia, took an Arab name and Arab nationality and worked for King Ibn Saud, doing far more damage to British ruling class interests than his son ever accomplished, by turning the Wahabbbites towards the United States rather than Britain when it came to the allocation of oil concessions.

➡

MAY 16   *Aptos*
GOT THE PHOTOS back of me in J.'s clothes, taken by J. with my old forties Leica. They're wonderful.

➡

MAY 17   *Aptos*
LAST YEAR, POLICE CHIEF Darryl Gates gave homeless people seven days to get off the streets and then started sweeps of the skid row area, carting off makeshift lean-tos, furniture, stoves, etc. He spoke harshly of the 'so-called homeless' and proposed that 'the vast majority are there because of their indulgences ... These people could be given a limousine ride to another area ... They'd come right back here. This is where they want to live.'

Since the early 1970s, unemployment in the South-Central neighborhoods has risen by almost 50 percent while purchasing power has fallen by a third. Since 1981, federal housing assistance has been cut by 70 percent. Not a single unit of public housing has been built in Los Angeles over the past thirty years.

➡

MAY 18   *Aptos*
A TERRIFYING BOOK about the photographer Garry Winogrand. His final phase is very strange. During his last years in Los Angeles he shot 8,522 rolls of film,

made more than 300,000 exposures he never looked at. In his introduction, John Szarkowski says that in these L.A. years Winogrand 'made thousands of pictures from his car, from the right hand seat, while being driven round by Tom Consilvio or another friend on his mysteriously dreamlike daily rounds. As a pedestrian he had come to shoot at anything that moved and from the car everything that moved ... Much of this is difficult to comprehend, or perhaps incomprehensible. If an explanation is necessary one might venture that he photographed whether or not he had anything to photograph, and that he photographed most when he had no subject, in the hope that the act of photographing might lead him to one.'

In the successful images among those hundreds of thousands (which partly gain their strength from one's knowledge that they are successfully seized moments from among precisely such innumerable failed moments), there is the purest essence of Winogrand's instrusive, solipsistic art: the people – man with wallet, girl with snake – are in an absolute state of Otherness, even though temporarily captured by Winogrand's insatiate curiosity. Hence Winogrand's repetitive desperation.

➨

MAY 23   *Aptos*
IS THIS WHERE it is all going to end, the heritage of October, the tradition of Tukhachevsky and Dimitrov, with bilateral commissions adorned by a former chief of the CIA and the head of Novosti, jointly denouncing 'adventurism'? It's enough to make one sympathize with another Leonid, one of the Russians withdrawing from Afghanistan: 'I'm really afraid that the Afghans will start to fight even more fiercely among themselves now and that the bloodshed will be tremendous ... Mine may not be a popular opinion back in Moscow, but I think we did a great deal here for the Afghan people ... They have come to depend on us as they build socialism, and now we are getting out, largely for our own reasons, and leaving them to face a situation even more difficult and complex than that in 1979. Is that fair?'

➨

MAY 27   *Aptos*
ANOTHER THING GORBY might do, apart from asking Raisa Maximovna to give Arbatov and the others a quick refresher course in Lenin's thought, is brisk up his own conversational style. Those great paragraphs he comes out with, billowing like a sultan's knickers, make one yearn for the crusty apothegms of Nikita K.

On May 22 the *Washington Post* published, across many, many pages, what must be the most boring interview in the whole history of journalism. On one side of the table was General Secretary Mikhail Gorbachev and on the other Chairman Katharine Graham, flanked by a horde of subordinates from *Newsweek* and the *Post*:

> GRAHAM: Mr. Gorbachev, the interest in the party conference is so great, could you not perhaps, even in more general terms, discuss your hopes for this meeting, which is obviously such an important event?
> GORBACHEV: I certainly think that my expectations coincide with the expectations of our whole society. First of all, we want to take stock of what has happened over these three years, to sort out the history of *perestroika*, and, of course, we want that analysis of this period to be a critical one. We want to draw lessons – perhaps that will be necessary. And based on that analysis, we may have to take some corrective measures in what we are doing with *perestroika*. But I think the central question is the question of how to deepen this process, how to move forward with *perestroika* and make it irreversible. Therefore, the main questions at the conference will relate to deepening the economic reform and to deepening the democratization of our party and society. This is the main thing.

Really. Chairman Graham and her team were so pleased with this blather that they published a special six-page section to accommodate it, with two whole pages of direct transcript of the ninety-page interview, plus an indirect rehash of this same transcript, plus two more pages of Gorby's written responses to written questions. These are veritable Exocets of ennui.

➤→

MAY 28   *Aptos*

THERE'S PLENTY OF evidence to support my view that the input of Nancy to the nation's business was beneficial. Don Regan reports in his memoir *On the Record* that 'oddly enough, it was Nancy Reagan who brought me into the process.' This 'process' was the formulation of economic policy, an activity from which Secretary of the Treasury Regan had previously been excluded. In the course of a phone call in which the First Lady inquired of the secretary why he had not answered a letter from a friend of her stepbrother worrying about the health of the savings and loan industry, the two fell into a discussion of the economy, and Regan told Mrs. Reagan that bugetary cuts, including defense, were necessary. 'The First Lady agreed, saying that she was upset with the Defense Department and Cap Weinburger. In her opinion, Cap was greedy for funds and had no idea how this was hurting the economy.' Nancy listened some more and then said that Ronnie should be hearing such talk for himself. The next day Ron called up Don, and the President and the Secretary of the

Treasury – this was some time in 1982 – had their first substantive talk about economic policy, which of course revolved around the usual insoluble problem of how to depose the true ruler of the country, Paul Volcker.

➤

JUNE 13   *Aptos*

J.'S PHOTOS OF me dressed in her clothes have come out in *Zeta*. I told Mike and Lydia to print them with no captions. They're going down very well. A chipper young lesbian told me today, 'But they're so *respectful*.'

➤

JUNE 14   *Aptos*

ANDREW V. UPSET about *Zeta* photos. He says, What about Mama? I tell him he's been living inside the beltway too long.

➤

JUNE 18   *Aptos*

ALMOST NOTHING IN life requires more artful preparation than a public apology. Whatever Jane Fonda thought she was doing with Barbara Walters, most Americans, particularly those who did not watch the show, thought she was saying she was sorry she'd been against the Vietnam War, and that since she was speaking as a representative of what used to be called the Movement, there was now unanimity throughout the nation that the war was a good thing. This is the trouble with apologies. Once you start, people never let you stop.

➤

JUNE 21   *Aptos*

HERE AT THE ADOBE MOTEL the problem is the *Zeta* pictures of me in girls' clothes. I showed them to S., the builder downstairs, and he mentioned them to the chap who lives in No. 3, who has me tagged as a child molester as a result. They call their children inside when I appear on the stairs.

➤

JUNE 24   *Aptos*

A FLIGHT ATTENDANT with Philippine Airlines tells J. about an encounter with Imelda Marcos outside a supermarket in Honolulu. Mrs. Marcos was trundling a shopping cart. She looked to be about 200 pounds, but her hairdo was impeccable. She hailed the flight attendant, who had worked many of her flights during better days, crying out, 'And how are my people?' The flight attendant said she just smiled. 'What was I going to say', she pondered later. 'They're better off without you?'

➨

JUNE 29   *Aptos*

HUEY LONG WAS WRONG. Fascism won't come to America dressed as anti-fascism. It will come dressed as a health campaign. New York commuters have beaten up a smoker at a train station, and airlines pummel passengers with announcements of possible legal sanctions against smokers trying to take a puff in the john. Hitler was a rabid anti-smoker and health nut, even though his doctor had him on twenty-eight different drugs by the end of the war. He nibbled his beansprouts while ordering the gassing of Jews.

I quit a three-pack-a-day habit five years ago, and though I can't say I'd die for the right of the man next to me to blow smoke past my face, I don't greatly mind that he does.

➨

JULY 16   *Aptos*

I'VE BEEN BANGED on the knuckles for saying that Harvard doesn't rule in the sense of a ruling class as defined by a Harvard diploma. I missed out the graduate schools. In his book *Who's Running America*, Thomas Dye identified 5,416 elite positions in US society, with the individuals filling those positions being defined as the 'national institutional elite' .

Dye does not give a school-by-school breakdown. But he says that 55 percent of all government leaders are graduates of twelve universities – Harvard, Yale, Chicago, Stanford, Columbia, M.I.T., Cornell, Northwestern, Princeton, Johns Hopkins, Pennsylvania and Dartmouth. Harvard would probably be ranked first if an individual breakdown was made.

➨

JULY 18   *Atlanta*

THE DELEGATES HERE for the Democratic Convention have only to read the Atlanta skyline to understand the way we live now, together and apart. Mies van der Rohe once declared that the destiny of modern architecture was to translate the will of the epoch into space. Whose will has triumphed over Peachtree Street?

The city is appropriate to its guests. The hopes, fantasies, discontinuities and self-deceptions of the Democrats are well set forth on this center stage of New South boosterism. To the newly arrived in Atlanta, heading into town from the airport up I-85, the downtown core suddenly swings into view behind a *cordon sanitaire* of half-completed highways, wastelands of urban clearance, ramparts of concrete and curtains of plate glass: Hyatt, Marriott, Westin Peachtree, Center Omni.

Day into night, from the warm bathwater of street heat the delegates pass through the glass doors into the air-conditioned cool of the expanding internal frontier of the American economy, the bright towers of downtown. Dukakis is at the Hyatt, Jackson at the Marriott, and though they talk of other Americas, forgotten Americas, they are securely lodged in the America of real estate's go-go years in the great construction bubble financed by oil rents, Third World debt, military production and the global rush of fugitive money to its last, best sanctuary.

Those bright towers: sanctuaries, above all, is what they are. With their vast interior 'spaces', their arboreta, glass-covered plazas, fountains, walkways, and malls, they mime the public city of the past, holding the real inner-core city at bay.

➡

JULY 19   *Atlanta*
THE DEMOCRATS IN search of unity are celebrating it in the apotheosis of privatized space, epitaph to the idea of urban reform. Meanwhile the press celebrates, too, the notion of a city that has somehow solved the racial problem, under the governance of cultivated and accessible black people like Mayor Andrew Young, a man in whom the spirit of boosterism breathes so deep that this year he issued an offer, ultimately rescinded, to the military police of Guatemala to come and train in the city 'too busy to hate'.

➡

JULY 20   *Atlanta*
JIMMY CARTER TAUGHT the press to think kindly of Atlanta back in 1976 when he came north with a late edition of the ever-unwinding saga of the 'New South'. In 1978 Bob Scheer went to Atlanta and brought back a rather different story. Carter was wrong, Scheer announced in the *Los Angeles Times:* 'The queen city of the South is a 60 percent black city that floats in a sea of white suburbia whose inhabitants desperately avoid contact with the untouchables – the minority poor that are increasingly segregated off in America's cities ... Despite a huge black middle class and a trickle of white professionals returning to the inner city, Atlanta is increasingly a holding cell for society's rejects ... while the

new, good jobs – and the whites who hold them – congregate in the suburbs.'

Today, beneath the vault of the Marriott's atrium, I bumped into Scheer and he remembered the uproar his article had caused in Atlanta, where the boosters became frantic at the thought of West Coast CEOs planning to relocate their businesses in Atlanta, then reading Bob's article and changing their minds. The head of Georgia-Pacific, about to move his managers from Oregon to Georgia, had to get personal assurances from Atlanta's police chief that his people would not be mugged at the end of their long commute in from the white enclaves of Guinnett County.

➡

AUGUST 3   *New York*

IN THE STORIES I'VE either read or watched about beggars lately the name of Ronald Reagan has barely been mentioned, as though no known connection existed between slashing funds for public housing, attacking welfare programs of one sort and another, and the consequent effect on the targets of these cuts.

A second remarkable quality of these stories is the tremendous hostility expressed toward the homeless. Like many unpleasant media trends, this one appears to have originated with *The New York Times*, whose editors and reporters have to complete their journey to work by walking through the seedy Times Square area, soon to be purged of its riff-raff by developers cheered on, naturally by *The New York Times*.

Today a *Times* editorial laments the fact that the beggars of yesteryear – 'the legless man propelling himself on a little wheeled platform and the sightless man asking for help to buy a seeing-eye dog' – have been replaced by a more aggressive type: 'Unlike the legless and sightless, who merely shook their tin cups, the new beggars speak right up. "Give me a quarter", they order, or "Help me out, lady."' There is a real note of nostalgia, as though the old-style beggars – man on platform, man in need of dog – belonged to some ordered universe now gone. They'll probably show up in wax soon at the Museum of Natural History.

AUGUST 11   *New Orleans*

I CAME ACROSS a marvelous scene-setter for this Republican convention in an essay by Fred Jameson:

'Faceless masters continue to inflect the economic strategies which constrain our existences, but no longer need to impose their speech (or are henceforth unable to); and the postliteracy of the late capitalist world reflects, not only the absence of any great collective project, but also the unavailability of the older language itself. In this situation parody finds itself without a vocation; it has lived, and that strange new thing pastiche comes slowly to take its place. Pastiche is, like parody, the imitation of a peculiar mask, speech in a dead language, but it is a neutral practice of such mimicry, without any of parody's ulterior motives, amputated of the satiric impulse, devoid of laughter and of any conviction that alongside the abnormal tongue you have momentarily borrowed, some healthy linguistic normality still exists. Pastiche is thus blank parody, a statue with blind eyeballs.'

➡

AUGUST 12   *New Orleans*

VELAZQUEZ PAINTED THE Spanish court in the tones of twilight; flesh, even when pink, carried intimations of the grave. Videotape does not like depth of field or shadow, that is to say, a sense of history or decay. The images of our politics are bright or they are nothing, and we lurch through a depthless present, itself only defined as the anticipation of what is coming next week: Iowa caucus, New Hampshire primary, convention, Election Day. Not life but shelf life is the timekeeper.

New Orleans is a fine place in which to consider such things. Only now is its past being irreversibly overwhelmed by pastiche-as-past. It may be a decade before Disney fully claims the Vieux Carré, though a local civil liberties lawyer told me today that one of her frequent tasks is to bail out itinerant street musicians jailed by police on the urging of the saloonkeepers. The cops, this lawyer said, take care to drop and dent the musical instruments as they book their owners. Less than a decade ago the NOPD was putting plastic bags over suspects' heads and letting them suffocate to death.

➡

AUGUST 13   *New Orleans*

THE FABLES OF THE CITY may revolve around jazz, masked balls and Mardi Gras, but the animating essence has always been oil, and throughout Louisiana, Texas and Oklahoma the oil business is on its ass. The consequences will be immediately apparent to any delegate strolling through the French Quarter, where the most conspicuous signs on Burgundy, Perdido, Basin and other streets that evince the early history of jazz are FOR RENT and FOR SALE.

Night after night the Republicans tell each other how well the American dream has fared under their patronage. They shovel down the oysters, go for riverboat rides, stroll decorously through the French Quarter. The city smiles on them with nervous geniality, like a panhandler who cannot believe his luck and is unsure how long it will last. Indeed, the city has decided to remind delegates tactfully not to wander too far from the beaten track. New Orleans is a desperate city. Some 26 percent live below the poverty line and about 50 percent could be classified as poor. On any measure of a city's socioeconomic welfare, New Orleans almost always appears at the bottom of the 'good' indexes and near the top of the 'bad' ones. The statistic the city sometimes likes to flaunt is that it has the highest number of millionaires per capita among America's fifty largest cities.

➤

AUGUST 15   *New Orleans*

LAST NIGHT, a glowing evening, I walked up Chartres Street toward Jackson Square. In a yellow mansion with neoclassical portico on my left, Paul Morphy, the first American chess champion, was born in 1837.

New Orleans, the greatest port city of the New World, crested just as Morphy was conquering the chess salons of Europe. According to Lyle Saxon's *Fabulous New Orleans*, which I found today, the last great season came in 1859: the largest receipts of produce, the heaviest and most profitable trade the city had ever done. The total river trade that year was valued at $289,565,000.

On April 24, 1862, New Orleans fell to the Federal forces: Farragut's fleet managed to penetrate the blockade at the river's mouth. News came that Federal ships had passed the two forts below New Orleans. The wildest confusion followed. Lest they fall into the hands of the enemy, 12,000 bales of cotton were rolled from the warehouses and set on fire. Next, tobacco and sugar depots were put to the torch. Ships on the Mississippi, loaded with cotton, were burning too, and the sparks leaped to the steamboats. The Mississippi was aflame. As Saxon puts it, 'Gutters flowed molasses; sugar lay like drifted snow along the sidewalks.' New Orleans was sacked by its own people. The years of poverty and misery began.

With misery came more masks, though it had actually been in 1857 that some young men from Mobile paraded during Mardi Gras as the Mystick Krewe of Comus, thus augmenting the traditional *bals masqués* of the Creoles. In 1870 came the Twelfth Night Revellers. Then, in 1872, Alex Alexandrovich Romanov, brother to the Czar-apparent, was in town for carnival. They organized a parade for him, headed by a makeshift monarch, 'Rex', parody of the real thing. In honor of the signature tune of a music-hall queen favored by the Russian prince, they sang, over and over, 'If Ever I Cease to Love'.

The krewes swelled as the years slipped by: 1890, the Elves of Oberon; 1897, the High Priests of Mithras. In 1916 the first black krewe, the Zulu Social Aid and Pleasure Club, in skirts, mimicked the mimicry of Rex by making the Zulu King's royal way the Basin Street canal, and his imperial float a skiff.

As in the 'life upside down' banquets of the Middle Ages, the parades and the masks parodied or at least underlined the actual nature of things. The young men from Mobile back in 1857 explained their name – the Mystick Krewe of Comus – as representing 'the Demon Actors of Milton's Paradise Lost'. At least that's what the local paper reported. In late Greek mythology Comus was the god of festive mirth. Milton gave him Circe and Bacchus as parents, the deities of sorcery and wine that can make men reveal themselves in their lower natures. As Errol Laborde, historian of Mardi Gras, describes it, 'In the waning moments of the Carnival season, Rex and his queen greet Comus and his queen. Carnival custom recognizes Rex as the symbol of the people and Comus as the symbol of tradition and high society. It is more than symbolic that in this ceremonial conclusion of Carnival, Rex bows to Comus – in this act, the people bow to society.'

The original mask was that of the sorcerer, presentiment of magic and terror, and however nonchalant by comparison, the mask still carries an aroma of the uncanny with its mocking commentary on nature and the 'unnatural', society and the antisocial, the perverse modes of player king and drag queen. From demonic possession to rational mime, the mask celebrates, like Velázquez, depth of field and shadow: I was what I am not now, nor am I now what I will be. At the heart are defiance and challenge, whether in the Quadroon Balls of the last century or the Gay Balls of today, where 'memento mori' stalks the halls.

➡

AUGUST 16   *New Orleans*
FROM MASK TO PASTICHE, from the street where two homosexuals were animatedly discussing their costumes for next year's carnival to the Superdome last night, where I spent some time, at a distance of twenty yards or so, scrutinizing the masks of Ron and Nancy Reagan. Simulacrum and 'reality', smile and greasepaint grin, merriment and the mime of a 'hearty laugh', have become so overlaid that one is not watching the fleeting history of emotion and thought but rather a series of mimetic adjustments. The President's body sat there, not at all like a human frame reposing in the moments before public oratory, but as Reagan-at-rest extruding not a tincture of emotion until impelled by some unnoticed command into Reagan-amused, the briefest of smiles soon being dismissed in favor of the somber passivity one associates with the shrouded figure in some newly opened tomb before oxygen commences its mission of decay.

Nancy Reagan presented herself as face-enjoying-a-speech, eyes akimbo and lips strained back slightly though not parted. It, too, wore no intimations of the pleasures or sufferings of life, even though my pocket held a proof sheet from a new book suggesting in retrospect more strenuous adjustments of the lips. 'I can remember', Patricia Seaton Lawford writes in *The Peter Lawford Story,* 'when Peter was watching the news right after Reagan was elected. He went over to the set, laughing and calling Mrs. Reagan a vulgar name. I was shocked and wanted to know what was bothering him. He laughed again and said that when she was single, Nancy Davis was known for giving the best head in Hollywood. Then Peter told of driving to the Phoenix area with Nancy and Bob Walker [according to Lawford, an *amour* of Nancy at the time]. Nancy would visit her parents, Dr. and Mrs. Loyal Davis, while Peter and Walker picked up girls at Arizona State University in Tempe, a Phoenix suburb. He claimed that she entertained them orally on those trips, apparently playing with whichever man was not driving at the moment. I have no idea if Peter was telling the truth, though I have to assume that he was because Peter was not one to gossip.'

Mrs. Lawford's purpose in advancing this startling and not unattractive proposition about Mrs. Reagan was to describe a similar passage from history to pastiche, from the leaven of experience to the blind eyes of those statues gazing out across the floor of the Superdome. By the early 1940s, the studio publicity department was already turning R.R. into a war hero. By day he would work in 'Fort Wacky' in Culver City, where they made military training films. Experts would take old stock footage of Japan and then edit it as though viewed through a gun sight. This not only helped gunners in planes about to make sorties over Japan but was also used as live-action 'newsreels' for American audiences craving combat footage. The fanzines discussed the loneliness of R.R.'s first wife, Jane Wyman, her absent man (a few miles away in Fort Wacky, home by suppertime) and her knowledge of R.R.'s hatred of the foe. 'She'd seen Ronnie's sick face', *Modern Screen* reported in 1942, 'bent over a picture of the small swollen bodies of children starved to death in Poland. "This", said the war-hating Reagan between set lips, "would make it a pleasure to kill."'

Forty years later R.R. would tell Yitzhak Shamir, then foreign minister of Israel, that he had helped liberate Auschwitz, had returned to Hollywood with film of the ghastly scenes he had witnessed, and if in later years anyone controverted the reality of the Holocaust over the Reagan dinner table, he would roll the footage till the doubts were stilled. Of course, R.R. never left Fort Wacky, which has led cynics to suggest that the Auschwitz–Fort Wacky conflation truly establishes R.R. as the first postmodern President. Just as postmodern history signifies pastime and culture by appropriating stereotypical emblems (the French Quarter slowly becoming a 'French Quarter', the masked 'Rex' becoming Bob Hope, Cajun cooking blackening into 'Cajun cooking', the volcanic ash garnishing the Pompeian culture of the Reagan age), so, too, do the postmodern politicians appropriate signage and emblems suitable to their pretensions but utterly divorced from the reality of their lives.

The heartening, unpostmodern aspect of R.R. was that he was after all an actor, and everyone knew it. Fort Wacky was there large as life on his C.V., which is why, try as they might to invent him as the most popular President and potent communicator, the media could never compel the American People to forget that R.R.'s log cabin was Fort Wacky.

➤

AUGUST 18   *New Orleans*

REPUBLICAN WOMEN, in their proximate physical aspect, have an undercurrent of erotic violence or ill-pent sadism that doesn't really come through on camera. Rooted under the rostrum and peering up into Jeane's Kirkpatrick's flaring nostrils, I could see planes of her face normally flattened out in the bland imagery of videotape. She was talking of 'national security' with her lips puckered in a *moue* of delicious cruelty as she foretold how Dukakis and the Democrats would leave America bound and helpless beneath the Russian jackboot. The only jackboot I could keep in mind was hers: Jeane lashing savagely at the cuffed and whimpering body of effete liberalism; I Bloom to her Bella. Bow, bondslave, before the throne of your despot's glorious heels, so glistening in their proud erectness. What is it about these conservative women, Kirkpatrick, Schlafly, Thatcher, Angela Lansbury in *The Manchurian Candidate* – queen bees throbbing in the hive? Perhaps conservative men can accept women in politics only when set in a Victorian psychospiritual frame – the demon mother – and when women of humane outlook start gaining too high a profile, the men hold their sides and start talking about Fonda and Abzug.

It's mostly a matter of camera angles, and even here an original sight line – a 90-degree downward look at a white-faced Dan Quayle marching down a corridor behind his bodyguard – does not last long because there is not much of a backstage in postmodern politics. Larry Speakes describes, in a memoir of his life as White House press secretary, how one evening he made his way up to the Reagans' private quarters, entered silently and found them in their dressing gowns, wearing spectacles, watching television coverage of Oliver North. Mrs. Reagan was muttering 'Not funny, sonny' at North's image as Speakes entered, which gave him a 'backstage anecdote', but the larger truth is that R.R. and Nancy were just feeding at the same image trough as everyone else.

➤

AUGUST 19   *New Orleans*

EMPTINESS IN LANGUAGE reflects emptiness in soul. The last time a political convention augured any serious challenge to business as usual, to the American corporate state, was nearly a hundred years ago, the 1890s; and language had vigor and content. The Populist platform of 1892, written mostly by Ignatius Donnelly, began, 'The conditions which surround us best justify our co-operation; we meet in the midst of a nation brought to the verge of moral, political, and material ruin. Corruption dominates the ballot-box, the Legislatures, the Congress, and touches even the ermine of the bench. The people are demoralized ... The newspapers are largely subsidized or muzzled, public opinion silenced, business prostrated, homes covered with mortgages, labor impoverished, and the land concentrating in the hands of capitalists ... The fruits of the toil of millions are boldly stolen to build up colossal fortunes for a few, unprecedented in the history of mankind; and the possessors of those, in turn, despise the Republic and endanger liberty. From the same prolific womb of government injustice we breed the two great classes – tramps and millionaires.'

A hundred years ago it seemed remotely possible that Rex could menace Comus. In fact it was already too late. The rural Populists would have had a chance of replacing the Democrats only if they could have formed an alliance with the Knights of Labor. Efforts had been made to this end, but by the late 1880s the Knights had been crushed. In 1896, in their convention in St. Louis, the Populists nominated William Jennings Bryan, already designated by the Democrats two weeks earlier as their man to run against the Republican McKinley. At that convention in Chicago, Bryan made what was probably the single most powerful speech at any convention before or since, concluding with the famous lines against the gold standard: 'You shall not press down upon the brow of labor this crown of thorns. You shall not crucify mankind upon a cross of gold.' Immediately after this, Bryan stood for a full five seconds in the posture of a crucified man as the audience sat transfixed by his performance.

People who remember only the lines about the cross of gold should study the rest of the speech to see how public political oratory has slowly shriveled and dried in the century following the defeat of Bryan by McKinley, in an election that Lawrence Goodwyn called 'the triumph of the corporate state'. For with the end of the Populists came 'the last substantial effort at a structural alteration of hierarchical economic forms in modern America.'

➤

AUGUST 20   *New Orleans*

THE FINAL IMAGE on the rostrum at Atlanta was the irruption of family – Dukakis's, Bentsen's, Jackson's, even unto the last cousin and unto the third generation. The Republicans took it as a serious political challenge and last night stocked the stage in the Superdome with a hatch of Quayles and a veritable herd of Bush kin: large white ones, 'little brown ones' stampeding in, wave upon wave, in demonstration of genetic brio.

This is Family, this is America, said the Omni and Superdome stages, as if in answer to two central topics of the age of Reagan: AIDS and family violence, notably child abuse. Bruce Anderson's brother, Ken, writes in the *AVA* about 'psychiatric child care' at Trinity School in Ukiah and describes (under pseudonyms) some of the boys: 'D.C. spent two years at Trinity before he finally ran away for good. This bright, intelligent fourteen-year-old was a victim long before he got to Trinity, suffering frequent beatings and sexual abuse in his lower-working-class home. Compounding his problems was an almost fanatical "Christian" family facade, within which incessant "religious" conversation and activities hid the reality of this child's twisted, painful life. Partly because of an incestuous relationship with a sister, and mostly because of the contorted guilt that his "Christian" family managed to inflict on D.C. for the things that happened to him, D.C. was a confused, complex mess. While at Trinity, he exhibited a warm and lovable empathy for others, in addition to bizarre, self-destructive behavior. He often injured himself (cuts, broken bones, bruises from pounding his head against the wall, etc.) and he had numerous sexual encounters where he "gave head" to other boys ... He entered as a "disturbed" twelve-year-old and he left as a "disturbed" fourteen-year-old.'

'Lee', Ken Anderson went on, 'is a twelve-year-old black boy from a California city. His mother tortured, whipped and beat him regularly for years. Lee ... fears and hates authority figures, especially women ... We fear his rages, but much of the time he is talented, bright and lovable ... If he doesn't get serious therapeutic help before he is a grown man, he will go on to become a rapist and a murderer. I don't want to say that, but it's so. Gene is a Trinity "success story". Coming from a background of sexual abuse and beatings ... his "passive-aggressive" personality was easily channeled into Trinity's program, which places high value on obedience and servility ... Still, Gene is a walking time-bomb of anger and resentment – not a healthy way to go through life.'

But what of Jackson, the only major politician in America with any serious words for, or rapport with, D.C. and Lee and Gene? In Atlanta, his speech had elements of jive, and also a potent theme of religious quietism with its celebration of his mother's quilt and its message of unity (or, as the Anglican hymn similarly put it, more crudely, 'The rich man in his castle/the poor man at his gate / God made them high and lowly / God gave them their estate'). In Atlanta as in New Orleans, Rex had doffed his cap and given Comus his due.

➡

AUGUST 21   *New Orleans*
THE REPUBLICANS HAVE headed home. Ron Ridenhour and Mary Howell took J. and me for a late-night tour. We swung by some of the better housing projects – Iberville, St. Thomas – scheduled for demolition. The boosters look forward to the day when the whole shoreline will be a monument to the social and aesthetic values of the Raus Corporation, with the poor driven away into hinterland ghettos.

I'd talked to Ridenhour earlier in the year, on the twentieth anniversary of the massacre at My Lai. The anniversary hadn't attracted too much attention. That trench filled with 583 bodies – Vietnamese men, women and children systematically killed by soldiers in Charlie Company over a number of hours starting at 7:30 a.m., March 16, 1968, recorded later that day by US Army photographer Ron Haeberle – did not figure much in retrospectives of the 1960s. But My Lai became the war crime of choice, and its ultimate exposure in the United States was due entirely to Ridenhour's courage. Without Ridenhour there would have been no Army investigation, no Seymour Hersh, nothing; except perhaps the memorial in Vietnam listing the 583 victims by name. The NLF had reported the massacre right away, but no one in America paid any attention.

'Did we learn anything?' Ridenhour said to me. 'A lot of Americans learned, a lot of middle-class people learned, "Gosh, these guys will do anything." I learned that. The motherfuckers will do anything. There really are no limits.'

Ron works here for a magazine called *City Business*. He just won an award for local reporting, on graft in the city government. In March of 1967 he was twenty, living in Arizona, and had just been drafted. He had shipped to Hawai'i in September and trained in long-range reconnaissance with men who ended up being assigned to Charlie Company, under the command of Lieutenant William Calley. Ron was assigned to helicopter observation in Vietnam and later to a recon unit.

'Right after My Lai', he recalled, 'a lot of these guys in Charlie Company started to transfer back into long-range reconnaissance. The first guys I ran into, I said, "Hey, what have you guys been doing?" And they said, "Oh, man, did you hear what we did at Pinkville?"

'I said, "No, what's Pinkville?" It was a village; that's what they called My Lai at the time, Pinkville. He tells me this story about how they went in and massacred all those people. When I heard that, I was horrified; my response was pretty much instantaneous. I wanted to get away from it, and I thought the only way I could do that, not be part of it, would be to discover whether it was true, and if it was true, to denounce it. To act against it in some way.

'I proceeded to do that. Every time I ran into someone who had been with that unit, I'd say, "Hey man, what happened?" These young men were traumatized and horrified that they had been involved in this. Now, all the time I was compiling this information I didn't have anyone I could – it was a very precarious situation, as you can imagine.'

'Did you think someone might kill you?'

'Well, I didn't know. I mean, these guys had just been involved in a massacre.'

'You were making notes?'

'I was keeping a notebook in my head. I did go down to 23rd Division office and obtain the official account of that action, which of course was quite different from what actually occurred. I took some notes on that. Everything else I just kept in my head.

'For my first five missions four of the people I went out with were veterans of My Lai. Two were good friends and two not such good friends, and I didn't know what their reaction would be if they knew what I was intending to do, so I just didn't tell anybody. About two weeks before I left, I ran into a friend who had been in the unit in Charlie Company. I'd heard from other friends that he had been opposed to what happened, had seen what was coming and had not participated. He was in a hospital with a terrible case of jungle rot, waiting to go home. I went over to the hospital and we conversed for a while until we sort of decided we were both coming from the same place. We agreed that we would try to get an investigation going, that we would stay in touch, and if they came and asked him questions, that he would tell the truth.'

A few weeks later Ridenhour shipped home. He tried to figure out what to do and consulted friends. Most of them told him to forget it, but in the end someone suggested that he write a letter to his local Congressman. Ridenhour decided to write such a letter, detailing what he knew, how he came to know it; to demand an investigation; and to send the letter to a whole lot of people. In December 1968 he had a relapse of malaria. When he got out of the hospital he began to write. The letter took six weeks to complete. Someone proofread it; someone else typed it. Ridenhour made 200 copies and sent out 30 of them on March 29, 1969. One went to his Congressman, Mo Udall, whose office responded almost immediately. Udall's administrative assistant asked permission to circulate the letter to the House Armed Services Committee, of which Udall was a member. Its chair, Mendel Rivers, was requested to demand a Pentagon investigation.

By April 30 the Pentagon, which claims it was acting on receipt of a copy of Ridenhour's letter and not under pressure from Rivers, had appointed an investigating team, headed by a colonel.

'I was in Arizona, waiting to go to school and working in a popsicle factory', Ridenhour said. 'They came and interviewed me, and then some of the people I mentioned in the letter – maybe five other soldiers – gave them more names. It sort of bumped and grinded along from late April to September, when they charged Calley. I was convinced there was a cover-up going on, that these guys were not sincere in pursuing the business. They stopped accepting my calls. Then they called me and said they arrested Calley. I waited to see what would happen, and then, when no one else was arrested, I knew what they were going to do. They were going to flush Calley, claim that this was the act of a wild man and then let it go. That's when I started trying to get in touch with the press.'

He talked to a man from *The Arizona Republic*. Nothing got published. The Army had put out a brief statement – two paragraphs long – saying that it had charged a lieutenant, Calley, with the murder of an unknown number of civilians. The Associated Press carried the story, but no one picked it up. Then Seymour Hersh interviewed Calley, who was being held at Fort Benning.

Hersh's first story prompted *The Arizona Republic* to print its article, which Hersh, in turn, saw. He flew out to talk to Ridenhour, who gave him the names and addresses of the people who had been at My Lai. Hersh asked Ridenhour to hold the story from anyone else for three days and went about his business. 'I was glad to give him the three days', Ridenhour said. 'He was the first person to respond. He went off and started finding these other kids, and they told him these horrible stories.'

Ridenhour wanted to make a point. 'The important thing is, this was an act of policy, not an individual aberration. My Lai didn't happen because Lieutenant Calley went berserk. There were similar acts of policy all over the country. I mean, every once in a while they decided they would make an example. If you read about the cover-up, you'll see that above My Lai were helicopters filled with the entire command staff of the brigade, division and task force. All three tiers in the chain of command were literally flying overhead all morning, while it was going on. It takes a long time to kill almost 600 people. It's a dirty job, you might say. These guys were flying overhead from 7:30 in the morning, when the unit first landed and began to move into those hamlets. I think the command units didn't get there till 9 a.m. They were there at least two hours, at 500 feet, 1,000 feet and 1,500 feet.

'So did we learn anything? Yes, we learned to have brown boys pull the trigger instead of good American boys. The policy continues. We continue to make war on civilians across the world. We've got black boys killing black people in Africa. It's our money that's paying for it. That's the lesson the Pentagon, the policy-makers learned. Like I say, a lot of Americans learned, the motherfuckers will do anything.'

As we drove along through the New Orleans streets some garish murals hovered into view. These have been painted by prisoners under the care of Criminal Sheriff Charles Foti, who conceived the idea of decorating his prison with displays of wars of aggression in the history of the United States. Apparently, for this reason, seemingly, World War II is not featured. Subsequently, Sheriff Foti launched his charges on a new project: depictions of enormous faces of women – chilly bitch goddesses, exquisitely painted by captive men.

At the foot of Canal Street near the Spanish Plaza, we came upon a landmark celebrating the Battle of Liberty Place. Early in 1874, a group of anti-Reconstruction zealots formed the White League, dedicated to the return of white supremacy. In August they murdered six Republican officials in Red River parish, and in September they launched an insurrection. On September 14, 3,500 White Leaguers defeated an equal number of black militiamen and police officials. They occupied City Hall, the Statehouse and the arsenal and withdrew only when President Grant sent Federal troops to the scene.

The monument records this episode. On its sides are four different descriptions of the battle and references to 'colored troops' and the glories of 'white supremacy.' Unsurprisingly, the Klan has long used the monument as a focus for its rallies. Not so long ago there were demands from the black community that the monument be torn down. The city rose to the occasion in an appropriately postmodern manner, covering the offensive text with granite slabs. But the plaques have been pulled off and the words are visible once more.

➤➔

AUGUST 28   *Houston*

MY FAVORITE PHOTOGRAPH of the campaign so far is of Lloyd Bentsen dandling an infant in his arms, a spectacle that in and of itself carries about as much pastoral authenticity as former Secretary of the Interior James Watt kitted out in a flannel camping shirt pretending in his hour of crisis to be Jim Bridger reborn. The infant held a stethoscope and was seemingly trying to discern a heartbeat within the suited bosom of the chairman of the Senate Finance Committee, now Vice Presidential candidate.

The actual effect of Bentsen on Dukakis has been for the former to define the latter's campaign by dint of negative gravitational force. Dukakis's only strategy is the one that earned him the nomination: waiting for other people to make mistakes and not being Jesse Jackson. He refused to mention the three slain civil rights workers, even though he was speaking in Philadelphia, Mississippi on the twenty-fourth anniversary of their murder. Admirers of Dukakis like to say that deep down he is a doughty liberal, puissant in principle, ruby-eyed in ardor. Once installed in the White House, with 'Reagan Democrats' lured to his banner, he will tear off the false whiskers of Bentsen and become the 'real Mike Dukakis'; but as we know from Roland Barthes, who castigated the bourgeois passion for thinking in essences, there is no real Dukakis any more than there was a real Reagan or a real Jimmy Carter. They are what they are at each successive moment of self-definition of what they feel they should be, just as with Cressida when she shuttled across the lines at Troy, in my favorite Shakespeare play.

➤➔

SEPTEMBER 1   *El Paso*

THE IDEA THAT DEEP DOWN, under the greasepaint of the Reaganista, there's a 'good' Bush is to make this mistake of supposing that each person has fundamental characteristics which stay with them from cradle to grave. Particularly in politics you are what you become.

The thing you notice pretty soon about George Bush is that he does shameful things in that peculiarly upper-class shameless way which stems from the useful sense that it's not really him – Bush – who is doing these awful things, but some other false-Bush, momentarily pinch-hitting for true-Bush.

➤

SEPTEMBER 2   *Boonville, California*
Dear Mr. President:
As you obviously know, there are many of us who consider you the anti-Christ from the Book of Revelations because (1) it says his name would number 666, and your three names each contain 6 letters; (2) it says he would cause everyone to carry a mark with the number of his name in their hand, and, when Governor of California, your administration introduced the now ubiquitous Universal Pricing Code, subliminally encoded with the line designation for the number 6 at the beginning, middle, and end of every single UPC mark. Finally, why did your friends buy you a retirement home in Los Angeles at 666 St. Cloud Street as reported in the *San Francisco Chronicle* 4/30/87? Well, whether you are 666 or not, you certainly are a beast, and your kingdom, a whore!
                                    May you be sucked out the ozone hole,
                                                        JonEric
                                                        Fort Bragg

I never knew the thing about the pricing code. The Beast is everywhere.

➤

SEPTEMBER 4   *Aptos*
SO DAN QUAYLE DODGED VIETNAM. In times of war you learn quick enough who has got money in the bank. At the time of the Civil War, draftees could buy their way out by purchasing substitutes to do the fighting for them. The going rate was about $300 in 1860s money, just under $4,000 today, which isn't too bad. The word used to be that no Congressperson's son ever fought in Vietnam, though I can't say I have checked this. Fred Gardner tells me that only two major league athletes ended up there: Garry Maddox, an outfielder for the Giants, and Rocky Bleier, a running back for the Pittsburgh Steelers.

➤

SEPTEMBER 5   *Aptos*
ACCORDING TO MIDNIGHT NOTES #9, done by Peter Linebaugh and friends in Massachusetts, if we distinguish two major American postwar eras – 1947-73, when the weekly wage rose 2.3 percent a year on average, and 1974-87, when

the weekly wage fell 1 percent a year on average – and then calculate the average percentage of estimated worktime in 'days idle' because of work stoppages involving 1,000 or more workers per year in each period, we get .17 percent for the earlier period and .08 percent in the later one. Roughly speaking this constitutes a 53 percent drop in workers' militancy. There's a correlated rise in drug abuse and murder, which is now the fourth-ranked cause of death in the United States, after heart attack, cancer and accidents. Capitalism obviously prefers murders to strikes. Most murders are committed by the poor against the poor anyway.

➻

SEPTEMBER 8 *Paris*

BY NIGHT, in honor of the impending anniversary of the French Revolution, one of the networks is running American films about the events of 1789. I watch a bit of the 1938 *Marie Antoinette*, with Robert Morley playing Louis XVI. There were gnarled sans-culottes howling for his head, and there was Tyrone Power trying to save the doomed queen.

Membership in the Happy Enders Club compelled me to switch off before the royals got nabbed on the flight to Varennes. Under Happy End rules settled by me and my brother Andrew you can root for the king in the cliff-hanger of the flight to Varennes, even though on the larger scale you root for the larger Happy End of the overthrow of the monarchy. The film was directed by W.S. Van Dyke, known as One-Take Woody, and the script was tarted up by Donald Ogden Stewart. It was Morley's first film, and he became no stranger to the pasteboard crown, later playing Louis XI and George III. Of course the jewel of his histrionic career was the role of Peterson in *Beat the Devil.*

➻

SEPTEMBER 10 *Paris*

THE NOVELIST DANIELLE MEMOIRE peered shyly around the Closerie des Lilas and confided that as a matter of fact her husband, Guillaume des Forêts, was the great-great-great-great-nephew of Charlotte Corday. When Danielle was a schoolgirl her grandfather in the Perigueux used to close the shutters of his house on July 14 and wear black on January 21, the anniversary of Louis's ascent to the scaffold. 'So far as I can remember', Danielle said sourly, 'Lenin died on January 21, and if my grandparents ever invite me again I'll say I'm wearing black to honor Lenin.'

I told Danielle that when I was growing up, a staple of the library of my prep school was the novels of Baroness Orczy relating the deeds of the Scarlet Pimpernel. Danielle nodded. 'Maybe things have changed, but for schoolchildren of my generation, now in their forties, there was a kind of cult round the revolution. I think I had the two sides of the story. The horror, the death of the King and of Marie Antoinette – these were the staples of the illustrated right-wing magazines. In the left-wing press appeared edifying stories about the characters of the revolution. The French Communists took Robespierre, Saint-Just and Marat as their heroes. At our school we heard a lot about Danton.'

'What do your children learn today about the revolution?'

'Not much. They don't favor French history as much as they used to. In my youth a large proportion of the professors at the *lycées* were Communists passionate about political history, so they taught it. But they're slowly becoming extinct. You know, school was a kind of republican idea, so the revolution had a kind of mythical status in our elementary school classes.'

Danielle laughed. 'I know some Maoists. They had a conference on the French Revolution, and their main speaker was a reclusive philosopher who'd spent years studying the period. He went to the podium, said nothing for the longest time, and then announced, "There was only one revolution – the French Revolution." There was thunderous applause.'

➤

SEPTEMBER 11   *Paris*
IT WAS ROBESPIERRE who said, 'If the basis of popular government in time of peace is virtue, the basis of popular government in time of revolution is both virtue and terror: virtue without which terror is murderous, terror without which virtue is powerless.' This is not at all what a bunch of Social Democrats running France in the age of the Fifth Republic want to be quoting this year and next. The official program has a lot of virtue and positively no terror, at least on the evidence of their calendar of upcoming events.

Among such events: March 21, symbolic planting of the Liberty Tree, 'renewing', as the bicentennial prospectus says, 'the tradition of symbolic ceremonies of the revolution'. Back in the early 1790s earnest Jacobins, who nourished their Liberty Trees and held solemn neoclassical ceremonies in support of the Supreme Being, had to protect these trees against devout Christians. The believers liked to urinate on them and, if given half a chance, pull them up. Many trees had little fences round them. The de-Christianization campaign was pushed along by such men as Joseph Fouché, a former teacher from the south of France and one of the few principals of the revolution to die in bed. He ended up as Napoleon's chief of police. During the revolution, Fouché ordered the words 'Death is nothing but eternal sleep' to be put by the gates of every cemetery in France.

In Strasbourg's Feast of Reason, on 30 Brumaire, Year II of the revolution (November 30, 1793), citizens led by girls dressed in white carried a bust of

Marat into the cathedral (renamed the Temple of Reason), over whose doors were placed the tricolor and a placard reading LIGHT AFTER DARKNESS. In the nave was a symbolic mountain with statues of Nature and Liberty on top and on the sides monsters with human faces half-buried in rock, symbolizing the frustrated powers of superstition. The 10,000-strong gathering sang a hymn to Reason, and then there was a bonfire on the altar of the remains of saints beatified by the Court of Rome and a few Gothic parchments.

'June 1989', the prospectus continues piously, 'will be the month of frater-nity, in memory of June 1789, when people expressed the desire for modern-ization and democratization.' You could put it like that. What Laignelot bellowed at the Jacobins of Brest was, 'The people will not be truly free until the last king has been strangled in the entrails of the last priests.'

The prospectus: 'From April 1 to November 15 in the Tuileries there will be masques, games, spectacles designed to evoke what happened between 1789 and 1799, putting the accent on institutional reform, which marked the progress of parliamentary democracy.' This would have made Saint-Just smile, given his pithy view that 'long laws are public calamities'.

'There were never so many plays in Paris as during the revolution', Bruno Villien told me. 'If you left a basement empty it turned into a theater. Lots of plays were about current events, on a day-to-day basis. The storming of the Bastille was performed on the stage two days later. Some of the actual partici-pants in the storming turned up and played their roles. People jumped up on the stages a lot and argued about what was being said. At Talma's first big hit, *Charles IX*, there were huge riots.'

It was like a newsreel. People went to the theater to find out what was happening and to swap news. The practice continued under Napoleon, who was an ardent theatergoer, dropping long memoranda on Talma about technique and tragic theory. Before the curtain went up they would announce the outcome of battles and the names of casualties.

➤→

SEPTEMBER 12   *Paris*

THE FRENCH GOVERNMENT seems to have decided to remember a revolution occurring between 1789 and 1792: Mirabeau, Danton and the Girondins who, with a little touch-up here and there, can be made to look like decent moderate social democrats of the late twentieth century. Robespierre, Saint-Just and the great Committee of Public Safety, who presided over the Terror and saved the revolution, have not been invited.

Lizzy Lennard has tracked down busts of Robespierre and Saint-Just. She talked to the keeper of monuments. It turned out to be as difficult as finding a statue of Trotsky in the Soviet Union. Lizzy said there was, by the sound of it, a sensational bust of Robespierre in the Musée de la Revolution at the Chateau de Vizille, a few kilometers outside Grenoble.

➤

SEPTEMBER 13   *Grenoble*

WE WENT TO the Gare de Lyon and mounted a *train de grande vitesse*. France – rural, succulent, remote – flicked past our window as we surged southeast toward Grenoble, birthplace of Stendhal; toward Vizille, sometimes described as the 'birthplace of the revolution', since a 'prerevolutionary event', leading up to the meeting of the Estates-General, occurred there in 1788.

The chateau looked as though it had been devised by a Hollywood designer as a suitable spot for the revolution to have got under way, amid mountains – the Belledonne, Vercors, Chartreuse; mist rose from the river. Ducks swam in the pond. In the distance was the gap through which Napoleon marched on his way from Elba to Paris.

Greeted by Philippe Bordes, bilingual director of the four-year-old museum, who was educated at Stanford, the Courtauld, and the Sorbonne. He led us along stone-flagged passages to the bust, which was indeed sensational. Normal portraits and busts of Robespierre portray the 'Incorruptible' as a prig, self-satisfied beneath his wig. In fact this bust, by a Jacobin called Claude-André Deseine, deaf and dumb from birth, is the only one of Robespierre from life, modeled while he addressed the Jacobin club.

In the late afternoon light, with snow drifting onto the Belledonne, Robespierre looked humorous and human, the orator of the great speech on democracy of February 5, 1793: 'We wish to substitute in our country morality for egotism, probity for a mere sense of honor, the empire of reason for the tyranny of custom ... May France, illustrious formerly among people of slaves, eclipse the glory of all free peoples that have existed, be the terror of oppressors, the consolation of the oppressed, the ornament of the universe; and in sealing our work with our blood may we ourselves see at last the dawn of universal felicity gleam before us. That is our ambition. That is our aim.'

Bordes is one of the younger generation of art scholars interested in excavating the revolution as a period of immense artistic ferment – an enthusiasm, he remarked, stemming from his years at Stanford in the late 1960s. 'I don't think one can understand Romanticism without taking into account the Terror. If you look at our catalogue on the iconography and history of the guillotine, there are very strong, frightful images that come from having lived through the Terror. There was an intensity in that period that destabilized the emotional equilibrium of people living through it, and at the same time there was a loss of faith in rational procedures for change, of rational hopes for a better life. The Terror is an *échec*, a failure of the Enlightenment's efforts to reorganize society.

Out of all this disillusion comes a sensibility that is very important for Romanticism.'

As with the theater, in art the revolution changed the rules of the game. Before it only artists at the academy were fully regarded as 'artists'. With its onset hundreds of artists emerged, submitting work on their own initiative.

The revolution inaugurated restaurants, too, since chefs of the fallen nobility had to make a living. Lizzy and I ate at a particularly miserable representative of the great gourmandizing tradition in Grenoble, spearing limp flanges of duck with increasing gloom.

➤➤

SEPTEMBER 15   *Paris*

'I LOVE THE ARISTOCRATS and I understand very well the revolutionaries.' The playwright Bernard Minoret proudly cradled Marie Antoinette's head for Lizzy's Leica. It had once adorned a shop, smirking somewhat, with a thyroid look that nicely evoked the Queen's impenetrable stupidities that had so helped to bring the Bourbons to ruin. 'Intelligence was on the side of the revolution', Minoret went on, 'but on the other side was something – six hundred years of civilization – and when it disappears it's sad. There were two revolutions, and all the good things were done in 1789. I love Mirabeau.'

Bernard Minoret's decorous pantheon pales beside what has been going on in French history. The days when scholarship on the revolution was in the hands of a Robespierrist like Mathiez, or men like Lefebvre and Soboul, are long gone. The bookshops are now piled high with the words of Furet, of Chaunu, of Secher and of Sedillot, who claim variously that (a) there never really was a revolution so much as a linguistic gust of national self-levitation, a 'discourse' that people have somehow mistakened for a revolution, or (b) if there was a revolution – which is doubtful – it was then betrayed by the sans-culottes, Hébertists, Committees of Public Safety, the spirit of proto-Stalinism and (c) it led to genocide, perpetrated by Frenchmen on Frenchmen, particularly in the Vendée, thus demonstrating that (d) in any event, it was most definitely a dreadful blunder and left the French people worse off than before.

A lot of this stuff is still an attack on the French Communists, part of the frenzy of French intellectual life in a period of reaction. Some of it is a useful corrective, but in the main – particularly with the use, by Secher in his book *Le Genocide franco-français*, of inflated figures – it does not approach in scholarship the work it seeks to demolish. A similar reaction occurred in the US in the 1950s, when a revolution that had once been extolled as the close relative of the American Revolution was suddenly deplored as the precursor of the Russian Revolution. Some of the most interesting American writing on the revolution, like R.R. Palmer's *Twelve Who Ruled* (1940), was done before this shift.

The number of people killed in the Terror came to about 17,000. The historian Charles Tilly says that he'd be 'surprised to discover that for France as a whole the number of deaths directly attributable to revolutionary struggles was greater than 100,000, and this includes military deaths in the civil war, retaliation, armed struggle among civilians and so on.' Greer's statistical study, *The Incidence of the Terror*, written in 1935, shows that 666 nobles were executed in Paris during the Terror and 1,543 throughout France.

A revolution is not a tea party. Neither is a counterrevolution. After the overthrow of the Paris Commune in 1871, some 20,000 Communards were executed immediately, more than the total during the Terror, though no one makes much of a fuss about that.

➡

SEPTEMBER 16   *Angers*

LIZZY FOUND SAINT-JUST in Angers, in a museum devoted to the works of David d'Angers. Yesterday we took the train west into the Loire Valley. The *musée* turned out to be wonderful, presided over proudly by Madame Viviane Huchard. Formerly a church, burned in the revolutionary period, the *musée* is now adorned with a glass roof and houses the *oeuvre* of David d'Angers. A sculptor and enthusiastic republican born in the year of the revolution, active mostly in the second quarter of the nineteenth century when the demand for public monuments was great, exiled by Louis Philippe, he did many of the busts that have become part of our iconographic furniture: Balzac, Victor Hugo, Goethe, von Humboldt. At the door of the *musée* there is an enormous statue of the dying General Bonchamps, titled *Freedom to Prisoners*. Bonchamps was a Vendéen leader who, when mortally wounded, uttered as his last command an order to spare the republican prisoners, including David D'Anger's father.

We walked along till we confronted the bust of Saint-Just, still in his twenties when he was guillotined along with Robespierre in Thermidor, on July 27, 1794. 'And what do you think of Saint-Just?' I asked. 'He's handsome, no? The angel of the revolution!' Madame Huchard cried enthusiastically. 'In our French mind we prefer Saint-Just because he was *intégre*, honest to the end, and he doesn't have the same *tâche* as Robespierre, who ordered the massacres.'

It's the only bust of Saint-Just, a man whose ideal republic certainly had its Spartan aspects. In his notebooks David d'Angers recounts how Madame Lebas, a daughter of Dupleix, who was Robespierre's landlord, had lent him a pastel of Saint-Just done from life, from which he modeled his bust. Then David asked Madame Lebas to look at his finished work. 'She came to my studio and the memories of the young representative of the people drew tears from her eyes. 'Poor young man', she said. 'It's as though I'm looking at him now, leaning against the foot of my bed when I was putting my little girl to sleep. He was beautiful, Saint-Just, with his thoughtful expression from which shone great energy, tempered with sweetness and candor.'

We spent the morning with Madame Huchard and then had a lunch at the Salamandre which completely restored the honor of the cuisine of postrevolutionary France. In a large private room just behind us, twenty veteran prisoners of war, presumably of 1939–45 vintage, campaigned gallantly through an enormous feast. We headed back toward Paris through a provincial France created in large part by the revolution and evoked by Eric Hobsbawm in his *Age of Revolution:* 'That impregnable citadel of small and middle peasant proprietors, small craftsmen and shopkeepers, economically retrogressive but passionately devoted to Revolution and Republic, which has dominated the country's life ever since ... Both big business and the labor movement were long doomed to remain minority phenomena in France, islands surrounded by a sea of corner grocers, peasant smallholders, and café proprietors.'

➤

SEPTEMBER 18   *Paris*

THE BICENTENNIAL COMMISSION has organized a 'Revolutionary Train' to tour France, adorned with images of the period, traveling 15,000 kilometers and visiting eighty-six towns. That man at the Maoist meeting who said, to tremendous applause, 'There's only one revolution, the French Revolution', was right in the sense that you can't read the history of any subsequent revolution without seeing the paradigms of the twenty years after 1789: the peasantry betrayed and insurgent in the Vendée and the Ukraine; the Girondists with their descendants in Kerensky's Duma. For the Terror read subsequent bloody, more bureaucratized horrors; Thermidor after Thermidor. The French Revolution set the mold. Those first revolutionaries had no one to look to but themselves and the virtuous Romans they took as their spiritual advisers.

Will the train, as it tours France, evoke the texture of the revolution: the people marching on Versailles who freed the animals from the royal zoo, whence they fled into the forest; the Jacobin club at Auxerre, which ordered all the ex-priests not working at some useful occupation to be exiled unless they showed signs of repentance by getting married; the Jacobin club at Beauvais, which held a session of Jacobin self-criticism in which one *citoyen* was rejected because he 'lacked the degree of warmth necessary for a real republican', prompting another in the defense: 'If his physique was cold, his morals were warm.'

The Jacobins at Limoges agreed that to be a republican one had to have passed 'through the crucible of perilous circumstance', which is what France did in 1793 and 1794 under the leadership of the Committee of Public Safety, directing a revolution that changed human history for the better (not incidentally, though this is hardly mentioned by the historical revisionists, ending slavery in its dominions, too). Do you know what kind of government was victorious in 1794? asked Jeanbon St. André, a Jacobin member of the Committee of Public Safety, later one of Napoleon's prefects, and he answered himself: 'A government of the convention. A government of passionate Jacobins in red bonnets, wearing rough woolen cloth, wooden shoes, who lived on simple bread and bad beer and went to sleep on mattresses laid on the floor of their meeting-halls when they were too tired to wake and deliberate further. That is the kind of men who saved France. I was one of them, gentlemen. And here, as in the apartments of the Emperor which I am about to enter, I glory in the fact.'

➥

SEPTEMBER 19   *Paris*

AT THE BRASSERIE Bofinger's last night I looked across a great mound of choucroute at the 35-year-old architect Bruno Barbot and asked him what he thought about the revolution. 'I'm from Brittany', Bruno replied. 'My father was a Communist, my grandfather was a farmer, and his father was a farmer. My father worked on the railroads, and when he got kicked out of the CP he joined the Maoists and visited Albania twice.

'So how do I feel about the revolution? The French people have a guilty conscience about the King, because when you come down to it the French are not bellicose. When Vercingetorix came to Rennes they gave him part of the town. They're happy eating well and sleeping with their beautiful women. Marseilles is not part of France. Lyon is not part of France. Amiens is not part of France. Paris is France.'

'Who are your heroes of the revolution?'

'Robespierre and Saint-Just.'

➥

SEPTEMBER 20   *Paris*

KEN TALKS WITH CHARLES TILLY, now the revolution's best historian.

Defense of the Revolution: First point: The revolution did occur – that is, control of the French state did change between 1788 (yes, 1788) and 1795. It may be obvious, but it's disappeared from the debate.

Bourgeois France did, through its own networks, seize power of the state machinery and transform it and set the conditions for a different kind of state. It happens that the same process allowed for a Napoleon, and some of his allies, to install a much more powerful and centralized state than had previously existed and such a state did not always serve bourgeois ends. The struggle for control over that state, after the allies defeated Napoleon, resulted in the more powerful state being in the hands of a monarchy. It's important to see that a centralized, administratively coordinated French state grew out of the reaction to the early improvisation of the revolution.

What would the alternative have been without the revolution? A lot of people lost their lives – 'but how many people would have been oppressed, would have lived shorter lives, would have been in misery, without this change? Many people didn't die under state repression who would have otherwise. My judgement is that on the whole the French set the model for states in which it was legitimate for citizens to claim that they were sovereign, even in the face of the centralized French state – they had a voice. In the name of the revolution, in 1830 and 1848, French citizens said that if the people disagrees with the state, the people who are governing have to change.The revolution installed in an irrevocable way a kind of popular voice that provided the model and precedent for a form, a limited form, of democratic government, in the rest of the world. That's a new principle that had no meaning until 1789 – a very important accomplishment.'

Two great accomplishments of the revolution: (1) It reduced the power of the landholding aristocracy that otherwise would have held power much longer. (2) It durably installed some form of popular sovereignty and power for peasants, workers, the petty bourgeoisie, etc., that had exercised very little power on a national scale until that time.

As for slavery: Indirectly, the insurrection in Haiti resulted from the revolution and it's also true that the French were precocious in abolishing slavery in their own domains. They maintained, for a while, the distinction between their colonies and metropolitan France, but they were still precocious.

Could the French monarchy have been toppled without a revolution? Key question. Hobsbawm makes an interesting point in this regard:

'... absolute monarchy, however modernist and innovatory, found it impossible – and indeed showed few signs of wanting – to break loose from the hierarchy of landed nobles to which, after all, it belonged, whose values it symbolized and incorporated, and on whose support it largely depended ... To take an obvious example ... few rational thinkers, even among the advisers of princes, seriously doubted the need to abolish serfdom and the surviving bonds of feudal dependence ... Yet in fact the only peasant liberations that took place from above before 1789 were in small and untypical states like Denmark and Savoy, and on the personal estates of some other princes. One major such liberation was attempted, by Joseph II of Austria, in 1781, but it failed in the face of the political resistance of vested interests and of peasant rebellion in excess of what had been anticipated, and had to remain uncompleted. What did abolish feudal relations all over Western and Central Europe was the French

Revolution, by direct action, reaction, or example, and the revolution of 1848.'

➤

LOTS OF MAIL waiting for me, forwarded.

Dear Alex,

I trust this letter will eventually reach you in Watsonville, Key West, Kabul or wherever ...

Do you know the Saguenay-Lac St. Jean region? Sophie and I are here with my daughter for ten days, admiring the great fjord with its Yosemite-like scenery, beluga whales and picturesque villages. The Hudson'S Bay Company kept this region closed until the 1840s, when it was settled by loggers and nationalist colonies of *habitants* led by their priests. Apparently most of the heartrending epics of Québecois literature are set in the grandeur and melancholy of the Saguenay.

In the 1930s US capital, especially the Mellon interests, poured $300 million into the region (probably the largest single US imperial investment of the time, larger than the Rockefellers in Venezuela) to develop its hydroelectric potential to refine bauxite from Guyana and turn pulp into newsprint. Arvida was the largest company town in North America; the corporations, the CIO and the semi-fascist Catholic syndicates fought bloody three-way battles. Later, of course, this became a wellspring of the PQ – their first seat outside Montreal – and they are still influential in the region, along with a growing NDP, although the Conservatives won the last election.

This is also the Lake Wobegon of French America. The big news this week – throwing the region into a tizzy – has been the attack of the killer black flies. Seriously. Two blueberry pickers in the last fortnight have been killed by black fly swarms. One became delirious and walked off a cliff, the other passed out and was slowly nibbled to death. The local clericalist yellow rag – *Quotidian* – had a macabre frontpage picture of the last victim, his face blackened and swollen by hundreds of black fly bites.

I have been using the vacation, after teaching summer school in Ottawa, to make some progress on my L.A. book (*City of Quartz*). While it has been easy enough to clink glasses and shoot eight-ball with the local Québecois working class, the intellectual left in Canada seems rather arduous. The Montreal intellectuals I have met are all absorbed in their 'morosité postmoderne', while the great achievement of the English Canadian new left seems to be to have saturated the baby-boom petty bourgeoisie in almost noxious nationalism. Someone actually told me the other day that they had stopped listening to jazz because of the obligation 'to support Canadian music'. Needless to say I wasn't much of a party hit when I suggested, on 'Canada' (aka 'Dominion') day, that it was too bad that the forces of revolution under the command of Benedict Arnold hadn't taken Quebec in 1775.

for War Communism,
Mike Davis
L'Anse St. Jean
Saguenay
Quebec

Dear Mr. Cockburn,
You said in your column that only two professional athletes fought in Vietnam. You forgot Al Bumbry, former outfielder for the Baltimore Orioles.

Vivian Martin
Baltimore

➤

SEPTEMBER 23   *Ardmore*
Dear Mr. Cockburn:
I have been to Haiti twice in the past five years, and I plan to go again later this year. I have friends there who tell me of the constant oppression of their government.

One of my friends who is twenty-five years old works in a restaurant in Petionville and earns $60.00 a month. He works twelve hours a day, seven days a week. My friend is very lucky – there are literally hundreds of people waiting to take his job if he should quit. This friend tells me that every week dead bodies are found on his street. No one in the government seems concerned. The disappearances and deaths continue. My friend is terrified to walk in the streets, but he must in order to get to his job.

As you can tell Mr. Cockburn I am not a writer, but if I was I would visit Haiti. A good writer would see the genocide that is taking place in this country. A good writer would see filth, slums, diseased dogs roaming the streets, malnutrition everywhere, sickness, the lowest forms of housing of any society, and polluted water everywhere. A good writer would see the men in the blue clothes with their UZIs and carrying out their terrorism on the people. A good writer would write of the truly 'invisible' Haitian people. A good writer would trace the involvement of our government in the affairs of Haiti. A good writer would realize that Haiti's drug connections are ultimately connected to us.

The last time I was in Haiti I was with a Haitian friend in the beautiful town of Jacmel along the coast. We were discussing the many problems of the Haitian people. After an hour or so our discussion drew to a close with an abrupt silence. A few minutes later my friend whispered, 'Why won't your country help us ...

we are friends, aren't we?'

I think the people of the United States need to be asked these questions. Unfortunately, my Haitian friend and I are not writers.

Sincerely,
Terry Hatch
Lancaster, Pennsylvania

➥

SEPTEMBER 24   *London*

THE REMEMBERED SMALL CHANGE of daily life: a certain indentation in the pavement at the corner of Dean and Carlisle Streets, observed across two years' worth of dutiful ploddings to an office nearby; the way the elevator drops to subway level at Holland Park and, heading southwest on the curve and dog-leg of the Circle and District lines, the vexed matter of the missing apostrophe in the underground sign for Earls Court.

The issue of missing apostrophes unplugs another trickle of memory. My first job in London was at the *Times Literary Supplement*, then housed in Printing House Square, opposite Blackfriars tube station. Soon I learned to scratch out the apostrophes inserted into *Howards End* and *Finnegans Wake*.

Each morning I travelled to Blackfriars from Turnham Green, thus having a statistical probability of encountering my sister Sarah, who would step aboard at Hammersmith, on her way to chambers at Lincoln's Inn. She smoked – indeed, still smokes – though more aptly in her incarnation as Sarah Caudwell, mistress of crime – a pipe, and as I would spot her down the carriage I could see her neighbors viewing with interest the tampings, attempted incinerations and transient bonfires associated with her enjoyment of tobacco. Sometimes a passenger would point either nervously or with exaggerated gesture, at a No Smoking sign and she would hastily fling the pipe, sometimes still smoking, into her handbag.

As I approached she would spot me and pause from the sucking-and-flaring involved in pipe ignition and shout, 'Alexander darling, good morning' and commuters hitherto rivetted by Sarah the pipe-smoker would swivel their heads to scan someone who, seconds before, had been a comfortable, anonymous particle in the great mass making its way east to Blackfriars and the City but who was now isolated and indeed marked out as an eccentric and potentially disruptive element by his newly exposed status as intimate of the lady pipe-smoker telling loudly and with expansive gestures unsuited to the crowded carriage her adventures of the evening before.

Sarah, under the name Sarah Caudwell, has written a number of excellent detective stories, including *The Quickest Way to Hades* and *The Sirens Sang of Murder*. She was previously a barrister at the Chancery bar and then senior tax adviser to a London bank. Among her admirers (as a writer) are George Will and Judge Bork. Bork turned up at a talk by Sarah in the Washington, D.C. bookstore Chapters, spotted the pipe, heard her spirited allocution against capital punishment, and left without coming forward to salute the great author in person.

➡

SEPTEMBER 26   *London*
CAME UPON AN astonishing piece by Norman Cantor, professor of history, sociology and comparative literature at New York University, which openly laments the failure of the Reaganauts to consolidate a fascist intellectual framework for their plan.

Cantor says it all boils down to confusion and lack of guts. No ordering hand had settled upon the Reagan mix, which Cantor conveniently lists as including 'the Friedmanite market economists; neo-Darwinian sociobiologists; neo-1920s modernists; traditional believers in inequality and hierarchy (who never found an effective theoretical spokesman); traditional Roman Catholics; evangelical and "born-again" Protestants; Zionists; exponents of Victorian "liberal" humanism, and the Bork-Meese constitutional fundamentalists.'

In Cantor's estimation these were all wandering sheep, seeking the fold of a robustly fascist philosophy. 'It is conceivable', he writes, 'that a theory could have been developed to bind all these intellectual traditions in a cohesive doctrine. For example, in interwar European Fascism, there were ingredients for such a comprehensive rightist doctrine, especially as propounded by thinkers on the French right like Charles Maurras.' (Maurras was a notorious anti-Semite.)

Cantor adds, 'But the discrediting of intellectual Fascism by World War II, Vichy, Mussolini, Nazism and the Holocaust meant that recourse to this intellectual reservoir was never attempted. And in the early post–World War II years, there was some effort to build upon T.S. Eliot's amorphous brand of English rightism, but nothing important came of it.'

Nostalgia for fascist thought is not confined to Cantor. Carl Schmitt is once again being given a turn around the paddock by social scientists, just as he was in the early days of the cold war. Schmitt, a student of Max Weber, was a paid-up Nazi – director of the University Teachers' Group of the National Socialist League of German Jurists – whose core idea was the notion that states are organized not for the mutual benefit of all but as enterprises directed against an enemy, said enemy being aliens, Jews, Bolsheviks, etc.

This was the philosophy of 'decisionism', and recently Schmitt has been finding some fresh support, *inter alia* among the pages of a special issue of *Telos* in the summer of 1987. From Schmitt we can then travel to the German historians' debate, discussed by Roderick Stackelberg in the Winter 1988 issue of *Radical History Review*.

With this debate, launched by Ernst Nolte in the summer of 1986 in the *Frankfurter Allgemeine Zeitung*, we are back in Bitburg country. The assumption offered by Nolte and others is that Nazism, so far from being an expression of German civilization and culture, was actually an import from Russia, which, in both its Czarist and Soviet incarnations, furnished the anti-Semitic and totalitarian strains infecting the pure stream of German thought. Andreas Hillgruber takes this proposition to its logical conclusion, arguing that German soldiers fighting on the Eastern Front were defending Europe against the Bolshevik hordes.

This was the true meaning of Reagan's mission to Bitburg.

➳

SEPTEMBER 27   *London*

TO GERMAN CAPITALISTS using slave labor in the Auschwitz industrial park the situation was normalcy, in the sense that it is the imperative of capital to minimize costs and maximize profits. In their minds they were, from the moral outlook of shareholders and accountants and market forces, doing the 'right thing'. The 'disaster' – the extermination of Jews and gypsies and Slavic prisoners of war – was, from the point of view of these capitalists running Buna and the other enterprises, the extension of normalcy.

➳

OCTOBER 17   *Oaxaca*

THE CHINANTECS LIVE about eight hours' drive north of Oaxaca, amid the crests of the Sierra Madre, and are about to have a way of life, maintained for nine centuries despite the onslaughts of Aztec and Spaniard, ended by the final consequences of multilateral loans. In this instance the Interamerican Development Bank, run jointly by tidy-minded people who brake for animals and men in sharp suits with gold at wrist and neck, has financed a regional program – under the Papaloapan Commission, something akin to the TVA – to the tune of more than $50 million for a dam that has already directly and indirectly destroyed more than 250,000 acres of Mexico's rapidly disappearing tropical forests and the cultures that survive them.

Who gains from these mad 'development' projects? The analogues of the people who have been shoveling money into the Bush and Dukakis election campaigns, namely Brazil's and Mexico's construction industries. These, in conjunction with their governments and multilateral lending agencies, underpin the political economy of tropical devastation. Such Third World Bechtels make the most money with the least risk, are powerful lobbies and have been able to capture the benefits of the indebtedness brought on by the stratospheric borrowing of Brazil and Mexico. With much of the rest of the population crammed into hovels, these corporate groups cavort in *Fortune*'s International 500, emblems of the aqua-military-industrial complex.

In any tropical development the luscious trove is 'infrastructure': the Machu Pichus, the Tikals, the Monte Albans of today's tropical world, pharaonic reveries conceived by their sponsors as monuments to their will. Infrastructure development – roads, hydropower, other forms of civil construction – absorbs 50 to 60 percent of regional development, the rest going to government bureaucracies, graft, and some services and credits for the 'target' populations.

➡

OCTOBER 25   *Aptos*
DAVID BARSAMIAN: What are some of your literary influences? Tell our listeners about Orwell?

AC: I don't particularly like Orwell and I never have. I would concede that certain essays of Orwell are stimulating, but I find his intellectual appeal extremely limited. When I grew up, if you ever, at school, tried to come up with the slightest radical statement or exhibited radical hopes, some idiot would always bring out *Animal Farm* and say, 'Some people are more equal than others', or a kindred tag line. The reactionary effect of Orwell was just awful. I actually hated him for years and years and years. I can admire his article on comics, but I think that plain, blunt man approach of his is very limited. So I'm no fan of Orwell's, to be frank with you. I was much more influenced by great columnists and writers like Flann O'Brien, not to mention my father, who disliked Orwell and vice versa.

➡

OCTOBER 27   *Aptos*
THE LIBERALS ARE in a panic. Yesterday the *New York Times* ran a full-page ad with 'A Re-Affirmation of Principle' in great big black letters. Top-drawer liberals followed in fine array.

'We speak', the text began, 'as American citizens who wish to reaffirm America's liberal tradition. At our founding, the spirit of liberalism suffused the Revolution, the Declaration of Independence, the Constitution and the Bill of Rights. We regret that the Vice-President of the United States has taken the lead in vilifying one of our oldest and noblest traditions. He made sport of "the dreaded L-word" and continues to make "liberal" and "liberalism" terms of opprobrium.'

Among the signatories, the Bundy brothers, who in the sixties defined liberalism as practiced in Vietnam, via Robert McNamara at the Pentagon, by the Kennedy Administration. In the early seventies, from his position at Lazard Frères, Felix Rohatyn was pioneering many of the merger techniques that today he deplores when advocating assaults on the deficit, usually through 'bipartisan' commissions beyond democratic reach or intervention. By the mid eighties, Robert Silvers was printing Robert Leiken's labyrinthine rationales for funding the Nicaraguan *contras*. And at the root of this historical tree is George Kennan, who, in his famous 'long telegram' from Moscow to the State Department in 1947, urged a policy of containment aimed at the Soviet Union, meanwhile ensuring that senior Nazis were forgiven. Two of these signatories, J.K. Galbraith and Irving Howe, are self-proclaimed socialists.

➳

NOVEMBER 14 *Aptos*

JULIA REED OF *Vogue* wants me to review cars. We discuss a pseudonym. I decide on Sandy Loveday, which has a breezy timbre to it, though Mama would probably also say it was a bit motorcad-ish. Also a reference to *Mr. Loveday's Little Outing*.

I picked up the car for review, a Cadillac Sedan de Ville, in San Francisco. The people at the Adobe Motel think I've struck it rich.

➳

NOVEMBER 22 *Aptos*

GOT STOPPED BY THE California Highway Patrol on the hill between Santa Cruz and San Jose. A warning. Lent the car to my neighbor S., who promptly dinged it. Julia a bit vexed.

➳

NOVEMBER 27 *Aptos*

SENT OFF MY Caddy piece. I think that's it for my career as car correspondent. I have the impression from Julia that this is not quite what the *Vogue* advertising department was looking for.

The Cadillac was once a synonym for all the especially good things life had to offer. Cadillac did not mean merely money. It spelled pizazz and innovation: the beautiful '53 Eldorado convertible in which Ike rode on his inauguration day; the '57 Eldorado Brougham; the clean cars of the sixties.

For years the breadwinners of the Cadillac division have been the Coupe de Ville and Sedan de Ville. It's now the fortieth anniversary of the Coupe de Ville, a two-door hardtop launched in the 1949 model year and powered with the new overhead-valve, short-stroke V-8. In Los Angeles, Eugene Jaderquist wrote in the later 1940s, 'Cadillac fever is of epidemic proportions. Dealers are now becoming acquainted with the "pool". Two, three, and sometimes five or six people of moderate means pool their resources for the specific purpose of buying one Cadillac ... actual use of the car rotates in whatever pattern the members have been able to agree upon.' Jaderquist added that you could get into the main parking lot at Ciro's only if you drove a Caddy.

Actually, the '49 Coupe was one of the slickest-looking Cadillacs ever made. The four-door Sedan de Ville came along in 1956 in time to join the fin-de-fifties madness. A few years ago, I picked up a '63 Sedan de Ville. The fins were still there, down but more sharply sharklike than the cultic, gross '59s. GM had supplied the '63 with a staggering 143 interior choices and a subtlety in social grading that would have dazzled Proust.

Older people buy Cadillacs. (The median age of the Caddy buyer is between 55 and 60; thus, not surprisingly, 85 percent of Caddy buyers are married and 35 percent are retired.) Those people seek solid, safe presence, like immense nineteenth-century armoires or leather club sofas. And that's the trouble. For the flush young professional the word Cadillac summons the intimations of 'mature' in all the doleful senses of that word.

⇒→

DECEMBER 10   *Aptos*

FOG HANGS OVER Aptos, more specifically over the Adobe Motel. Fog always hangs over the Adobe. Move a few yards to the left or right and the northern California sunshine sparkles down. It took me a while to realize that this was not bad luck for a day, but a fixed micro-climatic condition.

Fogbound, I read the *New York Times*. R.W. Apple, Jr. announces with great excitement on the front page that George Bush has 'signaled' republican leaders and something Apple knowingly calls 'the broader political community' that he intends to 'adopt a much more energetic and deeply involved Presidential style than that of the man he has served under for eight years, Ronald Reagan.'

They pay Apple to tell us this? Simply by getting out of bed in the morning Bush will display deeper involvement in the diurnal round than a man whose idea of a major political initiative is to switch on the television set; whose torpor has been so Oblomovian that halfway through his second term senior aides contemplated use of the Twenty-fifth Amendment to prise him out of bed and office. But I'm not sure that Bush's determination to get to his desk before noon will be popular. People liked Reagan's rigorous schedule of long lie-in, mid-morning nap, post-prandial snooze, forty winks over the TV dinner and early bed. It meant less chance for him to do something stupid.

I drove to San Francisco to speak at a fund-raiser on the occasion of the fortieth anniversary of the founding of *The Guardian*. As I entered the hall a bit late, a speaker was lathering up the crowd with a prospectus of George Bush's impending villanies. He painted a grim future, but one not nearly so grim as that drawn by the New Right, to whom Bush has come as a godsend. Viguerie & Co. can now send out mailing after mailing urging the faithful to send dollars to beat back the schemes and sellouts of this Trilateralist hellspawn of Nelson Rockefeller.

John Trinkl, who introduced me at the *Guardian* event, was kind enough to quote a latter from Cedric Belfrage, one of the founders of *The National Guardian*, saying that a major influence in causing him to start the paper had been my father, Claud. It was one of those weeks where the old boy's name kept popping up. Someone had just sent me a silly piece from *The Village Voice* making the rather belated discovery that he was one and the same as the Frank Pitcairn lashed by St. George (Orwell) on POUM. Anyone wanting a dose of realism about POUM should read Luis Buñuel's reminiscences.

Also in my pocket at that meeting was a speech by Steve Nelson, commander of the Veterans of the Abraham Lincoln Brigade, on the dedication of artist Roy Schriffrin's Barcelona Monument to the Intenational Brigades, October 28. Among other things Nelson said this:

'There is ... another monument, the one in Bitburg, Germany, on which President Reagan placed a wreath. Two days after his homage to this Nazi monument, President Reagan came to Spain. He said that the Lincoln Brigaders and others who fought for the Republic were on the wrong side ...

'This monument standing before us represents the right of all people to determine their own destiny, for a democratic rule of their own choice. When the governments of the Western democracies chose to sit on their hands as bleeding Spain called for help, it was the common people who said, We cannot be neutral. Many who were released or who escaped from the hell of fascist prisons found a way to reach Spain. Some 45,000 men and women from fifty-three countries rushed to aid the Republic and said, We are with you. More than 10,000 lie in the soil of Spain. In the words of Ernest Hemingway, "No men ever entered earth more honorably than those who died in Spain."'

⇒→

DECEMBER 12   *Aptos*

AMID THE CHARITABLE supplies pouring into earthquake-stricken Armenia are some dogs supplied by Israel. Only a couple of days ago five of their canine comrades lost their lives in southern Lebanon, in a mission scarcely merciful.

In fact and fantasy the accounts of animals in wartime are interesting, re the imperial and colonial imagination. There is a story about SS men being ordered, as a final *rite de passage*, to murder with their bare hands the dogs that had been training with them. The North Vietnamese used bees. And by the weekend Israelis were saying that the Hezbollah had been known to use bomb-laden donkeys.

It was the Spaniards, though, in their conquest of the Americas, who appear to have made the most systematic use of dogs as offensive weapons. Mastiffs and greyhounds would be put through their drills at an academy or 'finishing school' in Cuba. There, according to Jeannette Johnson Varner, who with her late husband, John Grier Varner, wrote *Dogs of the Conquest,* the hounds would be presented with mannequins dressed as Indians and smeared with Indian blood. Once trained, the dogs would precede the army into battle. Cloaked in chain mail surplices, they would pace forward, held fast by their handlers, yapping and growling until the order was given for them to be unleashed upon the Indians. From the Caribbean to the west coast of South America down to Peru, and then up through Central America and into Mexico, the Varners found evidence of these canine janissaries. As the land and the local populations were subdued, the dogs' duties shifted from attack on indigenous warriors to pursuit of runaway slaves.

➤

DECEMBER 14   *Aptos*
THE NATION FINALLY publishes letters about my attack on Gorbachev.

Dear Nation:
In his scathing and uninformed commentary on a joint US–Soviet statement on ending the cold war, Cockburn seems to imply that a Soviet pullout from the Third World (as part of a joint US–Soviet nonintervention policy) would be bad for Marxist regimes and national liberation movements. Now, I understand and appreciate where his sympathies lie – with the progressive forces of the Third World. But his comments reveal considerable ignorance of the nature of US–Soviet competition in Third World areas.

To wit: First, the major recipients of Soviet arms in the Third World are not Marxist regimes and national liberation forces but authoritarian Arab regimes that have systematically liquidated their internal opposition (whether left or right); second, in many cases the Soviet Union has refused to arm genuine national liberation movements, or has even, in some cases (e.g., Eritrea), armed the wrong side; and third, in any sustained competition to arm Third World forces, the West, with its superior resources and technology, will always be able to outperform the Soviet Union, thus placing Soviet allies at a relative disadvantage (a point that Gorbachev has taken some pain to emphasize in his comments on Soviet relations with the Third World).

Beyond these rather straightforward points are some basic questions of principle:

First, is it, on the whole, beneficial for the Third World for the superpowers to play out their own power struggle there? I would say that the answer is clearly no, even if the left has won some occasional victories. For it has been the introduction of East–West conflict into internal Third World struggles that has led to some of the greatest bloodbaths of modern times, including the Korean War and the Vietnam War. Without cold war justifications, moreover, the US government would find it much more difficult to arm the *contras*, give aid and comfort to the defenders of apartheid or to maintain various Third World dictators in power. If the United States and the Soviet Union were to extricate their own conflict from Third World struggles, therefore, the potential for liberation would increase, not decrease.

Second, is it right and proper for the Soviet Union to assume the white man's burden by bringing a civilizing mission to unruly Third World countries, as Cockburn suggests is needed in the case of Afghanistan? While I agree that the Soviet withdrawal from Afghanistan could be followed by a bloody civil war, the days are over in which any Northern power, whether sanctified by God or Marx, can legitimately exercise a paternalistic (that is, imperial) role in the countries of the South.

It seems to me, on final balance, that a mutual US–Soviet nonintervention pact would favor the Third World, not harm it as Cockburn suggest.

Michael T. Klare
Amherst, Massachusetts

Dear Nation:

In all my years of reading *The Nation*, I have not read a more senseless and petulant article than Cockburn's childish polemic against Mikhail Gorbachev. If it had not appeared in *The Nation*, it would not be worth challenging. Cockburn loves to quote Lenin, so let me say that Lenin has defined positions such as Cockburn takes as 'infantile petty-bourgeois leftism'.

What does Cockburn call for in this silly and shrill denunciation of Gorbachev? He suggests that to halt the bloody regional conflicts between the United States and the Soviet Union would be a betrayal of socialism. He damns Gorbachev for having a reasonable conversation with Katharine Graham. Would he prefer that Gorbachev cuss her out and denounce her as a wretched capitalist? He cynically recommends Donald Regan's book, and puts more weight on the President's foolishness than on the splendid – and I emphasize the word – achievement of finally, at long last, beginning a process of atomic disarmament. And he bewails the Soviet retreat from Afghanistan.

Cockburn calls with nostalgia for the goals of the 1930s. 'Is this where it is all going to end?' he asks, bringing up 'the heritage of October, the tradition of Tukhachevsky and Dimitrov.' Let me recall another heritage, the heritage of Stalin, the tortures, the beatings, the mass murders, the lunatic and endless killing, the savage orthodoxy that put back the cause of socialism and world peace for generations.

The position Cockburn has taken is not only snide and confusing, it is dangerous. For the first time in my lifetime – a bit longer than Cockburn's – a crack appears in the wall that has separated this country from Russia, not simply détente but a real possibility that a new generation will join our two countries with China and begin the process of civilization. It is like two great peoples beginning to laugh together for the first time, a joyous, lively occasion. The most reactionary and dangerous elements in America are already damning it and pleading with us not to be taken in by the Gorbachev charm. How very sad to see Cockburn joining them!

One more note: Not only does Cockburn bring me back to the days of my youth and a Communist Party so narrow and knuckle-headed that it destroyed itself as a willing gift to Truman and the FBI, but I am sure that whatever splinters of that party still exist toast Cockburn's denunciation of Gorbachev.

Howard Fast
Redding Ridge, Conn.

My answer:
For a time I thought I'd managed the historic feat of uniting the entire American left, or what passes for it. This outrage abuts on a Gorby cult (or in Fast's case a Gorby-Reagan cult), and my midsummer joke that if Ligachev was bundled off to Siberia, Gorbachev's champions would hail it as a triumph of the 'new thinking' was not so wide of the mark.

It's easy enough to trash Brezhnev, but the new Soviet world was not reborn the day Gorbachev became General Secretary and sneers at my remark about Brezhnev's 'golden age' for the Soviet working class are silly, as I'm sure many of the promoters of *perestroika* in the Soviet Union would readily acknowledge. An egalitarian wage structure, guaranteed employment and basic food prices steady at 1962 levels tend to be appreciated by workers and regarded by them as not at all incompatible with economic reform.

I'm all for *glasnost*, obviously, but that does not mean abdication of political perspectives or of criticism.

Klare's snooty letter is a marvelous example of the syndrome I was attacking: that of academics and foundation types shuttling from one comfortable conference to the next, drawing up ten-point programs to end the cold war.

Yes, of course the Soviet Union has been more concerned with national interest than proletarian internationalism, and of course it has supported regimes such as Iraq, Sudan and Nasserist Egypt (not to mention Argentina), which have jailed, tortured and butchered their internal Communist opposition. There are general tendencies to be considered. Where the Russians have been dealing with regimes under pressure or attack from the United States they have tended to look the other way if any indigenous movement is being suppressed. As noted above, they have pursued their own interests over international solidarity but have tended to support anti-imperialist national liberation movements, as in Algeria, Cuba, Vietnam, Angola and Nicaragua. In those cases where a Third World movement has been seeking to alter national boundaries (Biafra, Eritrea/Ethiopia, even Pakistani dissidents in Afghanistan/Pakistan) the Russians have not been supportive.

The wars in Korea and Vietnam were not byproducts of superpower rivalry. In both instances the United States wanted to crush indigenous revolution. What does Klare think 'conflict' (even the 'final' one) is all about? The United States seeks to establish hegemony in the Third World and has used anticommunism and anti-Sovietism as the propaganda equivalents of the older 'white man's burden'. If Klare thinks some decorous conference of twin souls in the Committee on US–Soviet relations can terminate the fundamental, inevitable antagonism between the United States and the Soviet Union and prompt, in some spirit of bipartisan tolerance for Third World self-determination, the withdrawal of the United States from, let us say, its bases in the Philippines, he's nuts and should be stayed from contact with impressionable youth in the area of the Five Colleges. He should also know that if it were not for the Soviet Union, the revolutions in Cuba, Vietnam, Nicaragua and Angola would not have survived. If he thinks authentic indigenous revolution or even reform can succeed without support from the socialist or even social democratic countries, he should study the economies of Latin America.

As Ligachev told the comrades in Gorky oblast at the start of August, in talking about 'the correlation between general human and proletarian-class interests ... we proceed from the fact that international relations are particularly class in character ... The struggle for peace and for the survival of mankind is indeed also the struggle for the interests of the working class, for the right of the people to choose their own road and to decide on their own fate.' So, yes, I rather wish that Gorbachev had asked Katharine Graham a few pointed questions, such as why, in 1987, the nine top executives at the Washington Post Company pulled down $7.28 million, against persistent mean-spiritedness toward the paper's unions and employees. He'd have done a lot more for the international class struggle than he did with the cubic hectares of hot air I complained about.

1989

➡

The Argument

IN WHICH I am discovered in the Adobe Motel, reading about the death of Bohemia. A conversation with James O'Connor about the Green movement's mistakes; the 'victory' of capitalism discussed; a visit with Helmut Newton; perversity and Nazism; 'what if' and *Hamlet*; a conversation about socialism with Paul Sweezy and Harry Magdoff – 'Mao's the boy!'; excursus on Patrick Moynihan; a trip to Belém; a hasty return to Ireland; the censoring of *Babar*; Ginsberg and the Beats and Connolly's *Horizon*; the Loma Prieta 'quake; the New Left defended; the Berlin Wall falls. Of my mother's death and an era's end I sing.

JANUARY 1 *Aptos, California*

THE MAIN ENEMY of urban Bohemia is the rising price of real estate. In America at least, we can have rural Bohemia. University towns are something else again. Too serious these days to be Bohemian. Peter Sloterdijk describes it well in his *Critique of Cynical Reason.*

'In the bourgeois epoch, the years at the university were for the students a time when they could defer the serious things in life, when they could take liberties before going on to careers and an orderly life. But it is eerie to be confronted by a young generation that is too cool for that nonsense and that, precociously cynical, gets straight to the heart of the matter. The twentieth century has known several such cool generations, starting with the Nazi fraternity in which a troupe of cool snot-noses mingled with the populist idealists; later they became fighter pilots or jurists in the system, and still later, Democrats. Following them came the "Skeptical Generation" of the fifties, which stands today at the helm, and following them, the generations of the seventies and eighties ...

'Research has established that there were only a few long-term Bohemians ... If we look today at these nurturing soils and living spaces in which deviation and critique, satire and cheekiness, cynicism and willfulness thrive, it becomes immediately clear why we must fear the worst for embodied cheeky enlightenment. Before our very eyes, cities have been transformed into amorphous clumps where alienated streams of traffic transport people to the various scenes of their attempts and failures in life. For a long time now carnival has meant not "inverted world" but flight into safe world, of anesthesia from a permanently inverted world full of daily absurdities ... These mutilations of cheeky impulses indicate that society has entered a stage of organized seriousness in which the playgrounds of lived enlightenment are becoming increasingly clogged.'

'Cheeky enlightenment'? Not a bad goal.

JANUARY 2   *Aptos*

DROVE UP THE ROAD to interview Jim O'Connor, prof. at Santa Cruz and founder of *Capitalism, Nature, Socialism*, 'a Journal of Socialist Ecology'.

COCKBURN: You say that the practical sign that human ecology and environment may become the dominant issues of the next century is the rapid growth of social movements fighting the trend toward destruction of nature.

O'CONNOR: There are very few people any more with an understanding of economic development or capital accumulation who think that such processes can be divorced from environmental issues. And here 'environment' is defined in the broadest possible sense, to include not just external nature – rainforests, for example – but also such things as urban space, human health and well-being: that is, all those things Marx called 'conditions of production', the definition of which is everything that's not produced as a commodity. These conditions of production are being destroyed.

AC: Why?

JO: My own view is that since the long economic crisis began in the early 1970s, capitalism has really been good at increasing efficiency, creating flexible production systems, at the level of the factory, the bank and the Safeway – in other words the circuits of capital. And just as capitalists and right-wing capitalist governments for the past ten years have been obsessed with such strategies for reducing costs, they have neglected the conditions of production, meaning things that aren't organized capitalistically, including everything from the education system to wildlife management, to forests and parks, rivers, water quality.

But when it comes to analyzing material life – which is after all most of life, in that it's what most people are concerned with most of the day, most of their waking hours, and in that it's the major activity of capitalist societies and not religion or play, which are all commodified anyway so they become part of material life – it's very important for a socialist, not to say Marxist, to begin if not end with the category of exploitation of labor.

Environmentalism had lots of power in the 1970s. Then there was a counterattack. The state restructured. Capitalism restructured. New technologies were introduced, regulations weren't enforced and so in the 1980s we had a new environmental crisis that came out of the contradictions and indeed environmental victories of the 1970s. In the present crisis capital is perfectly willing to bring back DDT or sweatshops in the home, if it can get away with it.

So here we have an environmental movement faced with a problem to a large degree of its own making, because it didn't calculate the effects of its own existence on capital, costs, and profits. Nor did labor. Capitalism is like ... mercury. If you attack it one place, it will displace the crisis into some other place. There are thousands of examples of this, of which the biggest and most obvious is the displacement of the crisis from the First to the Third World, to a large degree because of the success of the environmental and labor movements in the occupational health and safety fields.

So you've got a governing ideological content of pluralism and individualism which is very hard to transcend, with a lot of people doing a lot of good work, which has unintentional effects which are self-negating, meanwhile feeling good about themselves. Thus you have a political trend which is unfavorable to real environmental restoration, which is what I would call socialist reconstruction.

The environmental movement did have huge success: fifteen or twenty major pieces of legislation passed: all kinds of regulation; and indeed what I think was the movement's greatest victory achieved almost without realizing it, namely new democratic forms within the capitalist state in the shape of the EPA and OSHA, which were organized relatively democratically.

But of course this success contained its own failure. It turned out to be a multifront assault on capital. By the mid 1970s business was getting very angry at this. Business organized political action committees and decided to regain the political initiative. Business published lots of studies estimating how much all this clean-up and risk containment had cost it. The Council on Environmental Quality and the Labor Department put out studies saying this is pretty costly, not just in money terms but on the key issue of the flexibility and variability of capital. Environmental regulation made financial planning not just uncertain but constrained, and ditto with investment planning. Business was told when and when not to do things and business just doesn't like to be told this. It made the whole system less flexible, more ossified, and this in my view was more important than the quantitative costs of pollution abatement devices and stuff like that.

AC: Well, they sort of did face it, by saying, why not have a new industry, a pollution abatement industry providing jobs and profits.

JO: Yes, and that leaves out the crucial heart of the beast, which is (a) if that's the case and since business is not in the game of ruining nature just for the hell of it, then why hasn't business got into this area; no, because (b) these things just add to costs, they don't produce surplus value, because they don't reduce the cost of reproducing labor power.

AC: Wait a minute. Why can't I as a businessman produce my anti-pollution gadget?

JO: Of course you can, so long as there's a market for it, which in boom times like the 1960s there was. People bought pollution abatement devices, but not because they thought they would increase their profits by buying them. If they bought something to put on their smokestacks, they were going to make a local community happy, but that's a cost, not a profit. In a crisis period, business is less interested, so then your pollution abatement business isn't looking so great, and indeed in the 1980s such expenditures are way down. And as I've said, excepting DDT and lead in gas, everything is now worse than it was in the 1970s.

AC: So in terms of political debate, unless you can plan capital, make democratic investment plans, lay out a whole program ...

JO: Yes, unless you can plan imports-exports, have import controls – always a sign that radicals are taking over – have democracy in the Federal Reserve System so you can do financial and money planning in accordance with the needs of production, as opposed to the needs of banks ... Unless you go all those radical steps further down the path, then you are going to end up in the situation where we are right now, where your national environmental leadership is trying to cut private deals in semi-secret without even going through Congress and your base members are getting completely pissed off.

AC: You know, it is exactly like those people who say, cut a billion here or a billion there out of the military budget, convert this factory to peaceful production, like Grumman making aluminum canoes instead of F-14s, without thinking the whole thing through and realizing that military spending is essential to capitalism and if you are going to talk about cutting it, then you have to think pretty radically about what to put in its place. To end war production you have to end capitalism, so to speak.

JO: I don't think capitalism can reconstruct itself without socialism. For a democratic state, you elect politicians and they have to implement the laws they make. That's the way you get responsible legislation. My radical friends back east say that we have political democracy and we need economic democracy. I think that's horseshit. We don't have political democracy. The state is undemocratic. The Congress is undemocratic.

I had a talk the other day with a guy who runs the newspaper recycling program. I told him I didn't recycle my newspapers. He was appalled. I said, where do the recycled newspapers go? He told me they are sold to three or four paper companies in San Mateo. I asked him if the companies were getting them – the paper, that is – cheap. He said yes, maybe a quarter of the price it would be if they were cutting down trees in Canada and buying materials from a pulp mill. So by recycling newspapers to these paper companies we're saving trees.

Just think what you're saying, I said. You're lowering the costs of production for these companies, giving them this free labor and going around trying to get my free labor by making me stack my newspapers. If these companies lower their costs, then their profits are going to go up. If their profits go up, then their accumulation rate is going to go up and that's going to have a positive effect on whole economy. What you're doing is really causing problems someplace else.

AC: Because the exuberant capitalist will rush off and do some exploiting someplace else?

JO: Exactly. Then I said to the newspaper recycler, is there any element of new progressive social relations coming off this enterprise, apart from this conversation between you and me? He was pretty shocked. And then he remembered that there was a Gray Bear operation in Live Oak, between here and where you live in Aptos, in which old, retired people come and organize their own labor in this newspaper recycling business. They load the trucks and have coffee when they want it. And I said, that's interesting. That's the important part of your recycling project: to promote alternative production relationships. Little models.

I finally said to the man, if you set up a recycling project where your outfit helps to organize, to create the conditions to organize social relations of production that make sense, that have to do with fraternity, equality, liberty, and justice, etc., etc., then I'll recycle my newspapers. Come back and tell me when you have done that.

AC: What do you do with your old newspapers?

JO: Throw them in the trash. What do you do with yours?

AC: I throw them in the trash. Back in Ireland with my mother we leave them out for the man from St. Vincent de Paul who takes them away for some charitable purpose, thereby maintaining social relations in the sorry state they are today, imploring the poor to pray for relief from heaven. And needless to say, the poor people of my home town are very glad to have St. Vincent de Paul bail them out in their hour of need.

➤➤

JANUARY 18   *Aptos*

EVERY FOUR YEARS THE plump and ruddy visage of Senator Edward Kennedy appears on the nation's television screens, just as it did last summer, amid respectful commentary about the senator's symbolic role as guardian of the great traditions of F.D.R., the New Frontier, the Great Society, etc., etc. But much of the theoretical groundwork for Reagan's regulatory counterrevolution came out of Kennedy's office, and many of his former aides are now toiling profitably for Continental Airlines.

In the mid-to-late seventies Kennedy's rent-a-thinkers began to tout deregulation as the answer to low productivity and bureaucratic and corporate inertia. Famous at the time was a screed by his chief counsel Stephen Breyer quantifying such things as environmental pollution in terms of assessable and fungible 'risks', which could be bought and sold in the marketplace.

The two prongs of the Kennedy deregulatory attack – now decorated with the political label 'neoliberalism' – were aimed at airlines and trucking, and Kennedy's man Alfred Kahn was duly installed by Jimmy Carter at the Civil Aeronautics Board to introduce the cleansing winds of competition into the industry. By and large, airline deregulation went down well with the press and, for a time, with the public, who rejoiced in the bargains offered by the small fry such as People's Express, and by the big fry striking back. The few critics who said that within a few years the nation would be left with five or six airlines, oligopoly and higher fares were mostly ignored. No one ever really wrote about the terrible effects of trucking deregulation, outside the left press. It was certainly the most ferocious anti-labor move of the seventies.

Meanwhile the best and the brightest from the office of the Massachusetts senator are making money hand over fist trying to break unions on behalf of Frank Lorenzo, the Texan entrepreneur who runs the Texas Air Corporation and its properties, Continental Airlines and its subsidiary, Eastern.

➤→

JANUARY 20   *Aptos*
IT WAS ALWAYS EASY to laugh at Reagan and to underestimate him. The East Coast elite distrusted him even as late as the 1980 campaign, trying to head off his nomination by running Gerald Ford again. Learning of the Ford bid, Reagan turned to an aide and cried, 'What have they got against me? I support big oil. I support big business. Why don't they trust me?' Probably because they thought he would blow them up, along with everyone else. He didn't, but they never did trust him, though they had a hell of a party while he was around.

The people who did trust Reagan were mostly white men, small businessmen, rednecks, some (sometimes many) union people, construction workers, many ordinary folk up and down the map who wanted a world much as it had been in the 1950s. Them he betrayed.

➤→

JANUARY 21   *Aptos*
AS REAGAN SHAMBLED toward the stairway of Air Force One at Andrews Air Force Base on Inauguration Day, Bryant Gumbel mused to Tom Brokaw that this seemed to him 'quite remarkable'. It turned out that Gumbel was mightily impressed that the 78-year-old Reagan had not sought to stave off retirement by mounting a coup d'état. All around the world, Gumbel said, leaders 'cling to power', whereas here in the US they head off for the old folks' home without a whimper.

➤→

JANUARY 22   *San Simeon, California*
DRIVING WITH MAMA DOWN Route 1 to Los Angeles, we stopped at the Monterey Bay Aquarium. The aquarium, funded by the Packard millions and therefore a benign extrusion of the military-industrial complex, is nicely done and free of the cutification of the natural kingdom that makes the San Diego Zoo so offensive. The signs near the panda cage in that frightful place ('Sex and the

Single Panda') still make me tremble when I think about them.

Even so, an improperly instructed child gazing at the large central tank in the aquarium at the end of Cannery Row could nourish the sort of illusions that prompted poor little boys in Brooklyn to sneak into the polar bear pit at the Prospect Park Zoo to play with the furry white mammals. Round and round the Monterey tank glide a number of fish normally averse to being next to one another. A plump black sea bass nonchalantly nudged past a shark. But this calm is ensured by the regular, generous provision of food, without which the tank would soon be the scene of strife unsettling to the onlookers.

⇒

JANUARY 25 *Aptos*

BRUCE ANDERSON is in the county jail on a charge trumped up by Jim Spence, the scoundrelly superintendent of education in Mendicino, against whom the *Anderson Valley Advertiser* has been waging a fierce campaign. Bruce has written a good description.

'Many of the inmates here think of their home as a cave. I think of it as a grotto, meaning a half-submerged cave. Most grottoes are cleansed by the tides. This one has the deep-down grime of a decade of neglect. No tides clean it. Water runs constantly though from unrepaired showers and faucets. Stale, nicotine-pregnant air is perpetually recirculated, the captive oxygen being probably the oldest in the country. The ceilings around the heating ducts are black. This place would be an ideal testing site for the effects of secondary smoke inhalation. It's as if it were designed for contagion. At night, lying on my steel military rack, I listen to the running water, the steady hiss of the poisonous circulating air, and the idiotic, inescapable braying of canned laughter from the always-on television set. "Soul Train!" yells one faction, "FBI!" screams another as the almost daily programming dispute breaks out in the day room. Some choice. I thought I hated television before I came to jail, but now I plot assassinations of network executives. This is a place that takes some getting used to. It isn't Wellspring.'

⇒

JANUARY 31 *Aptos*

Dear Mr. Peretz,

Do you wish to sell the *New Republic*? May I know your terms? I am one of a small group whose members are eager to buy the *New Republic* and restore its credit as a liberal journal. We suspect that you may be ready to sell from the vacancy and desperation of recent articles, which I at least associate with the moral and material bankruptcy of the state of Israel.

I am the editor of this magazine, but none of my associates is in the magazine publishing business.

Ben Sonnenberg
Grand Street

Peretz has told *Newsday* that the magazine is not for sale, certainly not to the man Sonnenberg and his associates, self and Edward Said included.

➤→

FEBRUARY 1   *Aptos*
'LESS THAN SEVENTY-FIVE YEARS after it officially began, the contest between capitalism and socialism is over: capitalism has won. The Soviet Union, China, and Eastern Europe have given us the clearest possible proof that capitalism organizes the material affairs of humanity more satisfactorily than socialism ... the great question now seems how rapid will be the transformation of socialism into capitalism, and not the other way around.' – Robert Heilbroner, *The New Yorker*

Heilbroner takes the view that here in the United States capitalists don't run the show. As he sees it, there is 'verticality of wealth' and 'horizontality of democracy'. In this benign geometry the 'polity bows to the general electorate' and 'the vote of the millionaire counts for no more than that of the beggar'. He's writing from New York after all, where the wealthy are usually vertical and the beggars, equally puissant in democratic principle, horizontal on the sidewalk.

It's amazing how often one encounters people of sound reputation and widely advertised intellectual prowess who seem never to have opened a newspaper or garnered by any other means some inkling of how things actually work. In *Economics in Perspective* Galbraith points out that many Japanese business leaders were Marxists in their youth and that though they have evidently forsworn any revolutionary vocation, 'the Marxian influence does have a significant consequence: it relieves Japanese economic and political thought of the notion of a social dichotomy, even conflict, between the private market economy and the state, a theoretical conflict that has a strong hold on all conventional American and British economic thinking. In Japan the state is indeed, as Marx held, the executive committee of the capitalist class; this is normal and natural.'

George Bush, who has probably never read a page of Marx or Lenin in his life, unless the CIA's library has their works in one-page digest form, has a better grasp than Heilbroner of the role of the state as e.c. of the capitalist class.

FEBRUARY 5   *Aptos*

ASSIGNMENT TO INTERVIEW Helmut Newton. The Dutch ladies who live next
door to me here in the Adobe ask me what I'm reading and I try to shield them
from all the pictures of women with saddles on their backs and the rest of
Newton's stuff.

➤

FEBRUARY 9   *Monte Carlo*

THE GREAT NEWTON STRUCK a suitably *mondaine* note by greeting me affably,
then speeding back to the telephone. 'Look around', he cried over his shoulder.
'It's a very important guy in Paris. I must ...' He disappeared into his study.
The apartment was the sort of place successful journalists in the sixties used to
favor: an Eames chair, plenty of polished glass and metal, a bookshelf that
looked as though it had been designed in Milan. Through the tenth-floor
window of a modern high rise perched on the Monaco mountainside I looked
down on Monte Carlo, then out across the Mediterranean.

'Catherine Deneuve est d'accord', Newton's voice boomed down the corridor. 'Elle est ravie ... Fouquet's, c'est très bien. Elle va rester au diner avec un
ami de son choix.' There were some blowups of Newton photographs on the
wall, Stieglitz and Rodchenko. There was a picture of an enormous bull in the
sauvage German style. Newton called for me to join him in his little study.

Newton's photographic career began when he was twelve. He took seven
pictures with his new box camera in the Berlin subway, none of which came out.
The eighth was of the Berlin radio tower, and there it was in the print, standing
up like a toothpick.

'Do you think photographers are happy?'

'I don't know, most of them are boring.'

'Who are your heroes?'

'Brassai, always.'

Newton's eyes were darting glances at the telephone and he finally seized it
up. 'I've got to see my princess today, and I'd better see if she's there. I'm not
bragging, but I'm responsible for her ballet photography.' He dialed between
increasingly cryptic sentences. 'Ballet's her baby, because of her mother.'
Someone in the palace of the Grimaldis evidently picked up the phone. 'Oui,
bonjour, c'est Newton.' The word 'Newton' was said on a note of rising,
confident affirmation. New-TON. Across the desk Newton looked at me with a
trace of irony before proclaiming into the mouthpiece, 'Est-ce-que la princesse
Caroline est la?' But the princess wasn't at home. Newton left word she should
call back.

We went back to talking about photographers. Another great idol of his had
been the photographer Yva, to whom he had been apprenticed at the age of

sixteen in Berlin. 'I worshipped the ground she stood on. She did wonderful work, mostly fashion. Very sexy. She was a lesbian.'

He brightened as June, his wife of forty years, entered the room. 'I've hundreds of things to tell you', he shouted, 'but not in front of *him*.' He pointed at me warningly and then fell into strategic planning on where we should all have lunch. Rampoldi's? Perhaps too stiff. What about La Pinède down by the sea? Perfect. He seized the phone. 'C'est New-TON.' Reservations were made, and with Helmut impetuously at the wheel, we plunged through the streets in a VW Golf.

The conversation turned briefly to a well-known Hollywood actress famed for her drinking. 'I like the physical aspect of her now', Newton said thoughtfully. 'A big ass, those beautiful legs. The skin that is white, but not quite fresh.'

'Oh, Helmy, not quite fresh, how can you say that!'

'But good skin. Very interesting.'

'Bruises all over', June concluded by way of finale.

'I never knew prudery as a young man', Newton mused. 'At fourteen at the swimming club in Berlin I fell madly in love. We wanted to make love but didn't know how to do it. Then she had to go away for a swimming contest for the weekend, and when she got back, I'd found out what to do. I had my own room with its own entrance and we went ahead and did it. Then I went into the kitchen and I was starving and I told my mother everything. She was a little bit upset, but she said, "I'm going to increase your pocket money so you can buy French letters. I don't want you bringing home stuffed pigeons", meaning a girl who was pregnant.'

'So none of your fooling around with perverse erotic themes comes from guilt?'

'No, but I do like the concept of sin, of what is forbidden but not forbidden.'

By this time we were sitting comfortably under an umbrella by the side of the Mediterranean looking at a sea that, as Newton pointed out, was as black as the plastic Fellini used to represent it in his film about Casanova. Discussion of the Venetian lover led to the fundamental issue: are men nicer than women or vice versa?

Me: ' I think women are nicer than men. More romantic.'

June: 'I think men are nicer than women.'

Helmut: 'I agree. I like men's company and I don't get much of it because of my job, but I've never been one to go out with the boys.'

June: 'But you do have a lot of woman in you, don't you, Helmy?'

By now Newton was staring over my shoulder at a neighboring table. 'Look at that woman in the earrings', he hissed excitedly. Squinting back I could see what had caught his eye. The earring lady was very Newton, having the middle finger of her left hand carefully bound up in a long splint and bandage.

'It's been doing a lot of work!' June whispered, then, glancing at the earring lady's older companion, added, 'He's someone else's husband.'

'How do you know about these things?' Newton muttered, beckoning a waiter. 'It makes me wonder.'

He had a low-toned colloquy with the waiter and then reported that the couple came to the restaurant every Saturday and that the man who was somebody else's husband was probably a gangster. We kept the bandaged finger under observation as we ate our fish soup.

The conversation turned to voyeurism. I told them the story related in Kenneth Anger's *Hollywood Babylon*, of how Princess Caroline's mother had once agreed to undress in front of a lighted window while Hitchcock spied on her through a telescope.

'But it's Schnitzler's *Fraulein Else*!' Newton slapped the table. 'It's a story about a young girl of fifteen or sixteen who's staying in a grand hotel with her aunt. The mother writes to the daughter that the father is being bankrupted because of some dishonest thing he's done. In the hotel is an elderly man who tells the girl he will save her father's reputation if he can have her. In the end he's in the game room, and the daughter comes down the stairs with nothing on but a fur coat and he gets to see her naked. So he's there in the shadows and she just walks through the room. It's marvelous! I understand that, you see.'

I could indeed see why he understood it, since Newton has just given a glowing evocation, courtesy of his beloved Schnitzler, of the *mise en scène* for a Newton photograph. It had long seemed to me that a lot of Newton's work refers, mostly in irony or parody, to the Nazi culture and aesthetic from which he escaped. Newton readily agreed, citing his famous photographs of large blondes as having just those antecedents in Nazi iconography of Aryan supergirls. 'My pictures are always based on reality. Like Edvard Munch, who said, "I don't paint what I see, I paint what I saw." I photograph what I saw. I don't do that S and M stuff anymore', he added with a hint of nostalgia. 'My car used to have chains, always chains in it. I used to tie up girls all the time.'

'When did you start the perverse stuff?'

'In French *Vogue* in the early sixties.'

'It's not so long ago', June broke in, 'that Helmut did that photograph of a model sitting in a long dress but with her knees apart, and she was looking at a guy walking past. And there was a dog involved, but just sitting at the girl's feet. It was in an American magazine and people cancelled their subscriptions. Journalists called up to ask why the dog was there.'

'It was in 1975', Newton added. 'It did me a lot of good.'

Newton was peering again at the lady in the earrings with the bandaged finger and the boyfriend in the *milieu*. 'She has a very interesting leather bracelet', he reported.

'You seem a happy sort of fellow.'

'I am. I love God. He looks after me and I look away when he's bad.'

'When do you feel despair?'

'In London.'

The lady with all the accoutrements had long since gone and the Mediterranean slapped wickedly against the sea wall, tossed up by an east wind. We headed back into town. Somewhere, higher up on the mountain there was a house my mother used to stay in back in the thirties. It had belonged to a member of the Swedish royal family. One day he looked down on the winding corniche and seen a car skid, go over the edge. Stricken by the loss of wife and children he fled back to Scandinavia. Three quarters of a century ago Proust said that Monte Carlo was unacceptable. It's for people who have arrived but are never entirely sure how long the yacht will rest safely in its birth.

➤

FEBRUARY 18   *New York*

THE POLISH DIRECTOR Andrzej Wajda writes in his little memoir about moviemaking, *Double Vision*, that once he started directing *Hamlet* and realized the whimsical, arbitrary quality of the plot, the hardest thing was to relate onstage the sequence of events in proper order, from Hamlet's first meeting with his mother and the king to Fortinbras's victorious entrance in the final scene. That sequence of events could have been different if:

1. Hamlet had come to terms with his uncle, the king.
2. He had refused to believe in his father's ghost.
3. He had not succumbed to Ophelia's charms.
4. He had succeeded in killing the king while he was at prayer.
5. He had not killed Polonius by mistake, thinking he was the king.

Plus a whole lot of other 'ifs'.

And yet, Wajda goes on, 'we have to admit that *Hamlet* has a steel-like logic.' One thing just inevitably leads to another.

As with art, so with life. If in 1881 Alexander III, new Czar of all the Russias, had not made life even harder for the Jews, then the family of Louis B. Mayer would not have left Lithuania; Louis Zelznick (later Selznick) would maybe have stayed in Kiev and William Fuchs (later Fox) in Tulcheva, Hungary; the Warner family might have stayed loyal to Krasnashiltz, Poland; Adolph Zukor to Ricse, Hungary; Carl Laemmle to Wurtemberg; and Schmuel Gelbfisz (later Sam Goldwyn) to Warsaw. But Alexander III did not care for the Jews, so the whole gang listed above, born within a 500-mile radius of Warsaw, saw the writing on the wall as did about 1.5 million other Jews in the same period, and headed west.

You could say that Czar Alexander III founded Hollywood. He hanged Lenin's elder brother, too, and so maybe there would have been no Russian Revolution either. This Czar made the world the way it is today.

Wajda also tells a good story about something that happened the day the French left Algiers. People took to the streets and, in the course of events, still in a state of euphoria, arrived at the television studios. The gaping, empty studios, the television cameras and equipment scattered here and there, did not in the minds of the surging crowd seem to have any connection with what they conceived as television – that is, at least until the moment that someone in the know plugged in the cameras. Suddenly the blank screens of the monitors lit up, and the demonstrators saw their own bodies and faces on-screen. At first they were amused. Then they were emboldened. Hey, we're on TV! They realized if they could see themselves on the monitors, the rest of the population could also see them on sets throughout the city. Maybe even farther. They began to sing, dance, recite. The result was an uninterrupted television show that for once was completely authentic. It finally ended, as do all such spontaneous demonstrations, with the arrival of the police and armed forces.

All the same, Dr. Johnson differed with Wajda on Hamlet's 'steel-like logic'. 'The poet ... may be charged with equal neglect of poetical probability. The Apparition left the regions of the dead to little purpose; the revenge which he demands is not obtained but by the death of him that was required to take it; and the gratification which would arise from the destruction of a usurper and a murderer, is abated by the untimely death of Ophelia, the young, the beautiful, the harmless and the pious.'

➤

FEBRUARY 20 *Aptos*
THE FACT CHECKER for the Newton story says that since I can't supply the names of the gangster and the girl with a splint on her finger in the restaurant they should be cut. I say that this is completely absurd, and there's no way they should be identified.

Then the checker calls back after an hour and says that the descriptions of the couple might be libellous and so should be dropped. Her only obsession is she might somehow be held responsible for something. Finally the unknown couple are dropped, my story destroyed. This whole checking thing is lunacy.

➤

MARCH 1 *Topanga, California*
MY MAIN BEEF WITH Rushdie is that he apologized, offering an expression of regret that he may have caused offense to 'sincere followers of Islam'. This obviously would not propitiate Khomeini and was manifestly untrue anyway. Rushdie wrote a consciously blasphemous work, so the 'sincere followers' were precisely the people he desired to piss off.

MARCH 9   *Topanga*

FOR YEARS the great pleasure of looking at *Country Life*, the *Illustrated London News*, or *Tatler* (old style) was to study the role of retrievers, cocker spaniels, pugs, borzois, Jack Russells, chows, etc. in family portraits of the upper class. Dogs provided the *élan vital* for the otherwise spiritually consti- pated assemblies facing the camera and burdened with all the usual griefs of kinship, entail and estate taxes.

Of course, many people love dogs more than men or women, for all the obvious reasons. Then there's 'Love my dog, love me.' When I was growing up, girls knew this very well, burying face and golden curls in Towser's ruff. Dogs are jealous too, as adulterers know, pawing at the afternoon sheets, woofing angrily.

➤

MARCH 14   *Topanga*

THE MACHINISTS' STRIKE against Eastern provokes the usual sort of hostile coverage. Take the notion of 'the public'. In mainstream press reports of the strike something called 'the public' is gravely inconvenienced. This public is interviewed at airports and tends to be traveling to Florida for the family's first vacation in twenty-one years on tickets purchased by the accumulated life savings of the grandmother – now in an emergency room fighting for life after being insulted by a picket; tended by relatives who, after six days without food or water in a waiting room at the Atlanta airport, 'just want to go home'.

This same public does not include families of machinists thrown out of work by Frank Lorenzo's strategies. When Lorenzo closed down Eastern's Kansas City hub operation back in September, some 4,000 workers were inconven- ienced but somehow failed to make the 'member of the public' status necessary to earn sympathetic coverage.

➤

MARCH 16   *Topanga*

I'VE HAD A LETTER from Edward Abbey sitting in the big pile on my desk for the past three months and now I won't have to answer it, since Abbey died on Tuesday at the age of sixty-two. There always was a cranky survivalist tincture to his thought, and hence prose – but mostly in *Desert Solitaire* and above all *The Monkey Wrench Gang* it was a tolerable component in something magnifi- cent. You can still see 'Hayduke Lives' buttons around the southwest.

The argument of *The Monkey Wrench Gang* is that when push comes to shove, legal means are not enough:

The view from the knoll would be difficult to describe in any known terrestrial language. Bonnie thought of something like a Martian invasion, the War of the Worlds. Captain Smith was reminded of Kennecott's open-pit mine (world's largest) near Magna, Utah. Dr. Sarvis thought of the plain of fire and the oligarchs and oligopoly beyond: Peabody Coal, only one arm of Anaconda Copper, Anaconda only a limb of United States Steel, US Steel intertwined with the Pentagon, TVA, Standard Oil, General Dynamics, Dutch Shell, I.G. Farbenindustrie, the whole conglomerated cartel spread out upon half the planet earth like a global kraken, pan-tentacled, wall-eyed and parrot-beaked, its brain a bank of computer data centers, its blood the flow of money, its heart a radioactive dynamo, its language technotronic monologue of numbers and printed on magnetic tape ...

'See what I mean?' Hayduke says. 'Simple as shit. We place a charge here, a charge there, unreel a hundred yards of wire, set up the blaster, put Bonnie's little white hands on the plunger – '

➤

MARCH 23   *Rio de Janeiro*

THE BRAZILIAN SOCIALIST LEADER Lula defines the situation:

'The Third World War has already started – a silent war, not for that reason any the less sinister. This war is tearing down Brazil, Latin America and practically all the Third World. Instead of soldiers dying there are children, instead of millions of wounded there are millions of unemployed; instead of destruction of bridges there is the tearing down of factories, schools, hospitals and entire economies ... It is a war by the United States against the Latin American continent and the Third World. It is a war over the foreign debt, one which has as its main weapon interest, a weapon more deadly than the atom bomb, more shattering than a laser beam.'

The hut is sinking in the mud near the bridge over the River Guaibe in Porto Alegre, Brazil. A woman social worker is welcomed by five children, the oldest about eight years old. The parents have gone out foraging in the garbage heaps. Noticing how poorly the children look, the social worker asks them whether they have eaten recently. 'Yes, miss, yesterday Mummy made little cakes from wet newspapers.' 'What? Little cakes from what?' asks the woman. 'Mummy takes a sheet of newspaper, makes it into a ball and soaks it in water and when it is nice and soft kneads it into little cakes. We eat them, drink some water and feel nice and full inside.'

In Chile, laboratory of 'free market' policy, the Pinochet regime takes a creative approach to the statistics of hunger. Instead of measuring malnutrition in relation to a person's weight and age, as is usual, it looks at weight and height.

So a stunted child is not counted as malnourished, and thus is not eligible for food supplements, because her weight falls within an acceptable range for her height. 'Peru supplies some of the most disgusting food stories I've ever heard', Susan George writes. 'There's Nicovita, a fish-meal flour used for fattening chickens, manufactured under extremely dubious sanitary conditions. The good news is that (at least in the late 1970s), a lot of Peruvian shanty-town dwellers were subsisting on Nicovita. The bad news is that, as the once finance minister, Silva Ruete, put it, "They don't even have chicken feed to eat regularly."' George reports that in 1981 Oscar Trelles, former president of the Peruvian Senate, declared that 'it was healthier to eat less, that thin women were far more attractive than fat ones and that Jewish children who had gone hungry in the concentration camps had not become stupider as a result.'

Economically the African continent is in a state of virtual collapse. From the early to mid 1980s twenty African nations had economies that remained stagnant or declined. Structural Adjustment Facilities, new projects to realign economies through the joint efforts of the IMF and the World Bank, had by mid 1988 entrapped almost thirty of the world's poorest countries, the majority in Africa.

On average over the past decade the Third World has exported to the First about $20 billion a year; $44 billion in 1988. When it comes to the matter of whether capitalism is 'winning', trust the evidence of our senses. Look at the miserable shacks along the riverbanks in Santiago. Or the *favela* Rocinha, sprawling up a hillside not 200 yards from the high-rise residential fortresses of Rio de Janeiro's middle class. Or the bodies bundled in niches on New York's streets and lodged amid the bushes under the Los Angeles freeways. This is victory?

➤

MARCH 27   *Rio Branco*
SUSANNA AND I are here in the western Amazon for the meetings of the rubber tappers and the Indians. All grist for *Fate of the Forest*. Today we talked to Osmarino, one of the tappers who took over the union after Chico Mendes got murdered. The feds have given Osmarino two bodyguards, but he says they can't afford bullets. He reckons he has a 2 percent chance of staying alive through the rest of the year. Ailton Krenak, almost only extant member of his tribe, is very funny about anthropologists. Says they used to make up the most fantastic stories about kinship relations, all solemnly writen down by the anthrops. Ailton reckons Indians should get a cut of the royalties of all these books.

APRIL 5   *Porto Velho*

DRIVE WITH WIM and Susanna along BR 364, the road. Wim wants to start a tree farm, part of a project to help small settlers amass a little capital (tropical hardwoods) and fruits. There's land with good soil for sale, but Wim says it will take months to crank money out of a foundation. Susanna and I each give him $500 and are now co-founders of Green Hell Farms. Wim is a huge Dutchman. He must be six-foot eight and broad in proportion. He says he once stayed with an Indian tribe and left a pair of trousers behind. Subsequent travellers reported seeing these immense pantaloons strung up aby the Indians to show that giants walked the earth. We argue about cows. Wim takes the role of prosecution. Cows are stigmatized as ravishers of forest, etc., etc. Susanna speaks for the defense, cow as small peasant's asset of last resort.

Dinner beside the Madeira River, where the US venture capitalist Farquhar built the railhead for his line into Bolivia. Lots of *caipirinhas* – a kind of margarita made with *cachaca*, a sort of rum. Very elevating.

➤

APRIL 7   *New York*

WHY DID MUMFORD GIVE his biographer, Donald Miller, access to his notations and sketches of the sexual organs and capacities of his wife, Sophia, and his most significant mistress, Catherine Bauer? Or to the innumerable letters setting forth in detail his erotic preoccupations? He comes out of it all very badly.

When Mumford and the beautiful Sophia decided to become lovers, an investigative preliminary to marriage, both were virgins with limited knowledge of anatomy or sexual procedures. He thought the vulva was set horizontally. She did not know what a penis was and feared impregnation after being clasped tightly by a black man on the dance floor. Though set upon a long-term relationship with Mumford, Sophia wanted to experiment. Mumford was opposed to this. He spoke of 'conquering' her, which meant in essence that she was to have no other close associations and no separate life or career.

Mumford's preoccupation with regionalism, and hostility to the decadent metropole, had much to do with his fear that in New York his young wife 'will endeavor to extract from metropolitan existence all that it offers – which means the end of our marriage.' Sophia fought against this for a while. 'I don't want to be submerged in the personality of one who has a definite sphere', she wrote early on. But she got beaten down.

By this time, on the other hand, Mumford had discovered himself eager to grow and start an affair with Helen Ascher. Guilt rendered him impotent, but he saw his decision to be unfaithful as a 'genuine step toward emotional maturity: I had faced the man I was, and I had dared to do what Sophy had only dreamed of.' He came to suspect that the big problem of his marriage with

Sophia was that they were physically 'mismatched ... for the purposes of sexual intercourse' and that she would have been happier with someone with 'a larger and more insistent penis'. 'As to your orgasms', he wrote to Catherine Bauer, 'I count them along with *The Golden Day* as the only two really successful works of art I have produced so far.'

➤

APRIL 10   *New York*
BOWLES'S PENIS WAS, ON his biographer's account of it, far less intrusive or unruly. Sex does not appear to have been a big item on his agenda. Virgil Thomson reckoned Bowles had a lower 'power of ejaculation'. He married a lesbian, Jane, who threw herself into innumerable disastrous passions, most notably with the Moroccan woman Cherifa.

Bowles's dad, Claude, was one of those fathers from whom one can never run too far. He was a dentist and seems to have hated Paul from the first. Two of Bowles's most chilling stories are one in which a son seduces his father, and 'The Delicate Prey' (which Tennessee Williams warned Bowles was too strong to see print), in which a bandit slices off the boy Drib's sexual organs, stuffs them in a hole he cuts in Driss's belly, rapes him, and then slits his throat. In the war for Mummy's heart one takes no prisoners. The etymology of Bowles is truly summed up in the word 'expatriate'.

He visits Stein and Toklas in the Rhone Valley: 'At home, Bowles was assigned the duty of giving Basket his daily run. The ritual, like the bath that preceded it (given to the dog by Toklas), had to be performed at a certain hour every morning. For some reason it required Bowles to don lederhosen. Once outfitted, Bowles would proceed to run about the garden with the dog trailing behind. The quick pace had to be maintained or else Basket would overtake his exerciser, scratching the back of Bowles's exposed legs. All this was done to the accompaniment of Stein's commands of "Faster, Freddy, faster." Stein obviously greatly enjoyed the session, and Bowles, almost in spite of himself, did too, for it seemed to him "a sign of the most personal kind of relationship".'

➤

APRIL 15   *Aptos*
THE MARCH 24 SPILL from the *Exxon Valdez* was a 'disaster', but as George Bush was eager to point out, one 'disaster', caused by a supposedly drunk captain, does not mean you have to beef up measures to protect Alaska.

'Disaster' is actually normalcy perceived at the level of symbolism. The 500-plus wells on the North Slope produce 840,000 gallons of waste each year. The Alaska Department of Environmental Conservation recorded 953 spills involving oil and other liquids on the North Slope in 1985 and 1986. The contents of more than 250 reserve pits, each filled with 13 million gallons of toxic pollutants, are pumped onto gravel roads or the tundra each year. The whole coastal plain has been turned into a series of toxic cesspools, and each year the North Slope emits more nitrogen oxides than the cars on the streets of Washington, D.C.

This is normalcy. The *Exxon Valdez* merely highlighted it. Even if the oil had not spilled out into Prince William Sound, it would have made its way down to the terminals in Long Beach and then ended up in the air over Los Angeles, San Francisco and other conurbations. This too is normalcy, no longer defined as disaster. A lot of what is described as 'news' is really a series of mild doses of anesthetic, habituating you slowly to the new order of things.

Smog over Los Angeles used to be a disaster, but now is normal, whereas a clear day on which you can see the San Gabriel Mountains is now a stroke of good fortune. Normalcy in Alaska is now a series of toxic dumps, and soon Prince William Sound will become an 'ordinary' commercial channel like the Houston Ship Channel, which periodically bursts into flames, just like the Cuyahoga River in the Randy Newman song.

APRIL 24 *Topanga*

NO NEED TO HASTEN to Braunau, as so many journalists have, to find material for reflection upon the centennial of Hitler's birth. A simple reading of the day's papers sufficed. The Syracuse *Herald-Journal* disclosed last week that twenty years ago the evangelist Billy Graham sent Richard Nixon a secret plan urging him to bomb dikes 'which could overnight destroy the economy of North Vietnam'.

Graham's memorandum to Nixon, declassified earlier this year, is dated April 15, 1969, and was drafted after the evangelist met in Bangkok with a group of missionaries who had traveled thither from Vietnam. These men of God said that if peace talks in Paris, by then eleven months old, failed, then Nixon should withdraw American troops but keep permanent bases in Vietnam, along with overwhelming air power. They also called for a buildup of the South Vietnamese Air Force, the arming of 'loyal' mountain tribes and formation of a government-in-exile to 'liberate the North'. Above all, they urged, with Graham's imprimatur, the bombing of the dikes.

In the final months of World War II the Nazis sought to delay the advance of Allied troops by opening the dikes in Holland. This stroke against the Dutch population was ordered by the German High Commissioner in Holland, Seyss-Inquart. By the end of 1944 approximately 500,000 acres of land had been flooded, leading to what Gabriel Kolko called 'the most precipitous decline in food consumption any West European country suffered during the war'.

Of the 185 Nazis indicted at Nuremberg, twenty-four were sentenced to death, of whom one was Seyss-Inquart. Kolko's observation came in testimony lodged with the Russell International War Crimes Tribunal, which in 1967 conducted hearings on US war crimes in Indochina. Seyss-Inquart merely opened dikes. On May 13, 1953, in Korea, as Kolko also testified, the US Air Force attacked and destroyed the Toksan dam near Pyongyang. The aim was to wreck the system irrigating three-quarters of North Korea's rice farms. Adjacent dams were bombed on succeeding days, while armistice talks went on.

In their book *Korea: The Unknown War*, Jon Halliday and Bruce Cumings present a USAF photograph of the ruined Chasan dam. They also quote from the main USAF study of the bombings: 'These strikes, largely passed over by the press, military observers, and news commentators ... constituted one of the most significant air operations of the Korean war.' The study remarks that 'attacks in May would be most effective psychologically', when the backbreaking labor of rice transplanting had been completed but before the roots became firmly embedded.

Flood waters bursting through the destroyed Toksan dam 'scooped clean 27 miles of valley below', drowned the civilians sheltering underground and sent floods into Pyongyang. The USAF study tranquilly stressed, 'To the Communists the smashing of the dams meant primarily the destruction of their chief sustenance – rice. The Westerner can little conceive the awesome meaning that the loss of this staple food commodity has for the Asian – starvation and slow death.' It also cited the frantic repair efforts 'carried out round-the-clock, with complete disregard to the delayed-action bombs strewn over the target area.' This was noted in another official military history as an example of 'oriental fatalism'.

And Vietnam? While all eyes were on the North, where irrigation damage was relatively minor, the USAF destroyed dam upon dam in the South, without reproach. In 1969 Henry Kamm reported that in Batanang Province southeast of Hue there had been a dike 'blasted by American jets to deprive the North Vietnamese of a food supply'. (The peasantry in the area, including refugees from My Lai, had been herded into a camp over which flew a flag bearing the words 'We Thank You for Liberating Us From Communist Terror.') Kamm returned after two years to find the dike unrepaired and salt water from the South China Sea submerging the fields where rice once grew.

In 1951, a couple of years before the spirit of Seyss-Inquart hovered above the North Korean dams, President Juan José Arévalo of Guatemala made a farewell address. 'I took over the presidency possessed with romantic fire, believing as always in the intrinsic nobility of man ... Roosevelt's speeches told us ... that the horror of the killing would return our liberties to nations and to men.' Then Arévalo described the conspiracies by indigenous mercenaries and 'banana magnates, compatriots of Roosevelt's'. That, Arévalo said sadly, 'was when the ingenuous and romantic schoolmaster discovered from the presidency of his country the extent to which brilliant international sermonizing about democracy and human liberties is perishable … I came to confirm that, according to certain international norms, … little countries don't have a right to sovereignty … The arms of the Third Reich were broken and conquered … but in the ideological dialogue … Roosevelt lost the war. The real winner was Hitler.'

➤

MAY 2   *Topanga*

Dear Alexander Cockburn,

It has come to my attention that you have been making false and malicious statements about my interviews with the late David Kennedy. I have consulted counsel about this matter and advise you to stop doing this. I am sending this letter to you to serve notice to you that if you intend to publish this, you and your publisher do so at your peril.

Sincerely,
David Horowitz
Los Angeles

➤

MAY 3   *Topanga*

I WEAR A 1925 OMEGA which is a seasoned practical joker, keeping perfect time for weeks on end and then tripping me up by standing dead still for an hour when I'm not looking, then starting up again. The quartz generation knows nothing of these pleasures, being intent only on having everything figured out, right down to the last nanosecond. This is the chronometric culture of refined capitalism. Time is money to a level of precision not envisaged even by Frederick Taylor, great herald of time-and-motion studies, who was admired by Lenin (who kept his own watch ten minutes fast). At the deathbed Taylor's loved ones heard his watch tick, then didn't hear it and knew that he was dead, since watch and heart were synchronous in their diachrony. An old watch says, Time is fun, time is beauty, but of course also, given the rising value of antiques, time is money. As always.

➤

MAY 7   *New York*

VANDERBILT SECURED the services of a Victorian writer, Earl Shinn, to concoct a pseudonymous paean to the glories of his new home. Shinn threw himself into the task. Viewing Mrs. Vanderbilt's bedroom, which had a mural by Jules Lefebvre on the ceiling, Shinn wrote, 'The painting represents the dream of a poet who, with an invocation to the goddess of night upon his lips, has sunk to sleep on a Summer evening under a starry sky. The departure of night and the coming of day are represented by Phoebus, with crescent moon upon his brow, retiring, while Aurora, in a silver car, rides over the scattering mists, and ushers in the opening day. The rising vapors melt away and disclose the edge of the rising sun.'

But the construction workers screwed up, and the painting was displayed backward with the sun rising from the west. Of course, these workers could have been making their own piece of social commentary, to the effect that the rich often wish time to stand still or run backward, in which hope William Henry Vanderbilt was disappointed, dying after relatively brief enjoyment of these luxuries.

Vanderbilt's $9 million birthday present to his wife, Alva, was the Marble House in Newport. But Alva later married Oliver H. P. Belmont, and the couple lived in his house, Belcourt Castle. Belmont wanted to be near his horses, who resided on the first floor with their grooms, while the quality lived above. The Marble House was reserved for laundry and ironing, making it the most expensive drop-off in the world, then and since. The stalls for Belmont's privileged quadrupeds were each marked with a gold nameplate and the horses supposedly bedded down with pure linen sheets embroidered with the Belmont crest. Small wonder that Alva needed an extensive laundry. Stuffed and mounted upstairs with armored mannequins were the remains of Belmont's two favorite horses. Stained-glass windows depicted medieval tourneys. The rich retained this passion for living in Gothic tombs at least until the end of the 1920s.

With Belmont's death Alva moved back into the Marble House and continued with her architectural diversions. She got Richard Howland Hunt, son of the man who designed the Marble House, to build a Chinese pavilion overlooking Rhode Island Sound. Alva enjoyed reposeful tea parties therein. These were grueling occasions for her servants, since the pavilion had no kitchen. They had to dash to and from the main house with fast-cooling infusions. Eventually Alva built a little railroad for the tea carriers to ride upon in style.

In their enormous palaces the rich had constantly to battle with this problem of getting the desired liquids to a tolerable temperature. The emperor Franz Josef groaned for years at the sight of his valet approaching his bath with only one pot of boiling water, which had scant effect on the icy pool in which he performed his ablutions. 'Why not two pots of boiling water?' cried the master of the Austro-Hungarian Empire.

The servants of Frederick Augustus Hervey, fourth earl of Bristol and bishop of Derry, would have similarly wished for the age of steam to come to their rescue. The earl-bishop, insatiate in his constructions, spied the Temple of Vesta at Tivoli and liked it so well he tried to buy it from the innkeeper on whose property it stood. The innkeeper was firm in his refusal, so the earl-bishop got his friend Michael Shanahan to build him a replica. It stood on the cliffs of Derry, lashed by winds so powerful that the servants could get back to the main house only on their hands and knees, cursing Lucretius as they did so. The entablature on the 'Mussenden Temple', as it was called, carried an inscription from the Latin poet: 'Sweet it is, when on the high seas the winds are lashing the waters, to gaze from the land on another's struggles.' Mariners, irked by Lucretius's inconsiderate hexameters, could recite the lines maliciously while the servants up on the cliff tacked and beat against the wind.

➤

MAY 10   *New York*

I WENT TO THE *Monthly Review* and interviewed Paul Sweezy and Harry Magdoff.

HM: Back in 1949, at the founding of *Monthly Review*, Paul and Leo said, We've got to talk about the socialist idea. Now again we have to explore fundamental socialist ideals. You cannot create a decent society with emphasis on growth alone. The question is, What kind of growth? For what purpose? We have to go back to the basic principles of socialism, out of which Marx and Engels grew: utopian socialism.

PS: Socialism is now perceived by most people who call themselves socialists as removing the worst excesses of capitalism. That's understandable, but totally wrong in the sense that what is needed is the negation of capitalism, not the removal of its excesses. Excrescences and excesses are not the essence of environmental degradation here. It's the system itself. You have to have people in charge who care about things other than making profits; and the people implementing the policies have to care too.

HM: Which means economic, political and cultural revolution.

PS: Mao had the right ideas. Probably it was impossible to carry them out.

AC: How do you think Mao looks these days?

PS: I think he looks great.

AC: You don't think he destroyed the party with the Cultural Revolution?

PS: He probably destroyed the party because he had to, because it was a lousy party.

HM: There *was* a capitalist road!

AC: That's true. How do you think Fidel looks?

PS: I don't know. I haven't followed too closely. I sympathize deeply with him for standing for what he believes. He's headstrong and he's made a lot of mistakes, flew in the face of common sense. But what the hell, that's probably the way human history has to go anyway.

AC: Why do you think Mao looks so good?

PS: Because he said the kind of things – believed them and really inspired people to believe them – which have to be done to have a decent society. 'Serve the people.' 'Public service, not private gain.' Marx, if he had come back alive, would have said Mao's his boy ... I haven't seen anything in Marx that isn't good. I think he's got better and better, I really do. Mao is the only real Marxist at the leadership level in the post-Marx period.

AC: Leaving Vladimir Ilich out of this, are we?

PS: Well, his problems were so different. I think that if he'd lived he might have become a Maoist, in the sense of attacking the party and bombarding the party headquarters out of necessity to change the whole thing around.

HM: Mao challenged the idea that economic planning would dissolve conflicts of interest among the people. He saw it more dialectically: conflicts between intellectuals and manual workers, between the city and the countryside, stratification in the party and society. He said it was necessary to struggle to overcome these differences, whether it takes 100 or 500 years. But now within the framework of socialism – which is really social welfare in a social democratic framework – all they want to do is get the kind of economic growth of the capitalist world. It can't be done. It creates the same kind of problems as in the capitalist world.

PS: If we had a revolution here, in this rich country, we'd have to change our whole way of life.

➤

MAY 24   *Aptos*

J. IS INCENSED ABOUT a Falk piece for *The Nation*. In her capacity as Managing Editor she sent Victor a memo, which of course he will not answer.

Victor:

I am astonished at Richard Falk's editorial, its incredible lack of thoughtfulness and simple respect for the English language. You ask anyone on the street how they would define 'revolution' and I bet the vast majority would say something that would come down to a profound, fundamental change in the structure of a state or the basic contours of consciousness. Falk's use of the word indicates how slack usage has become since people started saying things like 'the Reagan Revolution'. This is more than a simple linguistic point. Start with the sentence 'In country after country "people power" has demonstrated its potency against entrenched forces of dictatorial rule.' The allusion is to the Philippines, and we are meant therefore to see that country's experience as a model for the new 'revolutionary politics'. If the Philippines had a revolution with the ousting of Marcos, then one can have no optimism any more in the transformative vision of revolution. 'Entrenched forces of dictatorial rule'? Where in the Philippines has been the break-up of the oligarchy? the submission of the armed forces? Aquino is slavish to her class and a puppet of the army. People who challenge that setup are being killed throughout the islands with her blessings (she after all encouraged the formation of vigilante squads). There have been more abuses of labor under Aquino than ever recorded under Marcos. Yet Falk writes weakly, 'Aquino has been unable to deliver on the promises to protect human rights and end corruption that she made during the great popular victory that swept her to power in February 1986.' Why is this? Perhaps because the Philippines never had a revolution; it had an election – a tumultuous one, to be sure, one that drove the dictator from his palace and brought throngs of people into the streets. But those people were never truly mobilized for a political project beyond turning the dictator out, and Aquino had no intention of mobilizing them. She was merely the convenient person on whom they pinned their hopes, and she is incapable now of delivering on her promises of '86 because for those promises ever to have been real she would have had to embark on a revolutionary course, a true revolutionary course, and that she is incapable of.

It seems that for Falk all anyone has to do is challenge 'actually existing socialism', from whatever perspective, to be classified a revolutionary and a radical. All is leveled. The socialist critic of the Polish state is on par with the fanatically nationalistic and anticommunist Papist. In the end though for Poland revolution seems to equal elections and a legal trade union. Are we to assume that the Soviet Union had half a revolution because it too just had broader elections? This is just silly.

J.

➤

JUNE 2 *Aptos*

PIOUS FOLK RECOMMEND a war on waste, and lament the waste of war, which constitutes a double slur on two fine American words. The American system – capitalism – needs war (or the permanent war economy) *and* waste. Without the stimulus of war, mankind would not have had the production line (first designed by the British Navy in the Woolwich arsenal at the start of the 19th century), radar, or 1950s furniture. Eames developed his techniques for the shaping of laminated wood from the techniques used to make prosthetic limbs for servicemen wounded in the Second World War. An exception is the non-stick frying pan – the NASA program borrowed the non-stick idea from Corning to put on the nose cones of its rockets. Without cold war fever we probably – not so soon anyway – would not have the interstates, which were conjured into being under the Defense Highways Act of the mid 1950s.

As for waste: our system is based on the production of commodities. If people slacken in their desire for and purchase of commodities, then the system collapses. We have an inherent puritanism that tells us not to waste. This is very wrong-headed from the point of view of sustaining the capitalist system of commodity production. If you don't throw it away, you won't buy a new one. If you don't buy a new one, the system will fall apart.

The system inaugurated forty years ago with Truman's NSC 68 installing economic stimulus through military spending has lasted more or less intact until now, surviving several 'peace threats', though none so grave as the one posed today. You cannot have a 'good' capitalism without militarist underpinning. Take away that underpinning and it falls apart – unless you urge something else: like redistribution, a reordering of the priorities of the economy. These are not acceptable within the present system. To tell people they will do better in a peacetime economy, without simultaneously telling them what this would involve, is to lie to them.

If the left is going to provide any vision in the years ahead, it has to think seriously about what 'ending the cold war' actually entails. Military Keynesianism is failing anyway. In the 1950s the deficit as percentage of GNP was 0.4, in the 1960s 0.8, in the 1970s 2.0 and in the 1980s 4.3. More deficit spending is needed in every decade to keep the show on the road. Even a $300 billion defense budget is insufficiently stabilizing.

➤

JUNE 5   *Topanga*
BUMS IN L.A. GET HOUNDED by the sheriff's deputies, rousted, pushed along till they go along. Most of the time they don't get shot, unless they make some mistake, like Marcus Donel. No bum, he was parking his car in his driveway in South Central as the police searched for a suspect, described as a Mexican of slight build. Donel was a black American of medium build and was rash enough to tell the deputies to piss off when they told him to put his hands up. They blew him away. Later a spokesperson for the sheriff's department said that even if he didn't commit the robbery, 'he probably shouldn't have been doing what he was doing', viz., parking his car in his own driveway.

Those wielding state power are always on the edge of psychosis. With his friends at FEMA, Oliver North planned to throw thousands of Americans in concentration camps if the United States invaded Nicaragua. God knows what North was on the lip of. A journalist visited North's Pentecostal church in the Washington suburbs not so long ago, hoping to catch a glimpse of North in executive session with the One and Only. A man slid into the pew beside him: North. When it came to the bit where they all speak in tongues North clung to him, roaring unintelligibly into his face.

JUNE 15   *Topanga*

MIKE DAVIS AND I DESCENDED to ground level and crossed Alameda for a closer
look at the Metropolitan Detention Center, a high-rise jail for federal prisoners
which was designed by Ellerbe Becket of Pasadena and passed into the hands
of the Bureau of Prisons in November 1988. Life being mostly a matter of
resting up after coming from somewhere while waiting to go someplace else, the
airport terminals, hotels and jails of the twenty-first century will all blend into
one form, very well evinced in this particular ten-story jailhouse. An inmate
sweeping the flagstones of the nicely landscaped patio said the place wasn't so
bad. Inside, in the main lobby, there were the furnishings of lobbies everywhere: planes of flat pastels and glass; well-tended interior shrubbery; a
reception desk with two chic young black women in miniskirts, fingertips
resting on computer keyboards, asking for your name and what this is in
reference to; a tactful security gate on the alert for unwelcomed metal objects.
You wouldn't be ashamed to have your mother come looking for you here, not
the way you would at the old county jail a mile to the east.

The new federal detention center is the sixth jail within three miles of City
Hall. Downtown and East L.A. house the largest incarcerated population in the
US – some 25,000 inmates. Mike and I had a decorous conversation with Lynden
Croasmun, executive assistant to the prison's warden, Margaret Hambrick.
Croasmun was vexed that no one had told her about a UCLA Planning Depart-
ment exhibit in honor of the bicentennial of the French Revolution, in which
there is a model of the Bastille blending into the Bonaventure Hotel and also
some very beautiful night shots of the detention center.

➤➔

JUNE 19   *Topanga*

THE STRATAGEMS OF MAGAZINES seeking to win fresh subscribers border on
armed robbery. A reader in Houston tells me that *In These Times* offered him
a trial subscription for a brief period but when he declined to take up a sub
after the trial was over, he was instantly assailed with a dunning letter. 'Dear
Former Subscriber', Leenie Folsom, circulation director, wrote, 'We can no
longer carry this outstanding debt on our credit files ... Now. Today. You must
pay the amount due. Send your check immediately. We expect to hear from you
by return mail or we will be forced to take further action.' Chilling stuff. The
poor nonsubscriber lives in fear of Jim Weinstein ripping through his door with
an ax, shouting for greenbacks.

The Nation's approach is rather different, preferring to keep the customers
uncertain as to whether they have one subscription, two, or none at all. I've
stayed in houses where *Nation* fans, parched for knowledge, say that no copy
has arrived in months, and as they speak, a wadded block of two dozen *Nations*

thuds through the mail slot. This gives *Nation* subscribers a Crusoe-like take on world affairs. I stayed with a man in eastern Oregon last year who met me at his gate with pressing questions. Was the war in Vietnam over? Was Edmund Muskie President? It turned out he was entirely reliant on *The Nation* for his news, and though he had faithfully sent in his renewal checks over the years, no copies had arrived. I started to explain to him that the Muskie campaign had gone awry, but he raised a finger to his lips and implored me to be silent. Having waited this long, he said, he had found his utter ignorance about the state of the world deeply refreshing; now that I was about to tell him that the Muskie campaign had not met expectations he felt that perhaps, all in all, it would be better to wait for those *Nation*s and, in a way, to hope that they would never come.

⇒→

JULY 3   *Topanga*
READING CARL GINSBURG'S TERRIFIC analysis of Moynihan, there's probably no newspaper in the corporate mainstream that has not, at one time or another, whacked the black poor on the head with the bludgeon of Senator Pat Moynihan's views: the black family's 'tangle of pathology', the 'internal' nature of the black poor's problems, hence the need for self-help by the black poor and for merciless tough-mindedness on the part of whites.

The notion that poor people bring their suffering upon themselves is certainly a lot older than Senator Moynihan, but it's hard to think of another North American over the past quarter-century who has given the rich and their agents so much assistance in the task of keeping it respectably at the forefront of their minds.

Moynihan was at the Labor Department when he and his team drafted 'The Negro Family: The Case for National Action' and injected it into the nation's bloodstream in 1965, at precisely the moment that the propertied class needed to be let off the hook. Think about poverty, the report said, and you have to think about the black family. No meaningful change is possible until that family is strengthened 'from within'. Pauper, heal thyself!

Moynihan's thesis first crept into executive speech on June 4, 1965, when President Johnson spoke at Howard University. 'Negro poverty is not white poverty', Johnson told his audience. 'There are differences ... radiating painful roots into the community and into the family and nature of the individual.' Moynihan had apparently sent his report to Johnson's assistant Bill Moyers, who urged it as the basis for Johnson's speech. This was not the last time Moyers pressed Moynihan's thoughts upon the public. Tom Wicker's story next day on the front page of the *New York Times* praised the speech hotly, as did a *Times* editorial on June 6 and as did Mary McGrory in the *Washington Star*. The

Washington Post said with ominous vagueness, 'Implicit in his discussion is the fact that the government cannot reach all these sources of maladjustment, except in a remote way.'

In the months that followed, the chorus swelled. 'Promoting self-help', the *Wall Street Journal* announced in late July, 'must realistically appear as a large part of the ultimate answer.' In early August, *Newsweek* was invoking Moynihan's famous phrase 'tangle of pathology' apropos the black family and saying of the 'Negro family problem' that 'its very intimacy has excluded it from the public dialogue on civil rights; it reaches too deep into white prejudices and Negro sensitivities'. (Translation: all that racist talk about shiftless blacks is true; pass the word along.)

Sliding, with time, into Nixon's camp, Moynihan sharpened his message, urging that black have-nots be treated with 'benign neglect' and honoring the haves as he did so in a memo to Nixon 'leaked' to the press in the spring of 1970: 'We have almost deliberately obscured the extraordinary progress, and commitment to progress, which the nation as a whole has made, which white America has not abandoned, and which increasingly black America is learning to make use of.' From here the leap was not far to the theory that integration had achieved 'irreversible' momentum, and therefore did not need any further encouragement from the nation's government or courts.

➤

JULY 5   *Topanga*

MOYNIHAN WAS PROPELLED into his Senate seat in 1976 by the *New York Times*, nicely ensconced against the day of the Second Coming of his report in the Reagan years, when its comforting properties were once more in urgent demand. By 1987, while Reaganites extolled the breadth of general economic 'recovery', black unemployment still stood at 13 percent; in 1965, the year of the report, it was 8.1 percent. One out of every three blacks was poor. The median earnings of full-time black male workers fell 10 percent between 1979 and 1987. In the same period more than half of all new full-time jobs paid poverty wages ($11,610) for families of four. With this acceleration in the misery of the have-nots came a corresponding rise in resentment among the haves. George Will observed that 'millions of blacks are victims of many irresponsible blacks'. Twenty years after Watts, from the towers of a downtown reared by dollars withheld from any urban initiative for the poor, the *Los Angeles Times* ran a glowing feature about the virtues of self-help, replete with quotations from the conservative black economist Glenn Loury, a great favorite of the haves, calling for subminimum wages for teenagers and for enterprise zones, thus, as Carl Ginsburg remarks, aiming to solve a situation caused by exploitation by imposing further exploitation.

Today more black men are in jail than in college. The number of blacks attending college stands at 26 percent, down from 33 percent in 1976. College-educated black men have an unemployment rate four times greater than their white peers. In this painful hour Moynihan's constructs have been more potent than ever, and in January 1986 got their most ecstatic reiteration in a CBS documentary by Bill Moyers, Moynihan's salesman to Lyndon Johnson.

Moyers's evocation of the 'tangle of pathology', visited in this case on some black people in a poor section of Newark, was received by the haves with wild enthusiasm. The documentary, much of it eliciting from teen-agers detailed accounts of their sex lives, honed in resolutely on 'personal responsibility'. The *Boston Globe* called it compelling and quoted from the Moynihan report. In *The New York Times*, John Corry praised it for examining a 'culturally unpopular topic'. This theme of the courage of Moynihan and his epigones in grasping nettles, speaking the unspeakable, etc. is common to many articles, despite the obvious fact that the themes of the report were very popular with the dispensing classes, and that a courageous approach would have been to say that the condition of the poor and of many black Americans in particular was due to capitalism and the political agenda of the overclass.

By 1988, Pete Hamill was writing in *Esquire* that 'there is very little now that whites can do in a direct way for the maimed and hurting citizens of the Underclass.' In the *Washington Post* in April, Richard Cohen called for a 'war' in the inner city and denounced the 'pathetic lassitude' of 'the underclass' which militates against 'the dignity of honest work, the chance to move up the ladder'. Why the appeals to war, now symbolized in South Central Los Angeles by police battering rams? What's dignified about cleaning toilets in downtown hotels? Where's the ladder and the robust black middle class? In fact, as Ginsburg points out, 'blacks have been more "self-reliant", by any measure of social adaptability, having survived *despite* government *and* corporate policies aimed at perpetuating their impoverishment.'

After the rape and battery of a white woman in Central Park by black and Latino youths, Edwin Yoder wrote in the *Washington Post* that their actions could not be explained by 'environmental factors'. Yoder preferred 'the theological alternative to sociological or economic determinism'. Thus do we come to Original Sin and Noah's drunken curse on the children of Ham.

➥

JULY 14   *Topanga*

THE SUPREME BEING PROBABLY spared Robespierre and St. Just the pain of witnessing from on high the travesties of Jacobin ideals enacted in Paris. The festive aspects would not have distressed them. The Jacobins were fond of festivals. But the spectacle of all those economic royalists mustered behind their bulletproof glass on the Champs Elysées would have had the sans-culottes bellowing for the Committee of Public Safety to summon the tumbrils.

Reading Tomás Borge's *La Paciente Impaciencia*. It reminds me of one of Robespierre's speaches:

> We announce to all the world the true principles of our actions. We wish an order of things where all low and cruel passions are enchained by the laws; all beneficent and generous feelings awakened; where distinctions arise only from equality itself; where the citizen is subject to the magistrate; the magistrate to the people, the people to justice. Where industry is an adornment to the liberty that enobles it and commerce the source of public wealth, not simply of monstrous riches for a few families. We wish to substitute in our country morality for egoism, probity for a mere sense of honor, principle for habit, duty for etiquette, the empire of reason for the tyranny of custom, contempt for vice for contempt for misfortune; the grandeur of man for the triviality of grand society. We wish, in a word, to fulfill the couse of nature, to absolve providence from the long reign of tyranny and crime.

Borge was recalling the day he heard news of Che Guevara's death:

> Che is as irritating as Christ, as Quixote, as Bolívar, in as much as he mounted Rosinante, knocked down bishops and frontiers and was crucified on La Higuera; meanwhile, I thought of Velia wiping away my tears and hers.
>
> It is our obligation to rescue his thoughts, without writing marginal notes on his actions ... His sermon on the new man will be the ring of a bell, a fire. ...
>
> Material stimulus exists, but it is a trifle compared with moral stimulus. Into our consciousness come midgets who deposit their basketsfull of consumer appliances and salary hikes: thanks. Into our consciousness come giants with empty hands. They put a star in our palm and say: keep this forever.'

➨

JULY 18   *Topanga*

The *Evening Standard* wants my *Zeta* girl pics. I say no.

➨

JULY 19   *Topanga*

'O SUN OF '93, WHEN shall I see your light again', cried the old English radical on his deathbed amid the darkness of reaction in the 1830s. Read Isaac

Deutscher's last lectures on the Soviet Union's 'unfinished revolution', given in 1967. Deutscher remarks that when, in the eyes of the people, the miseries of revolution came to overshadow its grandeur, 'the result was restoration', but restoration – tragic though it could be – 'demonstrated to a people disillusioned with the revolution how unacceptable the reactionary alternative was. Returned Bourbons and Stuarts taught the people much better than Puritans, Jacobins, or Bonapartists could, that there was no way back to the past; that the basic work of the revolution was irreversible; and that it must be saved for the future.'

➡

JULY 29   *Topanga*

BEN SONNENBERG AND I keep swearing we'll send our mutual godchild, Alexander Hitchens, the Eleventh Edition of the *Encyclopaedia Britannica*. Now that I'm reading a book about Babar, maybe we should get this cycle instead, except Alexander's dad is very antimonarchist. The elephant king presented monarchy in its most genial aspect – solicitous of the public weal, nice to his family, well mannered and not given to ostentation. Babar was conceived by Cecile de Brunhoff, realized in watercolors and stories created by her husband, Jean, and then carried on by their son, Laurent. When Jean had Babar and Celeste, in *The Travels of Babar*, drift in a balloon and land on an island inhabited by cannibals, he produced, in the words of the new Babar historian Nicholas Weber, a 'depiction [which was] an unfortunate example of the sort of prejudice that marked French attitude toward the inhabitants of its colonies in the 1930s. They are fat-lipped, bug-eyed stereotypes.' Laurent edited out the cannibals in the 1981 *Babar's Anniversary Volume*, having been approached in the 1960s by his Random House editor, Toni Morrison, who protested similar stereotypes in Laurent's own *Babar's Picnic* in 1949.

I'm not sure that this retrospective editing is such a good idea. As Dr. Johnson said about prudish eighteenth-century editors of Shakespeare, 'If phraseology is to be changed as words grow uncouth by disuse, or gross by vulgarity, the history of every language will be lost.' If that was the way either of the de Brunhoffs saw things, then leave them be. Next thing you know, Jacobin elephants will be complaining that de Brunhoff stereotyped their kind as monarchists, thus ignoring the long tradition of republicanism for which elephants are justly renowned.

One day I will write a long political history of Babar's kingdom from a Gramscian perspective, showing how *Babarismo* ossified social relations in the kingdom and chained the productive forces. Babar's realm never had a bourgeois revolution and this evasion of history produced untold subsequent trouble.

AUGUST 2   *Topanga*

THERE'S BEEN a tremendous flap about ABC's simulated footage of the supposed passage of information from a US diplomat to a KGB agent. The flag
serves the same function as the corrections that newspapers run each day,
which imply that all the other stories in yesterday's edition were true. Almost
everything on network news is simulated and has been for years. Trained actors
known as 'the President', 'Secretary of State' and so forth go before the
cameras and act out carefully prepared scripts intended to demonstrate that
everything is under control. In the early days of television a disclaimer was
attached to such coverage, explaining that what the viewers had just been
watching was not true but merely a well-intentioned effort to show how the
country was being governed by the real President, who of course was too busy
to give hours of his day to these charades.

Gradually the disclaimers were discontinued, and now the public has got so
used to the actors that the people really running the country must do so in
complete secrecy, lest the shock of their appearance cause civic unrest.

➤

AUGUST 15   *Ardmore*

BIG FIGHT HERE over Merrell Dow's prospective pharmaceutical plant outside
Killeagh. Locals mostly against. I attack it in my *Wall Street Journal* column
right before Dow Chemical's AGM. Mama edgy and in poor sorts.

➤

AUGUST 20   *Ardmore*

PROFESSOR NORMAN STONE, no Soviet lover, writes of the Nazi–Soviet pact in
the London *Times* of August 16 that Stalin 'had no alternative, because the
western powers were not seriously interested in the alternative, an alliance with
Russia that would have given him "security" of a different kind.' Three days
later the *Times* published a letter from a man recalling that in 1938 the British
Ambassador to Berlin, Sir Nevile Henderson, wanted the paper to promote
Hitler as 'the apostle of peace', since war would only serve the purposes of
'Jews, communists and doctrinaires'.

➤

AUGUST 22   *Ardmore*

A WORLD RECORD WAS created in Ardmore last night when 704 people formed a
human centipede and shuffled their ways into the *Guinness Book of Records* as
part of a charity fund-raising event. Last night was the first occasion, in this

country, in which an attempt was made at breaking the human centipede record which stood at 552 people, and is understood to be held by an English group.

With their ankles firmly tied together the centipede, involving members of the Garda Siochana, bank officials, rugby, soccer, GAA and badminton players, as well as representatives from youth clubs, rowing clubs and the Civil Defence traveled a distance of 33 metres – three meters longer than the old record. The human centipede idea was mooted by Mrs. Currie Hosford as part of a fund-raising activity to complete renovations at St. Peter's Church in the village, the place of worship for three Church of Ireland families.

➤→

AUGUST 25   *Ardmore*
MERRELL DOW crumbles! The plant cancelled. General exultation.

➤→

AUGUST 27   *Ardmore*
READING ABOUT CYRIL CONNALLY and Allen Ginsberg in books by Michael Shelden and Barry Miles. Ginsberg's world was turbid with homosexual en-tanglement and obsession, punctuated by violence. He was still at Columbia when Lucien Carr stabbed Dave Kammerer to death, warding off undesired sexual advances. But Peter Watson, patron and publisher of *Horizon*, was very possibly murdered in his bath by his lover, Norman Fowler, who was discovered dead some years later in a similar state of semi-immersion.

The drugs most frequently seen around *Horizon*'s offices were tobacco and claret, but cocaine, heroin or morphine were available too. It's true that *Horizon* was lodged in the superstructure of the English class system. Its supplies of paper, rationed during the Second World War, were laid on by Harold Nicolson, who was part of the high command at the Ministry of Infor-mation. A fixture at *Horizon*'s famous parties was the indubitably dissolute, fervently drunken, crusadingly homosexual Soviet agent Guy Burgess.

The Beats were never disloyal like that. None of them believed in revolu-tion, and both Kerouac and Burroughs were conservative in political instinct. Ginsberg's is a more complicated and far more genuinely radical case. J. Edgar Hoover was not among his fans. You can parallel Ginsberg's faith in the virtuous strain in the American political tradition with a similar faith in England expressed by one of *Horizon*'s contributors, George Orwell.

It is hard to underestimate the inspirational effect of the sanctions against homosexual practices operating on both sides of the Atlantic. Connolly was heterosexual in his enthusiasms but Watson, who inherited an enormous for-tune amassed by his father in the margarine business, was obviously impelled to resist conventional use of this money by his sexual preferences, which led him to art, Bohemia, the demimonde, and ultimately to that fatal bath. Without Watson there would have been no *Horizon*.

Miles is brilliant at describing the intensity of the homosexual dynamics of Ginsberg's circle. Homosexuality was the motor of Ginsberg's and Burroughs's exceptionalism, and Ginsberg's self-defining moment was when he went public in 1956 in *Howl*, with enthusiasm for those 'who let themselves be fucked in the ass by saintly motorcyclists and screamed with joy'.

Rambling through Miles's book I began to think of Burroughs as a kind of cosmic satire on T.S. Eliot. Both men came from St. Louis and affected a formality in their attire. Eliot had his own engagements with Bohemia and insanity (his first wife's) before espousing convention with increasing fervor. Burroughs stands beside Eliot like some doppelganger. In 1946, hanging out in New York with Ginsberg and the others, Burroughs would conduct lay analysis sessions with them. He himself had been shrunk by Louis Federn (who had been shrunk by Freud) and by Leo Walberg, who hypnotized Burroughs and by this technique excavated the strata of his personality.

'The top layer was Burroughs', writes Miles, 'the distinguished scion of an old St. Louis family. Below that was a nervous, possibly lesbian English governess with a prissy, self-conscious, simpering personality. Below her was Old Luke, the tobacco farmer [who] ... had the personality of a psychotic Southern sheriff. Beneath them all was an implacable, silent Chinaman, sitting starving, skull-headed, on the banks of the Yangtze, with no ideas, no beliefs, and no words, the ultimate Burroughs persona.'

They would play charades featuring these personas. As the English governess, Burroughs would serve people tea and rap them on the knuckles, shrilling as he did so, 'Don't say those dirty words in front of everybody!' Then Ginsberg would play a crooked Hungarian art dealer in Paris, with Burroughs dressed as his lesbian countess shill and Kerouac in a farm boy's straw hat, acting the innocent American bumpkin. It's too bad there aren't photographs.

The English governess makes a return appearance eighty pages later, when Ginsberg describes his physical love affair with Burroughs. Allen did everything he could to please Bill, even though he preferred younger men. 'But I thought he was my teacher, so I'd do what I could to amuse him', Ginsberg said. 'In bed, Bill is like an English governess, whinnying and giggling, almost hysteric ... He liked to come while being screwed.' The governess fell violently in love and was finally rejected with Ginsberg's impulsive, hurtful cry, 'But I don't want your ugly old cock '

Probably no other literary group has had such enthusiasm for placing intimate matters on the public record as a matter of spiritual and social duty, and it's clear that Ginsberg wanted sexual encounters and his notions of sexual freedom to feature very strongly. Neal Cassady – original of Dean Moriarty in

On the Road – comes out badly. In the Beat world women as a rule were ignored, exploited, betrayed or even murdered (Burroughs shot his wife through the head, the bullet passing a few fatal inches below the glass she had balanced on top of it). Cassady's girlfriends reported his sexual sadism, as does Ginsberg, who also lured him from his mainly heterosexual preferences. He and his wife Carolyn were devotees of the psychic theurgist Edgar Cayce and attended meetings with other adepts, where they would discuss Gurdjieff, Atlantis and the Akashic records. Another person who comes out rather badly is Kerouac, unattractively tight with money, sullen, blustering and, particularly toward the end of his life, a drunkenly anti-Semitic right-winger.

The Beats pointed the way for Dylan, to the gay movement, to the politics and culture both of self-realization and the spectacle. They also pointed the way to a lot of very bad writing.

➤

SEPTEMBER 1   *Aptos*
CHAPMAN PINCHER REVIEWS W. J. West's book on Roger Hollis for *The Spectator.* It features Claud, and the usual speculations.

'West has looked into Hollis's friendship with people who were not only communists but dangerous revolutionaries and, in some instances, such as Philby, Blunt and Burgess, proven traitors. The most significant of the revolutionaries was the late Claud Cockburn, who wrote for *The Daily Worker* (now *The Morning Star*) mainly under the name of Frank Pitcairn. Many who knew Cockburn regard him as a jokey figure who could never have been of much consequence politically, but West's evidence proves that he was a leading revolutionary at a time when an overthrow of the elected Government after Dunkirk was considered by no means impossible in the minds of pro-Soviet Marxists dedicated to that cause.

'There is no doubt that Hollis was friendly with Cockburn when they were both at Oxford in the 1920s and that after he joined MI5 in 1938 and became responsible for countering communists he concealed this association, keeping his friend's file locked in his safe. West is convinced that he covered up for Cockburn who was also producing a seditious publication called *The Week* which, in Moscow's and Berlin's interests, campaigned for Britain's withdrawal from the war after Dunkirk by urging soldiers and factory-workers to take no further part in it. He claims that Hollis repeatedly refused to provide the evidence for Cockburn's prosecution which had been demanded by the wartime body called the Security Executive; also that he connived at furthering some of Cockburn's activities, such as helping to secure him a visa to Algiers in 1943 to assist in promoting possible revolution there.'

SEPTEMBER 4   *Belém*

AT THE MOUTH OF THE AMAZON. Susanna and I walked to the old fort, with fine cannon, on which the lovers perch at sunset, the boy astride. These guns look down on the docks that Farquhar built at such cost, financed by Cowdray, back at the start of the century.

There's a museum with some of the early maps of the Amazon. A sixteenth-century one shows El Dorado, with Amazons and cannibals and mountains of gold. The myths were there from the start.

Down in the old town there are streets of what was once marvelous Belle Epoque elegance at the peak of the rubber trade, just before plantation rubber in Ceylon kicked in, in 1907.

Inside one old store there's a double art nouveau staircase with a winged Victory at the divide, plus tulip lights. Upstairs it's as it was in the teens: ancient mannequins, hatboxes, impedimenta from the glory days. Nothing has happened in this room for seventy years.

➤

SEPTEMBER 7   *Belém*

BELEM IS THE CHIEF CITY of the Amazon, though when people talk about cities in the Amazon, they usually start with Manaus and this is a serious mistake. Manaus is a dreary place. Almost everything of interest has been torn down, except for the opera house which must be one of the most overwritten topics in the world. Belém by contrast is an extraordinary city, both for its role in history and for its vitality and beauty today as the capital city of the Amazon. It was one of the first points of contact between the old and the new worlds, as the late fifteenth-century travellers sailed about the vast mouth of the Amazon, where Belém is situated on the south channel running under the island of Marajó. Its seventeenth-century convents bear witness to the early Portuguese colonization. The Belle Epoque ironwork stands still as testimony to the hectic rubber boom that surged to its climax in the first decade of this century.

Belém was the launching point for the conquest of the Amazon and its cultural personality was forged by its role as garrison, entrepôt and market. Here came the slaves from west Africa, the de-tribalized Indians, the mestizos and the Portuguese masters of Empire. From Amazonia (stretching across an area as vast as the distance between New York and the eastern slopes of the Californian Sierras), from the borders of Peru, Colombia, Bolivia, Venezuela and Guyana come forest fruits, herbs, medical plants, pickled snakes and *drogas de sertão* – drugs of the backlands – to its market, one of the richest spectacles in Latin America.

It is a city that saw the Cabanagem revolt of the 1830s, one of the fiercest rebellions of nineteenth-century Latin America, where 30,000 died and where an Indian led the assault on the presidential palace and killed the president of Belém. It saw the rise of the rubber trade. Belém, by 1755, was waterproofing the coats and boots of the Portuguese army and 'rubberizing' the King of Portugal's galoshes. By 1830 it was sending 200,000 pairs of galoshes a year to Boston. By 1900 the rubber trade headquartered in Belém was one of the lynch pins of the industrial world, and British and American companies rushed there to get a cut of the action.

➤

SEPTEMBER 15   *Belém*
WE FLY TO THE ISLAND of Marajó at the Amazon's mouth. There's the markings of a town laid out seventy years ago in the expectation of being the Manhattan of Amazonia: wide boulevards, blocks marked out, every street empty save for buffaloes, waste land on either side, a few shacks.

➤

SEPTEMBER 16   *Belém*
PHONE CALL. MAMA IS BACK in hospital. I have to rush to Ireland.

➤

SEPTEMBER 19   *Ardmore*
MAMA IS IN THE Mercy Hospital. Cork, on the Lee, reminds me of Belém, just as Belém reminded me of Cork.

➤

SEPTEMBER 24   *Ardmore*
Dear Alexander,
Of course, you will have noticed that in the *Times* AP obituary of Sir Ronald Syme, who was almost my all-time favorite Englishman, he was said to have been an expert on 'the Roman Emperor Tacitus'. So your systematic denigration of Tacitus is carried out by others.

Love, Ben

➤

SEPTEMBER 27   *Ardmore*
TODAY I READ MAMA portions of an interview of Graham Greene by John Cornwell published in the *Observer*. It was on the subject of his beliefs. She

listened keenly, as did the other four ladies, all of them devout Catholics, in the small ward.

"'And what about Satan? Do you believe in the devil or in demons?'" I kept my voice low, not wishing to upset the rest of the ward.

"'No, I don't think so.'"

'What did Graham say?' Mama asked. 'I didn't quite hear.'

'He said, No, he didn't think so', I said more loudly.

"'Do you believe in hell?'" I read on.

"'I don't believe in hell.'"

'I didn't hear that either', Mama said.

'He says he doesn't believe in hell.' There was sepulchral silence in the ward.

"'Do you contemplate God in a pure, disembodied way?'"

"'I'm afraid I don't.'" I bellowed this, to spare Mama the inconvenience of asking me to repeat it.

Sister Joan came in and sank to her knees. It was the hour for her to lead the ward in reciting Hail Marys. My mother and I kept quiet in our corner of the room.

➤

SEPTEMBER 28   *Ardmore*

EACH DAY I DRIVE in to Cork to the hospital. Mama sleeps a lot, while I read a life of Jackson Pollock. When I'm not seeing Mama, I buy compulsively in the antique stores. Also I seach for someone to tan my boa skin from Belém. A butcher in the English Market takes me to a strange tanner on the Northside. He also sells me mutton, but it smelled to high heaven when I cooked it. He must have left the glands in.

➤

SEPTEMBER 29   *Ardmore*

TO ANDREW COCKBURN

WASHINGTON, D.C.

I DON'T KNOW what cats are coming to. Cormac has been throwing up and otherwise scandalizing polite society. I got the vet Chris Humphries in who felt C's pulse, wielded stethoscope, took temperature, peered in C's eyes, ran a breathalyzer, stared into his jaws and then said C hadn't been flossing properly and had terrible plaque build-up. Remember plaque? I think it cost you $15,000, didn't it? In C's case plaque build-up means sore gums, which in turn means he isn't chewing his food which in turn ...

So next Tuesday it's the dentist's chair for Cormac.

SEPTEMBER 29   *Ardmore*

THE BOOK ABOUT Pollock by Steven Naifeh and Gregory White Smith is good. Pollock and Walt Disney were both fathered by disappointed prairie socialists, followers of Eugene Debs. By the early 1930s Disney was soundly embarked on his life project of carmelizing the frontier imagination. Pollock, emotionally mangled by pressures of his family – strong mother, defeated father, working the western country roads as part of a maintenance crew – was teetering toward his achievement: the violent yet accomplished negation of the Disney version of the American, and particularly the western, experience.

Disney domesticated his own erotic sensibility and unresolved tensions through his obsessive cutifying of bottoms. Pollock's own homosexual inclinations (like those of his teacher, Thomas Hart Benton) were more violently masked by booze and macho posturing.

Actually, Pollock was scarcely the naive country boy. As the Pollock family struggled on a farm near Tempe, Arizona, his elder brother Charles sent back from New York copies of *The Dial* for young Jackson and his brother to pore over. In Los Angeles Jackson was involved with Communist and union organizers. In Ojai, he became a follower of Krishnamurti. Later, in New York, a Jungian spent hours explicating Pollock's work to him in an attempt at therapy.

Pollock's story does not inspire love. The car that he drunkenly crashed at top speed, sending him forty feet, ten feet off the ground, into a tree, carried two women, one of whom died in the wreck. He beat and otherwise abused his wife, Lee Krasner. He was manipulative, and a horrifying drunk.

�>➔

OCTOBER 4   *Cork*

IN THE MERCY HOSPITAL. Mama has been in a coma for two of the past three days. The Mercy was originally the mansion of the Lord Mayor of Cork. It's an eighteenth-century building. The wards are high-ceilinged, some of them with mouldings. None of the sterility of a modern hospital.

There are many statues of the Virgin. Late at night the visitors go but the sisters let me and my brothers sit in my mother's curtained corner.

There are four other beds, all curtained off if necessary. The ladies can keep an eye on one another. This is a public, non-paying hospital. The ladies are mostly working-class Irish women and gossip all day. A lot of the time it's filled with families. The Irish are great hospital visitors and no one pays the slightest attention to the sign: Visitors 2 – 4, 6 – 8.

I'm reading an odd life of Eric Gill, designer, typefounder, sculptor who, it seems, had a happy married life, plus affairs and incestuous relations with his sister and daughter. Ken Thompson, who carved my father's gravestone, knows one of the abused daughters and says she seems happy.

OCTOBER 7   *Ardmore*

THE VICAR SENDS ME the order of service, after Andrew, Patrick and I have decided on the hymns and the lesson. It's handwritten on a little piece of paper by the Rev. Sir Dickon Durand.

Funeral.

1. I arrive first at St. Mary's. I alight at the Main Gate and, on foot, I precede the hearse to the Church doors reciting the approved psalms.

2. The coffin is carried in as at Ardmore.

THE SERVICE

Hymn 504: 'O God our help in ages past'.

Psalm 130.

Lesson: St. Matthew 5. 1–10.

Prayers.

Hymn 511. The Lord Is My Shepherd.

I leave my reading desk and go to the coffin. The pall bearers raise the coffin and turn it.

I precede the coffin out while the congregation and choir sing the NUNC DIMITTIS.

We refused to allow passages from Revelation, which Dickon recommended.

➡

OCTOBER 9   *Ardmore*

THE PAPERS HAVE OBITUARIES. A good one in the Cork *Examiner*. Also Richard Ingrams in *The Independent*.

Cork Examiner

Report: Isabel Healy

'A fantastically interesting life'

One of the wreaths at the funeral of Mrs. Patricia Cockburn in Youghal yesterday was from the Ardmore Guild of the Irish Countrywomen's Association. Everywhere she had been in her 75 years, Patricia Cockburn had been an important part of the community, a major force and an inspiration.

From her birth in Rosscarbery in 1914 to the high society of London, to her beloved family home at Myrtle Grove in Youghal, to the Balkans and the Sahara Desert, the South Pacific and the Congo, and back to bring up her children in Ardmore, through the bubbly life of a debutante, to the Wall Street crash, through two World Wars and the hardships of poverty, social alienation and illness, Patricia Arbuthnot Byron Cockburn was a strong, optimistic woman, who only gave up when the cancer she thought she had conquered finally won her home on Thursday morning last.

Patricia Cockburn was buried under the weeping cherry tree her mother had planted in memory of her brother Teeny who was killed during the war. The grave, where her husband, journalist Claud Cockburn was buried in December, 1981, is marked by a limestone headstone carved by Ken Thompson, and in the shadow of a great oak tree which straddles the wall between the ancient Collegiate Church of St. Mary and the Arbuthnot family home, Myrtle Grove.

The service yesterday afternoon was brief. It was conducted by the Rector of St. Mary's, Rev. Sir Dickon Durand, who said that it was right that a funeral service should be formal and solemn, and it was, unlike Patricia Cockburn's christening ceremony when the Bishop of Cork went on strike and threatened to walk out of the church, if her mother insisted on calling the child 'Kawara Finbaragh Evangeline' and gave her instead 'Patricia Evangeline Ann' as she had been born on St. Patrick's Day.

The small and ancient church was full, with all kinds of people present, all classes of people, all of whom had loved and respected this extraordinary and beautiful woman. Mrs. Cockburn's three sons, Andrew, Alexander and Patrick, daughter-in-law Leslie, grand-daughter Daisy and grandson Henry, nieces and nephews, and her companion, Kitty Lee, were the chief mourners.

Patricia Cockburn was born to an upperclass Anglo-Irish family with unconventional nationalist sympathies. She lived in Youghal and in London, where she was presented at court as a debutante in 1931, and had her coming out party for five hundred in the family home with lobster, caviar and champagne. She married an underwriter at Lloyd's, Arthur Byron, and bored with high living, went to Westminster School of Art, before taking off on pioneering travels with her husband and lecturing to the Royal Geographic Society on her return. After the death of their small son Darrell, who contracted blood poisoning after getting a scratch in the garden, she took off to travel again.

In 1939 she met Claud Cockburn, who wrote under six different pseudonyms and was recognised as a radical journalist and scourge of the establishment. Her father warned her at the time, 'don't you realise Patricia, that if you go ahead with this mad plan, you will never be allowed into the Royal Enclosure at Ascot again.' The cutting off of her family allowance meant the couple lived on £7 a week from her husband's editing job on *The Daily Worker* and during the war, the £2 a week she earned working in the ARP.

In 1949 they returned to Youghal and later to Ardmore, where Claud wrote, and she bred, broke and trained hunters, horse dealing smartly with the Travellers. In the fifties Claud Cockburn's name was 84th on the McCarthy list of the 250 'most wanted men in the world'. Despite this brand of communist, locally he was known as 'a decent man'.

Her resourcefulness was again tested when at one time three of the five members of the family were extremely ill, either with TB or polio. She nursed them all back to health, including the youngest son, Patrick, whom doctors said would never walk, but who finally threw away even his walking stick when working in Northern Ireland for the *Financial Times*, as the stick might have been construed as a weapon.

The Cockburn home in Ardmore has a 'family bookcase' in which are only publications by members of her own family, by her husband and her children and their wives. Her own autobiography *Figure of Eight* came out in 1985, and the paperback of the book went into the shops last week.

Patricia Cockburn turned to making shell pictures in the Victorian mode when she could not afford to buy presents for friends, and it led to 14 one-woman exhibitions of her exquisite work, which she continued until the past months. She collected the only extant complete set of all the Irish shells.

In her autobiography, Patricia Cockburn recounted how her great aunt Molly sowed the seeds of Lilium Giganteum at the age of 94, and though she knew they would not flower for at least seven years, said 'I can't wait to smell their enormous blooms.' In the same spirit, a few years ago, she herself sowed the seeds of Lilium Giganteum and would not allow her illness of the past two years to stop her full participation in and enjoyment of what she told me was 'a fantastically interesting life'.

➡

OCTOBER 13   *Ardmore*
EVERYONE GONE. I LOOK THROUGH Mama's papers. There's a Westminster wedding certificate showing that she and Claud got married on March 20, 1978. Under 'address' the registrar put 90 Westbourne Terrace, London, which was Patrick's flat. This must have been when Claud was getting successful radiation treatment for throat cancer three years before he died. Under a heading on the form, 'condition', the registrar has written 'previously went through a form of marriage at Sofia, Bulgaria on the 2nd March 1946.' Probably a Russian general breaking a bottle of champagne over their heads. This means Andrew and Patrick but not me had been in the legit column, as I make haste to inform them.

➡

OCTOBER 14   *Ardmore*
SOME FUNNY LETTERS. One from Claud he sent her on March 17, 1944, when Mama and I (three) were in Northumberland, evacuated from the blitz.

Dear Patricia,
Mrs. B has just come in to say that travelling to here this morning she was wearing the bit of shamrock your mother sent her and a 'very posh man' kept

looking at her nastylike and when she got up to leave the train here he said 'Aren't you just a little bit ashamed?' and she said 'No I'm not because I'm a spy and in here', she said, waving her bag full of rabbits' food, 'I've got bombs', and he was dumbstruck and everyone laughed him to scorn.

Wednesday evening I had dinner – vile, at Young's – with Whitney of the San Francisco *Chronicle* and a new correspondent just arrived called Ira Wilfrid – he is famous, it seems, wrote a book called *Guadalcanal Diary*, has been a long time in the Pacific, also written novels. Jewish man from Brooklyn. He gave me a cigar and then five more. I protested. He said he 'esteemed it just a token of his regard for a man who had seen the truth in life and gone after it, straight as a die, clear through all obstacles, scorning all temptations.' I reminded him, he said 'of the thin American line going up to Chateau Thierry in 1917 through the broken ranks of a defeated Army.' All this on very thin tea. Embarrassing. They came out to the house afterwards being discommoded by the air raid and barrage – a very short one with hardly any bombs, I think. Mr. Wilfrid told me a funny story he had had from Admiral Muselier when he was at St. Pierre Miquelon. Muselier used to be a close boyhood and young man friend of Admiral Abrial. Political divergences occurred. In the beginning of the war M was commander of the fleet at Marseilles, A was his chief in Paris. They had some rows about M having bombed some Italian submarines which A, in order not to report the matter and annoy the Italians, said must have been whales, so M wrote a report to the zoo about the new sort of whales with conning towers and Italian machines inside. Then M wanted to go on a trip to Dakar and notified A who said he would put a special plane at his disposal. Plane arrived, pilot was old friend of M, confessed he had had orders to un-synchronise the motors so the plane (which M was to pilot himself) would somehow be pulled to pieces by contradictory vibrations and fall into the sea suddenly. M arranged to fly out very low, with the idea that then he would crash very gently and taxi back to port with the evidence. Just then a happy accident provided a better plan. Some high Italian fascists arrived in Marseilles by boat on their way to some big Franco-fascist fiesta at Madrid, but were late, and begged M for a plane. He said 'I will put at your disposal my special personal plane sent to me by Admiral Abrial' so they were delighted and flew off. M rang up A and 'formally notified him' that he was sending them. A gave himself away entirely, shouting 'No, stop them it isn't safe' but it was too late and the plane exploded in the air and dropped them all into the sea from a great height and they were killed.

➤➔

OCTOBER 15   *Ardmore*
MORE LETTERS. One from Graham Greene.

Dear Patricia,

(Will you forgive me calling you that, for you know how much I loved Claud?)

I have just finished your book and I enjoyed it immensely, though I was saddened at the thought of how little I had seen of him in post-war years. Our last real contact was when, with Muggeridge, we played a joke of mine – a secret unofficial visit of Kruschev to England (Claud was to be a scoundrelly butler v informer to the *Daily Mirror* and K. was to be played by the original Mr. Norris.)

I have also read for the first time that marvelous novel *Beat the Devil*. I must finish the other two Helvick novels. Couldn't you also edit a volume of his political journalism including Pitcairn in Spain?

> *Yours (again forgive me) affectionately,*
> Graham Greene
> *Antibes*
> *July 8, 1985*

Actually Claud wrote more than two other novels under the name James Helvick. Greene was probably referring to *Ballantyne's Folly*, which he subsequently did a foreword to when it was reissued with an introduction by Andrew, and *Jericho Road*, my favorite.

➤

OCTOBER 17   *Ardmore*

AN OLD LETTER TO ME.

June 8, 1953

My Darling Alexander,

I was most *dreadfully* sorry and upset to hear about your accident. Poor child, it must have been agony; what a terrible thing to happen. That horrible game cricket. Daddy was quite right about it, don't play it again, at any rate not in glasses.

I sent you your bath towel dressing gown please let me know as *soon* as it arrives as the shop sent it off and I must make a row if you don't get it. I also sent £3 for your birthday. I wish it could have been more but I am in the midst of the usual financial crisis with the threatened general stoppage of all cheques, but I expect we shall survive. Molly lent me her house at Ardmore the weekend before last and Patrick and I had a delightful weekend there, quite hot weather surprisingly enough. Otherwise nothing has happened of note. We went fishing in the Watson's boat and caught nothing. Patrick has been given a baby rabbit by a man in the E.S.B. Blacky has not had a foal yet, the lawyers are still arguing about my teeth. I have been gardening a lot and it has become such a mania that I go out at midnight with a torch hunting slugs.

I wish I could send you some strawberries we have a bumper crop this year, but I am afraid you will only be able to eat them in the form of jam.

Daddy is cheerful but dreadfully bored with his hospital. He has, thank goodness, made great friends with the man in the box next door, a lagoubrious, humorous civil servant, with literary and political interests. They exchange books, papers and malign gossip about the other prisoners.

Darling, please write and tell us how your eye is. Daddy and I are both so worried about it. And how about your spectacles, can't you get new ones from the national health? Are the frames of your old ones smashed to bits?

Lots & lots of love from
Mummy

➤

OCTOBER 18   *Ardmore*

HONEY WILLIAMS CALLS from Carmel Highlands. There's been a big earthquake centered near Santa Cruz. It seems my motel is still standing.

➤

NOVEMBER 6   *Aptos*

IT WAS HARD TO get news of the earthquake's damage directly from my motel, but secondhand reports indicated it was still standing. When I got back last week the kind Dutch ladies who live next door had cleaned everything up. In my kitchen there was a bucket full of broken crockery and the remains of Robespierre's head. I had had plaster of Paris bas-reliefs of Robespierre and Saint-Just hanging on the wall. At a shock of 7.1 on the Richter scale Robespierre, who believed in the Supreme Being, plunged from the wall. Saint-Just, who probably agreed with Fouché that the words 'Death is nothing but eternal sleep' should be posted at the gates of all French cemeteries, dropped too, but stayed in one piece.

A couple of days later I went for a walk round Watsonville with Frank Bardacke. You would not have known it from the daily newspapers – initially at least – but Watsonville, about eighteen miles from the epicenter in the Santa Cruz Mountains, has been hit the worst. Of 765 buildings destroyed in Santa Cruz County, 333 were in Watsonville, as were 553 of the 2,438 buildings countywide suffering major damage. We walked along Lincoln Street and at first all seemed well, aside from tumbled chimneys, announcing the folly of building with brick in California. Then there'd be a swath of disaster: boarded-up windows, porches askew, red tags on the front doors indicating that the places were done for. With a house as with a person, the dividing line between life and death can be almost imperceptible. We'd look at an apparently healthy house marked with the fatal tag, and only after a minute or two see the skewed twist to the roof that meant the quake had bounced it off its foundation blocks and broken its back.

For my mother's funeral my brothers and I had rejected the vicar's suggestion that lessons be taken from some ravings in Isaiah and the Book of Revelation. My brother Patrick read the parable of the sower instead. Its lesson of prudent husbandry was spelled out in Watsonville. Was it fate or carpentry that had stricken some houses and spared others? Watsonville is a Third World town, like west Oakland low on the news agenda as reporters preferred to cluster round the First World destruction in the Marina district of San Francisco. Being a Third World town Watsonville is cheaply built, and though the price of a handful of nails would have meant foundation posts securely toenailed in, a lot of the poorer houses were just resting on their pier blocks until the tremors pushed them off.

Prospect, where Frank and his family live, is a nice-looking street: typically working class in a mostly working-class farm town; single-story wood houses, a bit of lawn out front. On Frank's block the earthquake knocked out five houses, which had nine Mexican families living in them. By such a count you can reckon that Watsonville's population, officially 30,000, is probably almost twice that number. Throughout the town, garages behind Victorian and Maybeck-style houses had held families paying $400 a month to sleep among the vermin, getting their power from the main building, into which more families were crammed. So as the earth shook and the shacks fell and some of the working poor upgraded from garage slum to emergency quarters under canvas, even the local newspaper, the *Register-Pajaronian*, felt emboldened to concede that the earthquake, a 'natural' disaster, had merely highlighted the entirely human disaster of a town that had long ceased to provide affordable housing for the people from whose labor the wealth of the town derived.

➡

NOVEMBER 7   *Aptos*

IN WATSONVILLE after the earthquake some homeless workers planted their tents in Callaghan Park, right in the center of town, where visitors from Marilyn Quayle to Mick Jagger to Cuauhtémoc Cárdenas could spot them. City officials implored the people to remove to sanctioned refuge on the edge of town, out of sight and out of mind. The homeless stayed put. Here was the place people suspicious of government agencies could bring relief parcels. Here was the political pressure of visible deprivation.

I walked through the park with Frank. There was a crowd round someone who had come to hand out a load of supplies. Others were standing near the bank of public telephones where for a while after the quake people could make free calls to Mexico. Frank chatted in Spanish with a friend who told him that though they are spending their days around the tents, they are sleeping in a house across town. 'Why?' Frank asked. 'It's cold', the man answered matter-of-factly. As did many of Watsonville's astute inhabitants, he understands how to use symbolism. Here, with the unauthorized tent city, is an opportunity maybe to prize a trailer home out of FEMA, to coax opportunity from disaster.

Up the road in Santa Cruz the homeless similarly seized their chances. As the doors of an earthquake-relief shelter opened, they hurried in. Three days later officials booted them out, angered that a respectable disaster should be exploited in this disreputable fashion. In fact, as coverage of the earthquake in the *Workers Vanguard* for October 27 showed in colorful detail, a large part of official emergency procedures are exercises in containment of potential political upheaval. Vested authority understands the seditious solidarity generated by an earthquake, which reminds people as forcibly about social foundations as about the frailty of houses just resting on their pier blocks. The quakes in Managua and Mexico City attest to that.

West of Watsonville, along the sea's edge, is Sunset Beach, and the condo complex of Pajaro Dunes: mostly empty second homes of San Franciscans, sometimes rented out for corporate retreats. Between Pajaro Dunes and the town stretch artichoke fields worked by people who have nowhere to sleep but their cars. Everyone in Watsonville can see the class geography, and the quake has brought to the surface the earthly potential of an act of God. At what point should a town declare eminent domain and seize developments like Pennsylvania Drive and Pajaro Dunes to house its people? Saint-Just knew the answer.

➤

NOVEMBER 10   *Aptos*
THE EAST GERMANS have given up on the Wall, which is the logical outcome of Gorbachev giving up on the Eastern European sphere. Scenes of great rejoicing. I find myself thinking of one of Brecht's last poems, 'Things Change', written in East Germany's youth:

    I. And I was old, and I was young at moments
        Was old at daybreak, young when darkness came
        And was a child recalling disappointments
        And an old man forgetting his own name.
    II. Sad in my younger days
        Sad later on
        When can I be happy?
        Better be soon.

I remember my father a couple of days before he died in St. Finbar's Hospital in Cork in 1981. He was weak, but listened attentively while I told him about the latest maneuvering in Poland. 'Good', he murmured when I indicated that the government might have engineered a split in Solidarity.

Yet he wasn't enamored of that government, or the Eastern European Communist regimes. He knew when the game, so to speak, was up. About Hungary in 1956 he'd written, two years later, 'The crime, monstrous in its fact and in its implications, was that after nearly a decade of absolute Communist power, a majority of people was prepared to die rather than tolerate the regime. That rather than the military repression – there has been plenty of that on all sides at all times – is what gives the Hungarian events their crucial, permanent, jolting significance.' He was realistic about actually existing Communism, but he was realistic about Walesa and Solidarity too; could see where, most likely, all that was headed.

Mentally, he was up and running right up to the moment his physical clock ran down that December day, sipping at the air with those old lungs, till he was still and we all of us around, my brothers and my mother, knew he had gone.

By the late eighties my mother, seeing the way things were heading farther east, sometimes used to say she was glad Claud was missing the Fall. In other words he was spared the necessity of posing the question Had all the struggles, heroisms, deaths, been for naught?

But he took history as it came, would have seen the old Communist dictatorships of Eastern Europe for what they were, seen they had to go, but nonetheless been realistic about what the velvet revolutions, breached Walls, cold war's end, presaged.

➤➤

NOVEMBER 13   *Aptos*
A PROFESSOR OF PHILOSOPHY, Warren Steinkraus of SUNY, Oswego, wrote recently to reprove me for using the word 'ravings' to describe biblical texts from Isaiah and Revelation rejected by me and my brothers as passages suitable to be read out at our mother's funeral.

This letter prompts one from Israel Shahak:

Editor,
I hope I can add a few remarks on the question of whether there are 'ravings' as Alexander Cockburn claims in a recent column in the book of poetry included in the Bible ascribed to Isaiah, which I've known practically by heart for many years, in the original Hebrew. Most of your readers, I surmise, don't know the book in detail but may be interested to know that Isaiah went completely naked for a period of three years, as 'a sign' (Chapter 20).

Second, the book contains the most anti-female passage in the whole Bible, well worth the name 'ravings' (3:16–26). The Lord is represented there as being so angry with the manner of walking of the 'daughters of Zion' (very similar, to judge by the detailed description, to the walking of well-dressed women today) that He, so Isaiah declares, will punish them by shaving their heads and 'destroying their privy parts' (so in Hebrew; the English softens the expression). I have wondered for about forty years how exactly He is going to do that, and all the commentators whom I have ever consulted on this point could not enlighten me on the details of that threat, which still faces so many women. Also one can find there a detailed list of twenty-one kinds of textiles and jewelry used by women. All of them, including sheets, are regarded as wicked and as bringing a variety of punishments both to the women who use them and to everyone who allows them to indulge in this wickedness. The punishments culminate in the threat of death to many in war.

Although these passages, and the whole book of Isaiah, are written in wonderful Hebrew, I am of the opinion, even when enjoying the style of the book, that 'ravings' is a quite accurate expression to describe much of it.

Israel Shahak
Jerusalem

➡

NOVEMBER 15   *Aptos*
ONE OF THE ORGANIZERS of the Free Speech Movement, in Berkeley in the 1960s, was Frank Bardacke, who introduced me to the Adobe Motel and who lives down the road in Watsonville. He later went on trial as one of the Oakland Seven. He was recently again on trial as one of the packing-house strike's organizers, one of the 'Watsonville Nineteen', against whom all charges were finally struck down.

Not so long ago, Frank wrote me a letter in which he tried to set forth the terms for a better history of the New Left than some of the apologetics now creeping into print:

Dear Alex:
I take it that what you are combating is an emerging semi-official orthodoxy on the history of the New Left. It goes something like this. The wholesome, open, democratic movement of the early 1960s self-destructed when confronted by the horrors of the war in Vietnam, as many people went berserk, waving the NLF flag in riotous demonstrations, and otherwise indulging in irrelevant revolutionary fantasies. How tragic. If only we could somehow recapture the spirit of those early years.

This is nonsense. It neither gives the New Left its due, nor explains its demise,

nor offers us a guide for radical action today. A better history would include
the movement's remarkable successes – putting limits on America's ability to
wage the war in Vietnam (crucial to this victory were those very demonstrations
that so upset the disapproving historians), helping create political space for the
civil rights and Black Power movements, and sparking a drive for educational
reform (which although now nearly completely gutted did open up many new
paths of acceptable scholarship as well as provide many New Left veterans with
relatively cushy jobs).

In the midst of these successes many people developed revolutionary hopes.
They wanted not just to stop the war, nor just to help clear the path for blacks
into the land of equal opportunity, nor simply to loosen the grip of an uptight
boojie culture. They – oh what the hell, We – wanted to make a revolution. It
sounds funny now, but there's nothing particularly crazy about that hope. Nor
was it peculiar to the American New Left. In Paris, Prague, Tokyo, Shanghai,
Mexico City – throughout the world people were trying to 'put revolution on the
agenda', as we used to say.

As it turned out, of course, it was not a revolutionary period, especially not
here in the US of A. Our revolutionary hopes were not matched by revolutionary
conditions. Our attempts to take our message to what we hoped would be
revolutionary sectors of society – the working class or the youth ghettos or
whatever – fell flat because the vast majority of the American people were not
in revolutionary contradiction with our ruling classes, especially after those
rulers stopped sending our young men to kill and die in Vietnam.

But the attempt to develop a revolutionary strategy, to link up with people
outside of New Left centers in the major university towns, was neither crazy
nor unprecedented. Throughout modern history young intellectuals have left
the security of the academy and tried to take a revolutionary message to the
'people'. When the 'people' were in a revolutionary mood, when conditions
were ripe, when luck would have it, a few made significant historical impact.
Mostly, however, these attempts have ended in disaster and defeat. Were they
not worth the chance?

How easy it is now to go back to that period, to pick out the inevitable
posturing, intellectual excesses, and sectarian lapses, and to say that the whole
attempt was crazy, that it destroyed our lovely New Left. No, it wasn't crazy.
We made our mistakes, who doesn't! But our big mistake – the crucial and
decisive error – was only that we misjudged the period; that we, along with
much of the world's left, believed that we were living in truly revolutionary
times.

So what does all this matter? Is it just a question of how one regards his or
her past? Some silly people trying to figure out among all of us fools who was
the biggest? Yes and no. No, because lurking behind this popular history of the
New Left is a political judgement about current political choices.

Those who say we went crazy back then, that we lost the true way, would have us now make peace with the more conservative times. They hope to rebuild a reform movement, keep it comfortably in line with the American grain, avoid extravagant hopes and actions. You can find them all over, mucking around in the Democratic Party, slogging up the halls of Academe, making music with labor bureaucrats, tailoring their views and rewriting their pasts so they can remain on center stage long after their historical moment has passed.

My intention is really not to ridicule Tom Hayden and his ilk. That hardly helps. Rather, I would like to salute my fellow New Left veterans throughout the country, and to tell them that we were right when we came to the conclusion that only fundamental revolutionary change can save humanity from modern barbarism and eventual annihilation. Now our job is to figure out how to make that conclusion count in these non-revolutionary times.

Good Luck,
Frank

➤

NOVEMBER 16   *Aptos*
Dear Alexander,
So sorry to read of your mother's death. I offer the following from Herbert Marcuse:

> Remembrance alone provides the joy without the anxiety over its passing and thus gives it an otherwise impossible duration.
> Time loses its power when remembrance redeems the past.
>
> *Eros and Civilisation*

I hope you are well. Take care.

E.M.

➤

NOVEMBER 20   *Chicago*
THE MORNING AFTER THE six Jesuits, their cook and her daughter were tortured and murdered, the *Detroit Free Press* led on its front page with an AP story beginning, 'The United States condemned Thursday's slaying of six priests in El Salvador, asked for an investigation and said it was speeding delivery of military aid to the Salvadoran government.'

The politicians and the press were hailing the walk of East Berliners to freedom just a few days before the death squad strode onto the campus in San Salvador to defend the capitalist way. I left Detroit and came to Chicago to give a talk at the tenth anniversary of Guild Books, after which a man from the Amalgamated Clothing and Textile Workers Union told me he'd been to a rally for Lech Walesa that had taken place in Chicago a couple of days earlier.

'You'd think that Walesa would have said something about the American labor movement', he said sadly, 'but he didn't. He talked about American entrepreneurs and capitalism and how wonderful America was and how he wanted Poland to be like America, but he never said one word to labor. Here we have the miners on strike against Pittston, and Walesa could have said something about their struggle, but he didn't.'

➤→

DECEMBER 1   *New York*
SPENT A BIT OF Thanksgiving weekend at Camp Solidarity, set up next to the Clinch River near the town of Lebanon in southwestern Virginia by miners striking the Pittston Coal Group. This was about the time that President Bush, warming up for the Malta summit, was boosting Western values of free speech and democracy. The Polish labor leader Lech Walesa had just been given an ecstatic greeting by the President and by Congress. The pundits and network newscasts gave Walesa lots of play too.

About 1,900 members of the United Mine Workers of America have been on strike against Pittston since April 5 of this year. Five hours down the freeway from Washington, D.C. the American miners wait vainly for the big guns of the press to show. It wasn't as though there was a shortage of dramatic incident. At about 4 p.m. on September 17 two U-haul trucks drove up the road leading to Pittston's Moss Number 3 coal preparation plant and disgorged 98 striking miners who promptly occupied the plant. By 7 p.m. on September 20, 75 hours into the occupation, a US district judge had ordered the miners to vacate the plant and 5,000 supporters were ranged around Moss Number 3. At 9 p.m. the occupiers marched out and melted into the crowd. Such scenes in the Soviet Union or Poland send network executives scurrying to book costly satellite time to relay back the dramatic pictures. It was the first occupation of this sort in the US since 1937, but here was mostly ignored.

A couple of weeks before I got to Camp Solidarity. Jackie Stump, District President for the mineworkers, had won a victory that once again offered an opportunity for dramatic coverage by a press hoarse with reporting revolt from below in Eastern Europe.

Prior to the election on November 7, the local member of Virginia's House of Delegates had been Donald McGlothlin, Sr., a twenty-year veteran of the statehouse and father of circuit court judge Donald McGlothlin, Jr., who had fined the union $30 million for strike activities. The miners thought that McGlothlin, Sr. should have been doing more than announcing his neutrality in the dispute. Three weeks before the election Stump announced he would run as a write-in candidate. He won by a margin of 2 to 1. When a Klansman triumphs in a race for the Louisiana statehouse the press rushes to New Orleans. Stump's unprecedented write-in victory drew scarce a line.

➤

DECEMBER 9   *Minneapolis*

AS TESTIMONY WOUND toward evening on Tuesday last, Council member Walter Dziedzic intervened. In the past, Dziedzic said, he'd been opposed to council interventions into foreign policy. He'd been a policeman who had grown up in working-class northeast Minneapolis. He remembered the work there of church women like those murdered by the Salvadoran death squad. 'Now', said Dziedzic, 'I've gone full circle from cop to protester. I sat silent till the Jesuits were murdered and I'm not going to sit silent any more.'

Amid cheers in the chamber, Dziedzic said he supported the motion to break city ties with O'Connor and Hannen until that firm gave up working for Cristiani. Listening to Dziedic I felt the same way as I had after talking to Hicks back in Virginia. Here were a vet and a cop, part of the vast spectrum of voices mostly caricatured as 'the silent majority'.

➤

DECEMBER 16   *New York*

SPYMANIA CONTINUES. Someone sends me the letters in the *Spectator* on Claud and Roger Hollis, about whom speculation is raging. The Hollis Claud used to talk about was Roger's older brother, Chris.

Spectator, October 28
Claud and I
Sir: In your issue of 14 October ('Proven connection'), I learn that I am the sole witness, so far established, of that missing link, consistently denied by Sir Roger Hollis, between himself as DG of MI5 and Claud Cockburn, Marxist wit and Comintern agent, after their days together at Oxford. Reading West's article, and the new book *The Truth about Hollis*, as well as several other books on this exhaustively scrutinised topic, I begin to see how easy it is for almost any one of us whose lives, for various reasons, have been at all intricate or shadowy to be denounced for activities of which our accusers deeply disapprove, on the feeblest evidence, indeed little more than guilt by coincidence.

W.J. West has reproduced what I told him over the shaky and intermittent telephone lines across the Berwyn Mountains of North Wales with reasonable accuracy. However, he is not correct in reporting that I said that Cockburn had previously advised me that he would be getting in touch with anyone 'in MI5'. In preparing our special issue of *Private Eye*, we had agreed that, since our ages were 20 years apart, I should concentrate on my contemporaries, mainly those just making their names or three-quarters of the way up the management ladder, while he would search out his old chums who were now possibly over the top of their trees, with the leisure of semi-retirement to indulge their mischief and malice. His precise words were: 'I am going to re-activate some of my old contacts.' Full stop.

I did not think then, or for some time after, that this might include the security services. I had the feeling, now I can't think why, that his 'high-up' informants were most likely to be in the police. Claud's editorial system depended on both of us getting in touch with any and everyone we knew, or had once known, who owed us a favour, or might welcome what Claud delicately called a 'quid pro quid' for information unprintable in his or her own publication. He urged that we leave on the hob whatever stories every other paper was bringing to the boil, at least for the moment.

When we were parting at lunch-time, in the middle of the pavement on Old Compton Street, all I knew was that he was meeting someone 'high up' nearby, an important possible tip-off. The pink-faced, cherubic, dark-suited fellow who surged by glassy-eyed, remained stuck in my memory only because Claud cursed, even mildly, at not being recognised, then again at having to hurry in pursuit at a pace any swifter than his usual, slightly wavering lope. If West judges that Hollis of MI5 was strictly obeying 'correct secret service procedure', then surely Cockburn of the Comintern, playing the same game, should have behaved in the same way. Instead he made clear to me that he feared he must not have been recognised, and went so far against the rules as to name his source as 'Hollis', a name that meant nothing to me, but would have done to many others within earshot.

West also cites me as proof that Hollis went out of his way to meet Cockburn 'clandestinely'. But neither then nor, come to think of it, now, is Soho the place to be clandestine, for those to meet who do not want to be observed meeting. Claud in 1963 was an easily recognisable figure, a regular writer for *Punch* and *Private Eye*, author of half a dozen books, often on television where he stood out as Fu Manchu in Irish tweeds. Would any professional, let alone the DG of MI5, select this place and this man to plot subversion?

Alan Brien
Glyn Uchaf, Faerdref, Cynwyd, Corwen, Wales

DECEMBER 18 *Aptos*

Dear Sir,

In his article about a feud between *The Nation* and *The New Republic* published in *The New York Times* today your reporter Richard Bernstein states that last March I wrote a column in *The Nation* 'dramatically revising downward the number of deaths attributable to Stalin'.

This is a distortion of my column and one exactly in line with a distortion made not so long ago by the editor-in-chief of *The New Republic*, Martin Peretz. In the column in question, published on March 6, and in subsequent correspondence, published in the August 7/14 issue of *The Nation*, I reviewed the wildly varying estimates of how may people died in the famine of the Ukraine in the early 1930s and in the purges later in the 1930s. I noted the high estimates of Stalin's victims, such as the 40 million figure attributed earlier this year to the Soviet historian Roy Medvedev, and I also noted the famous very low estimate made by George Kennan years ago, of maybe 'tens of thousands' dying in the Great Purge. Although I was quoting a book by Merle Fainsod and Jerry Hough, who in turn were quoting Mr. Kennan, and although these citations were clearly noted by use of quotation marks, Mr. Peretz hastened to suggest in *The New Republic* that I had espoused the figure of ten thousand. Now Richard Bernstein – who recently wrote an admiring article about *The New Republic* in your newspaper – has made a similar sort of insinuation, though he contented himself with the vaguer phrase 'dramatically revising downward'.

As a matter of fact I did not offer any revision – dramatic or undramatic, upward or downward – of my own. The point of my column was to examine the various estimates and to suggest some reasons for their rapid revision upward in recent years. In a later exchange I remarked that what 'looked sensible to me' were the estimates of Professors Barbara Anderson and Brian Silver, respectively of the University of Michigan and Michigan State University, demographers whose numbers on the famine are in line with estimates by Soviet academician V.P. Danilov. Anderson and Silver, and also Professor Stephen Wheatcroft of Melbourne University in Australia, say that the evidence shows that 3 million to 4 million people died in the Ukraine famine, with a total population loss between 1926 and 1939, including the purge, of some 6 million.

I feel no particular surprise at being misrepresented in *The New York Times*, but since your proclaimed purpose in journalism is to set forth the facts fairly and with dispassion, I do think you should ask yourself whether a man who recently wrote a glowing account of *The New Republic* and its 70th anniversary was suited for the task of discussing a feud between *The New Republic* and *The Nation*, or whether quotations from Martin Peretz about my supposed tendency to 'soft peddle the crimes of Communists' should have been matched at least with an effort to contact me to get my views on the affair and on Mr. Peretz's charge.

Yours sincerely,
Alexander Cockburn

Never printed. Oh well.

DECEMBER 21   *Albuquerque*

TOURING WITH SUSANNA to promote *Fate of the Forest*. Lula has narrowly lost
the presidential election in Brazil. Had Lula won? Panic would have exploded
Brazil's inflated cruzado and sent tidal waves of capital fleeing north. Our man
would have taken the oath of office amid economic rubble and bankerly bellows
that his prospective irresponsibility had wrecked Brazil. What is the maneuvering room for a socialist party in today's Third World? Collor de Mello was
the man the rich guys wanted and now they have him.

Right next to the news about Lula came tidings of Poland's plans for its
economy. One prime artificer of this impending catastrophe for Poland is the
Harvard economist Jeffrey Sachs, hailed by the slash-and-burn crowd as the
man who put Bolivia back on its feet, reducing the country's majestic 25,000
percent inflation rate in a matter of days. Sachs was imported as an adviser
when VIctor Páz Estenssoro became President in 1985, at which time Bolivia
had virtually no official state revenues – the result of years of incompetent and
corrupt military rule, plus a collapse in the world price of tin and natural gas,
amid workers' demands for a living wage.

What Sachs did was shut down the Bolivian economy, in a manner that will
soon be familiar to Poles: public workers fired, subsidies eliminated, service
costs denominated in dollars. But what sort of an economic triumph is it to turn
the lights off? As Sachs himself remarked, 'If you want to be cynical about it
you could say Bolivia used to be a miserably poor country suffering from
hyperinflation and now it's a miserably poor country without inflation.' This
is all very well if you are teaching at Harvard, but not so good if you are a tin
miner or a government employee in Bolivia suddenly thrown into the street with
nothing to live on.

➤

DECEMBER 23   *Ardmore*

'YOU'RE NOT GOING to defend Noriega, are you?' a features editor cried when I
told him my topic would be Panama. I told him I'd certainly be happy to defend
Gen. Noriega against the charge that the stuff supposedly found by US soldiers
in his private quarters marked him as a deviant and sworn foe of all that
America holds dear. The stuff in question was sex items, a picture of Hitler, lots
of cocaine, bundles of cash, religious paraphernalia including plastic frogs and
a rotting tamale with Seymour Hersh's name on it.

Leaving aside the Hersh tamale and the fact that Gen. Noriega probably had
more coke and more cash on hand than the average Joe, there's nothing on that
list you wouldn't trip over in at least one in every four American homes.

KITTY GIVES ME as a present a framed copy of the poem Sean Dunne wrote for Mama:

THE QUILT STORY
(*for Patricia Cockburn*)

For years she's been making the quilt,
Gathering the clothes her family outgrow.
When her husband died, his shirts became
Bundles waiting in baskets for the quilt
To absorb them into its diamond world.
In this house nothing is wasted, no jars
Thrown out, no object dispensed with.
In time all waste is useful or antique.
And so the quilt grows, a maze to include
Old scarves and caps, the ironed lining
Of jackets that smell of cigars.
In small squares cut shirts are set
Like tesserae in a quilt mosaic, each
Square a single story from her life.
There is the sober check of her husband,
The after-school denim of her sons.
There are pieces of blouse and trouser-end,
The cuffs and collars of a work-shirt.
Cut any smaller they'd seem like relics.
It grows farther away and longer as she sews,
Stretching across the floor piece by piece,
Quilt stories, autobiographies, each patch a deed.
Perhaps one night she'll lay it on the bed,
A long parade of fashion in the dark.
Lying under it, she'll hear the flap
Of laundry on the line in her garden,
Her own clothes drying, and she'll lie
And wonder at the waste of it when she goes.
She will leave her quilt behind like a farm,
Her life sewn into its every seam.

1990

➤

The Argument

IN WHICH I am discovered commencing a campaign against the 'Satanic abuse' hysteria. Salem revisited; unkind words for Vaclav Havel; the Pogo fallacy examined; my self-defense against charges of rapacity; Woody Guthrie quoted; Patrick Cockburn on journalism, taxis, hotels, shop windows; the importance of cabbage; Midge Dector's begging bowl; the mysterious affair of the pigeon, the Bay Bridge and Fred Gardner's eye; my set-up by Ted Koppel; Redwood Summer; a letter from Charlton Heston; sharks championed; an essay on violent death; impending removal to Petrolia. Of time and its tricks, of 'accidents' and 'normalcy', of history and the devil's hoof I sing.

JANUARY 1   *Ardmore, Co. Waterford*

... SO RAVEN WENT to a place of dirt and rocks, but when he go to put them together to make the world they won't stick. Raven got one terrible temper so he kick them rocks, then he swear because he hurt his foot. Then he got a good idea and he get some water to mix with the dirt so it stick. He work long, long time on the world; he jab it and poke it and roll it around. That world gave him a real bad time. Mountains want to fall off and oceans run all over where Raven don't want them. Sometimes he get so mad he just kick the whole thing apart, but he always go back and try again. Long time later, he get that world together so it will stay. It was real rough looking with big lumps everywhere, and Raven wasn't too happy. But he was sick of working on it and he was tired. So he say, oh, the hell with it ... it's done. And that's the way it was.

Tlingit version of the Creation

➡

JANUARY 12   *Ardmore*

Dear Mr. Cockburn,

To talk of the Bible as 'bloodthirsty nonsense', and to refer to the Book of Revelation as mostly 'psychotic', is to ignore completely a hundred years of study which attempts to understand the Bible in terms of history, poetry, and metaphor. You are no more free of poetic imagery than anyone else, including the writers of scripture. I expect that polemic writers of two thousand years hence will be chastising you for your use of such phrases as 'a dreadful weakness for hot air', and 'on and on go the strophes of windy uplift'.

My condolences to you and your family on your mother's death. My own mother died in the past year. I found the passages from Revelation helpful, interpreted as apocalyptic imagery, although, paradoxically, my mother would probably have dismissed them as 'psychotic nonsense'.

Alan J. Broadhead, M.D.
Hartford, Connecticut

READING MENCKEN'S DIARIES and yet another book about E. Waugh. Both are
cursed by their admirers, young blimps on the make, looking round for role
models. Cultists latch onto the bullying snobbery displayed in Waugh's diaries
and letters, while imitators like Emmett Tyrell of *The American Spectator*
manage to ape Mencken's loutishness but without his fun or learning.

A prodigious worker all his life, Mencken lamented near the end that he had
not worked even harder. There was always something waiting to be written. 'If
I am alive two or three years hence', Mencken wrote in his diary in 1931, 'I
shall tackle *Homo Sapiens*, a large treatise on the human race setting forth all
my ideas on the subject. My plan is to document it heavily ... After that, what?
I scarcely know. I'd like to do a psychological autobiography, describing the
origin and growth of my ideas ... I'd also like to do a book on government ...'

In 1964, two years before his death, Waugh confessed to Christopher Sykes:
'My life is roughly speaking over. I sleep badly except occasionally in the
morning. I get up late. I try to read my letters. I try to read the paper. I have
some gin. I try to read the paper again. I have some more gin. I try to think
about my autobiography. Then I have some more gin and it's lunch time. That's
my life. It's ghastly.'

Mencken hated Roosevelt for his success in getting America into the war, but
I could find in the diary no admiration for Hitler and a few disobliging remarks
about Nazis. Alfred Knopf, publisher of Mencken's *American Mercury*, had
famously reproved Mencken for being credulous about Hitler. The diary's
editor, Charles Fecher, declares that the entries establish that Mencken was an
anti-Semite, a charge against which he had previously defended him.

Evidence for the anti-Semitism is mostly to be found in Mencken's constant
naming of people as Jews or Jewesses, but that is not the end of it. There is a
bland account of the eviction of a member of Baltimore's Maryland Club on the
grounds that he had concealed his Jewish origins, and a couple of other entries
suggest that Fecher was right. But he should have elaborated that by the same
token Mencken was prejudiced toward blacks and indeed crackers, out of
certainty, it seems clear, that they were of inferior genetic material. Mencken
was a keen eugenicist, but then so was much of the American liberal elite – more
so than the conservatives.

One of Mencken's most ferocious entries, made on July 19, 1944, concerns
the mountain folk of North Carolina near Roaring Gap, 'supposed to be
inhabited by "the only pure Anglo-Saxons left in the United States". They turn
out, on acquaintance, to be a wretchedly dirty, shiftless, stupid and rascally
people.' Mencken raves on about their predatory rampages through the homes
of summer residents of Roaring Gap, concluding with their 'hostility to all
growing things', which he contrasts with the 'more civilized' horticulture of
Negroes, who have very pretty gardens ('though their taste naturally runs to

the more gaudy colors') and who take good care of their houses, though 'the colors used are garish, but they are at least niggerish, and the occupants plainly take some pride in the appearance of their house. No linthead or mountaineers [*sic*] ever shows any feeling for beauty. They all live like animals, and are next door to animals in their habits and ideas.'

➤

JANUARY 19   *Topanga, California*
For Immediate Release:
Contact: Thomas R. Eddlem, Research Analyst, (414) 749-3780

BIRCH SOCIETY CLAIMS DECEPTION IN EASTERN EUROPE

The BRI report, entitled *False Liberals in Eastern Europe*, certifies that many of the supposed 'anti-communists' taking power in Eastern Europe are, in fact, not anti-communist at all. In Romania and Czechoslovakia, many are former high-ranking Communist Party officials.

The Birch Society is one of only a few major conservative organizations to claim that the recent changes in Eastern Europe are part of 'a major and deadly disinformation campaign'. This puts the Birchers at odds with such conservative luminaries as syndicated columnist Joseph Sobran, who has proclaimed 'the Cold War is over', and William F. Buckley's *National Review*, which termed the events 'stunning victories' achieved by the West over Communism.

Birch Research Incorporated
Appleton, Wisconsin

➤

JANUARY 24   *Topanga*

SIX DAYS AGO, on January 18, a jury acquitted Ray Buckey and his mother, Peggy McMartin Buckey, on fifty-two counts of molestation after deliberating for nine weeks over evidence presented to it across two years. On thirteen remaining counts against Ray the court was deadlocked and a mistrial declared. He could still be retried on those. In the summer of 1983 Judy Johnson, the mother of a two-year-old, had complained to the police of Manhattan Beach, a rich seaside city in greater Los Angeles, that her son had been sodomized by 'Mr. Ray'. This turned out to be Ray Buckey, a teacher at the McMartin infant school founded by his grandfather. The boy was examined and pronounced to be telling the truth. Buckey was arrested, released, re arrested and then spent four years in prison awaiting trial.

In the months following his first arrest panic convulsed parents in Manhattan Beach. The police had sent them letters asking for information about abuse. By the spring of 1984 Buckey, his mother, grandmother, sister and three fellow teachers had been arrested; later they would be charged on 208 counts involving forty-one children. The police announced they had thirty-six suspects as yet uncharged and no less than 1,200 alleged victims of abuse. Amid the hysteria seven other infant schools in Manhattan Beach had to close.

The charges made by the children were gothic in detail. The children said they had witnessed devil worship in a church; had been photographed naked; had had sticks, silverware and screwdrivers stuck up their bottoms; had been marched to mortuaries and cemeteries where they dug up corpses with shovels and pickaxes; had been flown in airplanes; had been given red or pink liquid that had made them sleepy; had been buried alive; had seen naked priests cavorting in a secret cellar below the school; had seen one teacher fly; had observed three abusers 'dressed up as witches'; had seen Ray Buckey kill a horse with a baseball bat.

At almost exactly the same time that Judy Johnson was making the charges that provoked the longest trial in US legal history (at a cost of $15 million), in June 1984 children in Sacramento told of witnessing orgies, cannibalism and snuff films. Two months later, in Miami, children reported being made to drink urine and eat feces. In Wilkes-Barre, Pennsylvania, in March 1985, two children said adults had forced them into having oral sex with a goat and eating a dismembered deer's raw heart. In November 1985 in Maplewood, New Jersey, a 24-year-old woman was indicted on 235 counts of 'repulsively bizarre acts' alleged by infants, such as assaulting children with tampons, playing the piano naked and licking peanut butter and jelly off their bodies. In April 1986 children in a preschool in Sequim, Washington, charged they had been taken to graveyards and forced to witness animal sacrifice. In Chicago children said they had been made to eat a boiled baby. A boy in a Memphis preschool said his teacher, Frances Ballard, had, among innumerable perversions, put a bomb in a hamster and blown it up after children counted to eleven. She was acquitted of fifteen charges but, in what seems to be an appalling miscarriage of justice, went to prison supposedly for kissing a four-year-old boy on his genitals. Children in more than a hundred cities came forward.

In a series in late 1987 two reporters with the Memphis *Commercial Appeal*, Tom Charlier and Shirley Downing, surveyed nearly two score investigations of 'ritual abuse' against children and compared the cases and the children's charges. Many of them have a venerable antecedent, going back at least as far as Roman accusations against Christians in the second century. Others belong to what these days is called urban legend – lurid tales endlessly recycled, like the one about the phantom hitchhiker.

Of the thirty-six investigations reviewed by Charlier and Downing, all launched after the summer of 1983 and most of them concluded by 1987, ninety-one people were arrested and charged, and of the seventy-nine defendants whose cases have been heard, twenty-three were convicted, mostly on lesser charges, some of which have been reversed.

Buckey's life has been effectively ruined. His mother is suing for wrongful prosecution. The woman who started it all, Judy Johnson, is quit of the case. She died in 1986 of an alcohol-related illness. She had also claimed that her son had been sodomized by an AWOL marine who she said had inflicted similar treatment on the family dog. Johnson, who had a history of mental illness, also said her son – age two, remember – had described sex rituals in churches and animal sacrifice.

Why did this hysteria commence? An immediate response, by no means improper, is that 'hysteria' is an unkind word for a long overdue concern with child abuse. More than 100,000 cases are reported each year, most involving incest. By the early 1980s American society had evolved sufficiently for it to confront with some measure of determination the sexual persecution of children. In 1984 the FBI circulated nationally an advisory on child sex abuse which, in retrospect, may have fueled the paranoia.

It's clear from reading accounts of the various cases that many of the adults bringing the charges felt they were deeply involved in a national cause. An important issue in the Buckey trial was whether some major players in the case had themselves been abused as children. But it's also clear that some terrible injustices have been done.

In a January series on press coverage of the Buckey case, reporter David Shaw of the *Los Angeles Times* wrote a deadly account of the media frenzy that took place after the accusations first surfaced, making it clear that the essential function of most of the press had been to act as a conduit for the prosecution. The reporter responsible for breaking the story of the McMartin investigation was Wayne Satz of KABC in Los Angeles. He had an intimate relationship with Kee MacFarlane, who worked as a 'therapist' for Children's Institute International and who interviewed the McMartin infants and promulgated their charges. Her only credential was a certificate as 'welder-sculptor' from an Ohio welding school. Satz's descriptions of the Hillside Strangler's killings, which he covered, may have eventually been transmuted into details in the testimonies of abuse coached by MacFarlane from the McMartin children.

In the hysterical atmosphere the prosecutors felt they could get away with anything, and journalists eagerly lapped up their charges. Preposterous 'experts' were dutifully quoted. One California doctor of the mind claimed to have identified symptoms in children abused by Satanic cults – said symptoms including 'fear of monsters', making farting noises and laughing when other children farted. In general most expertise was rickety, often absurdly so. Examiners would tell a child to bend over, and if their scrutiny was greeted by an 'anal wink' – i.e., contraction of the sphincter – they would pronounce the child abused.

Commie hunters and Satan hunters share the same paranoid mind-frame. The Memphis Police Department's supposed expert on satanic crimes, Sgt. Jerry Davis, known to his colleagues as Mr. Conspirator, was in the late 1960s head of a criminal intelligence unit infiltrating Memphis student groups in search of subversives.

The laws of this chase would have been the envy of the seventeenth-century prosecutors at Salem. The accusers were infants as young as two and three, permitted in fifty states to testify without corroboration from adults or physical evidence; without cross-examination in many states; to have their charges merely reported by adults as hearsay in many states. These infants had themselves been interrogated as many as thirty times by social workers or other investigators, told they would remain separated from their parents if they retracted their charges, held in sterile environments during questioning, to a degree that one critic described as kindred to 'brainwashing' in the Korean War. In the total war against child abusers Iowa officials sought but failed to obtain sanction to strip and probe children without parental permission in search of evidence of abuse.

So the nation went on the hunt for Satan, and the search rapidly took up the usual populist impedimenta: priests conducting perverted masses in cellars, gulping down children's blood and performing other tricks of the heterodox trade. Rocking chairs disappeared from infant schools so teachers would not be compelled to take children in their laps. Teachers took care never to be left alone with infants. Video monitors scanned playrooms, for teachers' protection. In this purgative frenzy many lives were destroyed.

➡

JANUARY 25   *Topanga*
NABEEL SENDS ME a letter the *NYT* didn't print.

Dear Sir:
Today's edition of *The New York Times* carries an erroneous translation of the Arabic text that appears in the photo on page six. The photo depicts a demonstration of Lebanese journalists 'protesting attempts by Gen. Michel Aoun, leader of the Christian militia, to censor news reports.' The translation of the demonstrators' sign in the caption below reads, 'In Allah's hands we are safe.' The actual Arabic text is something entirely different. Translated into English, it says 'Freedom of the Press / Yes to the [printed] word, No to Terror.'

Sincerely,
Nabeel Abraham
Dearborn, Michigan

FEBRUARY 1   *Topanga*

DID A COLUMN FOR THE *Wall Street Journal* on the satanic abuse madness.
Here's a conversation with a child by an investigator in a case in Memphis:

> Mother: How did the hamster explode? Was it stuck with a knife?
> Boy: No, she [Mrs. Ballard] put a bomb in it.
> Mother: Was it a firecracker?
> Boy: No, it sounded like it.
> Mother: Are you sure the hamster was real?
> Boy: Yes, I saw it and it moved. We could not touch it.
> Mother: Was there blood?
> Boy: Yes.
> Mother: How did she clean it up?
> Boy: With a broom.

If a child says he saw Ray Buckey kill a horse with a baseball bat (which one
did), and if this charge is disproved (which it was), then the child should be
indicted for perjury. If the parent supported the child in this false accusation
and can be shown to have abetted it, then the parent should be indicted for
perjury too. If the court then establishes that parent/child were lying, they
should be sent to jail, just as so many of their victims have been. A few well
publicized cases of imprisonment of children and parents (along with 'therapists' and social workers, it does without saying) and we would see an end to
these disgusting miscarriages of justice. Indict the children and their parents
with them!

⇒

FEBRUARY 17   *Joshua Tree*

MANHATTAN'S ANSWER TO *Götterdämmerung* is the fissure between the Trumps,
and its Wagner is Liz Smith. An age – the great eighties speculative boom,
particulary in real estate – is dying, and the atmospherics of this decline are
being appropriately reported in the genre revived in the mid seventies to honor
the great boom: gossip columns.

Trump flourished exactly in step with the reordering of resources and
consumption that began to take shape at the end of the seventies. From a
desperate city he exacted tax concessions, as did all other developers. To New
Money he offered sanctuary without shame. 'From day one', he wrote in *The
Art of the Deal*, 'we set out to sell Trump Tower not just as a beautiful building
in a great location but as an event. We positioned ourselves as the only place
for a certain kind of very wealthy person to live – the hottest ticket in town. We
were selling fantasy.' Trump gives an entertaining account of our times simply
by reporting who bought the 263 apartments on offer:

'At first, the big buyers were the Arabs ... Then, of course, oil prices fell and the Arabs went home. In 1981 we got a sudden wave of buyers from France ... François Mitterrand had been elected president ... After the European cycle, we got the South Americans and the Mexicans, when the dollar was weak and their economies still seemed fairly strong ... During the past several years, we've had two new groups buying. One is American – specifically, Wall Street types, brokers and investment bankers who've made instant fortunes during the bull market frenzy ... The other new buyers are the Japanese.'

Trump Tower stands at the center of an island that now famously displays its linked dioramas of wealth and misery: the rich in their castles, the homeless on the subway gratings and indeed in the old rail tunnels below the gleaming bulk of the *ci-devant* Commodore – one of Trump's early ventures.

There's always been harmony between real estate and the Fourth Estate. As Trump fondly recalls, the City Planning Commission once frowned on his plans for Trump Tower. Then he invited the *Times*'s chief architecture critic, Ada Louise Huxtable, to look at his model. On July 1, 1979, she wrote a column in the Arts and Leisure section that contained what Trump gratefully calls 'several terrific lines', including the observation that 'it is undeniably a dramatically handsome structure'. In Trump's view, 'perhaps no one had a more powerful influence', and four months later the City Planning Commission unanimously approved his plans.

➤

FEBRUARY 24   *Topanga*

SINCE 1980, IN EL SALVADOR some 70,000 have been killed: Guatemala, some 100,000; Nicaragua, some 30,000. The death toll from the Soviet invasion in 1968 was 92 dead, according to the present Czech ambassador to the US. The Hungarian Human Rights Foundation (N.Y.) says that 2,200 Hungarians were killed during the Soviet invasion. According to Western news reports at the time, up to 50,000 Hungarians were killed during the Soviet invasion. Arnulf Baring, in his book *Uprising in East Germany: June 17, 1953*, says that 21 East Germans were killed by the Soviet troops. The latest figure for those killed in Romania during the overthrow of Ceausescu (clearly supported by the US) was 689 according to a Rumanian count published in the *New York Times*.

UNICEF's 1989 figures for the mortality rates per thousand of children under 5: Guatemala 103, Honduras 111, Nicaragua 99, El Salvador 87, Czechoslovakia 32, Hungary 57, Poland 19, Romania 28, Bulgaria 20. Life expectancy: Nicaragua 64, Guatemala 63, Honduras 65, El Salvador 64, Czechoslovakia 72, Hungary 71, Poland 72, Romania 71, Bulgaria 72.

FEBRUARY 26   *Topanga*

IT TURNS OUT that 'Satanic abuse' or 'ritual abuse' is an article of faith among
the politically correct set. I'm getting lots of denunciations for attacking the
whole craze. Students at Reed College where I am supposed to be talking on
'perspectives for the left in the 1990s' have said that since I discount the
'reality' of 'ritual abuse' I'm not fit to instruct youth, but must participate in
a session where I will be confronted by a panel which will review my crimes.

What really set them off was my demand that the accusing tots should be
jailed for perjury. This has caused some 'alternative' papers to drop my
column.

>→

FEBRUARY 26   *Topanga*

PICKED UP THE paper and knew the result before I unfolded it. The opposition
won the election in Nicaragua.

>→

FEBRUARY 28   *Topanga*

THERE WAS NO victory for democracy in Nicaragua last Sunday. The victory was
for violence and the lesson was that violence pays. After more than a decade of
being bled dry by a powerful and relentless enemy – the United States – a
majority of Nicaraguans chose realism over nationalism and said Enough.

>→

MARCH 1   *Topanga*

CHOMSKY URGES ME to my doom:

Dear Alex,

As a good and loyal friend, I can't overlook this chance to suggest to you a
marvelous way to discredit yourself completely and lose the last minimal shreds
of respectability that still raise lingering questions about your integrity. I have
in mind what I think is one of the most illuminating examples of the total and
complete intellectual and moral corruption of Western culture, namely, the
awed response to Vaclav Havel's embarrassingly silly and morally repugnant
Sunday School sermon in Congress the other day. We may put aside the
intellectual level of the comments (and the response) – for example, the profound and startlingly original idea that people should be moral agents. More
interesting are the phrases that really captured the imagination and aroused
the passions of Congress, editorial writers, and columnists – and, doubtless,
soon the commentators in the weeklies and monthlies: that we should assume

responsibility not only for ourselves, our families, and our nations, but for others who are suffering and persecuted. This remarkable and novel insight was followed by the key phrase of the speech: the cold war, now thankfully put to rest, was a conflict between two superpowers: one, a nightmare; the other, the defender of freedom (great applause).

Reading it brought to mind a number of past experiences in Southeast Asia, Central America, the West Bank, and even a kibbutz in Israel where I lived in 1953 – Mapam, super-Stalinist even to the extent of justifying the anti-Semitic doctor's plot, still under the impact of the image of the USSR as the leader of the anti-Nazi resistance struggle. I recall remarks by a Fatherland Front leader in a remote village in Vietnam, Palestinian organizers, etc., describing the USSR as the hope for the oppressed and the US government as the brutal oppressor of the human race. If these people had made it to the Supreme Soviet they doubtless would have been greeted with great applause as they delivered this message, and probably some hack in *Pravda* would have swallowed his disgust and written a ritual ode.

I don't mean to equate a Vietnamese villager to Vaclav Havel. For one thing, I doubt that the former would have had the supreme hypocrisy and audacity to clothe his praise for the defenders of freedom with gushing about responsibility for the human race. It's also unnecessary to point out to the half a dozen or so sane people who remain that in comparison to the conditions imposed by US tyranny and violence, East Europe under Russian rule was practically a paradise. Furthermore, one can easily understand why an oppressed Third World victim would have little access to any information (or would care little about anything) beyond the narrow struggle for survival against a terrorist superpower and its clients. And the *Pravda* hack, unlike his US clones, would have faced a harsh response if he told the obvious truths. So by every conceivable standard, the performance of Havel, Congress, the media, and (we may safely predict, without what will soon appear) the Western intellectual community at large are on a moral and intellectual level that is vastly below that of Third World peasants and Stalinist hacks – not an unusual discovery.

Of course, it could be argued in Havel's defense that this shameful performance was all tongue in cheek, just a way to extort money from the American taxpayer for his (relatively rich) country. I doubt it, however; he doesn't look like that good an actor.

So, here's the perfect swan song. It's all absolutely true, even truistic. Writing something that true and significant would also have a predictable effect. The sign of a truly totalitarian culture is that important truths simply lack cognitive meaning and are interpretable only at the level of 'Fuck You', so they can then elicit a perfectly predictable torrent of abuse in response. We've long ago reached that level – to take a personal example, consider the statement: 'We ought to tell the truth about Cambodia and Timor.' Or imagine a columnist writing: 'I think the Sandinistas ought to win.' I suspect that this case is even clearer. It's easy to predict the reaction to any truthful and honest comments about this episode, which is so revealing about the easy acceptance of (and even praise for) the most monstrous savagery, as long as it is perpetrated by Us against Them – a stance adopted quite mindlessly by Havel, who plainly shares the utter contempt for the lower orders that is the hallmark of Western intellectuals, so at least he's 'one of us' in that respect.

Anyway, don't say I never gave you a useful suggestion.

Best,

Noam

Cambridge, Massachusetts

➤

MARCH 2   *Topanga*

'SUDDENLY IT BECOMES a lot clearer, doesn't it, that the Enemy *isn't* Us? Not unless we're to blame for trying to survive in the World-As-It-Is. The enemy is The Bank, isn't it, the system of corporate imperialism whose blind uncontrollable will to profit will be served even if it means the death of the planet? And its apologists. Like Pogo. The media whores that makesure the last thawt we hold as we're marched away to the gasovens is that WE'RE the Enemy, OUR hearts are the problem, inshort that IT'S ALL OUR FAULT.

'Is there no fyt left in the victims of the Banks war on the Earth? Not enuf to allow us even to … *name the Enemy?* … Can't do that, can we? Safer to blame ourselves.'

Tom Reveille: *Is Pogo Public Enemy #1*

The trouble with Pogo-ism and with the idea of 'empowerment' is that they imply we're playing on a level field. If we are all equally The Enemy and if we all equally *empower* ourselves, then suddenly the enemy will no longer be Us. In fact there'll be no Enemy and Us will hold power.

This is all balls.

➤

MARCH 3   *Topanga*
Dear Editor,
I resent the hell out of mad-dog Cockburn's assessment that 'the fact that MacFarlane has a degree in social work is about as relevant to her activities in the McMartin (child abuse) case as saying she has a degree in Frisbee flying.' True, most psychologists are a sour lot – most border on insanity – and I have managed a poor but mentally healthy existence despite contemporaries' claims

that I drag my drunken bones into the city to pay someone who masturbates three times as much as I do to listen to me talk about mom. What I can't abide by is the Frisbee-flying crack. I spent many an afternoon on the atavistic campus of Georgetown Preparatory School sailing Whammo discs among the red brick buildings where the Jesuits cursed our uncontrollable sexuality and drank themselves stupid. At first I detested 'Ultimate', or rather the concept of it as a bogus hippy approximation of Sport, but discovered that it was as comfortable with the Clash as with the (I'll be happy when you're) Dead. The most communal and socialistic of sports, Frisbee can be enjoyed without the oppressive fascism of football or the boorish billionaire boys club aura baseball exudes. I recently met a wonderful woman at a party because I was tossing the 'disc' in the street at about three in the morning. She came outside because what my friend and I were doing seemed unusual at that hour (yes, we were drunk), and she and I spoke pleasantly while taking turns throwing the Frisbee. She even kissed me good-night – a truly kinder and gentler denouement, possible because of a piece of plastic manufactured in East Bumfuck, Ohio. Maybe if Kee MacFarlane *did* have a degree in Frisbee flying she would resist that unbearable urge social workers have to overanalyze, and might even learn to catch one between her legs.

Mark G. Judge
Fairfax, Virginia

➳

MARCH 4 *Portland, Oregon*
EXCERPT FROM TAPE OF Portland radio show, March 2, 1990:

Lisa (caller from Salem): I don't buy that there are innocent people in jail.

AC: You don't? You think everyone in jail is guilty?

Lisa: It's a little reactionary but I tend to believe that if you're not guilty you don't get convicted and that ...

AC: Do you really believe that?

Lisa: I have personally been accused of child abuse. I have personally been hauled to see a [garbled] and because I was willing to cooperate, would do anything they asked me to do I came out of it all right. If you refuse to cooperate you're automatically assumed guilty, which I think is fine.

Show host: No, it's not fine. That's the absolute opposite of our legal system.

AC: This is terrifying.

Show host: Lisa, don't you see that that's the turning around of our whole basic fundamental system? ...

Lisa: I'm just saying that I felt that it worked. I felt that they were capable and qualified to make decisions and they did a fairly good job – in my particular instance, and I'm not saying that in every instance that's true.

AC: Suppose it hadn't gone that way? You might be sitting in jail yourself and be innocent. Doesn't that scare you?

Lisa: Not when it comes to that particular field, no. It's like I'd rather have a lot of innocent people in jail than a lot of guilty people out running around abusing children.

➤

MARCH 6   *Topanga*

THE NEW ENGLAND JOURNAL OF MEDICINE published a paper by four doctors titled 'Racial Differences in Susceptibility to Infection by Mycobacterium Tuberculosis'. It got big play in the newspapers and on television. The *Los Angeles Times* ran a long story about the TB paper, headlined 'Blacks' High TB Rate May Be Linked to Genetics'.

It's in their genes. There's nothing we can do.

I talked to Dr. Sam Epstein, now at the School of Medicine at the University of Illinois, Chicago. Epstein said: 'Neo-Shockleyism loves to shift the blame from maldistribution of resources to some genetic predisposition. Look at cancer rates in blacks. Five-year survival rates are, let's say, 38 percent for blacks and 50 percent for whites. Do you say that's because of genetic susceptibility, or because of limited access to health care for blacks? Blacks get the dirtiest and most dangerous jobs in industry, working for example on the top side of coke ovens, living in close proximity to mills, with maximum exposure to point-source discharge of atmospheric effluents, so they have high cancer rates.'

Dr. Epstein said that it was all very well for those four doctors to match their black and white populations at the time of the study, but there was, in the study, no consideration of a wide range of those prior variables: Where had the black people in the nursing homes grown up, what had they worked at, what had been their income levels, as compared to similar indices for the white patients. When you think about all this for minute you see the absurdity of it.

➤

MARCH 7   *Topanga*

FRIENDS BACK FROM NICARAGUA tell me that the day after the election most places were quiet, almost eerily so. There was hardly anything in the way of UNO victory rallies. The place was subdued, as though people who thought they had voted with their heads were suddenly feeling the heaviness in their hearts. Here too in El Norte there was true melancholy, and it took a while before people pulled themselves together and went out shopping for silver linings. A whole generation came to political maturity with the revolution in Nicaragua and efforts to defend that revolution as a focal point in their political and, often, personal lives.

A bright side: The solidarity movement in the United States had its successes. The Reagan administration came to power in 1981 and almost instantly promulgated a white paper that looked like a preamble to invasion. By 1985 the solidarity movement, through diligent grass-roots organizing, education and coalition building, had played a major role in forcing the Reagan gang underground, into clandestine, illegal activities which in turn led to the Iran/*contra* scandal that pre-empted the invasion that in my view was being planned for early 1987.

A dark side: The movement was never able to install 'End the embargo' as a central and persistent demand, but it was the trade embargo that helped bleed Nicaragua dry. This embargo was imposed by Reagan in 1985 with an executive order premised on the claim that Nicaragua was a threat to US national security. It has been renewed each year since on the same claim. The World Court declared the embargo illegal in its decision of June 27, 1986, confirming the illegality of the bombing of the harbors and US funding and support for the *contras*.

If you want to trace the point at which vital momentum was lost, go back to the fight over 'nonlethal' aid after military aid to the *contras* had supposedly been terminated. Enough liberal Democrats were able to argue that some measure of aid was essential to 'hold' the center, and the famous 'bipartisan accord' was hatched. The Democrats were then able to argue that the *contra* war was effectively over; the press complied; no one talked about the embargo; and a broad section of the left decided that the battle was won and we could look elsewhere, to El Salvador.

➤

MARCH 10   *Topanga*
Dear Bob Brenner and other friends in Solidarity,
Yesterday, as I waited to go and hear a panel in the *Against the Current*/Solidarity conference at USC and you said to one of your comrades behind the ticket desk that I was a speaker and could get in for free, she said loudly for the benefit of all in earshot: 'Oh, the guy who's being paid $300 to come and speak', in a tone suggesting that this suggested a mercenary disposition on my part.

You know, this pisses me off.

Three or four weeks ago you called me up and asked me to speak at this conference. As you will recall, I was rather reluctant. You said it would be really helpful if I came and that there would be some doubt about holding the conference if I didn't. So I said I would. To do this I drove down yesterday from Watsonville. Cost in gas (Chrysler V8, a '64) some $30. Sunday I had long scheduled a talk on Central America in Marin. Because I'm down here to talk to your conference I will have to fly up and back again. Cost, about $250. The Marin people can't pay travel. By the time you take out the expenses, I'm talking to your conference for some $20.

Last weekend I had been asked to go to Reed College to give a talk about perspectives in the '90s. I didn't want to do that either. Mike Conner, the fellow organizing the conference, said they wouldn't be able to hold the conference unless I came. So I said yes. As you know, the Reed people suddenly felt that because I have written about the fact that innocent people have gone to jail because of the daycare molestation hysteria I was no longer qualified to be the keynote speaker and said I could speak for ten minutes on a panel well stocked with people eager to denounce my daycare pieces. Active in all this was your fellow Solidarity comrade Chris Phelps, who edits the *Portland Alliance*. Last December I gave a talk (the one reprinted in the current *ATC*) in Portland which was a benefit for the paper, the *Portland Alliance*. As far as I can remember, it netted for the paper a bit over $2,000. I also have been giving my columns free to that paper, because I support that kind of journalism.

The weekend in Portland was extremely contentious. I would not go on the clearly 'set-up' panel, but had said that I would be happy to give the keynote and also to meet people bothered by what I wrote. Having been roundly insulted by Phelps on the local radio, and the advertising manager of the *Portland Alliance* once again having regaled the Reed people on my extortionate characteristics, Phelps told my associate Rich McKerrow in New York the next day that I should be giving my column free to everyone! McKerrow had said that since he was now running my syndication, the *Alliance* should – like everyone else who runs it – at least pay something.

Okay. Do you people think I have private means? I don't. My columns cost money to produce – quite a lot of money actually. I don't have a teaching stipend. I live by writing and, to a small extent, speaking fees. From each according to their means. If a university student union has big money to pay speakers I'll happily ask for it. If a small Central American solidarity group has nothing, I'll equally happily figure out expenses and some reasonable divvy of the take. I've given evenings in Detroit which are fundraisers for Solidarity/*ATC* on this basis. But you know, the only times over the years that I've been guilt-tripped by people about asking for money for expenses or a fee is by Solidarity/*ATC* people (Phelps and his colleagues in Portland, Dolores Treviso here in LA who was obviously voicing Solidarity sentiments).

I'm not a member of Solidarity/*ATC*. I actually disagree quite strongly with many of your positions. But like all of you I believe in trying to build a left. I push *Labor Notes* whenever I can. But every time I speak for you I'm not speaking somewhere else, or not writing something. Do you think I'm some sort of a charitable resource, whose name you can use as a commodity to get people in the door, and then dump on because I'm not donating my services for the good of the cause? How come Phelps thinks it's okay to pay the printer who makes a living doing printing, but not the writer who makes a living doing writing. Or does he think I'm meant to gouge the *Anderson Valley Advertiser* for the $25 he's not giving, because he's somehow doing 'more valuable work' than the *AVA*. Remember what Woody Guthrie said when the lady, stunned at his request for a fee to sing at some benefit, protested, 'But Mr. Guthrie, it's for a good cause.' 'Lady', Guthrie answered, 'I don't sing for bad causes.'

So why don't you people figure out your group's relationship to non-members whose services you hope to exploit. If you think you should be getting it all for nothing, then say so upfront. Don't chisel around with me, discuss among yourselves what a rapacious fellow I am and act generally as though the world owes you a living. I've got happier things to do with my time.

Best,
Alexander Cockburn

>+

MARCH 19   *Topanga*
WATCHED THE RESULTS of the East German elections: all those Christian Democrats braying in triumph. A member of German New Forum has complained that 'Of course, we in the New Forum are frustrated when the population rushes with colors flying from the dictatorship of the party to a dictatorship of the Deutsche mark.'

In 1946 quite a number of people thought there could be differing roads to socialism. In a famous, calculated indiscretion Stalin said as much to Harold Laski, member of a Labour Party delegation visiting Moscow. Klement Gottwald, Secretary of the Czechoslovak Communist Party, reported to his comrades on the Central Committee a similar exchange with Stalin, in which the latter said that the dictatorship of the proletariat was not the only way forward.

Later that year Gottwald publicly said the same sort of thing, as did Dimitrov in Bulgaria. Gomulka announced, 'We have chosen a Polish path of development of our own, a road of people's democracy, and we think that under these conditions, along this road, the dictatorship of the working class, and still more of a single party, would be neither useful nor necessary.' From France and Italy, Thorez and Togliatti spoke of 'new paths'.

Many Western historians have denounced all this as trickery to distract attention from the Stalinist master plan. More sensibly, in his *Stalin and the European Communists*, the Italian labor historian Paolo Spriano says that though there was obviously a propagandist element, 'these overtures genuinely corresponded to each country's and each leadership group's need to autonomy, to the desire of the Communist leaders to experiment with gradual evolution without losing the required political allies.'

In early 1947 the Hungarian economist Eugene Varga was writing about 'democracy of a new type' in Eastern Europe. It was over before it began to breathe, for 1947 was the pivot year, in which the full outlines of the cold war came into focus. Already in 1946, US Secretary of State Jimmy Byrnes had told the Russians that if they wanted reparations from Germany they would have to take them out of their zone, which they did, East Germany thus being the only part of the Third Reich to yield damages. By January the Soviet Union was braced for siege and battening down the hatches, starting with the fixed Polish elections that sent the Peasant Party leader Mikolajczyk, who probably should have won, into exile. By March, Truman was promulgating the doctrine of 'containment' and a month later commencing security vetting of government employees. By June, special measures were enacted in the Soviet Union against those revealing 'state secrets'. That same month came the Marshall Plan.

Both the Polish and Czechoslovak governments yearned to receive US aid under the Marshall Plan but bowed to Soviet pressure to reject it. As Spriano writes, once all hope of collaboration with America had collapsed, Stalin faced a choice: 'He felt that if he was to avoid acknowledging US international hegemony, he had to accept the risk of global conflict.' More than forty years later Gorbachev accepts US international hegemony, and Czechoslovak and Polish leaders make trips to Washington and to the bankers, urging a Marshall Plan and speaking sometimes, depending on their audiences, about a new path.

➤

MARCH 23   *Topanga*
JOURNALISTS ABROAD LOVE taxi drivers, hotels and shop windows. Between the three of them an experienced overseas reporter can soak up all the necessary social, political and economic analysis on the way in from the airport and after a brief stroll down the street. The hotel itself provides a further important source material for profound analysis.

The trouble is that taxi drivers – mostly either embittered small businessmen or struggling immigrants – are of limited sociological worth, however spirited the harangue that the journalist eagerly jots down. The hotel can be even more misleading. My brother Patrick, housed for four years in Moscow in the late 1980s as correspondent for the London *Financial Times*, observes in his excellent book *Getting Russia Wrong*:

> After a few months watching [journalistic] visitors it became obvious
> that their optimism or pessimism about *Perestroika* depended less on
> the enormous number of interviews they conducted than the state of
> their accommodation. Here the Hungarians handled things much
> better. At the same time as their economic experiment got under way

in the late sixties they constructed on the Danube, in central Budapest, three or four first-class hotels where the food was good and the waiters spoke English. The aim was to earn hard currency from tourists, but the effect was to impress visiting journalists and diplomats with the success of the Hungarian economic experiment. They wrote reports suggesting that here was real change just as correspondents in Moscow, who had failed to get their breakfast, were writing about the inflexibility of the Soviet system.

There's no more indignant economic critic than a journalist without a morning cup of coffee.

I remember Patrick telling me that there was one hotel in Moscow from which it was hard to make phone calls. Dispatches from journalists lodged there used to put heavy stress on the technological backwardness of the Soviet Union. Another – I think it was the National – was noted for the petty corruption of its waiters. From here would be filed stories about the moral collapse of the country. A third hotel was on the outskirts of town and journalists staying here would brood into their laptops about the degree to which Moscow and Mother Russia itself were cut off from the dynamic mainstream of world history.

The front shop window is the third great resource of a journalist, but here too the evidence can be misleading. The standard is simple. If the store has long lines and nothing much on display then the economic system under review – usually in the Soviet Union or Eastern Europe – is a failure. If there are no lines and plenty of goods out on the counter, then the journalist usually gives a upbeat economic diagnosis.

There are refinements that any connoisseur of shop-window reporting soon learns to expect. Journalists don't like cabbage. Woe betide the store that has them on offer. Expect derisive prose about 'a few moldy old vegetables', all bleakly indicative of economic backwardness. Exotic fruits on the other hand – kiwis or mandarins – usually elicit great applause and are taken as emblems of vibrant economic reform.

MARCH 26   *Washington, D.C.*

Dear Mr. Cockburn:

During an interview last week on the *Donahue Show*, former White House astrologer Joan Quigley said that one of her duties was the charting of favorable times of day when Air Force One and any helicopters carrying President Reagan should take off and land.

This comment sparked a memory regarding the *Challenger* disaster, when one of the very first television news reports mentioned that there had been discussions about scratching the launch when engineers expressed concern about the effect of low temperatures on the O-rings. According to this news report, NASA was pressured by The White House to keep to its schedule, regardless. This interference was later seen merely as an attempt to accomplish a political coup for the president, as he was to make an address that day on the subject of education and wanted to tie-in a reference to a school teacher being on board the *Challenger.*

Yet, in view of Joan Quigley's comments, I am wondering if there was a more sinister reason behind The White House's insistence on a specific launching time: favorable astrological computations?

If you should consider this question worthy of a follow-up, I'm sure your reports on the subject would be of interest of readers of *The Nation.*

Sincerely,
Ruth Elizabeth Ramsey
Epworth, Georgia

➥

MARCH 28   *Washington, D.C.*
KENNAN'S SELF-REHAB has been one of the wonders of our age, and amazingly successful. Not conspicuous in his memoirs are such important aspects of his service to the State as his salvaging of war criminals for US purposes, or such documents as his wartime memo apropos future de-Nazification. Only Chris Simpson quotes it in his book *Blowback:* 'Whether we like it or not, nine-tenths of what is strong, able and respected in Germany has been poured into those very categories which we have in mind' for purging from the German govern-ment – namely, those who had been 'more than nominal members of the Nazi Party'. Rather than remove 'the present ruling class of Germany', as he put it, it would be better to 'hold it [that class] strictly to its task and teach it the lessons we wish it to learn.'

➥

APRIL 2   *New York*
Dear Alexander,
I've heard (and read) that you've taken some flak for your opinion on the California sex abuse trial. As a psychologist, I must say that I am in agreement with your analysis. I've worked with sex offenders and their victims and many mental health professionals and the latter are the worst! I have seen them create victims of both children and 'perpetrators'.

Beware mental health workers in general. Many are nuts who possess power to ruin lives, as you pointed out. And also be aware that some sex offenders are the most cunning and dangerous people alive. Still, it's clear that no good will come from further prosecution of the McMartin case.

The nutty mental health workers are partly responsible for 'empowerment'. It's simply psychobabble partly motivated by their fear of talking about obtaining political power. I imagine liberals at a rally for recycling shouting EMPOWERMENT TO THE PEOPLE! RECYCLE YOUR NEWSPAPERS NOW!

Sincerely,
K.H.
Oregon

➤

APRIL 4   *Topanga*
I SUPPORT LITHUANIA'S right to national self-determination. Its case is probably nearly as strong as those that could be advanced by nationalists in Hawai'i, Alaska or Mexico's stolen territory, Texas. People seem a bit vague about Lithuania's history all the same, imagining that it has been one nation, free (and most definitely under God) for centuries, governed from Vilnius. But Vilnius was once Vilna in Byelorussia, as the Byelorussians are now pointing out, and in my 1906 *Century Atlas* you can't find Lithuania, only a slab of terrain called West Russia, which is not surprising, since Lithuania was absorbed into the Czarist empire at the end of the eighteenth century.

If Eastern Europe is going to be recast in a prewar mold, we might as well have a clear idea of what the political cartography was like back then. The interwar Lithuanian Republic was scarcely democratic, being a right-wing dictatorship under Antanas Smetona, who seized power in a coup in 1926. The feudal knight-and-horse coat of arms raised by the Saljudis movement this past March 12 was the symbol of that anti-Semitic regime.

The last time Lithuania declared independence was the day after Hitler invaded the Soviet Union on June 22, 1941. The slaughter of Jews that followed was mostly accomplished by Lithuanians, with the German *Einsatzkommandos* awed by the ferocity of their helpers.

➤

APRIL 15   *Topanga*
Dear Friend:
People have lately been challenging us with the question, 'Well, what are you people going to do *now*?' We all know, of course, what they mean: since Communism is being rejected even by the Communists, is there any purpose left for an organization like the Committee for the Free World to fulfill?

I am writing you now, as a friend of the Committee, to give you our answer – and, it being springtime once again, to ask you to give us the financial support we need in order to continue our work.

Communism may be dead and the cold war as we have known it during the past decades may be over; it turns out, however, that Soviet weakness does not, spiritually speaking, mean American strength. Whatever the admiration for American democracy in Eastern Europe and the Soviet Union, here in the United States neither the media nor the schools nor many of the most fashionable intellectuals and celebrities have moderated their steady chorus of disaffection toward their own country and its political and social institutions. Mikhail Gorbachev they hail as a great statesman – *Time*'s 'Man of the Decade', if you please – while the United States continues to be the object of their weary litanies about imperialism, racism, and grinding the faces of the poor.

But as long as the media demoralize us with their smug, lazy, ignorant misreporting; as long as the schools miseducate our children on the racist assumption that real standards of achievement are inherently unfair to expect of minority children; as long as the universities are permitted to defraud their hard-pressed consumers by purveying anti-intellectual formulas packaged as learning; as long as the arts and publishing industries continue to demand the kind of conformity of which theocracies only dream; as long as such conditions persist, American freedom is not secure.

That is why we feel we still have a great deal of work to do. We have always said that nothing would make us happier than to witness the day when we would be deprived by history of a role to play.

Alas, that day has not yet arrived. So I am appealing to you now to help us hasten it by giving us the means to continue our campaign against the anti-Americanism of America's most spoiled and peevish citizens – those whom we have dubbed the 'brats of liberty'.

Won't you please fill out the enclosed card and return it to us with your contribution? As you probably know by now, the Committee issues an appeal for funds only once a year. We hope you will wish to respond.

Best regards,
Midge Decter, Executive Director
Committee for the Free World
New York, N.Y.

➤

APRIL 17   *Topanga*

ROBIN SENDS ME a good quote from Trotsky:

'The October revolution has been betrayed by the ruling stratum, but not yet overthrown. It has a great power of resistance, coinciding with the established property relations, with the living force of the proletariat, the consciousness of its best elements, the impasse of world capitalism, and the inevitability of world revolution.

'In order better to understand the character of the present Soviet Union, let us make two different hypotheses about its future. Let us assume first that the Soviet bureaucracy is overthrown by a revolutionary party having all the attributes of the old Bolshevism, enriched moreover by the world experience of the recent period. Such a party would begin with the restoration of democracy in the trade unions and the Soviets. It would be able to, and would have to, restore freedom of Soviet parties. Together with the masses, and at their head, it would carry out a ruthless purgation of the state apparatus. It would abolish ranks and decorations, all kind of privileges, and would limit inequality in the payment of labor to the life necessities of the economy and the state apparatus. It would give the youth free opportunity to think independently, learn, criticize and grow. It would introduce profound changes in the distribution of the national income in correspondence with the interests and will of the worker and peasant masses. But so far as concerns property relations, the new power would not have to resort to revolutionary measures. It would retain and further develop the experiment of planned economy. After the political revolution – that is, the deposing of the bureaucracy – the proletariat would have to introduce in the economy a series of very important reforms, but not another social revolution.

'If – to adopt a second hypothesis – a bourgeois party were to overthrow the ruling Soviet caste, it would find no small number of ready servants among the present bureaucrats, administrators, technicians, directors, party secretaries and privileged upper circles in general. A purgation of the state apparatus would, of course, be necessary in this case too. But a bourgeois restoration would probably have to clean out fewer people than a revolutionary party.

Trotsky: *The Revolution Betrayed*, 1937

➢→

APRIL 18   *Berkeley*
TODAY I SAT IN BERKELEY waiting to have lunch with F. He was late and arrived wearing dark glasses. He'd been coming up an on-ramp for the Bay Bridge from the San Francisco side when he got smashed in the head, as though someone had thrown a brick through his car window. He looked down on the floor, where a pigeon struggled to regain its composure before fluttering off through the window again.

F. showed me the scratch on his eyeball made by the pigeon's beak. I said to look on the bright side and that the pigeon could have blinded him. F. stressed the downside, that he had been the victim of a freakish accident. I remarked – and F. agreed in general principle, while swabbing his eye – that the idea of an 'accident' is mostly bourgeois. Newspapers, almanacs of bourgeois thought, love accidents because they ratify the idea of order. The *Exxon Valdez* had an 'accident' and covered Prince William Sound with crude oil. 'Normalcy' would have been for the ship to proceed to Long Beach, California, and unload its crude, which, duly refined, would then have been vented through car exhaust pipes over Los Angeles.

So the encounter between man and bird was not fortuitous. In fact it was the product of extraordinarily precise scheduling. Had not F. delayed in his office for two minutes; then stopped to chat with his son, whom he saw parked on Oak Street? A thousand factors could have caused the pigeon to miss F.'s car and perhaps, in an amazing 'accidental' twist, fly into the window of the Chinese-American driving twenty feet behind, who overtook F. seconds after the impact, making theatrical gestures of sympathy.

An 'accident' is normalcy raised to the level of drama.

➡

APRIL 27   *Topanga*
Dear Alex Cockburn,
Thank you for your letter in regard to the interview which appeared in *Issues Monthly*. I must say it was somewhat of a jolting shock to receive a letter from a writer and an intellectual whom I hold in extremely high regard.

That said, when I wrote that 'your reputation was secure among Stalinists', I obviously meant this as an oblique and overstated reference to your locking horns with your colleague Christopher Hitchens. From the interview, any dolt would realize that you, as you put it, don't 'yearn back to the days of Joseph S.' In the same sentence, the laud for your work is quite apparent. I wrote that *Fate of the Forest* is held 'quite high among the crowd who have read it'; I also wrote that you have been 'defamed' by the likes of Martin Peretz, the editor of the *New Republic*; and I also said that your reputation is 'quite solid among those who have delved into his *Corruptions of Empire* for confirmation of their own opinions'. If I had known that Adam Hochschild had a strong financial interest in American Metal Climax, of course I would not have accused you of hyperbole when you wrote that he has the 'politics of a 19th century mill owner'.

With regard to the typos and the transcription of the interview into what you deem to be 'gibberish', I have no excuse, save for pointing an accusing finger at our copy editor and my and my co-author's endemic carelessness. To say that I will be more wary in the future certainly won't ease your mind as the damage has been already done; but let me say that I have gained tremendously from your insight and that I find your work to be a welcome relief to the current, pitiful tone of political discourse.

Andrew Rubin
Providence, R.I.

MAY 2   *Topanga*

YESTERDAY, MAY DAY, the telephone rang and a voice asked if I would be prepared to go on Ted Koppel's *Nightline* that same evening. I asked what the theme was going to be. The voice, belonging to the Koppel show's Tracy Day, said that Koppel and his guests would be addressing the theme 'Is Communism Dead?'

By late afternoon in Los Angeles, Tracy called from New York. I'd be on with Angela Davis and Melor Sturua, a Russian columnist for *Izvestia* on leave at the Carnegie Endowment.

I drove east across Los Angeles toward the ABC studio. At the studio they make me up and sit me down. The drill with Koppel is that you look into a camera and listen to your earphone. You can't see what's happening on the show. You have to keep looking at the camera because you don't know when Koppel, the only person who can see all the people on the show, who controls everything, is going to call you. Swivel your eyes away from the camera and millions will think you have something to hide.

Suddenly we're off. I can hear the soundtrack of some footage, of people hammering down the Wall, denouncing communism. Then I hear Koppel saying, ' ... the state of distress in which communism finds itself ... seems easier for some Soviets to accept than ... for left-wingers like Alexander Cockburn or leaders of the American Communist Party like Angela Davis.'

So it's a setup: the viewers have been invited to watch scenes of collapsing communism, then here's Koppel cutting to the last dinosaurs, clanking into the studio dragging their ball and chain of dead ideas.

This was the trend of the show. Koppel got increasingly testy. Why, he asked, did I keep bringing up capitalism? We were meant to be talking about communism. It became a dialogue of the deaf. I said that in order to understand why millions of people around the world are still fired with radical ideals you have to understand that if actually existing communism was and is abhorrent to some, actually existing capitalism is abhorrent to others.

I was going to add that on the same May Day that Russian workers were booing the Soviet leaders, workers in the Philippines were demonstrating against the regime and the US bases, and in South Korea striking shipyard workers were still battling police.

No time for this though. By now Koppel was saying that I was putting words into his mouth and Prof. Davis was trying to explain that capitalism was not working too well for black people here in the US and Sturua was saying that Karl Marx was right when he said that theory was gray but green the tree of life. From the corner of my eye I saw a copy of *Business Week* featuring on its cover the best-paid executive of 1989, Craig McCaw, weighing in with $53.9 million. Why didn't I just hold it up to the camera and say that against salaries like this, how could the ideals of socialism ever die? But it was all over. I didn't even have time to tell Sturua that Goethe not Marx said the thing about the green tree. At least he had Marx associated with living things.

➤

MAY 9 *Topanga*

Hi,

I have been reading Pavese. P. is wonderful on childhood – somewhat like Adorno. I wonder what is it about these Europeans who lived through the war with their sensitivities intact despite their claims to cynicism. They are sweet about childhood, griefstruck about love. It is wonderful to read but always a little sad, suggesting that 'maturity' must mean the passing of all delicate senses. There is also a distrust of women, worse – far worse – in Pavese than in Adorno. Such sentiments always ruin what start out as promising passages on love. But then Pavese killed himself finally, and all his writing seems to have been preparation for that. You once marked out a passage when you were reading this at my house: 'All passions fade and die away except the oldest, those of infancy. The ambitious or libidinous dreams of childhood are insatiable, because maturity – the only age that could satisfy them, has lost the opportunities, the fresh sensitiveness, the means, the true setting in which those passions originally come to the surface.' I suppose I resist the truth in that, and perhaps you do too, which is why you try again and again to re-create your childhood.

P. says some things here that I thought might come in useful in some future discussion of Eastern Europe. You can read them almost in sequence, in expectation of the future, but they were all written quite far apart. The best is the most immediately applicable: 'While resistance was undercover, all was hope: now all is a prospective of disaster.' (1947) Then another: 'Having regained their liberty, the liberals no longer know what to do with it.' (1946 – July 5, around the time of what, this year, will mark German reunification) And finally: 'The proof of your own lack of interest in politics is that, believing in liberalism (i.e., the possibility of ignoring political life), you would like to enforce it autocratically. You are conscious of political life only at times of totalitarian crises, and then you grow heated and run counter to your own liberalism in the hope of quickly bringing about the liberal conditions in which you can live without bothering about politics.' (1940) That last actually suits American life quite well, I think. It is also, interestingly, not far from what that State Dept. guy was dubiously celebrating as the end of history, the culmination of democratic liberalism.

J.

New York

MAY 20   *Aptos*

Dear Mr. Cockburn:

As the news came through the pipelines about the adventure of the Americans in Panama and Noriega at the papal nuncio's house, I recalled my years in South America and the *institution* of political asylum. One could, I suppose, question it, but in the days before the Yanks managed to establish national security states it worked quite well. It gave defeated politicians a way to resign, and their exiles were arranged on at least the tacit acceptance of non-interference (for the duration of their status) in the affairs of their own country. The Nunziatura in La Paz was one of the favourite places, since the grub was good and they were in fact fairly immune to political pressure. Governments would give a safe-conduct and the Nunzio would drive them to the airport in his Chevrolet and they would fly off to a well-deserved rest in Peru or Paraguay. At its best, the institution did not involve any judgement as to the justice of the cause (if any) espoused by the persecuted politician. The Vatican, in its Latin American presence, was good at that, and as Italians schooled in the tradition of Machiavelli, they knew better than to sort out the murky rights and wrongs of Bolivian politics.

No one, to my knowledge, ever sought refuge in the US Embassy. It was rumoured that they would not be welcome, but it may also have been that involvement with the Yanks would really put an end to a political career, much more than a week or two in the Nunziatura or the Italian Embassy and a year or two in Peru. The British Embassy was equally inhospitable. It is possible that neither the Brits nor the Yanks were willing to involve themselves in the messy little intrigues of dago *politiqueros*, although the Brits at least did not moralise about it.

Why should I bore you with all this? Perhaps because not even in the Canadian media (although the *Ottawa Citizen*, a conservative newspaper, unequivocally condemned the Panama invasion and the Mulroney government's indecent arse-kissing over it) was there any recognition of the Latin American tradition of asylum. It may in fact be a thing of the past.

It is not, of course, enough to try to sort out criminals from political refugees. Most active politicians have been into something that could be qualified as criminal activity. You may recall the Archimandrite in Waugh's *Put Out More Flags:* 'I have been telling your office clergyman about my expulsing. The Bulgar people say it was for fornications, but it was for politics. They are not expulsing from Sofia for fornications unless there is politics too.' I assume that Noriega's real crime was treason, or, an attempt to refuse to conform with the wishes of his Yankee masters. The rest is fornications.

Best,
Jordan Bishop
Ottawa

JUNE 3   *Ardmore, Co. Waterford*
Dear Cockburn:
I was very happy to hear the news of your mother's death. As a Jew, whenever I hear tragedy befall an evil person, I quote from Proverbs 11:10.

For a Jew-baiting goy like you it means 'And when the wicked perish there is joy.' May you goyim who attack and criticize Jews and Israel suffer even more.

Joel Green
Toronto

➥

JUNE 6   *Ardmore*
MY BIRTHDAY. 49 years old. I bend all sinews toward extracting a favorable insurance settlement.

28th May 1990. Your ref. DC/BD.
Mr. Dominic Creedon, B.C.L.,
Philpott, Creedon & Co.,
43 - Grand Parade,
CORK
RE: Alexander Cockburn, Rock House, Ardmore, Co. Waterford.
Date of Birth = 6-06 1941

Dear Mr. Creedon,
This is the medical report, which you requested on the above named client.
DATE OF ACCIDENT: 12-01-1990
HISTORY OF ACCIDENT: Mr. Cockburn was driving his car on a round-about, when his car was struck on the left rear side, by another car. This second car came from a side road without warning, and Mr. Cockburn had very little time in which to brace himself for the impact. He had his seat belt on.
INJURIES SUSTAINED: He was thrown about by the impact. He did not lose consciousness. There were no obvious injuries at first, and he didn't seek any medical help at this stage. He noticed a muscle tenderness developing over the next few days, around the neck and upper back area.
1/ Soft tissue type sprain to the muscles of the neck. Examination confirms that there is tenderness over the trapezius muscles on both sides, with some limitation of movement. This area of tenderness extends approximately half-way down the back.
2/ There is a tingling sensation down the left arm to the palm of the hand. This occurs intermittently, in a random manner. It also affects the feet.
There is no objective evidence of CENTRAL NERVOUS DEFICIT, on examination.

The power and tone in upper and lower limbs is normal, and there is no superficial or deep sensory loss noted. The reflexes are all present and normal. PHYSICAL EXAMINATION: This is otherwise normal, and there is no other past history of relevance.

PROGRESS: Mr. Cockburn consulted with two Physicians in the US, a Dr. Joel Botkin in San Francisco on the 9th. March, and a Dr. Tom Jacobs in New York on the 29th. March 1990. They both confirmed the diagnosis of soft tissue type injury to the neck and upper back area. This injury has resulted in the tingling sensations which he has been experiencing.

I have prescribed a course of PIROXICAM - 20 mgs. daily. This is a nonsteroidal anti-inflammatory agent, and Mr. Cockburn has reported that he has got good symptomatic relief on this medication. I have advised that he continues this treatment for three - four weeks, and then review the situation. The PROGNOSIS in this case should be very good, and I would expect him to make a complete recovery from his injuries within the next four weeks. It is, however, difficult to give an exact prognosis.

I shall be glad to forward any further information you may require, on request.

Yours sincerely,
Dr. Joseph Meehan

➤→

JUNE 17   *Ardmore*
HERE IN IRELAND on the last Saturday in May, Chief Hollis Roberts of the Choctaw Nation led a thousand people along the Trail of Tears – where 600 men, women and children died on a trek in search of food in 1849.

On their own Trail of Tears, in 1831, they were deported from southern Mississippi to Oklahoma. Along that forced march, 500 miles in the dead of winter, 14,000 Choctaws perished. In 1847, in the Oklahoma Territory town of Skullville, the Chocktaw heard of the famine devastating Ireland. They raised $710, an immense sum for people themselves almost destitute, and sent it across a continent and an ocean.

In fact, the great famine of 1845–49 was one of the most determined tests of 'free-market' economic discipline in human history. In those days, Ireland was a nineteenth-century equivalent of El Salvador today, overcrowded with 8 million inhabitants, most of them on the edge of starvation. With their land largely in the hands of the British and used for export crops – a familiar story throughout Latin America today – the Irish were forced to rely on just one staple grown on the tiny plots that remained to them. When the potato blight struck, Irish peasants starved to death as their masters, braced by liberal free-market theory, continued to export the grain that could have saved their lives, while proclaiming their concern that the victims of famine not become welfare clients, their moral fiber sapped by government handouts. A million died.

➥

JUNE 27   *Ardmore*

Dear Alexander Cockburn,
Thank you for your kind mention of *The Sixties Papers*. Let me add that the book was co-authored by my wife, Judith.

It's great that you're getting on the Panther story. I've spent much time going through Cointelpro files and have come up with some interesting findings. I did this work a few years ago and my source for files was the Charles Gary law office on Market Street.

If you have a special category called 'THINGS I WOULD LIKE TO SHOW PRESIDENT HAVEL', I would offer the Huey Newton files. To get to the point – the FBI as an explicitly stated matter of policy, decided to bring about Newton's complete mental collapse. They had his apartment bugged and listened in on his phone calls. They knew what was bothering him, what he was afraid of, and of whom he was suspicious. The FBI had all it needed to attack Huey Newton's sanity. And attack they did. The government of the United States was officially dedicated to driving one man crazy. If you want to direct your researchers in this direction, their best bet when contacting the Gary office is Pat Richards.

By the way, from following your column, I've learned we have a good mutual friend, Frank Bardacke in Watsonville. I knew him from Berkeley in the '60s. Please say hello.

All the best,
Stew Albert
Portland, Oregon

➥

JUNE 28   *Topanga*

Dear Mr. Cockburn:
I was offended by your offhand comment about 'toxic Gaian odes to personal responsibility' at the beginning of your report on Earth Day. I assume your objection is to the notion that laying blame for environmental destruction at the feet of individuals is unconscionable in the face of our formidable corporate-government-military complex. So it is!

My objection is to the fact that Gaian consciousness as a feminist response (not the only one) to global destruction seems to fall on hostile male ears without a fair hearing; that patriarchy still infects the so-called progressive movement; that men like yourself seem unable to genuinely hear women's voices even as you cover yourselves by supporting abortion rights!

Let's struggle for equality and genuine respect within the progressive movement so we'll learn how to establish it everywhere.

Thank you for listening to this: Personal responsibility means we must each and every one of us act politically in whatever ways we can – from home to work to street. Personal responsibility IS political responsibility.

Sincerely,
Kath Schomaker
Columbus, Ohio

➳

JULY 1 *Garberville, California*

SOMEWHERE ABOUT LEVEL WITH Leggett, heading up 101 into California's north country, the colors change and the grasses, by this time in the summer dried farther south to pale gold, still ripple green on the open slopes below the trees. At Garberville we pulled the car off the highway and went into a bar to figure out the back road to Honeydew, the Earth First! base camp for the start of Redwood Summer.

A fellow with a bashed-up face, who looked like a meth-head, gave guidance and we swung west into cool lanes lined with wild foxglove. A lot of this area was logged in the 1950s. Then a man called Bob McKee bought slabs of land and sold off pieces to hippies and kindred souls at bargain-basement rates.

At sundown we found the base camp, on federal BLM land in a curve in the Mattole River. There had already been a couple of stories on the TV news about naked frolickers, and as we clambered out of my 1957 Plymouth station wagon I remarked to F. that with both of us heading round the curve into our fiftieth year I could imagine how grizzled FBI snoops felt back in the summer of love, pulling tie-dyes down over their beer bellies, flashing the peace sign and heading hopefully toward the love-in.

In fact the Earth First!ers were sitting in a big circle debating tactics for the next day's action, aimed at blocking the main gate of Louisiana Pacific's lumber export plant at Samoa, twenty miles north over the hills, outside Eureka.

The Italian Marxist Labriola said, 'Men, living socially, do not cease to live also naturally ... nature is always the immediate subsoil of the artificial terrain of society, and is the ambience which envelops us all.' Marx took the view that 'the nature that preceded human history no longer exists anywhere', which has its truth but became the animating proposition for central planners savaging nature in the name of 'human history', *aka* annual growth targets. The next day, looking across from the sand dunes at Louisiana Pacific's log export plant, we could see that L.P. executives are dedicated to proving Marx right. Extinguished nature here took the form of piles of logs, many of them barely more than saplings, ready to be chipped or pulped or trimmed and sent out of the country, often returning as finished goods.

Every five minutes or so a new logging truck would come hurtling along the Samoa road.

'What a perfect scene', a man standing next to me on a sand dune exclaimed. It was now after noon and to my eye the scene was far from perfect. Aside from the scene in the L.P. plant, a plume of toxic smoke coming from Simpson Paper next door, and the day's outflow of 40 million gallons of L.P. and Simpson effluent pouring through a waste pipe into the Pacific behind us, the police were at that moment arresting people who had stopped a logging truck from entering the plant. One fellow from the sheriff's department, amid chants of 'the whole world is watching', failed to prize an Earth Firster, Ian Baitz, from the truck's cab, finally kneed him in the balls and then maced him.

'It doesn't seem perfect to me', I said, and alluded to the features described. 'That's all part of creation', he insisted with complacency, as we watched Baitz being dragged off. 'Well, as a religious posture', I began, but the man cut me off. 'It's not a religious posture. I'm just saying that it's part of creation and therefore perfect.'

Later that day F. and I gave a lift to a youth in a tie-dye shirt from Boulder, Colorado, on his way to a Grateful Dead concert in Eugene. He said he carried only a Bible, and I began to take God's name in vain just to see how the land lay. He said he thought God meant well but was no match for the darker forces. 'Which darker forces?' I asked.

'Lucifer, most beautiful of all the angels.' Later, in Arcata, we had a precise description of this same Deadhead from a musician who'd paid him $25 for acid tabs, all of which turned out to be useless.

Back at the demonstration the police ended up arresting forty-four. Earth Firsters certainly know how to have fun on an action. A good band – Clan Dyken – played through the arrests, and a couple of drummers pounded away as young protesters danced only a few inches from the boots of the helmeted officers of the Humboldt County Sheriff's Department and the California Highway Patrol. Louisiana Pacific plans to export not only its wood but its jobs too, building a plant near Ensenada, Mexico, where it can hire labor for about 74 cents an hour.

We pulled away from Samoa and turned toward Trinidad, a beautiful fishing village just south of Patrick's Point. I wanted to look at the graveyard, where someone had told me there was an interesting stone. And there, at the back of the little cemetery, it was:

E.B. Schnaubelt

Born April 5, 1855, Died May 22, 1913

Murdered by Capitalism

Sid Dominitz, editor of *Econews*, down the road in Arcata, told me later that
Schnaubelt's brother had been involved in the Haymarket bombing. E.B. had
set up a lumber mill as a workers' co-op but then the big companies cheated
him out of the land where the mill stood, though he still owned the plant. One
night Schnaubelt, living nearby, thought he heard someone messing with his
machinery. He went to investigate and a watchman hired by the companies shot
him dead. His widow put up the stone and moved away. Local radicals now toast
Schnaubelt on red-letter feast days.

➡➜

JULY 2   *San Francisco*
SENDER GARLIN HAS SENT me a couple of pages out of Van Woodward's book on
Tom Watson, the agrarian rebel. Sender puts a note saying that Watson 'forges
a black–white popular alliance in Georgia. Later he turns viciously anti-Negro.
In that period, elected to Congress, he defends the Russian revolution in floor
debates.'

'As an example of [Watson's] juristic technique and forensic methods, there
is the case of Jack Peavy. This case came fairly early in his career; in itself it is
relatively unimportant and little known; it is not selected to illustrate Watson's
legal skill, but for what it may reveal about the lawyer himself, his methods, his
clients, his juries.

'Peavy, it seems, had boarded a train in an intoxicated condition and made
himself such a nuisance that the conductor had ejected him from the train.
Whereupon, it was charged, Peavy attempted to shoot the conductor, but
instead was shot by the conductor. Peavy then escaped. Discovered later by a
constable's posse he was again wounded, this time by an incredible number of
buckshot, placed under arrest, and later tried for assault with intent to murder.
Watson was appointed to defend him. It appears that Peavy did not enjoy an
enviable reputation in Warrenton, where he was tried, and that public sentiment was strongly against him. It was, naturally, Watson's first concern to
propitiate and if possible to convert this prejudicial atmosphere into one
favorable to the defendant. He began with what appears to be an unconscious
travesty upon Anthony's oration on the fallen Caesar "baring the wounds" of
the victim. *Pianissimo*.

Why, gentlemen, Jack Peavy has been shot till his hide wouldn't hold
shucks. If he was a cow his skin wouldn't be worth tanning. His coffin
will be a lead mine. It's a wonder to me all the little boys who are
learning to shoot don't practice on his carcass. The law certainly would
not interfere ... No! Let the brave work go on! Barnett shot *him* and
the law accuses Peavy. A constable's crowd shot him without warning

till the wife of his bosom might have tracked him seventeen miles by the life blood as it drained his veins. And the law makes no complaint.

This having taken effect, he proceeds with another trend. *Crescendo.*

The further we go the more clearly will we see one of these cruel class differences that disgrace the justice of men.

Suppose Gen. Toombs passing on this Washington train had cursed. Is there man on the jury who believes that this young conductor would have collared him and have spoken to him as he did Peavy? How absurd. Toombs, sacred by reason of his class, his cloth; powerful in the golden strength of his hundreds of thousands ...

But Peavy! That's another matter. Slouch hat and homespun dress inspire the youth with no such awe. Hear how his conduct speaks: 'I will collar him like I would a slave, speak to him as I would to a slave and if he dares resent either I'll shoot him like a dog. Such men have no rights that I am bound to respect.'

And finally for the "grand spread eagle". *Fortissimo.*

Peavy answers the shaking of the pistol in his face by saying, 'You, You — damned son of a bitch', and is shot. At least he had endured all he could and his whole nature rose up in arms. 'You have collared me as if I were a cur. You have talked to me like you would a servant. You have insulted me before all the passengers, put me off the train after I had bought my ticket and now you threaten me while I am down. I'll stand no more. Your rank and your riches give you no right to wipe your feet on me. God Almighty breathed into my nostrils as well as yours. My blood came from the dust and so did yours. I throw my defiance in your teeth and meet you face to face —

What tho on homely fare we dine,
Wear hodden gray and all that;
Give fools their silks and knaves their wine —
A man's a man for all that.

'Jack Peavy was cleared. "By the time I had spoken half an hour", wrote Watson, at the end of the above account, "the popular tide was with us and many a manly eye was dim."

'Out of such victories as this – and it was multiplied a hundred-fold – was built the legend of his invincibility. It became a widely prevalent belief that there was a sort of rule, or at least an agreement of honor, that Tom Watson should not assist in the prosecution of one charged with murder, for if he did, it meant certain death for the defendant. His talent was reserved for the defense. He was a tribune of the people, and hundreds had found shelter within his voice.

'And might not a whole people find shelter there likewise? Were not they all so many Jack Peavys in "slouch hat and homespun"? Were they not forever being collared and booted about by arrogant young conductors of the railroads who charged them such outrageous rates to carry their cotton? Or by some upstart millionaire of Wall Street, "sacred by reason of his class"? By city folk in general? And might they not, with the words Tom had put in Jack Peavy's mouth, some day rise in their wrath and say, "I'll stand no more"? And with such a voice and such a tribune for their leader, might they not become so many Jack Cades?'

➡

JULY 10   *Topanga*

SF Focus: What makes you so critical of the national park approach as a way to save wilderness areas? Isn't that what we've done here in California?

Cockburn: National parks are a terrible model for saving the Amazon. People don't understand what happened to the Native Americans here in the move to establish national parks. The Indians had to be removed from Yosemite before it could become a park.

SF Focus: Wait a minute. Yosemite became a national park around 1890 through the efforts of John Muir, who no one has accused of being an Indian killer.

AC: Actually Muir hated Indians. But the move to turn the valley into a park actually began much earlier. The Miwoks were the largest Indian group north of Mexico and they lived in the Yosemite area. Their destruction began with the gold rush. The miners came in, fouled their rivers, stole their livestock, murdered their chiefs, and sent the Indians off to live on reservations.

Extermination and deportation of Indians went hand-in-hand with nurturing tourism. By the middle 1850s, Yosemite was a tourist area. It became a state park in 1864, long before Muir came around. This is exactly what is happening in the Amazon right now. You get the people who live there evicted, and you get rich people with cameras enjoying the resulting park.

SF Focus: Do you have some paranoid vision that someone is censoring every newspaper in America?

AC: No, it's not as though there were some kind of secret committee sending out the marching orders. But there is a unanimity, and it is achieved in scores of different ways.

SF Focus: Such as?

AC: For example, newspeople love to say, 'The boss never intervenes' or 'You never see so-and-so on the editorial floor.' But that is all meaningless. People know what the boss thinks without him or her being on the floor.

SF Focus: Is there any newspaper you do respect?

AC: The *Anderson Valley Advertiser*, which comes out of Mendocino

County. It's a tremendous paper, written in really popular, uncondescending language. Bruce Anderson, the publisher and editor, is a good writer. He talks to people, addresses their concerns, and doesn't mystify them. You read local reporting in the *Anderson Valley Advertiser* and you prefer it and its community reporting to that in any other paper. My friend Fred Gardner does a great weekly column for it from the Bay Area.

It is so rare that you find good, strong writing about the institutions of our everyday lives. Who writes well about school board meetings? The *AVA* does. When Bruce goes for a walk, he'll write about people he sees, and they become real. He talks about local corporate power in a strong fashion, the Georgia Pacific or Louisiana Pacific lumber companies. It's not romantic, radical bullshit when he talks about clear-cutting, about the people whose jobs depend on cutting down trees: these are poor dudes who need to make a living.

SF Focus: You live down in Aptos, quite far away from any media center, and not even near the Anderson Valley. Don't you have trouble writing your commentary from so remote a place?

AC: You can sit in Watsonville down the road from Aptos and be involved in local politics and see – right in Watsonville – the national economy, the impact of Reaganism and the Pan American economy in terms of who's working where. You can see the housing crisis because half the people who work in the fields have to sleep in their cars. You see everything, as long as you know where to look.

SF Focus: You're one of the last unreconstructed, non-apologetic left-wingers around. Ever find it embarrassing to be a socialist, with the collapse of communism in Europe coupled with the Sandinista loss, and the terrible Chinese crackdown on the students?

AC: Embarrassing? No. I think people want me to do or say things that I just don't. Before the killings in Tiananmen Square, I thought that China was, effectively, a fascist government. You had 'market economics' and state coercion you could call it 'market Stalinism' . And I wrote so; it didn't make any difference. After Tiananmen Square, I got attacked by Mike Royko, who's a drunken fraud, and people all over the place for being an apologist for the Chinese leadership. And if I say, 'Well, okay, I'm glad that the repressive Stalinist regimes finally fell apart under the weight of their own repressiveness', that doesn't mean I'm going to suddenly go kiss Alan Greenspan's feet or worship at Market Central.

People somehow are angered by this. Look at Eastern Europe. Everyone implied that when these old Stalinist bureaucracies crumbled, some sort of justice was commencing. Now, they're silent as reality continues in a new guise.

SF Focus: What do you think about Marxism? What's ahead for it?

AC: Marxism, when it becomes rigid, and fails to take reality into account, is doomed to the trashcan. But to treat Marxism as some kind of catalogue of ruins is absurd. The spirit of Marxism is made of quite good stuff. If you go

back and read Marx, a lot of it is as strong as ever. My father used to say that
if I felt demoralized – like I was a teenager unlucky in love or something, or
spited by the world – he'd recommend a few pages of Marx to cheer me up.
There's a lot of truth to that.

SF Focus: How do you view your own contributions to changing the world
through your writing?

AC: I try to get things on the agenda. I feel a sense of satisfaction. So many
people I know are boiling with frustration, because they know bullshit when
they see it, but they don't have the venue to get it out. I do, and it makes me
feel great.

➤

JULY 12   *Topanga*
IN 1948, THREE LEFT JOURNALISTS, Cedric Belfrage, James Aronson and John T.
McManus, were founding *The National Guardian*. Belfrage and Aronson had
met in Germany, where they were trying to carry out Eisenhower's orders to set
up a post-Nazi German newspaper with people who had resisted fascism. Of
course such resisters included German Communists.

Since the actual purpose of postwar US policy was to make sure that West
Germany was not de-Nazified in any meaningful sense of the word, Belfrage and
Aronson's efforts later counted against them, as did the existence of *The
National Guardian*, which along with *Monthly Review* (begun in 1949) was a
lonely voice in those days. In the high crest of McCarthyism, Belfrage, a British
citizen, was deported. He eventually settled in Cuernavaca, where he died on
June 21 at the age of 85.

I never met him. To a fundraiser for *The Guardian* in San Francisco in 1990
at which I was a speaker, he was nice enough to send this message: 'Your celebration means a lot to me as the first editor of *The Guardian*. I was particularly glad
to hear from John Trinkl that your speaker tonight is Alexander Cockburn ...
because he is the son of my old friend Claud, who can also take some credit for
tonight's affair. For in the early Hitler years before World War II, when I was a
respectably non-political movie critic in London, I was one of many journalists
and others influenced to the left by Claud. I truly believe that had I not got to
know Claud at that time, the *Guardian* might never have been launched – at
least not by me as one of the founding trio.'

The same gang boosting the Cockburn–Hollis connection are saying that
Belfrage was similarly Moscow's pawn in espionage. Since the man is dead it's
easy to say it and useless for his relatives to issue denials, if they feel so inclined;
circumstantial or substantive evidence or even common sense is irrelevant in
these issues. In my father's case, when the war was over he left the *Daily Worker*
without undue fuss and headed to Ireland to begin a new phase of his life writing

fiction. Stalin was busy shooting his close friends like Mikhail Koltzov, and another buddy, Otto Katz, was hanged in Prague, saying before his death that he had been led into the path of counterrevolution by Colonel Claud Cockburn of the MI5. My father said he later reckoned Katz had been asked to denounce someone and thought that he, Claud, was unlikely to suffer painful consequences if Katz gave his name to the executioners.

➤

JULY 14   *Topanga*
K.K. CALLS ME. Andy Kopkind has been diagnosed as having bladder cancer. He'd been feeling sick for four months before. Chemo, then an operation.

➤

JULY 23   *Topanga*
Dear Mr. Cockburn:
We view the world from different perspectives, and thus often disagree. Still, I'm delighted to applaud you for nailing the media on the terms they've chosen to describe Soviet politics since the collapse of the Evil Empire.

The phenomenon you note seems simple: Gorbachev has been officially certified as the good guy. To the media, good guys are liberal democrats. Ergo, Gorbachev's a liberal democrat, his opponents are conservatives and other dissidents are uneasily categorized as 'radicals'.

All this is nonsense, of course. Gorbachev and his remaining allies in the Communist Party are Marxists. Surviving Stalinists are the most radical, those advocates of a market economy are obviously, by Western standards, conservatives. The *Washington Post* finds this indigestible, of course. Thanks for pointing it out.

Cordially,
Charlton Heston
Beverly Hills, California

➤

AUGUST 1   *Topanga*
Dear Mr. Cockburn:
I enjoy your columns more than any I have read. West Virginia is a lonely place for people who believe in the ultimate victory of socialism. My father was a candidate for the West Virginia House of Delegates on the Socialist ticket in the early 1920s. In some ways, things were better then than they are now.

My father left little in the way of material things, but he left me something much more important: a love for literature and an inordinate hatred for injustice. I can remember when I was a young boy, at least 60 years ago, hearing my father quote two poems, one of them he told me was written under the nom de plume of Sir Ragner (sp) Redbeard, who he said was a former Roman Catholic priest. I only remember parts of it, but it starts: 'In Northern climes the Polar bear protects himself with fat and hair ... but lo some people odd and funny, some people without a cent of money, arose and slew the bear, ate his fat and wore his hair ... the millionaires there weren't any ...'

The other poem:

> Cain's knotted club's a scepter still and the rights of man are fraud
> Christ's ethics are for creeping things; true manhood smiles at God.
> So what's the use of dreaming dreams that each shall get his own,
> By the priceless vote of the meek-eyed thrall that will blindly sweat
>   and moan.
> No, curses on their cankered brain, their very bones decay,
> Go trust your fate in the iron game – tis the logic of today.

I have tried to find something about these poems without success. As you probably know, a lot is lost when one's father passes. I wonder if you have ever come across either of these poems in your reading and research.

Keep up the fine work!
William L. Dodd, Jr.
Charleston, West Virginia

➤

AUGUST 3   *Topanga*

IT'S SHARK-PANIC TIME AGAIN. Given the amount of fear they generate, sharks injure or kill amazingly few people. They cause bodily harm to about 100 humans worldwide each year, killing about 25. Bees kill more. So do elephants.

But outside of some intelligent islanders in the South Pacific who hold them in high religious esteem, people detest sharks. They lurk as monsters in the great sea of the unconscious. The very word comes from the German *Schurke* or 'villain'.

For every human killed by a shark, about a million sharks are killed by humans, making an annual shark slaughter of about 25 million. Even though there are about as many sharks on the planet as humans, various of the 350 species of shark are dwindling rapidly and may soon be extinct.

The sharks' problems is that they are what ecologists call 'k-selected': they are slow-growing, late-maturing and produce a few well-formed young in which the mother invests a lot of resources. Remind you of anyone? Over-fished species of shark can't bounce back like the prolific mullet.

Samuel Gruber and Charles Manire, biologists at the University of Miami, found recently that lemon sharks have almost disappeared off the Florida Keys. Manire tells me that the porbeagle shark, 'exquisite, warm-bodied, speedy and powerful' – and, alas, also considered a delicacy by Italians – had, by 1968, been almost wiped out by the Norwegian fishing fleet. The Californian and Australian soupfin shark, the Scottish-Norwegian dogfish, the Californian thresher-mako, the Virginian sandbar shark and the Florida pelagic shark are similarly in trouble.

Right now the Asian economic boom poses yet another menace to sharks already enduring the worst pressures from commercial and recreational fishing in their 400-million-year evolution. Asians prize their fins as soup flavoring or as an aphrodisiac and are happy to spend $40 to $85 a pound at the market for dried fin. Fishermen often just hack the fin off a shark and throw the fish back to die.

We need a better image for sharks. As Gruber and Manire write wistfully in the newsletter *Chondros*, 'Sharks must be seen as good, not evil; sensitive and delicate, not indestructible "eating machines".' The shark, like the lion or the wolf, is an 'apex predator', up at the top of its food chain. Wipe it out and discord follows.

The South African government tried to protect white bathers by killing sharks. After fifteen years of slaughter, Gruber and Manire report, 'The diversity of the shark fauna was reduced, accompanied by the veritable explosion of one species, the dusky shark, to the exclusion of most of the others.'

Science and medicine have much to learn from sharks. They are highly resistant to cancer; serious wounds heal within 24 hours; a lacerated cornea remains clear and functional and soon heals. And they're not only smart but relatively safe. It's far more dangerous to get in your car than wallow about with a chondrichthyan. Think of it this way: More people probably have died of heart attacks watching Pat Buchanan on *Crossfire* than have been killed in the entire recorded history of shark attacks.

AUGUST 24   *Aptos*
JOANN AND I DO a piece on violent death.

Violence in New York has been sawing away at people's nerves all summer long. Bullets from machine pistols have smashed through tenement walls to kill children in their beds. From July 22 to August 22, ten children were shot by what have been called 'stray' or mistargeted bullets. Five of them died.

The memorials pictured in the paper, graffiti messages on walls or sidewalk, with bunches of flowers and sometimes plastic crucifixes set before them, are reminiscent, though in cruder form, of a memorial on East 13th Street to two little girls who were killed on July 1, 1990, when the metal supports to the stoop they were playing on gave way, causing the stairs to collapse and two large marble columns and an ornate concrete lintel to crash upon them. The girls were 10 and 11 years old, Jenny Quiñones and Evelyn Leon. Their friend Christine Martínez, 12, survived but now walks with a limp.

When accounted for, deaths of children like Jenny and Evelyn are not placed in the category of 'violence' but rather in the category of 'accidents'. Building inspectors do not check whether metal supports under concrete stairs are solid; neither do landlords. And even when they do check for dangerous housing conditions – faulty wiring, obscured passageways, poor exit opportunities, peeling lead paint, rodents, lack of window guards – a citation does not necessarily mean the situation is corrected, as becomes clear from any trip down to housing court. Deaths from these sources do not make the news with the same regularity as do deaths from 'violence', but in fact 'accidents' are the largest single cause of death of New York children between the ages of one and 14. In 1987, the last year for which data are available, 17.6 percent of the children who died did so because of accidents. Homicide was in fifth place, claiming 7 percent.

So the term 'violence' should not be so narrowly interpreted. On '87 figures, after accidents, the killers in order are malignant neoplasms, AIDS, and congenital abnormalities. It is a known fact that poor children (like poor people in general) are more prone to cancers, that AIDS in children usually means one of their parents is a junkie who uses dirty needles, and that congenital abnormalities can relate to prenatal care and the general environment in which the child was conceived. The infant mortality rate is a useful guide here as well, since one can assume that in central Harlem, for instance, where the infant mortality rate is 22 percent – equal to that of Romania and higher than that of Chile, Trinidad and Tobago, Jamaica, Kuwait, Bulgaria, Poland and Cuba– the child mortality rate will be similarly higher than it is in New York's fancier neighborhoods.

The problem, however, comes in trying to quantify what one can pretty much assume. Jenny and Evelyn lived in a working-class (though gentrifying) neighborhood of New York on Manhattan's lower east side. The 'accident' that killed them could perhaps not have been predicted, and the next day the landlord began construction to remove similar decoration from the building next door and replace the staircase. But it was an old building in a row of old buildings where rents, except for newly 'renovated' or 'market value' apartments, are relatively low, and therefore services, including building improvements, limited. Yet there are no data at all on dangerous housing conditions as a factor in childhood death or injury.

Frederick Rivera, an expert on child injuries and the co-author, with Beth

Mueller, of an essay in the *Journal of Social Issues* titled 'The Epidemiology and Causes of Childhood Injuries' (1987), says injuries are the leading cause of death in children, accounting for 'about one-half of the deaths of those under four years old, and more than one-half of the deaths of those aged five to 14'. 'Injuries' designates a very broad category, the result of fires, auto accidents, pedestrian accidents, poisoning, suffocation, drowning, falls, etc. In New York, fires are the leading cause of death from unintended injuries to children ages one through four.

Buildings that burn are mostly not on Park Avenue; they are sent up in flames because of arson or faulty wiring or poor storage of combustible materials or unsafe heating methods tricked up by those who have had their heating turned off, or because of the careless actions of people who sleep in or conduct business in the hallways. Fire bells are usually the alarums of poverty.

Returning to the story of Jenny and Evelyn: At the time they were killed they were playing ball, tossing it, according to the superintendent Jimmy Jones, between themselves and some friends across the street. The streets were their playground, so it would not be wildly speculative to say that on that day they also risked being killed by an oncoming car, the second leading cause of death for children of their age group in New York City. And in the same way that they risked a traffic accident and the revelers at the Happy Land Social Club risked death by 'accidental' fire, so at least two of the children shot this summer risked suffocation. Both were under four, and at this age suffocation is the second leading cause of 'accidental' death. When they were shot (one is still alive) they were asleep in their apartments, one in bed with his grandmother, another on a couch with his sister. The most likely reason for such sleeping arrangements is overcrowding. It is well known that today in New York there are somewhere between 75,000 and 100,000 homeless people. The number of 'near-homeless', those who double up with their relatives, is less well known and even less precise, but can be safely put at about one million.

One final note. The mural in memory of Jenny and Evelyn now dominates a wall of a little playground across the street from where they lived. Back in 1988 this playground was an empty lot, its pavement cracked and horrible, broken glass everywhere, dog excrement, old refrigerators. It has now been reclaimed by the community and until recently was in sight of a banner proclaiming, 'Drug Dealers Get Out!'

➥

SEPTEMBER 13   *Topanga*
PHILIP MORRIS ANNOUNCED THAT it will supply the Soviet Union with more than 20 billion cigarettes by the end of 1991. A company news release proudly describes it as 'the largest single export order in the company's history'. RJR

Nabisco will send a further 14 billion. After the first 20 billion cigarettes from Philip Morris, the company will continue to supply 'significant quantities of cigarettes' between 1992 and 1995, also technical assistance to help modernize Soviet cigarette factories.

The US shipments replace a shortfall in domestically produced cigarettes in the Soviet Union, and in the estimate (which he calls conservative), of Dr. John Seffrin, chairman of the National Board of Directors of the American Cancer Society, the 7,000 Russians who would have been killed by the home product will now perish from the substitute US imports.

➤

OCTOBER 4   *New York*
THE UNIFICATION OF THE Germanys was a fairly somber affair, as well it might be. Discussing his dog Harry's ear mite problem with Ben Sonnenberg when Germany was fourteen hours old (E.D.T.), I picked up a copy of Adorno's *Minima Moralia* on his desk and came across this passage: 'Fascism was the absolute sensation: in a statement at the time of the first pogroms, Goebbels boasted that at least the National Socialists were not boring.'

Seldom can the birth of a nation have been greeted with more wariness. When Germany was two hours old (G.M.T.), I was at a meeting at Montclair State College in New Jersey discussing the Gulf crisis. An East German of mature years stood up and with emotion stated that while its leadership had been awful, East Germany hadn't been as bad as they're now saying and hadn't ever attacked or invaded anyone. After a while he choked up and sat down.

➤

OCTOBER 10   *New York*
THE WAR FEVER over Iraq seems to be fitful. Bush keeps casting around for the right motivating tactic to inflame people.

➤

OCTOBER 15   *Topanga*
THE USUAL INGREDIENTS – a hungry daughter, liberated girlfriends – refined my interest in cooking. There's nothing like a decree nisi or the women's movement to propel that animal called man toward the stove.

When I moved to the United States in the early seventies, shortly after the above-mentioned decree, most men were still trying to get by on their sauce vinaigrette and steamed sweetcorn. By the second half of the decade it wasn't at all unusual to arrive for dinner and find the woman of the house doling out the drinks while her mate battled with the Cuisinart and Julia Child's *Mastering the Art of French Cooking*. Several summers spent on Cape Cod, plus a lot of driving to and fro across America in old cars, gave me a taste for outdoor cuisine in various forms. Over the eastern shores of the Atlantic, at least when I was living on them, this sort of cooking amounted to charcoal potatoes and marshmallows *brûlés*. There wasn't much else unless you count tail-gate lunches at the races.

The trick is not to buy one of those fancy barbecues that soon fall apart, but mix a bit of concrete in the bottom of an old metal wheelbarrow and let it harden. In this mobile and visually not unpleasing container you can burn your wood, grill food over the embers and then trundle the thing off into obscurity.

These days I try for the light-hearted and off-hand in cooking. A sure way of keeping the folks amused is to cook something on the exhaust manifold of your car. Using a 1967 Chrysler convertible with a nice big manifold I recently drove from one side of greater Los Angeles to the other (Topanga Canyon to Riverside, a distance of about eighty miles), in an hour and a half and arrived with a perfectly cooked, one-inch-thick port chop, plus corn on the cob. The surface of the manifold is at about 220°F, the temperature of a slow oven.

If manifolds are beyond you, try the dishwasher. Put, for example, the ingredients of Georges Blanc's *bouillon de légumes parfumés selon Marc Meneau* in a sealed Mason jar, set it among the dishes and let the washer do the rest. Theorists of energy conservation call this cogeneration. On big nights, for that flamboyant gesture, you can always bring the duck into the candlelit dining-room and then give it the final crisping with a portable propane blow-torch.

➤

October 26   *Topanga*
To Meg Devine
For Karen Marta, *Allure* Magazine
From Alexander Cockburn
Proposal, October 16, 1990, on Victoria's Secret

ARTICLE WOULD DISCLOSE author's enthusiasm for Victoria's Secret, laying out reasons of catalogue's appeal with digression on popularity of knicker catalogues among women and men, as against skin mags, *Playboy*, etc. Then deeper disclosure of author's particular admiration for the Slut character and distress at increasing prominence being given Wasp Wife at expense of Slut, reflecting, in author's view, tensions in Victoria's Secret re overall thrust and appeal of the catalogue. Dangers of enjoyable publication becoming sort of Smith and Hawken of the knicker world. Article having disclosed author's pov in first half as formulated by eager consumer untethered by actual facts would then disclose who models were, perhaps review on basis of interviews what is really going on in minds of Victoria's Secret editors ad marketeers.

Approximately 3,000 words, delivery date mid November.

➤➤

NOVEMBER 9   *Aptos*
I WAS CITED by a CHP officer on Rte. 17 at 7:30 a.m. The citation (attached) says 7:30 p.m., which is wrong. He claimed that his radar had a reading of 67 mph. At the time he made the claimed reading I was driving in the slow lane, on a mildly descending gradient in the region of a sign for a reservoir. I was driving at the legal speed of 50 mph behind a truck about 100 feet in front of me. Even though it was 7:30 on a Saturday morning, there was substantial traffic in both directions. At the time the CHP officer made his radar observation there was traffic overtaking me in the fast lane, also cars moving rapidly in the other direction. The officer's car was almost directly in front of my car, taking readings of cars coming toward us. 17 is a dangerous road and my Valiant is 29 years old and I was driving it with prudent attention. I am certain that the officer had a reading on a car in the fast lane, or, since there was none at that point, a car going in the opposite direction.

My plea of not guilty, sent in to Santa Clara County Court.

➤➤

NOVEMBER 11   *Sacramento*
UNTIL YESTERDAY I'd never see the Vietnam war memorial in Sacramento. The bronze statues and reliefs are strong: a nurse with an i/v bending over some poor fellow who's just had his arm sawn off; a B-52 with 750-pounders trickling earthward from its bomb doors; a GI reading a Dear John letter; a P.O.W.

The names of California's dead in that war run the circumference of the memorial's outside walls. A parks worker was wiping the dust off them with a swatch of newspaper, watched by three men who looked like Vietnam vets. It made a striking tableau: the names, the parks man stretching to freshen up the top row; the flag through the trees in the background on top of the Capitol.

The day before I'd read another call from Henry Kissinger for the United States to go to war in the Gulf, with bombers heading for Baghdad and those 'surgical strikes' Kissinger loves to summon in his prose. Many of the names on the wall in front of me belonged to men who died in Vietnam after Nixon came to power in 1969, Kissinger in tow.

I walked round to see if San Clemente, whence flowed some of the orders

that ended in those deaths, had paid some human tribute to Nixon's and
Kissinger's concepts of national security and honor. There were two: Lieutenant
Whynaught, Jeffrey L. 22 and S.P.4 Goodman, Greg F. 22. One often forgets
how young are the soldiers sent to war. Whynaught and Goodman were senior
to many of the names around them, hundreds of boys in their late teens.

➡

NOVEMBER 13   *Aptos*
Dear Alex, Hodding and Mike:
January will mark the 10th Anniversary of the Viewpoint column, completing
a decade of strong and provocative stories. During that time all of our other
weekly columns have been replaced or changed hands, and I've had a growing
sense that the time is coming to try a new concept with Viewpoint as well. So this
letter is to let you know that we plan to drop the column to which the three of
you have contributed regularly, substituting one that solicits the views of a wide
variety of writers.

   I'd particularly like to see all of your bylines continuing in some form because
I really do think Viewpoint has been a success, and wouldn't want you to take the
change as any sort of judgment on what you've written for us. Perhaps you'll
think we're carrying our term limitation campaign too far, but I hope you'll
understand our thinking, accept our assurance that we appreciate the contributions you've give us, and continue to think of us as a place to express your ideas
in the future.

Best regards,
Robert L. Bartley, Editor
The Wall Street Journal

➡

DECEMBER 12   *Aptos*
I WISH PEOPLE would stop writing to remind that in the 1930s leftists of prinicple
– Trotsky and Togliatti are two favorites cited by my correspondents – sup-
ported feudal Ethiopia against the invading Italians. The inference is that today
leftists of principle should espouse the cause of Iraq and eschew criticism of
Saddem Hussein. This is Marxism-Leninism-Bonkerism. There is one clearly
identifiable difference between Ethiopia then and Iraq now, namely that the
former was invaded by Italy and the latter invaded Kuwait. Would Togliatti and
Trotsky have been rushing forward with expressions of solidarity for Haile
Selassie if the latter had been invading Eritrea in the 1930s?

   One writer invoked Saddam, admittedly with what he called 'hesitant'
emotions, as a 'Ba'athist Bonaparte', assigned the historic task of uprooting

feudalism in Arabia just as Napoleon did in Europe. Absent further admonitions about the role of the external proletariat or Bonapartist substitute for same, let me quote to the Not-a-Word-Against-Saddam crowd some passages from a letter I received from a woman who signed her name Haneen:

'I was heartened to learn that not everyone who is generally on the left has to be tongue-tied when it comes to condemning Saddam for his invasion of Kuwait and demanding that he leave. I am speaking as a Lebanese who believes wholeheartedly in and has worked many years for the Palestinian cause. I also happen to have grown up in Kuwait and I do oppose US hegemony and policies in the region and elsewhere. But I have felt alienated from the various coalitions against US intervention in the Middle East, particularly because they would not articulate a direct position against Saddam's invasion.

'The fact that these coalitions cannot take such a stand as part of their platforms seems to me a bankrupt position and one which is hypocritical, particularly if they talk of 'linkage'. If they in fact do not call for Saddam's occupation of Kuwait to end, how then can they link the two issues if the only purpose is to liberate Palestine. Why are the Palestinians more entitled to a homeland than the Kuwaitis?'

Ingeniously finding a way to outflank this admirable position, the Bonkerists insist that Saddam and Iraq not be criticized, thus instantly placing themselves in an immoral and tactically impossible position. The Bonkerists also see the UN purely as a cat's paw of the US. The result of this is the denunciation by the Bonkerists of anyone approving of sanctions or critical of Iraq as 'tools of imperialism' – their imputation when men like Eqbal Ahmad and Noam Chomsky insist that Iraq's invasion should be denounced, even as US war plans should be resisted.

➤

DECEMBER 15   *Aptos*

IT WILL BE GOODBYE next year to Aptos and the Adobe. It looks as though I will be able to buy the house in Petrolia on the Mattole River, in Humboldt County, just south of Cape Mendocino. It must be the genes. My fathe quit the city life for rural life in Ireland when he was in his early forties. I'm forty-nine, but I haven't really lived in a big city since the middle eighties. Motel life is okay, but the drug trade here at the Adobe is getting dangerous.

1991

➤➤

The Argument

IN WHICH I am discovered in County Waterford at a hunt ball, remembering my youth. The bombing of Iraq; origins of aerial bombardment; 'a lively terror'; more dog's abuse; some history about prisoners of war; Los Angeles described; my father and Graham Greene's Catholicism; 'coincidence' again, and a grievous wound sustained; the true history of Ulagu the Mongol; uproar over political correctness; the female orgasm discussed; Mark Boxer remembered; the question of Iraqi dead; *finis* to Communism; an outing with the Yurok. Of Communism's end and American fears I sing.

JANUARY 2   *Ardmore, Co. Waterford*
WENT TO the annual hunt ball of the West Waterford Hunt which took place
last night in Dungarvan, eight miles along the coast. Class divisions have
certainly receded. Back in the 1950s when I used to hunt and go to such things,
the balls were very Anglo-Irish affairs and held in such fastnesses as Lismore
Castle, Irish seat of the Duke of Devonshire and now available for rent from
his grace at $12,000 a week.

The bash in Dungarvan took place in a modern hotel amid great apprehen-
sion, since the Gardai (police) are conducting a ferocious antidrunk driving
campaign, stopping one driver in three and giving them tests. That morning a
farmer had been torn from his tractor and arrested after gasping fragrant
billows of Paddy into the bag. After eleven, I switched to barley water and in
this sober state looked across to the young folk at the next table, who were
raising a great din.

They were mostly drunk, but not in that beefy, red-faced way I remember
in the hearties of my generation. One young man did get up on the table and
shyly lowered his trousers for a moment, which would not have happened in my
time. There were harsh words about this at the lawn meet the next day. The
girls were less hefty too. The poet Betjeman, who loved not only Dungarvan but
also big girls, would have been sorely disappointed.

> Pam, I adore you, Pam, you great big mountainous sports girl ...
> See the strength of her arm, as firm and hairy as Hedren's,
> See the size of her thighs, the pout of her lips as, cross,
> And full of pent-up strength she swipes at the rhododendrons,
> Lucky the rhododendrons ...

I know how Betjeman felt. A big girl named Ann used to muck out the stables
in the days when my mother bred horses. Just the memory of her powerful arms
holding a pitchfork load of straw and horse dung still makes me go weak at the
knees. These days she's married to the manager of a tea plantation in Zimbabwe
and writes to say life's fine.

Red hair she had and golden skin,
Her sulky lips were shaped for sin,
Her sturdy legs were flannel-slack'd,
The strongest legs in Pontefract ...
Oh love! for love I could not speak,
It left me winded, wilting, weak
And held in brown arms strong and bare
And wound with flaming ropes of hair.

➤

JANUARY 15   *Ardmore*
ANDY KOPKIND and John Scagliotti have been staying in my old apartment on
Central Park West, while K.K. is in Florida. After a long session of chemo Andy
has had his operation and it's a success. Things look good.

➤

JANUARY 16   *Ardmore*
TRUTH IS THE FIRST casualty, people always say gloomily at the prospect of war:
Just how rapidly this happens can be illustrated by the case of the premature
Kuwaiti babies, supposedly left to die last August by Iraqis who then removed
the incubators to Baghdad.

   There are, of course, thousands of examples of such Iraqi brutality. But the
baby horror is untrue. The charge received its first quasi-official imprimatur
in a report late last year by Amnesty International. Reviewing what it termed
extra-judicial executions, Amnesty International said, 'In addition, over 300
premature babies were reported to have died after Iraqi soldiers removed them
from incubators, which were then looted.' The report quoted an unnamed Red
Crescent doctor as saying that 312 premature babies at Maternity Hospital in
the al-Sabah Medical Complex died after being taken from incubators and that
he personally had buried 72 in al-Rigga cemetery.

   Amnesty International was remarkably off-hand in offering news of what
would be one of the most gruesome crimes of the age. Over 300 babies, and just
forty-six laconic lines deep in its report! Is it likely that any hospital in Kuwait
would have so many incubators? County Hospital in Los Angeles, for example,
has 13. Is it plausible that doctors and nurses at al 'Addan hospital would have
stood by when those babies were dying on the cold floors, deaths that could have
taken place over several hours? The report offered no names, either of witnesses
or of the families of the victims.

   Kuwaiti doctors and nurses now in exile, some of them formerly in senior positions, dispute the story. One says that when she left in the first week in September eighteen babies at Maternity Hospital were in incubators, and that there were other incubators which had not been taken. (The highest figure offered for incubators at Maternity Hospital prior to the invasion is eighty.)

➳

JANUARY 19 *Ardmore*

IN IRAQ'S CASE the concept of bombing as an essentially wholesome liaison between morality and Western technological prowess goes back to 1919, when the Royal Air Force asked Churchill for permission to use chemical weapons 'against recalcitrant Arabs as an experiment.' Churchill, then secretary of state at the war office, rejected timid nay-sayers at the India Office. 'I do not understand squeamishness about the use of gas', he wrote. 'I am strongly in favor of using poisoned gas against uncivilized tribes ... It is not necessary to use only the most deadly gasses; gasses can be used which would cause great inconvenience and would spread a lively terror and yet would leave no serious permanent effects on most of those affected.' Chemical weapons, Churchill concluded, represent 'the application of western science to modern warfare ... We cannot in any circumstances acquiesce to the non-utilization of any weapons which are available to procure a speedy termination of the disorder which prevails on the frontier.'

Despite Churchill's urgings that the RAF use mustard gas, technological problems prevented such deliveries, but by 1920 the British army was using gas shells in Iraq 'with excellent moral effect'. Ordinary shells ('conventional weapons') were used when villages did not pay their taxes. The RAF, balked of its gas deliveries, urged the dropping of bombs with delayed action fuses. Since village children were already playing with dud bombs, one senior officer protested that the result would be 'blowing a lot of children to pieces'. What would be called in today's press briefings 'collateral damage' (dead and mutilated children) did take place because the RAF dropped the delayed action bombs to stop tribesmen from working their crops after dark. I remember Braudel saying in his book on the Mediterranean that some peasants reaped after dark, I think in Spain, to reduce the loss of grain.

Prominent among the British air force officers thus engaged was Arthur Harris, who rejoiced in the didactic war being waged on Arab and Kurd: 'They now know what real bombing means, in casualties and damage.' He later became known as 'Bomber' or 'Butcher' Harris, directing the bomber offensive against Germany in World War II, most notoriously against Hamburg and Dresden.

JANUARY 24   *Ardmore*

Dear Mr. Cockburn:

How sad! Oh, not your departure from the op ed page of the *WSJ*, but that you have lived with so much hate and devoted your career to disapproving of America.

As you slip ever more into your well deserved obscurity it's to be hoped that you will indulge in some fearless self-scrutiny and find the reason for your dislike of your nation, a dislike that has guided you, like most of your extreme liberal colleagues, into simply being wrong most of your life.

There was little in your final column in the *WSJ* that even approached the truth, or had any relation to reality. But my long observation of the workings of the extreme media liberal mind has shown me that their intellectual arrogance demands that they dissent, as a way to display their presumed intellectual superiority to we mere mortals.

And I sincerely pray that you will find peace to replace the hate that so abides within you and which spews forth so clearly in most of your works that I have seen. How sad for a presumably intelligent man to lead a life so distorted with rancor, mean-spiritedness and being so terribly wrong.

Cordially,
Ernie Kreiling
La Cañada, California

➤➤

JANUARY 27   *Ardmore*

Dear Nation:

I was disappointed to see Alexander Cockburn weigh in on the side of increased disunity and the split in the antiwar movement. His attack on the Coalition to Stop US Intervention in the Middle East only deepens the division at a time when he should use his pen to bring those forces together, so we could have had one large demonstration in Washington and not two smaller ones. I am dismayed that the Coalition and the Campaign for Peace in the Middle East were unable to agree on the date for a demonstration against the threatened war against Iraq. It is an outrage that the antiwar movement is engaged in divisive bickering.

Michael Ratner
New York City

I didn't think there was the slightest chance for one demonstration instead of two, so rather than write a pious paragraph urging 'unity' I suggested people go to the Campaign's, as a choice based on principle. After all, Hegel said a political party truly exists only when it is divided against itself. Maybe the same is true of the peace movement. I'd think more of Michael Ratner's ecumenism if I didn't remember his letter containing the lines 'Making criticisms of Iraq part of the progressive community's agenda, I believe, is outweighed by the mischief and obfuscation that could cause.' Try this:

'As an Iraqi expatriate who had experienced Saddam's brutality firsthand, I am appalled by the pro-dictator position some in the American left have taken. Do these people know what their fate would be if they lived in Iraq? No better than my friend's. Bahram's only crime was that he had Arabic translations of Lenin's *What Is to Be Done?* and Marx and Engels's *The Communist Manifesto*. Someone had passed the information to the secret police, who, having searched his house and found no more 'subversive literature', took Bahram away while he was teaching English at a high school. Weeks and months passed and his family was still not informed about his whereabouts. His mother petitioned Saddam and was told he wouldn't interfere in matters of 'national security'! Like other parents who had lost their sons in similar fashion, by now Bahram's parents' only wish was to get back their son's body. And what a body they got back! One summer night it was left in a sack on their doorstep: eyes were gouged out; genitals, fingers and tongue cut; chest splattered with blood. The mother died in horror.'

A. Miran (*a Kurd*)

JANUARY 28   *Ardmore*
ATTEMPTS TO OUTLAW BOMBING go as far back as 1928 and the Geneva disarmament conference, but were sabotaged by the colonial powers who found it a cheap way of policing the colonies. In 1937, after the Japanese had bombed Chinese cities, the League of Nations condemned the act as a crime against humanity. In 1938 the United States government, protesting also bombing of Spanish towns by the Franco forces (whose victory it was helping to accomplish) declared that the 'ruthless bombing' was regarded by the United States as 'barbarous'.

At the start of the Second World War, Roosevelt said the same sort of thing, echoed by Churchill. Long before Pearl Harbor, American and British planners had secretly agreed to bomb Axis cities. On November 19, 1941, Gen. George Marshall's staff drew up contingency plans for 'incendiary attacks to burn up the wood and paper structures of the densely populated Japanese cities.' Even then, though, the Americans were keener on the British in equating virtue with technology and putting more rhetorical investment into high altitude daytime 'precision' bombing. The fire-bombing of Tokyo in 1945 left a million civilians homeless and some 80,000 to 100,000 dead. It was the largest urban conflagration in recorded history. Canals boiled. What with this raid and the two atom bombs some 400,000 died in 'one of the most ruthless and barbaric killings of non-combatants in all history', as Brig. General Bonner Fullers, an aide to Gen. MacArthur, later put it.

➤

FEBRUARY 1   *Ardmore*

'THE PRINCIPLE ITSELF [of secession] is one of disintegration and upon which no government can possibly endure ... the central idea is the essence of anarchy ... if a minority will secede rather than acquiesce, they make a precedent which, in turn, will divide and ruin them; for a minority of their own will secede from them.'

And so the epitaph: 'He was a man neither to be browbeaten by adversity nor intoxicated by success, inflexibly pressing on to his great goal, carried away by no surge of popular favor, disheartened by no slackening of the popular pulse ... the world only discovered him a hero after he died a martyr.' This was Marx on Lincoln.

➤

MARCH 10   *Ardmore*

THE TREATMENT of their Iranian prisoners by Iraqi troops in the 1980s war was appalling, if only slightly worse than the Iranian abuses of Iraqi prisoners. The fury in mid January at the Iraqi treatment of US and UK pilots should nonetheless be seen as hypocritical, at least to the degree that it implies 'civilized western norms' have been breached by the agents of Saddam.

The treatment of Vietnamese prisoners by the US military and their South Vietnamese partners was often barbaric in the extreme, the most notorious example being the tiger cages on Con Son island. Anyone picking up the memoir of former CIA officer Frank Snepp, *Decent Interval*, will find a detailed account of the interrogation, brutal confinement and ultimate execution of Nguyen Van Tai, a North Vietnamese prisoner of war: 'in April 1975, a senior CIA official suggested to South Vietnamese authorities that it would be useful if he "disappeared" ... The South Vietnamese agreed. Tai was loaded onto an airplane and thrown out at ten thousand feet over the South China Sea. At that point he had spent over four years in solitary confinement, in a snow-white room with temperatures kept at a constant chill as part of the attempt to force him to talk.'

Some of the worst atrocities committed against the Vietnamese people by American soldiers are revealed in the testimonies of more than 100 Vietnam veterans to the Winter Soldier Project. The veterans' direct accounts were recorded on film, but the movie was considered too lacerating an experience for the American public and was never aired by the main networks.

The vets spoke of killing civilians, women and children, flinging POWs from airplanes, decapitating other captives, and contravening the Geneva Conventions with regard to treatment of POWs in every manner imaginable. Weapons were placed on murdered civilians and one officer was described as telling those under his command that, once dead, civilians became enemy combatants. Sgt. Michael McCusker from the 1st Marine Division was with the Informational Services Office and acted as an infantry reporter-photographer who spent all of his time in the field. He testified that 'these things in the field, the torturing of prisoners, the use of scout dogs in this torture ... by seeing all of these units, I discovered that no one unit was worse than another, that this was standard procedure.'

➤

MARCH 15   *Ardmore*

IN A SOLEMN RECITATION of the obligations to an enemy taken captive during war, the London *Daily Telegraph*'s military commentator John Keegan – invokes the Christian tradition, while remarking that other races and creeds – Muslims and Japanese included – take a different view. But in respect to prisoners the Japanese and Americans probably matched blood for blood. In the February 1946 issue of *The Atlantic*, the war correspondent Edgar L. Jones wrote, 'We shot prisoners in cold blood, wiped out hospitals, strafed lifeboats, killed or mistreated enemy civilians, finished off the enemy wounded, tossed the dying in a hole with the dead, and in the Pacific boiled the flesh off enemy skulls to make table ornaments for sweethearts, or carved their bones into letter openers.'

In US camps POWs were starved to the point of collapse, performed 20 million man-days of work on army posts and 10 million man-days for contract employers. Some were assigned to work for the Chemical Warfare Center at Edgewood Arsenal in Maryland. At the urging of Eleanor Roosevelt there was also a 're-education' program for 372,000 German POWs in the US, to return them to 'Christian practices' and to reject 'German thinking'. As time wore on the name of the program was changed to 'intellectual diversion'.

In the Korean War, there were atrocities on both sides. Korean forces executed hundreds of American POWs, and treatment of South Korean POWs is believed to have been worse. In their book, *Korea: The Unknown War*, Jon Halliday and Bruce Cumings wrote of the alleged massacre by North Koreans of some 5,000 to 7,000 people in Taejon. But the authors claimed that the truth of that story was unclear. An article by Alan Winnington in the London *Daily Worker* maintained that South Korean police, under the supervision of American advisers, killed 7,000 people between July 2 and July 6, 1950. Winnington spoke with twenty eyewitnesses who said police ordered local people to dig vast pits and then brought political prisoners for execution. These killings continued for three days and, according to the witnesses, US officers in two jeeps looked on. The US Embassy in London called the Winnington story an 'atrocity fabrication', but British officials in Tokyo said, 'There may be an element of truth in this report.'

➳

APRIL 9 *Topanga, California*

LOS ANGELES IS bright, hard, opaque. Even the astonishing sunsets one can see from Interstate 15, looking west towards Pomona, have a sepulchral flush to them as the red light filters through the foul air rolling towards Riverside and the desert seventy miles east of the Pacific. And when the Santa Ana winds blow the other way and clean out the whole basin there's nothing warm in the color tones even then just an eerie depth of field so clear throughout its focal range that it's hard to keep an accurate sense of perspective.

Most writers find their way to Los Angeles from somewhere else and the city has been refracted through the lens of their disenchantment, remorse, bad faith, or, in the case of the city's most brilliant new historian, native son Mike Davis, a relentless curiosity.

For every *noir* scrivener staring out across the Hollywood Hills under eyelids heavy with disillusion there's been a booster, starting with Charles Fletcher Lummis, who in 1884 took 143 days to walk from Ohio to Los Angeles and was hired on arrival by the *patron* of the *Los Angeles Times*, Colonel (later General) Harrison Gray Otis. Lummis helped to forge the booster image described by Kevin Starr in his book *Inventing the Dream:* 'a mélange of mission myth (originating in Helen Hunt Jackson's *Ramona)*, obsession with climate, political conservatism (symbolized in the open shop), and thinly veiled racism, all put to the service of boosterism and oligarchy.'

Lummis was an enthusiast for Southwest archaeology; indeed the cultural/geographical ascription 'the Southwest' started with him, as did the museum of that name in Highland Park now under threat from the city's culture tsars, who want to shift it over to the West Side. He began the magazine *Out West (Land of Sunshine)*, which published the cream of California's letters and ran a salon pleasantly devoted to promulgation of a fake past (the mission myth) and an ecstatic future. Boosterism finds its most meaningful expression in the joyous language of a real-estate promotion, such promotions then and now being the amniotic fluid of Los Angeles.

There's rarely been a city harder to 'see', through a windscreen caked with the alternative myths of the boosters and the *noirs*, nor one about whose history and geography its more prominent denizens have been more ignorant. 'I didn't know Los Angeles had a history', one movie mogul remarked recently, reacting to the launch of a public TV series on the city's hidden past. The culture industry is but one small segment of a vast terrain largely unvisited and unsung: the nation-state of greater Los Angeles, with 14 million individuals, 132 incorporated cities and an economy bigger than India's.

Here in Los Angeles County is the largest complex of military aerospace plants in the nation: Hughes, Lockheed, Northrop, TRW, McDonnell Douglas; here until a few years ago was a powerful manufacturing base with car and tire paints and, to the east in Fontana, the only integrated steel plant on the Pacific slope. Here are strange sub-cities like Vernon, a separately incorporated industrial enclave. By day some 45,000 men and women toil in the garment and furniture sweatshops of Vernon and then go home to some place else. By night the population of Vernon falls to 90. Meanwhile, Vernon's city fathers, democratically elected by their citizenry, supervise their demesne. The City Supervisor draws $165,804 a year, which makes him the highest paid city official in the state of California.

Los Angeles has an industrial working class of over a million blue-collar workers. They toil and often live in the string of communities south of Downtown and along the Los Angeles River. The good, high-wage jobs are gone, along with the auto, steel and rubber plants that closed in the seventies. The city has tilted back towards the nineteenth century. Now across the city there are 125,000 working in the garment industry, of whom 90 percent are women, 80 percent undocumented, and all on the minimum wage. Just a few miles west are Redondo Beach and the LAX corridor, where resides the largest colony of scientists and engineers in the world, plunged in despair at the end of the cold war.

Los Angeles is a city whose good fortunes are either under duress or running out. Its vast boom in aerospace was for many years financed out of net tax transfers from the rest of the country – above all, the Great Lakes states. At the peak moment Southern California was receiving 14 percent of all federal militaryexpenditures.

At its starkest, the political economy of Southern California, its agriculture especially, is comprised of too many people working too hard for too little, to support too many people consuming too much and doing absolutely nothing. If growth were perpetual the equation might survive. When growth slows or stops, as it is now doing, the eventual consequence will be serious social dislocation.

➤

APRIL 10   *Topanga*

IT'S DUMP ON NANCY TIME, but the only people to feel shame should be those who toadied to the Reagans for eight long years, meaning most of the press who went along with the charade, right up to the moment Chief Daryl Gates invited Nancy and a platoon of reporters and photographers down to watch the LAPD conduct a storm-trooper 'drug raid' in South-Central Los Angeles, while Chief Gates congratulated Mrs. Reagan on her courage.

Kitty Kelley sounds sharp because she is cutting into a butter mountain of balderdash about Ron and Nancy served up by publicists and faithfully reproduced by the press.

Many people liked Reagan's act, but this does not necessarily mean they believed in it. In fact most Reagan fans knew the truth all along, but backed him anyway, same as they backed Nixon even though they knew his relationship to the higher side of morality was unstable. I remember folks along Reagan's campaign trails in the late 1970s enjoying the old man's performance just they would some character in a soap opera.

The press corps never caught on to this. So when Reagan was caught in some amazing stretcher, like claiming he'd helped liberate Auschwitz (repeated twice, to Yitzhak Shamir and to Rabbi Martin Hier), they expected the heavens to fall in. But with Reagan the voters had already discounted for stretchers, having decided that between a man – Jimmy Carter – who swore he'd always tell the truth and a man who made no distinction between truth and fiction they'd opt for truth in labelling.

➤

APRIL 12   *Topanga*
SAD TO SEE Graham Greene go. He was one of my father's oldest friends. Greene's father, James, was headmaster of Berkhamsted, which both Graham and my father attended. I came across my father's description of Greene's conversion to Catholicism, as tape-recorded in our house in Ardmore by Greene's biographer Norman Sherry in 1977, four years before my father died in St. Finbar's.

'Quite early on, Graham said to me that he had fallen madly in love with this girl, but she wouldn't go to bed with him unless he married her. So I said, "Well, there are lots of other girls in the world, but still if that's the way you feel, well go ahead and marry her. What difference does it make?" And then he came back and said (this went on over quite a number of weeks), "The trouble is that she won't marry me unless I become a Catholic." I said, "Why not? If you're so obsessed with this girl, you've got to get it out of your system." He was rather shocked, because he said, "You of all people, a noted atheist", I said. "Yes, because you're the one that's superstitious, because I don't think it matters. If you worry about becoming a Catholic, it means you take it seriously, and you think there is something there." I said, "Go right ahead – take instruction or whatever balderdash they want you to go through, if you need this for your fuck, go ahead and do it ..." And then to my amazement, the whole thing suddenly took off and became serious and he became a Catholic convert. So then I felt perhaps I'd done the wrong thing.'

➡

APRIL 16   *Carmel, California*

A LETTER IN THE *New England Journal of Medicine* suggesting that on the basis of a survey of some death rates in Southern California left-handers have a mean life expectancy of 64. This means me. Instead of being a white male in privileged circumstances looking forward to an average stretch certainly not less than 74 years, I'm now in the same boat as black men who, according to the latest survey from HHS are ahead of the average if they get past their mid sixties.

The report suggests that lefties are peculiarly accident prone, since tin openers, corkscrews and slot machines are all designed for right-handers, otherwise known as ordinary long-lifers. Lefties also perish in traffic accidents because in emergencies they yank the steering wheel down with their left hand and thus plunge under the wheels of the truck coming in the opposite direction. I practised driving with my right hand, and yanking towards the ditch.

➡

APRIL 21   *Carmel*

I APPROACHED yesterday a 1968 Dodge Dart GT I'd bought last summer and which has been sitting locked in a canyon ten miles south of Carmel Highway, hard by the Blue Pacific, left there for me by the previous owner. I unlocked it and, reminding myself to steer only with the right hand, swung down into the driver's seat.

At first I thought I'd sat on a bare spring. Then, aware that something seriously damaging had scythed its way into my left buttock I looked down and saw a piece of glass lying on the seat. Later, trundled face down on a gurney into an emergency ward in Monterey Community Hospital I tried to deal with Dr. Keller's amiable badinage as he put several internal and twelve external stitches in my backside. This being the end of the Laguna Seca bike races, Dr. Keller was waiting for a tide of mangled bikers, and treated me as comic relief.

The next day I went down to the canyon. A piece of mirror was there in the seat of the Dart. The previous owner had installed one of those wraparound, multi-pane rear-view mirrors you occasionally see in taxis. At some time between August 1990 and 5 p.m., Saturday, April 20, this pane had dropped out, bounced off the steering wheel and wedged in the center of the driver's seat. If I'd swung three inches to the right things would have been much worse.

G. reminded me of his friend who, once in a while, would suspend all activity for ten seconds, just to throw predestination off track. Had I engineered my own fate by popping the trunk, before I opened the driver's door? Maybe that thunk of closing trunk lid had sprung the mirror free of its last shard of glue. And why was I opening the trunk? To put in the plates I'd just taken off the car, numbers 666, the number of the Great Beast.

➤→

APRIL 26   *Topanga*

Dear Nation:

I regret Alexander Cockburn's attack on Amnesty International for its reporting on Iraqi abuses in Kuwait, especially because he cited the findings of Middle East Watch, a component of Human Rights Watch, in an effort to discredit Amnesty. I particularly regret Cockburn's imputation that Amnesty erred because it was 'politically convenient'. This is without basis and unfairly calumniates an organization that is scrupulous about not shaping its reporting for political purposes.

Aryeh Neier,
executive director
Human Rights Watch
New York City

Dear Nation:

Alexander Cockburn has attacked the factual accuracy, research methods and political motivation of Amnesty International. He called the reports of mass murder of infants in Kuwait a 'myth' and implied that Amnesty had been propagating 'tales' of atrocity, and he accused the organization of producing 'sloppy ... politically convenient work'.

All those charges are unfounded. For thirty years, Amnesty has based its work, within the framework of its well-defined mandate, on strictly observed principles of impartiality, balance, fairness, consistency and, above all, accuracy. It has built an impressive reputation for applying the same international human rights standards to all governments regardless of political ideology.

Winston Nagan,
John G. Healey,
Amnesty International USA
New York City

It's naïve to imagine that human rights organizations are immune to such political calculations. Outfits like Amnesty and the Rights Watch groups survive by the favor of financial contributions from donors who themselves often have strong political opinions. These groups need respectability so that their researches will be reported in the press. The more ample the coverage, the more constant the flow of necessary funding. The fiercer the allegations of liberal bias from the State Department – as aimed against Americas Watch, for example, in the mid 1980s – the more sensitive the human rights organization will become and the more prudent in locating the median line of respectable opinion, as did Americas Watch at a crucial moment in the *contra* war.

None of this should be surprising or even discomfiting, so long as it is borne in mind that human rights organizations have biases (e.g., against definitions of human rights that might have too 'political' a content) and inhibitions (e.g., against being consigned to the editorial dustbin as being 'radical' or 'anti-West'). So the spectrum of the permissible is narrower than might be initially supposed, and the desire for a sensational press release on occasion greater.

Take Amnesty's report on Iraqi abuses in Kuwait. By December, nineteen weeks into the occupation, Amnesty had put out an eighty-page document. Fully twenty-three years have elapsed since Israel's occupation of the West Bank, and Amnesty has yet to produce as comprehensive a single report. Why the urgency only in the case of Kuwait?

Such prudence is not confined to Amnesty. Middle East Watch has a very poor record when it comes to human rights abuses by Israel.

➥

MAY 2   *Rochester, N.Y.*
MEMORIES OF WAR here, as in most towns across the country, are beginning to fade. The yellow ribbons around trees along suburban avenues have slipped down and look tired next to the magnolia, forsythia and cherry.

On the campus of the University of Rochester some students were hard at work drawing chalk lines on the brick wall of the Wilson Commons building, which houses the student union. Four vertical lines on every brick, with a fifth diagonal line running through them. By the end of Saturday the wall was covered with 53,000 of these little lines. Along one course of bricks, about ten feet up, were written the words, 'Each slash has a face, a mother, a father, someone who misses them.'

The students, part of a group called United Student Activists – high school and college kids from all over the Rochester area – had an announcement they were passing out: '100,000 … and counting', in which they expressed the hope that the chalked wall would remind people just how bloody and devastating the Gulf War was. Valerie Metzler, who had spent eight hours drawing chalk lines, said she'd found it a rather somber experience.

A couple of miles from the campus, in Highland Park in the southern part of town, union leaders and labor activists were also talking about dead and wounded, though these were casualties unhonored by yellow ribbons or presidential oratory. Spring brings with it May Day, the workers' day. Here in the United States last Sunday was named by the AFL-CIO as Workers Memorial Day, in honor of the moment twenty-one years ago when, on April 28, 1970, President Nixon signed the Occupational Safety and Health Act. With the act came a new federal agency – OSHA – under the umbrella of the Labor Department; also came an expectation among workers that at last safety and health standards in workplaces would be vigorously enforced.

As one of the speakers at the rally in Highland Park I was able to tell the crowd in this home city of the famously non-union Eastman/Kodak Corporation that since the passage of the act – as with the passage of the Environmental Protection Act, another creation of that time – the trend has been downhill all the way from the high hopes of the Nixon years.

This is no irony. Nixon signed OSHA and EPA into law at a moment when public support for federal regulation was high. Soon came the corporate counterattack of the mid 1970s and under Presidents Ford, Carter, Reagan and Bush such regulation has got steadily more lax. In the twenty-one years since the Occupational Safety and Health Act was passed, some 200,000 American workers have lost their lives on the job. Another 1.4 million have been permanently disabled in workplace accidents and as many as 2 million have died from diseases incurred from workplace conditions. In the same period some twenty employers have been prosecuted and just one – a builder in South Dakota – sent to jail, for forty-five days.

Throughout the 1980s the casualty graphs climbed, as businesses fought to preserve profit margins by increased productivity, meaning speed-ups and more corners cut on safety standards. Repetitive motion diseases are now particularly conspicuous on these rising graphs, both among so-called pink-collar workers in the computer-dominated service sector and also among line workers, as in the auto factories in Detroit.

➤→

MAY 3   *Rochester*
WOKE UP AFTER a talk, and found a copy of Colette's *Thousand-and-One-Mornings* in my hosts' kitchen. C. wrote these pieces for *Le Matin*, edited by her lover. On the Gioconda: 'She who lacks for nothing and yet has no eyebrows.' Familiarity: 'Nothing is really new in the little shops on the boulevard. The shoe-polish is supreme, the mother-of-pearl stud for detachable collars at its post, like the ever-lasting nougat and the visiting card while you wait.' The Spectacle: 'This disgusting spectacle spirit takes hold of me, the same spirit which takes women to bullfights, boxing matches and even to the foot of the guillotine, the spirit of curiosity which so perfectly replaces real courage.'

The only thing it is usually impossible to find in a strange kitchen are the coffee filters.

➤

MAY 10   *Topanga*

I LIKENED THE DESTRUCTION wrought by the bombing to what the Mongol Ulagu, brother of Kublai Khan, did to Baghdad in 1258, destroying the irrigation system 'that was the basis of Abbasid civilization and hence its military capacity.' Now Professor Israel Shahak writes from Jerusalem to tell me that this is poor history; that though Ulagu slaughtered almost all the inhabitants of Baghdad *after* the surrender of the Caliph (thus prefiguring the slaughter on the Basra road at the end of February 1991), his destruction of the irrigation system is a myth.

Shahak then cites M.A. Shaban's *Islamic History, A New Interpretation* for its description of the late Abbasid empire, from A.D. 850 on:

'The government saw all its duties and responsibilities in terms of enforcing tax-collection, the revenues of which were to support a growing and corrupt bureaucracy and an almost useless army. When it came to public services the government did not seem to consider that these fell within the realm of its responsibilities. Even necessary repairs to the delicate irrigation systems which had been previously paid for by the government were now charged to the users who had to pay for them over and above the required taxes.'

Shaban also recounts how huge swaths of land were given by the later Abbasids to absentee generals, further degrading the irrigation systems and much else. Shahak goes on to say:

'In fact, this Iraqi cataclysm myth contains (as in other cases) only a grain of truth. Goths did not destroy the buildings of Rome; it was the Roman neglect (and pillage) that was chiefly responsible. For every destruction caused to Ireland by foreign invaders, much more was caused by internal Irish wars. More Jews were killed by each other than by the Romans during the Great Rebellion of 66–70 A.D., and so on. But in modern times, the romantic nation-alists, who do not want to blame their own infatuated peoples and the tyranni-cal governments of the past which they consider 'theirs' because the tyrants used their language, invent myths in which *all* the blame, instead of merely some less significant part of it, is ascribed solely to the foreign conquerors. Had more of the Arabs paid attention to what their own scholars were saying about the grim realities of the Abbasid Empire, or of other Islamic states of their past … their infatuation with the myth of their past, which was the basic cause of the Gulf War, would not have had such results. Incidentally, the right-wing

Jews in Israel and many of the Jews in the US suffer from the same disease which may cause similar results.'

The Abbasid decline commencing in the ninth century can be traced at least in part to overexploitation of water-intensive agriculture, leading to salinization. The same thing now threatens the agriculture of California's Central Valley.

In the realm of romantic nationalism nothing is more tragic than the spectacle of Pol Pot, in postwar Paris earnestly studying the fantasies of nineteenth-century French historians of the ancient Khmer civilization centered at Angkor Wat. They hypothesized an aquaculture of straight canals, and Pol Pot sent hundreds of thousands to their deaths, trying to revive these imaginary public works.

I'm not so sure about Shahak's Irish history. When Cromwell invaded Ireland (headquartering himself for a period in Youghal, the town in which I grew up), the consequent war, starvation and disease claimed some 620,000 people. In the Great Famine in the mid nineteenth century, about a million Irish died due to the English landlord system and England's refusal to grant relief to meet the scale of the disaster. By contrast no more than 4,000 Irish died in the Civil War of the 1920s, and less in the war in the North.

➤→

MAY 20   *Washington, D.C.*
THE WAR OVER 'political correctness' is entering a surreal phase with the commotion over 'The West As America' exhibition at the National Museum of American Art, part of the Smithsonian Institution in Washington, D.C.

Senator Ted Stevens of Alaska has worked himself into a fine froth about the P.C. horror, as deployed by the Smithsonian. 'To see that exhibit', he shouted at Smithsonian Secretary Robert McC. Adams during a hearing of the Appropriations Committee, 'I'll tell you, that really set me off ... Why should people come up to your institution and see a history that's so perverted?'

I visited the infamous exhibition. Billed as a reinterpretation of images of the frontier, 1820–1920, it's a fairly decorous attempt to gloss the paintings and photographs of Bierstadt, Remington, Moran, Jackson and the others with commentary derived from the historical and moral concerns that got such a useful shove forward in the radical 1960s.

Slabs of prose mounted next to the images invite visitors to conceive of a march to the West more compromised than the art suggests. Some of this commentary even indicates that the opening of the West involved the destruction of native peoples and that painters and photographers had been complicit in such destruction. It's all a mite preachy, in the P.C. manner; the term 'politically correct', after all, got its start among the left as a joke on those who took commitment to the far side of self-righteousness. More riveting by far is the Comment book in which Daniel Boorstin has scrawled a denunciation. Its pages bulge with recrimination and applause. 'Where are the "Buffalo Soldiers"? Again blacks have been left out', one visitor has written. 'A relentless sermon of condescension', snaps the historian Simon Schama.

The comments are about two-thirds unfavorable. The book as a whole was encouraging. Most exhibitions consist of people standing numbly in line to get in, numbly in front of 'important' works, then numbly in the museum shop which is usually the beating heart of these institutions, unless you count the trustees' cocktail parties. Here, for a change, is an exhibit that puts visitors on their toes, eager to get in on the act.

➥

MAY 21   *Washington, D.C.*

SAMPLES FROM the Guest Book at the 'West As America' Exhibition:

If I want Freud, I'll go to a hospital/clinic. If I want Indians, I'll go West.
*

This show is very biased against Western culture. It has absolutely nothing good to say about America. It should explain in the first room that the Aztecs in the painting were prodigious *cannibals*. The show is just another banal exercise in the 'politically correct' 'oppression study' movement.
*

How very un-American to examine our past critically.
*

How nice! According to your commentaries the world is filled with racist white males and their hapless victims. Grow up!
*

Some people won't want to accept any of this. Manifest Destiny lives on. Right on!
*

Such wonderful art – and such damn stupid analysis – the propaganda crap reads as though it came straight from Bankrupt East Berlin. Will the 'experts' ever learn?
*

Deconstructionist B.S.
*

Above commentary is overdrawn, overwrought, too 'politically correct'. What happened in America happened also in India, Africa, Australia – the morality is impossible to conclude in absolutes.
*

After viewing these paintings, it's clear that progress was inescapable. Interpret that as you wish.

MAY 25 *New York*

POLITICAL CORRECTNESS has come of age as a national bogy. Not a bad showing for something that is largely imaginary, though in the minds of its foes it is all-pervasive, like that other exhalation of *fin de siècle* American paranoia, child abuse in day-care schools. Indeed the uproar over P.C. and the destructive mania about 'ritual abuse' and child abuse in day care address similar terrors, about the theft of innocence, the intrusion of alien molesters into the natural rhythms of an American upbringing. The Satanists who coaxed children onto broomsticks and thence by rapid aerial locomotion to a lonely cemetery and unspeakable acts become, amongst the P.C. cohort, the heirs of St. Just or the Red Guards, tossing the Great Books of ancient wisdom on the pyres of the new intolerance.

➳

MAY 26 *New York*

MUCH OF THE PRESS has located the clearest representation of the P.C. impulse in restrictive speech codes imposed by colleges – inhibitions on students from speaking their minds freely, as the young love to do and as some fraternity 'Crows' at Syracuse University recently demonstrated by wearing T-shirts with the words 'Club Faggots Not Seals' and a cartoon of a crow wielding a spiked club above a prone and faceless figure. In February of this year Brown University expelled a student, Douglas Hann, under 'hate speech' provisions after he shouted, 'Fucking niggers ... What are you, a faggot? ... Fucking Jew'; told a black woman, 'My parents own your people'; and had to be restrained from provoking a fight.

Many universities have such 'hate speech' codes, among them Stanford and Wisconsin, the latter of which had experienced a rash of racist incidents including a 'slave auction'. Foes of P.C. who see its adepts as being oversensitive to the ethnohustle of today's campuses skim over the actual violence there. In December 1987 some Asian-American women at the University of Connecticut were spat upon by football players shouting 'Oriental Faggots'. At the University of Massachusetts in 1986 a white mob of 3,000 chased and beat anyone in its path who happened to be black. The National Institute Against Prejudice and Violence reported racial incidents at 115 campuses in 1989.

The P.C. barrage has also elided important initiatives from the story of campus sex and race relations. Wisconsin's speech codes and ethnic studies requirements have been mentioned frequently in the press, but the 'Madison plan', significant because it budgets $4.7 million to double minority faculty and otherwise diversify at the fourth-largest school in the country, is mostly unnoticed. Dinesh D'Souza, the Ahab of the P.C. hunt, has attacked Duke University's 'opportunities appointments' program, which mandates searches for qualified minority faculty by every academic department. He calls it 'the victims' revolution', astounded at the discovery that this is what revolution used to be before Reaganites appropriated the word. Hampshire, Purdue and Williams have similar recruitment programs – attempts to create a critical mass of minority scholars who need not feel threatened or turned into tokens or obliged in some silly fashion to represent the 'viewpoint' of their race.

➥

MAY 27   *New York*

BULKING LARGE IN the bill of indictment against P.C. is the claim that it undermines 'qualifications'. An article by D'Souza in *The New Republic* was interchangeable with the National Association of Scholars advertisement appearing on the opposite page. Both deplored 'the admission of seriously underprepared students' to universities, conflating affirmative-action candidates with these same 'seriously underprepared' at every turn. Conclusion: P.C. is out to undermine every measure of excellence, thus ushering in dreaded 'relativism' and hence the downfall of all we hold dear.

Shackled to 'relativism' in the P.C. case file is 'multiculturalism', honored in *The New Republic* as 'one of the most destructive and demeaning orthodoxies of our time.' 'Multiculturalism' here means race essentialism. Any reasonable person would object to essentialist doctrines, which propose race as the primary determinant of human behavior, but it is grotesque to see the demand for proportional hiring of minorities and curricular diversity denounced as a 'dogma of race and of a revolution'.

The diversification of the academy has ushered in a long-postponed conflict between the explaining and the explained classes, with the P.C. conflict as part of the fallout. On *This Week With David Brinkley* on May 5, for example, Stephan Thernstrom, a Harvard professor of history and an 'expert' on poverty, related 'political correctness' to what he termed the 'minority mismatch problem', a 'degree of frustration on the part of many minority students who have been placed through affirmative action in institutions where they're not doing very well on average.' What kind of atmosphere does it create in the classroom when a professor believes that minorities are 'mismatched' to higher education? What sort of conflicts ensue when a culture-of-poverty adherent faces a classroom with people whose lived experience contradicts his expertise? Professor Adolph Reed says, 'You can't just pick out the narratives of the people in charge and call it American history anymore.'

The final charge of the P.C. hysterics involves 'politicization', what *The New Republic* calls the distraction of 'the university from its central task of open-ended disinterested inquiry', though what university has ever practiced this is not recorded. In accurate translation this means fashioning of minds suffi-

ciently deadened to reason and history to allow the dominant ideology to reproduce itself from generation to generation. This is the silliest part of the whole
uproar. Part of the cry of 'politicization' stems from the notion that there has
been a slash-and-burn assault on core courses in Western civilization, allowing
ideological critiques and non-Western canons to sprout and multiply. Education
Department figures show that from 1972 to 1984 only about 20 percent of college
students elected to take Western civilization courses in the first place.

Academia is diversifying, albeit at a glacial pace when it comes to faculty. In
the early 1960s ten of the top history departments in the country had 160
professors, all of them men, and 128 assistant professors, four of them women.
Ten years later there were 274 professors, two of them women, and 317
assistants, 314 men. By the mid 1980s, 11.7 percent of all full professors in the
country were women. Only 2.2 percent were black. So 'glacial' is the word.

➡

MAY 28   *New York*
ON THE SUBJECT of quotas: last year my brother Patrick was confabulating with
a *New York Times* reporter in the coffee shop of the Al-Rashid Hotel in
Baghdad. The *Times* man commenced by denouncing Saddam Hussein at such
a volume that Patrick squinted round nervously to see if any Iraqi security
types were lurking nearby. This outburst concluded, the man leaned across the
table and, after a furtive glance about him, began to discuss ethnic hiring
patterns at the *Times* in a voice so low that Patrick could barely make out what
he was saying over the clatter of coffee cups – something about the paper's
editorial staff being now about 70 percent Jewish.

The final twitch of P.C. *grand peur* has to do with the age-old fear of
antinomian beastliness, lesbians holding deconstructionist black masses over
copies of Derrida and so forth. This brings us back to the other big fear, about
molestation of infants in day-care centers.

As in other scares, P.C. becomes shorthand for many anxieties. We are
nearing the point in the cyclical pattern of academic appointments at which
some one-third of American professors will retire. Many of these, themselves
tenured in the chill of the 1950s, see their values threatened by the younger
cohort moving up in seniority. What could be simpler therefore than to detect
and denounce the insidious menace of P.C. just as their forebears denounced
the Red Menace forty years ago? And the P.C. horror is good soundbite politics,
conflating every left cause imaginable, from Palestinian self-determination to
vegetable rights, and justifying counterterror by the academic right, whose
members have launched their own echo of the Vendée, swarming through the
bookstore at Duke, calling for the removal of all books with Marx in the title.

There's an element of career opportunism involved too. Amid the *grand peur* all the usual suspects muster on the talk shows and Op-Ed pages – William Bennett, Roger Kimball, Donald Kagan, Jeffrey Hart. The younger right-wing high-steppers, looking for preferment at the Heritage Foundation or on the editorial pages of the *Wall Street Journal*, lack issues. Communism is pretty much dead, and supply-side economics a shambles. The answer, as more than one high stepper like D'Souza has found, is race. So the enemies of P.C. can whack away at affirmative action, racial justice and civil rights while claiming that they are speaking in the name of tolerance and free speech.

Race, the core of all the fuss, is no doubt why George Bush, on the edge of his 1992 campaign, has turned his attention to P.C., with Willie Horton's equivalent in '92 being 'extremists' eroding Western values with their multiculturalism and contempt for Great Books (though Brendan Gill was once at Bush's place in Kennebunkport and, insomniac, tried to find something to read, discovering after investigation of the entire mansion only *The Fart Book*).

➡

JUNE 3   *Topanga*

IN THE AMERICANS: THE DEMOCRATIC EXPERIENCE Boorstin writes of Western ranchers: 'Their great opportunity was to use apparently useless land that belonged to nobody.' Whose history is perverse and inaccurate? Boorstin's nonsense is drawn from the same poisoned well that proposed a Yellowstone uninhabited before the white man came. The natives, so the story went, held the geysers in 'superstitious awe' because of their rumble and hiss, 'which they imagined to be the wails and groans of departed Indian warriors suffering punishment because of their earthly sins.' This rubbish was made up in the late 1870s by the park's first superintendent, Philetus Norris, who had lobbied for the expulsion of such Shoshone, Crow, Bannock and Blackfoot as remained, hoping thus to avert 'in future all danger of conflict between those tribes and laborers or tourists.'

In the same 1973 book Boorstin celebrates the grasses of the Western plains for their ability to survive low rates of rainfall. He sees this as a God-given phenomenon, awaiting exploitation by the ranchers. There's a vast literature about the role of Indians in creating and maintaining North American grasslands, particularly across the Great Plains. In *The Roots of Dependency*, his book about the Choctaw, Pawnee and Navajo, Richard White describes how planned burning for livestock management had a marked effect on the initial growth of prairie grasses: 'By eliminating the previous year's growth and excessive ground mulch, fire allows the sun to warm the earth more quickly, with the result not only that, in spring, growth comes weeks earlier, but also that yields are significantly higher from March to July, exactly the period when the Pawnees needed the grass.' White adds that one grass in particular, Indian grass (Sorghastrum nutans), almost certainly benefited from burning since 'this tall grass of the prairies greatly increases its range with regular fires.'

One of Alfred Jacob Miller's paintings from the 1830s (not in the Smithsonian exhibition) shows Indians in a village threatened by an approaching prairie fire, using blankets and brands to control backfires around their entire camp.

➡

JUNE 4   *Topanga*

TYPING THESE LINES two days shy of my fiftieth birthday I pause in search of uplifting sentiments, and my eye falls on Rob Anderson's column about the press in the *Anderson Valley Advertiser*. He cites a book review in *The Washington Monthly* by a fellow named Eric Alterman calling me 'the world's ... most infuriatingly rigid Marxist journalist.'

I search myself for signs of rigidity, finding only a certain stiffness in the lower back, no doubt caused by years stooped over my desk memorizing *Capital*. I remember Alterman. He once invited me to speak at Yale. Quarter cheeky-chappie, three-quarters brown-noser.

It's hard to imagine what an infuriatingly rigid Marxist does to win the title, aside from demanding that everyone commit the *Eighteenth Brumaire* to memory. I'm flattered all the same and call the confectioner to stencil the phrase on my birthday cake. It will ease the sadness caused by the Soviet Union's decision to drop the word 'Socialist' from its name. So it's no longer socialist in self-styling, probably doomed as a nation, averse to soviets. Next thing you know they'll be installing a czar. Maybe Mama was right, and it was best my father died when he did. I miss the old boy, but at least he was spared the sight of the Kennedy School devising the Union of Soviet Sovereign Republics' new economic program.

➡

JUNE 10   *Topanga*

Dear Alex,

Locally, the native grasses could not stand up to cattle trampling them year after year. 'Sturdier' grasses were imported from Spain and Europe. But these are not very drought resistant – hence die off with no rain. Letting the weeds take over.

Best,
Jim O'Connor
Capitalism, Nature, Socialism
Santa Cruz, California

JUNE 12   *Topanga*

MAYBE I'M BEING too pessimistic. Late last year *Moscow News* ran the results of a poll conducted in September and October by the All-Union Center for the Study of Public Opinion. The sample included 1,848 people in seventeen regions of the country.

Asked to agree or disagree with the statement that the October Revolution expressed the will of the populace of the Russian Empire, 39 percent agreed, 36 percent disagreed and 25 percent replied that it was hard to say. 'Imagine', the poll asked, 'that the October Revolution is happening before your eyes. You would ...' It turned out that 22 percent would actively support the Bolsheviks; 21 percent would cooperate with the Bolsheviks in some way; 13 percent would try to bide their time, taking no part in events; 10 percent would emigrate; and 6 percent would fight the Bolsheviks. 26 percent thought it was hard to say. No less than 46 percent thought a revolution was necessary to achieve the Bolsheviks' aims, as against 32 percent who thought there could have been a peaceful way to power; 52 percent thought armed seizure of power was necessary.

His statue may have been toppled in Addis Ababa, but Lenin still has admirers at home. He came out on top of the list among names that aroused greatest sympathy, getting the thumbs up from 64 percent – well ahead of the surprise runner-up, Felix Dzerzhinsky, founder of the Cheka, who got 41 percent.

What the people most definitely did not care for was the closing of other parties' newspapers (56 percent said it was unnecessary), the armed suppression of peasant uprisings (64 percent said it was unnecessary) and the execution of the czar's family (the largest group in the whole poll – 77 percent – thought this was a rotten idea).

➡

JUNE 16   *Topanga*

IN AMERICA IT'S mostly legal to go on strike. It's simply illegal to win one. Exercise your right to strike and the boss can hire scabs immediately. If these scabs are still in place after a year they, and they alone, can vote whether to keep the union.

You can't do much in the way of picketing either. The law makes it impossible to interfere in any way with scabs on their way into the plant. Frank Bardacke, who took part in a strike – ultimately victorious – against a packing house in Watsonville, told me they were allowed just three pickets at the plant gate. Everyone else had to stay at least a hundred yards back. Of course the employers had plenty of highly interfering pickets – in the form of police – right by the gates.

Often the only way to win a strike, or even put some pressure on the owner, is to get other workers to support you. The law takes care of that one too. Sympathy strikes are illegal, as are 'hot cargo' strikes, meaning that workers can't refuse to handle stuff made by scab labor. Solidarity is against the law.

➤

JUNE 26   *Topanga*

IN BRITAIN THE RHETORIC of 1940 is never far away. Mrs Margaret Thatcher, campaigning against the specter of full economic and political European union, draws on the emotional capital of those months in 1940 and 1941 when, on the edge of a continent swift to collaborate with the Nazi invader, Britain stood alone.

The truth is less romantic, though rarely stated. Before the war the British ruling class was mostly eager to cooperate with Hitler, sending the Wehrmacht and the SS battalions east against the Soviets. During the early part of the war a substantial faction remained eager to sue for peace and there is evidence to suggest that had the Germans managed to cross the channel (the failure to do this had less to do with the supposedly vital Battle of Britain than with Hitler's view that Britain was never really the true enemy) most Britons would have collaborated with the Germans as placidly as their continental neighbors.

In June the KGB disclosed a very interesting file to do with the Hess case. On May 11, 1941, on the eve of the German invasion of the Soviet Union, Rudolf Hess, Hitler's deputy, flew to Scotland, landing at the estate of the Duke of Hamilton. His plan was to make contact with the peace faction and inaugurate talks, leaving Germany free to attack the Soviet Union, disencumbered of any threat from the west. Fear of such a treaty was what had pushed Stalin towards his own pact with the Fuehrer.

Hess was arrested and ultimately committed suicide in Spandau prison in 1987. The new documents disclose the passionate interest Stalin and his colleagues took in the Hess flight. Lavrenti Beria, head of the NKVD – forerunner of the KGB – communicated personally to Stalin the reports of agents in London, including Kim Philby. According to Philby, Hess had been set up, lured by letters purportedly from the Duke of Hamilton but in fact written by Churchill's agents in the security services.

British archives remain far more firmly closed on this episode than those of the KGB and will remain so until 2017. The reason is almost certainly that the archives would reveal Churchill's fears that the pro-German peace faction whose most conspicuous representative was the Duke of Windsor – formerly Edward VIII – would overwhelm his government and negotiate surrender terms with the Germans. Some Churchill supporters, particularly in 1940, even feared a coup d'etat. So the Hess operation (coded by the Russians 'Black

Bertha' after Hess's nickname in gay circles in Berlin) was a trap, set to abort maneuvers to produce a government amenable to Hitler, such as had run Britain till Munich.

By the time of the Hess flight, the Germans had actually occupied British territory, in the form of the Channel Islands. Most of the inhabitants collaborated with the Nazis. The local governments of the islands thoughtfully printed a guidebook for their new rulers, and passed anti-Semitic laws without delay. Lists of Jews were also provided. Those thus betrayed were deported to their deaths. A death camp for prisoners of the Germans was set up in Alderney in which 7,000 captives were starved, tortured and thrown over the cliffs.

A recent British law requiring investigation of war crimes committed by British citizens (or those given British citizenship in the war's aftermath) is already leading to fresh disclosures as Scotland Yard detectives pursue enquir ies in such areas as the Channel Islands. Newly unearthed documents show Victor Carey, head of Guernsey's civil administration, zealously promulgating the Nuremberg laws and other anti-Jewish edicts. In one 1940 letter to the Nazi field commander Carey wrote, 'Regarding the registration of Jews ... I can assure you there will be no delay as far as I am concerned.' After the war there were no prosecutions in the Channel Islands for collaborating with the enemy. Indeed Carey was made Bailiff of Guernsey and knighted.

My father, himself on a Nazi death list (the relevant page may be found reproduced in Alan Moorhead's *Invasion, 1940*), asked the man who ran his local pub, who visited the Channel Islands after the war, why the inhabitants had behaved in this disgusting fashion. 'But Claud', the friend answered matter-of-factly, 'they thought the Nazis were going to win.'

➤

JUNE 28   *Topanga*
Dearest Alexander,
I looked out my scribbled notes on the female orgasm and decided, on reflection, that they were a little too raw and personal to photocopy and post to you. Fortunately my guardian angel seems to have intervened and caused them to be lost in the US postal system.

However, this is the gist of the theory. It is better to travel hopefully than to arrive. Orgasm, though, of course, very wonderful, has a certain predictability to it (which is why masturbation is so dull) and the most exciting stage of an affair is before orgasm becomes automatic. The best state to be in is one of insane lust and unsatisfied desire. Once a man can satisfy you, he can also bore you and, within the orgasm, lie the seeds of ennui. There are no more surprises.

Of course, this is a bit devious for most men. The whole business of the F.O. is a total mystery to them and has assumed an importance comparable to that of the Holy Grail which is why those who haven't learnt better always ask 'Did you ...?' And, as I was reminded only recently, by my friend Carla's nanny, if you give a truthful but negative answer, as she did, the chap goes into a decline and, in her case, rang up the next day and said that he thought they had better break off their relationship.

L.
U.K.

➤→

JULY 1   *Topanga*

WHAT IS IT ABOUT MACHINERY – these days they like to call it 'high tech' – that causes *Nation*-types to go weak at the knees? Even arms company flacks sounded demure next to leftists proclaiming the efficient horrors of the 'electronic battlefield' back in the Vietnam era, and the same is true today in the wake of the Gulf War: the war with Iraq conducted between January 17 and February 28 supposedly marked a triumph for technology, suggesting a new phase in military affairs.

There were differences in emphasis. Alvin and Heidi Toffler have spoken with the rhetoric of Herbert Spencer spliced into Defense Department handouts. In yet another chapter in the long tradition of American technological utopianism the Tofflers imagined new machines that are both magnificently violent and redemptive, atoning for the excesses of the twentieth century with a return to warfare that 'minimizes wasteful destruction'.

In contrast to this balderdash the *Bulletin of Atomic Scientists* and the *Nation* authors dwell on the novel powers of devastation recently displayed, citing at luxuriant length claims made by arms manufacturers and the Pentagon for cluster bombs, fuel-air explosives and other munitions. Even so, all authors were united by faith in the machine. Man barely enters the picture.

No achievement of technology was more hailed during and after the war than the Patriot missile. But the Patriots performed very poorly. From information coming out of Israel, it now appears that 157 Patriots were fired at 51 Scuds within Patriot 'coverage' – the numbers vary slightly. Few of those Scud warheads were prevented from hitting either a structure or the ground and then exploding. Moreover numbers of Patriots, some fired at Scuds and some launched upon radar false alarms, came down and exploded, adding to the casualties and the damage.

At one point Israeli sources were alleging that only one Scud warhead was destroyed in midair. Currently published figures show that Israeli casualties per Scud fired increased by 80 percent after the Patriots started 'defending' Israel. The number of apartments damaged per Scud increased by 400 percent.

The hoopla about laser-guided bombs was equally hollow. On the evidence of General Schwartzkopf's briefing of January 30, twenty-four sorties were needed to get one hit on a bridge. Not long after the briefing an RAF officer said that only one-third of the thirty-three bridges hit had actually been destroyed, so it took seventy-two attack sorties to destroy one bridge, indicating a success rate of rather less than 1.5 percent.

Pilots claimed 90 Scud launchers destroyed. The Air Force said later that the real number was zero. Of the 2,633 Iraqi Scuds destroyed, only 10–20 percent were hit by air-delivered munitions. Bombs and missiles were effective against big, fixed targets like power stations and refineries, not against stuff that could be camouflaged or moved. Carolling the triumphs of advanced weaponry in the gulf is not mere vainglory, since arms manufacturers are battling for procurement funds from a diminishing military budget.

➳

JULY 4 *Topanga*

NO ONE HAS ANY clear idea of how many Iraqis were killed by bombs and missiles. Among civilians the figure may well have been around 4,500, and though Schwartzkopf said 100,000 Iraqi soldiers may have died, this could be a considerable overestimate. The number of wounded Iraqi soldiers does not suggest losses of this magnitude. Prisoners of war from two Republican Guard divisions reported 100 and 1,000 casualties, respectively. The rate of desertion was also high, so there is no hope of ever resolving the matter with any pretense to accuracy.

As against the estimated 110,000 tons of bombs dropped by all 'coalition' forces in the Gulf War, the Allies dropped 3 million tons of bombs in World War II, and US forces dropped 4.6 million tons on Vietnam. General Schwartzkopf said that if the US-led coalition and the Iraqis had exchanged weapons the results would have been the same. Indeed, the Iraqis had many similar sorts of weapons. But aside from innovative tactics, what the US-led coalition had was the most potent weapon of all, the common sense of the Iraqi fighting man, who refused to fight. The left, mesmerizing itself with Defense Department handouts and arms company brochures, is forgetting – as Schwartzkopf did not – the maxim of Napoleon that in war the physical balance of forces is only 25 percent of the story; the rest concerns 'des affaires morales' – i.e., nonmaterial factors.

➳

JULY 10 *Topanga*

DAVID HOROWITZ AND PETER COLLIER: A couple of career opportunists who have been getting things wrong most of their lives, particularly Horowitz. He started life as a Trotskyist and made a name for himself with a couple of books on the cold war, using the works of Fleming and others. Then he came back from London to San Francisco and joined forces with some people still operating under the name of the Black Panthers, at a time when everyone with a brain in the Bay Area knew that these so-called Panthers were thugs pure and simple. Amid Horowitz and Colliers' stupid alliance a woman got killed, and instead of blaming themselves, H. and C. have been blaming the left ever since.

Then they decided to become right-wingers and jumped on the Reagan bandwagon at more or less exactly the moment it ran finally out of steam. Since then they have gone around sucking money out of right-wing foundations in the cause of something called Second Thoughts. The less people have any interest in what they say, the crazier they've become, which is usually the case with self-advertising turncoats.

➤→

JULY 16   *Topanga*
BETWEEN 1941 AND 1945 some 30,000 Jews and 750,000 Serbian Orthodox were murdered in a Catholic crusade, and some 240,000 Orthodox forcibly converted. Aside from the rampages of the Spanish in the New World it was probably the most blood-stained religio-racial crusade ever.

With Pavelitch installed as leader, the zealous Catholics of Croatia knew their hour had come. The focal center for the forced conversions and massacres was a Franciscan monastery in Herzegovina. A memorandum presented to the United Nations by three exiled monarchist Croatians described how in 1942 one young student at the monastery won a prize in a competition to see who could slaughter the most Orthodox. He slit the throats of no less than 1,360 Serbs with a special knife and was duly awarded a gold watch, a silver service, a roast suckling pig and some wine.

Curzio Malaparte, the Italian fascist journalist, described in *Kaputt* how he visited Pavelitch in his office in 1942 and saw behind the dictator what appeared to be a basket of shelled oysters. 'Are those Dalmatian oysters?' Malaparte asked. 'No', answered Pavelitch, 'that's forty pounds of human eyes, a present from my loyal Ustashe in Bosnia.' The Ustashe were the Catholic Croat murder gangs and the eyes those of the Serbian Orthodox.

After the war, when the Yugoslav government was seeking to extradite organizers of these horrors from the United States and other countries the Catholic Church and other anti-Communist zealots attempted to portray the forced conversion campaign as something denounced by the Croatian hierarchy. This effort had some success, though its pretensions were utterly without merit. Archbishop Sharitch of Bosnia wrote an ode in 26 verses to Pavelitch and published it in the ecclesiastical papers of his own diocese, and those of Zagreb. It contained flights such as the following:

Embracing thee was precious to the poet
as embracing our beloved Homeland.
For God himself was at thy side, thou good and strong one,
so that thou mightest perform thy deeds for the Homeland...
And against the Jews who had all the money,
who wanted to sell our souls,
who built a prison round our name,
the miserable traitors...
Dr Ante Pavelitch! the dear name!
Croatia has therein a treasure from Heaven.
May the King of Heaven accompany thee, our Golden Leader!

Some Croatian ecclesiastics thought the zeal of some of the converters counterproductive. Dr Mishitch, the Bishop of Mostar, wrote to a colleague that though the time was indeed opportune to 'save countless souls' the sad fact was that 'outsiders' were spoiling the conversion program in his parishes by seizing newly converted Serbian peasant 'mothers, girls and children under eight', transporting them by rail to the station of Surmanci, 'where they were taken out of the wagons, brought into the hills and thrown alive, mothers and children, into deep ravines ... The sub-prefect of Mostar, Mr Bajitch, a Moslem, publicly declared (as a state employee he should have held his tongue) that in Ljubina alone 7,000 schismatics have been thrown into one pit.'

When it became clear that the Allies would win the war the organizers of the forced conversion campaign carefully stored the records and the treasure of their efforts. The state documents were placed in the Archbishop's palace in Zagreb and the gold from dentures, watches and the like – hidden under the deaf and dumb confessional in the Franciscan monastery (a Franciscan had been commandant of the death camp at Jasenovac).

After the war Pavelitch made his escape to South America where he lived openly under his own identity. His interior minister, Artukovitch, moved from a Franciscan safe haven in Switzerland to another in Ireland where he stayed for a year before going on to California. In 1986 this Eichmann of the Croatian conversion campaign was finally extradited to Yugoslavia. By then he was 86 and suffering from delusional paranoia. He was sentenced to death in May, 1986 but does not appear to have been executed.

Growing up in Ireland I knew a bit about Artukovitch. A brave scholar, and Protestant, called Hubert Butler, from a distinguished family in Kilkenny, re-fused to tolerate the propaganda line of the Catholic hierarchy, which was that the suffering of the Yugoslav Catholics under Communist Tito could be com-pared with the suffering of the Irish under British rule. Naturally no mention was made of the dreadful conversion campaign only recently concluded.

Butler had made journeys to Croatia in the war's aftermath, and translated many of the most damning documents. His research and writings form the basis for the foregoing. At a famous meeting in Dublin he rose to refute the Catholic apologists. The papal nuncio swept from the room. Butler was the subject of abuse in the Catholic press. So fierce was the vendetta that he was even forced to resign from the secretaryship of the famous Kilkenny Archaeological Society, which he had revived. Butler described the whole affair and his investigation, in an essay called 'The Sub-Prefect Should Have Held His Tongue', later published in his collection *Escape from the Anthill*.

➨

JULY 18   *Topanga*
Dear Mr. Cockburn:
Brutus Hamilton was the track coach at the University of California in 1946 when I was an undergraduate and a close friend of his daughter, Jeanne. Brutus had a reputation for impeccable integrity and was not a man given to jest or offhand remarks. It is inconceivable to me that Brutus could ever have made an untrue statement or taken license in stretching a fact.

This is what Brutus Hamilton told me then.

He had recently been in the British Isles and had talked with the head of his family, the Duke of Hamilton. The Duke told Brutus that he was both perplexed and amused by Rudolf Hess's uninvited wartime visit to his estates near the border in Scotland. The reason why the Duke was graced by this visit was obvious to him. He had met Hess officially in his capacity as Chairman of the British Delegation at The Olympic Games in Berlin in 1936.

The Duke was not even home at the time Hess dropped in on him. He was a Group Captain in the RAF and told Brutus he was in an underground control room in Whitehall. He further remarked that he had absolutely no political power, and said laughingly that if he had talked with Mr. Churchill about pulling out of the war, he probably would have been certified to Colney Hatch.

The Duke was amused that the Deputy Fuhrer would take an official, perfunctory meeting as a pretext to discussing state matters of a probably treasonable nature with him. He was perplexed to think that the second political leader of Germany could be so badly misinformed and deluded about the British political system as to think that a Duke merely by his social status could order or advise The Prime Minister in and out of wars. It was not only Hess. There was an opinion floating about that Hess appropriated the aircraft with Hitler's either tacit or expressed connivance. (This is my recollection. I do not attribute this to Brutus or the Duke.)

Sincerely yours,
George R.L. Green
Castellammare, California

JULY 25   *Topanga*

Dear Mr. Cockburn,

Please, please, please, receiving a letter from this part of the country may not necessarily imply a KKK assault upon an Unchristian heathen. My wife and I have been readers for years, possibly the only ones in the upstate, but who cares as long as we know you're out there, somewhere, hearing the different drummer.

Once we lived in N.C. (that's Northern California), Lakeport on Clear Lake, to be precise, where my dear wife of 37 years, a nurse, helped deliver more Indian babies than white ones, but we still lost! In those days the Lakeport rightwing postmaster hated my immigrant guts because besides the pinko school principal I was the only other subversive in town who subscribed to the *Guardian* which, during the hateful days of Vietnam, was enough to get my European balls exorcized. Yahweh, what glorious days!!

After I became assistant director of OEO for Lake and Mendocino counties (there's more woolly stuff), I became good friends with the father of one of the Indian babies my wife helped deliver, Ed Simon, a Pomo Indian. This letter concerns the white annihilation of the Pomo tribe:

Two Irish prospectors discovered quicksilver on Mount Konocti, Indian holy mountain of Clear Lake. They forced the Indian males at gunpoint to labor 16 hours a day in the mines and the stuff was picked up by mule trains from below. While the Indians sweated in the mines, one of the whites watched them with his rifle while the other, on a regular basis, went to the village to rape the wives and girls. One day, the Pomos called it quits and cut Finley and Kelsey in tiny little meat ribbons. Today their graves are located on a road intersection outside the town of Kelseyville.

When the news of the white demise reached the S.F. military authorities, the US army entered the fray. An iron ship was dismantled in San Francisco and hauled in parts by mule train into Lake County by either Hopland grade or St. Helena pass, and reassembled on Clear Lake, because the Indians, who had noticed the scouts sent prior to the campaign, had established sanctuary for themselves on an island in the lake. American soldiers assaulted the island and killed everything on it except the few who managed to hide in tall reeds. Today a boulder with a brass plaque recalls 'Bloody Island'! The iron boat was left to rust in the water and eventually sank to the bottom.

I believe Lakeport library has much detailed data relating to the murderous incident; I know Ed Simon (then Middletown res.) does, but he doesn't talk a lot.

Best wishes, best luck and many thanks,
Robert Stein
Inman, S.C.

JULY 27   *Topanga*

I ASKED THREE Southern California women (two of them from somewhere else, which is the usual average) about their notions of the typical Southern California man. They drew a portrait of a fellow with a great body, twenty-three different types of sneaker, a hi-fi system unworkable without an advanced degree in electronic engineering from Cal. Tech., enough toys to fill all portions of his garage not already occupied by the Porsche 912 or Targa, and an unquenchable appetite for talking about real estate.

I asked them who they went out with and it emerged that there was Jaime the sensitive Chicano teaching in Cal Arts and Jet who divided his time between construction work, hiking in the Sierra, and political work in the Salvadoran community.

Denise, a peppy young thing doing post-grad studies in tropical ecosystems at UCLA, told me she was going out with a surfer, and at last I thought I was going to hear tell of the sun-baked zombie of legend. But Cal turned out to be a sensitive fellow deeply involved in environmental activism both idealistic and self-interested since no surfer wants to swim around in sewage.

Cal had a friend who had just been attacked by a shark, and his reaction from his hospital bed to the reporters clustering round had been to denounce anti-shark hysteria as foolish and immoral. 'Hey man', he said, nursing his wounds, 'it was me who was in the shark's space, not the other way around.'

➛

JULY 30   *Ardmore*

ONE OF THE BIG broadcasting successes this summer in Europe has been Radio Finland's weekend newscast in Latin on shortwave radio. I picked it up at 11,750 kilohertz and understood about a quarter of it as the phrases hurried by: 'Germani limitem inter ipsos ... Poloni autem ... se iura minoritatis Germanorum in Polonia habitantium ... nationibus potentissimis ... nuclearibus ...'

The Slovenes themselves have made haste, amid celebrations of newfound nationhood, to declare an amnesty for collaborators with the Axis powers. A few hundred miles north the Slovakians are dusting off their own proud heritage, evoking the salad years of Father Jozef Tiso, Catholic wartime leader who Aryanized the property of Jews and arranged with Hitler for their transport to death camps farther north.

It's enough to make one yearn for the Austro-Hungarian Empire, which did impose upon large portions of Middle Europe some kind of transnational respect for minorities, as did the Communists in the postwar period now concluded. Of course, the Austro-Hungarian Empire didn't seem so great to many of its inhabitants. 'From the charnel house of the Vienna cabinet', cried Louis Kossuth in 1848, 'a pestilential air breathes on us, which dulls our nerves

and paralyzes the flight of our spirit.' Metternich's dominions were known as
the prison house of nations, and the saying was that forbidden books were the
only ones read and forbidden newspapers the only ones believed. On the other
hand, the Habsburgs did bring Sacher torte wherever they extended their rule.
They made a dessert and they called it peace.

➡

JULY 30   *Ardmore*
THOUGHT OF THE LATE George Vesel after my brother Andrew and I spent a day
with him in Monterey in the mid 1980s. As a teenager Vesel had stood, on June
28, 1914, in the main street of Sarajevo as the Archduke Franz Ferdinand and
his wife drove by. Then Vesel's schoolmate Gavrilo Princip fired the shots that
killed the imperial pair, bringing World War I five weeks later.

The Sarajevo conspirators were Croats, Serbs and Muslims, and they desired a nation in which the diverse people of Yugoslavia should live in free and
equal union. It was racism, not nationalism, that undermined Yugoslav unity
after the new state was set up by the Serbian King. Butler argues in *Escape from
the Anthill* that it was 'because nationalism lacked a philosophy that in the early
twenties it began to decay and racialism took its place. The first signs of this
degeneration came in 1923, when by the Treaty of Lausanne in exchange for
Turks from Europe over a million Greeks were moved from the coast of Asia
Minor, where they had lived for three thousand years. This ghastly crime was
committed so efficiently under the auspices of the League of Nations that it won
universal applause. What Churchill was later to call "the disentanglement of
populations" began to seem a sensible and modern way of solving finally an
ancient problem.'

In 1944 Churchill called expulsion 'the most lasting and satisfactory
method' of dealing with the 7.5 million Germans of the East. The Germans,
naturally enough, took a different view. 'To drive men out of their homes',
went the Exiles' Charter, 'spells spiritual death ... Hence we feel called upon
to demand that the right to one's home be recognized as one of the basic rights
given by God to man.'

In the midst of his reminiscences Vesel, discussing his plans for a book, asked
if I thought publishers would turn him down because he was a Jew. I said I didn't
think so. He was, said Vesel, the son of the chief rabbi of Sarajevo. When the
Emperor Franz Josef had himself once come to Sarajevo he had been welcomed
by dignitaries including Vesel's father, and then the Emperor had kissed young
George on the head. Vesel touched his bald crown at the memory.

AUGUST 1   *Petrolia, California*
Dear Mark,

I'm glad to hear you are organizing a book about Mark Boxer. At least it won't be pompous, unless you are planning a work of fiction. You ask if I have anything to contribute.

Actually I didn't see that much of him here in America. The first time was somewhere in the mid 1970s when I was renting a vast mansion, built around 1910, on Buzzards Bay, overlooking the western end of the Cape Cod Canal. Mark arrived for the weekend, bringing with him Jane Bonham Carter. I had a boat and asked them if they wanted to go fishing, which in this case meant rowing a couple of hundred yards from the house and bumping a line up and down on the bottom, hoping for flounder. Jane was keen on the idea, Mark less so. So we left him reading a book by the edge of the water and rowed off.

The fishing didn't go too badly and of course I was happy to be the seasoned commander showing Jane, whom I'd never met, how to put worms on her hook, free a fouled anchor and so forth. After two hours of this we rowed back with our haul and found Mark stamping up and down on the shore, gnashing his teeth. It turned out that he had been keeping us under very close scrutiny and every time our heads vanished below the side of the boat imagined we were embracing. It would have been pretty forward work on my part. What was actually happening when we disappeared was the unromantic business of me playing the Ernest Hemingway role with the worms and the hook, as Jane followed with keen attention. No good trying to explain this to Mark, Jane reported later. Fishing was off for the rest of the weekend.

Then, a few years later, jealousy struck again, this time from a different angle. Mark came to New York with Anna Ford and we all met up at a dinner party in some highrise overlooking the East River. At that time Anna, whom I'd never met, was just making the transition from newscaster to commentator and was eager to inform herself about the political situation. I think the 1980 elections must have been just coming up. While we were standing about having drinks before dinner she fixed me with an unwavering gaze and commenced detailed interrogation about the farm vote, possible defection of western governors and so forth.

Of course I was eager to show I had the whole situation at my fingertips, and held forth at length while Anna drank in my learning. Finally I remembered the Cape Cod fishing imbroglio and not wishing to excite Mark's fury again suggested to Anna that I introduce her to some heavy-hitter on the other side of the room. As I led her off I caught sight of Mark and was pleased to see that he was sunk in quiet conversation with Mary MacDougall and not glaring at me for suspect behavior.

The dinner passed off reasonably enough and at the end of the evening I rode down in the elevator with Anna and Mark, who both seemed in amiable spirits.

In the early hours of the morning Mark phoned in pitiable condition. No sooner had I said goodbye to them than Anna embarked on the most tremendous bollocking, accusing him of flagrant infidelity right there in the drawing room. All the time that I had imagined her following with unwavering concentration my sermons about the farm vote and the intriguing poll recently held in Des Moines, etc., Anna had in fact been monitoring the conversation, taking place at a distance of about thirty feet, between Mark and Mary MacDougall. If she actually heard any words passing between them it must have been one of the great eavesdropping feats of all time.

But words weren't the point. I gathered from Mark that it was the way, beastly, he had been talking to Mary that had caused offense, being the way Mark always talked to women, in that intimately conspiratorial fashion. Somewhere around 2 a.m. Anna had told him it was all over and why didn't he just bugger off, after which moment Mark had been pacing the streets until he called me. He was scheduled to come over to breakfast but never showed, so I assume he patched it up with Anna in time for his scrambled eggs. So that evening was the last time I saw him.

As ever,
Alexander

➤

THE GANG OF EIGHT should have read their Lenin, assuming copies of his works are still available in the Moscow public library. If you plan to seize power, then seize it. Don't sit around all day watching CNN and complaining that Boris Yeltsin is getting too much airtime.

The night before the Russian Revolution in 1917 many of the comrades began to shift around in their seats, saying maybe this wasn't the right time to seize power after all. Lenin walked halfway across the city in the middle of the night to stiffen the spine of the Bolshevik central committee. Maybe it would have been better if Lenin had stayed home in bed. That way we would have been spared the final, farcical outcome of so much tragedy and sacrifice: Western ambassadors supervising the restoration of constitutional order, while Boris Yeltsin thanks George Bush for his support in these difficult hours.

The Gang of Eight seem to have thought that it would all be an easy rerun of the way Khrushchev got dumped: solemn talk about the Motherland, tanks rolling into Red Square, a new line up on the reviewing stand while Gorbachev embarked on lifetime convalescence in a well-guarded nursing home.

As the Gang stated, 'Torrents of words and piles of declarations and promises only underline the scanty and meager nature of their [i.e., the Gorbachev crowd's] practical deeds.' True enough. 'Whereas only yesterday', the Gang's proclamation went on, 'a Soviet person finding himself abroad felt himself a worthy citizen of an influential and respected state, now he is often a second-rate foreigner, the attitude to whom is marked by either contempt or sympathy.' True, too.

And besides, the Gang said, there was all this sex and violence, which the statement described as 'the octopus of crime and glaring imorality.' The Gang felt outrage at the pass to which things had come.

What the Gang didn't have was a plan. They haven't had one since the mid eighties, in contrast to the liberal agenda of people like Gorbachev's old comrade-in-arms Aleksandr Yakovlev, who said, as he was being expelled from the Communist Party, 'Our task is to enter the international division of labor so that foreign investors accept us as a normal country, so that Western capital sees us as a place with laws. Our psychology here is still different. All the normal layers of society here were exterminated: the aristocracy, the merchants, business people. Now everything has to be built up again.' Come home, Prince Yusupov, all is forgiven. But this is at least a strategy.

All the Gang could offer in response was nostalgia.

The trouble is that even before it was willfully disassembled by reformers naïvely hoping that 'market forces' would come to the rescue, the old command economy was hopelessly constipated. In Stalin's time the planners were supervising allocation of about 300 essential items. By the eighties this had risen to more than a million.

Try to supervise the distribution of a million commodities of one sort or another and you've got bureaucrats shifting at least 10 million forms in triplicate from one desk to another. Their In and Out trays were the size of warehouses.

The Gang of Eight probably had the Tiananmen precedent in mind, but they didn't study the whole menu. When Deng Xiaoping and his colleagues decided to clamp down, they went all the way. They wouldn't have given a Chinese Boris Yeltsin the chance to harangue the crowd from a tank in front of the Gate of Heavenly Peace. But the Chinese leadership also had an economic strategy, embarked upon in the late seventies, which may or may not have much to do with socialism but which has now produced a growth rate of 10 percent, the highest in Asia.

The Gang of Eight had no strategy. They also had no sense of history. They didn't realize that whatever their economic travails, Soviet citizens cared passionately about the political reforms and had no yearning to turn the clock back. If they had been reading their Marx, the Gang would have known that, but then they were probably too busy watching CNN.

AUGUST 25 *Petrolia*

THEY SAID TUESDAY that the line in front of Lenin's tomb was longer than it had ever been, country folk visiting Moscow to catch a glimpse of the old fellow before they clear the mausoleum, pending conversion to a trade mart, Pizza Hut or some kindred symbol of the new dawn.

When Lenin was in exile in Zurich during the First World War, before the sealed train brought him back to Russia in 1917, he used to visit a restaurant frequented by bohemian types, Dada painters and poets, and low-lifers of one sort or another. A young Romanian poet called Marcu later wrote an account (to be found in Robert Motherwell's *Dada Documents*) of a chat he had with Lenin there.

"'You see", he said, "why I take my meals here. You get to know what people are really talking about. Nadezhda Konstantinovna [Lenin's wife, Krupskaya] is sure that only the Zurich underworld frequents this place, but I think she is mistaken. To be sure, Maria is a prostitute. But she does not like her trade. She has a large family to support – and that is no easy matter. As to Frau Prellog, she is perfectly right. Did you hear what she said? Shoot all the officers!"

'Then Lenin said to me, "Do you know the real meaning of this war?"

"'What is it?" I asked.

"'It is obvious", he replied. "One slaveholder, Germany, who owns one hundred slaves, is fighting another slaveholder, England, who owns two hundred slaves, for a 'fairer' distribution of the slaves."

"'How can you expect to foster hatred of this war", I asked at this point, "if you are not in principle against all wars? I thought that as a Bolshevik you were really a radical thinker and refused to make any compromise with the idea of war. But by recognizing the validity of some wars, you open the doors for every opportunity. Each group can find some justification of the particular war of which it approves. I see that we young people can only count on ourselves ..."

'Lenin listened attentively, his head bent toward me. He moved his chair closer to mine. He must have wondered whether to continue to talk to this boy or not. I, somewhat awkwardly, remained silent.

"'Your determination to rely on yourselves", Lenin finally replied, "is very important. Every man must rely on himself. Yet he should also listen to what informed people have to say. I don't know how radical you are, or how radical I am. I am certainly not radical enough. One can never be radical enough; that is, one must always try to be as radical as reality itself."'

That last line has always been one of my favorites, and I hope to be using it long after the last bust of the man Reagan insisted on calling Nikolai has been ground down to talcum powder.

AUGUST 26   *Petrolia*

AT THE VERY MOMENT in the 1970s and 1980s that capitalism was learning to be hyperflexible – to the cost of workers and peasants the world over – the Soviet Union became more rigid and inflexible. As I once remarked, to the great rage of many, the Brezhnev years were a Golden Age for the Soviet working class. But in terms of economic advance they were (just as the fifties and sixties were for their white North American counterparts). They couldn't last, and now those workers' sons and daughters will face diminishing expectations as neoliberal market norms take them by the throat.

Long since, the Communist Party became the expression of a corrupted elite, a spoils allotment system. Just as the allocation system presided over by Gosnab had become hopelessly unwieldy and choked up, so too had the party suffocated initiative and creativity.

After the Second World War Soviet industrial growth ran at an average of just under 10 percent a year through the 1950s. By 1956 Khrushchev was telling the West, 'We will bury you', and the words did not seem lunatic. A decade later the Soviet economy began to slow.

Now comes accelerating Balkanization of what was formerly the Union, strife between the republics, looting of resources by foreign powers, and extension of German influence up to the Urals meeting the Japanese coming the other way, in conclusion of what Hitler started in 1941. A year or two from now Boris Yeltsin may be able to stand atop the converted mausoleum and view the parade of new times: Soviet lumbermen under the command of Georgia Pacific and the Japanese; oil drillers bearing the standard of Conoco; long battalions of unemployed under the discipline of the Chicago School.

➤

AUGUST 27   *Petrolia*

THE SOVIET UNION defeated Hitler and fascism. Without it, the Cuban Revolution would never have survived, nor the Vietnamese. In the postwar years it was the counterweight to US imperialism and the terminal savageries of the old European colonial powers. It gave support to any country trying to follow an independent line. Without it, just such a relatively independent country as India could instead have taken a far more rightward course. Despite Stalin's suggestion to Mao that he and his comrades settle for only half a country, the Chinese Revolution probably would not have survived either.

It was Communists who spearheaded the fight for civil rights for black people in the United States in the 1930s; and without the threat of the Soviet model in the competition for the loyalties of the Third World, Truman probably would not have felt the pressure to desegregate the Army when he did, though of course there were domestic pressures on him too. Without the threat of the Soviet

Union there would have been no Marshall Plan. The CIA would never have retained my friend Ben Sonnenberg or sent Gloria Steinem to the World Youth Festival in Helsinki. Ben wouldn't have been able to tell the story in his wonderful memoir, *Lost Property*. There wouldn't have been ... Well, write your own list. There would never have been the International Brigades, the workers who had crossed the Atlantic or ridden the rails across Europe to Spain.

Outside a few enclaves of state-assisted capital around the world the trend-lines are now all down, as the tensions and desperation rise. For the future of Lenin's heritage we need only study what is happening in Yugoslavia and imagine those horrors on a far vaster and more savage scale.

➤

AUGUST 28   *Petrolia*

A COUPLE OF DAYS into postcommunism a friend of mine said he was off to the hypnotist to stop smoking. While he was at it, he said, he might as well get the whole Communist era wiped out as well. It would be soothing, a straight transition from Kerensky and the Duma to Yeltsin and the Russian Parliament, with everything in between a blur. Whatever happened to that nice Czar Nicholas? Collectivization, what's that? Joseph who?

Russians, hauling down the statues and cleaning out the mausoleum, seem keen on wiping out their history all over again, just as they have so many times in this century – very much the reverse of what Boris Kagarlitsky remarked to me in Moscow in 1987 as we chatted underneath a statue of a czarist general, a hero of Pamyat: 'People are crazy about history and eager to get the empty parts of the past filled in.' Four years later it seems to be ending with more chunks of history being sent off to the cellars.

Almost since the moment the Bolshevik-led soldiers of the Petrograd garrison, sailors from Kronstadt and the workers' Red Guards stormed the Winter Palace in the early night hours of November 8, 1917, tens of thousands of books – many of them covertly subsidized by the state – have been written in the capitalist West dedicated to the proposition that it was all a very bad idea, a detour from the proper course of history. This is an inane game. To say that the Russian Revolution was a bad idea is also to say that the First World War was a bad idea. In the latter case it was, but it happened; and because it happened, the revolution happened. The revolution wrought some bad things, but some good things too.

My father often talked to me about the If Only fallacy. Discussing the pact between the Soviet Union and Germany in 1939, he wrote in his memoir *Crossing the Line*, 'Nobody can judge whether an historical event, an order to an army, a diplomatic maneuver, was a catastrophe or otherwise unless he is prepared to say at the same time what *would* have happened if that thing had *not* happened. And since nobody is in a position honestly to make such a statement about what the alternative would have been, the question is in the nature of things unanswerable and otiose.'

It all happened, and at this juncture I'm reminded of what the Vietnamese Dr. Vien wrote: 'If a world front of capital is being founded, its counterweight, the democratic popular front on a world scale, is also in formation.' We have a history to carry forward, so long as we remember what Lenin said to the young poet in Zurich seventy-five years ago.

➤

AUGUST 29   *Petrolia*

THE WEEKEND THAT Gorbachev resigned as party leader and plumes of smoke began rising from party archives across the country I was at a conference on anticorporate environmental strategies, hosted in Los Angeles by Labor/Community Watchdog. There were plenty of intelligent, radical people there. There was much talk and analysis of the victory of Salinas de Gortari and the PRI in Mexico, about the need for internationalism and building of ties in the new era of the *maquiladora* and the unending corporate search for cheaper labor and laxer laws. I barely heard the Soviet Union or the collapse of the Communist system mentioned until I brought up the matter myself in the course of some remarks on the last day. A friend who'd gone that weekend to a conference of the Union of Radical Political Economists in upstate New York said the same thing happened there.

The Soviet Union's disintegration, the end to what electrified the world and horrified capital three-quarters of a century ago, didn't seize the imagination of these conference-goers (or maybe, for some in the older crowd, it was a matter of just preferring to talk about something else, because there wasn't too much to say).

➤

AUGUST 30   *Petrolia*
Dear Alex,

I met your brother Patrick in Baghdad, and he was kind enough to give me an hour of his time. I found myself very influenced by his interpretation of the war, his low casualty estimate, and his notion that the war was stopped by the Iraqi soldiers. In a week of traveling I saw only a couple of people who were clearly war wounded. On the other hand last week the Ramsey Clark operation was in town, and I had the bad luck to be given ten minutes to talk immediately following his fifty-minute oration. He and the lady preceding him assured the audience that the entire Iraqi industrial infrastructure had been destroyed and that it would take a generation to repair, and that more babies are dying of malnutrition now than died during the bombing, and so on. I had ten little minutes to make the anticlimactic remarks that we saw lots of industry in operation, that the public hospitals have half the beds empty, that one way or the other everybody is drinking good water now, and eating. It reminds me of the early days of the Vietnam War, there was an English exchange student in Berkeley who used to sit around and listen to the American pacifists lament to each other about how the poor helpless Vietnamese were being ruthlessly massacred, and then infuriate them by announcing, 'They're going to win, you know.' There is a certain kind of American pacifist who is willing to say that he is *against* US power, but can't stand the thought that that power is anything less than omnipower.

I understand you are living in Petrolia part of the time now. Say hello to the Paffs and the Simpsons if you see them.

Sincerely yours,
Doug Lummis
Tsuda College, Tokyo

➡

SEPTEMBER 1   *Petrolia*

'FOR AT LEAST eight years American law enforcement has been aggressively investigating the allegations of victims of ritualistic abuse. There is little or no evidence for the portion of their allegations that deals with large-scale baby breeding, human sacrifice and organized satanic conspiracies. Now it is up to mental health professionals, not law enforcement, to explain why victims are alleging things that don't seem to be true. Mental health professionals must begin to accept the possibility that some of what these victims are alleging just didn't happen and that this area desperately needs study and research by rational, objective social scientists.'

Kenneth V. Lanning, FBI

In the Fittanto case last year in Chicago, John Fittanto's five-year-old next-door neighbor accused him of forcing her to participate in the 'ritual abuse' and sacrificial murder of five girls. No forensic or physical evidence was ever found. Gerry O'Sullivan, co-author of the Committee for Scientific Examination of Religion's 1990 report, *Satanism in America*, and Paul Ciolino, a staff investigator with Komie and Associates, debunked the prosecution's key witness, Pamela Klein. Klein was then director of the Child Advocacy Center and a self-styled expert in Satanism and 'ritual abuse'. She'd been called in as an expert witness in several other abuse cases, two of them supposedly involving

'Satanic abuse'. The state relied on her so completely that the police were instructed by the State Attorney's office to turn over their investigation to her.

She was a fraud. Kleid has a $250,000-a-year consulting practice in Chicago, a new green Jaguar every year, and a partnership in England, where she was much in demand on the lecture circuit. Ciolino produced affidavits showing that parts of her resume were false; in sworn depositions both the BBC's 'Child Watch' staff and the Thames Valley Police Department claimed never to have heard of her.

An Illinois judge finally ruled that Klein was 'not a legitimate therapist', which was news in Britain, where she'd organized two large conferences on child abuse (featuring 'adult survivors' of Satanic cults), developed courses for the Police Staff College at Bramshill in Hampshire, and enjoyed an adulatory profile in *The Maidenhead Advertiser*. This was before twenty children were taken from their families in pre-dawn police raids in Rochdale, where no evidence of Satanism ever surfaced. Rosie Waterhouse reported in *The Independent* last September that over a six-month period, in Manchester, Yorkshire and Rochdale, fifty-two children had been rounded up and made wards of the court, ostensibly to protect them from a conspiracy of hell-bent abusers. The Satan scare spread from Liverpool to Manchester, Rochdale to Glasgow, and even to the Orkney Islands; Klein's English consultancy and a well-organized network of evangelical seminars paved the way.

Fittanto was acquitted on civil charges earlier this summer, but 'Satanic' criminal charges against him are still pending in Illinois. The Illinois state legislature, meanwhile, concluded hearings last week on a bill disallowing cross-examination of child witnesses. It also authorizes closed-circuit and videotaped testimony. In the last few weeks, five similar bills have been introduced in the North Carolina state legislature. The bills are designed to protect child witnesses, authorizing closed-circuit TV testimony and severely limiting cross-examination.

Satan-mongering is an industry of sorts, well-served by look-tough legal efforts such as these. But there are more concrete reasons for the epidemic daycare scare of the past few years. With daycare panics in more than a hundred cities across the country, the scare seems to reflect something more than the mischievous preoccupations of shut-ins, pay-TV preachers, and fundamentalists. Satan may be trying to subvert American families, but so is Washington. The result has been the erosion of the American middle class, and with it, the traditional ideal of the family nucleus.

Daycare is so much in demand because of the rising number of families in which both parents work. This is at least partly the consequence of the sharp increase in the ranks of the working poor that began with the Reagan era.

Some states' 'workfare' legislation actually requires poor mothers to place their children in authorized daycare centers while they work menial jobs. Their benefits are docked if they stay home with their own children, but if they hand their kids over to an institution, they can be paid to scrub floors by the state while the state pays the institution. Lesson: poor women raising their own kids are lazy welfare queens, but poor women raising somebody else's kids are gainfully employed.

➤

SEPTEMBER 2   *Petrolia*

DR. NGUYEN KHAC VIEN is one of the most distinguished figures in the Vietnamese revolutionary movement. Today, at the age of seventy-eight, he heads the Center for the Study of Child Psychology. Dr. Vien's militant career began in 1943, when he enlisted in the anti-French nationalist movement. Soon he joined the French Communist Party and spent two decades in France. A Trotskyist in the immediate postwar period, he rejoined the Communist Party in 1949, criticizing Tito and the Trotskyists, though apparently without the slanders employed by many of his party colleagues.

In 1963 he returned to Vietnam and joined the Communist Party there in a senior position. He edited *Études vietnamiennes*, regarded as a journal of high quality. By 1981 he began to agitate for reform of the party, sending a public letter to the National Assembly attacking the bureaucratism and Maoist heritage of the VCP. By 1986 he was writing hopefully of Gorbachev. Today, weak (for most of his life he has had one lung), highly articulate, Dr. Vien has continued to evolve his thought. This letter, from a translation published in *International Viewpoint* for April 15, was addressed to Nguyen Huu Tho, president of the Patriotic Front, explaining why he was not attending the meeting to discuss draft texts for the 7th Party Congress.

The party apparatus, Dr. Vien wrote, is today 'plunging society into disorder and preventing any development.' The reason: its direct hold on power. 'If in the past to join the party was to voluntarily join in its struggles and risk imprisonment, today it is no more than a way of getting promotion.' The population has lost all confidence in the party leadership, which, he said, with the average age in the Political Bureau at seventy-four, is rooted in the past.

Dr. Vien proposed a shift of functions from party to state, with mass retirement of those heading the party's various organs:

> The private economy is going to develop and foreign firms will invest in Vietnam. This is a tendency that cannot be resisted and which will allow scientific and technical progress and will permit some people to use their abilities. The national bourgeoisie and foreign capital are going to make an alliance to exploit the resources and labour force. To service this economic structure there will be a threefold apparatus: the apparatus of economic management; the state apparatus of govern-

ment (administration, police); and the cultural apparatus (which controls the media).

Now, from the moment when there is a market economy, profit is king, and talk of humanity is out of the window. Furthermore, humanity is not the hallmark of bureaucratic apparatuses. Faced with such an economic/political/ideological apparatus, which is both national and international (in that a higher cadre of this apparatus will consider him or herself at once as Vietnamese and as belonging to Mitsubishi, Toyota or Philips) the people must form a democratic front as the counterweight and defend:

- Democratic liberties.
- Social justice (to assure reasonable pay for the workers; avoid excessive social differentiation; assure education and health; defend culture).
- The environment.
- Peace.

Such a front, while rejecting armed struggle, must put to work all forms of democratic struggle to obtain, above all:

- The freedom of the press and of thought.
- Freedom of association to organize its own activity free from apparatus dictates.

It was through a constant 200 year struggle that the populations of the developed capitalist countries were able to establish a regime that we have wrongly qualified as 'bourgeois' democratic. Democratic liberties and social rights were torn from the bourgeoisie in struggle and should thus be called popular liberties, if the real meaning of the development is to be understood. If a world front of capital is being founded, its counterweight, the democratic popular front on a world scale, is also in formation. Our people cannot stay on the sidelines. It is not only in the so-called socialist countries that we have friends. The moment will come when limits will be imposed on the apparatus, which will be bound hand and foot, when the words capitalism and socialism will no longer have any importance. The democratic front will have changed its nature. Freedom of the press, of association, of petition, of demonstration, to strike and of election are the forms of struggle of our epoch; they are proven means that can lead to profound reforms.

➵

SEPTEMBER 4   *Petrolia*

I DIDN'T MUCH CARE for the theory and practice of 'outing' – exposing someone as homosexual, that is – when the subject first came up. Over the past couple of weeks the issue has gone critical with the fuss about the outing of Pete Williams, the ranking Pentagon flack and longtime associate of Defense Secretary Dick Cheney.

I called up my friend John Scagliotti, maker of the famous historical documentary *Before Stonewall*. The test for outing, John said, should be 'Has the person benefited from being in the closet in careerist terms, in the sense of actively pretending to be something he or she is not? There's a difference between a passive closet, in which you simply survive and hope for the best, and the active closet, which involves putting on a heterosexual mask and promoting yourself as such, which is in ethical contradiction to your actual life. You've made the choice. You're living an actual lie, bringing girls to the company ball and so on.

'So, think about a gay actor who has made the decision to advance his career by pretending to be heterosexual. But by doing that he is insulting and oppressing all those who are already out. Take Barry Diller, who is in a position of enormous power at Fox. Why doesn't he push for a gay and lesbian TV show, which I could produce, which would be a gay version of *In Living Color*? Now, no one wants to out little people, gay teachers and so on – unless gay teachers are publicly anti-gay – but I would out people who are gay and yet are promoting heterosexuality.

'I believe as a general proposition that people should come out. It would be better for them. But at the same time I understand that such a public coming out might hurt or confuse children, parents, etc. But just as there's a difference between being passively and actively in the closet, you can be actively or passively out. In the former case, you are publicly espousing a cause, and in the latter, passive case, you are attempting to live a gay or lesbian life within the limits of what's possible for you and not too hurtful to parents, children, etc. One of the reasons straight people don't understand outing is that they don't understand what it's like to be gay. It's all more complicated than they think.'

J. Edgar Hoover used the gossip columnist Walter Winchell to out Commies. Gossip usually has a repressive function in the mainstream press, which is why outing has to remain a subterranean, countercultural activity. Yet even in the counterculture, or at the level of the offbeat and unofficial, gossip always has the twin function of being liberating – letting the sunlight in – and repressive, in the sense of exposing the personal and the private, naming names and hurting people. Gossip represents visible fault lines at the social surface, reflecting subterranean, gradual shifts in our social attitudes. Although the liberating and repressive functions are both at work, given the structure of media ownership and control, the repressive function is usually dominant.

Outing, which itself is shifting from a kind of anarchic dada to something else, has clearly changed consciousness. Williams's boss, Cheney, has been compelled to distance himself from traditional Pentagon policy toward gay people, something he certainly would not have done, or been pushed toward by the press, before Signorile began the journalistic exercise of outing Williams. This does not mean that the repressive aspect of the practice could not easily become dominant, as the mainstream press would dearly desire.

➤

SEPTEMBER 5   *Petrolia*

AMONG THE BRIEFERS during the Persian Gulf war was a Navy man from the Defense Intelligence Agency called David Harrington. During his tour as a naval attaché in Moscow back at the start of the 1980s Harrington won first prize at the US/UK military attachés' drag ball, appearing in the humble vestments of a Russian maid. One US military attaché who witnessed Harrington's triumph says that he had had no idea how seriously some officers took the event. He merely borrowed his wife's nightdress. But others imported glorious costumery from Helsinki. On the big night a fleet of cars transported the gowned participants from their domestic quarters in central Moscow to a dacha on the outskirts. If the KGB had been on its toes, the cold war might have gone the other way.

➤

SEPTEMBER 6   *Petrolia*

MARGARET, A YUROK INDIAN I'd met in Los Angeles at a conference on the environment, invited me up to spend a day with her family at the mouth of the Klamath. She said they'd be catching salmon.

I loaded up my old station wagon, a 1964 Newport, and headed north toward Eureka. Down off the mouth of the Mattole, the river that flows past my front door, there were trawlers scooping up the salmon massed off the sandbar: fish politics in action. Salmon season had just begun, and these trawlers have a two-month window in which they are permitted to net north of Shelter Cove up to Trinidad. In practice this meant the Mattole and the Eel, rivers already under severe stress. They can't fish off the mouth of the Klamath because the Yurok, at some twenty-five hundred the largest Indian tribe extant in California, have recently won the right to fish the Klamath, and the trawlers are held south of Trinidad.

In the fish store on the way into Eureka, opinion was strong against the Yurok monopoly on netting in the Klamath. 'What makes them special?' the fishman asked as he filleted northern halibut.

I picked up Margaret in Arcata. We bought a few cases of beer and bowled north on 101. The highway wound through the coastal hills. At least three times this century, the place had been logged out, and except in some strips of state park, the trees were on the skimpy side. South of Orick I kept an eye out for a scenic rest area which, according to a memoir by his wife, Theodora, had once been the site of a cabin owned by Alfred Kroeber.

It's through Kroeber that the Yurok made their way in the world of learning, their lives distilled into monograph and footnote. In 1900, Kroeber, the father of academic anthropology in California, began a series of encounters with the Yurok that lasted many years. Many of these Q&A sessions were at this cabin formerly located in the scenic rest area where I was now peering under the hood of my wagon, trying to figure out why my brakes had stopped working.

Here, at the place known as Sigornoy, Kroeber would interrogate Indians, chiefly Robert Spott, a Yurok theocrat. Their conversations eventually had academic consequence in such works as *Yurok Narratives* and figured in Kroeber's dispassionate reflections on the supposed 'character' of the Yurok, scattered through various works. The Yurok were, he wrote on one occasion, an 'inwardly fearful people ... the men often seemed to me withdrawn.' Kroeber mused that 'for some reason, the culture had simply gone hypochondriac.' Kroeber never got around to mentioning that between 1848, the start of the gold rush, and 1910, the Yurok population in the region was reduced from about two and a half thousand individuals to about 610. Disease, starvation and murder had wiped out 75 percent of the group. It is as though an anthropologist studying the inward fears of Polish Jews never mentioned Auschwitz.

In his *Handbook of the Indians of California*, published by the Bureau of American Ethnology in 1925, Kroeber wrote that 'there is one Indian in California today for every eight that lived in the same area before the white man came.' Then he mused that 'the causes of this decline of nearly 90% ... are obscure.'

Kroeber, eager to dignify American anthropology in terms of 'millennial sweeps and grand contours', had little patience with the shorter chronological span encompassing the extermination of most of the Californian tribal groups he was presuming to study. As he put it, 'the billions of woes and gratifications of peaceful citizens or bloody deaths' were of no concern. He visited the desperate native Americans of California, writing these tranquil ethnologies, sometimes, after only a couple of weeks with a group, all but ignoring the end of history elapsing before his eyes.

This posture bothered some of Kroeber's professional associates. The linguist Edward Sapir wrote to him in 1938, 'You find anchorage – as most people do, for that matter – in an imaginative sundered system of cultural and social values in the face of which the individual has almost to apologize for presuming to exist at all. It seems to me that if people were less amenable to cultural and social mythology, we'd have less Hitlerism in the world.'

In the back of my station wagon I had the special 1989 California issue of *The American Indian Quarterly*, in which Thomas Buckley discussed Kroeber's attitude to the Yurok and his relationship with the Yurok aristocrat, Spott. Buckley described how Kroeber was once asked why he hadn't paid any attention to recent Yurok history and acculturation. Kroeber answered that he 'couldn't stand all the tears' that these topics elicited from his Yurok informants.

Not that Kroeber was indifferent to pain. He'd been through a fairly harrowing time in the century's second decade, suffering from Menière's disease and psychic ailments, undergoing some lengthy sessions with a Freudian psychoanalyst. He also corresponded with Freud himself. Kroeber's remark about the tears reminded me of a sudden outburst from Freud once, to one of his intimates, about the filthy and despicable lives of the people who ended up on his couch in Bergasse 19. There may be a secret text here. A fellow who had it from a Yurok once told me Kroeber was a closet gay and Spott was his lover.

Freud fortified Kroeber's addiction to the sweeping cultural judgment. 'Among other things', Kroeber wrote in his big work *Anthropology*, 'Freud set up oral and anal types of personality ... The personality of anal character is orderly, economical, and tenacious; or, in its less pleasant aspects, pedantically precise, conscientious, and persistent; miserly; and obstinate to vindictiveness ... Now, just as the anal-type description fits certain individuals quite strikingly, it seems to agree pretty well with the average or modal personality produced under certain cultures. This holds for instance for the Yurok of native California and their cotribes of the same culture. It holds also for certain Melanesians ... On the contrary, within Oceania, Polynesians, Indonesians, and Australians are wholly unanal in character, the Australians in fact standing at a sort of opposite pole of living happily in disorder, in freedom from possessions, and in fluctuations of the moment. And the Siamese are certainly oral if the type has any validity at all.'

Kroeber was basing his perceptions of the Siamese on the work of Ruth Benedict, who had never been to Siam but was keen on majestic generalizations about native traits, having begun her career by contrasting two American Indian cultures, that of the Plains bison hunters and that of the Southwestern Zuni and other Pueblo farmers, as being respectively Dionysiac and 'Apollinian' (to use Kroeber's spelling). During the Second World War, the US government commissioned Benedict to write a study of Siam and she responded speedily enough, stating in her book that much in Siamese politics and society could be explained by early child nurture, during which period infants were permitted to manipulate their genitals freely.

Spott was once reproached by his nephew for spending so much time with Kroeber, whose work didn't do the Yurok much good. 'Ah, Harry', Spott answered, 'white man hurt so much. We have to help him.'

The brakes on my station wagon were barely working at all, but the hills weren't too bad and we made decent progress up toward the Klamath, swinging west off the highway in midafternoon, down a smaller road, which eventually ran alongside the estuary inside the sandbar that all but blocked the river's mouth.

Like other Yurok families, Margaret's sons had scraped out a little landing at the estuary's edge, with enough space for a campfire and a small jetty. The whole expanse of the river mouth, about a mile across and a mile up till the river narrowed, was dotted with boats: white anglers with their fishing poles, Yurok with their 100-foot nets.

Margaret's two sons and her granddaughter were just pulling their nets when we got down to the landing stage. A couple of minutes later, Margaret's son Liam, back at the dock, was talking to me about the real predators of salmon, namely the Japanese and Russian factory ships with their drift nets, out across the horizon. Liam? I spend a few weeks each year back in Ardmore, County Waterford, my home village in Ireland, listening to fishermen with names like Liam complaining about rules that prevent them from fishing with monofilament nets such as the Yurok use, and also about the real predators, Japanese and Russian factory ships out across the horizon. I remembered that Margaret had told me that many of the Yurok had Irish blood in them.

We were all drinking Budweiser at a pretty rapid clip. Liam's brother Rex went out to haul another net with his fourteen-year-old daughter, Carrie. Carrie was smart and pushed her father around as he cranked up the Evinrude. 'Asshole' and 'idiot' floated to us across the ripples. They were pulling in a twenty-pound salmon, the first – and last, as it turned out – of the day.

Liam and Rex were delighted, since it would feed the family reunion down in Eureka on Labor Day Sunday. Carrie began to clean the fish, throwing the guts up to the birds. The overseers began to swing by. First a Yurok-appointed river cop checked out the length of the nets and recorded the catch. Then a young man from State Fish and Game landed to take a sample of the salmon's scales. From one scale, he told me, the biologists back at the lab could figure out how old the salmon was, its feeding and migratory patterns.

Out in the river, Liam was cursing an Anglo with a pole who'd hooked into his net. 'Cut your fucking line, asshole.' 'Fuck you.' Rex's wife and adolescent daughter joined us, and we went on swallowing Budweisers, the cans mashed down in the dirt in a way that would have bothered Kroeber in his analysis of Yurok anality. Rex's wife, Donna, who was mad at him for a whole series of specifically listed crimes, described how next morning she'd cut off Rex's dick, slice it up, and cook it for breakfast. An eagle flew overhead.

'See that eagle?' Rex said. 'Last week we watched him catch a fish and cook him. Down in the water he came, blam, and up he went with the fish and flew up and over to the sandbar and set that sucker down in the full sun. He flew up again, then an hour later he comes back and turns the fish over to cook on the other side. He leaves the fish for another hour, and only then he starts eating it.'

'Where's your Volvo?' Patricia, the teenage daughter, asked me.

'I haven't got a Volvo.'

'Well, your BMW, then.'

'I hate BMWs.'

'Well, Eric, I sure thought you'd be driving a Volvo.'

'You know how to hurt a man.'

The Eric thing became the running joke of the evening, and I was Eric, Albert, Hugo, Archie, William, as the hours slipped by. Liam said we should get driftwood from the sandbar. We chugged down in the dusk and began to collect. Liam said he could figure out what people were like from the notions they had of what the wood shapes represented.

'So, Eric, what's this?' He held up a piece of twisted wood, bleached out from a summer's sun.

'I think it looks like an egret's neck.'

Liam didn't say anything and went on picking up driftwood.

Back at the landing stage, as the fire burned higher, the boys converted a couple of Budweiser cans into dope pipes, knocking a little dent in one side, making a hole there. The smoker would put some grass on the hole, hold a match to it, and then suck through the top of the can. Between puffs, Rex told me about their battle a little less than a decade ago to assert Yurok fishing rights.

'We just started fishing with the nets. They said we couldn't and that we'd run down all the salmon stocks. So we said, How come the trawlers just the other side of the sandbar can fish out the salmon with nets and we can't? And of course that's the question they could never answer. We went ahead and did the netting, and then we started to sell them commercially. So they said we couldn't do that, and we asked, How come the trawlers can sell their catch just the other side of the sandbar and we can't? And of course they hadn't any answer to that either. So they arrested some of us, me among them, but in the end they gave up.'

'Wheee', shouted Margaret. She'd jumped into the water and was hanging on to the edge of the landing stage.

'Fuck it, Grandma', Carrie cried. 'You know you can't swim.'

Liam was describing how he'd been driving along a sandbar higher up the Klamath and an old white man had said he was trespassing on his land.

'So I said, Listen, old man, I'm a Yurok, and you're driving on *my* land. At that he leans down in his truck cab and pokes out a forty-four magnum, right at my chest. So I say, Pull the trigger, old man, and then I drive round him. Imagine.'

'I think we should bond', said Margaret, who'd hauled herself out of the water and was sitting by the fire. I said to Liam that maybe we should run down to the sandbar again and get more driftwood. We headed down through the twilight, past an abandoned motel on the north side, then a rock shape known as the Squaw. The actual mouth of the river was way over on the south side, nearer to the marina. Yurok fires spotted the north edge.

'I love being in this place', Liam said suddenly.

During the week, he worked in a lumberyard in Eureka. Earlier in the day, when we were driving up 101, Margaret and I had talked about the Columbus quincentenary. She said she was thinking of raising a memorial on Indian Island, where a massacre occurred in 1860.

In January of that year, a volunteer company of settlers formed in southern Humboldt because 'the fishing season was over and many men were out of employment.' After killing forty Indians along the south fork of the Eel River, they applied to be mustered into service (and thus paid) by the governor of the state. He refused.

The company 'thereupon met and resolved to kill every peaceable Indian man, woman, and child in Humboldt county', an executive decision recorded in Chad Hoopes's *Lure of the Humboldt Bay Region*. The Indian Island massacre outside Eureka duly followed, on February 23, 1860. One anonymous reporter of the time, probably Bret Harte, observed in its wake that 'out of some sixty or seventy killed on the Island at least fifty or sixty were mercilessly stabbed and their skulls crushed with axes ... Old women wrinkled and decrepit [*sic*] by weltering blood, their brains dashed out and enveloped in their long gray hair. Infants scarcely a span long, with their faces cloven with hatchets.' Though there was quite an uproar in the press and though Eureka was referred to for a while thereafter as Murderville, no one was ever brought to justice. The names of the killers were known.

Back at the landing stage, the party was beginning to break up. Liam and Rex hauled their boat out of the water and hitched it to the truck. I said I'd better drive alone, as I had no brakes and didn't want any Yurok companion to go flying through the windshield if I went off the road. 'Goodbye, Eric', they shouted, and they invited me to the reunion and salmon feast next day. Everyone headed south. For me it was relatively flat and easy going down through Eureka to Ferndale. I didn't want to try the mountains over to the Mattole in the dark with no brakes and slept in the back of the wagon amid Ferndale's Victorian fretwork.

Next dawn, through the mists and brilliant sun, I made my way home.

➤

SEPTEMBER 21   *Petrolia*

A MAN WORTH listening to on collaborators is the historian Moshe Lewin, author of original and prophetic works on the Soviet Union, and a Red Army soldier based in Lithuania after the war. From the University of Pennsylvania:

'The rehabilitation has nothing to do with what the Soviets did or did not do.

It has to do with the phenomenon of Lithuanian nationalists trying to recover their past and to restore pre-1939 conceptions.' Lewin said that since the rise of the Saljudis movement the terms in which the past is discussed have begun to frighten Jews, many of whom have left the country, as Lithuanian nationalists 'try to present whitewashed history, saying Jews were Soviet secret police and so on.'

Lewin described how upon returning to Lithuania after the war his military unit camped on a beautiful spot in the hilly countryside outside Vilnius. Later they found they had been camping on a mass grave of 100,000 Jews killed by special units of Lithuanian collaborators in 1942–43. Lewin began to gather accounts from survivors. The victims had been rounded up from all over Lithuania. One of Lewin's cousins had been among the condemned. Feigning death amid the corpses, she later made her escape to the Vilnius ghetto (itself liquidated in 1943) and reported what had happened, and how Lithuanians had been the killers.

Lewin had a friend who served in the NKVD, equivalent at that time of the KGB, as an investigator after the war. He heard much from this fellow about the process of punishment of collaborators: 'These guys [the accused] were not treated kindly. They were forced to confess. But these were bloody murderers. A collaborator is someone who sold people out, who gave his friends away; people who did it willingly. Someone who collaborated under menace, that's a different story; the petty collaboration, that doesn't interest me here. I'm talking about officials, secret policemen, killers.

'What's going on now is the phenomenon of recovering an ugly past. Even in Russia – restoring St. Petersburg. St. Petersburg was built on the bones of masses of people! Stalin liked Peter the Great for exactly that reason.' (Lewin's friend was later kicked out of the NKVD – 'police work was not for him' – and became a teacher, a pedagogue, winning the Lenin Prize for his pains.)

But while the Russians may have been overzealous in their prosecutions of collaborators after the war, it is also necessary to remember that not too much later the United States was mobilizing Nazi collaborators in assassination squads in the Baltic States. The strategy of using indigenous groups to kill foreign officials was begun during World War II, according to Simpson, when the OSS supplied thousands of pistols to partisans in France and Yugoslavia specifically for assassinating collaborators and German officials. By 1951 the CIA's chief of covert operations, Frank Wisner – who developed paranoid delusions, ultimately killing himself – estimated, according to Simpson, that 'some 35,000 Soviet police troops and Communist Party cadres had been eliminated by guerrillas connected with the Nazi collaborationist OUN/UPA in the Ukraine since the end of the war, and that does not include casualties from other insurgencies in Lithuania and the Muslim regions of the USSR that were also receiving aid from the United States and Britain.'

Explaining why Jews would have disproportionately favored the Communists in Eastern Europe, Moshe Lewin said, 'Jews like anyone who is not instituting pogroms against them. When the Lithuanians came in there were pogroms. When the Latvians, the Estonians, the Ukrainians, came in there were pogroms. When the Poles came in there were pogroms. When the Soviets came in there were not pogroms. Under Stalinism the net was cast very widely, and arbitrarily. It didn't involve nationalities as a matter of course. Stalinism was a microbe that killed anything in its path, but here is the difference. If I were a Jew in Lithuania during the war, I would have been killed. If I were a Jew in Germany, I would have been killed. In the Soviet Union, I might have been killed, but I joined the Red Army, I was a citizen, I didn't get caught in the net. In the Soviet Union Jews were citizens; by definition they were not condemned to die.'

➤

OCTOBER 10 *Petrolia*

Alex,

I have before me, as writers are wont to say, the October 7 issue of the *Nation*, the jump on Alexander issue. And I have a few thoughts on critic H.'s attack on your article on the attempted coup and your general attitude toward the 'big C' (that's Communism, not Cancer). This is something I have done some thinking about (I assume that doesn't make me much different from every other Leftist in the world). How do we think about what was the Soviet Union? What is the answer to critic H. when he says, 'What possible reason can there be for nostalgia at the closure of this abysmal system?'

Well, it depends on what time frame we are talking about, doesn't it? Is H. glad that the soviet experiment that began in 1917 came to grief? If not, then when did it start being an 'abysmal system', and why? It is one thing to welcome the failure of the coup, and quite another to try to understand exactly what went wrong in Russia, and what it means for the future of socialism in the world. H. offers no thoughts on either of those questions.

Was the problem Lenin's conception of the party? Was it Stalin's criminal confusion of ends and means? Was it some inevitable bureaucratic degeneracy of any triumphant revolutionary movement? Was it a failure to recognize the inevitable role of markets in human affairs? Was it, as Lummis thinks, the substitution of economic development for radical democracy?

This question goes back a long way. Emma Goldman split with Lenin and Trotsky in 1919, I believe, partly over the question of Kronstadt. And one could march right through the years, specifying who split when and why. I am not a scholar of the Russian Revolution, but there is a whole tradition of debate about what happened in Russia that every Leftist thinker knows a little about, and it

seems wrong to me to try to talk about recent events without some reference to
that 70-year-long 'conversation'. Now that the whole thing is over, are we going
to forget all those arguments?

My own view is that the key error was the substitution of the party for the
working class as the agent of history. The Revolution began to ebb when the
slogan 'all power to the soviets' was replaced by 'all power to the party'
sometime in the early 1920s. The beginning of Thermidor was the CP destruction of the soviets. This is not a Trotskyist position by the way – Trotsky
supported the Party versus the Soviets, I believe. I think this position makes
me what is called a Council Communist, with intellectual roots in Gramsci (who
I never read), Luxemburg (who I read with pleasure), and Arendt, of all people,
who has some terrific things to say about all these questions, but who is not often
considered part of the Left conversation. Another way of stating this position
is that Lenin's idea of the party was too undemocratic to nurture a revolutionary
movement from the bottom. It was good for seizing power, but not for building
revolutionary working class power. Trotsky later in his life, sometime in the
thirties, put it like this: 'The Dictatorship of the Proletariat becomes the
Dictatorship of the Party becomes the Dictatorship of the Central Committee
becomes the Dictatorship of the Dictator.' (The Old Man had a way with words.
I don't think this was a development he foresaw, but he understood it when it
happened.)

But if a Leninist party cannot nurture real revolutionary power among the
people in a post-revolutionary world, we are in a bad fix. Because it seems very
hard to achieve the first steps in a revolution (seizing state power) without one.
I don't know what to say to this. Before the recent events I would have said that
revolution in the First World would not look like the seizing of state power, but
like the breakup of state power into little units of local power (soviets all over
the place). But 'current events' make me less sanguine about the abilities of the
local units of power to get along – to say the least. Of course one could answer
that the local units of power must be democratic ones, not like the Croatian
National State. I don't know.

What does H. have to say about any of this? Would he say that this whole
debate is out of date? These questions are not rhetorical. I really don't know.

As to the four points around which he frames the debate with you. Jesus
Christ, the way he talks about them, you would think nobody in the world ever
thought about these questions before. Actually there are three points in his
argument: Russian foreign policy, the role of the American CP, and Spain.
About Russian foreign policy he is mostly wrong – the Russians have been a
shield from some good things happening in the world (Cuba, Vietnam) although
that doesn't mean that at the same time they didn't do a lot of dirt (in the name
of getting along with the imperialists). This was the very first political discussion
we ever had together. I think I said that the Russian shield was just the product

of a bipolar world and that in any bipolar world small powers might be able to take advantage of big power rivalry. You gave me some historical answer to this, and I was convinced at the time, but I can't remember it now. Actually, on this question I like Perry Anderson's argument at the end of his book on 'historical materialism'. He said something like this. Stand the traditional Trotskyist view on its head. (The traditional trot view being that domestically the Soviet Union – a worker's state, degenerate tho it may be – was worth defending, but internationally that state was reactionary.) Well, Anderson argued (he wrote it in the '80s I think) that currently the situation is reversed. Domestically the Soviet Union has become a horror, but internationally it supports movements against American Imperialism. As to the second issue: the American CP. Very much a mixed bag. What year are we talking about? Arguing about their role in the labor movement and the civil rights movement would take more than a couple of sentences. On the question of Spain I agree with H. and the Trot view. We talked about this before when we argued about Orwell.

So what have I said? It is easy to cheer the defeat of the coup. Everyone (or almost) around the world is doing so. But if you are rooted in a Left tradition, or in a socialist tradition, then while you cheer the coup, you are obliged to tell us what went wrong in Russia, because supposedly we were all champions of the Russian Revolution when it began.

That's point one. Point two is this. For a political development to deserve our unmitigated praise you would think it would not only have to do away with a bad thing, but lead to a better thing. Where are the changes in Russia and Eastern Europe leading? Early indications are not good. What does H. say about that? 'They [the Russian and Eastern European people] will discover the limits of nation and capital in the same way as we have – by experience.' (This argument is a more sophisticated repeat of the infamous Stalinist slogan about Hitler, except this time it goes like this: 'After Yeltsin, Us!') Leaving aside the empiricism of the remark (people don't learn just by experience, they have ideas in their heads that lead them to interpret their experience in this way or that) the question is: 'when, baby, when?' As long as the Spanish had to wait to learn about (and get rid of) Franco? Because of his eagerness not to have any second or third thoughts about what is happening in Russia, H. falls into what I consider Marx's greatest intellectual 'mistake' (one that he shared with all the liberal 19th Century political philosophers): the idea of progress. That is, somehow, some way, things are going to get better.

What if most Russians and Eastern Europeans are now going to live in dramatically worse conditions and suffer intermittent ethnic civil war for the next two generations? And after that no promise of anything better? Sure we could still say that the CP bureaucracy got its just deserts. And we could champion that. But we wouldn't be quite so joyous about it. (By the way, I see every indication that most of the old bureaucracy is going to survive in a privileged position under capital – the capitalists will use them as middle managers – and only a few of them are going to get their 'just deserts'.)

This is what I was trying to say so inarticulately on the phone, when I was talking to you about the coup. I am almost always for people against tanks (Almost!). And surely it is a good thing that the coup failed. But, my god, what a horrible situation when the choice is between Stalinism and capitalism. And that was the choice in the last go around in Russia. A pox on both their houses, I say. All power to the soviets.

> *And all the best to you,*
> *Frank Bardacke*
> *Watsonville, California*

➤

OCTOBER 21   *Berkeley, California*

THE WORST URBAN FIRE in California's history: I drove last night across the Bay Bridge from the San Francisco side at around 9 p.m. and met the warm, slightly acrid smell of wood smoke about halfway over. Directly ahead, through the superstructure of the bridge, I could see a glow up the hillside, red at its heart and then darkening into a smoky crimson at the fringes, like a Turner watercolor.

The airports around the bay were reporting near-zero wind velocity, and though this meant that humid sea breezes weren't blowing in from the Pacific, the flames were no longer being whipped by Northeasterlies – Santa Anas – coming in from the Central Valley, through the canyons and ravines at forty to fifty miles an hour, driving down the humidity as low as 10 percent, leaving acre after acre of some of the highest priced real estate in Northern California ready to explode.

The neighborhoods of Claremont, Montclair and Rockridge contain expensive houses, creeping up the hillsides, perching over narrow ravines, patchworking themselves up toward the ridges. Decade upon decade the Bay Area's realtors have grazed off the dreams of the upwardly mobile. The Claremont Hotel itself, featured all through Sunday as the point of desperate resistance to the fire's westward march, was completed in 1908 as a giant billboard to advertise the joys of high-priced East Bay real estate. Realtors would put up clients in the hotel as their homes were being built. It was right here, around 1910, that exclusionary-use zoning was born. The fortunes of those now homeless from the blaze – the old rich, the new rich, those who inherited and those who amassed their wealth in the Reagan-Bush years – were points on a speculative curve that began to rise a century ago.

Earthquakes tend to favor the rich, whose houses have secure foundations. The shacks and tract houses of the poor jump off their piers and break their

backs. After the Loma Prieta earthquake of October 1989, which rippled out
from its epicenter in the Santa Cruz mountains, one could see clearly in a town
like Watsonville how prudent but necessarily more costly foundations could
save a house. The rich in the Marina district in San Francisco who lost homes
did so because the real estate industry had exploited unsuitable landfill and
because budgetary cutbacks had reduced maintenance crews capable of turning
off gas mains and the like. But though one would not have known it from most
of the press, the rich were not the prime victims of Loma Prieta. Fires hurt the
poor more too. People are always being burned alive in tenements, though the
news stories are always about wildfires menacing big homes.

⇒

OCTOBER 23   *Berkeley*
THE VILLAIN OF THE HOUR is the eucalyptus, a name whose etymology ironically
evokes covering, concealment, even protection. The state's geographic ecology
– Mediterranean chaparral – is fire-adapted, with many plants and trees
requiring intense heat for the germination of their seeds. In the natural order
of things fire is essential for processes of regeneration. In former times the
landscape had to wait for lightning or spontaneous combustion. Today a
cigarette or campfire ember does the job.

Eucalyptus globulus was first imported from Tasmania in 1856 as an orna-
mental curiosity. Within a quarter of a century it had become the object of a
speculative mania. There were already worries about a timber shortage. The
speculators touted eucalyptus plantations as a means for selling both land and
wood. In Southern California the trees were planted as windbreaks for citrus
plantations, in Central California as sources of fuel, furniture and timber.
Railroads saw the quick-growing wood as a raw material for ties, and the bark
was advertised as a cure for malaria. The University of California issued a
handbook about the tree's virtues.

The eucalyptus bubble burst just as Bay Area real estate was beginning to
boom. It turned out that there were more than 700 species of eucalyptus, and
the species blanketing California by the millions was the wrong one. The twisted
wood was commercially useless. Oily and volatile, it was also a serious fire
hazard. A cold snap could make it die back, leaving a dried-out trunk and leaves
as a natural firebomb.

The eucalyptus of California claimed its first major disaster in 1923. A freak
snowstorm left broken branches strewn about, and an ensuing fire burned down
half of Berkeley. Only a change in the wind saved the other half. The neighborhood associations in places like Montclair and Rockridge failed to study the
pyrophoric history of the eucalyptus. As the East Bay fire was raging I heard a
well-informed citizen on a call-in radio show say that these associations made

rules strictly limiting the cutting of such trees, along with other timber and shrubs. No doubt their members cherished the sense of wildness in their urban sanctuaries. The trees protected, embowered, soared in the gray-green silhouettes of *rus in urbe* and became the agents of inferno.

A dry eucalyptus doesn't so much burn as explode. That Sunday afternoon and evening the fire leaped from tree to tree, all parched as paper on a hearthstone. In the end some 1,770 acres were incinerated and with them more than 3,000 houses and apartments. The beautiful and the vulgar blazed alike, wood-shingled structures with shake roofs built by Maybeck, many of whose masterpieces went up in 1923; spec palaces of more recent vintage. One mansion shown extensively on television as it fell to the flames, and perceived by many to be a venerable pile, turns out to have been raised within the year and was still awaiting its owner. To these costly residences, crammed up the hillsides, the fire trucks could scarcely penetrate and when they did the firemen stood with dry hoses in their hands, the reservoirs already emptied.

➤→

OCTOBER 24   *Berkeley*
DICK WALKER, WHO TEACHES at U.C. Berkeley, outlined to me some of the social geography of the disaster. His neighbor came by looking for decongestants. He was sheltering a refugee, Rand Langenbach, an architectural historian and co-author of *Amoskeag*, an elegy to the nineteenth-century mill town of Manchester, New Hampshire. At 1:30 that afternoon Langenbach – someone who had campaigned fiercely to protect earthquake-damaged brick buildings from the wrecker's ball – had watched helplessly as 35,000 photographic slides of nineteenth-century buildings burned blue when his house went up and, as was happening all around the East Bay, his history turned to ash.

No one will ever know – though the insurance adjusters will get nearest the truth – how much history went up in smoke. In the days that followed I heard of one major private collection of pre-Columbian objects that had gone, of some libraries stuffed with rare things. Fire is final. Even the ancient history submerged by such dams as Aswan exists beneath the waters. But a pot once carried by an Aztec, a vase from the Ming Dynasty, are forever gone. And that abrupt termination of their presence on earth and in history has poignancy. Here was the Aztec pot, entombed, uncovered, smuggled, bought, resold, hoarded in its East Bay fortress, traveling down through time in all its manifold reincarnations, suddenly volatilized at 1,200 degrees Fahrenheit, conclusively part of *temps perdu*.

NOVEMBER 5   *Petrolia*

Dear Mr. Cockburn:

I am writing you to inform you that in the most recent edition of *Utne Reader* your name appeared in a special section which, in an attempt at humor, sought to depict a cartoonish 'American Political Landscape', in which you were portrayed as a risible and marginal extremist.

I am telling you this because I assume you don't read such frivolous and self-indulgent periodicals as the *Utne Reader*. I only receive it because it was given to me as a gift (a kind, but poor, choice on the part of some of my friends).

Perhaps this information will incite you to launch some invective against this contemptible neo-theosophist, consumerist publication.

I have been enjoying you for four years now. You are the only columnist that I know of in this country who consistently reveals and analyzes the contradictions of current political dialogue. My friends and I greatly appreciate your column.

With respect,
Allen Frank
Bloomington, Indiana

I looked. I get the *Utne Reader*. Allen is correct. It's one of those colored maps *Esquire* used to be fond of. I'm in a sort of sewage color, at the bottom, next to Lyndon LaRouche. Chomsky appears in a green swatch next to the environmentalists, which seems unfair, considering that I write about the environment and co-authored a book on the Amazon.

➤

DECEMBER 1   *Petrolia*

CALIFORNIA REPRESENTATIVE Bill Dannemeyer is up here in Humboldt County addressing several hundred local businessfolk mustered at the Eureka Inn.

'We should understand', Dannemeyer told the crowd, 'that this environmental party has in its objective a mission to change this society, to worship the creation instead of the creator. You have to understand their theology. I can't prove this by empirical analysis, but my gut reaction to their thoughts is simply this: If you go through life and you don't believe in a hereafter and all you see before you today are trees, birds ... if anybody begins to consume those things, you can get excited about that because it's your whole world. And this is where the militancy comes.'

To be an environmentalist is to be pagan, like the Druids assailed by both Romans and early Christians for rites amid the sacred groves. To cut down a tree is somehow a Christian act.

1973, Dannemeyer told Eureka's business people, was the year the Endangered Species Act was passed; also the year abortion rights were guaranteed at the federal level.

'That same law on the books today results in the death of more than 1.5 million each year', Dannemeyer exclaimed. 'The Endangered Species Act is in business for protecting the lives of animals, little critters and birds.'

The theological construct unleashed by Dannemeyer upon the massed denizens of the Redwood Empire is based on God's word:

> And God said, Let us make man in our image, after our likeness: and let them have dominion ... over all the earth, and over every creeping thing that creepeth upon the earth ... Be fruitful and multiply, and replenish the earth and subdue it. – Genesis 1:26–28

In a famous 1967 essay, 'The Historic Roots of Our Ecologic Crisis', Lynn White Jr. interpreted this text as meaning 'God planned and fashioned all the natural world explicitly for man's benefit and rule: no item in the physical creation had any purpose save to serve man's purposes.' White concluded that 'we shall continue to have a worsening ecologic crisis until we reject the Christian axiom that nature has no reason for existence save to serve man.'

In the nineties, in *Tikkun* for March/April 1990, Jeremy Cohen discussed the passage from Genesis, keen to prove that rabbinical interpretation of the verse displays Judaic environmental consciousness embodied in the notion of *bal taschit* – rejection of the 'needless destruction of anything.' But the rabbinical exegesis he quotes would not have been shocking to Dannemeyer, since it casts the preservation of trees within the construct of utilitarian militarism:

> When in your war against a city you have to besiege it a long time in order to capture it, you must not destroy its trees, wielding the ax against them. You may eat of them, but you must not cut them down. Are trees of the field human to withdraw before you under siege? Only trees which you know do not yield food may be destroyed; you may cut them down for constructing siegeworks.

➤

DECEMBER 14   *Petrolia*

AMID THE FIFTIETH ANNIVERSARY of Pearl Harbor, the press has been full of discussion of whether Japan should apologize for the surprise attack. Excluded has been any scrutiny of US diplomatic and trade offensives against Japan, commencing with the London Naval Treaty of 1930 (denying Japan naval hegemony in its own waters) and culminating in the August 1, 1941, total US embargo of all shipments of oil to Japan and the terms for Japanese trading subordination as laid down by the Americans in the Hull-Nomura talks. Also shunted swiftly out of sight has been the issue of US guilt for dropping nuclear bombs on Hiroshima and Nagasaki, not to mention the thousand-plane air raid launched after the Japanese surrender had been announced, though not yet officially received. Secretary of War Henry Stimson recorded that it was 'appalling that there had been no protest over the air strikes we were conducting against Japan which led to such extraordinarily heavy losses of life.' He thought 'there was something wrong with a country where no one questioned that.'

This season brings another anniversary, about which remarkably little has been heard. It's generally reckoned that US intervention in Vietnam began thirty years ago, on December 11, 1961, when, on the orders of President Kennedy, two companies of thirty-six Shawnee helicopters and 370 officers and men of the US Army, together with seven T-28 trainer combat planes, landed in Saigon.

In fact the United States had begun its unofficial intervention before the ink on the 1954 Geneva Accords was dry, but in 1961 the descent into the vortex began in earnest. In June of that year came the mission of Eugene Staley, president of the Stanford Research Institute. The Staley Plan as disclosed by the North Vietnamese in 1962 (though scanted by the 'Pentagon Papers') called for 'pacification' of South Vietnam within eighteen months, sabotage of the North, displacement of up to a million peasants into 'strategic hamlets' and new 'prosperity zones' in the Mekong Delta.

By January 1962, as Kennedy's counterinsurgency expert Roger Hilsman later regretfully noted in his book *To Move a Nation*, by a 'tragic error' US planes had bombed a Cambodian village. The error was duly rectified when the correct Vietnamese village was bombed, with severe loss of civilian life.

Eleven years later the United States withdrew, leaving behind three destroyed countries and about 2 million dead. Apologize?

1992

➤

The Argument

IN WHICH I am discovered in dispute over *JFK*. The notion of a conspiracy
attacked; a member of the Warren Commission interviewed; first sighting of Bill
Clinton in New Hampshire; the Clintons' friends and circumstances in Arkansas discussed; the mystery of Mena; a bizarre conversation with Web Hubbell's
son-in-law; earthquake in Petrolia; flight of Euclid; a gang manifesto for
post-riot L.A.; Jerry Brown and his flat tax; fury of the chess players; the
Republicans in Houston; why Chomsky grinds his teeth; Prozac and the
invention of a depressed America; the impossibility of liking Clinton; his world
foretold. Of the search for happiness, by conspiracy resolved, by ballot box
achieved, by Prozac induced, I sing.

JANUARY 1   *Topanga, California*

THE STONE AGE ARTISTS used true paint, it turns out. The cave paintings near Tarascon in the Pyrenees had a red made from the iron oxide haematite. Black came from charcoal or manganese dioxide. The extender which made the paint stick to the wall and not crack was from four different minerals – potassium feldspar with biotite was one recipe.

They planned the paintings carefully, starting with charcoal sketches, and they were created over long periods of time.

➼

JANUARY 3   *Topanga*

WHETHER J.F.K. WAS KILLED by a lone assassin or by a conspiracy has as much to do with the subsequent contours of American politics as if he had tripped over one of Caroline's dolls and broken his neck in the White House nursery.

Of course many people think otherwise, reckoning that once it can be demonstrated that the Warren Commission was wrong and Oswald was not the lone killer, then we face the reality of a rightist conspiracy engineered to change the course of history. (After the first hours, the idea of Oswald as a leftist conspiracy of one or more has perhaps fortunately never had the popularity one might have expected.) This is the view taken by Oliver Stone.

The core of this vision of history is put by Kevin Costner in his role as New Orleans District Attorney Jim Garrison:

> We have all become Hamlets in our country, children of a slain father-leader whose killers still possess the throne. The ghost of John Kennedy confronts us with the secret murder at the heart of the American dream. He forces on us the appalling question: Of what is our Constitution made? What is our citizenship – and more, our lives – worth? What is the future, where a President can be assassinated under conspicuously suspicious circumstances, while the machinery of legal action scarcely trembles? How many political murders dis-

guised as heart attacks, cancer, suicides, airplane and car crashes,
drug overdoses, will occur before they are exposed for what they are?

Stone wrote those words himself (and at one point even planned to have the
ghost of J.F.K. appear to Garrison as he stood in his kitchen making a chicken
sandwich while watching news of Bobby Kennedy's assassination). It's an
important passage, for in its fascist yearning for the 'father-leader' taken from
the children-people by conspiracy, it accurately catches the crippling nuttiness
of what passes amid some sectors of the left (admittedly a pretty nebulous
concept these days) as mature analysis and propaganda: that virtue in government died in Dallas, and that a 'secret agenda' has perverted the national
destiny.

➡

JANUARY 5   *Topanga*
OLIVER STONE LOOKS upon the assassination as the coffin of all the bright hopes
of the early sixties. To get a truer insight all you have to do is go to a junkyard
or an auto museum and look at the colors. Bright hopes were really being born
in the mid fifties, with Detroit palettes of desert rose, aqua, even paisley. By the
time of the New Frontier the colors had darkened into the dreary greens, tans
and drab blues of combat. With their prophetic three-year lead times, the
colors told the story. Kennedy had betrayed the hopes of people like Stone
before he had stepped off the inauguration stand.

Kennedy, having fought the 1960 election partly on an imaginary missile
gap, then acted as if this missile gap were genuine. In his vivid account in *High
Priests of Waste*, Ernie Fitzgerald suggests that the military spending surge of
the Kennedy years definitively undermined all rational standards of productivity and cost control achieved in the preceding seven decades (though an old
autoworker from the Chrysler plant in Newcastle, Indiana, once remarked to
me that such declines could be traced back to the cost-plus contracts of the
Second World War). The idea that Kennedy was methodically tilting toward a
full-employment civilian economy is preposterous.

The real J.F.K. backed a military coup in Guatemala to keep out Arévalo,
denied the Dominican Republic the possibility of land reform, promoted a
devastating cycle of Latin American history, including the anticipatory motions
of the coup in Brazil, and backed a Ba'athist coup in Iraq that set a certain
native of Tikrit on the path to power.

Thomas Paterson, the editor of the 1989 collection *Kennedy's Quest for
Victory*, put it well. Only out of respect for history 'emerges unpleasant reality
and the need to reckon with a past that has not always matched the selfless and
self-satisfying image Americans have of their foreign policy and of Kennedy as

their young, fallen hero who never had a chance. Actually, he had his chance, and he failed.'

➡

JANUARY 16   *Topanga*

A YEAR AGO THIS MONTH, most American reporters had cleared out by the time the first bombs began to fall on Baghdad. The first week in January the Al-Rashid Hotel was stuffed with news people; then, as the January 15 deadline drew near, the numbers swiftly thinned out.

Marie Colvin of the London *Sunday Times* recalls this deadline eve as 'a moment that made one think. I remember watching Patrick Tyler of the *New York Times* and Scott MacLeod of *Time* … packing their bags and checking out. The atmosphere was conspiratorial. They'd say, "We have information Iraq is going to be bombed. You're mad to stay."'

The Americans told their European colleagues that their editors were getting calls from the White House telling them to get their people out. 'I really believe', Colvin says, the Administration 'didn't want anyone to report what was going to happen. They themselves didn't expect a low body count.'

Many of the American correspondents had arranged for their home offices to send code phrases such as 'The baby is being delivered', which would signal the bombing was about to start. These phrases began to come in on the night of January 16. Demoralization increased.

Some American reporters tried hard to stay. Others were eager to leave, while protesting that though they yearned to remain they were reluctantly following orders from home base. Two reporters from a current affairs show left, but their cameraman stayed. The two who left got him fired, but he was promptly hired by another organization desperate for footage. My brother Patrick Cockburn of *The Independent*, who stayed, remembers the cameraman spending a night in the garden of the Al-Rashid to film the bombing and lurching in at dawn, bitten by every mosquito in Baghdad.

'The result of the flight of so many journalists', Patrick recalls, 'was that the war was dehumanized. Most of the TV shots were going to be what the pilots were seeing. And despite the presence of CNN or ABC, TV is easily deniable. Anyone (i.e., government officials) counterattacking can produce lots of detail, which only a print journalist can refute.'

➡

JANUARY 17   *Topanga*

ON HIS USUAL REGIMEN of Halcion, the jet-lag drug, Bush flew to Hawai'i, jogged; flew to Sydney, jogged; flew to Singapore (very humid), held a news conference in full sun; flew to Seoul (very cold), played tennis with President Roh Tae Woo in 34-degree temperature on an indoor court; flew to Kyoto, played *kemari* (in which a flaccid deerskin ball is kicked about by elderly aristocrats); then back to Tokyo where the 67-year-old itinerant played doubles tennis with the Emperor Akihito and his son (lost 6-3, 6-3). Then, suffering a tummy upset and taking Tigan, on to the fateful rendezvous with Saumon Frais Mariné à l'Aneth au Caviar (pickled raw fish), which he consumed shortly before vomiting on the Japanese prime minister.

FEBRUARY 3 *Manchester, New Hampshire*

HAVING READ SO MUCH about recession-torn New Hampshire, I half expected, at the border crossing from Vermont near Lebanon, to encounter scenes reminiscent of the Soviet Union: throngs clamoring for bread, Jeffrey Sachs handing out pamphlets about the joys of a cauterizing plunge into the free market, whiskered peasants lofting icons of George III. Andrew Kopkind, John Scagliotti and I peered around hopefully, but all seemed placid. Hard times in the countryside exact a covert toll, mostly in the form of alcoholism, wife beating, child abuse and other versions of the pastoral condition. The most of sociological interest to be espied from Route 4 were hunter-gatherers ice-fishing in their little shelters on the frozen lakes.

Our objective was an Arkansas pig roast for Bill Clinton, organized by a couple who had moved to Meredith, an hour or so north along Interstate 93 from Manchester. Reporters and locals were mustered in force, swaddled in goose-down against the savage cold. A charred pig revolved slowly on a spit. Mary McGrory was interrogating one couple about stories of Clinton's expansive sex life. They said it didn't bother them. What about Gary Hart? That hadn't bothered them either. I asked them about J.F.K. What about a President sharing his mistress with a Mafia chieftain? They said that was probably a bit much.

Clinton and his wife, Hillary, arrived. He looks like a big frat kid, with a meaty face, poised on the verge of midlife bloat. Hillary is trim and very self-assured. The night before, in Bedford, New Hampshire, she'd been asked in a public meeting whether she thought a candidate's personal life was fair game. 'We've been hit with all kinds of accusations', she answered. 'The kind of accusations that are in the tabloids next to the people with cow heads and the like. In any marriage there are issues that come up between two people ... that, I think, are their business.' Then the payoff. If anything about marriage is important to the people of New Hampshire, she said, 'it's whether or not they'll have the chance to keep their own families together.' Prolonged and stormy ovation.

People will always cheer someone stomping the gutter press for unwarranted intrusion, even if it's the Marquis de Sade, a protective arm wrapped around Justine, beefing about the slanders and low talk put about by his enemies.

Journalists love Clinton. In a typical passage in the *Los Angeles Times*, Robert Shogan recently hailed his 'serious and well-documented problem-solving approach to national issues rather than dependence on traditional liberal formulas expressed in impassioned rhetoric and based on sweeping federal programs.' Item One on Clinton's proposed economic agenda is that emblem of the nontraditional, anti-porkbarrel way of thought: road building. More or less everything else turns to mush at the first encounter with reality.

Actually Clinton hasn't got an economic program; rather, rhetorical bric-a-brac courtesy of Robert Reich, Derek Shearer, Bob Kuttner and other up-thrusters last seen in Atlanta licking their lips at the prospect of traveling to Washington with Dukakis. Clinton has plenty of fine words about training, education and so forth. He says nothing about what those nicely equipped Americans will do once they leave the classroom and the training shop. The high-tech jobs supposedly the preserve of First World workers brimful of costly instruction might be done just as well and far more cheaply by Third Worlders. The reality of Clinton's 'good job' is some underpaid, nonunion checkout clerk in a Wal-Mart in Arkansas, burdened by a regressive sales tax and getting slowly poisoned to death by the toxins and kindred hazards of a state ranked by the Institute for Southern Studies as forty-eighth in environmental practice.

Clinton stopped pouring words into the faces of potential voters and came out with Hillary to stand in front of the pig. Then they went off. We took a closer look at the pig. The cold had kept it raw. Saved from trichinosis, we all headed down to Manchester.

➤

FEBRUARY 20   *Topanga*
THREE DAYS AGO, for the benefit of television viewers in Australia, I found myself squaring off on the subject of *JFK* against Fletcher Prouty and Carl Oglesby. Perched on a stool beside me in a Los Angeles studio was my ally for the evening, Wesley J. Liebeler, a sixty-year-old professor of law at UCLA. Originally from North Dakota and conservative/libertarian in political outlook, Liebeler was one of the staff counsels on the Warren Commission. Yesterday, after *JFK* got eight Academy Award nominations, and when Richard Heffner, a Rutgers professor who is also chairman of the motion picture industry's film rating system, announced in the *Los Angeles Times* that *JFK* marked the end of the Gutenberg era and the dawn of a new way of telling history, I drove up to Zuma Beach and interviewed Liebeler.

AC: What about the speed at which Oswald would have had to fire his

Mannlicher-Carcano? Critics of the Warren Commission say Oswald could never have loosed off the shots in so short a time.

WJL: The clock for the whole thing is the Zapruder film, which runs at 18.3 frames a second. The film shows only two shots striking the people in the car. A time fix on the first shot can't be precise, for reasons I'll come back to. But the time of impact of the second shot that struck is precise. That was at frames 312–313 of the Zapruder film. At frame 313 the head just explodes. Either at 312 or 313, which is practically the same instant. And that's the last shot for which there is any evidence of anything in the car being struck.

The first shot hit, in the view of the Warren Commission, between frames 210 and 225. The commission came to that conclusion based on the Zapruder film, which shows that at a certain point Kennedy was reacting to a shot. He raises his hands up. During part of that time the limousine is behind a road sign, so it can't be seen for about nine-tenths of a second. So you can't tell how long before the reaction the shot actually struck.

The House Assassination Committee (1978) said the first shot struck around frame 190, which is a little sooner, about a second. To establish the time frame the Warren Commission subtracted either 210 or 225 from 312, and divided that by 18.3. Let's say 210. This gives us 5.6 seconds. Take 313 and subtract 225, and divide that by 18.3 and that gives 4.8 seconds. So the commission said that the time lapse between the first shot that hit and the second shot that hit was between 4.8 and 5.6 seconds.

If we assume that three shots were fired, you have the question of which shot missed. The House committee concluded that the first shot missed. The Warren Commission never decided on the matter. The evidence is consistent with the proposition that the first shot missed. If so, all Oswald had to do was fire one more shot. So in fact he would have had from 4.8 to 5.6 seconds to fire one shot, not three shots.

AC: So, on that explication, he's waiting with his gun aimed. The car comes along, he shoots and misses. But there's no time fix as to when he might have fired that shot. It wasn't in the famous 4.8- to 5.6-second interval. He reloads and then fires the shot that hits the President in the neck between frames 210 or 225 according to the Warren Commission, or 190 according to the House committee.

WJL: Right. Now he has to reload (which takes a minimum of 2.3 seconds), work the bolt once and fire the third shot that's fired (the second shot that strikes). And he has, according to the Warren Commission, 4.8 to 5.6 seconds. That is even time enough to fire twice, which he would have had to do if the second shot missed. If, as the House committee said, the first shot that hit was fired at frame 190, then Oswald had 6.72 seconds to fire either one or two shots. That is 313 minus 190, divided by 18.3. There was enough time.

You know, people harp on about the Warren Commission, which is fine. But the House Assassination Committee confirmed every single finding that the Warren Commission made – every one, except on the conspiracy question.

AC: Well, what about that?

WJL: The only evidence for conspiracy that the House committee had was a Dictabelt tape that recorded police radio transmissions. That was discovered long after the event in a file cabinet in the Dallas Police Department. There were two different radio frequencies that the Dallas Police Department used to transmit messages back and forth among the police. Both those frequencies were separately recorded. The Warren Commission didn't know anything about this evidence. When you listen to the Dictabelt there's no sound of shots at all. But the House committee took this Dictabelt and gave it to an audio consulting firm in Boston that did an analysis and found some pulses. The Dictabelt had been recording from a motorcycle somewhere that had its microphone stuck open. The consultants claimed they could distinguish four different pulse phenomena, three of which could be made to correspond to the shots we've just talked about, if you pushed the first shot back to frame 190. And there was a fourth pulse.

So the consultants went down to Dealey Plaza, set up microphones, fired off rifles and established what they called an audio footprint, and said initially that there was a 50–50 probability of a shot fired from the grassy knoll. This was in September of 1978. Then in December, right before the House committee closed up shop on the hearings, the audio consulting firm came up with a 95 percent probability on this same shot. So on the basis of that evidence the House committee concluded there was probably a conspiracy, that there was a guy on the grassy knoll shooting, though he didn't hit anybody. Robert Blakey, the committee's chief counsel, then gave the Dictabelt to the Justice Department to be analyzed further. Later he wrote a letter to *National Review* saying that if the Justice Department's investigation of the tape didn't bear out the 95 percent probability of another shot, he'd retract the whole conspiracy theory.

Well, the Justice Department turned all this over to a panel of acoustic experts set up by the National Research Council. They figured out that sounds on both Dictabelts could be matched, and since the one had a time reference, they could fix the time frame on the other Dictabelt as well. The NRC acoustic committee then concluded that the sounds on the second Dictabelt were recorded more than a minute after the assassination occurred. So they didn't have anything to do with the shots in Dealey Plaza.

AC: The other thing that seems to cause people a lot of problems is the 'single-bullet theory' – the first shot that hit Kennedy and also John Connally.

WJL: The first shot that hit went through the top of Kennedy's back, came through the throat to the right of his trachea, didn't hit any bones. Governor Connally was struck right below the right armpit in the back. The bullet went down through his chest cavity, came out just below his right nipple, struck him on the back side of his right wrist at the joint, broke the wrist and came out the front of his wrist and entered his thigh, making a very shallow hole.

The pathology panel of the House committee and also the Warren Commission concluded that the damage to Connally was done by one bullet. Work it backwards. If his hand was on his thigh, which is consistent with the Zapruder film, you know that the bullet wasn't going very fast when it came out the underside of the wrist, which has implications about how fast it was going when it entered the wrist. If it had already gone through Connally's chest cavity and the President's neck it had been slowed down. A wounds ballistic expert testifying to the House committee established that there's a range of velocity within which a bullet will break a bone without hurting the bullet, provided it's not going too fast.

Warren Commission Exhibit 399 is the so-called 'magic' or 'pristine' bullet. It is neither one. It is in good shape, but eight of the nine forensic pathologists on the House committee medical panel agreed that it had gone through the President's neck or upper back and then inflicted all of Connally's wounds. Ask yourself where the bullet went after it came out of the President's neck if it didn't hit Connally. After coursing downward through the President's body, where it hit no bone to deflect it, either it's got to hit Connally, who is sitting right in front of him, or it's got to hit the car. It didn't hit the car.

The Warren Commission did a re-enactment of the assassination which showed that the President and Governor were located in a way that the bullet would have gone directly from the exit wound in the President's neck into Connally's back. The House committee used a different method of calculating the trajectory and unequivocally confirmed the Warren Commission findings that one bullet – CE 399 – did go through the President and inflict the Governor's wounds. The House committee said flatly that the trajectory it established supported the single-bullet theory.

Oliver Stone's treatment of this question is simply a lie, and he knows it. The House committee confirmed the Warren Commission's findings on this point without qualification. But with the conspiracy Stone has fabricated, the addition of the House of Representatives won't cause any further problems. He's got half the country in on it now.

I have challenged him to debate the validity of the Warren Report. Naturally he issued a press release saying he'd be happy to do it, but he never responded to me. He's engaged in scholarship by press release. I repeat my challenge.

AC: In the Zapruder film, at frame 313, when the second bullet strikes, Kennedy's head jerks back convulsively, and people have reckoned this implies a shot from the front.

WJL: If you look at Kennedy's head, right at frame 313, just as the bullet strikes it, it doesn't move backward. It moves slightly to the left and downward, just for two or three frames, which is consistent with a bullet striking it from behind, because the momentum of the bullet is imparted instantly.

Then shortly after frames 312–313 the President's body goes backward. The House committee said there are two explanations. One is the jet effect, caused by the skull and brain exiting and forcing the head back and to the left. Combined with that effect, the committee said, was a neuromuscular reaction. The medical evidence is the best way to determine the direction of the shots that hit the President. Take the skull. The entry wound in the back of his head is 'coned' on the inside of the skull. What can be constructed of the exit wound from the skull is coned on the outside. The House medical panel all agreed to these conclusions, and also that the wound on the President's upper right back could only be an entrance wound. Eight of the nine pathologists on that panel concluded that the President was struck by two *and only two* shots. The medical evidence excludes the possibility that the President was struck by a shot fired from any direction other than behind him.

AC: Why didn't the Warren Commission have access to the autopsy photographs and X-rays?

WJL: Warren didn't want to press Bobby Kennedy, who controlled them, for their release. The worst consequence was the idea that someone was trying to hide something. Without these materials the autopsy surgeons described to the commission their recollection of the wounds, and their medical artist drew the diagrams showing the entrance wounds in the wrong place.

AC: What happened to Kennedy's brain?

WJL: The brain was under Robert Kennedy's control when it disappeared. It is widely believed that he destroyed it. He was afraid that these materials might end up on public display.

AC: Do you think the Warren Report was flawed?

WJL: It was too oracular, overwritten. Also I think it relied too heavily on eyewitness testimony. The problem is that people will testify to damn near anything. So the commission had one eyewitness testifying that he saw Oswald sticking a rifle through the sixth-floor window ...

AC: But there was another witness next to him who saw Oswald and another man beside him.

WJL: Right. That's the problem. The only way you can avoid that is to look at evidence that can be replicated. Evidence that is here today, will be here tomorrow and 100 years from now: the autopsy photographs; the autopsy X-rays; the ballistics tests. The bullet that was found on the stretcher was fired from Oswald's rifle to the exclusion of all other rifles; the two big fragments in the car were fired from that rifle to the exclusion of all other rifles; that rifle was on the sixth floor of the School Book Depository; it had Oswald's print on it; there was a brown paper bag there that had Oswald's palm print on it; it was a long bag that would have held a rifle.

At this point it would be nice to have an eyewitness who said that when he gave Oswald a ride to work that morning he had the bag with him, and there was one.

But fine, never mind how the bag got there. We know it was Oswald's rifle because he rented a post office box and his handwriting is on the application; he ordered the rifle and his handwriting is on the paper he ordered the rifle with; he wrote out a money order and his handwriting is on that; and the rifle was sent to his post office box. There are a number of pictures of Oswald with a rifle. The House Assassination Committee, with improved enhancement techniques that the Warren Commission didn't have, was able to prove it was the same rifle. The negative was found and it had been taken from Oswald's camera to the exclusion of all other cameras. George de Mohrenschildt had a copy of that picture with Oswald's handwriting on the back. There's no evidence of tampering on the negative; the scratch marks are the same. The picture was taken six months before the assassination. We have photographic evidence, like the Zapruder film. On the Tippit shooting, we've got forensic evidence that shows clearly Tippit was killed by bullets from the gun Oswald was carrying when he was arrested. You can make out a good case just on the basis of the physical evidence.

Why did Oswald kill the President? The man was a malcontent, not happy, not stupid by any stretch of the imagination, but unhappy and discontented. I guess your typical liberal [laughs]. Not that. I guess he would have as much contempt for liberals as you or I. He was a revolutionary of one form or another. I drafted a psychological profile of Oswald for Chapter 7 of the report. It was reviewed by a panel including the chief of psychiatry at the Mayo Clinic, who threw my draft down and said, 'This is very interesting stuff, but it tells me a lot more about you, Liebeler, than it does about Oswald.' So how the hell do I know why Oswald killed the President?

➤

FEBRUARY 27   *Boonville, California*
BRUCE ANDERSON and Fred Gardner and I do our quasi-annual state of the nation show at the Casper Inn. I do a monologue on Clinton's hair, which goes down well. Fred sings his 'Here & There in Mendocino County'. Bruce savages the audience.

HERE & THERE IN MENDOCINO COUNTY

Where the Rossis sell the hardware
Where the faux professors raise goats
Where LP is waging warfare on the trees
There's a man going 'round takin' notes.

Who makes the beds at the inns out on the coast?
Who makes the breakfast they serve?
Who prunes the vines on the beautiful rolling horizon

Tell it like it is, brother, tell it like it is
Brother you got a lot of nerve.

Nailed Bosco for a sellout sellout sellout
And thAt quasi-fascist Crazy Jack
And the De Vallians so liberal so respectable so mellow
– An all too familiar pack

Here and there in Mendocino County you think you got it bad
But it's just the same nationwide
Hey, Bruce, where's the party, I'm ready tonight
Count me in one more time for the ride.

Here and there in Mendocino County you think you got it bad
But it's just like everyplace else
That's why it's good to know there's someone speakin' for me
Just muttering to himself.

Who makes the beds at the inns out on the coast?
Who makes the breakfast they serve?
Who prunes the vines? Who bottles the wines?
Tell it like it is, brother, tell it like it is
Brother you got a lot of nerve.

➤

FEBRUARY 28 *Petrolia*

STONE TRIES TO HAVE things both ways. He maintains that *JFK* is all true until someone demonstrates forcibly that it isn't. Then he tilts the other way and claims he is trying to construct an alternative myth. We should leave this 'alternative myth' talk to the deconstruction industry. Myth making is a two-edged sword. Disraeli promoted a Jews-run-the-world theory; not so many years later the authors of the *Protocols of the Elders of Zion* happily adumbrated the theme. The wizardry of the film lab, which can produce a grainy news film of L.B.J. making deals with the masterminds of J.F.K.'s assassination – part of Stone's mythic truth – can also produce Arafat urging Sirhan to kill R.F.K.

Every artist deals in myth, but anyone arguing for Stone's manipulation of history should be aware of the morally tricky terrain and of the downside of myth making. There's no 'golden key' (e.g., the 'truth' about the Kennedy assassination; 'proof' that George Bush flew to Paris on October 20, 1980) that will suddenly render the overall system transparent and vulnerable. People who look for golden keys are akin to those poor souls who thought history could be decoded by certain measurements in the Great Pyramid.

MARCH 13 *Petrolia*

SINCE AMERICANS CARE LITTLE for economic theory but know all about chemotherapy, Tsongas has adroitly conflated the two. Everyone knows someone who went through the pain and horror of chemo, threw up hour after hour, had their hair fall out. Now here's Paul Tsongas saying that the economy has cancer and has to have chemo. And who better to guide us through the pain than a man who has faced what all Americans fear and has (thus far) survived?

As a matter of preference, I hope Jerry Brown continues to prosper, given that he's the only candidate you could find yourself next to on an airplane without having to hide behind the in-flight magazine. Liberals get hung up on his flat-tax proposals on the grounds that it surrenders the principle of progressivity, which it does.

In an interview in *Challenge* magazine, Jeff Faux remarks that the problems with the US economy took on a structural cast in the early 1970s, when wage and income growth stopped. But just as growth was stalling, the Democratic Party began to steer toward economic conservatism, retaining a measure of liberalism on social issues. The assumption was that private enterprise would continue to deliver growth for the foreseeable future, and government should take a back seat.

Thus began a hostility toward government, reflected in Carter's own philosophy and campaign in 1976. Jimmy Carter actually lost his re-run for the presidency in 1980 back in December 1976. After his election, Democratic leaders in Congress came to him and offered a routine re-authorization of wage-price controls. Carter held a press conference in which he expressed opposition to wage-price controls and support for the free market to take care of any inflationary problems. So, in 1979, with the consumer price index rising at 13 to 14 percent, and things out of control, Carter could have stopped the hemorrhaging just the way Nixon did in 1971. Indeed, Carter threw away the government tool he had. If you look at the post-election polls of 1980, most people had voted against Jimmy Carter because of inflation.

A neoliberal Democrat opened the door to Reagan, and hence to all those Neanderthal judges and Republican bureaucrats. Accept the terms of the system, and you get the system.

MARCH 12 *Petrolia*

WE'RE LOOKING INTO Clinton's Arkansas background. On the question of Clinton's favors to his friends, Larry Nichols – the man fired by Clinton from the Arkansas Development Finance Authority, and the original source of the Flowers story – claims that connections to Clinton are practically a requirement for companies seeking loans from ADFA. ADFA, which grew out of an agency

offering low-interest loans for housing construction, was vastly expanded by
Clinton in 1985 to attract capital to the state for the purpose of economic
development, offering companies long-term loans financed through the sale of
tax-exempt bonds. And, indeed, names appearing in ADFA documents bear the
aroma of Clinton's circle. Among underwriters of the bond issues we have
copies of, Stephens Inc. features prominently. The company's chairman, Jackson Stephens, and his son Warren have helped Clinton raise more than
$100,000 for his campaign. In January the bank Stephens has a controlling
interest in, Worthen National, extended to Clinton a $2 million line of credit.
Another familiar name on the bond issues is the now-defunct Lasater and Co.
Dan Lasater, who headed the company, is a longtime friend of Clinton and his
brother, Roger. Both Roger and Lasater were busted for cocaine, the former
on a stiffer charge.

Then there's the Rose law firm, Hillary Clinton's firm, whose name adorns
both bond issues and loan agreement papers. Hillary Clinton has represented
a company owned by Stephens Inc. in litigation. Rose partner Web Hubbell
represented the recipient of the first loan that ADFA made, a company called
Park on Meter, or POM, whose name has cropped up in talk about Mena, the
odd airport in western Arkansas. Hubbell had been secretary of POM in the
early 1980s. Hubbell's client in the ADFA deal was Seth Ward, Jr., the current
president of POM, known as a friend of Clinton. The Worthen bank appears
among institutions that have from time to time had liens on POM.

Then there's the drug-smuggling trail that leads to Mena, the town and
airport in western Arkansas. Clinton can't claim ignorance of the fact that
Arkansas served as a nexus for international drug operations. One of his state
prosecutors, Charles Black, brought this to his attention in 1988. For five years
before that there was a federal investigation into drug money laundering in
Arkansas – an investigation joined by Clinton's own State Police. As part of that
a federal grand jury was assembled. This grand jury was eventually dissolved,
and the local press carried reports that members of the panel had been
prevented from seeing crucial evidence, hearing important witnesses and even
seeing the 29-count draft indictment on money laundering drawn up by an
attorney with the Justice Department's Operation Greenback. In 1989 Clinton
received petitions from Arkansas citizens demanding that he convene a state
grand jury and continue the investigation. Winston Bryant, now the state
Attorney General, made the subject of drugs and Mena an issue in his campaign
in 1990.

Yet with all this knowledge, Clinton has done nothing. The state Attorney
General does not have the power to conduct an investigation, but the state
prosecutor does. When Charles Black urged Clinton to allocate funds for such
an investigation, Clinton ignored his request. The State Police were taken off
the case after the federal government scrapped its investigation. Now the ball

is back with Clinton, and he continues to do nothing. Congressman Bill Alexander says that it was clear to him that the only thing holding up an investigation at the state level was the absence of a commitment toward funding. Last fall Alexander arranged for Congress to allocate $25,000 to restart an investigation in Arkansas. Since then the money has been held up behind a wall of bureaucratic excuses in Little Rock.

➨

MARCH 28   *Petrolia*

AT A CRUCIAL STAGE in the *contra* war in Nicaragua being sponsored by the Reagan administration, Governor Bill Clinton's personal creation, the Arkansas Development Finance Authority, made its first industrial development loan, in 1985, to POM Inc., a parking meter manufacturer based in Russellville, Arkansas. POM, it has been alleged, was under secret contract to make components of chemical and biological weapons for use by the *contras*, as well as special equipment for C-130 transport planes. Such planes were at that time ferrying drugs and weapons in and out of Mena, a town not too far away in western Arkansas. POM's lawyer during those transactions was a partner in the Rose law firm, of which Hillary Clinton was, and is, a member. Clinton's state thus appears to have been an important link in the *contra* supply chain at a time when military aid to the *contras* had been banned by Congress.

About a mile north of the airport in Russellville, on Highway 331, sits the headquarters of POM, a low building made of corrugated metal. POM – the common name for Park on Meter – has been at that location since 1976, when it bought the premises from Rockwell International. Back then POM controlled about thirty-six acres; a series of real estate transactions has since divided the land among other holders. And today, on a plot immediately northwest of POM's property, you can see a building occupied by the 354th Chemical Company of the 122nd Army Reserve Command.

We come now to Michael Riconosciuto, a former contract employee of the CIA who says he worked at Mena on and off between 1980 and 1989. Riconosciuto was arrested shortly after being named as a witness in the Inslaw Corporation's case against the US government for the latter's alleged unauthorized use of software Riconosciuto wrote for Inslaw. He was arrested on ten drug-related charges and has been convicted on seven. Riconosciuto claims he was set up. He is being held, pending sentence, in a county jail outside Tacoma, Washington. Federal prosecutors are seeking a life sentence under the new drug laws.

POM, according to Riconosciuto, was not merely in the business of making parking meters. He says that beginning in 1981 the company also made ferry drop tanks – i.e., external fuel canisters – for use on the C-130s. These tanks, attached to pylons on the wings and jettisoned when empty, are necessary to fuel long-range transport missions of the kind that would have been necessary in *contra* resupply/drug transport flights. While standard on military aircraft, they are virtually unknown in civilian use. Drop tanks are essentially nothing more than aerodynamic metal containers – well within the productive capabilities of a company set up to make parking meters.

By 1983, Riconosciuto says, it was clear to US intelligence that the *contras* were unable to inflict serious damage on the Sandinista troops and needed a tactical advantage – either through new technical equipment or through unconventional weaponry. To this end, he says, POM was enlisted in a project with Stormont Labs of Woodland, California, and the Wackenhut Corporation to develop chemical and biological weapons that could be deployed in guerrilla warfare, with POM assigned the task of producing delivery systems that could be easily carried and used by troops. Stormont confirms that in the early eighties it was approached by Wackenhut in connection with the development of biological weapons but denies anything went beyond the talking stage. Wackenhut denies any involvement with Stormont, POM or Riconosciuto.

According to Riconosciuto, the 354th Chemical Company, which even before leasing property across from POM had maintained a facility in Russellville, had an arrangement to provide POM with chemical agents once the prototype carriers for those agents had become advanced enough for testing. These were meant to be fairly simple devices – a hand-held grenade, a mortar shell, a small bomb – all of which could have been produced with the machinery on hand at POM.

Two years after entering into this chemical weapons project, by Riconosciuto's account, POM became the first company to receive an industrial development loan from the Arkansas Development Finance Authority (ADFA). This loan, for \$2.75 million, was rushed to completion at the close of 1985.

After speaking with a receptionist and her superior, who claimed variously that POM was and was not engaged in classified activities, my colleague Bryce Hoffman reached POM's president, 'Skeeter' Ward. Ward said POM had contracts with the military through US Atlantic Corporation and other intermediaries, and that details were classified.

He acknowledged knowing Bill Clinton socially but said he was not a friend. As regards POM being the first company to get an industrial development loan from ADFA: 'That is just not true.' Bryce told him we'd got this information from Bob Nash, ADFA's president. 'Well', said Ward, 'talk to their vice president. He's the one that handled the loan.' Bryce said we had the same information from him. Ward insisted POM had not been the first. All the ADFA records we have show that it was.

'And you say', Skeeter Ward exclaimed, 'that Web Hubbell and the Rose law firm handled our ADFA loan application; that isn't true either.' Bryce asked him why Hubbell's signature adorns the loan documents. 'You see, he is our corporate lawyer, and he's my father-in-law, so what'd you expect?' Bryce then asked Ward if he was manufacturing delivery systems for chemical or biological weapons. The parking meter manufacturer said this was ridiculous: 'What we make is re-entry nose cones for the nuclear warheads on the MX missile and nozzles for rocket engines.' Bryce told him there are allegations that POM also made casings for chemical weapons. When he denied this, Bryce asked about POM's affiliation with the Army Reserve unit across the street.

'Oh that? That's the armory. We don't have anything to do with them. I don't see how it matters anyway.' Bryce told him that it was not an armory, that it was a warehouse maintained by a chemical warfare unit. 'Well, see, someone's been lying to you again. That's just the Army Reserve.' Bryce informed him that it is, specifically, the 354th Chemical Company of the Army Reserve and added that all of this information had come from the unit itself (he had checked it that morning). 'Well, that's all news to me. Shoot, I'd have been a little worried if I'd known we had chemical weapons stored over there.'

Next, Bryce asked Ward if POM had ever manufactured aircraft drop tanks. 'No, we've never done any of that. I told you we made re-entry cones and nozzles. We have got a contract with McDonnell Douglas to make aircraft parts, but I don't even know what that's about.' Bryce asked how, if he did not know what kind of aircraft parts they made, he could be so certain that these did not include drop tanks. 'I don't know – but I know we didn't make those at all. Now you've got the truth, right from the horse's mouth.' In parting, Ward reminded us to put in a good word for his parking meters.

According to the Federal Aviation Administration, it is legal to use drop tanks on ex-military planes in civilian use (though it is illegal to drop them). Manufacture of the tanks is a different matter: legal but only with an FAA permit, and with the manufacturing facilities subject to inspection. POM is not among the FAA's authorized suppliers. When Bryce called the FAA in Washington, the official with whom he spoke apparently misunderstood his question on drop tank regulations and assumed he was a prospective manufacturer. 'Oh! So you must have one of those Southern Air Transport contracts.'

➻

MARCH 30   *Petrolia*
SADLY, I MUST REPORT the death of Harry, who loved to put his nose under women's skirts. His master, Ben Sonnenberg, commemorates him thus:

STAY

Harry 1981–92
I was a bad dog and didn't obey
Any command, until today.

APRIL 21   *Petrolia*

Dear Nation:

What we see [in Alexander Cockburn's interview with Wesley Liebeler] is a merging of the far right and the far left for entirely different agendas. Liebeler's operating principle is fairly simple and human: Cover your ass. Cockburn's is philosophical. His dialectic view of history precludes the possibility of individual choice affecting the outcome of events – thus, the very thought that Kennedy might have betrayed his capitalist upbringing by halting the war in Vietnam is unbearable. As Cockburn puts it: 'The effect of *JFK* is to make people think that America is a good country that produced a good President killed by bad elites.' While that is exactly what I believe, it's a veritable nightmare for Cockburn, who is convinced that a democratic country cannot be good, and could not elect a leader who wasn't merely another link in the inherently evil system.

As a selling point, controversy helps, but please, don't misinform the public in the name of commerce. The public is not stupid. As the polls show, a strong majority know the evidence does not support the fantasy that a lone nut shot and killed the President of the United States. Journalists (like Cockburn) and journals (like *The Nation*) should be our protection against official untruths. But in this unique instance, the media have bought wholesale the lies and distortions passed down from Washington. *The Nation* and Cockburn trivialize the event of November 22, 1963, by dismissing it as nothing more momentous than an accident. That will not do. As the record shows, Mr. Cockburn, J.F.K. did not trip on Caroline's doll. He was murdered – and history changed – by parties still unknown.

Oliver Stone
Santa Monica, California

Stone's admonition to me not to 'misinform the public in the name of commerce' is matchless effrontery. The film from which he stands to make millions is undoubtedly one of the most willfully error-riddled pieces of 'historical reconstruction' in the history of cinema. Like all demagogues Stone is now a full-blown megalomaniac given to such sentiments (announced grandly at a Nation Institute symposium at Town Hall) as 'Even when I'm wrong, I'm right.' So far as historical scruple goes, Stone makes Cecil B. De Mille look like Braudel. One of the most squalid aspects of the whole affair is that Time Warner plans to distribute 'documentary materials' about the assassination to schoolchildren.

In tune with the fascist aesthetic of his movie, Stone now mounts the traditional fascist defense: he, like Kennedy, is victim of a gigantic conspiracy, and 'the media have bought wholesale the lies and distortions passed down from Washington.' Passed down by whom?

But then whining has been a characteristic of Warren Commission critics down the years. Ever since the late 1960s they have successfully dominated debate, yet they still pretend that theirs is the persecuted and unpopular posture. I interviewed Liebeler because I think that the commission's conclusions, particularly in light of the 1978 House inquiry, are a good deal more plausible and soundly based than is commonly supposed. Most conspiracy mongers are either imbeciles or mountebanks, as I discovered when I did several months' research, back in the early 1970s, on the murder of Robert Kennedy. In that case the 'critics' couldn't even be bothered to find out which way R.F.K. was looking when he was shot. Absent this basic information, they invented another gunman in that crowded kitchen alley.

What was striking in the wake of the Liebeler interview was readers' outrage that I had presumed to take a Warren Commission lawyer seriously, coupled with attacks labelling me a Stalinist. (This latter term is being devalued with relentless speed. Before me is a letter savagely denouncing me as a Stalinist for my support of Jerry Brown.) But the commission staffers were conscientious people, of widely varied political opinion. They have been steadily libeled down the years, culminating in the oafish abuse by Stone, who espouses the most preposterous theory of all, aside from anything else requiring total suspension of disbelief, seeing as how not one among the several hundreds if not thousands party to this imagined conspiracy has ever surfaced, even on deathbed or in post mortem testimonial, to admit participating in the mighty plot.

Inference: because the credibility of the Warren Commission is low, its critics must be right. This claim is endlessly popular: 'Seventy percent of the American people now believe there was a conspiracy, the Warren Commission was wrong', etc., etc. According to a 1991 Gallup poll, 81 percent of Americans believe that the Bible is 'the inspired word of God'. Only 9 percent of Americans believe that man has developed over millions of years from less advanced life forms without divine intervention; 47 percent of Americans believe that God created man in essentially the present form all at one time within the past 10,000 years.

➤

APRIL 28   *Petrolia*
CATS AND DOGS SENSE an earthquake's imminence, or so they say. Euclid, orange tomcat, veteran of at least two major quakes, snoozed through that golden Saturday morning on my garden step, his mind on mice and dying squeak of captured vole or bird. The wind rustled lightly through the cottonwoods and willows alongside the Mattole, not sixty yards from Euclid's peaceful nose.

Across the river from my house, hanging over the road to Honeydew in far northern California, six hours' drive from San Francisco, is a cliff face some 300 feet high – a constantly changing testament to the subterranean upheavals that make this region the most seismically active on the North American continent. In the quiet of night I lie in bed and often hear the rattle of stones tumbling down this cliff as, far below, the North American tectonic plate strains against the Gorda plate to its north and the Pacific plate to its west. The region is Elysium to geologists. This summer will see 2,000 Friends of the Pleistocene swarming over the Coastal Range, chipping away with their hammers.

Back at the start of March there'd been a shake. I was up in Oregon at the time and got back to find that the tremor had shoved the sewage pipes up a few inches and thrown the water out of the lavatories, a well-known portent of Satan's arrival if you believe the infernal guidebooks. I reckoned then that the earthquake account for 1992 had, so to speak, been settled and that Petrolia was in the clear for a year or so. It rained for a few days after that shake. Dirt and trees slipped down the cliff face, and all day long our remote valley echoed with the crunch and grind of bulldozers and their cautionary whistles as they backed up to take another bite out of the shale at the foot of the cliff. I began to take daily photographs to see, at the end of the month, how much had moved without one noticing. Time's footfall can be so stealthy: a tree, already sprawled at an angle on the cliff face, dropping a couple of feet; a tail of scree starting higher on the hill. A few years ago some artists began rephotographing the Western vistas taken by Jackson and other pioneers who had lugged their 8x10s over the mountain ranges a century earlier. The artists worked out a complicated formula to get their own cameras and tripods in exactly the same positions as the ones adopted by their predecessors. I used to gaze at the old and the new vistas side by side. Often they seemed exactly the same until, somewhere in the new frame, I would realize that a rock had rolled a few feet or yards, a tree was missing, a scarp subtly altered in contour, and there was the sense of some immensely leisured, tranquil calibration of infinity.

No stone rolled down the cliff that Saturday morning, and I left Euclid snoozing on the old redwood step, about 10:50 a.m., and headed off over the bridge to Lighthouse Road, which runs along for two or three miles south of the river, through to the mouth of the Mattole and the northern tip of the King Range. I stopped off at Jim Groeling's place – a fine barn he's fixed up – to discuss some architectural drawings with him. We looked at his stone fireplace, cracked horizontally about six feet off the ground from the March quake, and moved over to a drafting table.

The first spasm seemed like a pistol crack but was perhaps a board or beam snapping, or just the urgent creak of wood under extreme pressure. There was a pause, and I saw Jim looking at his fireplace. Then it came again, and the barn shook like a dicebox.

One, two, three, four seconds. It didn't stop. We jumped for the door. It stuck for a moment and then we were outside. 'Shit', said Jim, 'I only just took out earthquake insurance.' There's a limbo period before the policy cranks in.

We took a step back toward the house and the ground shook again, strongly. Later a radio interviewer from KQED asked me if I'd been frightened and I said, truthfully, no, adding that maybe I was just too slow and stupid. I've been in hurricanes on the Florida Keys and there's plenty of time to flirt around with fear. The radio keeps telling you that the eye of the hurricane is here or there, getting nearer anyway, and you try to figure whether to leave the windows open a crack or tape them, and you remember that the highest point of Key West is only sixteen feet above sea level and how the great hurricane of 1936 caught a train halfway up the Keys filled with refugees from Key West, drowned them all, and you can get nervous. The earthquake is nowhere, everywhere, gone. Later people spend hours reconstructing that brutal transition from the nowhere to the everywhere, when nature can destroy you.

Jim and I walked back through his house. The windows were sound, the fireplace worse. His shop was a mess. But nothing of what we could see in the landscape around us spoke of serious damage. It was like Bruegel's painting of the fall of Icarus, about which Auden wrote his great poem about suffering and the Old Masters. Only we couldn't perceive that bit of the panorama in which Bruegel had shown Icarus drowning. We couldn't sense that a few hundred feet above us up the ridge, David Simpson and Jane Lapiner's house had shaken apart, that rocks had thundered down the cliff face opposite my house, that a mile to the north at the precise moment that I was spreading out the blueprints on the hood of my car to continue our conversation, an overturned coffee machine in the Petrolia store had already started a blaze that would finish off the store and the adjoining post office in about forty-five minutes.

Gaby Cohen came bowling down Jim's driveway in a truck. A boiler had fallen over; they couldn't close off the water. Did I think that maybe under my house the gas line from the propane tank had fractured, that gas was accumulating, that the pilot light was on? I thought of no such possibility. Driving to the bridge, back toward my house, I saw a black plume of smoke. This was the first time I felt a stab of personal anxiety. Was it my place? The road twisted and turned; I got my bearings and realized it was farther north and west, probably in the town itself.

It concentrates the mind when you find yourself approaching a final few yards round a bend, up a driveway, not knowing whether your house is up or down. Mine was up. The windows were whole. The redwood garden step was empty. I remembered my father describing to me what happened after a German V2 rocket had hit our house in St. John's Wood in London during the Second World War. My mother and I were evacuees in Cumberland, a few hundred miles north. My father was out. The cat was in sole occupancy. The rocket destroyed the house and blew the cat's fur off. Returning home from work, my father met the poor creature, who fled at his approach. Who to blame for the explosion? In the cat's mind there was only one candidate. As the Gnostics feared, God had turned out to be on the wrong side.

Bomb blast does famously strange things. My mother used to lament the heavy marble table blown to powder by the V2. Yet till the day she died she put the tea tray down on a lighter table that had survived next to the heavy one that hadn't. The quake had been similarly sportive. I have seventy-five-pound lead weights on my stereo speakers. They had been tossed four feet away. A glass pitcher on a wooden divider had moved five inches. Nature had been absent-mindedly destructive, sparing a glass bowl, breaking a clay pot from New Mexico, kicking over a hurricane lamp, above all leaving the house up on its blocks which, a year before, had been underpined with bell-shaped concrete piers sunk in the earth, strengthened with rebar and crowned with metal ties holding the house down. In 1989 the Loma Prieta quake had a force of 7.1. This new one was rated at 7.0. Memories of that earlier quake lay on the floor as I walked through the house: porcelain survivors of 1989 done in by 1992, along with two cups I had bought in Cork on the eve of my mother's death and of Loma Prieta, smashed in a final appointment in Samarra. Every now and again the house would shudder in an aftershock.

I drove into town. At the bottom of the black plume was the Petrolia store, now almost gone, with picture-book red flames licking its remains against the backdrop of the coastal hills and a foreground frame of eucalyptus. The firehouse, a few yards to the right, was intact, its crew away at a firefighting clinic in Guerneville, a couple of volunteers squirting water in the direction of the store. Later the person from KQED asked me to 'describe the town of Petrolia.' I said there were a few houses, a school, a church, a community center and the store. The focal point was the store, now volatilized by Fahrenheit 451 on upward. No gas, no milk, no friendly chats with Cynthia, Renée, Trish.

Renée walked by, pale and shaken. A woman in a Camaro pulled up. She'd been driving over the Wildcat, the route from Ferndale forty miles north over the mountains, and the quake had blown her off the road. There were rock slides everywhere. I had to leave later that day and asked if the road was drivable. People do what they always do in disasters. Silent staring, action updates, hash and rehash of the moment when. Talk as stipend, comfort and anesthetic. I took some photographs of the dying store and the living firehouse beside it. Back at my house I finally remembered to turn off the gas.

I drove along the north side of the Mattole, up toward Conklin Creek to see if Dan Weaver was O.K. I knew his wife, Tally Wren, was away in Garberville. The road was very bad and I had to get out of the '67 Chrysler 300 to clear rocks. Nature, aside from the mess in the road, seemed only slightly askew. It would take a hard rain to reveal what toll had been taken in terms of weakened banks, loosened trees, masses of earth or stone kept back by only a root or snag. Dan, who had stood in the kitchen through the quake holding the doors of his glass cabinet shut, said the dogs had taken it badly but the horses had danced.

On the hearth lay a big undamaged crucifix from Mexico amid the fragments of a glass candlestick. An hour later Tally came walking up the driveway. She'd been trying on a bra in Changes in Garberville and had run out in the street with her shirt open. The road back hadn't been a problem.

I cleaned up, talked to my neighbor Carlos Benemann, who also has a house in Ferndale. He described the mess over there, and how the Best of the West horse parade had ended ten minutes before the quake hit. A woman had fallen off her horse and broken her pelvis, the worst casualty. Then at 7 p.m. I set off on the drive to San Francisco. The earthquake finally registered on my nervous system. Fifteen miles south of Garberville my eyes began to close and I pulled over and slept for half an hour. I had to take two more roadside breaks and got into the city at two in the morning, taking off for Texas at dawn.

➤

APRIL 29   *Houston*

TALLY CALLS FROM my house. There'd been another quake at 4 a.m., a 6.5 shock. My place was O.K. David and Jane's house was definitely gone and they were in their new barn, cynosure of the Mattole, originally intended for horses below and dancers above. Emergency crews and supplies were flooding into Petrolia, but there weren't too many customers. Tally had told them there were plenty of homeless people in Eureka, an hour and a half to the north.

My plaster of paris plaque of Robespierre had smashed in the 1989 quake, thrown from the wall of my sitting room in the Adobe Motel. I almost asked Tally to check whether the other plaque, of Saint-Just, was still safe in the garage, but let it go. She said there was no sign of Euclid.

➤

APRIL 30   *Houston*

I FACE AN AUDIENCE at the University of Houston, talking about the L.A. riots and the election. I described the grinding of the tectonic plates up in Humboldt County. When the pressure gets too great, you get a quake. The audience listen with interest. Petrolia has been on the news. I draw a parallel between the grinding plates and the grinding, unresolved pressures underlying this election year. Reduced to simile, nature is safely on its chain again.

➤

MAY 24   *Los Angeles*

IN A MONTH OR SO, when the camera crews have left South Central and Pico-Union and weeds begin to poke their way up through the asphalt in the burned-out lots along Crenshaw, Vermont and Western, it will be easy enough to see who was just talking and who had a genuine plan. The only plan that breathes the concrete expectations and desires of people in South Central is one issued under the name of the Bloods and Crips. It's a coherent outline of community needs, with a price tag of $3.7 billion over and above existing appropriations. Excerpts:

BLOODS/CRIPS PROPOSAL FOR LA'S FACE-LIFT ($2 billion)
Every burned and abandoned structure shall be gutted. The city will purchase the property ... and build a community center. If the structure is on a corner lot or is a vacant lot, the city will build a career counseling center or a recreation center, respectively.

- All pavements/sidewalks in Los Angeles are in dire need of resurfacing ... Our organization will assist the city in the identification of all areas of concern.
- All lighting will be increased in all neighborhoods. Additionally, lighting of city streets, neighborhood blocks and alleyways will be amended. We want a well-lit neighborhood. All alleys shall be painted white or yellow ...
- All trees will be properly trimmed and maintained. We want all weeded/shrubbed areas to be cleaned up and properly nurtured. New trees will be planted to increase the beauty of our neighborhoods.
- A special task force shall be assigned to focus on the clean-up of all vacant lots and trashed areas throughout the deprived areas. Proper pest control methods shall be implemented by the city to reduce the chances of rodent scattering. The city will declare a neighborhood clean-up week wherein all residents will be responsible for their block – a block captain will be assigned to ensure cooperation.

Continue with an education plan that – besides demanding rehabbing and resupply of schools, a new minimum salary of $30,000 for teachers and re-elections for the School Board – reflects the concerns, and even more frivolous desires, of people who want to learn in dignity:

BLOODS/CRIPS EDUCATIONAL PROPOSAL ($700 million)
All schools shall have new landscaping and more plants and trees around the schools; completely upgrade the bathrooms, making them more modern; provide a bathroom monitor to each bathroom which will provide freshen-up toiletries at a minimum cost to the students. ...

- A provision for accelerated educational learning programs shall be implemented for the entire Los Angeles Unified School District to provide aggressive teaching methods and provide a curriculum similar to non-economically deprived areas. Tutoring for all subjects ... will be mandatory for all students with sub-level grades.

- In these after-school tutorial programs, those students whose grades are up to par will receive federally funded bonus bonds which will be applied to their continued education upon graduation from high school. They will also receive bonus bonds for extra scholastic work towards their fellow students ...
- High achievers in these areas [math and science] shall be granted a free trip to another country for educational exchange ...
- The LAUSD will provide up-to-date books to the neglected areas and enough books to ensure that no student has to share a book with another ...
- LAUSD will remove all teachers not planning to further their education along with teachers who have not proven to have a passionate concern for the students ... All teachers shall be given a standard competency test to verify they are up-to-date with subjects and modern teaching methods. Psychological testing will also be required for all teachers and educational administrators, including the Los Angeles School Board, every four years.
- All curriculums shall focus on the basics in high school requirements ... inundated with advanced sciences and additional applied math, English and writing skills.
- Busing shall become non-existent in our communities if all of the above demands are met.

As part of their human welfare plan, the gangs propose three new hospitals, forty health care centers, and dental clinics within ten miles of each community, as well as the reconstruction of city parks; and then deal with a topic on which the quackery of the Haves has exceeded all bounds:

BLOODS/CRIPS HUMAN WELFARE PROPOSAL ($1 billion)
We demand that welfare be completely removed from our community and these welfare programs be replaced by state work and product manufacturing plants that provide the city with certain supplies. State monies shall only be provided for invalids and the elderly. The State of California shall provide a child welfare building to serve as day care centers for single parents ...

GIVE US THE HAMMER AND THE NAILS,
WE WILL REBUILD THE CITY.

JUNE 3   *Topanga*
SUSANNA HECHT AND I do a piece on the eco-summit.

As Rio de Janeiro prepares for the Earth Summit by paving the road to the airport and placing in detention the abandoned children regularly preyed upon by death squads, the inhabitants of a city mangled by a disintegrating national economy braced themselves for the windfall of some 30,000 visitors.

For some of these transients – international bureaucrats, environmentalists, representatives of citizens' movements – Rio is the final milestone in a protracted itinerary of preparatory conferences, interim minisummits and drafting sessions that sent them in costly caravans from Paris to New York to Caracas to Nairobi. But as they all came once again to earth in Rio, most of them knew that here is not a summit that in any meaningful construction of the word will settle the world's environmental and developmental agenda.

Rio's origins go back twenty years, to a world still ripe with optimism about Third World development. The participants of that conference in Stockholm still saw only promise in the Green Revolution, whose dark side – social inequality, genetic erosion, environmental damage – had yet to be widely displayed. With growth rates of 8 percent a year, countries such as Brazil seemed to have soundly embarked upon 'takeoff'.

The agenda in that 1972 Stockholm conference was profoundly influenced by a sharp re-emergence of Malthusian thought in the developed world, as represented by Paul Ehrlich's *The Population Bomb* and Garrett Hardin's 'The Tragedy of the Commons', both appearing toward the end of the 1960s. Both blamed population increase for environmental degradation (with Hardin linking this to nonprivate forms of property), and thus fed the fears of the Haves that the gains of postwar development would be drowned in a flood tide of humans in that familiar guise – the infinitely fertile and pullulating Have-Nots.

Ehrlich's Malthusian premises were swiftly condoned by the Club of Rome, with its *Limits to Growth*, which coupled anxieties about population growth to a critique of industrial development, stressing that pollution, along with food shortages, was another global constraint. This technical modeling exercise (it was the first widely read book that included the *frisson* of computer modeling, thus helping to initiate an entire genre) left its readers with the omen of world populations pressed against limited resources, while generating ever-increasing amounts of poison. Population and pollution controls and the expansion of capitalist property were the sole means of avoiding doom.

The Third World national delegations congregating in Rio have a mien very different from the spirited profile apparent in the mid 1970s, when the calls for a New International Economic Order were at their zenith. Amid collapsing economies, stratospheric debt and stringent austerity programs imposed by the International Monetary Fund, these delegations have been brought to heel.

Simultaneously, their very standing as sovereign states has been increasingly compromised in the eyes of their own civil societies, which see them as predatory and corrupt domestically and, internationally, as servile executors of the First World's economic agenda. The Earth Summit's host country, Brazil, is testimonial to these developments.

Hopping to the tune of international donors, such states have become less the providers of benefits (except to their corrupt elites) than enforcers of 'stabilization' and 'structural adjustment reforms.' This has been accompanied by a fierce ideological attack, with neoliberal and monetarist reformers blaming the erratic performance of Third World economies on statist interventions that have distorted the free functioning of markets.

Nowhere can reliance on the market be seen so clearly this year as in the World Bank's World Development Report, which focuses on the environment and was compiled under the authority of Lawrence Summers, the bank's chief economist and vice president. The premises of the document ignore a generation's worth of work on environmental issues. The value of the environment as a 'good' is placed effectively at zero, so its destruction has no cost and no negative implications for current or future production.

The World Bank views environmental problems as the outcome of the 'three Ps' – population, pricing problems and (faulty) property rights. Hence, the solutions offered pivot on the reduction of population by putting women to work, the elimination of pricing 'distortion' by creating tradable pollution permits, and the elimination of common property. Familiar patterns of Malthusian thinking (pollution is consequent upon population pressure, not patterns of consumption) are harnessed to data-free analysis, since in Brazil the highest levels of deforestation occur in areas held as private property. In countries such as Malaysia, traditions of commonly held property kept forests intact, until these were replaced by impeccably 'private' logging concessions.

Lunatic assumptions flit across the report's intellectual horizon: soil depletion is the consequence of a lack of development (a thesis that can be confuted by anyone with the curiosity to visit California's Central Valley); the market in pollution rights will proceed smoothly, beyond politics or the exercise of bribery.

But if the Third World states have ceded most initiative to First World institutions, their frailty has also made possible more positive perspectives for political action. Weakened, corrupt, delegitimized, their impotence has opened up considerable room for the elaboration of new civil-state relations. This terrain has increasingly come to be occupied by civic associations (housewives, peasant leagues, environmental groups) pressing demands on the state through the 'politics of claims' or seeking to find solutions to collective problems without the intervention of the state. It is here that the origins of an 'alternative' Rio lie, and why there is such suspicion about state-to-state agreements when the state is seen as either irrelevant or pernicious.

The structure of environmental debates and proposed 'solutions' to the environmental crises of the tropical world are skewed in an ideological construct of conservation and development that is largely removed from the historical and economic realities of most of the Third World. In response to this, and to the declining living conditions of many of the poor, national political and social movements have increasingly moved into the sphere of 'political ecology', where the hope is to redefine the environmental agenda in terms that address more fundamental questions of resource distribution and access, political rights and processes; also to consider larger philosophical issues regarding the nature of property (ranging from usufruct to intellectual property rights), the nature of nature (untrammeled Eden or artifact and habitat), and technical and development alternatives. Environmental issues are but one component in a broader range of activities, and the central focus is on social justice. While there is an argument to be made about the value of indigenous knowledge and management of tropical resources, the environmental dimensions of these concerns have largely been appropriated by mainstream environmental movements, while international attention to the legitimacy of pressing claims for social justice has been scant.

➡

JUNE 6   *Petrolia*
GEOFFREY DE SAINT CROIX once explained to my brother Andrew the semantic trend of the Latin word *suffragium*. In the Roman Republic it meant a vote. In the Roman Empire it meant a favor and, as things went steadily downhill, ended up meaning simply a bribe.

Just as *suffragium*'s career reflected the increasing weight of money in the Roman political system, so Perot's initial announcement told us everything we need to know. He would, Perot proclaimed, spend 'all the money it takes'.

➡

JUNE 15   *Ardmore, Co. Waterford*
ONE REFLECTION OF THE Lloyds insurance crisis is the fact that no less than a third of a million acres of prime Scottish sporting land is now up for sale, with many of the vendors being Lloyds Names trying to dispose of their grouse moors, deer forests, salmon rivers and kindred expositions of the good life. Lord Kimball, for example, a Lloyd's council member, is offering for £7 million the 47,650 acres of his Altnaharra estate in the far north of Scotland. Not all such sales are Lloyd's-connected. Some merely reflect the outfall of the go-go years. The island of Gigha, in the archipelago west of Glasgow, is being sold for some $8 million by the Swiss bank Interallianz, which repossessed it after the

collapse of Malcolm Potier's property empire. The former Olympic bobsledder Keith Schellenberg is selling the island of Eigg after protracted legal unpleasantness with his former wife, Margaret de Hauteville Udny Hamilton.

There can be few places in the world where feudal property rights hold more uninhibited sway than in these vast Scottish estates, whose clearances in the eighteenth century and substitution of sheep for peasants were so memorably recorded by Marx. When Queen Victoria and Prince Albert set the fashion for Scottish sporting holidays, the sheep were in their turn disposed of, in favor of deer, whose function was to give pleasure to these new Actaeons, resplendent in their freshly invented tartans and kindred antic drapery.

Professor Hugh Iltis of the University of Wisconsin, a botanist, claimed to me recently that, ironically, these big Scottish landowners had been among the great preservers of biodiversity. (Iltis also claimed that Hermann Goering's taste for hunting had been similarly constructive in preserving some ancient German estates as prime habitat.) Such a view is not shared by Drennan Watson, an environmental land-use consultant, who says, 'The highlands have been devastated. Forestation, for example, is not about wall-to-wall sitka spruce. Few examples of naturally diverse forest are now left. And huge deer populations mean that once the ecosystem is ruined, they'll be the only bloody thing left to shoot.'

➤

JUNE 16   *Topanga*
Dear Alexander Cockburn,
Re Jerry Brown's flat tax proposal, which you've been attacked for supporting. Congressional Budget Office statistics show that the poorest 20 percent pay 8.7 percent of their income in taxes. The flat tax would require them to pay 13 percent. However, people from this population group normally rent their homes, which under the flat tax (and not the present tax code) would be a tax deduction. In Los Angeles, people at that income level pay about 60 percent of their income for rent. This would make their actual flat tax rate 5.2 percent.

The quick assumption that corporations would automatically pass on the VAT to the consumer is likely in the short run. However, in the absence of income taxes and in the presence of at least some competition (there is still some left), prices would drop back down to some degree. Let's assume a 6.5 percent rise in prices caused by a VAT. The 5.2 percent tax would increase to 11.7 percent.

Finally, let's analyze the expenditures of the poorest 20 percent. Most of their money is spent on rent (60 percent). Assuming that rent would not be subject to VAT (what's the value added?), the tax would decrease to 7.8 percent. This is a lower rate than any in the present system.

Although my assumptions are no less valid than Doug Henwood's, our conclusions are much different. Conclusions are only as good as the assumptions used to reach them. So why beat up an idea in its embryonic stages? Can anyone really defend the current tax system?

Mark Howmann
Aliso Viejo, Calif.

Many on the left do. Bob Pollin and I continue to defend Brown and a Pollin-drafted version of his flat tax proposal. Brown was alone in taking the left seriously as a constituency and advancing ideas congenial to it. He has denounced the dictatorship of the money/incumbency party. He has argued for union rights and insisted that the L.A. riots be seen in an economic context, pointing out the effects that globalization and downward wage pressure have had on working-class life.

True, as we openly recognized in the *Wall Street Journal*, the plan as initially drawn up fails on progressivity grounds. Brown himself has acknowledged this many times in public appearances. But as we also showed, it could be fixed through simple measures. Indeed, part of the beauty of Brown's plan was that through simplicity, one could achieve the desired ends without having to get lost in the labyrinth of loopholes. This became increasingly clear in Pollin's work on revising Brown's plan with Max Sawicky of the Economic Policy Institute.

Consider only one such loophole, perhaps the most popular of all, the tax deductibility of mortgage interest on owner-occupied homes. This is almost universally embraced as necessary to promote home ownership and stable middle-class living standards. In fact, it is a vast subsidy for the rich.

A 1991 study in the *National Tax Journal* by James Follian and David Ling found that the total federal revenues lost through the mortgage interest deduction on owner-occupied housing amounted to $81.1 billion in 1988. Neither the homeless, renters or even homeowners who do not itemize their tax deductions receive a penny of this subsidy, whose magnitude far exceeds all other federal housing programs combined.

Among the homeowners who do itemize, the housing deduction is equivalent to an average subsidy of $6,680 for households with incomes over $100,000 but only $444 for households with incomes between $15,000 and $30,000. The reason is simple: The higher your tax bracket and the more you spend on housing, the greater your tax savings. But again, what politicians would be willing to have themselves photographed handing a $6,680 check to a Beverly Hills movie producer to finance a new Jacuzzi while 2 million Americans live in streets, parks, alleys and subway stations?

If the mortgage interest subsidy were cut by only half, this alone could finance all the Conference of Mayors' proposals and leave $6 billion to spare. Thus, an obvious revision that Pollin and Sawicky proposed on Brown's initial plan, which was consistent with the spirit of the initial proposal and to which

Brown immediately agreed, was to cap the mortgage deduction at $15,000 per household.

It is crucial to keep in mind that the goal of left economic policy is progressive outcomes, not merely progressive taxation. Tax policy is just a means to progressive ends. Indeed, if the choice is between, on the one hand, a mildly progressive tax and pure market-supported expenditures and, on the other, a proportional (flat) tax, where tax revenues go for spending on a genuinely left agenda that changes life opportunities for the majority – child care, public schools, infrastructure, national health and full employment – the choice should be clear. The aim of left policy should not be merely to protect a few handouts for the poor but to eliminate poverty, and to increase working-class living standards.

➥

JUNE 17   *Petrolia*

ONE OF MY FAVORITE examples of the British aristocracy's sometimes narrow focus on land use and agricultural practice comes in the chapter on partridge in *Shooting* (Field and Covert), by Lord Walsingham and Sir Ralph Payne-Gallwey, published in 1889 in the Badminton Library of Sports and Pastimes, edited by the Duke of Beaufort.

'Another agricultural change has been the substitution of the scythe, and still later of the mowing machine, for the old-fashioned sickle. In the days of reaped stubbles, which were habitually left long, uneven, and not unfrequently weedy, birds could be approached, not only during the first half of the day, but equally well at a later hour when they had retired to their feeding grounds, the stubbles affording sufficient cover to hide them and to prevent them from noticing the approach of sportsmen. This is now no longer the case. No stubble in these days is high enough to prevent birds from seeing men and dogs the moment they enter the field, and where the birds are at all wild they will not allow themselves to be approached.'

So much for the combine harvester. They have some interesting records of the slaughters achieved by the time this book was published. The largest bag of grouse ever made in a day by one shooter was on the Blubberhouse Moor in 1872 when, on August 27, Lord Walsingham, one of the authors, killed 842 birds. In 1876 the Maharaja Dulap Singh personally shot 2,530 partridges across nine days on his estate of Elveden in Suffolk. All this rather pales before what happened at Chantilly, outside Paris, on October 7 and 8, 1785, when the two Princes de Condé and the Prince de Conti, with twelve other guns, killed 2,580 partridges, 1,593 hares, twenty-four rabbits, twelve pheasants, two fieldfares and two larks. One of the Princes de Condé thought he was going to be reincarnated as a horse, which is why today Chantilly boasts one of the most grandiose stables in the world. Susanna and I visited them, and a tiny circus featured a woman perched on a horse (perhaps the reincarnated Prince) went round the ring to Wagner's Valkyrie music. Maddening. Susanna had to hold me back.

➡

JUNE 25   *Petrolia*

EUCLID RETURNS! He no longer believes in me. I try to reconcile. He eats voraciously.

➡

JULY 8   *Petrolia*

FROM ADORNO:

Les Adieux: To be lastingly apart and to hold love fast has become unthinkable. 'O parting, fountain of all words', but it has run dry, and nothing comes out except bye, bye or ta-ta. Airmail and courier delivery substitute logistical problems for the anxious wait for the letter, even where the absent partner has not jettisoned anything not palpable to hand as ballast. Airline directors can hold jubilee speeches on how much uncertainty and sorrow people are thereby spared. But the liquidation of parting is a matter of life and death to the traditional notion of humanity. Who could still love if the moment is excluded when the other, corporeal being is perceived as an image compressing the whole continuity of life as into a heavy fruit? What would hope be without distance? Humanity was the awareness of the presence of that not present, which evaporates in a condition which accords all things not present the palpable semblance of presence and immediacy, and hence had only scorn for what finds no enjoyment in such simulation. Yet to insist on parting's inner possibility in face of its pragmatic impossibility would be a lie, for the inward does not unfold within itself but only in relation to the objective, and to make 'inward' a collapsed outwardness does violence to the inward itself, which is left to sustain itself as if on its own flame. The restoration of gestures would follow the example of the professor of German literature who, on Christmas Eve, held his sleeping children for a moment before the shining tree to cause a deja vu and steep them in myth. A humanity come of age will have to transcend its own concept of the emphatically human, positively. Otherwise its absolute negation, the inhuman, will carry off victory.

FOR THE THIRD TIME Andy Kopkind and I do our quadrennial state of the
Democrats piece.

The electoral system in America is now being convulsed by the broadest,
fiercest voter insurgency in perhaps 140 years, and the left is watching from the
sidelines. But the reality thus far is bleak. The two formerly major parties are
a shambles, institutions of government and the press despised, political authority disdained, and every measure of popular anger overflowing. And yet those
who have long expected this transformative moment to come, have organized
and struggled for its arrival, are – if they are realistic – confronted primarily
by their own irrelevance to this historic hour.

The social culture that has congealed around Clinton – the first such afflux
to a Democratic presidential candidate in three decades – excludes the diversity
that an expanded Democratic electorate would present. The contours of the
Clinton culture are generational and ideological, and its purposes are both the
advancement of careers and the confirmation of identities. In the think tanks,
research institutions, nonprofit foundations, campus towers and editorial offices that house the neoliberal cavalry of the Democratic Party there are people
at the apex of their careers who have been waiting twelve years for access to
executive power. The thrust of the Clinton culture was perfectly expressed by
one of Clinton's Washington acolytes: 'It's *our* turn.'

It's difficult to convey the feel of the Clinton culture. Like the Kennedy
culture thirty years ago, it is a stir-fry of blatant self-promotion, unexamined
idealism, cynical sophistication, suspect intellectual certainty and an arrogant
race and class snobbery that can be oppressive to those without the necessary
credentials. It comes on as hip and liberal, but it panders to the right (Clinton's
embrace of the death penalty) and abhors any person or movement to its left. It
is suffused with a gestural sentimentality about racial harmony, but its commitment is to white privilege. Its adherents protested the Vietnam War, if they were
old enough, but they hold no internationalist values and, like Clinton, are ever-
willing to sacrifice principle to 'political viability within the system' .

The salient feature of the political year so far is the spectacular deconstruction of the two parties. The coalition of white ethnics, middle and high subur-
banites, God-fearing reborns, neoconservatives and stalwart country-club
Republicans that Reagan led into the White House has come unstuck in the late
years of Bush. David Duke and Pat Buchanan dislodged part of the package,
and various Democrats – Paul Tsongas, Jerry Brown and Clinton himself – were
able to co-opt elements during the primaries. The result is that Bush has an
unsure base. It should also be stressed that the Republican Party is still a
immensely powerful institution, part of the glue holding together most of the
significant (Western chapter) of the world's ruling class.

The Democratic Party is in a far more advanced stage of decay. Only Jerry Brown tried to speak to the interests and further the agendas of the party's basic constituencies. It was he, not Clinton, who was most able to expand the Democratic base. His support in the Michigan primary, where his final arc of success began, was among white workers who had voted for Reagan and Bush. It was the same in Connecticut.

➳

JULY 20 *Petrolia*

Dear Alexander Cockburn:

Although your book on chess is now seventeen years old, I thought you would be interested in reading the controversy it rekindled on the LINC computer network, which is frequented by serious chessplayers. Attached is a printout, showing how fondly they recall your book.

I am sending you the computer messages for your enjoyment. But if you care to fashion a response, I would be happy to post it on the LINC computer network. As a reporter and chessplayer, I thought the book was a delightful tweak at the game and its personalities.

By the way, out here in Northern California you are better known as the roving columnist for the *Anderson Valley Advertiser.*

Best Regards
Bleys W. Rose
Santa Rosa

The following notice was posted by: EXETER on JUL07 09:50PM

> Next, does anyone have a review/thoughts/comments on IDLE PASSION: CHESS AND THE DANCE OF DEATH by Alexander Cockburn?

The following notice was posted by: JASON. on JUL08 06:45PM

> Re 'Idle Passion': I remember thinking that the book was a piece of garbage. I borrowed a copy from the library; I refused to buy the book on principle. The author hated chess and chessplayers. I remember that a reviewer in 'Chess Life' ripped the book to shreds. It seems that the author's dislike for chess began when his father taught him how to play and then beat him. I recall the author saying that this game, played when he was a child, was the only game of chess he ever played. For some reason, he thought this qualified him to write a book about chess.

The following notice was posted by: DOUG on JUL08 06:51PM

> Yeah, I came to the conclusion that Cockburn's unwarranted dislike of chess must have come from getting beat earlier in life.

The following notice was posted by: BURTSKY on JUL11 06:39PM

Cockburn's sick book

Jason has hit the nail on the head regarding Cockburn's 'Idle Passion': it is a potboiler of no value designed to exploit the interest in chess generated by Fischer. The reviewer who tore it to shreds in 'Chess Life' was the editor of that estimable magazine at the time: Burt Hochberg.

The following notice was posted by: H.W.R. on JUL11 06:57PM

Cockburn Book

Is there a hardy soul out there who would like to do a responsible review of this book. I do not have it and could not get to it for a while even if I did. "Responsible" does not mean you have to like the book, it just means reasonably even-handed. If you still hate it, c'est la vie. Here's Burt Hochberg's account of a daytime TV debate with Cockburn.

During the program the two women interviewers, both ignorant of chess, persistently questioned Mr. Cockburn about the sexual peculiarities of chess players (an area in which Mr. Cockburn was assumed to be an expert), displaying precisely the prurient curiosity his book was intended to arouse in the layperson. The two ladies pointedly asked me whether I was a homosexual, while they pointedly avoided asking Mr. Cockburn to announce his sexual orientation. Since he is not a chess player and is therefore presumed to be 'normal', the question apparently did not need to be asked.

The following notice was posted by: H.W.R. on JUL13 07:48AM

Review of *Idle Passion*

Per my request for someone interested in doing a review about Cockburn's 'Idle Passion...' I have received a generous offer from David Burris to do it. The review should be even more insightful inasmuch as Mr. Burris has some training which may help in shedding some light on the quasi-psychological aspects of the book.

A previous posting inquired why waste time on it. I think the reason is because the book targets our game/science/art and apparently comes up with some damning, even if unfounded, conclusions.

➤→

AUGUST 2   *Petrolia*
I'VE BEEN WRESTLING with this damned piece on lips. My heart just isn't in it. Chris Krom sent me a little memo plus some odd stuff in Ernst Kris's essay on the sculptor Messerschmidt, who went mad in the eighteenth century.

Alex:

Here are some recent articles in the media that talk about the new Big Lip esthetic (not just observed in Kansas):

Lynn Norment: 'They took our music ... now they're taking our lips; as beauty standards change, some white women are seeking large, voluptuous lips with injections and cosmetics.' *Ebony,* April 1991

'Reverse Liposuction', *The Economist,* Jan. 21, 1989

'Liplifts: Is Bigger Better?' *Vogue,* Sept. 1989

And a couple of articles in *Health,* Feb. 1991

I'll go look for the Hollander book as soon as I fax this. Finally, a chance to put my art history degree to work. Here's Ernst Kris on Messerschmidt's busts of demons:

> It is indeed highly plausible that we are here confronted with an image of the demon in his role as persecutor and seducer. In these busts, as in the others, the lips are the center on which attention is focused. However, they are not only pressed together as they are on the other busts; they are pulled out and elongated in a protruding and pointed shape as if they were made out of dough. A phallic impression, a general sense of activity and directedness, is thus evolved. This activity, we may venture to assume, is attributed through projection to the demons as persecutors. But on closer inspection, a second and more convincing interpretation is suggested by the very appearance of the busts and by the content of the delusion--at least if we try to supplement by general clinical experience the information conveyed by Nicolai: What on one level may impress us as activity is on another a break-through of the passive feminine fantasy, which the tightly closed lips of Messerschmidt's other busts seem to have warded off. We gain the conviction that what the busts represent can be conceived of as direct illustration of fellatio, to which the demons invite Messerschmidt and which they force upon him. A glance at the rectangle of the neck in the frontal view confirms the impression that the features of the human head have been distorted or stretched in order to combine or include both male and female sexual organs.

And then there's John Berger on Rodin:

> Judith Cladel, his devoted biographer, describes Rodin working and making notes from the model.
>
> 'He leaned closer to the recumbent figure, and fearing lest the sound of his voice might disturb its loveliness, he whispered: "Hold your mouth as though you were playing the flute. Again! Again!"'

AUGUST 8   *Houston*

THERE WAS A MARCH the Sunday before the convention from the Fourth Ward
to River Oaks, which is about as drastic a transition from shack to mansion as
can be made anywhere in the United States. The Fourth Ward, tucked in at the
edge of Downtown, is the old Freedtown, where former slaves moved after the
Civil War. The neighborhood reminded me of Key West in the 1970s, before the
real estate boom hit: scruffy and intimate, with wooden homes clustered along
narrow streets and lanes. Hurricane Andrew could have chewed it up in a
couple of minutes.

Houston started with cotton and slavery; cotton money lured the railroads,
the banks and the lawyers, establishing the infrastructure that gave Houston
its edge over other gulf cities as regional HQ of the oil industry, whose capital
is still New York. Here grew up Jim Baker, grandson of the man who founded
the mighty Houston law firm of Baker & Botts. Thither, on his way to Odessa,
came Cap'n Bushy, actually a recently demobilized lieutenant, with agreeable
credentials from the Rockefeller interests in New York for whom his father,
Senator Prescott Bush, sedately labored.

The Downtown interests hate the Fourth Ward and yearn to relocate its 7,000
African-American inhabitants somewhere else, far far away. The precedent for
such ethnic cleansing came in the Fifth Ward, which used to be a vigorous black
community until it was crucified by asphalt in the 1980s, with Interstate 10 and
US 59 scything through the 40,000-person neighborhood.

➤

AUGUST 17   *Houston*

FIVE MILES SOUTH of River Oaks sits the Astrodome, rising like a tumor from
the vast asphalt parking lot. Adjacent to it rises the lesser tumor of the
Astrohall, temporary home to the Fourth Estate. To get from the latter to the
former you have to go through a stringent security check. Dan Quayle was
certainly well guarded. I counted a retinue of seventeen cars, plus six outrider
H.P.D. motorcops plus ambulance, to take him from the Astrohall to the north
entrance of the Astrodome, a distance of maybe 400 yards.

The fact that most of the press stayed in front of TV sets in the Astrohall
contributed to the usual misperceptions of the convention among the national
audience. By midweek friends across the country were calling to ask me in
hushed tones what it was 'like in there', expecting me to describe something
akin to the A.H. rallies in Nuremberg.

I stood under the podium while Pat Buchanan addressed the hall. In the first
part of his speech the applause lines got their reward, but by the end – the racist
coda about the lads from the 18th Cavalry fighting off the rioters on behalf of
the old folk in the retirement home, which turned out to be fake – Buchanan

had lost his audience. The applause was tepid, though the TV screens showed Buchanan banners lofted amid the hoarse roars of the Beast Unchained.

➥

AUGUST 21   *Houston*
THE CHRISTIANS SAVED the convention from being a complete flop. Inside the Astrodome, Pat Robertson's Christian Coalition dominated the platform debate, stayed late, captured the ground and dug in for 1996.

These Christians, at least the ones I encountered on the convention floor, seemed different, less feisty, than the old right-wing populists of the 1970s, brandishing their Duck Paper tracts and denouncing Bush, then Reagan's rival, as the agent of Bilderberg, the Trilateral Commission and, behind it all, the Rockefellers.

The Republican fantasy of self-help and individualism is indestructible. Hour after tedious hour they hurled their curses at Big Government, eyed from the Distinguished Visitors' section by millionaire Houstonians whose environment is one mighty testament to the therapeutic power of the federal dollar: the Lyndon B. Johnson Space Center, the Texas Medical Center, the Port of Houston, the Metro Authority – all of them plump with government handouts.

They hurled their curses, and cheered dutifully when Cap'n Bushy gave a terrible speech. The balloons popped and then the lights went down. Next day the Dow fell 50.79 points and the dollar dropped through the floor. Wall Street had read Cap'n Bushy's lips and didn't like what it saw. He'll have to kill Saddam with his bare hands, and even then the Republicans most likely will lose.

➥

SEPTEMBER 1   *Petrolia*
MISSED THE DEADLINE for Lips. Shelley is furious. I just couldn't do it, which is unusual.

➥

SEPTEMBER 3   *Petrolia*
CHOMSKY WENT TO THE DENTIST, who made his inspection and observed the patient was grinding his teeth. Consultation with Mrs. Chomsky disclosed that teeth-grinding was not taking place during the hours of sleep. When else? They narrowed it down quickly enough to the period each morning when Chomsky was reading the *New York Times*, unconsciously gnashing his molars at every page.

I asked Chomsky why, with the evidence and experience of a lifetime, he kept
hoping against hope that the corporate press, particularly the *New York Times*,
was going to get it right. Reality should long since have conditioned him to keep
his jaw muscles relaxed. Chomsky sighed, as if in anticipation of all the stupid
perversions of truth he was condemned to keep reading for the rest of his life,
jolted each morning into furious bouts of grinding.

People will go to a talk by Chomsky partly just to reassure themselves that
they haven't gone mad; that they are right when they disbelieve what they read
in the papers or watch on TV. For hundreds of thousands of people over the
years – he must have spoken to more American students than any other person
alive – Chomsky has offered the assurance, the intellectual and moral authority
that there is another way of looking at things. In this vital function he stands in
the same relationship to his audience as did a philosopher he admires greatly,
Bertrand Russell. Chomsky's greatest virtue is that his fundamental message is
a simple one. Here's how he put it in an interview with Fred Gardner in the
Anderson Valley Advertiser.

'Any form of authority requires justification; it's not self-justified. And the
justification can rarely be given. Sometimes you can give it. I think you can give
an argument that you shouldn't let a three-year-old run across the street.
That's a form of authority that's justifiable. But there aren't many of them, and
usually the effort to give justification fails. And when we try to face it, we find
that the authority is illegitimate. And any time you find a form of authority
illegitimate, you ought to challenge it. It's something that conflicts with human
rights and liberties. And that goes on forever. You overcome one thing and
discover the next.

'In my view what a popular movement ought to be is just basically libertarian: concerned with forms of oppression, authority and domination, challenging
them. Sometimes they're justifiable under particular conditions, sometimes
they're not. If they are not, try to overcome them.'

➤

SEPTEMBER 14   *Topanga*
FROM THE LOOK of the one car in it, *The Field* is set in the fifties. It would be
hard to tell otherwise, since before the early sixties many a village and small
town in Ireland looked more or less the way they did at the turn of the century.
When I was going to Protestant parochial school in 1950 in Youghal, a donkey
cart would trundle me and my companions to lessons and my mother did all her
shopping in a horse and trap as did all the country people coming into town.

Land hunger is *The Field*'s theme and here the agony of Bull McCabe both
about the possession of land and the inheritance of land is vividly true to life.

There's nothing unimaginable in Bull's passion for the three or four acre field he's nourished with seaweed, nor his murderous fury that though he's worked it as a renter it's not legally his and can be sold from under his pitchfork.

There are plenty like the Yank in the movie, an Irish-American come back to Holy Ireland after making his pile the other side of the Atlantic. You see them all the time, particularly in the summer, looking up their ancestors in the church registers, asking locals where the McSomeones or the O'So-and-So's used to live. The house outside Youghal I grew up in was owned by a man called O'Keeffe. In 1947 his father had been about to sell the old Georgian pile to my parents for eighty pounds but he died and young O'Keeffe inherited and refused to sell.

He was a policeman in Los Angeles and gradually rose from the ranks to become sheriff in one of the cities in East Los Angeles. Eventually he said he wanted to come back. We moved over to Ardmore, my mother nearly as angry as Bull that this man was going to be strutting the earth she'd tended so long in the walled garden. She took six truckloads of topsoil with her for the new place and never went back, even to pass the house that had sheltered us for thirty years. O'Keeffe never came. It was just a dream he had over those same thirty years. The house stayed empty and within five years looked as though it had been abandoned for a century. Eventually it was bought by a vet who knocked it down to build his own pile.

At *The Field*'s heart are themes of madness, sexual frustration, suicide. One of the Bull's sons has killed himself and the other, Tadgh, is a bit cracked. The lunatic asylum - 'the mental' – was a familiar landmark when I was growing up. My father was in a TB hospital for a couple of years in the 1950s and when he and his fellow patients, mostly farmers, got rowdy, the sanction of the hospital, carried out from time to time, was to threaten the troublemakers with being carried off to the mental.

Back in 1960 Ireland had the highest figure in the world for people hospitalized for mental illness, at 7.3 persons per 100,000. Sweden was the distant runner-up, with 4.8. On any given day in 1971 two out of every hundred males in the west of Ireland was in a psychiatric hospital or institution, most of the celibates between the ages of 35 and 50.

There's a lot of dispair, particularly in the West. The main business of one hotel near Knock airport is hosting wakes around the bodies of Irish people flown home to be buried in the family plot. In her brilliant, depressing 1979 study of mental illness (which she traced to the broken culture consequent on Ireland's colonization, and emigration) in rural Ireland, *Saints, Scholars, and Schizophrenia* the American anthropologist Nancy Scheper-Hughes describes a conversation with one bachelor farmer being shown a picture of a boy looking at a violin on a table:

'He feels down and out.'

'Why?'

'It's broken, anyway.'

'What's the future?'

'He's thinking about his future as a fiddler.'

'What about it?'

'There is none.'

This could have been Tadgh talking.

A friend of mine, the wonderful artist Robert Bates, moved a few years ago to the village, Castle Gregory, on the Dingle peninsula where Scheper-Hughes had done the field work for her book. In his first couple of years, he told me this summer, he'd found the melancholy atmosphere and indrawn natives so overwhelming that he'd walk the long strand for hours each day, weeping. He told me this as we looked out across the misty dawn waves at a couple of trawlers looking for the body of a young fisherman who'd fallen overboard the night before. He couldn't swim. Many Irish fishermen reckon it's bad luck to have a swimmer aboard. These are the waves which receive the victims of the field and across which so many others have had to flee.

➤

OCTOBER 3   *Petrolia*

IT'S A MEASURE OF CLINTON that he should be muddying up the most visibly principled political act of his life – namely, his opposition to the war in Vietnam. He hops about, telling one silly fib after another, till he's managed to convert principle into something devious. Why be apologetic for refusing to napalm peasants, shoot old women in paddy fields or herd villagers into concentration camps while dumping Agent Orange on their forests?

➤

OCTOBER 12   *Petrolia*

EVERYONE FULL OF Columbus quincentennial musings. When he was colonial governor of the Bahamas, my Irish great-grandfather Henry Blake found out what island C. landed on. My cousin Shirley gave me the text of his talk at the Athenaeum about his findings:

For days they ploughed through the thick mass of golden weed that filled the Sargasso Sea spreading as far as the eye can reach, like a field of ripe grain. Away beyond it, with the steady northeast trade winds filling his sails and the blue waters of these southern seas dancing in the sunlight, but sunlight and blue water would not satisfy the sailors who daily murmured more and more ...

... At 2 a.m. on the morning of Friday, 12th October, Roderigo de Triana, a sailor on board the Pinta sighted the land and gazing, as I have gazed upon that very strand, glittering white in the bright southern moonlight. I have pictured for myself with what gratitude and joy the sailors and their great leader saw before them the prize for which they had ventured so much. Now, ladies and gentlemen, that is a short sketch of the events that up to the discovery.

Of all the writers who have so exhaustively written upon the landfall of Columbus, not one has visited the spot while I have sailed over the course of Columbus with his diary in my hands; noting what he noted and comparing his description with the lakes and woods and beautiful capes and everlasting verdure spread before me. Meanwhile Mrs Blake had not been idle with her brush in transferring to paper the scenes described by him.

I have for three years made careful enquiries about the mysterious currents and tides that make the Bahama Banks even now the most dangerous spot to approach in the whole western Atlantic and I think I have satisfactory grounds for the conclusion at which I have arrived.

That the island upon which he landed was Watlings Island and that the coral strand presented here is the very strand upon which the flag was first unfurled that brought in its train such dire destruction to the unhappy inhabitants and opened a new world to the westward rush of restless humanity.

The facts are that the Guanahani was a large and populous, therefore fertile island with a large lake or lagoon in the center; that it was surrounded by a reef; and to the north a very large harbour within the reef and a peninsula that was almost an island; that he was able to proceed from his anchorage round the north north east point to observe all this and return the same day so early that having set sail for the south west he saw an island which was about 20 miles from Guanahani which he had now given the name San Salvador. Now, without following Columbus any further, let us examine these five islands, Turks, Mayaguana, Samana, Cat Island and Watlings, and see how far the description tallys with these statements. Turks Island is a mere sand bank, six miles long, and two and a half miles wide. It possesses no soil and would not support a score of people. It is entirely dependent upon its salt pans. That could not have been Guanahani. Mayaguana is a large island containing some fertile land but there is no lake in the center, nor is there such a harbour and peninsula as he describes, besides had Columbus sailed south west instead of reaching another island within twenty miles he would have sailed for a hundred and fifty miles and seen no land until he reached the coast of Cuba. Samana I visited last year after a very hard passage of 24 hours to beat thirty miles to windward against a heavy head sea. It is enough to say that the small cay is everything that Guanahani was not. There is no soil, no water and the island is simply a mass of bare rock with low scrub. So desolate is it that not an acre has been sold by the Crown.

We are therefore reduced to the choice between Cat Island and Watlings. The reason why Cat Island is the popular favorite is on account of the name,

San Salvador, that has been lately assumed by the inhabitants but in the official records of the Bahamas I find that the island now called San Salvador was always called Cat Island down to 1795. In 1794 the member of the House of Assembly was returned for Cat Island and in an Act for defining parishes in 1802 the Parish of San Salvador is defined as the island of San Salvador, commonly called Cat Island. Curiously enough Watlings Island was the name of the Parish of St. Christopher but there is still stronger proof that Cat Island is not Guanahani.

In a map published by Diego Ribero in 1529, that is only thirty seven years after the discovery, a copy of which I have in my possession (1) the names of Lucayos or Bahamas Islands are given and among these names the five that may be identified; the island of Bashama, Bimini, Magua and Mayaguana are still the same. I need not tell you that Guanahani is also shown upon this map and in the position of Watlings. Therefore Mayaguana cannot have been the landfall. There is another long island on that map in the relative position of Cat Island and the name of that island is Cigato; now as *gato* is the Spanish for cat I think there is no difficulty in accounting for the derivation of the name and as Cigato and Guanahani are two different islands, then Cat Island cannot be Guanahani which was named San Salvador by Columbus.

Cat Island is sixty miles long, it has not a reef all round nor indeed at any point except at the southern shore. It is the most hilly island in the Bahamas and here the land reaches its greatest elevation.

Lastly Columbus could not have pulled round to north of the island in one day and had he done so he would not have formed a harbour there. So by process of exhaustion we have come to the point that Watlings is the only island of the five left for comparison. Now let us see what kind of an island this is. And how well it agrees with the description given by Columbus.

Watlings Island is about thirteen miles long and eight wide. About one-third of its area is occupied by a lake or lagoon of brackish water. It is very fertile and capable of supporting a large population, so much so that in the days of slavery when cultivation was systematic, it was called the garden of the Bahamas. It is almost entirely surrounded by a coral reef, about ten miles from the anchorage on the south east side proceeding to the north north east we come to Grahams Harbour, formed by a great sweep of the reef and about seven miles long by four miles wide with a narrow entrance and close by a promontory attached to the mainland by a very narrow neck.Now if you call to mind the short description of Columbus you will see how completely this island, only, tallys with it. Twenty miles to the south west there lies Run Cay and from a position about three miles north of it I have seen from the rigging Conception Island to the northwest, while to the west and south west the tops of the hills of a long island rose like numerous islands of various sizes and shapes.

OCTOBER 20   *Petrolia*

AMERICA IS ON THE EDGE of a free trade agreement with Mexico, following an earlier one with Canada. Workers in all three countries will be locked into a downward spiral of low-wage, low-skill jobs, with uninhibited movement of capital and a ratcheting down of social and environmental standards.

The function of states like Arkansas has been to maintain that bludgeon of a low-cost nonunion work force over the labor movement in the northern tiers. And as we stand on the threshold of NAFTA, Arkansas represents not the past but the future. From the point of view of capital, Governor Clinton has spent his political life thus far in the proper rehearsal room.

Among Business Leaders for Clinton is Robert Haas, Chairman and CEO of Levi Strauss, supposedly one of America's more enlightened firms. On January 16, 1990, 1,150 textile workers at the Levi Strauss plant on South Zarzamora Street in San Antonio were told that the plant was closing. The first group of about 300 workers were to clear out that afternoon; within three months the rest would be on the street. The Zarzamora plant, which had had record profits in 1989 and which overwhelmingly employed Mexican-American women, was Levi's largest operation in Texas; its closing was the last in a series of at least twenty-six Levi plant closures nationwide since 1985.

The company moved its Zarzamora operation to Costa Rica, where it now benefits from reduced US import tariffs on goods re-entering the country. Conditions at Zarzamora were familiar: nonunion low-wage workers (one woman employed for eighteen years was earning an average of \$5.24 an hour), paid on a piecework basis, performing repetitive actions at high speeds (at the time of the shutdown, at least 10 percent of the workers suffered from carpal tunnel syndrome) and deterred from reporting injuries for fear of being assigned to slower, lower-paying jobs.

'Our sense is we do more than anyone in our industry and more than almost anyone in American industry', a Levi spokesman said later. This may be true. Levi paid severance – one week for every year worked. But in October of 1989, even as managers assured worried workers the plant would stay open, its engineers went around to every sewing machine and added a task that slowed down the operators and thus lowered their pay. When it came time for calculating severance pay, the rate was set on the basis of the average from October to December, reflecting the lower amount after the machines were jigged.

The company claims it has paid out more than \$1 million for retraining, education, social services and emergency assistance. But \$770,104 of that came as general charitable payments in San Antonio stretching back more than two years before the plant closed. As you might expect from the neoliberal pact between business and government, volunteer organizations are left to pick up the pieces (Clinton's basic reaction to the L.A. riots). The city of San Antonio, which lost 10,000 jobs in 1990, received \$468,000 for general support services.

Even then, an officer of the Department of Economic and Education Development said it was a 'drop in the bucket'. Money for tuition, books and other materials for retraining came through federal programs. Not all the workers were eligible for these classes, which in any case were conducted only in English – a problem for the Levi workers, 90 percent of whom spoke only Spanish. As for training for 'high-skill, good-wage' jobs – Clinton's mantra – only thirty-five of the workers were able, with federal assistance, to attend college. Most of the others languished in English and high-school equivalency classes, prerequisites for retraining. 'The few that received retraining, such as cosmetology people', Fuerza Unida, the laid-off workers' organization, reports, 'were put to work cleaning the floors and bathrooms. When they completed their training, they had not learned what they needed.' About 700 have found some sort of work, most at lower pay.

Every Thanksgiving the women stage a hunger strike in front of Levi Strauss headquarters in San Francisco. Fuerza Unida is suing Levi and calls for a boycott and other actions.

➤

OCTOBER 21   *Petrolia*

IN THE FIRST DEBATE Sandy Vanocur asked Bill Clinton how he proposed to deal with the chairman of the Federal Reserve, a man with more power over the economy than the President, yet accountable to no one.

Clinton hastened to assure the vast television audience that he had no problem with the Fed. President Bush and Ross Perot chorused agreement with each other that there be 'separation' between the Bank and elected government. That was it. Nothing more about Alan Greenspan, the present chairman of the Fed. So much for Fed-bashing, which used to be a decent national sport.

➤

OCTOBER 22   *Petrolia*

A BUNCH OF KEYNESIANS are exulting over an experiment in mind control they've been attempting for months. Each week they join hands around a copy of *The General Theory*, close their eyes and imagine they are inside Bush's head, jostling against the bric-a-brac of his interior life. Success came last week. In the course of a disastrous trip to Vermont and New Hampshire in which local Republicans openly spurned his caresses, the President said at a fundraiser in Burlington, 'We have a sluggish economy out there nationally. That's one of the reasons I favor this deficit so much.'

The Keynesian coven has been a bit indiscreet in its boasting, and now the Secret Service is investigating.

OCTOBER 30   *Petrolia*

ELI LILLY AND COMPANY, one of America's biggest drug companies, maker of the antidepressant Prozac (and earlier in its career, heroin medicine and LSD), gazes mournfully at the departing Bush-Quayle Administration, offering us a vivid paradigm of the intersections between government, the press and a powerful corporation.

After he left the CIA and before he began to run for the 1980 Republican nomination, Bush worked for Lilly. Later, he dropped the Lilly directorship from his resumé and failed to disclose his holding of Lilly stock. As Vice President, Bush continued to lobby on behalf of Lilly, whose first Washington lobbying office was set up by Dan Quayle's uncle, back in 1959.

Lilly's headquarters is in Indianapolis, and synergy with the Indiana-based Quayle clan was inevitable. The fusion between 'public service' and toil for Lilly has been most egregiously symbolized in the person of Mitch Daniels, who shuttled between the Reagan and Bush White House and Lilly as vice president for corporate affairs, overseeing government lobbying. In November 1991, Daniels co-chaired a fundraiser that collected $600,000 for Bush-Quayle, including $12,500 from Lilly executives.

After the 1988 victory Bush gave Quayle the Council on Competitiveness, charged with taking calls from corporate chieftains and their lobbyists and jumping to their commands. Ultimately the council asked Lilly to review the government's plan to revamp the Food and Drug Administration's approval procedures. Lilly, which had already won exemptions from the Clean Air Act, received its finest gift in the FDA's expedited approval of new drugs. This, in effect, would lengthen the time that a drug company can maintain product exclusivity (seventeen years from granting of the patent), hence reap more profits before competitors can bring a generic version on the market.

Here we come to the antidepressant drug Prozac, a product of immense importance in propping up Lilly's bottom line, placed on the market in 1987, and by 1990 doing $760 million in sales. In July of 1990, Lilly faced a Prozac crisis. Already in May the company had been warning doctors that problems associated with Prozac included 'suicidal ideation' (a muffled way of saying 'wanting to kill oneself'), and on July 17, Rhoda Hala of Long Island sued Lilly for $150 million in damages, charging that Prozac had impelled her to self-destructive acts.

Among the most formidable opponents of Prozac has been the Church of Scientology, whose affiliate the Citizens Commission on Human Rights is assiduous in collecting evidence of Prozac's impact. The Scientologists have long been hostile to 'psychiatric drugs' like Prozac or Ritalin, a Ciba-Geigy product against which the church has carried out a prolonged and admirable campaign. By the end of July the Citizens Commission was urging Congress to take Prozac out of circulation. Between June and August, Lilly's stock dropped by 20 percent, a $5.8 billion decrease in overall value.

Eight months later the tables were turned. On April 19, 1991, after a series of matter-of-fact articles about the Prozac furor, the *Wall Street Journal* published a violent front-page attack on the Church of Scientology by Thomas Burton. It conflated the life of Scientology's founder, L. Ron Hubbard, its theology and its onslaught on Prozac in paragraphs greeted with delight in the public affairs department of Eli Lilly and the company's P.R. firm, Burson Marsteller (among its former clients, the Argentine junta), which is where a cynical reader of the *Journal* might have supposed Burton's article to have been inspired.

On April 28 came release of *Time*'s cover story on the Church of Scientology by Richard Behar, a discursive onslaught depicting the church as a predator on the disturbed and the unknowing, devoid of virtue. The so-called exposé was larded with errors – not unusual for Behar – including a misstatement of the church's 1987 income as $503 million instead of $4 million, a blunder with which *Time* has said it is 'comfortable.' Lilly bought an extra print order of 250,000 copies of this edition of *Time* and distributed them to doctors across the country. In May, Lilly offered doctors indemnification against lawsuits if they would continue to prescribe Prozac.

Meanwhile, the Lilly White House was doing its bit. In its new policy of letting the fox into the barnyard, the FDA had mustered an advisory committee to study Prozac; five of its eight members had serious conflicts of interest, including substantial financial backing from Lilly. The September 20 hearing on Prozac was favorable to Lilly.

The Church of Scientology did not get too much sympathy for the press assaults against it. The church is reckoned to be a 'cult', and in most journalism, mainstream or underground, cults as opposed to 'religions' are fair game. In his *Journal* piece, Burton had rich sport with Hubbard's quasi-Gnostic constructs of 'thetans' and 'engrams.' By contrast, Bush, Quayle and many officers of Eli Lilly and indeed of the Dow Jones Company, which publishes the *Journal*, are adherents of the Christ cult, about which journalists are uniformly deferential.

The Church of Scientology has made many cogent points about the campaign mounted by Lilly and its publicists to defend Prozac. There is the matter of tie-ins, translating into the many tentacles of Lilly. Mitch Daniels worked for Lilly, Reagan and Bush. Richard Wood, who is Lilly's chairman of the board, president and chief executive officer, serves on the board of Dow Jones. We also have the two Nicholas brothers, one of whom – Nicholas J. – was until this year chief executive officer of Time Warner, and the other of whom – Peter M. – was senior executive at Eli Lilly, married to Ruth Virginia Lilly.

Then there is the matter of the P.R. firms. In the wake of the *Time* attack, Lilly and other pharmaceutical companies forced the P.R. firm of Hill and Knowlton to drop its valuable Church of Scientology account, believing (erroneously) that Hill and Knowlton was responsible for the church's effective anti-Prozac campaign. Hill and Knowlton is a subsidiary of the London-based WPP Group, run by Martin Sorrell. In their vigorous and amusing counterattack on *Time*, run in paid space in *USA Today*, the Scientologists pointed out that WPP, after a series of highly leveraged buyouts of such conglomerates as J. Walter Thompson and Ogilvy and Mather, faced a financial abyss. Soon after WPP acquired J. Walter Thompson, the latter lost the Burger King, Goodyear and *Los Angeles Times* accounts. Lilly is a JWT client.

I hope the Scientologists take *Time* to the cleaners. Right now Bush is probably shoveling Prozac down his throat along with the regular Halcion dosage. He'd better watch out for 'suicidal ideation'.

➥

NOVEMBER 1 *Petrolia*
COUNSELED BY FRIENDS of mature judgement, I try to like Clinton. It's impossible. Listening to him is like having a pillow stuffed into one's mouth. He just can't stop talking.

He must have had a terrible childhood. The other day I was reading Adorno and Horkheimer's essay on stupidity in *Dialectic of Enlightenment* and came across the following:

> Every partial stupidity of a man denotes a spot where the play of stirring muscles was thwarted instead of encouraged. In the presence of the obstacle the futile repetition of disorganized, groping attempts is set in motion. A child's ceaseless queries are always symptoms of a hidden pain, of a first question to which it found no answer and which it did not know how to frame appropriately. Its reiteration suggests the playful determination of a dog leaping repeatedly at the door it does not yet know how to open, and finally giving up if the catch is out of reach.

There is something doglike about Clinton, smacked on the muzzle, always coming back for more. Woof woof.

➥

NOVEMBER 4 *Petrolia*
ANOTHER JOYLESS ELECTION. Doug Lummis put it very well, at the conclusion of a manuscript on the philosophy of radical democracy:

> 'Hannah Arendt has described eloquently how, when political action succeeds in generating real power, the participants experience a happiness different from the kind of happiness one finds in private life.

'Public happiness is not isolating but shared. It is the happiness of being free among other free people, of having one's public faith redeemed and returned, of seeing public hope becoming public power, becoming reality itself ... The experience of public happiness is an exceptional one in the politics of our time, but not such a very rare exception. It has been known in many countries in this century, on every continent, in societies of every kind of political, economic and cultural configuration. It has been felt, if sometimes only momentarily, everywhere, and therefore it is possible everywhere.'

Probably the most intense moment of public happiness this political year was experienced by those people who rose up in Los Angeles. You can't go through life just holding your nose.

➤→

NOVEMBER 6   *Petrolia*

CLINTON WON for the reasons many said he would win. He won because the economy is uppermost in voters' minds and the economy is bad, at least in the minds of a decisive slab of these voters.

The press favoured Clinton. Unusually for a Democrat, he got more editorial endorsements than Bush. Clinton's neoliberalism and pro-business patter went down well in the editorial offices and, more importantly, the boardrooms of the major newspapers and news magazines. The press protected him amid the Flowers sex scandal, insistently belittling the 'uncorroborated allegations' of the tabloids.

Every politician accumulates IOUs, but Clinton has them by the truckload, starting with Wall Street. The herald of 'change' is utterly traditional in his fealty to the traditional lobbies, starting with the military-industrial complex.

Clinton's preternaturally keen eye for the political main chance elicited a majestic refusal to endorse him by the main newspaper of his own home state. The week before the election, the Arkansas *Democrat Gazette* unleashed some of the harshest abuse that the governor had ever sustained.

The editorial asked what Governor Clinton's record could teach us about President Clinton: 'A purely rhetorical approach to issues that may please all, coupled with a tendency to side with those interests powerful enough to do him some political good ... his tax policy in Arkansas has been to hand out exemptions to large corporations and soak the middle class.'

After painting a desolate picture of Clinton's failures as an administrator, the editorial concluded thus: 'Finally, and sadly, there is the unavoidable question of character ... it is not the duplicitous in his politics that concerns so much as the polished ease, the almost habitual, casual, articulate way he bobs and weaves. He has mastered the art of equivocation. There is something almost inhuman in his smoother responses that sends a shiver up the spine. It is not the compromises he has made that trouble so much as the unavoidable suspicion that he has no great principles to compromise.'

➵

NOVEMBER 10 *Petrolia*

WELCOME TO CLINTON'S WORLD. I wish I felt better about it. I feel sorry for poor people, sometimes known as the underclass. Let them work or let them starve, as Bill put it so pithily in North Carolina three days shy of the election. And if there's no work available, let them starve anyway.

Expect, in the neoliberal future, increasing respectability for the notions of Malthus and furtive versions of eugenics, these taking the form of phased reduction of the underclass by voluntary sterilization under a system of market credits. Would-be mothers will be able to purchase child credits from those less fecund than themselves and thus exceed the litter limit. Poor mothers will be unable to afford the credits and thus will have to accept Norplant (voluntarily, of course) and kindred impediments to pregnancy, on pain of losing whatever pitiful allotment of public subsidy remains to them after Clinton's reforms take effect.

➵

NOVEMBER 12 *Petrolia*

ONE EAGER STUDENT of strategies for reduction of the dangerous classes was Winston Churchill. As Home Secretary in 1910 he secretly proposed the sterilization of 100,000 'mental degenerates' and the dispatch of tens of thousands of others to state-run labor camps, so as to save the 'British race' from inevitable decline as its 'inferior' members were allowed to breed.

In the decade after Churchill entered Parliament, in 1900, elite policy planners were concerned that Britain was sliding into decline, losing industrial pre-eminence and world market share to Germany and the United States. A cult of national efficiency flourished, with diverse schemes for improving output, education, training and the nation's gene pool.

A Royal Commission recommended to the Liberal government in 1908 that Britain's lunacy laws be expanded to cover not merely the insane but also the 'feeble-minded' – those incapable of 'competing on equal terms with their normal fellows or managing themselves and their affairs with ordinary prudence', meaning simply that they were less educated, less intelligent and less adept in social skills. The commission reckoned there were some 105,000 people in England and Wales in this category.

In the view of one commissioner, Alfred Tredgold, these feeble-minded folk were impeding the advance of the nation and hence its ability to compete in the world economy. Worse, they were breeding almost twice as fast as the national average and, if this was not checked, the time would come, 'if it has not already come', when the nation would contain a 'preponderance of citizens lacking in the intellectual and physical vigour which is absolutely essential to progress' and which therefore 'must inevitably end in national destruction'.

Churchill urged fundamental change: forced sterilization of these saboteurs of Britain's ability to compete. He buttressed his case with a booklet, *The Sterilization of Degenerates*, by Dr. H.C. Sharp of the Indiana Reformatory in the United States.

In the first couple of decades of the twentieth century American elites were also much concerned about the national gene pool (the founders of Cal Tech were rabid eugenicists) and about national efficiency. Between 1907 and 1913, starting with Indiana, twelve states put sterilization statutes on their books. Indiana's Governor, J. Frank Hanley, signed a law authorizing the compulsory sterilization of any confirmed criminal, idiot, rapist or imbecile in a state institution whose condition was determined to be 'unimprovable' by a panel of physicians.

Churchill argued to dubious officials in the Home Office that sterilization was a merciful act, it being 'cruel to shut up numbers of people in institutions for their whole lives, if by a simple surgical operation they could be permitted to live freely in the world without causing much inconvenience to others.'

Churchill simultaneously urged 'proper labour colonies', where tramps and wastrels could be sent 'for considerable periods and made to realise their duty to the State.' He had already set up the first labor hiring halls, not as a social reform but as an efficient way of organizing the labor market. The colonies, or gulags, were a logical extension of the plan. The feeble-minded would be part of this corvée.

The plan was rounded off with a series of mandatory sentencing instructions whereby second offenders (for any crime) could be declared criminally weak-minded and compelled to submit to medical examination. If the doctors upheld the diagnosis, the offender could be sent to a labor camp for an indefinite period.

In 1960 the Maryland Senate passed a bill that made it a felony to bear more than two illegitimate children, but the bill was thrown out by Maryland's House of Delegates. Twenty years later the Texas Board of Resources put forward the plan of mandatory sterilization for all welfare recipients. In 1981 a Houston member of the Texas legislature asked his constituents whether or not they favored sterilization for women on welfare with at least three children. Out of just over 6,000 respondents, 60 percent answered in the affirmative.

The shape of things to come in this field can be summed up in the term 'neogenetics', being eugenics decked out in the respectability of modern technology. First you knock out embryos with Down's syndrome and similar ailments, then you widen out from this beachhead. Negative Population Growth, based in Teaneck, New Jersey, with Joanne Woodward on its board, reckons the optimal US population to be 150 million.

➡

DECEMBER 10   *Petrolia*

NATIONS, LIKE PRIESTS, should be trusted least when they are at their most self-righteous. President Bush's plan to dispatch about 28,000 US troops to Somalia to protect relief efforts has won general approbation.

Clinton and his crew are ominously eager to put the world to rights. Liberal columnists have been urging intervention in such areas as the Balkans, imposing mercy by any means necessary.

Troops will not go in and out of Somalia within a week or a month. Their arrival will affect rivalries, systems of pillage and black-marketeering, as well as the bargains arranged by relief organizations in the field – particularly the International Committee of the Red Cross and Save the Children (UK). So they will be challenged and will either kill or be killed and probably both.

The US military commander will inevitably be drawn into his own political negotiations, thus intervening in struggles that have continued in Somalia since the flight in 1991 of Mohammed Siad Barre, the country's tyrant for twenty-one years.

➡

DECEMBER 24   *Petrolia*

SO WHY NO PARDON for Gen. Manuel A. Noriega? If George Bush is going to behave like a Latin American dictator on the way to the airport, signing pardons for his secret police and kindred underlings and accomplices, how can he forget the Panamanian who aided and abetted his secret war and is the only one of the gang who has ended up in prison?

In the bitter words of Special Prosecutor Lawrence Walsh, reacting to the pardons, 'The Iran-Contra cover-up, which has continued for more than six years, has now been completed.'

The men Bush pardoned on Christmas Eve – former Defense Secretary Caspar Weinberger, National Security Adviser Robert McFarlane, former Assistant Secretary of State Elliott Abrams, and CIA men Dewey Claridge, Clair George, Alan Fiers – were mostly accused of deceiving Congress.

But deception of a Congress that was agreeable to being deceived was but a minor facet of a secret terrorist war in which tens of thousands died. The men who are now breathing easier were involved in plans and operations aimed at destroying a country, Nicaragua. They hired torturers from Argentina, drew up an assassination manual, ordered the mining of harbors, the destruction of health clinics, the killing of peasants and social workers, all in defense of US and international laws.

Already there's a tumult of rage over the pardons. But as they clamber up on their high horses, Americans should remember that the terrorist war against Nicaragua was a bipartisan affair in which senior Democrats connived at the illegalities by ignoring the trails of evidence pointing to the illegal covert operations.

At least the pardons will finally put to rest the theory that, deep down, there was a 'good George Bush' yearning to be free. These pardons are entirely in character, are in fact the appropriate bottom line on his resumé. He always believed in covert operations and hence in the lying, law-breaking and deceptions of Congress that accompany secret government. If he believed in the operations, then he logically believed that the executives and subordinates carrying them out must, in the larger sense, be innocent of crimes. As he said when he issued the pardons, the men he was forgiving were patriots all.

1993

➤

The Argument

IN WHICH I am discovered amid the flood waters of the Mattole, contemplating the beginning of Clinton time. Janet Reno's past as a 'Satan cult' prosecutor; the Queen Mother's affair with a Leninist revealed; the lesbian moment evoked; the killings at Waco; career of 'Jolly' West and untimely death of Tusko the elephant; end of the Clinton administration; Irving Howe memorialized; evocation of Mesmer and the sociology of the parasciences; gays in the military; the Pajaro Valley and the importance of local history; the chant of Hawaiian nationalism; mystery of Olaf Palme's murder; the benefits of multiple personality explored; Lee Harvey Oswald, man of the left; the great Oakland fire; Karl Popper and the march of science. Of the decay of liberalism I sing, and sing.

JANUARY 1   *Petrolia, California*
OF THE CRUELTY OF MEN:

'Creatures shall be seen on the earth who will always be fighting one with another, with the greatest losses and frequent deaths on either side. There will be no bounds to their malice; by their strong limbs a great portion of the trees in the vast forests of the world shall be laid low; and when they are filled with food the gratification of their desire shall be to deal out death, affliction, labour, terror, and banishment to every living thing; and from their boundless pride they will desire to rise towards heaven, but the excessive weight of their limbs will hold them down. Nothing shall remain on the earth, or under the earth, or in the waters that shall not be pursued, disturbed, or spoiled, and that which is in one country removed into another. And their bodies shall be made the tomb and the means of transit of all the living bodies which they have slain.

'O earth, why dost thou not open and hurl them into the deep fissures of thy vast abysses and caverns, and no longer display in the sight of heaven so cruel and horrible a monster.' – Leonardo da Vinci: *Notebooks*

➳

JANUARY 2   *Petrolia*

'FUNDAMENTAL CHANGE' is not the phrase that comes to mind while contemplating the features of Senator Lloyd Bentsen, nominated by Clinton as his Secretary of the Treasury. Like a desert landscape, those folds and tucks and dewlaps speak to terrifying continuity, exactions of time and climate presenting themselves with the bleak clarity of landmarks along the entropic path.

➳

JANUARY 15   *Petrolia*

UNUSUALLY LUNATIC PIECE on the *WSJ* editorial page, even for them. David Brooks reverently quotes that old idiot Max Beloff: 'The post-colonial countries that are doing well are countries that had a long apprenticeship under the colonial administration The countries that are doing badly are those that had a brief experience with colonialism.'

Japan?

➡

JANUARY 20   *Petrolia*

FOR THE FIRST TIME in six years, the storm window off the Pacific coast has opened. The jet streams drag monsoon weather in from the south Pacific and northwesterly gales down from the Gulf of Alaska. In Honeydew, fifteen miles upriver from my home, ten inches of rain fell in one night and the river rose a foot every half-hour. Tracing its rise, moving our cars and trucks to higher ground, I and some neighbours – marooned above the flooded river road – caught snatches of the inaugural phrasemaking in Washington. Clinton calls for 'a government for our tomorrows, not our yesterdays'. Clinton is a man of many tomorrows. The Fleetwood Mac line, 'Don't stop thinking about tomorrow', has become his mantra.

New Hollywood has mustered in Washington today, just as old Hollywood did in 1981, when Reagan took over. Indeed, the symbolic transition this time is not from Bush but from Reagan. Reagan invented a past, Clinton a future. The outcast in both cases is history, and a psychobiographer would no doubt point out that each man had the experience of a drunken parent in their earliest years. The real past is pain, *bonhomie* the eternal mask.

The Clinton cohort wants everything on its terms. 'We force the spring', said the new president in the second paragraph of his address. As any gardener could tell him, forced bulbs bloom only once.

Even so, most people I talk to feel benign about the day.

➡

JANUARY 25   *Petrolia*

I'm attacked as a Goebbels-type for being rude about Clinton. The *Statesman* has run an amazingly silly piece by someone called Philip Gould urging Clintonism as a model for the British Labour Party, and lashing me as beastly to Bill, misrepresenting him as a self-serving slave of the corporate agenda instead of a noble populist and lefty.

There's obviously a big push to sell Clintonism in the UK. There was a conference chaired by Martin Walker of the *Guardian* and stocked with a rum lot from the States like Don Stillman of the UAW, Jeff Faux of the Economic Policy Institute and the pollsters all lauding Clinton. Gould quotes Faux as stating 'It's not true that Clinton became a centrist to win the election' and

Stillman as saying Bill is a big friend to labor. God knows what rubbish Walker was preaching about his pal. The Goebbels charge came as a consequence of Gould deriding my view that Clinton will punish the poor.

What planet do these people live on? What do they think Clinton's talk about 'ending welfare as we know it' really adds up to? Do they think that appalling mess dreamed up by the insurance industry and Alan Enthoven is 'universal health care'. I suppose Faux feels he might as well start off on the right foot. I can't imagine he believes that rubbish. Walker is writing incredible drivel in the *Guardian* about Clinton as Roosevelt, and Dennis McShane is doing the same thing every time he gets a chance in the *Statesman*.

In its effective aspects, the Democratic Party is the creature of lawyer/lobbyists in Washington, who now crowd Clinton's cabinet (fourteen lawyers) and the upper tiers of his government.

I must admit to one spasm of annoyance. Gordon Marsden – who, I'm glad to see, was rejected by the voters of Blackpool South last year – was respectfully quoted by editor Steve Platt as denouncing 'the tired anti-Americanism that Alexander Cockburn too frequently peddles.'

For some reason, the British find it far easier than Americans to label as 'anti-American' any view of America that happens to differ from their own. Unlike Marsden, I live among Americans and have done so for twenty years. Like these Americans around me, I honor much in America and deplore much else. Again, like many Americans, I do not particularly honor Bill Clinton, or the political tendency he represents. Bill Clinton is prolific with promises, meek to vested power. Thus far, he's running true to form. Only those who argue (many do) that progress in America is rated by the freedom with which a woman can be urged to have an abortion can hold that a fresh wind is blowing down Pennsylvania Avenue.

➤

FEBRUARY 2   *Petrolia*

CHARLES: The trouble is I need you several times a week.

CAMILLA: Mmm. So do I. I need you all the week. All the time.

CHARLES: Oh God, I'll just live inside your trousers or something. It would be much easier.

CAMILLA: [laughs] What are you going to turn into, a pair of knickers? (both laugh) Oh, you're going to come back as a pair of knickers.

CHARLES: Or, God forbid, a Tampax. Just my luck! [laughs]

CAMILLA: You are a complete idiot! (laughs) Oh what a wonderful idea.

CHARLES: My luck to be chucked down a lavatory and go on and on forever swirling round on the top, never going down.

CAMILLA: [laughing] Oh darling!

In Britain there's been a good deal of clucking about this destroying the last vestige of popular respect for the House of Windsor. In line with the symbolism of the Wars of the Roses, Carlists should sport little Tampax pins on their lapels, while the Diana party could wear tiny silver lemon slicers, in memory of the implement with which she supposedly stabbed herself amid the torments of her loveless union.

Queen Victoria, following the loss of her consort, Prince Albert, in 1861 when she was forty-two, emerged from a period of bereavement to a new love. Her manservant, the former Scottish gillie John Brown, was always at her side. Popular ditties soon speculated upon the nature of Victoria's passion. Tariq Ali, who's just interviewed E.P. and Dorothy Thompson, has passed on the latter's info.

The Queen addressed Brown in letters as 'Darling One'. One note, fished out of Brown's wastepaper basket by a footman, contained the aside – amid instructions for the management of the estate – 'Oh, forgive me if I offend, but you are so dear to me, so adored, that I cannot bear to live without you.'

Brown and Victoria shared a taste for whiskey (she mixed it with claret). Edgar Boehm, who sculpted Brown on the Queen's command, told to his mistress, Catherine Walters (*aka* 'Skittles'), who in turn told Wilfrid Scawen Blunt, that 'John Brown had unbounded influence with the Queen whom he treated with little respect, presuming in every way upon his position with her. It was the talk of all the household that he was the Queen's stallion.'

In September 1866, the *Gazette de Lausanne* reported that Victoria had married John Brown and borne his child. A detailed version of the story appeared in 1873 in a pamphlet by Alexander Robertson, a tax collector in Scotland who had been trying to levy a toll on the Atholl family. The Dowager Duchess of Atholl said that if he, Robertson, persisted, she would let the cat out of the bag. The cat in question was the presence of Brown in a certain bedroom in Dunkeld House (a home of the Atholls) during a royal visit, and the implied role of the Duchess as midwife in a delivery in the same house nine months later. The child was allegedly placed with a Protestant pastor in Vaux, Switzerland.

Brown died of drink in 1883. A vast portrait of him in full Scottish regalia hung in Balmoral. On the Queen's death her son Edward, now on the throne, gazed at the portrait with hatred and then stuck his walking stick through Brown's heart.

➤

FEBRUARY 4   *Petrolia*

DURING WORLD WAR II, Balmoral was a hothouse again, as Elizabeth, consort of George VI and today the aged Queen Mother, was seized with a passion for one of the military detachment based there. Her lover was a married man who before the war had attended the London School of Economics and there became a member of the Communist Club, confessing to the club's secretary, J.B., that he had read no Marx but all the works of Lenin. With the invasion of the Soviet Union he volunteered and was subsequently posted to Balmoral, where his love affair with the King's wife commenced. He told his wife of it. She was not pleased but remarked that at least she could be sure the relationship had no future.

As did many leftists of the period, the couple had adopted a Basque baby orphaned in the Spanish Civil War. At the funeral of her mother years later, this young woman told intimates that finally the great secret could be disclosed. Widowed in the early 1950s, Elizabeth conceived a passion for Cointreau, for at least one other military man and, some say, for Bourguiba of Tunisia, exchanging the dour surroundings of Balmoral for pleasures amid the ruins of Carthage.

My grandfather Jack Arbuthnot, an officer in the Scots Guards, used to visit Scottish fastnesses such as Balmoral and Glamis, home of the Queen Mother's family, the Bowes-Lyons, early in the century, and the future consort of George VI used to commandeer him as her steed, perched on his back and galloping him around the drawing room. Perhaps this formed the foundation for her later predilections.

I shall wear a little Tampax pin with pride. As dear Jack Finnegan used to boast in his Scottish accent as thick as John Brown's, 'Finnegan, ML – Monarchist-Leninist'.

➤

FEBRUARY 6   *Petrolia*
THE RATIONALES FOR PREJUDICE don't alter much down the years. In April 1948, Dwight D. Eisenhower faced Congressional questions about desegregation of the armed forces. Senator Richard Russell of Georgia (later a mentor of the young Sam Nunn) stirred himself:

Russell: The question of segregation is one that is always painful for me to discuss, and particularly unpleasant for me to ask the questions that I shall now, but ... more is involved than racial prejudice. It goes directly to such vital factors as the morale, discipline and health of the troops.
You are familiar, I am sure, with the ratio of crime among Negro troops compared with white troops in the service, are you not?
Eisenhower: It was higher.
Russell: You are familiar with the reports that indicated the incidence of venereal diseases, are you not?
Eisenhower: Yes, sir.

Russell: I am sure you are familiar with the figures among the men examined for the draft. The incidence of venereal diseases, gonorrhea and syphilis, was 252 per thousand among the Negro race, as compared to 17 per thousand with the white race.

Russell believed that the races should not mix, in peace or war. Forty-four years later, Lieutenant-Colonel William Gregor (US Army, retired), who had done extensive work for the Joint Chiefs of Staff on the issue of gays in the military, gave expression on CNN's *Crossfire* to his view of the problems caused by ending discrimination against gays.

Lieut.-Col. Gregor: I suggest you look at the studies of the attempts to induct active venereals during World War II ...
Michael Kinsley: What does that have to do with homosexuals?
Gregor: Well, precisely as a public health concern ... Let's imagine for a second, you've gone through training and developed a habit of universal precautions ... Now you go to the battlefield ... The question is, if a penetrator courses through a turret and amputates a gunner's arm, will the tank commander, having developed this habit of universal precautions, instantaneously and swiftly grab that bloody stump to save the life of his friend? Or will he hesitate and allow the life of his buddy to slip away?

In 1948, Eisenhower responded to Russell that he believed that improved living standards and education among Negroes would eventually dissipate the senator's concerns. In 1992, Rep. Barney Frank (D-Mass) pointed out to Lieut.-Col. Gregor that all applicants to the armed forces are tested for AIDS and, if they carry the virus, are not admitted. Reform comes as a matter of political calculation. In 1948, Harry Truman was trying to steal the desegregationist thunder of Henry Wallace, his presidential rival running on the Progressive ticket. In 1992, Clinton was similarly trying to capture a helpful political constituency.

➤

FEBRUARY 22   *Petrolia*
JANET RENO USED a seventeen-year-old undocumented Honduran worker to help her win a fierce re-election battle for Dade County prosecutor back in 1984. Ileana Fuster, the young woman in question, received a ten-year prison sentence as a reward for testifying against her husband, Francisco, who pulled six life terms plus 165 years.

Troublesome here is the manner in which Clinton's nominee for A.G. pressured Ileana to turn against her husband. If outlined in a human rights report the methods endorsed by Reno would justly be called brainwashing. They included isolation, quasi-hypnosis, conditioned response and kindred mind-bending techniques.

Having presided over the reduction of the young Honduran woman to psychic flotsam, Reno then huddled next to her, holding her hand while the prosecutor's hired 'psychologists' guided Ileana through the catechism that produced her own confession and her husband's ruin.

The Country Walk case in Miami was a benchmark in the 'ritual abuse' persecutions that have landed scores of innocent people in prison with hard time. It began less than a year after the McMartin preschool case started in Los Angeles in 1983. Debbie Nathan sent me her account.

In 1984 Francisco Fuster, a 36-year-old Cuban immigrant, was running a home-based babysitting service with Ileana in the wealthy Miami suburb of Country Walk. The case began when a three-year-old boy asked his mother to 'kiss my body. Ileana kisses all the babies' bodies'. As a Miami-based anthropologist, Rafael Martinez, consultant to the Dade County Medical Examiner's Office, told Nathan, in traditional Latin American cultures 'kissing and hugging is common with children up to three and four years old. It is common for females to kiss children all over the place – including on the genitals.'

In the North American culture of those early Reagan years, on the other hand, adults were learning that kissing and hugging of young children, or even more genteel contact with them in a day-care center, could swiftly lead to charges of oral copulation, sodomy, forced consumption of mind-altering drugs and alcohol, anal penetration with a crucifix, obscene magic ritual, unregulated transport of minors by broomstick across state lines, etc.

All this lay in store for the Fusters, whose clientele were soon being interviewed by Joseph and Laurie Braga, retained by the state as 'expert' interrogators of children, though their skills were most conspicuously displayed in hectoring their tiny subjects and forcing them with remorseless leading questions into following a predetermined agenda of incrimination.

Nathan's transcription of one such interrogation – in which four-year-old 'J.L.' bravely insists, in the face of outrageous leading questions by Mrs. Braga, on the Fusters' kindness and proper behavior – is searing. Bullied and cajoled, 'J.L.' finally accepts the prepared script.

The Dade County prosecutor's office soon found out that Francisco had done time in New York for manslaughter, and had also been convicted of lewd assault for fondling a nine-year-old girl. On the other hand, his ex-wife denied he had exhibited any pedophilia, and other family members said his relations with children were affectionate, nonviolent and nonsexual. With one exception, no child lodged at the Fusters' displayed any physical sign of sexual molestation. The exception, Francisco's son, was deemed to have examined positive for gonorrhea of the throat. I say 'deemed' because Nathan reports that the testing method then in vogue has since turned out to be utterly unreliable. Three years after Fuster's conviction researchers at the Centers for Disease Control showed that the test could not distinguish the gonorrhea culture from others occurring normally in both adult and juvenile throats (irrespective of sexual activity). When the CDC tested samples from children who had supposedly tested positive for the bacterium that causes venereal gonorrhea, more than a third of the samples turned out to contain a different organism. The Fuster child's sample was destroyed before a retrospective analysis of it could be made.

Throughout the interrogations the Fusters vehemently insisted on their innocence, and the case was threatening to become a political liability for Reno. In her re-election campaign against a strong challenger she was promising 'justice' – that is, convictions.

Nathan gives an admirable account of how Reno's political emergency dovetailed with a crisis for the Fusters' defense attorney, Michael Von Zamft, who was finding that public hysteria over the Country Walk affair was imperiling his larger career ambitions. His solution was to sever Ileana's case from Francisco's and 'persuade' her to confess that yes, she was an abuser, but only because she had been acting under duress. Francisco's defender thus became his prosecutor.

The only inhibition to this agenda was Ileana. She told a chaplain at the jail where she was being held that the district attorney and her lawyer wanted her to say things about her husband that weren't true. Ileana was terrified of being held in solitary. She'd already experienced such treatment during the first seven months of her imprisonment, sometimes being kept naked under a suicide watch, and she found it unendurable. By the summer of 1985 she was back in isolation again. Although she had now been separated from her husband for a period as long as they had been married prior to her arrest – eleven months – Ileana, eight weeks into solitary, insisted on his innocence.

A psychologist was mustered who duly declared that Ileana was a 'needy child' under Francisco's domination. He announced that he could 'get her to respond in any way that I pushed her … and she would be interested in pleasing me, so I wouldn't be mad at her.' All that was now required was a confession, and Von Zamft recruited another psychologist, Michael Rappaport, who with his partner, Merry Sue Haber, ran a Miami business called Behavior Changers. You could say that Rappaport had experience in the field, having done time in Fort Leavenworth for adultery and sodomy with two women he was counseling. He himself was ordered by the Florida Department of Professional Review to be under the supervision of a psychologist – namely his partner, Haber.

Rappaport visited Ileana in her cell at least thirty-four times, putting her through 'visualization' exercises, contrasting the lenient treatment she would receive consequent upon a confession with the dire punishments ahead if she were uncooperative. 'It's a lot like reverse brainwashing', he later told Nathan. 'We just spent hours and hours talking to her … It's kind of a manipulation. It was very much like dealing with a child. You make them feel very happy, then segue into the hard things.' While this exercise in applied mental disintegration was going on, Ileana was, according to Rappaport, receiving a surprising number of visits from prosecutor Reno, whose involvement in the case had become fanatical.

Ileana broke on August 21, stating during a polygraph test that she and Francisco had molested the children. Confessions were conjured out of her in subsequent depositions, often with Reno holding her hand while Rappaport hugged her. As Nathan puts it, 'When viewed chronologically, Ileana's 'confession' depositions also suggest that many of her statements were confabulations or fabrications cued by her jailhouse visitors.'

The material in the confessions echoed many of the staples of ritual abuse charges. The Bragas were enthusiastic missionaries for the 'discoveries' about such 'ritual abuse' then being elicited in the McMartin case in Los Angeles. Reno, similarly obsessed, had already been active in urging changes in evidentiary law to allow the admission of videotaped charges leveled by children and other star-chamber innovations advocated by the ritual abuse lobby.

Ileana, prompted and coached by Rappaport, had been led into a world of fantasy. She said Francisco had hung her in the garage by her hands and his son by the ankles, and that he had also rubbed feces on her legs and put snakes on both her and the children's genitals. When a lawyer probed this accusation, she answered, 'Well, I remember a snake.' 'What about a snake?' the lawyer said. 'Having bad dreams about it', responded Ileana. If she failed to recollect an atrocity on the stand, Rappaport would take her aside for private counseling and then return her to give the appropriate responses – that she remembered 'a tool thing' or 'crowbar' Francisco put 'around' her vagina; that Francisco took a gun and placed it on Ileana's vagina and fired it.

In her statement to the judge Ileana set her confession in perspective: 'I am not pleading guilty because I feel guilty ... I am innocent of all those charges. I wouldn't have done anything to harm any children ... I am pleading guilty to get all of this over ... for my own good.' She was sentenced to ten years, served three and a half, and was deported to Honduras, having divorced Francisco while in prison. As have many victims of these persecutions, she turned to Jesus, was born again and is now sequestered from journalistic inquiry by an evangelical group, although she is apparently about to recant her earlier confession. Francisco is in prison, still insisting on his innocence, while his nemesis, Janet Reno, heads for Washington.

Meanwhile, the Ritual Abuse Task Force, a subcommittee of Los Angeles County's Commission for Women chaired by 'psychologist' Myra Riddell and comprising therapists, alleged victims and religious leaders, recently claimed that Satanists are poisoning them, along with other therapists and survivors of Satanic abuse, by means of a pesticide pumped into their offices, homes and cars. They invited the county's chief of toxic epidemiology to listen to their allegations, which he categorized as 'outrageous'.

It's doubtful Reno will be given any trouble about the Country Walk case in her confirmation hearings, or about a later one involving a Dutch youth, who was similarly isolated for long months before being found innocent of abuse charges.

Guess who's behind all this ritual abuse? According to the lore of the ritual abuse lobby, a man called Dr. Green or Greenbaum is the leading promoter of Satanic child abuse in the United States. As a Hasidic teenager in a concentration camp he supposedly learned the essentials of the cultic lore from the Nazis, adding his own cabalistic embroidery. So, ritual abuse ends up as a subset of anti-Semitism. Pass that cup of Christian blood.

➡

MARCH 6   *Petrolia*
FROM TRANSITION MAGAZINE, March 1932, ed. Eugene Jolas
Questions on the future of collectivism for Alex – for your archives and enjoyment. An article called 'The Crisis of Man':

xx S.E.

MARTIN BUBER: Your question is very difficult. I envisage the evolution of individualism, in a collectivist regime, as revolutionary; and the evolution of metaphysics as partaking of the mood of the catacombs.

GERTRUDE STEIN: I don't envisage collectivism. There is no such animal, it is always individualism, sometimes the rest vote and sometimes they do not, and if they do they do and if they do not they do not.

H.L. MENCKEN: Your question leaves me in some uncertainty, but here is my attempt to answer it:

I do not believe that this is a collectivist epoch. It seems to me that the effort to set up collectivism in Russia is bound to fail, and that little will be heard of it by 1950, save historically. Such a man as Stalin is really not a collectivist. At heart he is quite as much an individualist as J. Pierpont Morgan. As for Mussolini, he is simply a passing phantasm. He will blow up anon, and be forgotten. There is always room in the world for individualists. If they are rare, it is only because courage is rare.

➡

MARCH 22   *Petrolia*
THE PUTSCH LAUNCHED by Yeltsin on March 20 was undertaken with the direct connivance and encouragement of the Clinton administration and is now being

cheered on by a bipartisan chorus of the US political and journalistic elite.

On March 12 'a senior administration official' confided to the press that 'Washington would not oppose a move by Yeltsin to suspend his Parliament or abolish the Soviet-era Constitution to put down political opposition.' This gave Yeltsin his green light.

The virtually unchallenged assumption in the US is that Yeltsin is the lone representative of democratic legitimacy, confronted by holdovers from the Soviet museum intent on steering Russia back towards a totalitarian past. Yeltsin owes both his own political ascendancy and the post which he now holds to the same Congress of People's Deputies whose credentials are now being derided here in the U.S. It was vice president Alexander Rutskoi's group in the Congress that pressed for a strong executive and it was parliamentary chairman Rhuslan Khasbulatov who stood shoulder to shoulder with Yeltsin on the balcony of the Russian White House, denouncing the putsch of 1991.

The Congress itself was elected in March of 1990. The Communists still ruled, but the conditions under which that vote took place bore no resemblance to the one-party rituals of the past. There were no reserved seats. Any candidate nominated by residents or by workers in a factory or institute could get on the ballot paper. Every prospective deputy had to face the voters, had to get 51 per cent of the vote.

This was at a time when the Communist Party was in utter disrepute, but when many of the most vociferous reformers were still formally party members, like Yeltsin himself, since Russia was still in a one-party system. In some areas, particularly the more rural ones, the old *nomenklatura* still held sway, and their representatives were uncontested. But elsewhere this was not the case. The March 1990 election saw victories for such famous dissidents as Galina Starovoitova and Father Gleb Yakunin.

➤

MARCH 23   *Petrolia*
CAME ACROSS a good note from one of the Woolf/Bell women, I think Virginia, though I wrote it down in a library and forgot to be precise.

February 11, 1925
Dearest ... I have had a most shameful and distressing interview with poor dear Tom Eliot, who may be called dead to us from this day forward. He has become an Anglo-Catholic, believes in God and immortality and goes to church. I was really shocked. A corpse would seem to be more credible than he is. I mean, there's something obscene in a living person sitting by the fire and believing in God ...

EVERY AMERICAN PRESIDENCY has its sexual correlate, and with Bill Clinton it looks as though the lesbians are finally coming into their own.

With something as impalpable as the *zeitgeist* evidence is necessarily anecdotal, but in the Clit Club, Crazy Fanny's and a thousand feminist bookshops across America where women dump their backpacks and browse through the erotica of Anais Nin, there is the fragrance of lesbian empowerment wafting down Pennsylvania Avenue.

The sense that somehow the dikes have taken over is swiftly substituting itself as demon fear among the Bible-thumpers who previously reckoned that male homosexuals were pulling the strings. The AM radio talkshow crowd says 'Hillary *Rodham* Clinton' (the first lady specifically requested the triple-decker handle) with enough innuendo to curdle the blood.

Lesbians, nosing through Blanche Cooke's cult classic about Eleanor Roosevelt's lesbian passions, hopefully recruit Hillary as a kind of honorary lesbian, with the same zeal that male gays used to suggest that every man of eminence since Adam was by essential nature and enthusiasm a son of Sodom. No one seems to have contemplated the reverse scenario. Bill has an affinity to lesbians. At Oxford he consorted with a famous switch-hitter. Together they would prowl the streets for young female prey, on whom the girl would batten, to Bill's disadvantage.

It's certainly chic to be a lesbian. *Mademoiselle*'s latest edition carries 'Women in Love' ('young lesbians: they're fresh, they're proud, they're comfortable with their sexuality ... they're now defining a new style'). Madonna, eye ever alert for trend and tremor, diddles with lesbian identities and her friend Sandra Bernhard plays a lesbian in America's most popular sitcom, *Roseanne*.

'Lesbians are hot', says my friend John Scagliotti, producer of the PBS gay and lesbian variety show *In The Life*. 'They're where the male gay movement was ten years ago. Women are now running the activist gay and lesbian task forces. One simple reason is that a lot of older gay men in the movement have died. The men from the boomer generation you'd expect to become leaders have gone.'

The lesbian culture now unfurling on shows like *In the Life* has been fermenting for at least a quarter of a century in its current cycle. Back in the late 1960s radical women, affronted by phallocrats coarsely putting them in their place, broke away into separatist movements, consciousness-raising sessions and kindred manifestations of Sisterhood. Some of these, fueled by Simone de Beauvoir, lysergic acid, Shulamith Firestone and other catalysts, developed into lesbian collectives.

Feminist teachers at colleges like Vassar fostered a new generation of lesbians who fanned out across the country and developed the famous sanctuaries of

Northampton (western Massachusetts, largest assemblage of lesbians in the world, recently surveyed by Barbara Walters and the *National Enquirer*), Santa Cruz (a kind of Pacific Northampton, home of the famous lesbian seminars of Bettina Aptheker, *rite de passage* of baby dykes without number), San Francisco and Manhattan.

Each of these lesbian *quartiers* has its own personality. Northampton and Santa Cruz foster the granola look, with lesbians in a uniform of plaid shirt, black trousers, boots or birkenstocks with obligatory backpack, or ragged skirt over leggings, against chic Manhattan or San Francisco where variants of the old femme/butch modes play out in lesbian clubs. Biker girls and cute nurses from the suburbs consort amid the whips and chains.

Lesbian culture has its heroines: Kate Millett, Adrienne Rich, k.d. lang, Martina Navratilova, all of whom are Out. There's somewhat less enthusiasm for the self-declared bisexual Camille Paglia who flails away at the PC crowd and likes to be photographed in a dominatrix pose, all beetling brows and pale fierce mien. A major heroine is the black poet Audrey Lord whose memorial service, after she died of cancer recently, was attended at St. John's in New York City by thousands of lesbians, many of whom described the service as a defining moment in their lives.

As usual there's the gnashing of teeth at the known lesbians who stop short of public affirmation. 'What lesbian revolution?' snorts my dear niece Laura Flanders, political organizer in New York. 'They can't even find a woman to put on the cover of *OUT* magazine.' Laura went on to talk in vexed terms about such icons of the lesbian crowd as Susan Sontag, Annie Leibowitz, Liz Smith and Iris Love. Even Lily Tomlin is coy about where exactly she stands in the matter of preference.

One encouraging sign is that dike comics are all the rage. The women's movement has famously been on the dour side (Q: How many lesbians does it take to screw in a light bulb? A: That's not funny.), but now lesbian comediennes like Kate Bornstein are on the cutting edge. Lesbian politics are getting friskier too, whether with the sex journal *On Our Backs* (a take-off of a famous feminist movement, Off Our Backs) or with the Lesbian Avengers, a New York group. The Avengers have dumped papier maché bombs on their foes and agitated for Alice B. Toklas to be conjoined to the new statue of Gertrude Stein in Bryant Park outside New York Public Library. (Gertrude is the first real woman to be the subject of public sculpture in New York. She joins Alice in Wonderland and the Statue of Liberty.)

The only shadow falling over this lesbian naissance is the question of the truly avant garde trend, which may have already made a dialectical leap over the dykes and into ... cross gendering.

Lesbians are defining themselves less in opposition to straight men, and more as people having a fine time sexually with each other and therefore more relaxed about men. Many of them are having babies too, courtesy of turkey basters and helpful gay male friends.

Which brings us back to the Clinton presidency. Lesbians, like gays, look to Clinton to expand the Civil Rights bill, thus giving them access to expanded legal protections. Everything in America begins in bed and ends in the law courts.

➤

MARCH 25   *Petrolia*

THE NEW IMPROVED STYLE of American environmentalism is predicated on the trade-off, as brokered by big groups such as National Wildlife, by foundations such as Rockefeller or Pew that give money to these big-time environmental groups, by business, and by government.

The theory of the trade-off is that inside every seemingly irreconcilable antagonism there's a compromise awaiting the skilled touch of the mediator. Downgrade the status of the California gnatcatcher from 'endangered' to 'threatened', throw in some uplifting talk about an ecosystemic approach and Lo! the governor of California declares that the lamb has lain down with the lamb, or in this case the gnatcatcher may flourish in the embrace of the coastal developer.

This union from opposing ends of the Great Chain of Being, brokered by Governor Pete Wilson and blessed by Babbitt, has been given the ultimate accolade of the mediator, a 'win-win' solution. The developer gets his teeth into coastal habitat and the gnatcatcher gets a bit of chaparral at the far end of a golf course now designated on the impact statements as 'open space' and by implication gnatcatcher-friendly. This is the kind of ecosystem a builder can live with. Whether the gnatcatcher can life with it is another matter entirely.

➤

MARCH 27   *Petrolia*

RICHARD GARDNER, a clinical professor of child psychiatry from Columbia University, wrote in the *Wall Street Journal* for February 22 that the child-abuse witch hunts of recent years represent the 'third great wave of hysteria' in U.S. history, following the Salem witch trials of 1692, which saw nineteen hanged, and the McCarthy persecutions. 'Our current hysteria', Gardner continued, 'is by far the worst with regard to the number of lives that have been destroyed and families that have disintegrated.' You can quarrel about exclusions – labor scares, other red scares, race hysteria, etc. – but the point Gardner makes is a fair one.

Dear Daddy,

Well, here I am planted in a small but cosy 'kvartiva' in the middle of what somehow feels like Clapham. I've only been here a week, during which gradual acclimatization I've had enormous meals twenty minutes apart and heated discussions with my landlady about knitting patterns and dogs. Televised politics – Yeltsin battling Khasbulatov – is not considered interesting in any way. Much preferred is the tv serial *Simply Maria* all the way from Mexico.

The family consists of Ma: 38, architect, modest, intelligent, wages 9000 roubles a month which right now is $15, Pa: head engineer, makes aeroplane parts, very thin, doesn't make conversation, but occasionally spits out wry witticisms, and daughter: 16, laughs openly at my grammatical mistakes and takes extreme pleasure in correcting me as often as possible. Apparently the most amusing thing I've said so far is 'cherepycha' which I innocently thought to be a tortoise (I was trying to explain the tortoise and hare syndrome) but which turned out to be an unidentifiable mixture of about three different, silly and rude words.

The little I have seen of Kazan amounts to this: slush, unimaginable dirt. Deep, fathomless puddles calling to mind the one enormous filthy puddle in Gogol's town of Mirgorod which generally reflects the baseness of that town's inhabitants. Apart from that it looks a lot like Youghal – similar colours. The colours on the whole are fantastic. One part of town consists of half derelict houses – pinks and greens mostly – filled with snow and crooked trees.

Every morning I have to catch a tram which is stuffed with vicious babushkas elbowing you as hard as possible, sighing and rolling their eyes. Tut-tutting in the English style gets you nowhere here. I'm trying to look as Russian as possible, silly hat, huge coat, etc., etc., but somehow look like a very old-fashioned soldier or safari guide.

Lessons at the Institute have so far been quite interesting and also cause for amusement. Many are the times it has been pointed out to me that Kazan is *not* a provincial town but in the 19th century was the cultural center of Russia where lived Tolstoi, Herzen, Aksakov. Pushkin once used the loo in a rich merchant's house, etc., etc.

I hope you love the Tartar national symbol here enclosed.

Love,
Daisy

Inside the envelope from Daisy successfully surviving the trip from Kazan was a plaster of paris medallion with a double eagle on it.

APRIL 16   *Petrolia*

Dear Mr. Cockburn,

I tardily read your piece 'Tales Out of School: More on Reno'. I don't mean to downplay the Salem witch hunts, the Red Scare, or the child molestation scare, but they pale in comparison against two of the biggest hysterias of our nation – Prohibition and the current Drug Wars.

While maybe a thousand got caught up in the Salem-type affairs, maybe tens of thousands in the Red Scare of the fifties, and perhaps tens of thousands in the child molestation scare, tens of MILLIONS have been ruined in the attempts at prohibition as well as a complete and utter corruption of our legal system and moral compasses. It is a more serious crime today to grow pot than murder!

It should come as no surprise that the same gang that brought us the child molestation hysteria ('a network of social workers, psychiatrists, psychologists and law enforcement officials') is pushing the drug wars today and making a load of money. One month at the local Charter House runs over $14,000. Most of the victims are forced to go there either by the law or their bosses. Of course, no cure is known, for as Dr. Thomas Szasz points out, there is no disease except a plague of politicians barking about not being soft on crime. Forfeiture has become a billion-dollar-a-year industry.

Berry Hickman
Placitas, New Mexico

➤

APRIL 20   *Petrolia*

WAS IT REALLY NECESSARY to send tanks into the Branch Davidian compound northwest of Waco, Texas, converting the place into a crematorium for over eighty people, including seventeen children?

The hostage rescue squad, Attorney General Reno explains, were getting tired, could not remain in place indefinitely. So both in its origin and its conclusion the Branch Davidian crisis saw deaths of men, women and children because the Feds can't sit still.

We live in the militarized police culture of SWAT teams, tac squads, elite storm units, Delta teams and kindred commandos. Don't knock on the door to solve enforcement problems, but break it down with a bulldozer. The President and his attorney general seem to have signed on to that culture with alacrity. From President Clinton, continued funding for the War on Drugs; from Attorney General Reno a go-ahead for the FBI's catastrophic final solution. Bill and Janet should count the bodies outside Waco and think again.

APRIL 22 *Petrolia*

THE NIGHT OF THE WACO holocaust Attorney General Janet Reno told Larry King that 'We are concerned for the children because there had been reports of sexual abuse of the children.' Well, they certainly put a stop to that! As Wesley Pruden wrote in the *Washington Times*, 'Any time you start the day by gassing women and children, you have to expect it to end badly.'

What really did in the Branch Davidians was the word 'cult'. You can do more or less anything to a cult.

After hiding behind Janet Reno's skirts in the immediate aftermath of the federally sponsored disaster, President Clinton sent out word that the Davidians brought it on themselves: there was evidence that the children were abused, even to instruction on how to 'clamp down' on cyanide pills. The FBI has conceded that there's absolutely no evidence for these chilling claims.

For six hours in Waco the FBI pumped CS2 into a compound containing children too small even to wear the gas masks allegedly stockpiled by the Davidians. It now seems likely that the M-60 tank knocked over the kerosene from the compound's lamps (which the Feds also knew about) and almost everyone was either gassed to death or burned alive.

This appalling event took place on the fiftieth anniversary to the day of the final Nazi assault, April 19, 1943, on the Jewish ghetto in Warsaw. Were those tank commanders and flame dispensers surprised that the ghetto mothers did not seize their children and rush towards the attackers in search of safety?

The Nazis too regarded 'cults' as ripe candidates for persecution. On July 20, 1937, the SS Reichsführer Reinhard Heydrich ordered the banning and persecution of small religious sects, including the Bahais, theosophical groups, New Salem Society and the Seventh Day Adventists. The Gestapo claimed that such action was required because of the sects' menace to society.

➤

APRIL 23 *Petrolia*

MAN GOES INTO A BAR, sees familiar-looking fellow at far end nursing a Becks Dark. He looks like Hitler, only older. Pepper-and-salt moustache. Certain stiffness in one arm. Man sidles along bar, finally speaks up. 'Excuse me, do you mind if I ask you something?'

Fellow raises hand wearily – 'I know what you're going to say. I look like Hitler. Well, I am Hitler! And I'm not sorry! In fact, I'm planning to do it again. Only this time I'm going to kill twenty million Jews and three acrobats.'

'Three acrobats?'

'You see!' Hitler screeches triumphantly, 'You've forgotten the Jews already.'

APRIL 24   *Petrolia*

I SUPPOSE I'M somewhere in the spy files accumulated by a former SFPD inspector, Tom Gerard, and by an ADL spy, who was also an FBI informant, Roy Bullock. Between them they held more than 12,000 names in their computers, ranging from Representative Ron Dellums to such outfits (this from Bullock's files) as Earth Island Institute, United Auto Workers, Jews for Jesus and ACT UP. Bullock's files included the category 'pinkos'.

Bullock was a particularly important member of a national ADL spy network run from New York. An FBI interview with Bullock discloses a curious history. From Indiana, and not himself Jewish, he offered to work undercover for the ADL after reading about an infiltrator of the Communist Party. Affinity for double-identity role playing might also have been fostered by the fact that he was gay. Dividing with Gerard $16,000 in new hundred-dollar bills from the South Africans, he told the San Francisco policeman, 'I may be gay, but I'm a straight arrow.' Gerard's briefcase, discovered in his police locker after he fled, disclosed evidence of a baroque physical and imaginative life: passports and IDs in ten different names, extensive info on death squads (Gerard had earlier worked for the CIA and spent time in El Salvador), a black hood and photos of blindfolded and chained men.

➤

APRIL 25   *Petrolia*

LIEUT.-COL. RALPH VAN DEMAN created an Army Intelligence network targeting four prime foes: the Industrial Workers of the World, opponents of the draft, Socialists and 'Negro unrest'. Fear that Germans could foment black grievances was great. Van Deman was much preoccupied with black churches as centers of sedition.

By the end of 1917 the War Department's Military Intelligence Division had opened a file on Martin Luther King Jr.'s maternal grandfather, the Rev. A.D. Williams, pastor of Ebenezer Baptist Church and first president of the Atlanta NAACP. King's father, Martin Sr., Williams's successor at the Ebenezer church, also entered the Army files. Martin Jr. first shows up in these files (kept by the 111th Military Intelligence Group at Fort McPherson in Atlanta) in 1947. He was attending Dorothy Lilley's Intercollegiate School, and the Army suspected Ms. Lilley of having Communist ties.

Army Intelligence officers became convinced of Martin Luther King Jr.'s own Communist ties when he spoke in 1950 at the twenty-fifth anniversary of the integrated Highlander Folk School in Monteagle, Tennessee. Ten years earlier, an Army Intelligence officer had reported to his superiors that the Highlander school was teaching 'a course of instruction to develop Negro organizers in the southern cotton states'.

By 1963, the Tennessee journalist Stephen Tompkins reports in the *Commercial Appeal*, U2 planes were photographing disturbances in Birmingham, Alabama, capping a multilayered spy system that by 1968 included 304 intelligence offices across the country, 'subversive national security dossiers' on 80,731 Americans, plus 19 million personnel dossiers lodged at the Defense Department's Central Index of Investigations.

A more sinister thread derives from the anger and fear with which the Army high command greeted King's denunciation of the Vietnam War at Riverside Church in 1967. Army spies recorded Stokely Carmichael telling King, 'The Man don't care you call ghettos concentration camps, but when you tell him his war machine is nothing but hired killers you got trouble.'

After the 1967 Detroit riots 496 black men under arrest were interviewed by agents of the Army's Psychological Operations Group, dressed as civilians. It turned out King was by far the most popular black leader. That same year Maj. Gen. William Yarborough, assistant chief of staff for intelligence, observing the great antiwar march on Washington from the roof of the Pentagon, concluded that 'the empire was coming apart at the seams'. There were, Yarborough reckoned, too few reliable troops to fight in Vietnam and hold the line at home.

The Army increased surveillance on King. Green Berets and other Special Forces veterans from Vietnam began making street maps and identifying landing zones and potential sniper sites in major US cities. The Ku Klux Klan was recruited by the 20th Special Forces Group, headquartered in Alabama as a subsidiary intelligence network. The Army began offering 30.06 sniper rifles to police departments, including that of Memphis.

Tompkins details the increasing hysteria of Army Intelligence chiefs over the threat they considered King to be posing to national stability. King was dogged by spy units through early 1967. A Green Beret special unit was operating in Memphis on the day he was shot. He died from a bullet from a 30.06 rifle purchased in a Memphis store, in a murder for which James Earl Ray is serving ninety-nine years.

➤

APRIL 26   *Petrolia*

SOON CLINTON'S FIRST 100 days will be up. What will the record show? Sold out the Haitian refugees (US press very cooperative in this regard, suppressing the recent OAS call on the United States to review its policy in light of international law); let a Bush appointee, Herman Cohen, run Africa policy, essentially giving a green light to Savimbi in Angola to butcher thousands; put Israel's lobbyists in charge of Mideast policy; bolstered the arms industry with a budget in which projected spending for '93 is higher in constant dollars than average spending during the cold war from 1950; increased secret intelligence spending; maintained full DEA funding; put Wall Street in charge of national economic strategy; sold out on grazing and mineral rights on public lands; is pushing NAFTA forward and is now neutering the side agreements that as a candidate he proposed would protect workers and the environment – a big sellout, this one; and, with Mrs. H.R.C. at the wheel, ignores the desire of about 60 percent of Americans for single-payer national health insurance, opting instead for some version of 'managed competition' that leaves the insurance companies in charge of the show.

I know. He's no friend of the unborn and unwanted, and that's enough to keep some liberals happy.

➤

APRIL 29   *Petrolia*
A LETTER FROM ROBERT GORHAM DAVIS, who is married to my father's first wife, Hope Hale Davis.

Alexander Cockburn quotes Richard Gardner, clinical professor of child psychiatry, as stating in the *Wall Street Journal* that the child abuse trials of recent years represent 'the third great wave of hysteria' in US history, following the Salem witch trials of 1692 and the McCarthy persecutions.

Neither Dr. Gardner nor Alexander Cockburn mention a respect in which the Salem witchcraft trials were strikingly like those of alleged child abusers. The Salem accusers, whose testimony, 'spectral evidence', was used to condemn those charged with witchcraft, were almost entirely children or adolescents – in the Salem instance all girls who had learned occult lore from a woman slave, half Carib, half Negro, owned by a local clergyman.

The more the youthful Salem accusers were believed by their elders, including some of the leading theologians of the Bay Colony, the Mathers, for instance, the more bizarre their behavior became and the more fantastic their accusations – very like those cited by Cockburn in the Florida Bobby Fijnje case. Finally they trooped from town to town, falling in pretended fits before persons they had never seen before, but whose possession by the Devil they could allegedly discern in detail. When the courts at last banned such spectral evidence, the trials ceased and the accused were released, all except the hanged. Accusations were even made by the children against other children. One boy of four was jailed for months, kept in leg irons.

Obviously the Salem evidence of such fantasy-making powers in children and their readiness to use them destructively is a reason for moving cautiously in response to child abuse charges though, Alexander Cockburn agrees, child-abuse does undoubtedly occur and more often than we like to think.

Robert Gorham Davis

MAY 1   *Petrolia*

AT THE FOREST SUMMIT in Portland they kept talking about 'ending gridlock'. Gridlock in defense of virtue is no vice. Gridlock can often be defined as holding the bastards at bay, and it's often the best that we can hope for. Every time I hear Clinton or Gore chirp about an end to gridlock and the need for people of good will to hammer out compromises my heart sinks. You can't broker everything. There was gridlock between the slave owners and the abolitionists. What's compromise here? a 4-lb. leg shackle instead of the 12-lb. hand-neck-and-ankle rig cherished by the slave industry?

It was at least amusing to see the rape-and-pillage crowd fumbling for words to indicate their empathy with the primal rhythms of Mother Nature, like Visigoths trying to recite the UN Charter from memory.

➤➤

MAY 2   *New York*

EDWARD SAID HAS his piano concert with Diana Takieddine. He did wonderfully. Beautiful Mozart sonata for two pianos in D major. I liked the Britten Mazurka Elegiaca though Ben disagreed. Diana had smooth motions of her hands. Edward had more flourishing gestures. He took off his watch with masterful theatricality. It was Edward's evening as a renaissance man, cheered to the roof by all his friends.

➤➤

MAY 3   *New York*

THE ONLY PERSON getting as good press as Reno is Babbitt, secretary of the interior. A recent McNeil-Lehrer profile presented him as a cross between Teddy Roosevelt, John Muir and the late Edward Abbey.

Indeed Babbitt is not averse to insinuating that he and Ed were buddies and liked nothing better than to kick back in the wilderness.

In fact Abbey loathed Babbitt.

'Not Babbitt the Rabbit!' bellowed Abbey on hearing news that Babbitt, after ten years as governor of Arizona, was running for president in 1987. 'Babbitt is nothing but a flunky for the developers and industrialists who are rapidly destroying what's left of Arizona.'

Many folks in Arizona hate Babbitt with a steely passion, having long suffered the hypocrisies of this Prairie Pecksniff. The discordance between national posture and local reality was comical. Babbitt the man who lashed out against over-grazing became Babbitt the man who apologized to the Arizona Cattle Growers Association two weeks later; Babbitt the custodian of precious resources was also Babbitt the advocate of the Central Arizona Project, a pork barrel scheme to run water backwards uphill for 370 miles across the Arizona desert to grow surplus cotton.

➤→

MAY 4   *New York*

STARTLING TO SEE Louis Jolyon 'Jolly' West being cited reverently in the press as an authority or 'expert' on cults. West is a psychiatrist at UCLA, renowned for his suzerainty over the Neuropsychiatric Institute.

Back in 1969 West leaped to prominence with disclosure of his plan to put electrodes in the brains of suspected violent offenders at a bureaucratic spin-off, the Center for the Study and Reduction of Violence. Public uproar forced West to abandon this scheme.

In 1973 West once again sought to set up a center for human experimentation at a former Nike missile base in the Santa Monica Mountains. In this pastoral setting the work of scientific experimentation would proceed undisturbed. 'The site is securely fenced', West wrote excitedly to a state legislator. 'Comparative studies could be carried out there, in an isolated but convenient location, of experimental model programs, for alteration of undesirable behavior.'

In 1975 West and his collegial mindbenders at the UCLA Institute were subjecting children to electric cattleprods and LSD as part of aversion therapy against homosexual tendencies. The experimenters had set up the following criteria to establish homosexual preferences: 1. Do you ever extend your fingers to their limit? 2. Do you ever stand with your hands on your hips? 3. Does your wrist go limp? 4. Do you flutter your arms up and down the way Nixon did? 5. Do you touch your palms to your back? 6. Have you ever moved your hand towards the outer surface of the forearm while the elbow is either fixed or extended? Yes to two of these behavioral traits got you aversion therapy, meaning a whack with the prod followed by a bracing dram of lysergic acid.

West had long worked with CIA chemists and kindred boffins on the use of LSD in altering human behaviour. Not just humans either. In 1962 West killed Tusko, a renowned elephant at the Oklahoma City zoo. He shot the mighty pachyderm full of acid and Tusko swiftly succumbed. West claimed that the zookeeper had brought him the elephant for treatment.

In the late 1960s and early 1970s neurologists and psychiatrists were much taken with the problems of urban violence. One of West's mentors was Dr. Ernst Rüdin, a Strangelove-type heading up the neurology department at the Lafayette Clinic who recommended psychosurgery and castration as appropriate medical technologies to apply to the dangerous classes.

Rudin equated 'dumb young males who riot' to oxen and declared that 'the castrated ox will pull his plow' and that 'human eunuchs, although at times quite scheming entrepreneurs, are not given to physical violence. Our scientific age tends to disregard this wisdom of the past.'

West made similar statements after the Watts rebellion, but for the castrator's sickle he recommended the substitution of cyproterone acetate, a sterilizing chemical developed by the East Germans ('Ve haff vays of making you squeak'). By 1972 West was suggesting the use of prisoners as 'subjects' in such treatment. There was a big stink about this and in 1974 statewide protests led to cuts of state funding to West's NPI.

In his *Operation Mind Control* Walter Bowart wrote that West is 'perhaps the chief advocate of mind control in America today'.

➤

MAY 5   *Ardmore, Co. Waterford*
KEVIN MYERS, the *Irish Times* columnist, refers to the 'excuse' of the penal laws used to account for Ireland's failure to become a fully fledged industrial power in the nineteenth century. He suggests that maybe the Irish appetite for whiskey is actually what accounts for the failure. Odd to find an Irish paper parroting the old British line that the Irish were shiftless sots fit only for export to Botany Bay. Foster's new history of Ireland takes the same sort of tack about the British effect. You get from it the notion that the famine was something a bit unfortunate, one of a phase of famines in the nineteenth century which weren't really anyone's fault. Certainly not the fault of English free market Malthusians saying that export crops from Ireland shouldn't be used to feed the starving peasantry. Incredible that this sort of drivel hasn't been put in its place. I wonder if some Indian historian of British colonialism there is making similar mumbles about the Raj's constructive role, and sneaking round difficult things like the breaking of the thumbs of all the weavers in Dacca so they wouldn't compete with the British textile industry.

➤

MAY 10   *Ardmore*
'IT WAS A THRILLING TIME recently for Ardmore, one event seemed to eclipse the other. There was the marvellous win of the u-14's over De La Salle and their emerging as Co. champions. There was Tidy Towns Day with attendant celebrations on the sea front before the unveiling of the plaque for the All-Ireland victory in 1992. But there was also the visit of professor Noam Chomsky and his wife to Ardmore, as the guests of Alexander Cockburn. He has been in Dublin all the week, lecturing in the Psychology Dept. of UCD: he is recognized as one of the minds of the 20th century, 'a theorist of language whose work since the late 1950s is so influential as to make him the equivalent in linguistics of Freud in psychology or Einstein in physics', according to Fintan O'Toole in the

Irish Times on April 30th last. He also says "on the other hand, as a persistent critic of American foreign policy, he is both an exemplar and a harsh critic of the American dream."

'He unwound in Ardmore over the weekend and distinguished himself by singing in O'Reilly's Pub, another first for Ardmore.'

Dungarvan Observer & Munster Industrial Advocate.

Carol Chomsky sang too. Michael O'Reilly was very pleased with everything.

➤→

MAY 11   *Petrolia*

I GAVE A PARTY the other night to celebrate the birthday of someone arriving at the age of 21. Legal at last. The next day people were kind enough to say they'd had a good time. Today the phone rang. It was Ellen Taylor. 'I was gardening', said Ellen. 'Then I thought about you and I want to ask you a question. I hope you don't think it's rude.'

'Maybe I will. Maybe I won't.'

'Did you come to Petrolia to kill yourself?'

'No, Ellen. I didn't. Why do you ask?'

'As a registered nurse I must tell you that on three separate occasions I've observed you drinking to excess.'

'But Ellen, I only had three margaritas.' I was going to add, '... and maybe one or two glasses of wine', but Ellen was plowing on.

'Oh good, so you came to Petrolia to be happy.'

Then she said she had to get back to her gardening and rang off.

After the suicide call I went back to a column I was writing. It had been a beautiful Sunday evening, young green leaves glowing in the setting sun. But now my concentration was jarred. I felt cross and I'm sure that if Ellen, digging away in her garden, had known that my mood had changed for the worse she would have felt contented that already I was taking the first timid steps towards rehabilitation.

➤→

MAY 26   *Petrolia*

THE CLINTON ADMINISTRATION is over. Oh, it will drag on in a thickening twilight of new beginnings and fresh tomorrows. The press corps will detect 'a new maturity', better yet an 'appreciation of the tough compromises' that Washington extorts.

But as an opposing, progressive challenge to business-as-usual the Clinton presidency has failed, even by the standards of its own timid promises. The recruitment of old Nixon/Reagan/Bush hand David Gergen as the President's new public relations czar signals the surrender.

As registers of liberal or conservative political potency American presidencies seldom coincide with the precise four-year terms that march reassuringly down the quadrennial calendar. By the official measure Jimmy Carter's administration stretched from 1977 through to the end of 1980. But the liberal arc actually extended from Richard Nixon's ouster in mid 1974 through to the successful counter-attack of the right in 1979.

In 1979, with Paul Volcker installed as chairman of the Federal Reserve and arms spending pulsing up in tune with the new cold war, the Reagan years truly began. The Clinton presidency got underway with the budget compromise of 1990, when President Bush abandoned his party's right wing and agreed to raise taxes. In terms of popularity and political strength Clinton peaked at the time of the Democratic Party convention in New York in July of 1992.

Decline was not long delayed. By the time of the official election last November the long sunset had already commenced. The big vote for Ross Perot was one augury. Clinton's post-election disclosure that there would be no tax cut for the middle class was another. By the time of the inauguration the Clinton administration was already low in the water. The President-elect and his advisers had destroyed their room for maneuver in the formulation of economic policy. They fanned budget-cutting hysteria by accepting the silly Republican claim that – surprise! – the prospective deficit was going to be more severe than expected. And they were trapped by the turn-of-the-year talk about an economic recovery.

By the time he gave his presidential oath, Clinton's presidency, as anything other than a vehicle for economic orthodoxy and Wall Street wisdom, was in the ditch. A few days later he pushed the wreck into the crusher by catastrophic handling of the issue of gays in the military. Inexperience and uncertainty allowed Senator Sam Nunn and Joint Chiefs chairman Colin Powell to seize the initiative. Before the week was out the Pentagon had its majority in Congress, and the Christian Right were trumpeting renewal and victory.

Clinton's economic program outlined the terms of surrender and defeat. Wall Street orthodoxy was duly acknowledged with a deficit reduction program that will assure continued stagnation. The 'forgotten middle class' has been duly remembered with tax hikes that will in all likelihood assure Republican victories in 1994 and 1996.

A modest stab at redistribution with raising of tax rates for the better off has been accompanied with a renewal of the loophole and tax shelter industry. So now, as a regressive bill heads to the Senate from its narrow victory in the House and David Gergen takes over the White House 'communications', we can bid goodbye to any thoughts (always scant) of a progressive agenda in what remains of the official Clinton presidency.

Today, the continued full funding of the 'drug war', the tough-on-crime posturings. Tomorrow, the evisceration of the Endangered Species Act, the caps on entitlements ... In short, the Republican administration officially to be inaugurated in 1997 already has begun. There were those of us on the left who said all through last year that this is the way it would turn out.

➤

MAY 27   *Petrolia*
DAISY REPORTS from Moscow a charming Russian saying: drink in the morning and you're free for the rest of the day.

➤

JUNE 1   *Petrolia*
THE SLUSH ABOUT Irving Howe is ankle-deep. Howe's prime function, politically speaking, in the last thirty years of his life was that of policing the left on behalf of the powers-that-be. The obits tells the whole story. In the 1960s Howe 'was denouncing the violent, authoritarian strains of the New Left' (Weinstein). 'About the authoritarian tendencies of the New Left, and the shabbiness of many of its notions, nobody was more withering' (Wieseltier). 'Howe rejected the New Left cults of youth and expressive violence in the '60s, the cults of Castro and Ho Chi Minh and Mao' (Dionne). 'He vigorously scolded the student Left for its intellectual laziness, authoritarian arrogance and occasional barbarism' (Clarence Page, *Chicago Tribune*).

In other words, Howe was a foot soldier in the ideological Cointelpro campaign to divert political currents electrifying America and supporting liberation movements in the Third World, the only significant general mobilization of a left in the United States in the second half of the twentieth century. In his later years he was wheeled onto the Op-Ed pages to announce what 'the left' thought of Dukakis or Clinton, but by that time his prime sociological significance was as a magnet for money from the MacArthur Foundation. As Josh Muravchik once pointed out in an entertaining piece, the chances of an American receiving a MacArthur genius award are about a million to one. Become a member of the editorial board of *Dissent* and the odds are ten to one.

➤

JUNE 2   *Petrolia*
'BUT THE GRASS *is* greener in England. There used to be quite a decent bit of grass round the Duomo in Pisa, but I can't think of anywhere else in Italy where it's a patch on ours.' – Letter in the *Independent Magazine*.

JUNE 3   *Petrolia*

A FAX FROM a Swiss translator after I'd sent an article (commissioned by them) on the Woodstock Festival (the original one). This was for *Züricher Allgemeine Zeitung*:

Dear Mr. Cockburn,

I do have some questions regarding your article.

p.2 line 9: I cannot find the word 'tractations' in any dictionary.

p.2 l.15: What does 'Humboldt country' mean?

p.3 l.4: from the bottom: 'generational self-consciousness', does this mean one becomes conscious of belonging to a certain generation, or does the generation become conscious of i.e. find itself?

p.3 l.2 f.b: 'Hobbesian sense of conscience': where does Hobbes define this, so I can look for the correct translation? Do you mean conscience in the strict technical/religious sense or rather in the sense of consciousness?

p.3 last line: 'The cash nexus was left on the Interstate.' Does this mean that everything was for free?

p.4 l.6 f.b: Woodstock was not just a blip = a flash in the pan?

p.5 l.16: 'San Francisco Lesbian supervisor': what is R.A. the supervisor of?

p.6 middle of page: I have never been able to understand that line from 'Me and Bobby McGee'. Does it really mean that only things which cost something are worth anything?

➡

JUNE 4   *Petrolia*

SOMEONE SHOWED ME an invitation to a wedding here in the Mattole Valley the other day. 'Join Us for a Circle of Magic & Miracles As Two Become One and Everything In the Light & Mystery of Sacred Spirit.' The two proposed to be united 'with the Blessings of the Gemini Lovers New Moon As the Great Goddess the Moon Herself Harmonizes with Mars-Man and Venus Woman.' Long life to them both.

The invitation was very precise in its times: Prayer Circle, May 21, 6 p.m. ('absolutely no alcohol & no drugs allowed'); Ceremony, May 22, 2:04 p.m.; Reception, 4:06 p.m.; Music, 7:11 p.m. It seems these times were all calibrated astrologically, when Gemini was entering the house of Mars and so forth.

Yesterday I met vexed wedding guests. The to-be-weds went to a sweat lodge in the morning and were sufficiently elevated by the experience to be four hours late for the wedding. Gemini had quit the house of Mars and, more to the point, the rabbi had left too after heroically entertaining the impatient guests with lively music. New Age Bummer.

JUNE 6   *Petrolia*

MY BIRTHDAY. Long live Geminis, 'flyweights of the universe' as someone unkindly called us. Nice astrologers say Geminis are impulsive, brilliant, leaping with sure foot from peak to peak. Less benign estimates have us as schizophrenic, vain as peacocks and with the powers of concentration of a gnat. Down the years a couple of astrologers, one of them the novelist Alison Lurie, have taken enormous pains to cast my horoscope, and of course one's constrained by the bonds of friendship from telling them what rot it all seems.

Americans are notorious for their belief in the parasciences of telepathy, astrology and spiritualism. But the French are just the same. A poll this year showed 55 percent of the heirs to Descartes believing in telepathy, 46 percent that astrological signs hold the key to character, 35 percent that dreams foretell the future and 55 percent that hypnosis and the laying on of hands cure sickness. Among Greens the numbers were higher by a factor of about 10 percent.

'Communists', the study reported, 'form the only group that is almost solidly skeptical of parascientific achievements, except where healing by hypnosis and laying on of hands is concerned.' Such enthusiasm amid leftists for hypnosis goes back to the important role played by Mesmerism in the evolution of European progressive/mystical thought.

Frederick Anton Mesmer was an Austrian doctor born in 1733 who developed an interest in astrology. He concluded that the force exercised by the stars on humans took the form of electricity or magnetism. He first tried to cure sick people by magnets, then concluded that occult force resided in humans and could be harnessed by the adept to heal the afflicted.

He moved to Paris just before the French revolution and excited a huge following, even though the medical faculty of Paris stigmatized him as a charlatan. His consulting rooms were dimly lit and sepulchral. Soft music played and patients sat around a vat in which strange potions bubbled and heaved. They all joined hands while Mesmer, dressed as a magician, moved among them, touching, looking or waving his hand.

Mesmer freely admitted that these trappings were flummery, but maintained that there was a force called animal magnetism, which could be benignly evoked. I suppose communists like such procedures because they imply a human mastering of the natural forces.

French sociologists, reporting the figures quoted above, believe that enthusiasm for parasciences can be matched to a sense of relegation to the social fringe, particularly among professions where social status is not clearly defined, as with teachers, social workers and intellectuals: 'The gap between their social expectations and the indeterminate reality of their situation gives rise to a fundamental uncertainty, a sense of being relegated to the fringes of the world, or of being unadapted to the world as it is, and this makes it easier to subscribe to other systems of representing reality.'

JUNE 7   *Petrolia*

FAX FROM Daisy Cockburn, Moscow
to Alexander Cockburn, Petrolia
Daddy:

1.) a.) The dog idea, *Dogs and Power*, which you say you and Ben Sonnenberg are working on, has no boundaries. My friend Peter needed a little prompting before a dog-based monologue filled the air. No difficulty with the concept of dogs and power, dogs and owners, hierarchy of dogs, dogs and communists, communist dogs – (Bull terriers; they may skip amiably alongside you by the banks of the Neva but nothing can alter their bloodthirsty course once they have decided to tear you limb from limb) ... Anyway, Peter's mulling it over.

I think Pavlov's dogs were run of the mill 'dvornyashki', i.e. good for nothing mongrels. Peter seemed unimpressed by my eager enquiries concerning Pavlov's pups – not interested and/or disapproving of experimentation with The Dog – who is a) more honest b) more CONSISTENT than the crooked swine the Human Being. 'Honest' here meaning I think the canine talent for recognizing at one whiff the social status of fellow dog in street.

2.) The sensation of potential blindness is due I think to the fact that microscopic dogs are the focal point for the entire family – rarely do they register each other. Also staring meaninglessly at a dog is akin to meditation, a sort of blind seeing. And, needless to say, the dog is indispensable in stilted situations when the least you can do is incline your head into a position of coy contemplation and avoid head-on collision with the human gaze.

Love,
Daisy

P.S. from *Minima Moralia:*
p. 48 no. 28

Paysage. – The shortcoming of the American landscape is not so much, as romantic illusion would have it, the absence of historical memories, as that it bears no traces of the human hand. This applies not only to the lack of arable land, the uncultivated woods often no higher than scrub, but above all to the roads. These are always inserted directly in the landscape, and the more impressively smooth and broad they are, the more unrelated and violent their gleaming track appears against its wild, overgrown surroundings. They are expressionless. Just as they know no marks of foot or wheel, no soft paths along their edge as a transition to the vegetation, no trails leading off into the valley, so they are without the mild, soothing, un-angular quality of things that have felt the touch of hands or their immediate implements. It is as if no-one had ever passed their hand over the landscape's hair. It is uncomforted and comfortless. And it is perceived in a corresponding way. For what the hurrying eye has seen merely from the car it cannot retain, and the vanishing landscape leaves no more traces behind than it bears upon itself.

Also a bit further on in the Theses against occultism – in section VI.

Wonderful to have a daughter who likes Adorno.

➤

JUNE 25   *Petrolia*
FAX URGENT, to Ben Sonnenberg, patient in Intensive Care Unit:

Daisy and I went to San Francisco and we went into Black Oak Books in
Berkeley to look for a second-hand copy of Berlioz's memoirs, which she had
been pestering me for after reading about them in YOUR book. As we went in,
we were handed tickets and it turned out a reading by Susan Sontag of her new
novel was impending. Susan came in, greeted us warmly, which got me points
with Daisy, murmured in my ear how beautiful my daughter was; and then,
there we were in the back, second-hand book part, as Susan read a longish
chunk of her book. But in the course of all this I took a look at the Berlioz
memoirs, which are wonderful. I particularly liked the bit when he hears his
mistress has been unfaithful, and resolves to return to Paris and gain access to
her house, disguised as a maid: 'I am shown the drawing room [on pretense of
delivering an urgent letter]; I hand over a letter and while it is being read,
produce my pistol and blow out the brains, first of number one, and then of
number two; and, seizing number three by the hair, throw off my disguise and
finish her off in the same manner, regardless of her shrieks. Then, before this
concert of voices and instruments attracts attention, I hasten to deposit the
contents of the remaining barrel in my own right temple; and if the pistol misses
fire (which has happened before now) I shall at once resort to my small bottles.
A charming comedy! It is really a great pity it was never put on the stage.'

Of course Berlioz loses the maid's costume on the way from Rome, gets
waylaid in Ventimiglia and that's the end of that. All this prompted me to listen
to his *Romeo and Juliet* which is lovely.

Alexander

➤

JULY 9   *Petrolia*
CLINTON FIRED A MISSILE at Baghdad on June 27. Michael Jansen on one of his
victims (in *Middle East International*):

'Leila al-Attar, who was killed in the US cruise missile attack on Baghdad on 27
June, will be remembered not only as a talented Iraqi painter but also as the
founder and director of the Saddam Art Centre, one of the largest and probably

the best art gallery in the Arab world. It houses the work of an array of Iraqi painters, sculptors and ceramists without equal in the Middle East.

She came from a wealthy and artistic family. According to Palestinian artist Samia Zaru, who knew her well, Leila Attar was best known for "portraying the suffering of women". Her work was both "impressionistic and individualistic. Her canvases are filled with light, as she was. Leila was a very optimistic person." And that was her tragedy. She had just moved back into her home after it was damaged by bombing during the Gulf war in 1991. Many of her paintings were damaged in that attack, as were many more in the one which killed her, since she exhibited very little of her work.

The Mansur district in which she lived is a better-off area near the racecourse, recently ingested by the sprawling suburbs of Baghdad. It was an unexpected target for attack, as one of her neighbours, Palestinian-born Jabra I. Jabra, celebrated essayist, novelist and translator of T.S. Eliot, told MEI.'

JULY 22 *Petrolia*

RAKIYA OMAAR, who runs Africa Rights out of London, tells of a pleasing exchange she had with the Belgian press. Her colleague Alex de Waal had reported from Somalia that the Belgian paratroopers under UN colors performing errands of mercy in the southern Somalian town of Kismayu had killed at least 200 Somalians under the lax rules of engagement espoused by the UN. When Rakiya put out a press release to this effect the phone in the Africa Rights office came alive with Belgian journalists wanting to know only one thing: were the Belgian troops Flemish speakers, or Francophone. 'I have no intention of becoming involved in your tribal politics', Rakiya said stiffly.

The Belgian ethnic and linguistic division between Flemings and Walloons produces outlandish absurdities. Recently a university hospitable to both factions was divided and the rivalry was so intense that when the library had to be apportioned into two, multi-volume sets were split down the middle, with one library getting the first vol. of Newton's work and the other getting the next and so on.

JULY 29 *Petrolia*

THE CLINTON COMPROMISE on gays in the military registers a shift in compass from religion to etiquette, as embodied in the Pentagon's statement that 'sexual orientation will not be a bar to service unless manifested by homosexual conduct.' Thus sexual orientation becomes a comedy – or tragedy – of manners. To the Christian Right this will always be anathema, since the guidelines accept the propriety of a homosexual essence, and invigilate not sin but tactlessness.

The erotic possibilities under the new guidelines are considerable, as indicated throughout history by kindred mannerist restrictions on the libido, and consequent mannerist expressions of that libido.

So for gay dogs in the military, think but don't look; look but don't sniff.

Blame for the squandering of political capital can be shared between Clinton and those gay strategists who urged him toward an executive order ending discrimination against gays in the military. That botched effort reflected the political naïveté of the President and the gay movement. It grossly underestimated the foe's institutional strength and overestimated Congressional support.

➤

AUGUST 4   *Petrolia*

HITLER JUSTIFIED the 1934 purge against Röhm – *aka* the Night of the Long Knives – by saying that the Brownshirts were rife with homosexuals. 'Why, in one room we found two naked boys', the Führer told Albert Speer in shocked tones. To be caught *in flagrante* in the Wehrmacht at time of combat was to be accused of *Wehrkraftzersetzung* – roughly, rot inside the virile body of the armed forces – and shot straightaway. In less fraught conditions it meant the concentration camp and a pink triangle.

➤

AUGUST 6   *Petrolia*

A CORRESPONDENT chides me for not answering his letter, which was an invitation to evaluate his novel, 644 pages in length. I'm a poor letter writer, it's true. I store letters in boxes by year and am now working my way through the 1991s.

In his book *The World of the Shining Prince*, about the *Tale of Genji* and the Japanese court a thousand years ago, Ivan Morris describes skill in the art of correspondence as a determinant of social reputation:

> First it was necessary to choose paper of the proper thickness, size, design, and colour to suit the emotional mood that one wished to suggest, as well as the season of the year and even the weather of the particular day. The calligraphy, of course, was at least as important as the actual message, and often the writer had to make numerous drafts with different brushes before producing the precise effect he wished. The nucleus of the text was usually a thirty-one syllable poem whose central image was some aspect of nature that delicately symbolized the occasion. Having finished his letter, the writer would carefully fold it in one of the accepted styles. The next step was to select the proper branch or spray of blossom to which the letter must be attached. This

depended on the dominant mood of the letter and on the imagery of the poem. It was also correlated with the colour of the paper: blue paper for a willow twig, green for oak, crimson for maple ...

So you see, it all takes time.

➤

AUGUST 7   *Petrolia*

A FEW YEARS BACK a French intellectual, Baudrillard by name, drove across the United States, spoke to no one and, having thus rapidly and silently traversed the continent, turned out a book called *America*, which enjoyed considerable vogue. Going about the country, driving into a new town, checking out the scene, I often think of Baudrillard careening through landscapes that only time and an expert guide can help one comprehend. Europeans love to repeat that silly line of the expatriate Gertrude Stein about Oakland, 'When you get there, there's no there there.' Of course Oakland is there, invisible or uninteresting only to those for whom America can be shrunk to a handful of cities genteelly advertised as being on the beaten track.

Often American intellectuals slide into a native version of the same snobbery, believing that thinking, writing or political work can only be conducted in a handful of metropolitan or campus habitats.

What would a Baudrillard or kindred transient make of Watsonville, maybe pulling off Highway 1, looking for a gas stop, heading east on Airport Boulevard, past Hector's, down Freedom Boulevard, along Main, out through some broccoli fields at the south end of town and then without further ado back on 1 with Castroville, artichoke heart of the world, next up on the route map.

The glazed tourist's eye might, even at a speed never dropping below 30 mph, pick out a few of the insignia of local drama: a church without a steeple, some of the south end of Main missing altogether. Watsonville got hit pretty bad in the earthquake of 1989.

But even at a walking pace it's hard to decipher the main streets and side alleys without detour and patient investigation. Take those snug-looking, single-story Maybeck houses. How many families are crammed in them? Two? Three? More? And the broccoli cutters, a raggedy line of figures in the middle distance. You can't tell anything about them at that range, unless through their old cars, sometimes their homes parked nearer at hand. How much are they making? Where are they from?

Actually Watsonville has its historian, or raconteur in the form of Frank Bardacke, whose *Liberals and Great Blue Herons* is now published by Jim O'Connor and Barbara Lawrence, as part of their *Capitalism, Socialism, Nature* enterprise. Frank gives the answers, same way they should be given for every town in America but almost never are. It's not easy to be a truthful, therefore radical reporter about the significant affairs of a town where – to use one of Frank's favorite images from Ivan Illich – you can see the surrounding field from the church steeple. The man you criticized in harsh terms yesterday is the man you meet on Main Street tomorrow.

You have to know what you're talking about. A reporter can make a mess of the street names in Mogadishu and be safe enough from rebuke. Err on a name, an event, a deal, a saga in Watsonville and your critics are outside the door or next in line at the post office.

That's why most local journalism is so unselfconsciously deadly, or if self-conscious, sentimental in the manner of Garrison Keillor. It's also why, when you read Frank or the *Anderson Valley Advertiser*, put out by Bruce Anderson two hundred miles farther north in Mendocino County, you can understand the explosive political potential of robust description and analysis of locality.

As it is, Frank tells how Watsonville works and how the farm land works and how the two evolve, according to the motions of the world economy. There are no closed horizons. At the other end of Main Street is Michoacán, whence so many of the workers came; is Irapuato whither so many of the jobs finally went; is London where some of the momentous recent decisions in the history of Watsonville were made.

Nothing stands still in Frank's Watsonville. The fingers of the world economy shape and reshape its destinies. The town's polar attraction shifts from the southward pull of Salinas, to the valley of silicon an hour's drive north. One of Frank's central themes is the movement of history, the fateful swerves of political economy.

'Imported water, argues Ivan Illich in his book *H_2O and the Waters of Forgetfulness*, converted Rome from a city to an Empire ... The Empire was built and the city was lost. Imported water will not transform Watsonville into an Empire. But it will fully integrate us into the Hydraulic Empire of the American West. And it will destroy the Pajaro Valley as a place.' So he takes us from Rome to Watsonville, in a marvelous swoop of political ecology.

AUGUST 9 *Petrolia*

BACK IN THE 1930s the Federal Writers' Project of the WPA produced the last attempt at a detailed guide to America. The volumes vary. Even though the guides were in part written by radicals in the depths of the Depression, class politics were entirely suppressed. In the California volume, one can find amusing entries for Aptos, and for Watsonville, and for the Pajaro Valley, the river of the bird so named, the guide says, 'because they (the Portola expedition) found on its banks a great eagle stuffed with straw by the Indians ... it is a vast sweep of apple orchards ... Watsonville's Plaza in the center of town was the scene of bull and bear fights and horse races were held in its main street in the days when the townsmen spent their Sundays – after dutiful attendance at early mass – gambling, dancing, and racing.'

That's about the best the zealously censored or self-censoring WPA writers could do, never rising above the level of the anecdotal. Imagine guides to American states written by people like Frank! A guide that told tourists rolling down Highway 1 who owns those fields, who the workers are and what happened to their union, their town, their lives. A guide that had humor, but also passion and politics.

➡

AUGUST 23   *Honolulu*

'E MOLIA AKU I NA KOLEA 'AIHUE EA ... Sacrifice the foreigners who have stolen our sovereignty ... Return to us the land ... Preserve and inspire your descendants until we are so old that we are bent with age, and our eyes droop like a rat ...'

Her chant to gods and ancestors concluded, Dr. Lilikala Kame'eleihiwa – director of Hawaiian Studies at the University of Hawai'i – plunges into a vivid account to nine attentive judges of the adverse impact of the United States upon her nation.

Over on the other side of Oahu from where Dr. Kame'eleihiwa is testifying in a Honolulu church, others are organizing demonstrations against a motorway – H3 – that is cutting through ancient burial and temple sites.

Go to the other islands in the archipelago and you'll find similar activism. On Hawai'i there's a struggle against a geothermal project that threatens to destroy a rain forest. On Kauai there are actions against the use of public lands for missile tests, part of a death twitch of the Star Wars program.

There are scores of other such political struggles under way. In back of them lies something that has been growing steadily in force for at least fifteen years, the reassertion of Hawaiian sovereign rights.

Earlier this year the sovereignty movement known as Ka Lahui Hawai'i (literally, 'the Hawaiian People') organized the largest gathering of Native Hawaiians in the past hundred years.

Fifteen thousand people mustered in front of the Iolani palace on January 17, centennial of the overthrow of Queen Liliuokalani by white settlers backed by the US Navy. The largest of the groups agitating for political and sovereign rights, Ka Lahui Hawai'i, has some 18,000 members, a constitution, a concise program and a respected presence in international gatherings of indigenous peoples. Ka Lahui is a nationalist movement but it is not seeking Hawaiian independence. As its head, Mililani Trask matter-of-factly explains, they are realists, and they reject violence. Their goal is the status of 'nation within a nation', with a land base made up of approximately 1.5 million acres, land formally held in trust for native Hawaiians or deeded to them.

By a fragrant mix of chicanery, legal hocus pocus and political corruption this land – some of it of immense value – has never been distributed to its rightful inheritors.

Thus, unlike other indigenous groups, the native Hawaiians have no land-base. As 'wards of the state' they have also faced near-impossible odds in trying to get legal standing in federal or state courts to sue to recover their lands.

When Mililani Trask and her colleagues finally extorted a modicum of such standing two years ago, a new state law decreed that no successful Hawaiian litigant could ever receive land as a consequence of a court victory.

Hawai'i is a rich salad of genes. Ask militants about their family backgrounds and one finds lineages replete with Celtic, Chinese, Japanese, Filipino and English as well as Hawaiian stock. To class as a native Hawaiian in the Ka Lahui constitution means having at least one ancestral line descending from pre-1778 Hawai'i, the year Captain Cook dropped anchor here. The movement also has honorary, non-Hawaiian members.

Over the past two weeks nine judges mustered to a tribunal from across the world have been listening to an indictment of the United States for its abuse of Hawaiian rights. The charges range from abetting the white settler coup d'état of 1893, through formal US annexation in 1898, imposition of statehood in 1959, appropriation of Hawaiian land and resources, to acts of genocide and ethnocide against the indigenous people.

There was a chair reserved for the accused, but no one from the US government has showed up, which is a pity since it would have added extra drama to the proceedings.

The 'judges' were in fact lawyers plus one theologian and two writers, an accurate rendition of cultural norms in the modern era, though .5 of a theologian and .5 of a writer, plus two more lawyers would probably be a more realistic count. Serving on the tribunal were a couple of eminent white law professors from the mainland, Richard Falk of Princeton and Milner Ball of the University of Georgia; Moana Jackson, a Maori lawyer from Aotearoa; and Sharon Venne, a Cree lawyer from Saskatchewan. By the end of the two-week session, after hearings on all the major islands, they issued an interim finding that sustained the indictment. The full record of testimony and judicial findings will come in a few months.

The disadvantage of such tribunals is their informal nature. Adverse judgement is not followed by the clang of the prison gate or the thunk of Uncle Sam plunging through the hangman's trap door. What's aimed at here is the furnishing of a competent record of what precisely was done to the Hawaiian people, also public advertisement of the strength of the sovereignty movement.

Of the latter there is no doubt. A powerful campaign for civil and sovereign rights is underway. The time is ripe for Ka Lahui Hawai'i. Already impatient Hawaiians so long on the margins of society, sleeping in old cars or on the beaches, are occupying lands. After over two hundred years of horror and a century of annexation, they are no longer prepared to see justice denied or even postponed.

➤

AUGUST 29   *Petrolia*

ST. MARY'S CHURCH in my hometown of Youghal in County Cork, Ireland, is a venerable pile dating from Norman times. Standing before the altar gazing down the length of the nave to the great west door one can detect, high above and slightly to the right, a small opening. From this vantage point many centuries ago the town's lepers, reaching the opening by a special entry, could peek out at the devotions of the notables and merchants mustered below. Hence the ancient name for such an opening, 'the leper's squint'. Such is the vantage point available to leftists in America today.

➤

AUGUST 30   *Petrolia*

BABEL ON WRITING: 'A sentence is born both good and bad at the same time. The whole secret lies in a barely perceptible twist. The control handle must be warm in our hand. You must turn it only once, never twice …

'No steel can pierce a heart so icily as a period planted in the right place.'

➤

SEPTEMBER 6   *Petrolia*

BAD NEWS FROM VERMONT. Andy Kopkind calls from Tree Frog to say the cancer is back.

➤

SEPTEMBER 7   *Petrolia*

SAY WHAT YOU WILL about Boris Yeltsin, at least he brought drinking back into superpower politics, a tradition best evoked by Shakespeare in *Antony and Cleopatra* when Antony, Pompey and the other fellow all get plastered. A friend of mine, covering the last face-off between Yeltsin and the Russian parliament, stood a few yards away from Boris, and observed that he was so drunk that aides had to hold him up.

Nixon drank heavily and so did Ford. Carter the prig brought jogging into international politics. In the old days the high and mighty stood at banquets sluicing down tumblers of firewater. These days they run about in their underwear. Who says there's progress in human affairs?

Whether he goes up or down Boris at least knew how to get his hand round a vodka bottle, in marked contrast to his predecessor, the slimy lawyer Gorbachev who was a dry. Meanwhile, it turns out the Poles have had enough of capitalism. Soon we can run all the newsfilms backwards and have the Lenin statues popping up on their plinths.

➤

SEPTEMBER 8   *Petrolia*

Dear Alexander,

I am relieved that you have not become a renegade. Your computer skepticism was needed among younger fanatics who seem to think that Absolute truth is just a mega-byte away and excel in showing off all the information that is available – except they have no history, no ideological perspective and therefore no questions to ask. As for unpaid work, there is nowadays a new trend in Sweden: not even the printer gets paid! Left-wing publications in particular – and the entire Social Democratic newspaper conglomerate of some 20 titles – have found it more convenient to go bankrupt and let the bailiff sort things out. Let's have lunch in Petrolia or in Malmö, next time we meet!

Palme's assassin has not yet been found. We were all upset a few years ago, when investigators tried to prove the guilt of Abominable Petterson, a small-time thief and drunk, extremely undignified. We want at least a major national or international conspiracy behind the murder, not some crazy individual who saw Palme outside the movie theater, went home to fetch his gun and then bumped him off, for no elevated reason at all. Palme deserves a plot by Pinochet, the CIA, South Africa or Israel. My own favorite is the strange coincidence between a telephone number in Stockholm where an old couple were rung up a few minutes after the murder to be told that Palme was dead and an absolutely identical number, but different area code, in Uppsala, where a South African, former secret agent and officer in Angola, used to live. This is too complicated for the Swedish police to look into, but they have at least the means and the resources. My late friend Ebbe Carleson (his obituary follows) pursued a different lead, a mad, grandiose vision of the Ayatollah scheming to kill our prime minister. Ebbe was totally off course, but he almost brought down the government. We've yet to see the bottom line.

All the best,
Björn Komm
Malmö, Sweden

SEPTEMBER 9   *Petrolia*

THE NOTION of multiple personality is all the rage these days. I'm not sure whether M.P. is dysfunctional or functional for the bourgeois state. A series of democratically participating personalities inside the same human envelope obviously raises serious legal questions of culpability.

On the other hand bourgeois society likes 'roles', since they multiply opportunities for the circulation of commodities. But bourgeois society likes the idea of many personalities ruled by a chief executive who can, so to speak, exercise the tyranny of the boardroom majority. Against this democratic centralism is what political groups of the left used to call the 'right to tendency' and faction. These days we have the numbing rituals of consensus formation, a collective act of brainwashing dictated, as always, by the most unstable participant, exercising the tyranny of the hysteric, the unhinged, anybody whom sensible people in the group decide it's not worth the trouble to upset. So there's consensus, since these more-or-less stable participants realize that their concerted objective is to please this weakest member, who obviously agrees.

Laura Nader, professor of anthropology at UC Berkeley, gave a striking interview in the *San Francisco Examiner* the other day in which she noted the growth of 'coercive harmony', a process she recognized from methods of pacification introduced by European missionaries during the colonial period to control indigenous villagers.

According to the article, 'Alternative dispute resolution', she said, 'was a response to the confrontation and litigiousness of the 1960s civil rights movement.' Spearheaded by former US Chief Justice Warren Burger, it aimed to free courts of cases that could be settled through mediation or arbitration. But in the pursuit of compromise, justice often has been forgotten ... and the pursuit itself has carried far beyond the justice system.

'It's basically a movement against the contentious in anything, and it has very strange bedfellows, from people with various psychiatric therapy movements, Christian fundamentalists, corporations sick of paying lawyers, activists who believe we should love each other ... and it's spread into different parts of American life.

'We are talking about coercive harmony – an ideology that says if you disagree, you should really keep your mouth shut.'

➤

SEPTEMBER 10   *Petrolia*

THINKING ABOUT multiple personality reminded me of Althusser's piece on Freud and Lacan which he wrote sometime in the early sixties. 'Since Copernicus we have known that the earth is not the "center" of the universe. Since Marx we have known that the human subject – the economic, political, or philosophical ego is not the "center" of history and even, in opposition to the Philosophers of the Enlightenment and to Hegel, that history has no "center" but possesses a structure which has no necessary "center" except in ideological misrecognition. In turn, Freud has discovered for us that the real subject, the individual in his unique essence, has not the form of an "ego", centered on the "ego", on "consciousness" or on "existence" – whether this be the existence of the for-itself, of the body proper or of "behavior" – that the human subject is decentered, constituted by a structure which has no center either, except in the imaginary misrecognition of the "ego", i.e., in the ideological formation in which it "recognizes" itself.'

Of course, given that Althusser ended up strangling his wife, all this kind of stuff has an eerie ring.

➡

SEPTEMBER 13   *Petrolia*
IT WOULD TAKE THE PEN of Swift to evoke the nauseating scenes of hypocrisy, bad faith and self-delusion on the White House lawn today, crammed as it was with people who for long years were complicit in the butchery and torture of Palestinians and the denial of their rights, now applauding the 'symbolic handshake' that in fact ratified further negation of those same rights.

In the shadow of an American President with the poise and verbiage of the manager of a McDonald's franchise, Arafat produced oratory so meager it made Rabin sound like Cicero.

Right now, Palestinians get the right to manage the world's largest prison, the Gaza Strip, plus one cow town. It's as though the Irish in 1921 got Tralee plus a few acres in West Cork, with the British holding the entire eastern half, Belfast, Dublin, Waterford, plus all the resources, with its army free to roam at will across the Irish enclaves, themselves fragmented by British highways and drained of water. There will be no Palestinian sovereignty and an economy completely subordinated to Israel's. As the Israeli economy gets internationalized, companies will set up sweatshops in Gaza and the West Bank, and the Palestinians will furnish the $6-a-day labor. Members of the Palestine Liberation Army, imported from outside the territories, will do the policing, just as the sepoys did for the British in colonial India. Arafat or some successor could end up running, with Israeli and American backing, a mini-Haiti.

➡

OCTOBER 8   *Petrolia*
THE JUSTICE AND TREASURY departments are now releasing their reports on the circumstances leading up to the incineration of eighty-six Branch Davidians

outside Waco on April 19. The Treasury's Bureau of Alcohol, Tobacco and Firearms, which is taking the main fall, deserves everything it gets, but should be joined in the scapegoats' gallery by the FBI and by Attorney General Janet Reno.

One of the outside experts recruited by the Justice and Treasury Departments to review the case and peruse internal documents was Professor Nancy Ammerman of the Candler School of Theology at Emory University. Ammerman gives short shrift to the ATF, and she confirms, after scrutinizing ATF and FBI records, that career 'cult hunters' were deeply involved in the government's assaults. Ammerman makes some sensible recommendations about treatment of religious groups, which could usefully be studied by the press as well as the Justice and Treasury Departments:

> [The agents] should have understood the pervasiveness of religious experimentation in American history and the fundamental right of groups like the Davidians to practice their religion ... They should have understood that many new religious movements do indeed ask for commitments that seem abnormal to most of us, and these commitments do mean the disruption of 'normal' family and work lives ... They should also understand that the vast majority of those who make such commitments do so voluntarily. The notion of 'cult brainwashing' has been thoroughly discredited in the academic community.

The deprogramming strategies of the Cult Awareness Network are highly reminiscent of the strategies used by Reno on supposed child abusers, breaking Ileana Fuster and trying to break Bobby Fijnje, coercing them toward mental disintegration.

➤

OCTOBER 9   *Petrolia*

CATHARINE MACKINNON'S Boy Toy may be Jeffrey Masson, but her horse toy is Horse Boy. She is being sued by a man who claims her 'dangerous, blooded and spirited' horse threw him to the ground. David Johnson is suing MacKinnon for an incident occurring on October 4, 1992, when he was renting MacKinnon's property in Half Moon Bay, south of San Francisco. He says he had arranged to ride MacKinnon's horse and that MacKinnon had represented Horse Boy as having a 'harmless' and otherwise normal disposition. But it seems Horse Boy was inclined to 'bolt, buck, throw and charge' and promptly unseated the novice Johnson, who fractured his hip and suffered severe emotional distress.

Further reports filter in of MacKinnon's performance at the Human Rights conference in Vienna. After her speech, outside the hall two Serbian feminists, who had been running a hot line in Serbia for women and children victims of physical abuse, protested MacKinnon's blanket denunciation of all Serbs.

Hearing their complaints, a sympathetic woman marched them up to MacKinnon and said that here were two women representing the Serbian opposition and that MacKinnon could at least acknowledge their existence. MacKinnon turned to the Serbians and said, 'If you were an effective opposition, you wouldn't be here. You'd be dead.' Let's get Horse Boy in the witness box. I bet he has a tale to tell. I assume he was gelded.

➥

OCTOBER 25   *Petrolia*
Dear Alex,

Just opened the 200th issue of *New Left Review* and read the first page, where Robin writes: 'Where the West has had a free hand, there the disasters have been greatest – above all former Yugoslavia and the Gulf. By contrast, in Central America, Namibia and Cambodia, where the power of the West is still qualified and counter-balanced by local democratic movements and political structures, more positive and effective forms of international action have developed.' So, in Yugoslavia, the West had a free hand (unconcerned by reactions in the Islamic world, Slavic nationalist fanatics, Serbia's possible expansion of the war, etc.), but in Central America, say, the US didn't have a free hand, because it was 'counter-balanced ...' so there was constructive international action. What dream world is this?

I needn't tell you, at least, that in Central America the US had more of a free hand than anywhere in the world, and the disaster is catastrophic. Local democratic movements scarcely function, and international action is derisory. As for Yugoslavia, is it really the greatest disaster? Worse than Angola, say? Hardly. Rather, it is a disaster that threatens the interests of rich white folks not too far away, and they can blame what's happening on bad guys – while in Angola it's just a bunch of blacks slaughtering each other somewhere off in the dark continent, Europe's interests are not threatened, and it would be necessary to pin the blame on the grand 'freedom fighter' lauded by Western ideologues. Not to speak of Afghanistan; Kabul has suffered more than Sarajevo, it seems, though coverage is so slight that one cannot be sure. I'd expect to see this kind of stuff in the *Daily Telegraph*, but in *NLR*? For the 200th issue, no less.

Noam
Cambridge, Massachusetts

➥

NOVEMBER 7   *Los Angeles*
LISTENED TO DENNIS HOPPER describing to the L.A. Drug Conference sponsored by Nation Associates his own exciting days in drug madness, putting

Amanita muscaria at the start of the menu. As often happens with those who've cleaned up, Hopper's eyes shone with fond reminiscence of excess, in contrast to his punctilious citation of clean living under the spartan regime of twelve-step programs.

I was hoping he would give a detailed account of how he fared with *Amanita muscaria*, the fly-agaric hallucinogen whose brilliant red cap, speckled with white, brightens the woody hillsides round my house in Humboldt County this time of year, living in mycorrhizal intimacy with pine and fir. Best not try it.

In his classic *Soma, Divine Mushroom of Immortality*, demonstrating that this mushroom was the 'Soma' of the ancient Aryan religion, R. Gordon Wasson describes how the Uralic and Paleo-Siberian tribes would have their shaman eat the dried *Amanita* and then would quaff his urine, which would pass on the hallucinogenic properties in safer, diluted form.

➡

NOVEMBER 8   *Petrolia*

BACK IN THE EARLY 1980s, here in Humboldt County and elsewhere in Northern California, before CAMP and MET began their war, the county sheriffs would seize about 50,000 plants a year and make forty to fifty arrests. This was achieved with a handful of local deputies and one fixed-wing plane.

But the marijuana plants back in those times were grown in full sun, could reach a height of twelve feet and yielded up to a pound of processed marijuana. Now growers are forced to cultivate in shaded areas to avoid detection from low-flying helicopters. Thus, a plant today might furnish an average of an ounce, even less from an indoor plant. Mel Pearlston of the Pacific Justice Center in the Humboldt County town of Redway, who defends people charged with marijuana cultivation and facing forfeiture of property, tells me that it's not uncommon to find several thousand plants in an indoor grow, and though the government claims they yield the same as a full-size plant flourishing amid the blaze of noon, the truth is that it may take dozens of these foot-tall plants to produce a pound of processed buds.

The government points to the raised price of marijuana – $2,000 a pound to the grower in the early 1980s, about $4,500 now – as evidence of a successful crackdown. Where the government has had success is in stopping imports of marijuana from Mexico and South America and of the Thai sticks of Asia. Smugglers now specialize in cocaine or heroin.

So enforcement has acted as a price support for domestic producers, in a fine example of import substitution, courtesy of the small farmer hailed in song and story. Mel's view is that the true function of the war on drugs has been to test the nation's tolerance for intrusive law-enforcement techniques, whether in Humboldt County or in South Central L.A.

Straightforward legalization, urged by many respectable citizens, has one unremarked flaw. In peasant economies across the world, in the Andean nations, in Southeast Asia, not to mention rural counties in California, cultivation of marijuana, coca or the opium poppy is either the main or sole economic standby. Often there are no realistic alternatives in an era when commodity prices have plunged.

Similarly, in today's blighted inner cities there are no realistic economic strategies to substitute for the drug commerce, which is often the only rational career choice for urban youth. Certainly the tycoon impresarios of Rebuild L.A. have come up with no alternative. Under the current terms of society, legalization would mean government licensing of monopolies to large corporations that would swiftly wipe out small producers and vendors.

A better answer would be to decriminalize drugs, apply the sort of fines and penalties attached to parking, speeding and drunken behavior, declare the war over and move on.

➤

NOVEMBER 17   *Petrolia*

Dear Sir,

Alexander Cockburn is up to his old tricks: he savages the opposition, or rather he savages *anyone* he disagrees with, or who is unfortunate enough to disagree with him. Not everyone on the opposite side of an issue is the absolute enemy; Cockburn really ought to learn to make common cause wherever possible.

Now his sexist underpinnings really flash. Right off, let me acknowledge that I am not a fond follower of Catharine MacKinnon's politics. I find myself more in disagreement than agreement with her. I am not her defender.

However, I find it disgusting and inappropriate and pointless to open a political discussion about MacKinnon at the Human Rights conference in Vienna with wholly irrelevant, snide, and one-sided comments about rental of her property in Half Moon Bay to a fellow who was injured riding her horse – named Horse Boy.

That, preceded by a reference to Jeffrey Masson as her 'boy toy', hasn't got a goddamn thing to do with Cockburn's gripe about her performance at Vienna. (Is Cockburn suggesting MacKinnon is 'keeping' Masson? Whose business is it, and what has it got to do with political journalism?)

I don't quibble with Cockburn's characterization of MacKinnon in Vienna. My point is the astonishing sexist finale to his little tw- paragraph item: 'I assume he (Horse Boy) was gelded', with which he falls into the old routine of men frightened of strong women; she's a ball buster, a ball eater, a deballer, an emasculator.

And that makes Alexander Cockburn, as well as a small-minded character assassin, nothing more than an old-fashioned sexist.

Sincerely,
Peter Albertson

➤

NOVEMBER 18   *Petrolia*
Dear Mr. Cockburn,
This is unsigned for reasons of 'security', yours and mine. Your remarks about CAMP and marijuana prices was close. Since 1975 I have been a hemp producer. Every year I produce (grow) and process about 160 lbs. of product. This operation gives a living to six families in two states. So far farming is good. Our price has been $2000 a lb. since we started (1975).

My observation has been that hemp is suppressed in the USA because Mexico produces and sells about 75–80% of product for American smokers. This is the giant sucking sound Ross hears.

American money from every small town and county in the USA is going to Mexico and then it comes back to Chase Manhattan to pay Mexico's debt. Simple as that.

You are right when you say 'enforcement has been price support'.

Your last two paragraphs are pretty insightful, except the youth in this area are not brainwashed by the PC crowd. I am truly amazed at the number of young folks that see through the fog.

Also, this is the first time in any blat that R. Gordon Wasson's *Soma: Divine Mushroom of Immortality* has been spoken of. You write as if you know of these things. If you don't, you should.

Thank you for well researched and *factual* writing over the years.

A. Hemp Meister
Somewhere in New York and Pennsylvania
PS. I also enjoy reading your brother Andrew. Tell him Hi.

➤

NOVEMBER 18   *Petrolia*
WHAT IS IT ABOUT AMERICA that demands total conversions? People have to be booze-free, or drug-free or even sex-free. Why not all these delightful addenda to the human condition in amounts sufficient to uplift but not to destroy? Today's *bien-pensant* youth are so brainwashed by the PC crowd that they are barely capable of the sexual act, lest it somehow be an expression of disrespect for womanhood. I made a joke about Catharine MacKinnon's horse being a gelding the other day. Letters have poured in denouncing me as fearing a

'strong woman'. The letters were all from men, no doubt reading their letters self-righteously to their helpmeets in hopes of an encouraging pat on the head.

➥

NOVEMBER 20   *Petrolia*

THE KENNEDY YEARS saw six military coups overthrow popular regimes. In those Camelot years the Central American death squads were conjured into being. Like Reagan, Kennedy was enamored of covert operations, nowhere more than in the attempts to assassinate Fidel Castro and topple his regime.

Kennedy courtiers have been eager in trying to claim that the President and his brother, Attorney General RFK, were shielded from the CIA's sponsorship of Mafia hit teams and other assassination bids. Years later, Winn Taplin, a CIA career operations officer, acknowledged that following the Bay of Pigs, the CIA's covert operation planning and control were taken into the White House and that 'there were few in the Agency operational offices in the early 1960s who did not know that Robert Kennedy was the driving force on the special group working to topple Castro.'

➥

NOVEMBER 21   *Petrolia*

THE NOTION OF OSWALD as a person who acted out of radical political motives runs athwart the propositions proposed by conspiracy buffs that he was an agent of the right. It also challenges what Warren Commission lawyers used to call the 'washing machine' construct of Oswald's personality, meaning that if only he had been able to afford to buy Marina a washing machine he would not have felt impelled to kill the President.

To ascribe rationality to Oswald is to invest him with a comprehensible mission rather than the homicidal petulance of a psychopath. In the immediate aftermath of the killing of Kennedy, the left was terrified that it would be scapegoated. Most people initially thought Castro was responsible. The National Security Agency's electronic intercepts assured Johnson and his advisers that Castro was stunned and indeed terrified by the killing, lest he be held responsible. Fearful of a stand-off producing nuclear war, the US elites insisted from the start that there was no international sponsor of the assassination. The first big cover-up was of any suggestion that the Commies had shot JFK. When the district attorney in Dallas wanted to charge Oswald with being the agent of a Communist conspiracy, the White House and Justice Department turned white hot in a successful effort to shut him up.

Oswald was a subscriber to such periodicals as *The Militant*. He described himself as a Marxist. In the brief period between his arrest and his murder by

Jack Ruby he had given the clenched fist salute. My friend Frank Bardacke vividly remembers the frightened outrage this caused to socialists in Berkeley on November 23, when they saw the Communist salute on television.

As Leon Day of Oakland recalled to me last year, 'The witch-hunt was barely over in 1963, and the Smith Act and McCarran Act were at hand if the government wished to use them. In liberal New York City the evening of the killing saw city police closing a legal and routine meeting of the Socialist Workers Party. Would the JFK killing provoke the internment of all radicals, as the Wall Street bombing had the Palmer raids of 1919? That night, none of us could be sure.

'For the first year or two after the killing most books and articles postulating a conspiracy came from left-wing publishers. This repeated almost exactly what the Louisiana Republicans had done back in 1935 after one of their fellows shot Huey Long. Not wishing to run as the assassination party, they spread the rumor that Long had really been shot by his own guards. Not only did this ploy work, but it's still working on some people to this very day, without a figleaf of fact to cover it.'

In all in the assassinology I've read or seen, Oswald is always unpersuasive. In *JFK* Oliver Stone hadn't the slightest idea how to portray him, which pointed up the weakness of his artistic insight and the preposterous premises on which it was based.

I see Oswald as one of those guys in the left-wing meeting who is by the door selling *The Militant* or pamphlet of choice as you go in. Then, in question time, he's up on his feet, asking WHAT SHOULD BE DONE? The people up on the platform haven't – as always – got much by way of convincing suggestion, and Lee goes into a tirade about THE NEED FOR ACTION and the urgency of defending the Cuban revolution and … This is where folks in the audience begin to say, What's the question? Ask the question, and finally Lee either sits down or fumes out of the room, goes home and reaches for the mail order catalogue for Mannlicher-Carcanos.

Of course no leftist is ever going to say that he saw Lee at a meeting. How many rolodexes in America after November 23 had Lee's name still lodged there? Never, ever heard of him.

Perhaps one day Oswald will be recognized as a leftist who came to the conclusion that the only way to relieve the pressure on Cuba and obstruct the attempts to murder Castro was by killing President Kennedy. In this calculation he was correct. A year and a half later after the killing in Dallas, Lyndon Johnson suspended the CIA's assassination bids. Oswald's ambush was one of the few effective assassinations in the history of such enterprises. Today this radical exponent of the propaganda of the deed is traduced by assassination buffs as a creature of the right, the pawn of the Joint Chiefs of Staff and of other right-wing forces supposedly trying to bring Kennedy down.

NOVEMBER 22   *Petrolia*

In her recent song about satanic abuse, 'Play Me Backwards', Baez has the words 'There's a sacrifice in an empty church / Of sweet li'l baby Rose / And a man in a mask from Mexico is peeling off my clothes.'

The notion that Satanic abuse came across the border from Mexico (paired with another version, having it imported by a Jew from Europe) goes back to the so-called WICCA Letters, discussed by David Alexander in *The Humanist* for March/April 1990. (WICCA here stands for Witches International Coven Council, the 'A' having no explanation.) These cognates of the 'Protocols of the Elders of Zion' surfaced in the early 1980s in a report for a fundamentalist periodical, *Exodus*, by Dave Gearin, a sheriff's deputy in San Diego who claimed to have decoded them. They supposedly record a meeting of the Covintern in Mexico in 1981, intent on subverting the United States and attaining world domination through satanic abuse in day care centers.

All we need now is an alliance between Baez and Catharine MacKinnon, who lives the other side of the Santa Cruz Mountains from J.B., in Half Moon Bay, home of Horse Boy.

Recently in *Ms.* MacKinnon offered a ghastly account of torture and murder in Serbian-occupied Croatia and concluded, 'Change the politics or religion, and victims of ritual abuse in this country [the United States] report the same staged sexual atrocities ending in sacrifice.'

➡

NOVEMBER 23   *Petrolia*

READING THE PHOTOGRAPHER Danny Lyon's fine *Memories of the Southern Civil Rights Movement*, published last year by the University of North Carolina. It has the uncensored text of John Lewis's speech at the March on Washington, August 28, 1963. Lewis was chairman of the Student Non-Violent Co-ordinating Committee.

His prepared speech had lines like 'We are now involved in a serious political revolution. This nation is still a place of cheap political leaders who build their careers on immoral compromise and social exploitation. What political leader can stand up here and say, "My party is the party of principles"? The party of Kennedy is also the party of Eastland. The party of Javits is also the party of Goldwater. Where is *our* party?'

Lewis went on to attack Kennedy for sabotaging civil rights legislation and for appointing racist judges. 'We shall march through the Heart of Dixie, the way Sherman did', he wrote for his finale. 'We shall pursue our own "scorched earth" policy and burn Jim Crow to the ground – nonviolently. We shall crack the South into a thousand pieces and put them back together in the image of democracy.' These lines were, as Lyons puts it, 'apparently unbearable to some members of the grand coalition that now rode the coattails of the movement.' They were cut. So was 'We Shall Overcome', considered too provocative for the official program.

Lyons also gives the minutes of the discussion in SNCC's Atlanta office on November 22 and 23 of JFK's assassination. For example,

Foreman: Johnson is taking over now, without hesitation. We can not be shocked, it slows our intellect. We can't delay ...

Price: From experience in this field, he knows that sentimentality can mess you up terribly. SNCC can not lose a week because of sentimentality ... In this case as in others, sentiments will develop either negatively or positively ...

Dinky: Only by taking the offensive will we prevent a purge.

Foreman: The rightists and birchists etc. will attempt to use this killing against the Civil Rights Organizations. We must take a positive stand ...

Shira: We are on the defensive, true. But the best defensive will be a strong offensive. While the country is in shock, we should come on with a strong offensive ...

Boy next to Iris: I do not want to demonstrate for a guy who sold out on Civil Rights, not demonstrate as if he had not sold out ...

Dinky: I want to use him and his death, not eulogize him. 2. The establishment will oppose us under any circumstance ...

Foreman: ... I was surprised the killer was not a rightist. Because he is a leftist, we can not take the position this was the same thing that killed Evers. We must take the position he died a martyr's death, like the others. Demonstrations will occur for the monument of legislation, not for the president alone ... After all our political discussions on tactics and policy, we must always remember that in the end, the highest considerations are moral principles.

➤

NOVEMBER 24   *Petrolia*

MY DWORKIN PROJECT lumbers along. More on Stoltenberg's penis:

Dear Alex,

Had a long chat with your Brooklyn informant, who described to me how Andrea Dworkin, occasionally sighted around Park Slope snacking on ice cream with her (undoubtedly flaccid) companion Stoltenberg, declines to take her frozen treats from a cone. No doubt, her penised friend has dissuaded her from any action that smacks of 'verticality'. After all,

'Manhood is a vertical palisades, perpendicular to a base line of female bodies ... Authentic human selfhood can only be horizontal ... [I'm happy to send to you copies of the accompanying diagrams.]

Stoltenberg is the founder of Men Against Pornography, a sympathetic formation cognate with Women Against Pornography. He has been living with Dworkin since 1974. He advertises his recent release, *The End of Manhood: A Book for Men of Conscience*, as 'a deliberate personal and political choice to apply the liberation theory articulated in [my first book] *Refusing to Be a Man* in everyday human interaction – to apprehend what we mean when we think and say "I", and what we mean when we regard one another as "you" ...' His aim is to promote what he calls 'loving justice – an act of intense desire for, and attraction toward, fairness ...' &c.

Informant claims that Stoltenberg is attempting to keep himself from having an erection, for the reason that there is no such thing as consensual heterosexual relations, and that the erect penis can only be understood as a tool of rape. Reading from his books, Stoltenberg's take on the habits of his member may be more complex than popularly believed. In a chapter entitled, 'How Can I Have Better Sex?', the author marries moral reasoning to scientific proof in his effort to undo penised men's enduring commitment to 'manhood mode' during sex. In a subchapter on 'Seven Mysteries of "Male" Sexual Anatomy (Or, Why Humans Don't Come the Way We Sometimes Think We Do')', Stoltenberg observes: 'Ejaculation and orgasm are not the same phenomena. They can be experienced independently of each other. Their neurological hookups are separate and enter the spinal cord in different neurological and vascular systems. They don't always come, and they don't always have to. So if you're keeping count, that's three independent bipolar variables; and that makes at least ten possible combinations of experiential events in a human with "male" sexual anatomy.'

– There can be penile erection without ejaculation and orgasm.
– There can be penile erection and ejaculation without orgasm.
– There can be penile erection and orgasm without ejaculation.
– There can be orgasm without penile erection and ejaculation &c., &c.

None of these bipolar variables is singled out as an acceptable option, though some are clearly preferable. That he is attempting to induce atrophy in his penis cannot, therefore, be deduced from the text. Seek empirical confirmation.

Michael

➤➤

NOVEMBER 28   *Petrolia*
FAITH IN TECHNOLOGY beats stoutly in many an American heart, *The Nation*'s editorialists included. The cover editorial for the issue dated November 22 headed 'Star Wars to Fire Wars' was an amazing piece of nonsense about converting 'the marvels of the electronic battlefield so recently exhibited in the Gulf War' into 'delivering payloads that put out fires instead of starting them'.

'How is it', the editorial asked, 'that the United States can engage in pinpoint night bombing over Iraq in the face of fierce enemy fire and yet cannot drop water in the dark over Topanga Canyon?'

This is a version of the old 'How is it we can put a man on the moon and yet' construction favored by every bar-stool pundit. It yokes faulty premise to silly conclusion. The American electronic record over the Iraqi battlefield was scarcely impressive. Not a single SCUD missile site located or hit, despite all-out efforts; Saddam's Winnebago mobile hq – the target at one time of up to a third of all US aerial sorties – either never located, or if located, never hit. Not a single Patriot missile found its mark.

This rousing record of achievement is to be transferred to pinpoint nocturnal water-dumping on firestorms in the Santa Monica Mountains, saving California's aerospace economy in the process. God save us from the techno-fix mentality.

Fighting wildfires could be a way of soaking up the ag surplus. Shift California's ag investment out of water-intensive cotton and rice cultivation and into tomato production. Scoop the tomatoes into giant spheres a hundred yards across and launch them into space, flying in geosynchronous orbit fifty miles above fire-risk areas of California. At the first sign of trouble, douse the hot spots in a shower of ketchup. It used to be my plan for Moscow in the Star Wars era, but with a nice little MacArthur grant – say, $300,000 over a couple of years from their 'peace and security' gravyboat – I'd be happy to redraw the plans.

⇒→

NOVEMBER 29   *Petrolia*
Anderson Valley Advertiser
Boonville, CA
Dear Mr. Anderson
Cockburn has finally taken the great leap forward and has propounded a theory of his own. And he's done nothing less than create a new Oswald for us. To the existing Oswalds – the disgruntled loner, the Castro/KGB/FBI/Mafia hitman, the radio-controlled Manchurian Candidate, the switched-in-Minsk Russian, the CIA/FBI/ONI agent, and the fall guy – Cockburn adds his own Oswald model: The Trotskyite dweeb.

Cockburn finds it telling that Oswald supposedly subscribed to the Trotskyite Socialist Workers Party newspaper, *The Militant*. Here's the problem. Remember the Judi-Bari-esque Oswald pin-up on the cover of *Life* magazine? Oswald is supposedly in his back yard posing with his weapons and two newspapers. Oswald was shown the original photo during his interrogation and said it was a falsification. Cockburn, as a believer, must, however, accept the photo as a true relic. Nevertheless, forget the analysis of the shadows and the unnatural way Oswald's body is poised in relation to his head. Here's the really weird part: Oswald is holding a copy of *The Militant* and a copy of *The Worker*.

First some quick background: One of the intense, bloody, and pointless political controversies of the 20th century is over who was the true messenger of Lenin: Stalin, or one of the original disciples Stalin had killed, Trotsky. The socialist *Militant* hated Stalin, the betrayer of the revolution; and the communist *Worker* hated Trotsky, the enemy of the people.

So why is Oswald standing there proclaiming conflicting ideologies? One can argue that high school drop-out Oswald was unschooled in the subtleties of Marxist/Leninist dogma. Very unlikely. Oswald spent two years in the Motherland, spoke Russian like a native, married the niece of a GPU officer, is reported to have read the primary works, and intelligently discussed the distinctions between Soviet Communism and Marxism/Leninism during a debate on New Orleans television. With that background, it's unlikely that Oswald couldn't decide whether he loved Joe or loved Leon. Of course, he loved neither. He wasn't a Trotskyite or a Stalinist. The pictures of Oswald in his back yard are fakes. The agent who doubled for Oswald and the agent who took the picture probably assumed that two commie papers were more damning than one.

Sincerely,
Jock Penn
San Rafael, California

➤

DECEMBER 3   *Petrolia*
Dear Bruce,
As a published author on the history of American Communism, as well as a former Marxist-Leninist, I would like to offer some comment, based on personal experience, to the Oswald debate.

Penn did not make clear – perhaps he does not know? – that there are two separate photos, showing two separate papers with the rifle, not one photo with the Trotskyist *Militant* and the Stalinist *Worker*, an argument that the photos must be faked, since, according to him, no leftist in 1963 would have stood on both sides of that historical divide, the Stalin–Trotsky fight.

He is completely wrong. I know whereof I speak because, as Bruce once pointed out, in 1963 I was one of the most obnoxious members of the CPUSA's youth wing, the W.E.B. DuBois Club.

In that period the disagreements between Stalin and Trotsky had long faded into rhetoric, if not irrelevance, for both groups. Beginning in 1956, after the 'secret speech' of Khrushchev on Stalin's crimes, a number of prominent CPers called for a united front and even a reunification with the SWP.

For example, in 1956 George Hitchcock, former educational director of the state CP and a close friend of my parents, publicly endorsed Farrell Dobbs, the SWP candidate for president; so, as I recall, did Vincent Hallinan, who had been the presidential standard bearer of the CP-lining Progressive Party in 1952. In 1958 there was a joint CP–SWP political effort in New York.

In 1963 Khrushchev was still in charge in Russia. He had presided over the rehabilitation of all the military figures killed in the Stalin purges and had either rehabilitated or partially rehabilitated numerous other old Bolshevik victims of the same massacre. At the time I joined DuBois, many people in the CPUSA thought the rehabilitation would extend all the way to Trotsky.

In addition, *de facto* united fronts between the CPUSA and SWP existed in two areas: the civil rights movement and Cuba. CPers and SWPers also worked more or less harmoniously in the student movement in Berkeley. In the anti-discrimination demonstrations in San Francisco at that time (Mel's, Auto Row, Sheraton Palace), the two groups worked together. CPers were well aware of the SWP's then-important influence with Malcolm X and other militants in the Black movement.

Most importantly, the Castro regime had taken a certain distance from Moscow in openly accepting support from Trotskyists (especially in Europe and the US) and Maoists. The Fair Play for Cuba Committee, to which Oswald claimed to belong, was in fact an SWP front group, to which the CPUSA deferred in Cuba work. When I inquired of the CP's leaders in San Francisco at that time about Cuba, I was specifically directed to a member of SWP which was considered closer to the Cubans and more active on that issue than the CP.

I do not think it was at all rare at that time for independent Marxists, which is what Oswald claimed to be, to feel that Stalin vs. Trotsky was ancient history and that both the CP and SWP, as well as the tiny Maoist tendencies in existence in the US then, were part of the same international Communist movement, each with a different contribution to make. Even a pro-CPer would be interested in the SWP's work if only because of Cuba. That, of course, was Oswald's main obsession, we are told.

I, like Oswald, read both *The Worker* and *The Militant* regularly in 1963, buying the former at the CP bookstore and subscribing to the latter as well as to the *Workers World*, then the only weekly Maoist-lining periodical in the US. (*Progressive Labor* had already started coming out at that time, but was a monthly.) Perhaps I was naïve to think of them all as more or less alike.

In my recollection that was the situation, anent CP–SWP relations, obtaining until the middle of 1964 and the launching of DuBois as a national organization, when DuBois and the SWP's Young Socialist Alliance (YSA) became serious and more hostile competitors. And, of course, when Khrushchev was replaced by Kosygin and Brezhnev, a re-Stalinization began.

Unfortunately the Trotskyist movement did not undergo a similar 're-Trot-skyization'. Trotsky, after all, had called for the overthrow of the Stalinist regime, a position from which the SWP retreated after his death, and to which they never returned.

Stephen Schwartz
San Francisco

➤→

DECEMBER 5   *Petrolia*

AMERICANS LIKE A GOOD SNIGGER now and then about English class systems. But Americans like to ponder those quaint English ways, courtesy of Masterpiece Theater or long articles in the *Wall Street Journal* about the House of Lords, partly as a way of avoiding the realities of their own class system which is different, but in many ways more drastic.

After all, as Jim Britell recently remarked to me, between 1965 and 1985 slavery was successfully reintroduced into the United States. In 1960 one college graduate with a C average could earn enough to buy a house with three bedrooms, a garage, basement and an attic; own a two-year-old Chevy; and raise four kids. Today it takes two childless wage slaves to afford the rent on a one-bedroom apartment. The upper classes have succeeded in enslaving the middle and lower classes. Or perhaps the older generation has succeeded in enslaving the younger.

The English have been at it longer, so the refinements of class distinction have been aging longer in the cask. Americans in the 1980s would sit in front of re-runs of *Upstairs, Downstairs* at the English Museum. Meanwhile a new American class was solidifying out of the magma of the Roaring Eighties before their very eyes.

Short of shooting every member of a particular group the old contours persist. And even efforts far more determined than any launched in English history have been doomed to failure. I remember touring Albania in 1965, a country led by Stalin-fan Enver Hoxha and widely advertised as having taken a stern, even blood-thirsty, line with the old order. Our official guide was a young fellow called Dino Bashkim who kept the nail on the little finger of his right hand untrimmed at a conspicuous three-quarter-inch length, thus signal-ling him as a man apart from the toilers. By now Dino is no doubt back in his townhouse in Tirana, the Hoxha years an increasingly blurred memory.

Back in the early eighties – 1880s, that is – Lord Derby urged a Parliamen-tary survey to refute 'wild and reckless exaggerations' to the effect that most of Britain was owned by a very small number of people.

Bateman's *New Domesday Survey*, later expanded as *Great Landowners of Great Britain and Ireland*, duly established, much to Derby's mortification, that no less than 75 percent of the Kingdom was owned by seven thousand people, with a quarter of England and Wales in the hands of 710 persons. Half the Scottish Highlands were owned by fifteen lairds, led by the Sutherlands immortalised in Karl Marx's account of the Highland clearances, who held 1.25 million acres.

Jeremy Paxman cited Bateman in his entertaining and informative *Friends in High Places*, demonstrating with a wealth of illustration the humbug of all talk about a new, classless Britain. The old gang was still running the show, and owning it too. After the holocaust of the First World War, and the tax and inheritance imposts of the pre-Thatcher governments following the Second, an examination by a Canadian scholar, Heather Clemenson, of five hundred families disclosed that 259 of them – 52 percent – still owned some of the land they possessed at the time of the *New Domesday Survey*. Nearly half the families owning ten thousand acres or more in the late nineteenth century still held most or all of their estates, as most happily symbolised by the Duke of Westminster with properties stretching from Mayfair to Hawai'i, and with the Duke himself recently flushed with success in beating off challenges to the inalienable rights of freehold.

➤

DECEMBER 8   *Petrolia*

GLOOMY ABOUT MORE OR LESS everything, I fell to browsing in Lenin's '*Left-Wing' Communism, an Infantile Disorder*, a pamphlet in which the old extremist was letting himself go on the period of reaction following the failure of the democratic revolution of 1905:

> Tsarism was victorious. All the revolutionary and opposition parties were smashed. Depression, demoralization, splits, discord, defection, and pornography took the place of politics. There was an ever greater drift towards philosophical idealism; mysticism became the garb of counterrevolutionary sentiments.
>
> At the same time, however, it was this great defeat that taught the revolutionary parties and the revolutionary class a real and very useful lesson ... It is at moments of need that one learns who one's friends are. Defeated armies learn their lesson.

➤

DECEMBER 9   *Petrolia*

NICK VON HOFFMAN called me and said he was doing an article for *The New Yorker* on *The New York Review of Books* on its thirtieth anniversary, and did I have a quote for him. The trouble with the *Review*'s Bob Silvers is that he's always wanted to be well received in polite society. It was either scruffy bohemia or the Council on Foreign Relations, and Bob chose the latter. Back in the 1960s it was a lot more fun, with articles from radicals like Noam Chomsky and Andrew Kopkind. When the sixties were over Silvers carefully cleaned up his act. I don't think there's been much in the *NYRB* to disturb conventional opinion over the past fifteen years, plus it has carried some truly awful muck about Central America and so forth. The *Review* ended up in dead-center mainstream liberalism, taking the place of the *New York Times* Op-Ed page, just as it took the place of the *Book Review* back at the beginning.

➤

DECEMBER 12   *Petrolia*
Dear Mr. Cockburn,

In your column in the *Nation* on December 13 you mention that you may seek a MacArthur grant to develop your ideas regarding giant spheres of tomatoes 'flying in geosynchronous orbit fifty miles above fire-risk areas of California'. This plan has the savor of genius! It is well-deserving of all that strings-free MacArthur cash. There is one tiny problem however, and I'm sure you only overlooked this in your burning desire to shed yourself of the 'techno-fix mentality'. Orbital velocity is a function of orbital radius, and hence the height at which a geosynchronous orbit exists is determined. Unfortunately (for the tomato plan) the height is 22,300 miles, not fifty. You and I know this is a footling objection, but grant reviewers are notoriously costive, and would use this faux pas as a pretext for dismissing the idea out of hand. Don't despair, though. I would like to offer my services to you as a science and math consult-ant. My fee? A mere 49% of all grant monies. I offer you the larger percentage in tribute to your imaginative and creative mind.

Adrian Riskin
Flagstaff, Arizona

➤

DECEMBER 27   *Petrolia*
PRESIDENT BILL IS troubled by TV violence, same way as, these days, he's troubled by Murphy Brown morals. He hails ex-veeplet Dan Quayle's re-nowned speech on moral responsibility as containing 'a lot of very good things'. Back in 1992 Candidate Bill said he was 'fed up with politicians in Washington lecturing us about family values'. Governors who get blowjobs in cars shouldn't throw stones. Of course, being Bill, he told his bodyguard he'd looked it up in the Bible and blowjobs didn't constitute adultery.

Japan poses a certain problem for the media-causes-violence school. The place is flooded with violent media – TV, comic books, etc. – including violent porn, rape fantasies, sadism fantasies, guns and swords. But according to Doug Lummis, who has lived there for over 20 years, this doesn't spill over into violence in the society. 'The streets really are safe. The people dressed up like punks are not scary. No violence from the homeless (though occasionally violence against them). A fair amount of date rape, I guess, but not the kind where you are dragged into the bushes by someone with a knife.'

Japan does have gun control, so people rely more on kitchen knives and baseball bats. The police system keeps everyone under very careful watch.

One big difference is that Japan hasn't fought a war for fifty years. Nobody under the age of 65 or so has ever shot a gun at anybody under the right of belligerency of the state. The society isn't shot through with people who have tasted First Blood in some foreign land, in uniform.

Bring this back to the US, Doug argued in a recent letter to me, and you have a very persuasive argument the other way around. 'The cause of the real violence in society is not fantasies of violence but other real violence. Has research been done on this? How many of the people convicted of crimes using weapons, first learned how to use those weapons in the military? Any relation between violence in the black community and the huge number of black men who go through the military training mill? Ok, not true of the kids, I know, but still the indirect effects can be there. Why shouldn't the breakers of law in Panama be the breakers of law in Pasadena? I think this argument is 1) probably right, and 2) has the potential of turning the fear and revulsion against violence in a completely different direction: from support your local police to a transference of fear and violence against Violence Central: the US military.'

➡

DECEMBER 28   *Petrolia*

'FOR FORTY YEARS', Dr. Milton Greenblatt told a meeting of the American Psychiatric Association in Miami in 1976, 'the therapeutic value of convulsive therapy has been recognized. My personal recollections go back to 1939 shortly after the introduction of metrazol when, as a medical student, I was allowed to inject metrazol into chronically ill patients at Worcester State Hospital – against their terrified and frightened resistance, which, I might add, was overpowered by several burly attendants. In those days we required only the approval of next of kin for this procedure, and had few qualms about proceeding against the patient's physical resistance.'

The title of the paper prepared by Dr. Greenblatt was 'Efficacy of Electroconvulsive Therapy in Affective and Schizophrenic Illness'. 'Those who now regard electroconvulsive therapy as barbaric', the doctor went on, 'will be interested to learn that when ECT replaced metrazol, it was hailed as a great humanistic triumph, for the patient no longer suffered the awful preseizure sensations that accompanied the metrazol injection and furthermore, with electroconvulsive therapy, they were fortunate to have a period of amnesia after the treatment.'

The 1950s found Dr. Greenblatt overseeing research into LSD, in a program funded by the CIA. One woman at the Boston Psychopathic (later renamed Massachusetts Mental Health Center) killed herself within hours of taking acid, hanging herself in a bathroom. She was about to be discharged when she was given the LSD, of whose properties and possible effects she was entirely unaware. One of Dr. Greenblatt's subordinates, Dr. Max Rinkel, threatened another psychotic to whom he had administered LSD, brandishing a knife at her to see how she would react while on acid. This patient had not been told what was in the glass of water she had been told to drink by Dr. Rinkel.

In his tract *The Poverty of Historicism* Karl Popper argued that 'science, and more especially scientific progress, are the results ... of ... the *free competition of thought*' [author's italics] and that ultimately such scientific progress 'depends very largely on political factors; on political institutions that safeguard the freedom of thought; on democracy.'

Yet even as Prof. Popper was writing these words in the mid-1950s, scientists like those involved in the LSD experiments, or injecting radioactive material into patients, or bombarding communities with whooping cough virus, or releasing mosquitos carrying yellow fever, or indulging in any of the other myriad programs funded and overseen by the Pentagon and CIA, were enacting the very antithesis of democracy. Their watchwords were secrecy, unaccountability. Their patients were kept in ignorance, and the larger public uninformed of the scientific investigations being carried forward in democracy's name.

Popper saw 'the human factors ultimately uncertain and wayward' as the mainspring of evolution and progress. Peering through his anti-communist spectacles he worried that 'no doubt, biology and psychology can solve, soon will be able to solve, the "problem of transforming man". Yet those who attempt to do this are bound to destroy the objectivity of science, and so science itself, since these are both based upon free competition of thought; that is, upon freedom.' So much for Popper's cherished 'human factor'. I found this in Peter Sloterdijk's *Critique of Cynical Reason*:

> The analogies between modern medical diagnostics and the machinations of the secret services (to the point of linguistic details) are glaringly obvious. The doctor undertakes, so to speak, somatic espionage. The body is the bearer of secrets and is to be shadowed until so much is known about its inner states that 'measures' can be decided on. As in secret diplomacy and espionage, in medicine, too, things are 'probed' a lot, listened in on, and observed. Medical apparatuses are 'infiltrated' into bodies like agents – probes, cameras, connecting

pieces, catheters, lamps, and tubes. With auscultations, the medico eavesdrops on the body. Reflexes are noted, secret(ion)s drawn off, tensions measured, organ data countered. Quantitative statements, whether they be about production figures, troop strengths, urine data, or diabetes points are particularly appreciated because of their 'matter-of-factness', here as there. For the doctor as well as the secret agent, there is often no other way than to rummage around in excrements and refuse because the investigations, as a rule, must take place indirectly, without disturbing the normal running of the body or the overheard corporate entity. Only artful and often disreputable methods lead to important information about the inaccessible secret area. To be sure, more recent methods of spying on the interior of the body shrink back less and less from direct and aggressive advances. In places, the distinction between diagnostics and intervention becomes blurred: Foreign substances are infiltrated into the body. For these reconnaissances and illuminations of the body, not only the medicos put great efforts into encoding their information so that the 'object' does not know what is known about it. Learned bluff and intentional concealment for 'therapeutic reasons' separate the doctor's knowledge and the patient's consciousness. Coding and secrecy characterize the medical secret service style. Both exercise formally analogous intelligence practices.

➥

DECEMBER 29   *Petrolia*

PEOPLE THROW AROUND the word 'penis' these days. Time was, people handled it gingerly, and you mostly came across it in court reports or autopsy records. Otherwise, folks scurried to the gentility of 'organ' or 'member'. Open the paper these days and there's someone talking about his 'penis'. 'Vaginal pride' is offered by some feminists as their slogan of choice, but the vagina is still recovering from the disrepute of the seventies, when its supposed role in orgasm was fiercely derided. Given P.C., almost no demotic term for the female sex organs escapes rebuke as demeaning to womankind – which most such terms indeed are. Tim Hermach, who did business in Arkansas in the early 1980s, tells me Gov. Clinton used the word 'snatch' as his favored metonym for the Second Sex.

➥

DECEMBER 31   *Petrolia*

JOE PAFF GIVES ME a poem by Wen Yi Tuo, who was murdered by the Kuomingtang in 1946.

THE DEAD WATER

Here is a ditch of dead and hopeless water;
No breeze can raise a ripple on it.
Best to throw in it scraps of rusty iron and copper,
Pour out in it all the refuse of meat and soup.

Perhaps the copper will turn green like emeralds,
Perhaps the rusty iron will assume the shape of peach blossoms;
Let grass weave a layer of silky gauze
And bacteria puff up patches of cloud and haze.

So let the dead water ferment into green wine,
Littered with floating pearls of white foam.
Small pearls cackle aloud and become big pearls,
Only to be burst like gnats and to rob the vintage.

So this ditch of dead and hopeless water
May boast a touch of brightness.
If the toads cannot endure the deathly silence,
The water may burst out singing.

Here is a ditch of dead and hopeless water,
A region where beauty can never stay.
Better abandon it to evil–
Then, perhaps, some beauty will come of it.

1994

➤

The Argument

IN WHICH I am discovered, for the third time, in a major earthquake, this time in Los Angeles. The continuing campaign to market 'America the depressed'; the question of unemployment, the end of Keynesianism and André Gorz's thousand-hour work year; myth of the teenage pregnancy boom; Gennifer's thighs and the hypocrisy of President Bill; the Zapatistas rise up; I claim some credit for the Disney defeat; my career statistics as an eco-warrior; a trip to Istanbul; Bosnia and the laptop bombardiers; bids placed at the Philby auction; an aside on cider making; harsh words for Bernie Sanders; a hike down the Lost Coast; my rules for camping; conversations with Noam Chomsky and Edward Said; Andrew Kopkind and the coming of the familiar stranger. Of Malthus and his progeny, of life and death I sing.

JANUARY 17   *Topanga, California*
EVERYONE IN LOS ANGELES has their earthquake story. They all start a few
seconds short of 4:31 Monday morning. If there's ever a dead time in this vast
city it's at that smallest of hours. At 6.6 on the Richter scale, it wasn't the Big
One. But then, the Big One is really a theological notion, End Time as the
revivalists call it.

But there's a patch of starry sky at the west end of the big second story living
room where the fireplace used to be in Susanna's house. The brick chimney has
crumbled. The house groans as the shock waves pound up against the foundation, torquing the floor joists, wall studs, rafters. Every book, plate, glass,
saucepan, picture is smashing down. Blunder across the glass-strewn kitchen
floor in bare feet. Outside at last.

When a quake, particularly a long one, stops there's a moment when the
whole world catches its breath. You feel your body finding its balance. Some
people laugh. Others cry. As for animals, it depends on the creature. My neighbor, Sam Weaver, watched three horses during the mid-morning earthquake in
April of 1992, in Petrolia. It was a force 7, but after the horses skipped to keep
their footing they went back to grazing. The dogs barked hysterically for long
hours after and the cat was gone months and never did quite forgive me.

Earthquakes bring out the best in folks. Outside in the street people are
checking up on their neighbors, hurrying to turn off gas lines from their propane
tanks. It's the aftershocks that unhinge people.

There's no power, no television, but everyone has their transistor. In the
dawn people sit in their cars, away from the mess in their houses, dozing and
listening to the radio. The function of the radio is half informational, half
therapy, a process of forging the disaster into a communal experience. A kind
of emotional grid replaces the electrical one.

What we learn in the morning is that the city's arteries have been cut, as
strategically as if sappers from some invading army had carefully carried out a
long-meditated plan to paralyze the most auto-dependent human settlement on
the planet. Everyone in Los Angeles knows the prison term announced in those

ten seconds: traffic jams, extra hours for the commute, extra tension on the highway, another long-term ratchet on nerves already stretched by last November's fires, by the riots earlier, by economic decay.

Earthquakes liberate people into sociability and cooperation. The post-tremble hours are a kind of high. Crooks turn into heroes. Nerds boldly direct traffic. Folks experience collectivity, as against the normal dog-eats-dog mores of the city. In the big Mexican earthquake of a few years back this shared sense of community changed the politics of Mexico City forever. People ignored the police who arrived only to loot. The Mexican president waited three days before making a public statement. The opposition to the ruling party represented by Cuahtemoc Cárdenas crystallized in that earthquake's aftermath.

Maybe Los Angeles is too far gone for that. The city is raw and bitterly on edge. Even so the earthquake offered an ironic unity to a city so deeply divided. Also a shared sense of the miraculous. Martin Luther King gave America a holiday which kept even the early commuters at home.

Soon people will go back to talking about the Big One.

➤

JANUARY 24   *Topanga*

DR. GOODWIN IS INTEGRAL to the promotion of America's new Great Depression, which was launched with tremendous hoopla at the start of December in the form of a study purporting to show that the cost of depression to America is just under $44 billion a year. A cascade of bogus statistics followed this bald calculation, including a grotesque estimate that America's 18,400 suicides in 1990 cost Uncle Sam $7.5 billion in lost productivity and that 60 percent of the self-slaughterers did so because of depression. And the other 40 percent?

The study was put together by people from the Sloan School of Management at M.I.T., a private outfit called the Analysis Group and someone from the National Bureau of Economic Research. Along with Dr. Goodwin, Tipper Gore, at that time the White House's anchor on mental health, promptly hailed the report as indicative of the vital necessity for a huge boost in the nation's health spending in this area.

Almost all newspaper, radio and TV accounts that I monitored failed to mention that the report and the press conference promoting it were backed by Eli Lilly, the pharmaceutical company that makes Prozac (and that, incidentally, also concocted LSD), now being promoted as the cure for the Second Great Depression. Goodwin's NIMH and Lilly worked together in the recent national TV campaign on depression. The NIMH claims that no fewer than 52 million American adults – a fifth of the population – have a diagnosable mental illness.

➤

JANUARY 26   *Topanga*

THEY MAKE A DESERT and they call it fun. First the good news. The Disney themepark outside Paris (three medieval villages razed to make space for it; four French cheeses lost forever that Mickey might flourish) is a disaster. The French don't like Disney work rules: no facial hair, no human affect, no bodily functions, no visible manifestation of cerebral activity. Crowds have been thin. The whole operation is a bust.

And the Disney plan to open a park/golf course/real estate development in Virginia is in trouble too. Local residents up in arms include bluebloods, retired mass murderers from the CIA, Civil War buffs and other fractious elements.

In California the Disney family needs one vote from Yvonne Burke, new member of the Los Angeles Board of Supervisors, to destroy Topanga Canyon, one of the last remaining decent habitats in the greater metropolitan area of LA. The real-estate scheme is scheduled for the summit of Topanga Canyon: 257 acres to contain up to 97 sites, selling for up to $750,000 apiece, with all future mansions, assuming any get built, appropriately gated and guarded. The whole *development* – another word they've stolen from us – will be anchored to a golf course and club house offering membership at $55,000 a pop.

The proposed golf course alone will require several times the daily water use of the community, up to 1.6 million gallons daily pumped up to the canyon's highest point to irrigate the toxic sump that any golf course inevitably becomes. These are among the costs that economists call 'externalities', meaning that the community at large will bear the environmental price.

And if the speculation fails, if the golf club – fulcrum of the project – attracts insufficient members, if the price of the sites is too high, there'll be no going back. The bulldozers will have gouged out the hills, bladed out the oaks, destroyed the ecosystem. The 'developers' will have moved on.

➡

JANUARY 27   *Topanga*

RIGHT AFTER THE EARTHQUAKE in Los Angeles the California Highway Patrol said only essential workers should use the roads. The earthquake poses a radical question. How essential are most of the jobs causing people to spend hours in jams dispensing and ingesting the poison fumes?

They're certainly essential in the sense of allowing wage-earners that all-important paycheck. But aside from that? Capitalism demands higher productivity, fewer workers. Capitalism causes unemployment, needs unemployment to keep wages down, demands a reserve army of cheap unemployed labor.

Neoliberalism as currently represented by Clinton denies the market logic of unemployment and offers chest-pounding talk about good jobs at good wages, plus hard times for those on welfare unless they get a job in two years. The jobs aren't there. Each year there will be fewer of them. The radical demand is for shorter hours plus a social wage, unhooking livelihood from jobs.

The French political writer André Gorz is eloquent on this subject. Gorz points out that about half the active population in industrially developed countries bounce between precarious, part-time, temporary or short-term jobs with periods of unemployment. Productivity gains in the manufacturing sector, as well as employers' preference for overtime rather than expansion of the workforce, reduces available jobs. Meanwhile, the only place where extra jobs – however make-work and unproductive – can be created is the service sector. The 'service' society is indeed a society of masters, mistresses and servants.

Gorz advocates two strategies that ultimately blend: a radical reduction in the working week, plus a social wage that unhooks livelihood from a permanent job. 'The six-day week and the eight-hour day were originally regarded as ruinous demands. The present social security system would have seemed completely unrealistic seventy years ago. At the beginning of the century, full-time employment meant working more than three thousand hours a year. [that is, 11.4 hours a day for a five-day week with no other days off.] In 1960, the figure was twenty-one hundred. In 1985, it was sixteen hundred, and yet this volume of work, which was twenty-five percent lower than the 1960 figure, produced a GNP two-and-a-half times higher.'

So the present system produces increasing wealth with a decreasing amount of work, yet the work is not redistributed in such a way that it is a source of social liberation, with everyone working less and better, without loss of income. Thus is the casualized and precarious half of the potential work force isolated: 'They are victims ... of a discrimination whose rationale is essentially ideological. They are used as an example to show that only time actually worked entitles a person to remuneration and therefore that working time must remain the measure of wealth and social usefulness.' Gorz proposes a new 'contract for society', centered on a reduction and redistribution of working hours.

'There is no reason why we shouldn't gradually get back to an average of one thousand working hours a year [÷ 365 = 2.7 hours a day; allowing weekends and holidays, 3.9 hours a day] – which was the norm in the eighteenth century – or twenty to thirty thousand hours over a lifetime, enabling everyone successively to adopt several lifestyles, jobs, careers or types of activity, without ever ceasing to receive a full wage ... It is the time in which paid work is done that has to become – and in fact already is – secondary in importance.

'Your pension fund already holds a record of the number of weeks and months you have worked and what you have earned over your lifetime. Instead of being paid from the age of fifty-five – or even fifty – onward for a period of complete inactivity that will continue until you die, why shouldn't you be entitled to spread that economically – but not socially – inactive period out over your life?'

We have, then, to conceive a way of financing all this that does not burden either the working incomes of individuals or the manufacturing costs of enterprises. Such could be the case with taxes on consumption, of the VAT type, which could be greatly increased on those industrial products whose relative prices are continually falling. These taxes would fuel a fund that would pay people their incomes during nonworking periods. But you could also envisage different types of money, for example, a 'circulation money' that couldn't be hoarded, a 'neighborhood money', for trading services, that could not circulate.

A political strategy centered on the reduction of working hours could allow an imaginative labor movement to seize the social initiative and also connect to the vast legions of nonunion part-timers, casually employed, barely employed and never employed, who are destined to bulk ever larger in the political economy.

➡

JANUARY 28   *Topanga*
Dear Daddy,
I thought I'd send you some original Leontiev. Yesterday I read some of the New York review and thought it was rubbish. You would have particularly disapproved of the review of a book called 'Smoking is Sublime' which elevates smoking to great kantian heights – anyway the whole thing was so stupid. Maybe you could send me some good papers like the *Anderson Valley Advertiser* which I've been asking you for yearly.

This photograph of you in the cave I think captures the darker and brighter sides of life – and Ben Sonnenberg's suit seems to be reliving its heyday. I'd love it if you sent me a few pictures. I had the best time possible in Ireland I really did. I'll write again soon, I'm going back to bed to try and shake off this flu thing.

Lots and lots of love,
Daisy
London

The Leontiev:

> Both in *War and Peace* and even in *Anna Karenina* (although much less in the latter), we can find examples similar to the two just mentioned:
> 'Nesvitsky, munching something in his moist mouth', calls Andrey Bolkonsky over to him. Of course, he could call him over without munching anything. After all, this is still that same 'excess of observation' about which I spoke at the beginning.
> As everyone's mouth is moist when he is healthy, it was not necessary to mention Nesvitsky's mouth. Well, all right, so be it, suppose his mouth was especially moist; but, after all, we knew this already – ever

since the time our men burned the bridge over the River Enns. This same staff officer, Nesvitsky, was there, too – and there, too, he was joking with the other officers and 'chewing a meat roll in his handsome, moist mouth.'

In all that has been cited here, there is, of course, nothing strange. People of different periods, different sex, and different aesthetic upbringing express themselves differently about one and the same thing. In a broader context, this difference is even noticeable in whole nations. The French prefer to make everything somewhat more lofty than life; this was particularly true in the past. The Russians of the most recent semi-Gogolian period (not yet finished) prefer to make everything as base as possible. The English take a middle course. Suppose, for example, it is necessary to say that one of the male characters was frightened. An Englishman would more than likely simply say, without exaggerating either one way or the other, either positively or negatively: 'Intensely frightened, James stood motionless', et cetera. A Frenchman: 'Alfred began to tremble! A deathly pallor covered his handsome face. He withdrew, but with dignity.'

The Russian writer would prefer to express himself thus: 'My hero, like a blackguard, got cold feet and trudged off home.' Perhaps even better: 'dashed off home'.

This all relates to the choice of individual words and whole phrases.

'"Miss, please come to tea", said the servant in a bass voice, upon entering the room.'

And it is good if it is only 'in a bass voice'. Sometimes it is in greater detail. For example: 'The door opened with a creak. The flies that had just settled down on it to rest, flew up in thick swarm. Bending sideways and slightly thrusting himself through the half-open door, Arkhip showed his grinning face ...' (or perhaps even his ugly pock-marked mug), et cetera.

I do not understand – what is the point of this?

➤

FEBRUARY 1   *New York*

SAW ANDY KOPKIND at the apartment on Gansevoort. First time since we covered McMuffin's campaigning at the pig roast in New Hampshire in early '92. He is cheerful, but the chemo has taken a pretty bad toll.

➤

FEBRUARY 2   *New York*

THE WHOLE NOTION of a (black) teenage sex epidemic, born of teenage 'irresponsibility', 'children having children', is bogus. Mike Males of Occidental

College did a useful paper on this, published in the *Journal of Sex Research* for November 1992.

As Males writes, less than one-eighth of all 'teenage' births and one-fifth of all births to school-age girls appear to fit the popular image of youths of high school age or younger – 'children' having children. In only about 20,000 births annually – less than 4 percent of all births among teenage girls and 1 percent of the total births in the US – are both partners minors under the age of eighteen.

In 60 percent of all births to school-age girls, the male partners are over the age of 20. Men aged 23 and older are more likely to father a child with a school-age girl than boys under the age of 19. Fewer than 2 percent of the total annual pregnancies in the US involve boys and girls under 18. Similarly more than 100,000 of the 150,000 annual cases of syphilis and gonorrhea among teenage girls appears attributable to post-teenage men.

Males adds that if there was an 'epidemic' in the growth of teenage parenthood it was mostly in the late 1950s and 1960s, coinciding with falling ages of puberty, rising postwar teenage populations and the 'sexual revolution'. Births among teenage girls peaked in 1987 and have declined since then. The difference between then and now is of course that pundit flaunters of the 'epidemic' are alarmed about a burgeoning 'underclass'. As so often, 'epidemic' is a code for class paranoia and oppression. As Males points out, the term 'teenage pregnancy', in most cases where it is labelled a social problem or assigned 'public costs' is simply a euphemism for the much larger category of 'low-income pregnancy'.

Poverty, not age, is the problem. A ten-year sample of some 12 million abuse and neglect cases from 1976 to 1985 shows the average age of the perpetrator to be 32. The average age of divorced couples at time of divorce is 35.

Contrary to pundit panic, a large majority of teenage parents, Males writes, 'appear to adapt well to parenthood'. Most unmarried mothers are married within five years, most have jobs and few receive welfare. Teenage childbearing creates more public costs than adult childbearing because teenagers are poorer, just as blacks are poorer. The pundit elite has turned everything on its head. A mythic teenage rutting boom fuelled by a supposed absence of 'family values' has produced a mythic baby boom in which mythically irresponsible teen mothers and their feckless teen inseminators (who mythically all flee the rocking cradle) are lodged on lifetime welfare (instead of remaining childless until that well-paying job as a symbolic analyst at Xerox shows up).

➤

FEBRUARY 3   *New York*
DOUG HENWOOD RUNS an urgent plea in his *Left Business Observer* this month. He wants ideas on what to call residents of the US who trace their origins to

Spanish-speaking countries or regions in the Western Hemisphere. Official-dom, such as the Census Bureau, uses 'Hispanic' or 'Hispanic-origin'. Many people find these terms offensive. In New York 'Latino' is preferred, but there are objections here too. It's imperialistic, it demeans the indigenous, non-European population, and so forth.

True enough. The Mayan Indians who recently launched their rising in Chiapas are neither Hispanic nor Latino, and would have every reason to dislike being called such.

'Maybe it's wrong to use a single label for such a diverse population', Henwood writes. 'Or is it too much attention paid to names at the expense of social relations?'

Two and a half thousand years ago the historian Herodotus had a single label for all the folks out there beyond the edges of Greek ethnic dominion. He called them 'barbarians', meaning they were un-Greek. Of course these people pre-ferred to be called people of Egypt, Scythia, Nubia, Bactria, Babylon, Thrace and so on, which shows just how picky folks can be.

Face it, there isn't a 'correct' word for Hispanic out there waiting its turn at bat. Big bureaucracies love uniformity. It makes filing easier. But back before Herodotus put the word 'barbarian' into play, Homer had people very carefully announce who they were, where they were from, plus genealogy going back to great-grandpa.

People sometimes call me a 'Brit'. This annoys me because I'm Irish, from County Waterford. Then they ask how come if I'm Irish I have an English accent. I explain that my father was Scottish (born in Pekin, or Beijing as Westerners now pretentiously call it, to the amusement of the Chinese) and my mother Ascendancy Irish, or Anglo-Irish, meaning that she was from the Protestant minority. Her roots went back to both the gentry and the bog Irish, as the latter Irish were slightingly termed by the colonizers. By the time I get through all this their eyes glaze over and they dismiss my history out of hand and go back to calling me a Brit.

I conclude from this in general that one should call people what they want to be called, however odd or illogical it may appear. For years liberals fought the term 'coloreds'. Now 'people of color' is the PC term. I teased Doug about his hunt for the perfect word and he replied that mostly what he was trying to do was to get people to talk about the difficulties and absurdities of legislated language.

'In PC circles in New York', Henwood writes me, 'using the words black or Hispanic labels you as heir to Bull Connor. Sandra Cisneros, no New Yorker, told the press sometime back that she will stop talking to someone who uses the word Hispanic. Who decides these things? Why did the late *Guardian* weekly (a left publication) capitalize Black but not white? How did African American (no hyphen, God knows why) become the preferred term? I think it happened when Jesse Jackson convened a press conference to declare it so.'

Jackson's intention, it seems, was to coin a phrase on the model of Italian-American – a bit of assimilationist Americana. But in PC usage the emphasis is on the African, which is anti-assimilationist. The Census Bureau, which falls under the aegis of Commerce Secretary Ron Brown, uses the term 'African American' on orders from Brown himself. Here we get to the bottom line on correct language. Sometimes it becomes a substitute for politics. After all, as Henwood concludeS, the Clinton administration won't do a thing about black poverty (except to stigmatize single mothers and hold their AFDC checks hostage), but they will do something about the language. It doesn't cost anything.

➤

FEBRUARY 5   *Petrolia, California*
Dear Mr. Cockburn,
In 1950 a story appeared in Britain that the Czech Government had claimed that the CIA had dropped beetles in the country to destroy the potato crop. Naturally the story was not believed by most people but when I went to Czechoslovakia in August 1950 with the National Union of Seamen party I was told by an Englishman living in Prague that the story was true and that he had seen some evidence of it. What do you make of that?
                          With Best Wishes, Yours very sincerely,
                                                    A. Wilcock
                                                    London

➤

FEBRUARY 7   *Petrolia*
'WE CAN'T RENEW our country unless more of us, I mean all of us, are willing to join churches', Clinton piously told the joint session of Congress. Then he talked about family, work, community. This from a man who spent slabs of the eighties with his nose between Gennifer Flowers's thighs and who can't even spend a Christmas vacation with his family without rushing to a conclave of powerseekers in Hilton Head.

Politicians who presume to lecture the people on fundamental values deserve to have their personal laundry aired on national TV.

➤

FEBRUARY 8   *Petrolia*
PRESIDENT BILL TRAVELED to the poor area of Anacostia in Washington, D.C., where the kids, ready with questions about NAFTA and the Clean Water Act,

were treated to his headline-seeking homilies about 'personal responsibility' and sex.

The effrontery of this documented philanderer grandstanding about sexual mores to impoverished, minority eighth-graders in a crumbling inner-city classroom almost beggars description. But using the most defenseless members of our society as stage props for a 'family values' campaign snitched from Dan and Marilyn Quayle doesn't bother our brave commander-in-chief. The 1980s Reagan-Bush paranoia against adolescents has evolved into 1990s Clinton hostility. When all else fails, even the most hack politician can get a headline by picking on teenagers as the source of all social ills, from dissolute welfare leeching to murder.

But don't expect consistency from the President. A week after his repulsive performances in Anacostia he visited a GM plant in Shreveport, La., where he raised some good-ole-boy laughs with a rib-nudging reminiscence about the Astroturf in the back of his El Camino pickup in the 1970s, and 'You don't want to know why.' No lectures about values to this crew, who were more likely than eighth-graders to ask Clinton what qualifies him to be a preacher.

The facts about the bogus epidemic can scarcely be secret to Clinton advisers on these issues, such as Marian Wright Edelman of the Children's Defense Fund, Hillary Clinton and Donna Shalala. Scholarly work by Edelman's group exposes the myth, even as Edelman chimes in with the opportunistic Clinton line, thus betraying the poor kids her organization professes to speak for.

At least two-thirds of pregnant teenagers have childhood histories of violence and sexual abuse in their homes. This makes Clinton's threat in the State of the Union to cut off teenage mothers from welfare and force them to live with a parent or grandparent doubly cruel.

When writer Jonathan Kozol visited a public school in Anacostia he asked the school principal what he found must frustrating about working with young people. 'On Fridays in the cafeteria', the man answered, 'I see small children putting chicken nuggets in their pockets. They're afraid of being hungry on the weekends.' And this President fresh from cutting public spending lectures them about responsibility. It should be the other way around.

➥

FEBRUARY 10   *Petrolia*
DAISY GIVES ME THIS sample translation of the rhetoric of Zhirinovsky, Russia's bad boy, describing the evolution of his philosophy:

'I thought, "Everything must be done so that the Russians really get going ... so that Russian artists will be recognized in the streets of the mangiest small towns in America, so that every black in Harlem knows that it is useless to mess with the Russian Mafia, so that every slut in Australia will go weak at the knees at the sound of the word 'Russian' because she knows that Russians are the most volatile, richest, generous people on earth." This is all possible if Russians don't shoot other Russians, not for any other reason. This is the point of my nationalism and my militant actions.'

⇥

FEBRUARY 11   *Petrolia*
PRESIDENT BILL ENDORSES the crime bill, with its repellent social architecture of boot camps for feral youth before they graduate to mandatory maximum terms in the adult slammers, whose construction will surge as we goose-step toward the third millennium.

Re TV and violence, Nancy Macdonald, at the University of South Carolina, Sumter, has provided me with an essay by Dane Archer and Rosemary Gartner, 'Peacetime Casualties: The Effects of War on the Violent Behavior of Noncombatants'. Their analysis of the five years preceding and following a war establishes conclusively that warring nations were more likely to experience homicide increases and that a majority of combatant nations have seen increases of at least 10 percent. The US murder rate surged 42 percent after the Vietnam War.

The increases occur, say the authors, after wars large and small, among the victors and the defeated, among veterans and nonveterans, among men and women. 'By a process of legitimation ... wartime homicide becomes a high-status, rewarded model for subsequent homicides by individuals. Wars provide concrete evidence that homicide, under some conditions, is acceptable in the eyes of a nation's leaders.'

The authors quote Justice Louis Brandeis pertinently. 'Our government,' he wrote in 1928, 'is the potent, the omnipresent teacher. For good or ill, it teaches the whole people by its example. Crime is contagious. If the government becomes a lawbreaker, it breeds contempt for the law.'

⇥

FEBRUARY 13   *Petrolia*
Dear Alexander Cockburn,
I can't believe that neither you nor your editors caught the error, but 'blowjob' is not two words, but one. Think about it: if you quit in the middle it isn't a blowjob, it's foreplay (also one word). Form and content are one.

Regards
Henry Gordon
Seattle

FEBRUARY 15   *Petrolia*

BEING 'IN RECOVERY' speaks to something very deep in the American soul, indicating vigorous spiritual transition. Reagan managed an entire political career on the claim he was a recovering Roosevelt Democrat.

➤→

FEBRUARY 16   *Petrolia*

SOME TIME IN EARLY or mid 1949 a CIA officer named Bill (surname deleted) asked an outside contractor for input on how to kill people. Requirements of the performance envelope – inferring from the contractor's response later that year – included the appearance of an accidental or purely fortuitous death suffered by the Agency's victim.

There's a certain bluff innocence in the letter of Bill's contractor friend, who seems from the style to have been a doctor. The noun-heavy bureaucratic tone of the fifties is not yet apparent. The timbre belongs more to wartime commando exploits than to the chill advisories that lay ahead, far down the pipeline, in the form of the Assassination Manual furnished the *contras* in the early 1980s.

The 1949 communication to Bill, which came just two years after the Agency was founded with a charter limiting its activities to gathering and analyzing foreign intelligence, shows assassination policy in process of evolution at a relatively early stage. Note that two methods favored by the CIA's consultant were already being inflicted on a very large number of Americans in lethal doses. Bill's friend suggests 'exposure of the entire individual to X-ray'; or tetraethyl lead 'dropped on the skin in very small quantities' – more dramatic than leaded gas, it's true, but not nearly as widely dispersed or so thorough-going in its application:

Dear Bill:

There are two chemical substances which would be most useful in that they would leave no characteristic pathological findings, and the quantities needed could easily be transported to the places where they were to be used. Sodium sluoacetate, when ingested in sufficient quantities to cause death, does not cause characteristic pathological lesions ... Tetraethyl lead, as you know, could be dropped on the skin in very small quantities, producing no local lesion, and after a quick death no specific pathological evidence of the tetraethyl lead would be present.

If an individual could be put into a relatively tightly sealed small room with a block of CO_2 ice, it is highly probable that his death would result and that there would be no chances of the circumstances being detected. It is highly probable, though, that there would be a period of hyperactivity in the course of such a death.

Another possibility would be the exposure of the entire individual to X-ray. When the whole body is exposed, a relatively small amount of radiation is sufficient to produce effects that would lead to death within a few weeks, and it is highly probable that sporadic deaths of this kind would be considered as due to blood dyscrysias.

If it were possible to subject the individual to a cold environment, he would freeze to death when his body temperature reached around 70 degrees, and there is no anatomic lesion that is diagnostic in such cases.

There are two other techniques which I believe should be mentioned since they require no special equipment besides a strong arm and the will to do such a job. These would be either to smother the victim with a pillow or to strangle him with a wide piece of cloth, such as a bath towel. In such cases, there is no specific anatomic change to indicate the cause of death, though there may be ... marked visceral congestion which would suggest strangulation along with some other possibilities.

I hope you will forgive the random way in which I have set these things down ... If I can be of any further aid to you, I hope you will call on me.

➡

MARCH 1   *Petrolia*

MARY COMBE: 'Man after man among the drinkers in her inn complained that she "put her hand into his breeches to feel what he had" and then proclaimed that "if it were ready to stand she was ready for him." On the highway she was equally direct. She ridiculed one man because "his prick would not stand" and claimed she had brought some starch and "would draw it out and starch it, to make it stand." She often "layed her down in the highway between Axbridge and Crosse, and called to all persons passing, by spreading her legs abroad, saying: "Come play with my cunt and make my husband a cuckold." Yet Mary Combe's activities are not that of the normal village slut. She provided more than her body. She deliberately encouraged and organized activities and sentiments opposed to traditional values. In 1653 she organized a drinking orgy to which only cuckolds and cuckold-makers, the outcasts of respectable society, were invited. When a respectable villager was ill, Mary visited him and tried to tempt him in front of his wife. She asked him "whether he was able to do her a good turn. And more plainly whether he would .x.x. her or not, which is unseemly to write." Before his wife could remove her she took up the man's underclothes and threw them in the fire. Whereas all the evidence points to sexual intercourse taking place almost exclusively by the male lying on top of the woman, Mary Combe was renowned for plucking up her coats and smock and sitting astride any man she found lying on his back. She wandered around the parish naked – another uncommon habit.' – G.R. Quaife: 'Wanton

Wenches and Wayward Wives: Peasants and Illicit Sex in Early Seventeenth-Century England'

➤

MARCH 3   *Petrolia*

THE ACT OF LOVE DEFINED: Masters & Johnson: 'effective intercourse' is 'inserting the penile shaft into the vaginal barrel, thereby resulting in the retraction of the clitoral hood by active thrusting and pulling by the coronal ridge.' This ranks with a German doctor's definition of laughter as a rictus of the naso-labial musculature.

About 6 percent of all heart attacks occur during sexual intercourse. Of such episodes about 90 percent occur during extramarital sex. Mostly, the man is stricken. He's about 13 years older than his partner and usually drunk. For further reading, see M. Ueno, 'The So-Called Coition Death', *Japan Journal of Legal Medicine*, Vol 17 (1963).

➤

MARCH 5   *Petrolia*

THE TZOTZILS, TZELTALES, Choles, Tojolabales, Mames, Zoques and mestizos of Chiapas may have been driven to the margins across nearly 500 years of oppression, but their fibers of resistance have remained strong. A broken people does not organize secret guerrilla armies and train for ten years, which is what the Indians in Chiapas did.

The Maya of Chiapas have changed the political face of Mexico and, beyond that, the mood of the hemisphere. Subcomandante Marcos is the mestizo EZLN spokesman whose witty, eloquent letters have transfixed Mexico and made him a national hero. Here's his reaction to Salinas's offer of a pardon. The translation, by Frank Bardacke, appeared in the *Anderson Valley Advertiser*:

'Why do we have to be pardoned? What are we going to be pardoned for? Of not dying of hunger? Of not being silent in our misery? Of not humbly accepting our historic role of being the despised and the outcast?... Of having carried guns into battle, rather than bows and arrows? Of being Mexicans? Of being primarily indigenous peoples? Of having called on the people of Mexico to struggle, in all possible ways, for that which belongs to them? Of having fought for liberty, democracy and justice? Of not following the example of previous guerrilla armies? Of not giving up? Of not selling out? Of not betraying ourselves?

'Who Must Ask for Pardon and Who Can Grant It?

'Those who for years and years have satiated themselves at full tables, while death sat beside us so regularly that we finally stopped being afraid of it?

'Or should we ask pardon from the dead, our dead, those who died "natural" deaths from "natural" causes like measles, whooping cough, breakbone fever, cholera, typhoid, mononucleosis, tetanus, pneumonia, malaria, and other lovely gastrointestinal and lung diseases? Our dead, the majority dead, the democratically dead, dying from sorrow because nobody did anything, because the dead, our dead, went just like that, without anyone even counting them, without anyone saying "ENOUGH ALREADY", which would at least have given some meaning to their deaths, a meaning that no one ever sought for them, the forever dead, who are now dying again, but this time in order to live?'

➤

MARCH 8   *Boonville, California*
DID SOME WINETASTING – *aka* drinking – with Bruce. One, a present to the AVA from a wealthy industrialist who'd picked it up on a recent visit to the Bohemian Grove, was a 1984 Nuits St. Georges Premier Cru, Clos de la Maréchale, shipped by Faiveley. The other was a red table wine from the Santa Ynez Valley, produced and bottled by the Firestone Vineyard, and called Prosperity Red. The Editor had bought it at a San Francisco wine store for just over $4 entirely because of the label, a striking piece of retro New Masses–type proletarian art featuring a brawny prole with basket of grapes up on one shoulder, red sans-serif lettering below.

The wine, given the price, wasn't bad at all. This is very smart marketing by Firestone, catering to the big market of old Commies, comsymps, IWW fans and kindred imaginers of utopias on hold. The fancy wine, which would no doubt sell in a restaurant for $100 or higher, was a sore disappointment. Even a final mouthful from the lees taken a full hour after opening was still wretched.

The Editor rounded off the evening with production of a singl- malt Scotch. It was okay, but malts are getting trashier by the year.

➤

MARCH 9   *Topanga*
FOR A WHILE the White House's Human Radiation Interagency Working Group was not including the Marshall Islands in its review of US government-sponsored radiation experiments. The reason? The Group held, in the words of one White House official, that 'there is not evidence that radiation experiments were ever conducted on humans living in those islands', which is all very well but for the fact that the tests themselves were in the nature of a rather drastic experiment.

A document has now been unearthed from the secret files of the Atomic Energy Commission's minutes, in a January 13–14, 1956 session of the AEC's

Advisory Committee on Biology and Medicine.

The author, a scientist, minuted as follows:

'We think that one very intriguing study can be made and plans are on the way to implement this – "Uterik" Atoll is the atoll furthest from the March 1st shot where people were exposed (and) got initially about 15 roentgens and then they were evacuated and they returned.

'They had been living on that Island; now that Island is safe to live on but is by far the most contaminated place in the world and it will be very interesting to go back and get good environmental data, how many per square mile; what isotopes are involved and a sample of food changes in many humans through their urines, so as to get a measure of the human uptake when people live in a contaminated environment.

'Now, data of this type has never been available. While it is true that these people do not live, I would say, the way Westerners do, civilized people, it is nevertheless also true that these people are more like us than the mice. So that is something that will be done this winter.'

➤

MARCH 10   *Topanga*

THE TRAITOR AMES apparently survived his CIA polygraph, though the polygrapher had doubts.

CIA Polygrapher: Alright, Mr. Oedipus, I'm going to ask you some questions, okay?

Oedipus: Okay.

CIA Polygrapher: Ever sleep with your mother?

Oedipus: What an extraordinary question. Of course not!

CIA Polygrapher: Hmm. Well, put it this way. Did you ever sleep with someone you didn't know was your mother but who turned out to be her in the end? That wouldn't be so bad.

Oedipus: You mean, is there someone, a woman I once slept with, who might have been my mother?

CIA Polygrapher: Take your time over it. No need to hurry yourself.

Oedipus: I'm just trying to think …

CIA Polygrapher: What has four legs, two legs and three legs?

Oedipus: That's an old one! Everyone knows that!

CIA Polygrapher: Getting back to your mother, you probably didn't see much of her when you were young.

Oedipus: Not really …

MARCH 12   *Topanga*

DISNEY HAS GIVEN WAY on Topanga. I like to think my *L.A. Times* column had something to do with this. So far my career triumphs are four. A park bench moved in Maida Vale. Ciba-Geigy helped out of the Toms River by my *W.S. Journal* column. Merrell Dow is frightened out of Killeagh, in Ireland, by another *W.S. Journal* column. And now this.

Susan Petrulas Nissman, a leader of the community's fight, discussed with me what it takes to win. She herself had been working eight hours, seven days a week for the past three years and only marginally less for the previous seven.

War has to be waged politically, bureaucratically and technically. This means lawyers, biologists, hydrologists, physicists, economists, archaeologists, resources experts, all of them preparing counter testimony, working on Environmental Impact Reviews, spending countless hours pro bono.

It means forging alliances and coalitions. It means calling up politicians, poring over campaign funding statements, picketing, getting harassed. It means being a monomaniac, year after year.

There are people fighting these kinds of battles all over the country.

This time our side won. Susan reckons it was the spirit of the Chumash Indians that gave them the will to fight; a local newspaper (very important); one county supervisor, Ed Edelman, adamantly opposed to the scheme; a developer perhaps worried that the name Disney was – given other Disney fights and reverses in Virginia and France – getting a bit too meshed in the public's mind with the eighth dwarf, Greedy, whose sign kids flourished at demos.

Long fights and, sometimes, victories.

Up at the top of Topanga these spring days have been gifts from the gods. The hillsides are greening up after the fires. The red-shouldered hawk circles above.

➤

MARCH 18   *Chico, California*

MY ASSIGNED TOPIC was 'Immigration' and I arrived after a prolonged drive through the mountains along route 36, nourishing more than usually positive emotions toward my fellow migrants, having been phoned at ten p.m. the previous evening by a young Mexican waitress who had discovered my wallet where I had dropped it outside the liquor store in Ferndale. My Chico host was Alioun, from Senegal. He said he liked Chico and had been there for ten years. He was studying agriculture, of which there is of course plenty in the environs of Chico.

Some years ago *Playboy* named Chico as among the top college party towns in America. So the inhabitants feel constant pressure to keep their standing in good order. St. Patrick's Day and they were lined up from dawn at the bars, drinking green beer and other abominations. An unusually large amount of women in Chico have red hair.

➡

MARCH 20   *Petrolia*

ANNE HOOPER'S *Pocket Sex Guide* tells that only 21 percent of men today know where the clitoris is. Do the other 79 percent even know what it is?

As with all home-improvement manuals, Hooper's preserves a tone of optimism and faith in human progress, like a nineteenth-century engineer explaining a piece of machinery.

It's touching to see Hooper's two graphs of sexual response – pink for her, blue for him – peak together at the 20-minute mark. I thought simultaneous orgasm was part of fuddy-duddy fifties sex theory, matching the 'mutual assured destruction' model of the nuclear war-gamers. This was no coincidence. Bernard Brodie, one of the Rand Corporation theorists in Santa Monica, was undergoing psychoanalysis at the same time he worked on strategies of nuclear destruction. He circulated a paper privately to colleagues such as Herman Kahn, likening 'withholding' full nuclear assault to withdrawal before ejaculation. Kahn later systematized no fewer than 44 rungs of nuclear escalation, from 'ostensible crisis' to 'spasms or insensate war', which was Brodie's G-spot.

But in the early 1970s, theories of mutual assured destruction gave way to 'preemptive strikes', and trendy sex guides duly followed suit, with advisories that it was OK to do your own thing in your own time so long as everyone got there in the end.

The girl–horse thing isn't about sex; it's about fear and about obedience.

➡

MARCH 22   *Petrolia*

JOBS AND THE WORLD ECONOMY: David Roche, who works for the investment banking firm Morgan Stanley in London, marries Marx to Maynard Keynes when he says, 'Investors love long dole queues as long as they're reducing costs and not damaging demand. But eventually there is a certain length of a dole queue which causes a reversal of this perception.'

High unemployment and stagnant wages precipitate declines in consumption and thus usher in deflation, as Keynes pointed out sixty years ago. Keynes didn't live to see the advent of the global economy, which renders moot his strategies for reflation and full employment in the industrialized countries. There are a billion new skilled workers in China, India and Brazil prepared to do the same job as European or North American workers, at 10 percent of the price.

Businessmen ruthlessly following market rules sometimes have a clear notion of where this ruthlessness is leading. Percy Barnevik, a Swede who heads ABB, the world's largest power engineering group, runs a transnational enterprise that operates freely across borders and which, in the admiring words of the London *Financial Times* 'is at home in all the 140 countries in which it operates, yet owes fealty to none.' Between 1988 and 1992 ABB shed 50,000 jobs while increasing sales by 60 percent, to $28.8 billion.

Barnevik predicted last year that the proportion of Europe's labor force employed in manufacturing and business services will fall from 35 percent to 25 percent by the end of the century and to 15 percent ten years farther on. 'Where will all those people go?' Barnevik said. 'Out they will go because we don't need them ...If anybody tells me, wait two or three years and there will be a hell of a demand for labor, I say, tell me where. What jobs? In what cities? What companies? ...We end up with permanent unemployment or under-employment, or with two classes of differently paid people. Both are social dynamite.'

Which brings us to Chiapas. The Indians in Chiapas rose up on New Year's Day because they faced economic extinction, what they called the 'death sentence' of cheap corn imports from the US and Canada permitted under NAFTA. So, is that rising the last of old-style Latin America guerrilla movements, or an augury of the new fissures opening up in the global economy?

Those strategists of new employment in Detroit and elsewhere had better think big, about shortened work weeks, about a social wage, about the coming permanent absence of jobs. 'Job', by the way, is defined in the larger Oxford English Dictionary as meaning only 'a small, definite piece of work', which doesn't last long.

So retraining isn't going to do it, as the capitalists for whom Reich works well know. The real strategy is prison construction, to provide a few jobs penning in the ever-growing desperate and dangerous classes.

➡

MARCH 25 *Petrolia*

Dear Alexander,

I'm sending separately the latest CNS, with an article called 'A Red Green Politics in the US?' I think you'll find it helpful when you write 'what is to be done' columns ...

Son Dan sent me your excellent column about world unemployment. This message should be in every paper in the country, every day. In Italy, up to now the CGIL has confined its alternative to short work weeks and more spending on infrastructure, etc. But there are elements within the CGIL, and many other groups and movements, which understand that the 1990s represents a radical break with the past, and that old Keynesian nostrums and social democratic–type solutions won't work in the global economy you describe in the article noted above. The line within these groups is, 'restore, maintain, preserve, etc. what we've got left, in the way of environment, ecosystems, household and neighborhood life, etc., before accumulating more capital.' This line opens the way for a reconceptualization of what kind of employment (non-wage labor, but worker coops, mixed enterprises, municipal enterprises, etc.) needs to be provided.

The Institute for Policy Studies line is – we need a global Keynesianism. How this comes about given the destruction and self-destruction of national Keynesianisms escapes me. The place to start is to attack the world ministry of finance (IMF), world ministry of public works (WB), world ministry of trade (GATT) as misguided, cruel, undemocratic, etc. My position is a) if the IMF and WB can't be truly democratized, they should be abolished, b) preservation first! c) global Keynesianism re: commodities that are internationally traded, and should be; not necessarily the same as those that are so traded today – I mean, there's lots of room for regional self-sufficiency, and a healthier and more equitable relationship between cities and their hinterlands, on the one hand, and cities and their bioregions and watersheds, on the other.

The problem of global economy, from the perspective of its own rationality, is not just that a massive realization crisis threatens, as you say, but that the process of 'accumulation through crisis' from the mid 1970s through late 1980s has led to a reallocation of labor time, money capital, technology, etc., from consumer goods industries to capital goods and services in the first world (esp. the Big Three). This is a perfect set-up for a disproportionality crisis, touched on but not developed by Marx, but brilliantly applied by Sid Coontz in his underground and out-of-print (what else?) classic, *Unproductive Labor and Effective Demand*, an explanation of the contradictions of the 1920s, leading to the Great Depression.

We both hope you are well,
Jim O'Connor
Capitalism Nature Socialism
Santa Cruz, California

➤→

MARCH 26   *Petrolia*
'ASK NORTHWESTERNERS to identify the three most important sectors in the Northwest economy, and most of them will say timber, agriculture and tourism.' Thus W. Ed Whitelaw in *Left Bank* #5 out of Oregon.

Whitelaw goes on to say that if we measure economic importance in the Northwest by total employment in Washington and Oregon, not one of these industries actually rank in the top three or even the top six. In these states the top five are health services (about 8 percent of total employment), educational services, schools and colleges (also about eight per cent) business and professional services (about 7 percent), wholesale trade (about 6 percent) and finance, insurance and real estate (about 5 percent). Agriculture leads timber and tourism, but each of the three sectors employs only 2 to 4 percent of the total.

This makes the Clinton-Babbitt Option 9 sellout to Big Timber and the Carpenters not only criminal but politically blind. Whitelaw ridicules the claim of Con Schallau, chief economist for the American Forest Resource Alliance, that forest products are still the dominant component of Oregon's economy. As Whitelaw points out, 'The number of workers in Oregon's lumber-and-wood-products industry *declined* by 17 per cent (13,500 jobs) between 1979 (the year preceding the national recession of the early 1980s) and 1989 (the year preceding the current national recessionary period and long before the spotted owl plan had any impact). By contrast, total employment in Oregon increased by 23 per cent (257,000 jobs) during the 1979-1989 period.

Combined, Oregon and Washington lost 27,227 jobs in lumber and wood products in the 1979–89 timeframe, while total employment in the two states increased by 26 percent in that same period.

Whitelaw attacks the export-or-die model of Northwestern states, which premised economic growth on export of timber products, as opposed to far more diversified manufacturing, services and so forth.

➥

MARCH 27   *Petrolia*

'ONE CONFESSES in public and private ... One confesses – or is forced to confess. When it is not spontaneous or dictated by some internal imperative, the confession is wrung from a person by violence or threat; it is driven from its hiding place in the soul, or extracted from the body ...Western man has become a confessing animal ... The confession was, and still remains, the general standard governing the production of the true discourse on sex.' – M. Foucault

Got a letter from Lawrence C. Jorgensen, a teacher and 30-year veteran of Los Angeles Valley College. Not so long ago a female student attended about 45 minutes of Jorgensen's first evening's introductory lecture on the American political system. She complained that she had been sexually harassed by the professor's response to an unidentified male student's question about the availability of extra credit. Jorgensen allegedly responded, 'No, I can't accept credit cards because I don't have a machine; I won't accept cheques because of the economy, and I don't accept sexual favors because of AIDS. So you will all just have to do the assigned work.' The unidentified female withdrew from the class and two weeks later filed a harassment charge.

Professor Farrel Broslawsky, 'designated representative' for Prof. Jorgensen, has written to Dean Thomas Oliver, sexual harassment compliance officer (sic) of Los Angeles Valley College, in part, thus: 'Your misconduct in Professor Jorgensen's case continues the pattern of your office over the past academic year. First your office encourages the filing of malicious complaints of sexual harassment so that your office can open secret files on the accused instructor. You deny the instructor the opportunity to confront the accuser, you refuse access to the files, you obstruct the efforts of the falsely accused instructor to be exonerated and if the accused instructor refuses to grovel and comply with your arbitrary demands that he attend 'est' seminars (emotionally sensitive teaching), you claim the matter will no longer be pursued, but you continue to maintain secret files containing the unsubstantiated complaint.'

Which brings us back to Foucault.

➤

APRIL 1   *Petrolia*

IN CHICO THE OTHER DAY a woman who said she was head of the 'population group' (or committee, I can't remember) of the Sierra Club in California asked why I was so hard on Malthus. Why was I discounting the menace of overpopulation?

As a political economist Malthus had to reconcile his theories of population with the problem of effective demand. Who were the consumers necessary to keep the system turning over? Malthus loathed the poor and rejected the idea of increased purchasing power among the laboring classes, arguing that under a system of private property 'the only effectual demand for produce must come from the owners of property', and that these affluent underbreeders would spare the otherwise inevitable visitation of misery on their own sector of mankind and secure 'to a portion of society the leisure necessary for the progress of the arts and sciences', thus conferring on society 'a most significant benefit.'

For Malthus, the poor – outside such workers as are necessary for production – are dispensable and should not be assisted in any way. Consumption – the exercise of effective demand – is mostly the purview of the wealthy.

In Malthus's era the answer to the problem of the poor was definitively given when the British did nothing to alleviate the starving to death of about one million Irish peasants in the mid-1840s. The welfare reformers of today have essentially the same perspective, for no 'reform' is possible within the terms of capitalism, so there won't be any, aside from endeavoring to make life worse for the wretched, for starters linking welfare to sterility.

APRIL 16   *Petrolia*

TWO CERTAIN WAYS of getting people of supposedly liberal bent truly angry is to
(a) to suggest that poor African-Americans have sound reasons to have babies
while in their teens and (b) to argue that shouts for full employment in the
modern economy are stupidly unrealistic, that we need less work, not more,
that most jobs are idiotic and that leftists should press for a guaranteed income
or social wage. One prosperous doctor was so angered by this latter proposition
when I put it to a group in Los Angeles recently that he began extolling the
virtues of 'hard physical labor' though he himself, still in his forties by the look
of him, was already retired.

I've been getting abusive mail and kindred counter-argument from Malthusians only matched in fury by the nose-thigh fuss re Bill and Gennifer.

➤

APRIL 17   *Petrolia*

THE TACTFUL WAY the press here is handling renascent Italian fascism has exact
parallels in the way the *New York Times* handled the rise of Mussolini himself.

Right after Musso's March on Rome in 1922, the *Times*'s senior foreign
correspondent, Walter Littlefield, wrote, 'It is easy to mistake, in times of
political turmoil, the words of a disciplinarian for those of a dictator. Like
Garibaldi, Mussolini is a severe disciplinarian, but no dictator ... The manner
of [the new government's] work is already being described in a way to arouse
sympathy, if not enthusiasm – the long hours of toil, the dispatch of business,
economy in Government bureaus ... If the Italian people are wise they will
accept the Fascismo, and by accepting gain the power to regulate and control
it.' An unsigned *Times* editorial six days earlier remarked that 'in Italy as
everywhere else the great complaint against democracy is its inefficiency ... Dr.
Mussolini's experiment will perhaps tell us something more about the possibilities of oligarchic administration.'

Thus the stage was set for the great myth that Mussolini made the trains run
on time. He never did. In 1936, George Seldes reported that while the big express
trains were mostly on schedule (though other travelers disputed even this) the
local trains had huge delays. But very intelligently, Mussolini's P.R. men fanned
the legend and millions of commuters round the world laud *Il Duce*'s memory
in consequence. Mussolini also took care to ban all reporting of railway accidents and delays. For their part, the Nazis touted the autobahns and the VW,
but their heirs face the problem that too many still remember that they ran the
death camps on time too.

APRIL 18   *Petrolia*

OVER THE PAST FEW YEARS Arline Geronimus of the School of Public Health at the University of Michigan at Ann Arbor has produced a wealth of epidemiological and sociological data suggesting that there may be very sound reasons for poor black women to see their teen years as more appropriate for mothering than the middle to late twenties (and increasingly thirties and forties) preferred by richer whites.

The import of her work, as I read it, is that owing to long-term socioeconomic disadvantage and racism, the health of African-Americans, especially those in poverty, deteriorates earlier than does that of others. Lead levels, for example, rise sharply in the blood of black women in their twenties, presenting increasing risks to infants in utero. Stress levels in these women rise as the care of looking after aging parents and ailing kin increases.

Geronimus tells me, 'High rates of teenage child-bearing have been a consistent pattern in impoverished African-American communities, regardless of pervasive ideological pressure suggesting teenage parenting is morally deficient. It is not merely a matter of the availability of contraception or abortion. I assume that women in all groups make reproductive choices and may – consciously or unconsciously – strategically time the birth of their children. Until proven otherwise, when we see differences, we should not assume they are doing it wrong, and should realize that they may be responding to circumstances we do not appreciate.' A child born to a poor black teenager is likely to be healthier, and to have a healthier mother, than if born to the same woman a few years later. The extended family and social network surrounding the teenage mother and child is also healthier. A decade later the wretched economic and social circumstances in which poor blacks live will be exacting their toll of disability and death.

So the 'cultural deficiency' lies in the economic arrangements pressing down upon those young mothers, not in the timing of their decision to bring their children into the world.

➤→

APRIL 20   *Petrolia*

IT'S A YEAR SINCE the FBI killed at least seventy-five people – men, women and plenty of children – in the Mount Carmel compound of the Branch Davidians outside Waco.

The weekend before the anniversary I got a call from Balenda Ganem, mother of a man who'd been in the compound that day. Ganem lives part of the year in Bangor, Maine, and part on the Greek island of Andros, where she co-owns a *taverna*.

'My son David Thibodeau was one survivor of the fire. He was married to David Koresh's sister-in-law, Michelle. They were married a year prior to the fire. She had three children already when she met my son. Serenity was 4 at the time of the fire and the little twin girls were 16 months. Michelle and her three daughters died.

'They were in what the FBI called a bunker. It wasn't a bunker. It was a storage area where they were eventually going to put big restaurant-style refrigerators. A good many of the mothers and children were in that area too.

'What's really important is that people understand that 400 canisters of CS gas [along with more than 1,000 charges of liquid gas] were lobbed into the Mount Carmel community in a three-and-a-half-hour period. CS is a riot-control chemical. CS was to be used outdoors. Indoors it is lethal. That community was gassed to death.

'The young mothers, with their arms full of kids – my daughter-in-law had three, my friend Julie had five children – these women were inundated, the children were overwhelmed; how was a mother supposed to maneuver her children through the debris?'

So fifty years after the Nazis' final attack on the Warsaw ghetto, the FBI gassed a religious community on national television, with the near total support of the press. Once you are officially designated a 'cult', the cops can burn you alive or drill you with machine-gun fire without much public demur. They could have fried the Scientologists or the Family and it would have been hats in the air from the liberals. You have to go to the far left (maybe) and the far right (more likely) to get some respect for citizens' rights in these situations.

➤

APRIL 27   *Istanbul*

IT COULD NOT BE SAID that Nixon's death has been received with any evidence of public interest or concern in the ancient city of Byzantium.

The person they would most dearly like to see flying at half mast is Tanzu Ciller, the Turkish prime minister who has just managed to destroy the Turkish currency by her acts of submission to the International Monetary Fund.

The bankers told her to impose austerity and this former economics teacher who did her doctorate in the US sprang swiftly to the task. The Turkish lira was devalued by 100 percent, giving an exchange rate of 33,000 liras to the dollar. Inflation eats away even at this, and so the value of what people have in their pockets drops day by day until there is another formal devaluation.

Small wonder therefore that the Islamic Party is doing well, having captured Istanbul and other major cities in the recent local elections. Between Ciller and the prophet Mohammed, who would hesitate between certain disaster and the possibility that Allah might have something better in mind?

APRIL 28   *Istanbul*

LEFTISTS HERE have a highly concrete knowledge of what repression means, since almost all of them were thrown into prison and often tortured in the coup of 1980 when the military took over to finish what they had embarked on in an earlier, less harsh coup at the start of the 1970s.

One woman doctor I met had spent eight years in prison, having been put away for her part in the kidnapping of a couple of NATO officers in 1971. Prison, she said, was the place she finally met the workers and peasants in whose name she and her student group had been acting. Then, after release she had been exiled and lived in Brussels for twelve years, which she said was worse than prison. Now she was back in Istanbul, working in a clinic and trying to alert Turkish people to the menace of AIDS.

The case load of AIDS victims thus far is extremely low; under 100 as I recall from what she told me. But take-off is quite likely, given the fact that Turkish sexual mores involve a good deal of homosexuality by men in heterosexual relationships at the same time. Only the passive male partner is regarded as being homosexual.

➤→

APRIL 29   *Istanbul*

OF THE TEN ORGANIZERS I met in one visit to a radical trade union syndicate – DISK – all had been imprisoned at one time or another. At least they are alive, which puts them several jumps ahead of their brothers and sisters in Central America.

Organizing is difficult, since any recruit to the union is promptly fired. After 1980 the military banned any formal connection between unions and political parties. So the Social Democratic parties in parliament agree with Ciller that the rules of the IMF game must be enforced, while workers get overwhelmed in the maelstrom of the imploding economy. Thus, you don't have to argue particularly hard on behalf of the Prophet Mohammed to get folks to sign up.

The head of the DISK labor syndicate – an older man – told me he reckoned the Islamic Party would never get more than 20 per cent of the electorate. But then, after he had left the room, his younger lieutenant said matter-of-factly that he thought this was nonsense and that in the not too distant future the Islamic Party would win a national election and take over. Workers had voted for the Marxists who'd done nothing for them; then the Fascists who had done no better, and so the workers were now ready to try their luck with the Prophet. Same as in Algeria.

When you read about 'a wave of fundamentalism' sweeping the world, translate this as mostly a statement that the 'masses' in whose name that woman doctor kidnapped the NATO officers conclude that the 'western-oriented' secular parties have nothing to offer. And indeed they haven't. So Islamic populism has a lot of appeal.

➡

MAY 1   *Istanbul*

WANDERING THROUGH the small streets of the old city I stumbled into a small shop where a well-built fellow was making horse harness. A Turkish friend translating my questions about Anatolian equestrian practices announced after half an hour that we were invited a couple of nights later to the weekly meeting of the man's Islamic order. This, it turned out, was the Cerrahi order of people who are orthodox Sunni Muslims, but also Sufis.

Along we went at the appointed hour to an ancient structure in the shadow of the Suleymaniye mosque. The meeting seemed to be a cross between a Rotary session, a soup kitchen and a revival meeting. There were small businessmen like our saddlemaker, plus poorer folk. The man next to me during the meal was a traffic cop. The meal consisted of lentil soup, then vegetable soup, then plain macaroni. Canned fruit salad at the end. I suppose that feeding a couple hundred people twice a week (Mondays and Thursdays) means you keep the victuals simple.

Dominating events was the order's chief, a sheikh in his sixties. He was in good trim, offering sage observation and comment to the punters, who hung on every word. There were half a dozen other foreigners present. Three of them turned out to be young German Catholic priests on vacation who had been invited by a blind man they had met somewhere. There were two American women, appropriately crowned with demure headgear. One of these gazed at the sheikh in rapture and was incapable of speech. The other told the sheikh a dream and asked for interpretation.

The dream material, as Freud would say, was rich. She had, she told the company, dreamed that she saw a large black chest, out of which emerged her Sufi teacher, whose fingers then turned into serpents with green eyes. What did this mean?

The sheikh said without hesitation that there were good dreams sent from Allah and bad dreams sent from the devil and that he most certainly wasn't going to offer any commentary or evaluation. The conversation moved on to other matters, and our saddlemaker told me the Cerrahi order had many recruits in America, including Harlem and San Francisco.

Later, as dervishes whirled sedately in front of us, the dreamer told me her name was Mahalia Pugach, from Mill Valley. She hadn't wanted to tell her dream but had been asked to do so by the man translating for her. I commented that Pugach sounded Hungarian and she said No, Russian and shortened from Pugachev. "The name of a famous leader of a Russian peasant uprising in older times', I informed her pompously. 'My great-great-great-great grandfather', she responded without any great show of family pride, and wagging her head in time with the Sufi chanting.

The musical part of the evening went on for about three hours, with dervish activity by eight young men for the final hour. The music was excellent, with the chanting reminding me from time to time of Celtic folk songs. But four hours were enough and finally Selim and I crept out. He told me that there had been polite attempts to recruit him to the order, with intimations that the association might also be of commercial advantage, alongside the spiritual benefits.

For my part, I told the saddlemaker I was a journalist and would pass the word along.

➤→

MAY 5   *Ardmore, Co. Waterford*
'WE HAVE NOW REACHED the point where every goon with a grievance, every bitter bigot, merely has to place the prefix, "I know this is not politically correct, but ..." in front of the usual string of insults in order to be not just safe from criticism but actually a card, a lad, even a hero. Conversely, to talk about poverty and inequality, to draw attention to the reality that discrimination and injustice are still facts of life, is to commit the new sin of political correctness. Anti-PC has become the latest cover for creeps. It is a godsend for every sort of curmudgeon and crank, from the fascists to the merely smug.

'Hate blacks? Attack positive discrimination – everyone will know the codes. Want to keep Europe white? Attack multi-culturalism. Fed up with the girlies making noise? Tired of listening to whining about unemployment when your personal economy is booming? Haul out political correctness and you don't even have to say what's on your mind.'

Fintan O'Toole, *Irish Times*

➤→

MAY 8   *San Francisco*
FLYING INTO SAN FRANCISCO I had the usual internal debate whether to admit on the customs form that I had food in my luggage. I had bitter memories of Cork Airport in Ireland a few days earlier whither the customs man, hearing I'd been in Turkey, promptly arrested my Turkish sausages. 'Foot and mouth disease in Turkey', he remarked and didn't flinch when I pointed out they were lamb and a lot better than the ghastly tubes of pork-flavored bread the Irish confuse with a sausage. 'Bread and water too', he remarked fondly of these Irish sausages as he bore the Turkish products off to the incinerator.

It must be a relict of the Ottoman onslaughts on Christian Europe, only finally repelled before the gates of Vienna in the late seventeenth century. Say the word 'Turkey' at any Western frontier and officialdom turns sour.

I told no lies on my US customs form, hoping the official would accept my unlabeled glass jar of caviar as Russian rather than Iranian, which is banned. He paid no attention to the form, began to quiz me on my suspiciously vast amount of baggage and then, on hearing my trade, moved into cheerful discussion of journalism before waving me through. The dispatcher of SuperShuttles wanted to discuss the art of the novel and Steve the SuperShuttle driver said he liked my work. Sometimes life conspires to make you feel good, and that's the way it was for me coming into San Francisco.

➡

MAY 10   *Petrolia*

FOR MORE THAN A YEAR each new twist in the saga of Bosnia has brought its war cries from a coalition, stretching, in the United States, from the *Wall Street Journal* through William Safire and Anthony Lewis of the *New York Times*, Jim Hoagland of the *Washington Post*, Michael Ignatieff in the *New York Review* and editorialists of virtually every newspaper in America.

Scarcely less urgent in their demands for throwing gasoline on the ethno-religious conflict have been conspicuous members of the liberal left and even self-professed socialists. Calls to arm the Bosnian Muslims have come from the Democratic Socialists of America (which also advocates 'massive airstrikes'). In *Against the Current* and *Monthly Review* (a March piece by Rabia Ali and Larry Lifshultz) we find the case argued for ending the arms embargo. In Britain a coalition running from Margaret Thatcher to the *New Statesman* calls for arming the Bosnian government and bombing the Serbs.

The 'arm the Bosnians' crowd has bought into a central claim of Izetbegovic's government: that it represents the will of all the Bosnian communities and that this government was annointed with legitimacy in 1992 – despite the refusal of the Serbian third of Bosnia's population to have anything to do with it – merely because the NATO powers gave it the thumbs up, diplomatic recognition. All the problems of how best to construct a post-Yugoslav Bosnia – problems best entrusted to an interim UN protectorate– are solved by the laptop bombardiers with terse advisories to rain down explosives or rush in arms. Can't they see the ironies inherent in the urgent requests of the Bosnian Muslim leaders that NATO bomb great slabs of their own territory?

Bombing won't do any good and will only fortify the resolve of the Serbs. Raising the arms embargo on the Muslims will mean the end of the UN presence and a lot more killing. The only way to save the UN peacekeeping role and, more important, the lives of Bosnians, is to have a much larger peacekeeping force, with Russian troops matching the Western contingent and no corresponding influx of Americans.

Genuine peacekeeping is a delicate affair, as dangerous as warmaking. Clinton does not want to commit American ground troops, fearing some will be killed. There are excellent political reasons for any sensible person not to want US ground troops involved. Such troops are always commanded by officers answering to the Pentagon and not to the UN chain of command, unless such a chain of command is itself entirely subordinate to the Pentagon. As the Somalia intervention showed most recently, US commanding officers are trained to fight wars, not to keep peace, and they are extremely sensitive to their domestic press bellowing for decisive action.

While Clinton may not be shoved in the dock for declining to send ground troops, he bears grievous responsibility for Bosnia's travails. He has fueled the war with bellicose pronouncements and threats of aerial attack that have not deterred the Serbs but only worsened the situation, as was shown when the F-16s were deployed over Gorazde, to the hurrahs of the laptop bombardiers, as Simon Jenkins calls them. Beyond that, Clinton has consistently kept alive the Bosnian government's hopes that the West will forcibly intervene on its side to assert control of all the territory it claims. Here's where Clinton and all those along the 'bomb the bastards' rainbow coalition join hands.

➡

MAY 14   *Petrolia*

Dear Alex,

You mention the Irish famine. A colleague of mine who does Irish history claims to have discovered documentary evidence of at least one shipload of grain that left Ireland during the peak of the famine, returned because no buyers were found, and then sailed out again.

Your remarks on Malthus also raise another question. Since the Reagan/Thatcher revolution defined itself I have had an increasing sense of *déjà vu* with respect to the history of the eighteenth century. Sir James Steuart, Adam Smith, and Malthus all assumed that the situation of the poor could not be improved (although Steuart thought the economy should be managed), that manufacturers were to produce luxuries for the rich (there is now some evidence that consumer demand was a factor in the cotton industry in England, even popular consumer demand), which much of it did. Wedgewood's special orders to Catherine the Great and Frederick the Great (molds broken afterwards) are only extreme examples of up-market production. Computers have made this possible again. And look at Moscow under the shock therapy. Good business for BMW, Mercedes, Jaguar. And here we regard Keynes as a prime shithead and note the end of Fordism and are quite willing to concentrate on up-market goods. As for the proles, 'Est-ce qu'ils on pas de orloone'?

Enough! Too much in fact. But do keep half an eye peeled for those enemies of a minimum wage who want to introduce programmes to top up wages. It does amount to a maximum wage.

Jordan Bishop
Ottawa

➵

MAY 19 *Petrolia*

BANGLADESHI TAXI DRIVER to J., after Nixon died:

'Islamabad, you see, was Nixon and Kissinger's friend. Only later did we learn that it was their secret broker to Beijing, and even while the army was killing us, the government in Islamabad was sending messages back and forth, to China, to Kissinger; so Nixon, he had to cover up what was going on. He could not anger Pakistan, and China was an ally with Pakistan against India, which supported us and which the US could never be sure of, so he could not risk losing his prize even before he had it.

'But the massacres were terrible. The army rounded up everyone they thought would be useful to our independence – political people, but also intellectuals, university professors, doctors, artists – and they machine-gunned them. They would take people into the stadium and shoot them. They would take people outside the city and tell them to dig, and after they had, to line up, and then they would shoot them too. Dig and then shoot; that's how it was. And the rapes – oh my God. They raped our women at gunpoint, and then after the rape, would torture them, cutting their breasts, their face, their pussy – oh God. My uncle worked for the government during the day and was very quiet, and at night he worked for the independence. He was killed finally. My cousin, he was tortured. Millions of people fled into India. Eventually your Congress stopped arms to Pakistan, but Nixon and Kissinger – Kissinger is really the one we hate most – they were very powerful. They could have stopped Islamabad at the start. But they looked away.'

As J. says, the eulogists miss out one thing. It is not for us to forgive. Nixon was America's man, and we can only atone.

➵

JUNE 1 *Petrolia*

MY FIRST WEEK as a syndicated columnist through Creators in Los Angeles; a very nice crowd. I keep trying to hold punditits in check. Remember the old rule: Comment is free, facts are expensive; meaning you actually have to produce some information.

JUNE 6　　　　　　　　　　　　　　　　　　*Petrolia*

ANDY KOPKIND CALLS to wish me happy birthday. He sounds very up these days.
He's working away on his collection, which J. will edit.

➤

JUNE 7　　　　　　　　　　　　　　　　　　*Petrolia*

PRESIDENT MCMUFFIN'S MARCH to the Normandy beaches repeats the antics of
an earlier Commander in Chief. Back in 1984 the fortieth anniversary of D-Day
was hijacked by Ronald Reagan's P.R. men as opportunity for martial posturings by the old actor.

As regards the defeat of Hitler, D-Day itself was, relatively speaking, and
not to downgrade heroism and sacrifice, a sideshow. The war had already been
won on the Eastern front by the Russians at Stalingrad and then, a year before
D-Day, at the Kursk Salient, where 100 German divisions were mangled.
Compared with those epic struggles, D-Day was a skirmish. The commonly cited
20 million figure for the Soviet Union's wartime casualties is now regarded as
probably an underestimate.

The D-Day landings had greatest effect for the postwar shape of Europe.
The German General Staff bore this as keenly in mind as the Western commanders. Hitler's generals knew the war was lost, and the task was to keep the meeting
point between the invading Russian and Western armies as far east as possible.

It's not fashionable these days to recognize that the Soviet Union had the
lion's share in defeating Nazism. The latest issue of *Time* represented this
aversion to historical reality accurately with its cover photo of Eisenhower
beside the headline 'The Man Who Beat Hitler.' Inside, Soviet participation in
the war was given only passing mention. At the fortieth anniversary Reagan's
people even doctored Eisenhower's Order of the Day to omit reference to 'our
Russian allies.'

If by chance he's still alive on some Argentine *estancia*, the aged Adolf must
be smirking with satisfaction at the shape of the world: a dismembered Soviet
Union; fascist renaissance in Italy; his wartime puppet state of Croatia promptly
recognized by Germany and then the United States, thus helping to precipitate
the Bosnian crisis. Even the Chairman of the Joint Chiefs of Staff is the son of
a Georgian who fought for the Nazis.

The Führer must be itching to get on the phone to Chancellor Kohl to ask
him how long it will be before Deutschland demands its lost Polish territories
and marches into Kaliningrad, the *ci-devant* Königsberg. 'In truth', Hitler
mumbles as he wraps a blanket round his skinny shanks, 'I really did win the
war.'

MOST POLITICIANS CLAIM the voters want a steady diet of throw-away-the-key sentences for malefactors, plus an end to welfare. Bruce Anderson, who has been running for Fifth District Supervisor in Mendocino County, says it's true. After weeks of candidate forums, campaigning in trailer parks, doing radio talk shows, he's found that people mostly do want to talk about crime and so-called welfare fraud, often parroting exact phrases from the nightly network news shows.

The supposed crime wave in Mendocino County is as mythic as it is almost everywhere else. As Bruce says, 'I read the sheriff's weekly printout for all the county, and what I see are the same drunks, crankheads and lowlifes doing the same self-destructive things, week after week. The full-time criminal population is virtually nonexistent except for a few methamphetamine manufacturers affiliated with the Hell's Angels in the Bay Area.'

The Anderson program calls for eminent domain takeover and local public management of corporate timber lands, rent control on residential and commercial property, reinvestment of county employees' pension funds in the county housing authority, plus no prosecution of families for growing fewer than fifty marijuana plants (the way it used to be with District Attorney Joe Allen back in the mid 1970s). Anderson's campaign mailer also calls for 'an end to the D.A.'s so-called welfare fraud unit, which basically persecutes and prosecutes welfare mothers for the crime of working to supplement their AFDC grants.'

Phrases about 'eminent domain' don't make much impact. But at a session with the International Woodworkers of America and the Carpenters' local in Fort Bragg, Bruce, who once – as he was reminded – called them fat, yellow-shirted corporate flunkies in the *Anderson Valley Advertiser*, did get a warm reception for the proposal that the holdings of Louisiana Pacific and Georgia Pacific be confiscated 'on the grounds that the short-term profit-taking has caused great harm to the people, streams and forests of Mendocino County, and Harry Merlo (chairman of Louisiana Pacific) should have been arrested for treason when he shipped our jobs, trees and mills out of Covelo and Potter Valley to Mexico.'

There's almost no radical idea you can't get a cheer for in America as long as you put it in terms people understand. Is there any political room these days for a socialist in the populist style?

Yes, Bruce says. 'The choice here is the same as at the national level, between the fuzzy pseudoliberals and the corporate surrogates. The ruling conservatives are all Farm Bureau types reading boilerplate manifestoes written for them by corporate timber, and the local liberals are all Clinton types – plenty of high-minded rhetoric, but behind it they're grasping and sanctimonious. I find that there really is a strong sympathy for left Populist ideas. The Democratic Party has conceded this whole terrain to the Rush Limbaugh right.'

JUNE 10   *Petrolia*

A MEXICAN WORKER up here in Humboldt County, in Northern California, was recently picked up in a sweep that filled every seat of a bus chartered for the day by the I.N.S., which duly trundled its cargo – including several children born in the United States – south to Tijuana.

He then met a friend who lent him the money to fly to Guadalajara to visit his girlfriend. Back a couple of days later in Tijuana, he climbed the border fence, was buzzed by an I.N.S. helicopter and duly picked up and thrown back across. Finally making it into San Diego, he was told that the *migra* were watching train stations, the airport and all roads north.

On the advice of another friend he'd bumped into, he got on a charter bus shuttling prospective gamblers to Caesar's Palace in Las Vegas. Thence, after brief review of the gaming tables, he made his way back to Eureka, passing on Highway 101 a procession marching to protest the deportations. A few days later he had one of President McMuffin's good jobs at good wages – time and a half, twelve hours a day, seven days a week, $1,500 in a fortnight – working for a company operating at a hazardous material site and happy to have its toxins breathed in by the lungs of workers unlikely to sue.

⇒→

JUNE 25   *Petrolia*

FOR FEEDING HOMELESS PEOPLE in San Francisco, Keith McHenry has been arrested ninety-two times since 1988, though never tried and never convicted. Lately, under pressure from San Francisco Mayor – and former police chief – Frank Jordan, the cops have changed their tactics. They have been hitting McHenry with trumpery charges of assault, which is a felony. These charges are contrived to fit California's new 'three strikes and you're out' law – a variant on the provision in the crime bill President Clinton is pushing at the national level.

McHenry faces life behind bars for giving food to the down and out. McHenry's latest charge stems from an incident that took place on Friday, May 13, when he and a companion entered the office of Supervisor Barbara Kaufman in City Hall to distribute literature about their organization, Food Not Bombs.

In San Francisco there's a Chamber of Commerce eager to have the city's homeless off Union Square, Civic Center Plaza and the parks; go someplace else, out of sight, out of mind, like Oakland. Anywhere from 6,000 to 15,000 people in San Francisco are in shelters, or flophouse hotels, or making do in alleys and parks. Jordan and his colleagues would have you believe these are drug addicts and dangerous drifters lured to San Francisco by the prospect of a cushy life on public assistance. In fact, as with most cities, they are a mixture of folk looking for work but not finding it, vets, people who should be in mental hospitals and so forth.

Jordan's Matrix program, launched in August 1993, saw them hassled mercilessly, their backpacks and carts tossed into garbage trucks. Harassment extended to McHenry and his fellows, who were trying to feed the homeless and to assert that homeless people are full citizens with full citizens' rights.

It's difficult to imagine McHenry ending up with hard time for trying to feed people. But then it's difficult to accept that the way many cities and states are confronting social misery is to criminalize poverty. Close down public assistance, close down welfare, close your eyes and hope the homeless, the single mothers, the down and out will disappear. Jail them and maybe sterilize them. America is a society hot for final solutions.

➤

JULY 13   *Petrolia*

THE ERROR IS TO SUPPOSE that zealous itemizing of Limbaugh's errors will make any difference. Anyway, the test is to find something he got right.

Ronald Reagan proved that once and for all. Year after year he trotted out his old favorites: welfare queens in Chicago shopping by limo; more environmental toxins put out by nature than by every industrial facility on the planet; more American Indians alive today than at the time of Columbus, etc., etc. (Many of these have been echoed by Limbaugh, 'that meteor formed by the vapours of putrifying democracy' to quote Dr. Johnson on Junius.)

There's almost no one out there fighting the political battles with Limbaugh in any kind of language ordinary people can understand and enjoy. If National Public Radio wasn't made up of a bunch of terrified elitist liberals with basically the same agenda as Limbaugh in more polite language they'd field a tough talk show with a radical democrat, with a small d.

Limbaugh is open to challenge, precisely because he's such a faker where it truly counts, not in his facts but in whom he claims to speak for. He says he's the champion of the ordinary Joe, which is nonsense. He speaks for the elites, which is why the Republican high brass love him so. He's a safe demagogue, sedately lunging about on the end of his chain, singing hymns to the innocence of the tobacco companies and assuring the small business people that the Reagan tide lifted them in the eighties along with the super-rich.

So why can't the liberals field their champion to go up against Limbaugh? The problem is that on issue after issue – welfare, military spending, crime – they're all in sync, which is why Limbaugh and the right have to invent or recycle all the personal gossip about Clinton to show there's a devil in the White House rather than someone who's doing basically what they want.

'WITH BATED BREATH, the entire civilized world is watching the bold experiment in mass sterilization recently launched by Germany. It is estimated that some 400,000 of the population will come within the scope of this law, the larger portion of whom fall into that group classed as inborn feeble mindedness ... It is estimated that, after several decades, hundreds of millions of marks will be saved each year as a result of the diminution of expenditures for patients with hereditary diseases.'

Thus, in 1935, Dr. J.N. Baker, State Health Officer for Alabama. He was addressing the legislature on a proposal for compulsory sterilization of a category of persons vaguely sketched as 'the feeble minded', but also including 'any sexual pervert, Sadist, homosexualist, Masochist, Sodomist, or any other grave form of sexual perversion, or any prisoner who has twice been convicted of rape' or imprisoned three times for any offense. Also scheduled for sterilization, subject to approval by county Public Health Committees and the superintendent of Alabama Insane Hospitals, were those 'habitually and constantly dependent upon public relief or support by charity.'

Before Hitler and his fellow Nazis (who said they had learned much from US sterilization laws and immigration restrictions) made the discipline unfashionable, eugenics and the prevention of socially unworthy babies were hot topics among American social cleansers.

The keenest of these cleansers were not Southern crackers but Northern liberals. Indeed, in the mid 1930s Alabama's Governor, Bibb Graves, vetoed a sterilization bill enthusiastically passed by the legislature. He cited the 'hazard to personal rights.' Around the country eugenic sterilization was most energetically pushed by progressive politicians, medical experts and genteel women's groups. States pioneering sterilization laws included La Follette's Wisconsin and Woodrow Wilson's New Jersey.

The argument of the social cleansers is that welfare mothers have babies to accrue more benefits. These babies ultimately repeat the cycle. Response: Curtail the babies by cutting the welfare benefits; end the cycle by ending welfare. Liberals begin at the former end, conservatives at the latter, and they meet in the middle.

We are at a critical stage in the evolution of these policies. In late April of this year Arizona and Nebraska both prohibited AFDC benefit increases for recipients who have additional babies while on the dole. Connecticut recently had a bill providing subsidies for AFDC recipients who accept Norplant ($700 for the implant, plus $200 annually), but it failed. A Florida bill also failing this spring – though it may soon reappear – offered $200 annually for contraceptive use by women who receive AFDC or are below 125 percent of the poverty line. New Jersey, active in the old sterilization crusade, has installed an exclusion policy eliminating the pathetically tiny increases for mothers having children while on welfare. Wisconsin, another sterilization pioneer, is experimenting with child exclusions. Georgia will commence doing the same next year, and NARAL reports that similar propositions are being considered in at least twenty-one other states.

Vicious myths fuel this legislative craze. Contrary to belief, welfare recipients average fewer than two children per family, and fertility rates of AFDC recipients are lower than among the general population. Illegitimacy rates are lowest in those states whose welfare benefits are the most generous, and highest where benefits are meanest. AFDC benefits have declined by 42 percent in real terms over the past twenty years. In every state the benefits are below the Census Bureau's poverty threshold.

As always, blame the victims – for the profoundest myth of all is that which makes poor, young, unmarried mothers responsible for drug abuse, slums, poverty, stagnation, the falling rate of profit, America's declining role in the world. And so, as with the vasectomist's knife, Norplant will turn things around. These are gas-chamber economics and social prescriptions. Behind it all is the Malthusian alarum that poor people are reproducing at a faster rate than rich ones or those endowed with 'high IQ' (as Garrett Hardin once fearfully put it). Hardin wrote in his hair-raising *Biology: Its Human Implications* in 1949, 'Either there must be a relatively painless weeding out before birth or a more painful and wasteful elimination of individuals after birth ... If we neglect to choose a program of eugenics, will the production of children be nonselective?' From there we travel to Paul Ehrlich's 1968 *The Population Bomb*, urging a cutback on government programs of 'death control' – i.e., public health – and thence to Nixon's Christmas 1970 veto of $225 million in funds for training family doctors on the same day that he authorized $382 million to 'control population growth'.

➤

JULY 17   *Petrolia*

ALLAN CHASE, in his *The Legacy of Malthus*, says that 63,678 people were compulsorily sterilized between 1907 and 1964 in the thirty states and one colony with such laws. But he also points out that these victims represent 'the smallest part of the actual number of Americans who have in this century been subjected to forced eugenic sterilization operations by state and federal agencies.' Chase quotes federal judge Gerhard Gesell as saying in 1974, in a suit brought on behalf of poor victims of involuntary sterilization: 'Over the last few years, an estimated 100,000 to 150,000 low-income persons have been sterilized annually in federally funded programs.' This rate, as Chase points out, equals that achieved in Nazi Germany. Across the twelve years of the Third Reich, after the German Sterilization Act of 1933 (inspired by US laws) went into effect, 2 million Germans were sterilized as social inadequates.

Gesell said that though Congress had been insistent that all family planning programs function on a purely voluntary basis, 'an indefinite number of poor people have been improperly coerced into accepting a sterilization operation under the threat that various federally supported welfare benefits would be withdrawn unless they submitted to irreversible sterilization. Patients receiving Medicaid assistance at childbirth are evidently the most frequent targets of this pressure.' Among the plaintiffs in this action was Katie Relf of Alabama, who fought off the advancing sterilizers by locking herself in her room.

Writing toward the end of the 1970s, Chase reckoned that probably at least 200,000 Americans *per year* were the victims of involuntary and irreversible sterilization.

➤

JULY 24   *Petrolia*
BEN SONNENBERG SENT me a copy of Sotheby's sale catalogue, which featured some of the contents of the late Kim Philby's Moscow apartment.

We discussed it over the phone. I asked Ben if there was something he'd like. He said he wouldn't mind the first edition of *Forty Years in the Wilderness* by Kim's father, Harry St. John Philby, published in 1957 and inscribed, 'For Kim H StJ B Philby 2/12/57 Ajahtan.'

This was estimated at £800 to £1,000. Through Quaritch in London, I sent in a low bid, plus one on an Azeri carpet featuring Lenin's head, presented to Philby in 1971 by an official in Azerbaijan. The catalogue note added that 'having accepted the gift with gratitude, however, Philby expressed astonishment to his wife that the Islamic tradition of rug-manufacturing had been perverted by the depiction of Soviet leaders and even local bosses (like the chairmen of collective farms).' This three-by-two rug was estimated at £400 to £500. The day after the July 19 sale, the trusted agent at Quaritch, whose nostrils had flared in fond reminiscence of Ben's rampages in his high book-collecting days, phoned to say that my low bids had proved futile. *Forty Years in the Wilderness* had gone for £1,300 and the rug for £1,000.

But by this time my interest had shifted from Philby's effects to a lot in an earlier portion of the auction, namely the library of Stanley Baldwin, British Conservative Prime Minister in the 1930s. Lot 318 was Hitler's 1935 Nuremberg speeches in English translation.

The Führer gave these to Baldwin's emissary, the civil servant Tom Jones. Jones recorded in his diary: 'May 17. Secret. I saw the Führer in his flat in Munich on Sunday morning, 17 May 1936 ... The interview lasted an hour and a half ... Finally he gave me a signed copy of his three Nuremberg speeches (Liberty, Art, Nationhood) to take to the Prime Minister. I observed that I felt sure Mr. Baldwin would be particularly interested in the address on Art as he was acutely sensitive to all forms of beauty, especially in nature and in language.'

Jones's *A Diary with Letters* quoted in the Sotheby's catalogue offers further context for the presentation. Jones told Hitler:

'Shortly after Mr. Baldwin returned victorious from the last election campaign he had told me that among the objects which he hoped to pursue were the following: to launch the young King, to get alongside Germany, and to hand over his Party united and in good heart to his successor. This reference to Germany obviously pleased Hitler ... What [Hitler] wished most of all [he said] was to achieve some solid piece of security in Europe, however limited, and that could be done in the West if the German proposals were adopted ... He repeated, with much animation and elaboration, his objections to attempting grandiose undertakings divorced from reality, urged the importance of an alliance with England, and his great desire to meet Mr. Baldwin. I pointed out that Mr. Baldwin was a shy and modest statesman who had never entirely gotten over his astonishment at finding himself Prime Minister ... The Führer smiled and interjected: "And I also."'

At the time that Jones was conveying Baldwin's compliments to Hitler, Philby was already a Soviet agent infiltrating pro-Nazi circles in Britain, before heading for Spain as a supposedly pro-Franco journalist. In 1941 his public pro-Nazi affinities recommended him to his British intelligence recruiters as politically reliable material.

≥+

JULY 30   *Petrolia*

NOAM CHOMSKY: You grow language in your head the way you grow arms and legs. If a child is in the right environment the language will grow. You can't do anything about it. It's something that happens to you and you end up with refined and highly distinctive conceptual abilities, and an astonishing capacity to express yourself in novel ways and over an unlimited range of situations. One major goal of linguistics is to try to find out what that capacity consists of. How much of it is part of our nature? How much of it is modified by experience? Ultimately we would like to know such things as its relation to physical mecha nisms, to other forms of human action.

There are similar enquiries to be made about human moral and aesthetic capacities. If people are capable of making systematic judgements in some area without having the relevant evidence, then the principles have got to be coming from inside. You and I can make systematic judgements about sentences in English. You never heard these sentences before, but you're understanding them right off, which means that you're making highly systematic and quite complex judgements about very intricate matters. Your experience is far too impoverished to determine these specific processes, so what you are doing must derive from your inner nature. Unless there are angels around, anything you do is the result of your internal nature, or some impact of experience. And experience is extremely impoverished. It has a limited effect on what you are. It modifies it a little bit, but as with your physical growth, where you couldn't have eaten different food and had wings rather than arms.

The same is true of intellectual development, and the same is true in moral life. You're constantly making choices and decisions and judgements – sometimes you don't know quite what to do, but over a wide range you know what's right. And even when you disagree with people, you find shared moral ground on which you can work things out. That's true on every issue.

Take a look at the debate over slavery; it was largely on shared moral ground. And some of the arguments were not so silly. You could understand the slave owner's arguments. A slave owner says, 'If you own property, you treat it better than if you rent property. So, I'm more humane than you are.' We can understand that argument. You have to figure out what's wrong with it, but there is shared moral ground over a range that goes far beyond any experience. And this can only mean – again, short of angels – that it's growing out of our nature. It means there must be principles that are embedded in our nature or at the core of our understanding of what a decent human life is, what a proper form of society is, and so on.

AC: So is there much work now being done on some kind of essential moral or progressive human capacity?

NC: I've written about it. Not in any particularly original way. It goes back to the Enlightenment, and the classical liberalism of Humboldt.

Rousseau actually tried to connect his ideas about the limits of Cartesian concepts of mechanism to a basis for human freedom. This is in the Second Discourse, which is the libertarian Rousseau. It derives from a kind of Cartesian basis, concerned with the limits of mechanism. The limits of mechanism in Cartesian philosophy are very closely related to observations about the creative aspects of the use of language. That's essentially the connection. It also appears in Humboldt, who was a very important linguist.

These elements of Enlightenment were much more advanced than modern thought, in my opinion. In these respects there's been a lot of regression. Structuralism, or contemporary behavioral psychology, or work on artificial intelligence lacks much of the sophistication of seventeenth- and eighteenth-century understanding.

AC: How much of that regression is related to the evolution of political structures?

NC: I have my own speculations. The idea that human beings are malleable and that people don't have an instinctive nature is a very attractive one to people who want to rule and to control. If you look at the modern intelligentsia over the past century or so, they're pretty much a managerial class, a secular priesthood. They've gone in basically two directions. One is essentially Leninist. Leninism is the ideology of a radical intelligentsia that says, we have the right to rule. Alternatively, they have joined the decision-making sector of state capitalist society, as managers in the political, economic and ideological institutions.

The ideologies are very similar. I've sometimes compared Robert McNamara to Lenin, and you only have to change a few words for them to say virtually the same thing. This is why people can jump so quickly from being loyal communists to 'celebrating America', to take the *Partisan Review*'s famous phrase back in the early cold war. All of this was predicted by Bakunin; probably the only prediction in the social sciences that's ever come true.

If you're essentially a manager of people, it's convenient to believe that they have no nature, that they are malleable. Then there's no barrier to coercion. In fact you can believe you are benefitting them by controlling them. On the other hand, if they have an instinct for freedom, then there's a severe moral barrier to any kind of management. You're injuring their fundamental nature, as with enslavement. So it's convenient to believe this isn't true. That could be one of the reasons why 'empty organism' theses, and malleability, are very attractive to intellectuals.

AC: I was reading a passage from Lévi-Strauss's *Tristes Tropiques* the other day, which quotes a phrase from Rousseau that seems to embody part of what you've been saying. 'Enthusiastic partisans of the idea of progress are in danger of failing to recognize – because they set so little store by them – the immense riches accumulated by the human race on either side of the narrow furrow on which they keep their eyes fixed: by underrating the achievements of the past, they devalue all those which still remain to be accomplished. If men have always been concerned with only one task – how to create a society fit to live in – the forces which inspired our distant ancestors are also present in us. Nothing is settled; everything can still be altered. What was done, but turned out wrong, can be done again. "The Golden Age", which blind superstition had placed behind (or ahead of) us, is *in us*.'

NC: Aside from the word 'everything' near the end, that's certainly correct. He's right about what we call primitive or pretechnological societies. They have great cultural wealth, including lots of scientific knowledge, the result of thousands of years of enquiry, experiment, plant-breeding and so on, which has led to an enormous wealth of knowledge, which the West is now trying to steal and establish patent rights over. And that's not even to consider other knowledge they developed, on how the world works, on language, human relations. The natural sciences have made enormous progress, but they tell us nothing about how to lead our lives.

AUGUST 4   *Petrolia*

DAISY IS IN New York and calls to say she had a wonderful evening with Andy
Kopkind and John Scagliotti. Then Andy calls to say that he and John have had
a wonderful evening with Daisy. Then Daisy calls again to talk about her
wonderful evening with Ben Sonnenberg and Ben calls to talk about his wonderful evening with Daisy. Compliments for each other pour out of the telephone receiver.

➤

AUGUST 5   *Petrolia*

FRANK BARDACKE AND HIS Watsonville committee's translations of Subcomandante Marcos' communiqués are out today in the *Anderson Valley Advertiser*'s
special issue. It looks terrific and everyone is very pleased. Joe Paff has read
through the whole 55,000 words and says it is as great as Malcolm X.

Bruce: 'Why would an obscure weekly newspaper based in a tiny town in
Northern California go to all the trouble to reprint the words of a Mexican
revolutionary thousands of miles to the south? Well, not to be too sentimental
about it, in a small way I hope it encourages the many Mexicans forced north
by global ownership to places like Mendocino County to know that there are
many thousands of Americans who will help them fulfill *all* the betrayed
promises of the first Mexican Revolution. Besides, it reads good, and it's often
very funny. Our own would-be subcomandantes up here could learn a few things
about how to talk to people in words they can understand and apply.'

➤

AUGUST 17   *Petrolia*

THE FIRES THAT HAVE been devouring forests from Colorado to the Pacific
Northwest coincide with the fiftieth birthday of Smokey the Bear. The timber
companies pushed the Forest Service – and thus Smokey – into big-time fire
suppression half a century ago because they didn't want their standing assets
– trees – to go up in flames. The result is that we now have over-fueled forests
that periodically erupt in lethal infernos.

Long before Smokey ever raised his priggish paw, these forests had known
a history of burning and intentional manipulation through fire. American
Indians were expert at it. The Forest Service's fire suppression program – a big
subsidy to the timber industry – promulgated the idea that forest fires are bad.
They're not. Many western species such as ponderosa pine are dependent on
fire for germination of their seeds.

Suppress the fires, and the ponderosa get out-competed by trees such as
spruce which are far more susceptible to insects and disease. Net result: dying

forests, as on the eastern slopes of the Cascades, overstocked with fuel and waiting for the first lightning strike or faulty muffler to set them off.

Forests do well with intermittent small fires which have a cleansing effect and create patches of different-age forests which enhance diversity of habitat. Such fires also clear out pests and brush and make nutrients available. The big blazes that result from long-term fire suppression have the reverse effect, consuming everything and reducing diversity.

➡

AUGUST 20   *Petrolia*

'THE PICTURESQUE is virtually invisible to those who believe concentrations of power are external. When they come upon Picturesque subsidence, they can only "take it straight". The doubt, the irritating uncertainty of the Picturesque completely escapes committed despots. One of the most striking proofs of this fact is the action that the Nazis took when they came upon a bridge in a palace garden outside Berlin. The bridge, built by an apprentice of Karl Friedrich Schinkel, crossed over an artificial waterway fed by a pump-driven waterfall. Its three and a half stone arches spanned only part way over the stream. The remaining gap was spanned by wooden planks. In the 1930s the Nazis repaired the 'damage' by 'completing' the masonry structure. Despotism cannot take any risks; any system working at full bore has no unused plenitude with which to amuse itself or entertain irony.' – Sidney K. Robinson, *Inquiry into the Picturesque*

➡

AUGUST 23   *Petrolia*

WHEN WE TALK ABOUT mainstream environmental politics, we always find ourselves talking about money, as dispensed by nonprofits, most of whom are mustered in the Environmental Grantmakers Association, which is dominated by the Rockefeller Family Fund and Pew, both of which have a long-term obsession with 'global population control', as the Pew annual report grandly puts it. (Pew money, like the Rockefellers', originally came out of the ground, as oil.)

At a recent association meeting, participants agreed that population issues were going to be a prime focus for the next three years. So now grant-seekers applying for a life-enhancing dollop of money will be sure to work population into their proposals. More torrents of astounding nonsense about population pressure and environmental degradation will duly pollute the rivers of public discourse.

SEPTEMBER 1   *Petrolia*

SLOWLY, SLOWLY dies this odd summer away. It seemed to go quicker than usual. Somewhere between about June 6 and July 4 I think the earth went through some sort of black hole. It's Clinton's fault. Most of the nation's political life revolves around the business of McMuffin trying to make up his mind. Will he aid Bosnia? Will he invade Haiti? Will he … You sit there fiddling about, waiting for the other shoe to drop and suddenly a month has dropped out of sight.

I find increasing difficulty in studying the national press: the fake debate about health care, the lunatic debate about crime. A reporter in the *New York Times* the other day managed to write an article presenting the US as victim of Cuba for the past 25 years. Meanwhile *The Nation* runs an endless discussion on whether the left should stop being nasty to McMuffin. What is one meant to say? Here's a man who has produced a health care bill worse than what Nixon proposed at the start of the seventies and what Bush proposed at the start of the nineties; a foreign policy towards Cuba that's far worse than Reagan's or Bush's; a crime bill beyond what George Wallace ever dreamed of.

By way of relief I've turned to cider making. Joe Paff and I built a press and barrel amid anticipatory hoots of derision from the better element, in the shape of Karen Paff and Susanna Hecht. The manufacture of hard cider elicits particularly vigorous winking and roguish badinage from passers-by, with fond reminiscence about drunken youthful encounters with the demon brew.

Never having had much luck with chemistry classes in my youth I much enjoy the practical work of jacking up the potential alcohol content (to around 8–10 percent), measuring acidity and racking the liquid from one container to another. The results have been benign thus far, with the stuff inducing (a) a genial tolerance towards mankind, mixed with laughter and beneficence; (b) drowsiness; (c) profound sleep; (d) a clear morning head and optimistic outlook toward the earth's affairs.

➤

SEPTEMBER 2   *Petrolia*

'(A BRITISH LORD, and subsequently a bishop, blamed Goethe for the epidemic of suicides provoked by *Werther*. To which Goethe replied in strictly *economic* terms: "Your commercial system has claimed thousands of victims, why not grant a few to *Werther*?")' – Roland Barthes, *A Lover's Discourse*

➤

SEPTEMBER 3   *Petrolia*

MILITARILY, YOU COULD SAY that bombs, detonated in the right place at the right time, did yield a political dividend.

The IRA has had two functions: defense of the Catholic communities in the North against sectarian attack; eviction of the British armed forces from the North and thus progress toward a united Ireland. Outside of its defensive functions, the IRA had until recent years been faring badly. A series of botched jobs, horrifying deaths of civilians and political ineptitude sank its reputation, hence its political clout, into the mud. Then a couple of years ago, a more supple Republican political strategy began to emerge. In the spring of 1993, Adams held talks with the Northern Irish nationalist John Hume. The well-advertised though private discussions ended the IRA's and Sinn Fein's political isolation and drew Dublin in. Albert Reynolds, Prime Minister of the Irish Republic, subsequently went to London in a visit that led to last December's Downing Street Declaration. This (albeit swaddled in contradictory verbal accouterment) let it be known that the future of the North was a matter for all Ireland to consider.

By this time, the IRA's military strategy had shifted from blowing up band boys and little old ladies in shopping malls, to attacks on the beating heart of British prosperity – London's financial district. In 1992, the bombing of the stock exchange; in '93, the National Westminster Bank and Bishopsgate.

On the eve of the cease-fire the London *Evening Standard* disclosed that after the big financial district bombings, the British Home Office received a letter of exquisite politeness from the Japanese Chamber of Commerce. Behind the courtesies there was a message alarming to the British government. The Japanese made it clear that unless the British government could guarantee its security, the Japanese banking and business community would move to safer climes elsewhere in Europe. The prospect of losing this highly lucrative presence compounded the already immense costs of British operations in Northern Ireland. The drain on the British Treasury amounts to $5.4 billion a year.

The British could not afford the war indefinitely. And at a fundamental level the status of the Protestants there had changed in the eyes of the English, who have been footing the bill for Ulster's loyalty to the crown. Every nation is an imagined community. The Ulster loyalists are no longer part of that imagined community. At this pregnant moment of historical evolution in the British posture, President Clinton allowed Sinn Fein's chief, Gerry Adams, a forty-eight-hour visa to the United States.

The effect of the Adams visa on Downing Street was electric. The fundamental diplomatic principle of any British government is: Don't offend the United States. John Major's regime managed to offend candidate Bill Clinton very deeply. It had cooperated with George Bush's re-election campaign in searching British security files for damaging material about Clinton during his Oxford years.

It could all fall apart. The long-term future of Ireland is in the hands of the European Community. It will supply the funds. It will supervise the federal power-sharing that may allay the fears of the Northern Protestants if the British are to go.

But after a 25-year war (in its most recent phase) that has left 3,168 dead and 30,000 badly injured; that has seen the British suspend all commonly recognized protections for the accused, run death squads, torture suspects, send people to prison for life on the unsupported word of informers; after all this the Republican movement has shown the capacity to recognize political opportunity, and the discipline to make the cease-fire decision.

➻

SEPTEMBER 6   *Petrolia*

I THOUGHT THE POINT of having an independent socialist in Congress was precisely that: to be an independent and a socialist. Instead of which we have Bernie Sanders (supposedly the 'independent socialist' from Vermont), hack Democrat. He voted for Clinton's budget, and now he's voted for the crime bill, a milepost in the development of the repressive corporate state.

This summer we passed, for the first time, the million mark for people in US prisons (not counting city and county jails). Steve Whitman of the Committee to End the Marion Lockdown calculates that the imprisonment rate for blacks is now 1,534 per 100,000, compared with a white rate of 197. The central aim of the crime bill, passed on August 25, is to lock up even more black people. In their book *It's About Time* the criminologists John Irwin and James Austin estimate that a set of laws akin to those just passed 'would mean that most of the nation's 5.5 million black males age 18 to 39 would be incarcerated.'

People designated as gang members can have their sentence for certain offenses (even those unconnected with gang membership) increased by up to ten years. Of course, it sometimes amounts to a death sentence or a beating for a kid to refuse to join the neighborhood gang. 'Affiliation' merely means the police put your name in a file. Mike Davis recently discovered that the cops in Compton had more names in their gang computer than there are male youths in the city.

There's no medical or scientific distinction between the two substances, but poor people use crack and rich people use powder. In 1992, 91.3 percent of those sentenced federally for crack offenses were black. Get five years for first-time possession of more than five grams of crack; get no jail time for possession of the same amount of coke powder. The crime bill did nothing to alter such iniquities.

This is to pass over the rest of the fascist panorama of the bill: the three-strikes provision, the enhanced mandatory sentencing, the stripping of federal judges of their power to enforce constitutional rights of prisoners, the ending of Pell grants which provide funding for prisoners to get higher education, the car searches, the hysterical and unjust treatment of sex offenders, and on and on, through to the expansion of the death penalty to cover more than fifty crimes.

Like the GATT treaty and the 'health' bill, the crime bill radically diminishes the powers of states, one of the reasons – along with the death penalty – that Senator Russell Feingold of Wisconsin voted no. Sanders voted yes. I asked him why and he faxed me four paragraphs of pitiful blather – almost all other 'Progressives' had voted yes; rejection of this bill would have meant a worse one down the road (this was always the cop-out of the yea-sayers for 'nonlethal' *contra* aid – 'We had to head Zyklon C off at the pass'); there was money in the bill for cities and towns and for battered women's shelters.

For over a decade I've listened to the rap from Sanders and the Progressive Coalition in Vermont about the need for an alternative to the two-party system. Some alternative! Sanders's record is scarcely more liberal than that of Vermont's Republican senator, Jim Jeffords. To their everlasting shame, not one squeak, so far as I can ascertain, was raised by the Vermont Pwogwessives about Sanders's crime bill vote. I suppose the money for battered women's shelters caused them not to notice one of the most rabid expressions of racism in the nation's legislative history.

➼

SEPTEMBER 12   *Petrolia*

Your report on the harassment by the San Francisco police of homelessness activist Keith McHenry was shocking, but not surprising. From the standpoint of history, it's a very old story. For instance, the historian Gaston Roupnel reports that citizens of 17th century Dijon were forbidden to feed the poor: 'In the sixteenth century, the beggar or vagrant was fed and cared for before he was sent away. In the early seventeenth century, he had his head shaved. Later on, he was whipped; and the end of the century saw the last word in repression – he was turned into a convict.' Of course, this kind of progress, like others, occurs more quickly now than it did three centuries ago.

Barry Schwabsky
Brooklyn, New York

➼

SEPTEMBER 14   *Petrolia*

BRUCE ANDERSON said a couple of months ago that he'd like to hike down the Lost Coast from Petrolia to Shelter Cove and I answered that I'd had the same thought myself. Karen and Joe Paff also wanted to go, though Joe now claims that I seduced them with all the talk about food, never reviewing the actual trek and kindred natural hazards.

I interviewed a few young hikers over the summer and they laid sinister emphasis on ankle supports. There was vague talk about big cobbles and soft sand. The Editor asked what to bring and I suggested a couple of bottles of whiskey to stretch over the two nights. The Editor confided to Carolyn Cooke that he feared a drunken amble, with Bly-like ravings round the campfire.

The Editor with Ling, who will command domestic HQ with Susanna, showed up with the whiskey but without ankle supports or even socks. His feet protruded through the sides of his Etonics. A packet of austere trailmix fell from his pack. My own pack was that of a fugitive sutler from the HQ of a gourmet general. In my view the two cardinal rules of camping are (a) cook nothing over a campfire, whose function is purely as decorative background and warming agent, and (b) stop at least 90 minutes before dark. Between us, the Paffs and I had roast chicken and roast beef, Karen's delicious pane forte, cheeses, smoked albacore, three types of jerky, smoked oysters, sardines, etc. etc.

The Editor had prepared spiritually by reading Walter Scott and said to me austerely before the hike that the highland sheepherders had moved through the Cairngorms sustained only by oatmeal. I packed some steel-cut oats and prepared porridge each morning.

The first bit of the walk was trying, though things looked up with the bottle of Glenlivet at the end of the day. Down through Spanish Flat, Big Flat and Miller Flat things looked up even further. Every mile or so an abundant creek burst from the King Range. We made camp at Shipman Creek six miles north of Shelter Cove. Next morning found the jerky hauled off a few yards before some disgusted rodent threw it aside. Tracks revealed that we'd been checked out before the mountain lion headed off on a leisurely nocturnal promenade down the beach.

Tramping into Shelter Cove twenty minutes late we met a couple clad from head to feet in late model North Face webbing, spandex, etc. coming the other way. They had three dogs, two of whom were burdened by custom packs. A third, unloaded dog looked worried. The couple were heading north and we watched them stop frequently to disentangle the dogs. I thought of the mountain lion but said nothing. Three-day trail veterans know when to hold their peace. The mighty Editor was first into the parking lot. On the way home in Joe and Karen's Goldrush van we saw some Roosevelt elk and a buck, which set some sort of finale to our own pleasant, 25-mile version of pastoral.

➤➔

OCTOBER 1   *Petrolia*

Alex,

'We must refuse the division of labor that is often proposed to us: between individuals who become indignant and speak out; and governments which reflect and act. The will of individuals must be joined, in an ongoing effort to challenge, in theory as well as in practice, every abuse of power, whoever the author, whoever the victims. After all, we are all governed – and, as such, we are in solidarity.' – Michel Foucault, 'Face aux gouvernements, les droits de l'Homme', *Libération*, July 1, 1984

Is this the meeting ground of the radical environmentalists and the Wise-Use Movement? I'm beginning to think it is. Resistance unites us.

Cheers,
Jeff St. Clair
Portland, Oregon

➤

OCTOBER 10   *Petrolia*

ANDY KOPKIND is back in hospital in New York. J. is visiting him and says there's a serious problem with liquid in his chest.

➤

OCTOBER 22   *Petrolia*

ANDY CALLS FROM the hospital. His voice sounds very thin and strained. I tell him I hear he's on the way up, and he says he is. We discuss the subtitle to his collection. We don't talk for long. Later he calls and leaves a brief message on this matter.

➤

OCTOBER 23   *Petrolia*

J. CALLED. Andy died this morning, suddenly, of an embolism. He'd been talking to John half an hour earlier on the phone, laughing and joking for the first time in a week. My oldest friend in America.

➤

OCTOBER 26   *Petrolia*

THE GUARDIAN called for an obit. J. and I write an editorial about Andy for *The Nation*.

➤

OCTOBER 27   *Petrolia*

'WHAT ABOUT THE BOMB on the bus in Tel Aviv?' I asked Edward Said a few hours after the Islamic fundamentalist group Hamas had taken credit for the explosion that killed at least twenty. Said broke with Arafat over the negotiations leading to the Oslo agreement and has been a harsh critic of the 'peace process' ever since.

'It's a catastrophe. It's criminal and also stupid. But on the West Bank the bombing has no doubt got a lot of support. They say, "At least the Muslim people are fighting." These are the same fundamentalists, more or less, who five days earlier stabbed the Egyptian writer Naguib Mahfouz in Cairo. To make a devil's pact with reactionary religious sentiment is a tremendous mistake. But with, if I may say so, the exception of myself, there is no credible Palestinian voice putting forward the non-Hamas critique of Arafat's actions and the so-called peace process.'

'Aside from terror, Hamas has absolutely no sane strategy of resistance. 'Take the settlements and continued expropriation of land – prime cause of contention between us and the Israelis on the West Bank. Just the other day they took another 3,000 acres. Most of the labor on these settlements and new roads consists of Palestinians working for the Israelis.

'Now, you'd think that the principal responsibility of a national authority or a coherent resistance would be in some way to mobilize the people against participating in the destruction of their own future. But they've never done that.

'Again, take Jerusalem, a core problem. It's now expanded to some 25 percent of the whole West Bank. There are dozens of Palestinians whose land has been taken away, but who cling on in little shacks and simply refuse to move out. They could become the focus of a mass struggle – strikes and so on – to stop the bulldozers, some of which are driven by Palestinians. The Israelis have made no secret of their plans for Jerusalem. They publish their plans all the time. But there has never been a Palestinian response. In the meantime we've become at best a bantustan and at worst an Israeli protectorate. In the meantime, Arafat has become a parody of a Latin American dictator.'

And if the Oslo agreement really falls apart, what do the Palestinians have to do?

'There has to be resistance at the grass-roots level. Then revive the popular committees of the *intifada*, which is really what brought the Israelis to their knees. I'm not saying they defeated them, but they made it difficult for the Israelis to rule the West Bank the way they wanted. Two demands: no Palestinian labor on the settlements of any sort; no compliance with the Palestinian National Authority, which is simply a Vichy government, a stooge.

'We have to restate the fundamental objective: self-determination for the West Bank, Gaza and the Palestinian people. You can't keep changing your objective. That's why I left them in 1991. To go from self-determination to limited self-rule, what kind of nonsense is that?'

OCTOBER 30 *Petrolia*

THE LATEST SEX SURVEY out of the University of Chicago claims that Americans are almost entirely straight (maybe 2 or 3 percent gay, at most) and the vast majority revel in the loyal married state and have sparse sex. Among women, conservative Protestants have the highest rates of orgasm, which gives us a new slant on religion and sublimation. The whole thing is deliberately sedative, controverting the sexually subversive Kinsey report. One of the authors said complacently that, in derogating the practice of 'hot sex' nationwide, the report would 'bring down the temperature a bit'. We get the sex surveys we deserve. Bestiality doesn't even show up in the index, unlike Kinsey, who reported torrid levels of intimacy (particularly in the West) between humans and sheep, kine and kindred significant barnyard Others.

On the whole, the Chicago report seemed to be a match with Francis Fukuyama's *End of History* reprise of Hegel and Kojève, with the bourgeois Christian ethic blissfully victorious after all those years of instability since Kinsey lifted the corner of the rug.

Even the gay movement seems to have ended with tenured academics opening up Departments of Queer Theory, with solemn stuff about discourse, anti-essentialist rejections of gender rigidity and, no doubt, Christmas charades in which de wimmin caper about with carrots pinned to the front of their trousers.

➤→

NOVEMBER 2 *New York*

MY EYE FELL ON a book about Patrick Hamilton, a dear friend of my father. In the thirties and forties Hamilton was a highly successful playwright who wrote *Rope* and *Gaslight*. But his best work was in two novels, *Hangover Square* and *The Slaves of Solitude*, also the trilogy *Twenty Thousand Streets Under the Sky*. He and my father were Communists, and sometimes they would hawk party literature along London streets, though I suspect they soon ended up in the pub. Hamilton was the poet of the shabby bed-sit and frowsy saloon bar. He had a wonderful ear. He'd sit in the pub, my father used to recall, and come back with a head full of at least a dozen meandering saloon bar palavers.

Drink did for him. He sank into terminal alcoholism during the fifties and died in 1962. Literary gents age badly in England. There's no cult of the body there, plus heavy drinking and smoking, so the senior citizens of Parnassus mostly look in very poor shape indeed, blotched and paunchy and physically incapable of much beyond a totter round the club or saloon bar.

At least up until the early seventies drink used to do most of them in, if my father's pals were anything to go by. His liver was saved by the fact that it didn't take more than a very few Paddys or Scotches to lay him out. But the hard drinkers usually ended up very badly, to and from the dry-out spas, going through spells of the D.T.s, tended by some martyred wife or girlfriend.

I don't know if anyone has ever done a proper historical aetiology of literary alcoholism in England. Most of my memories of the early fifties London through which my father shepherded me on my way to school are of people getting drunk, being drunk, passing out.

Acquaintances were often rated exclusively by their habitual drinking volume. So-and-so could 'put it away' (drunk a lot of the time), or 'drank like a fish' (drunk almost all the time) or – this usually said with an air of gravity – was 'a very heavy drinker' (blotto *ad inf.*). The word 'alcoholic' was reserved for people shackled to their hospital beds, screaming at the pink mice nibbling on their toes.

People were always falling down. I remember going to some donkey races at Fort William in Ireland with Conor Cruise O'Brien, Paul Johnson, my father and also Perry Anderson, who grew up forty miles from me in Waterford. O'Brien, Johnson and my father all tottered in the course of the afternoon, and Perry and I had to support them to the car. No one thought this particularly worthy of note. Admittedly, rural donkey derbies – dwarf donkeys at that – in Ireland are informal in social *moeurs*, but when I went to Oxford the same style was in evidence. Outside the senior common room there was a row of wheelbarrows into which the scouts would deposit dons (what would be called tenured faculty here) too drunk to walk and trundle them off to their rooms.

➤

NOVEMBER 5   *Petrolia*
DID MY FAREWELL piece about Andy:

In the late 1960s in England when I worked for *The New Statesman* I used to travel down to the printers at High Wycombe each Wednesday in the company of the editor, Paul Johnson, mad though not as mad as he is now. On the train Johnson would ruminate on issues and persons of the hour ('Tony Richardson, a homosexual sadist *of the worst sort*'). Relief from these explosive allocutions would come in the form of Andrew Kopkind's weekly dispatches from Washington, telexed overnight and waiting for us at the printer.

It would be hard to overestimate the impact of these pieces. They were collected in a Penguin edition published in 1969 called *America: The Mixed Curse* and in the days after Andrew died I leafed through my old copy. Andrew worked hard at his opening lines and after a quarter of a century I can still remember many of them: 'To be white and a radical in America this summer is to see horror and feel impotence' (1967); 'In America, the cult of personality is the faith of the outcast, the politics of salvation' (1967, on R.F.K.); 'History is full of last chances, lost opportunities and unperceived possibilities. The history of political liberalism in America for the past twenty years is composed of very little else' (1968, on the McCarthy campaign); 'There is a cord which is strung from the winter of 1948 until now, and along it hang the politics, the events, and the personalities of one long, cold season of history' (1968); 'I used to work for *Time*; or was it sell? A Lucemployee is always a salesman first, and then a journalist of whatever degree' (1968).

There was polish and wit in such prose, but the rhythms had a tempo that stretched beyond elegance or aphorism:

'The Movement is dead; the Revolution is unborn. The streets are bloody and ablaze, but it is difficult to see why, and impossible to know for what end. Government on every level is ineffectual, helpless to act either in the short term or the long. The force of Army and police seems not to suppress violence, but incite it. Mediators have no space to work; they command neither resources nor respect, and their rhetoric is discredited in all councils, by all classes. The old words are meaningless, the old explanations irrelevant, the old remedies useless. It is the worst of times.

'It is the best of times. The wretched of this American earth are together as they have never been before, in motion if not in movement. No march, no sit-in, no boycott ever touched so many. The social cloth which binds and suffocates them is tearing at its seamiest places. The subtle methods of co-optation work no better to keep it intact than the brutal methods of repression; if it is any comfort, liberalism proves hardly more effective than fascism. Above all, there is a sense that the continuity of an age has been cut, that we have arrived at an infrequent fulcrum of history, and that what comes now will be vastly different from what went before.'

This was Andrew, writing in August of 1967 in an essay on Martin Luther King Jr. for *The New York Review of Books*. I had a line about Andrew in the wake of his death that many people didn't like, to the effect that 'If it ever needed it, he gave extremism a good name.' I suppose the noun makes people nervous. But what extremism meant here was following a simple logic:

'Martin Luther King once had the ability to talk to people, the power to change them by evoking images of revolution. But the duty of a revolutionary is to make revolutions (say those who have done it), and King made none. By his own admission, things are worse in the US today – for white people and black – than when he began the bus boycott in Montgomery eleven years ago ...'

The tall fellow, rather Ivy-Leaguish in appearance at that time, who finally came into *The New Statesman* in 1968 was somewhat diffident, in contrast with the enormously assured prose I had been reading for a couple of years. At that time I was sharing an apartment with Perry Anderson, editor of *New Left Review*, and since Perry was away teaching in Brazil, Andrew came to stay.

In those days we European leftists were pretty impressed by our radical

American visitors. For one thing, they were – so to speak – coming from the front lines, of urban riot and civic insurrection. For another, they traveled confidently from one end of the world to the other, spending – to our provincial eyes – prodigious sums.

For their part our American friends thought us inheritors of a European socialist – Marxist – tradition that might at a moment's notice catch them at a disadvantage. They might have Dylan, but we had Gramsci, Sartre and the rest of the gang.

Andrew was well educated, but he wore it all pretty lightly. I don't often recall him with his nose in a book and as often as not it was an allusion, a half-quote or a glancing pastiche that made apparent the reading he must have done at some point in the past.

He did, on the other hand, like current movie and music culture a lot. Back at that time, after a stay of a couple of weeks, he left me by way of a thank-you two records – the Temptations and Country Joe and the Fish. He also left me the advice that things might be getting rough in the States, and it might be necessary to communicate under some conditions of security. We figured out a code whose key, I remember, was 'ce n'est qu'un début', which was the first half of the Paris '68 slogan, 'Ce n'est qu'un début, continuerons le combat.' It's only a start. We'll continue.'

I became the European correspondent of *Mayday*, later *Hard Times*, the newsletter he started with Jim Ridgeway and Robert Sherrill. After two or three years it was over. Andrew was on a farm in southern Vermont, had come out. He and his friend John Scagliotti came through London, not long before I decided to go to the States, in 1972. The next time I saw him was in Miami for the Republican National Convention, no longer Ivy-Leaguish but not diffident either. I stayed a lot at the farm, and we were under the same editorial roof often enough in the seventies, at *The Village Voice* and then finally from the early eighties at *The Nation*.

Every now and again I'll bump into someone who says, 'That piece you wrote in 1972' (or some such distant year), 'it was the best thing you ever did!' It's never very uplifting to hear this sort of thing, as twenty years of work are waved aside. Andrew may have felt that about his sixties writings. They did command their time, and formally speaking they had a poise to them that was almost dissonant with the disorder they were describing.

Writing – if you are a writer, which many people think they are when they're not – is a long-distance game. Andrew survived his sixties classicism and made the shift, formally as well as substantively, to new times and a more relaxed style.

An important part of this transition was his own shift from observer to participant. Of course, in the sixties, he was a participant in the sense that he sympathized passionately with the insurgents he was writing about. But auto-biography and radical project still lay athwart each other, not least at the level of sexual sympathies. His writing in the sixties had – or so I feel now looking back at it – the unnerving and, in a way, misleading clarity of those days in Los Angeles after rain.

We talked a lot, mostly on the phone. Every now and again we'd go on the road and do a joint piece for *The Nation*, around the presidential campaigns. The trips were fun.

Writing with Andrew was harder. Our sentences got in the way of each other, and in the end we'd settle for separate sections of the piece even though our political thoughts were in sync, as they were in most respects for the duration of our friendship.

He was ill for a long time. Later on the Sunday he died I spent half an hour trying to find the passage by Proust in *The Guermantes Way* in the chapter on the death of the narrator's grandmother:

> But it is rare for these grave illnesses ... not to take up residence in a sick person a long time before killing him, during which period they hasten, like a 'sociable' neighbor or tenant, to make themselves known to him. A terrible acquaintance, not so much for the sufferings that it causes as for the strange novelty of the terminal restrictions which it imposes upon life. We see ourselves dying, in these cases, not at the actual moment of death but months, sometimes years before, when death has hideously come to dwell in us. We make the acquaintance of the Stranger whom we hear coming and going in our brain. True, we do not know him by sight, but from the sounds we hear him regularly make we can form an idea of his habits. Is he a malefactor? One morning we can no longer hear him. He has gone. Ah! if only it were for ever! In the evening he has returned. What are his plans? The consultant, put to the question, like an adored mistress, replies with avowals that one day are believed, another day questioned. Or rather it is not the mistress's role but that of interrogated servants that the doctor plays. They are only third parties. The person whom we press for an answer, whom we suspect of being about to play us false, is Life itself, and although we feel it to be no longer the same, we believe in it still, or at least remain undecided until the day on which it finally abandons us.

Andrew must have had a premonition. The day before he died he called me to dictate the dedication to the collection. We discussed the suggested subtitle, 'Dispatches and Divertissements of a Radical Journalist, 1965–1994'. He said he had his doubts and wanted to think about it. Later there was a message on my machine. He changed Divertissements to Diversions, and apologized for sounding a bit stupid. 'Still', he said laconically before he rang off, 'stupid is as stupid does.' Next morning, though he had sounded perkier on the phone to John, he was suddenly gone with an abruptness that reminded me of nothing more than the way he'd end a phone conversation. He often found it hard to get out of a chat and would suddenly say goodbye, and hang up.

Afterword

➤➤

THIS IS THE JOURNAL of a working life, public and occasionally private. I write almost every day and much of it ends up published and some of it doesn't, either because it didn't work out, was chopped out, or wasn't meant to be published in the first place. Here, there's material from each category. I'm lucky, because I have long-term relationships with publications, particularly *The Nation* and the *Anderson Valley Advertiser*, where continuity of a journal can be maintained week after week, idiosyncratic and personal. The other place that was hospitable in this sort of way, within the time frame of this book, was Shelley Wanger's marvelous *Interview*, idyllic from my point of view.

A left journalist writing in *The Nation* or the *AVA* or the *Los Angeles Times* every couple of weeks, or in columns syndicated through my friends at Creators in Los Angeles, sets off rows and passions. I've tried to give a sense of this rattle of brickbats against the windows of the ivory tower, including the chap who wrote from Toronto saying he was glad my mother had died.

There are friends I talk to all the time, who set me thinking or who try to set me right, and anyone reading this book will find out quick enough who they are. Since 1984 no one has read more of my words, or more helped me shape them, than JoAnn Wypijewski at *The Nation*, immersed, as I was completing this book, in the task of editing my dear friend Andrew Kopkind's lifetime work into the magnificent *Thirty Years' Wars*. But she still found time to help me in the final furlong.

My loathing of the computer, complimented by Björn Komm in his letter (see page 344), means that I type on the instrument scorned by Bill Clinton in his State of the Union address of January 1995, a typewriter. (Variously, an IBM Selectric I, a pre-war Royal SX, and an Underwood 5.) This means plenty of inputting by my friends Carolyn Cooke in Point Arena, Mark Scaramella in Boonville and Sandy McCroskey in New York. Thanks to them and, for other bouts of inputting, to Gaby Cohen in Petrolia, and Barbara Lewis in Grant's Pass, Oregon. And thanks to Suzanne Edminster Reilard for her scholarship about the Golden Age.

In the final hours, as I lurched through pre-Cambrian cards for my index, Priya Rangan, who helped Susanna Hecht and me with *Fate of the Forest*, came to my rescue, and also demonstrated that Joe Paff's views about the golden age of cooking are true so far as south Indian food is concerned. To Steve Hiatt of San Francisco, who received the scrofulous boxes of manuscript in the tidiest office I have ever seen and readied them for the printer, I tip the hat of a typewriter man in a silicon age. A final wave to the designer, Deborah Thomas, who translated my seventeenth-century typographical dreams into reality, and to Robin Blackburn and all the folks at Verso.

Hobbes opened the *Behemoth* with the words, 'If in time, as in place, there were degrees of high and low, I verily believe that the highest time would be that which passed between the years 1640 and 1660.'

Some years between 1987 and 1994 were high times in Hobbes' sense, of concentration and intensity. I look back across them particularly to the fall of 1989, when my mother died. I'm not sure how much of this book she would have liked, or how soon she would have laid it aside before she went off into the garden, but I think of a line in the poem 'The Quilt' Sean Dunne wrote for her, which Kitty Lee gave me framed at Christmas of that year, and which appears on page 138:

'In time all waste is useful or antique.'

So it was with the makings of that quilt, so be it with this journal.

Index

➤

Abbey, Edward 18, 94–5, 185–6, 327
Abbey, Susanna 186
Abraham, Nabeel 146
Abraham Lincoln Brigade 14, 72
Adams, Gerry 413
ADL (Anti-Defamation League) 324
Adobe Motel 27–8, 186
Adorno, T. 283, 299, 335–6
AEC experiments on people 383–4
'African-American', PC questions
   375–6
Against the Current 18, 154–6
AIDS 1, 49, 180, 394
al-Attar, Leila 336–7
Albert, Stew and Judith 169
Alexander, Morton 17
Althusser, Louis 345–6
Amanita Muscaria 348–9
Ammerman, Nancy 347
Anderson, Bruce 29, 87, 262, 340, 401,
   415–16
Anderson, Ken 49–50
Anderson, Ling 415
Anderson, Perry 243, 420
Anderson, Rob 210
Anderson Valley Advertiser 29, 174–5,
   210, 340, 373
anthropologists 96, 235–6
Aptheker, Bettina 319
Ardmore, Co. Waterford, Ireland
   and Chomsky, Noam 329
   and Cockburn family 122–3
   and gin 23
   and the human centipede 113
   and Mayor Daley 23
Arendt, Hannah 242
astrology 334
Atlanta 41–3
Austro-Hungarian Empire 220
   and sacher torte 221

Babar (the elephant) 112
Babbitt, Bruce 327
Babel, Isaac 343
Baldwin, Stanley 406–7
Ball, Milner 342

Bangladesh, and Nixon 399
Bardacke, Frank 126–7, 130–52, 241–4,
   339–41, 353
Barthes, Roland 412
Bates, Robert 292
Baudrillard, Jean 339
Beast, The Great aka *666*, 55, 200
Belém 117–19
Belfrage, Cedric 176–7
Benedict, Ruth 236
Bonemann, Carlos 274
Bentsen, Lloyd 54, 307
Berger, John 287
Berlin Wall 128–9
Berlioz, Hector 336
Bernstein, Richard 135–6
big girls 189–90
Bishop, Jordan 166, 398–9
Blackburn, Robin 161
Blake, Henry 292–4
bohemia, decay of 81
Bonham-Carter, Jane 222
Boorstin, Daniel 209
booze 419–20
Borge, Tomas 111
Bornstein, Kate 319
Bosnia 397–8
Boulder, Colo. 12
Bowles, Paul 98
Boxer, Mark 222–3
Brecht, Bertolt 128
Brenner, Bob 154–6
Breyer, Stephen 85
Brien, Alan 134–5
Britell, Jim 360
Brown, Jerry 264, 265, 280–82
Buchanan, Pat 288
Bullock, Roy 324
Buñuel, Louis 73
Burgess, Guy 114
Burroughs, William 114–16
Bush, George 255–6, 288–9, 297–9, 303–4
   the 'good' and the 'bad' 54–5
Butler, Hubert 217–18, 221

Cadillacs 71–2

Cantor, Norman 68–9
capitalism
  and the environment 82–5
  and the Third World 95–6
  and the victory over Communism 88–9
Cardenas, Jeffrey 9
Carter, Jimmy 264, 343
Casper Inn 262
Central America 148, 348
Channel Islands 213
Chase, Allen 405
chess 285–6
Chico, Calif. 385
child abuse
  and American hysteria 320
  and Baez, Joan 354
  and class 179–81
  and the Country Walk Case 312–16
  and FBI study 229
  and frisbee flying 151
  and the Fusters 312–16
  and infant witnesses 147
  and Klein, Pamela 229–30
  and the McMartin Case 143–6
  and the *Memphis Commercial Appeal*
    144–5
  and political correctness 149, 152–3
  and Reno, Janet 312–16
  and Salem 145–6, 320, 326
  and social workers 159–60
  and Waco 323
  and WICCA 354
  and workfare 230
Chile 95–6
Chinantecs 69–70
Choctaw 168
Chomsky, Noam 149–51, 185, 289–90, 348
Churchill, Winston 25, 191–3, 212–13,
  221, 301–3
CIA
  and 1949 assassination memo 380
  and the Czech potato blight, 377
  and Oedipus 384
Ciba-Geigy 385
cigarettes 181–2
Citizen's Commission on Human Rights
  297–9
class, enduring strength of 360–61
Clinton, Bill
  ADFA 264–5
  and al-Attar, Leila 336–7
  Arkansas friends 264–8
  British claque for 308–9
  culture of 284–5

  and D-Day 400
  and *Democrat Gazette* 300
  economics of 257
  end of his administration 330–32
  Fed bashing 296
  first hundred days 325–6
  first sight of 256–7
  and gays in the military 337–8
  and Gennifer Flowers' thighs 377
  hypocrisy of 362
  and impending world 301
  the impossibility of liking 299
  inauguration of 308
  and IRA Ceasefire 413
  indecisiveness 412
  and lesbians, 318–20
  and Mena 265–8
  and NAFTA 295
  reasons for victory in '94 300–301
  and the 'teenage sex epidemic' 374–5
  and Vietnam 292
  visit to Anacostia 377–8
Clinton, Hillary 256, 265
cocaine 6
Cockburn, Andrew 12, 23, 40, 122, 221,
  279
Cockburn, Claud 14, 73, 116, 122, 123,
  125, 129, 134–5, 176–7, 198, 213, 419
Cockburn, Daisy 27, 122, 321, 332,
  335–6, 378
Cockburn, Henry 122
Cockburn, Leslie Redlich 122
Cockburn, Patricia 12, 23–4, 29, 86,
  118–26, 167, 291
Cockburn, Patrick 7, 122, 157–8, 208,
  228, 255
Cockburn, Sarah
  and Bork, Judge Robert 67
  aspersing Christopher Isherwood 26–7
  on her mother Jean as Sally Bowles
    26–7
  her novels 67
  and her pipe 67
'coercive harmony' 345
Cohen, Gaby 272
Cohen, Richard 110
Cold War 156–7
Colette 202
Collins, Michael 25
Columbus, Christopher, landfall of 292–3
Colville Vets for Peace 16
Combe, Mary 381
Connally, Cyril 114–16
conspiracy myths 263

cooking 182–3
Country Joe and the Fish 422
Creator's Syndicate 399
crime wave, myth of 401
Crime bill 414–15
Croatia 216–17
Croix, Geoffrey de St. 279

D-Day 400
Daily Worker, The 18
Daly, Sean 16
Dannemeyer, Bill 247
Davis, Hope Hale 326
Davis, Mike 65, 107, 196
Davis, Robert Gorham 326
Day, Leon 353
Decter, Midge 160–61
depression, marketing of 370
depth of field 44
Deutscher, Isaac 112
Dimitrov 38
disasters, as normalcy 99
Disney, Walt 120
Disney Company 371, 385
Dodd, William L., Jr. 178
Dogs, 7–8, 73–4, 268, 335
Druids 247
D'Souza, Dinesh 207
Dukakis, Mike 54
Dunne, Sean 138
Dworkin, Andrea 355
Dwyer, Kate 14
Dziedzic, Walter 134

Earth First! 18–19, 30–31, 170–71
Earthquakes
    and class 244–5
    Loma Prieta 126–8
    and Los Angeles 369–70
    and Petrolia 270–74
    and Watsonville, 126–8
Ehrlich, Paul 277, 405
Eli Lilly & Co. 297–9, 370
Eliot, T.S. 317
Elizabeth, Queen Mother
    and my grandfather 311
    love for Leninist 310–11
environment
    and capitalism 82–5
    and Rio Summit 277–9
environmentalism
    'gridlock' 327
    the Pacific Northwest 388–9
    and the Rockefellers 411

the theology of logging 247–8
    the trade-off 320
Epstein, Sam 153
Eucalyptus globulus 245–6
Euclid 270, 283

F. (Fred Gardner) 162–3
Falk, Richard 104–5, 342
family
    cult of 49
    truths about 49
Fast, Howard 75–6
Faux, Jeff 308–9
FBI 169, 323, 392–3
female orgasm 213–14
Field, The 290–91
Finnegan, Jack 311
fish
    hammerhead sharks 9
    sharks 178
    tarpon 9
Fitzgerald, Ernie 254
Flanders, Laura 319
flat tax 280–82
Flowers, Gennifer 264
Fonda, Jane 40
Ford, Anna 222–3
Foreman, David 18, 26, 31
Foti, Sheriff Charles, and his murals 53
Foucault, Michel 389, 417
French Revolution 56–65
    Baroness Orczy 56
    changing interpretations 60–65
    Charlotte Corday 56
    and films 56
    and Fouché 57
    the Girondins 57
    and the Jacobins 62–3
    and the judgement of history 63–5
    and Lennard, Lizzy 58–62
    Mémoire, Danielle 56
    and plays 58
    Robespierre 57, 58–9
    Saint-Just 61–3
    and the Terror 59–65
    and Tilly, Charles 63–5
Freud, Sigmund 345, 346
Fuerza Unida 296
Fukuyama, Francis 419
Fuster, Ileana and Frank, 312–16
Gamileya 18
Ganem, Balenda 392
Gardner, Fred 17, 31, 55, 162–3, 262–3
Gardner, Richard 320

Garlin, Sender 172
Gates, Darryl 37, 197
Gerard, Tom 324
Geronimus, Arline 392
Gesell, Gerhard 405
Gill, Eric 120
Ginsberg, Allen 114–16
Ginsburg, Carl 108
Goethe 412
Goldman, Emma 241
Gorbachev, Mikhail 19, 28, 39, 75–7, 177
Gordon, Henry, on blowjobs 379
Gore, Tipper 370
Gorz, André 372–3
Graham, Billy 99
Graham, Katharine 39, 75, 77
Green, Joel 167
Greenblatt, Milton 363–4
Greene, Graham 118, 124–5, 198–9
Greenspan, Alan 296
Groeling, Jim 271
Guardian, The 176–7
Guermantes Way, The 423
Guevara, Che 111

Haiti 66
Hallinans, Kayo and Ringo 17
Hamas 417–18
Hamill, Pete 110
Hamilton, Brutus 218
Hamilton, Patrick 419
Hardin, Garrett 405
Harvard and Radcliffe 25th Anniversary
　Report 31
Harvard
　and Bartolet, Terry 32
　and Birch, Eric 32
　and Branson, Roger 32
　and Burden, Carter 33
　and Gardner, Fred 33
　and Hougen, Edward Thomas 33–5
　and Murray, Eleanor Wahl 32
　and Rockefeller, David Jr. 32
　and Sokolov, Raymond 33
　and Stillman, Arthur 32
Havel, Vaclav 149–51
Hawai'i 341–3
heart attacks and sex 382
Hecht, Susanna 117, 137, 277, 283, 412,
　415, 426
Heilbroner, Robert 88
Henwood, Doug 375–6
Hersh, Seymour 53, 137
Hess, Rudolf 212–13

Heston, Charlton 177
'Hispanic', PC questions 375–6
Hitchens, Alexander 113
Hitler, Adolf
　as health nut 41
　and Tom Jones 406–7
Hoffman, Bryce 267
Hoffman, Nick Von 361
Hollis, Roger 116, 134–5
homeless, and Keith McHenry 403
homosexuality
　and the Beats 114–16
　and Hitler 338
　and the lesbian movement 318–20
　and the military 311–12, 337–8
Hopper, Dennis 348–9
Horizon 114–16
Horowitz, David, 9–10
Horowitz, Roger 13
Houston 287–9
Howe, Irving 332
Howell, Mary 50
Howman, Mark 280–81
Hubbell, Web 265, 267
human rights 200–201
Humphries, Chris 119

'if only'
　and 1917 227
　as fallacy 227
Iltis, Hugh 280
Indians, extermination of 235–9
Ingrams, Richard 121
IRA ceasefire 413–14
Iraq
　and bombing 191, 214–15
　and casualties 214–15
　and charges of incubator theft 190
　the flight of journalists 255
　and Rochester 201
　and torture 193
　and US Anti-War Movement 185–6, 192
Irish famine 168, 329, 398–9
Irish Times 329
Islam, in Turkey 393–6
Israeli–PLO Settlement 346, 350
Istanbul 393–6

J. (JoAnn Wypijewski) 36, 37, 40, 51,
　104, 165, 179–81, 417
Jackson, Jesse 50, 54
Jackson, Moana 342
Jameson, Fred 43
Jansen, Michael 336

Japan and violence 363
Jesuits, murder of 132
John Birch Society 143
Johnson, L.B. 108
Johnson, Paul 420
Johnson, Dr. Samuel 93
Jones, Tom 406–7
Jorgensen, Lawrence C. 389
journalism, art of 157–8

K.K. (Kathryn Kilgore) 177
Kagarlitsky, Boris 227
Kahn, Alfred 85
Ka Lahui Hawai'i 341–3
Kame'eleihiwa, Lilikala 341–3
Katz, Otto 177
Kazan (Tartarstan) 321
Kennan, George 71 159
Kennedy, Edward 85–6
Kennedy, John F. 254–5, 352–5
  assassination, 253–5, 257–62, 263,
  269–70, 352–5, 357–60
Kerouac, Jack 114–16
Key West 5–9
Keynesians 296
KGB 212–13
King, Martin Luther 324–5
Koltzov, Mikhail 176
Komm, Björn 344
Kopkind, Andrew 177, 190, 256, 284,
  343, 374, 417, 420–24
Koppel, Ted 164–5, 170–71
Kris, Ernst 286
Kroeber, Alfred 235–6

lang, k.d. 319
Langenbach, Rand 246
Law, Oliver 14
Lawrence, Barbara 339
Lee, Kitty 122, 138
left handedness 199–200
Left Business Observer 375
Lenin, V.I. 7, 12, 28, 104, 223, 225
  *'Left-Wing'Communism, an
  Infantile Disorder* 361
Leontiev on Moist Mouths 373–4
lesbians 318–20
letters, art of writing 338–9
Levi Strauss Factory 295–6
Lewin, Moshe 239–41
Lewis, John 354–5
Liebeler, Wesley J. 257–62, 269–70
Ligachev, Yegor 77

Liliuokalani, Queen 341
Limbaugh, Rush 403
Linebaugh, Peter 55–6
lips 286–7, 289
Lithuania 160, 239–41
Lloyds, Names and the crash 279
Long, Huey 41
Lord, Audrey 319
Los Angeles 196–7
  riots, Bloods–Crips Plan 274–6
Lost Coast 416
Love, Iris 319
Lowry, Glenn 109
LSD experiments 364
Lula, Inaçio 95
Lummis, Charles Fletcher 196
Lummis, Doug 228–9, 299–300, 363
Luxemburg, Rosa 242
Lyon, Danny 354–5
MacDougal, Mary 222–3
MacKinnon, Catharine 347–8, 350–51,
  352, 354
Madison (Wis.) 13
Magdoff, Harry 103–4
Major, John 413
Malaparte, Curzio 216
Males, Mike 374–5
Malthus, Rev. Thomas
  and class distinctions 390–91
  and Club of Rome 277
  and the Irish famine 390
  Malthusian ideas, 18
  and Norplant 404–6
  and the Sierra Club 390
  and sterilization 301–3, 404–6
  and World Bank 277–9
Mao Tse-tung 103–4
Marcos, Imelda 40–41
Marcuse, Herbert 132
marijuana 6
  farming, policing, economics of 349–50,
  351–3
Marx, Karl 194
McBride, Sean 24–6
McDonough, Mark 31
McGrory, Mary 108
McHenry, Keith 402, 415
'Me and Bobby McGee' 333
medicine and state security 364–5
Meehan, Dr. Joe 167–8
Mencken, H.L. 142–3
Merrell-Dow 113, 385
Mesmer, Frederick Anton 334–5
Miles, Barry 114–16

Militant 358–9
Millet, Kate 319
Mishara, Tanju 6
Monthly Review 103
    interview w/ Paul Sweezy and Harry
    Magdoff 103–4
Moyers, Bill 108
Moynihan, Daniel Patrick 108–10
multiple personality 345–6
Mumford, Lewis 97–8
Murray, Shirley 292
Mussolini, Benito 391
Myers, Kevin 329
My Lai 50–53

Nader, Laura 345
Naifeh, Steven 120
Nathan, Debbie 313
Nation, The 107–8, 135
National Museum of American Art 204–5
Navratilova, Martina 319
New Age 29, 333
New Left Review 348, 422
New Orleans 43–54
    Carnival 45–6
    and the Civil War 45
    economic hard times 44
    oil and 44
    Rex and Comus 45–6, 50
New Republic, The 135–6
New Statesman 420
Newsweek 109
Newton, Helmut 89–92, 93
    and Newton, June 90–91
Newton, Huey 169
New York 179–81
New York Review 361–2, 421, 422
New York Times 108, 109, 146, 148
Nicaragua 149, 153–4
Nichols, Larry 264
Nissman, Susan Petrulas 385
Nixon, Richard 399
Nolte, Ernst 69
Noriega, Manuel 137, 138, 166, 303
Norplant, 404–5
North, Oliver 48, 106
Northern Ireland 25

O'Brien, Flann 70
O'Connor, James 82–5, 210, 339, 387–8
O'Reilly, Henry 24
O'Reilly, Hugh 15
O'Reilly, Michael 300
O'Reilly's Bar 15

O'Toole, Fintan 396
Oakland fire 244–6
Omaar, Rakiya 337
Orwell, George 70, 73, 114
Oswald, Lee Harvey 17, 257–62, 352–5,
    357–60
'outing' 232–4

Pacific Northwest, employment in 388–9
Paff, Joe 1, 366, 412, 414–15, 426
Paff, Karen 412, 414–15
Paglia, Camille 319
Palestinian State 13, 417–18
Palme, Olaf 344
parasciences, 334
Paterson, Tom 254
Pavelitch, Ante 217
Paxman, Jeremy 361
Pearl Harbor 248
Peavy, Jack 172–4
penis 365
Peretz, Martin 87
Petrolia 186
Philby, Kim 36, 406
Philby, St. John 406
Philip Morris 181–2
picturesque 411
Pincher, Chapman 116
Pittston Strike 133
PLO 417–18
Pogo Fallacy 151
political asylum 166
political correctness 204–10, 396
Pollin, Robert 281–2
Pollock, Jackson 120
P.O.M., 265, 268
Pomos, massacre of 219
Popper, Karl 364
Populists, the 48
    and Bryan, William Jennings 49
Presley, Elvis 17
Princip, Gavril 221
prisoners of war, treatment of 194–6
Proust, Marcel 423
Prozac, 297–9, 370
Pugach, Mahalia 395
Purges, Stalin's 135–6

Quayle, Dan 55

racism
    and Atlanta 41–3
    and epidemiology 153
    and Moynihan, Daniel Patrick 108–10

and political correctness 206–10
and teenage sex 392
at U. of Wisconsin 13–14
Rather, Dan 16
Reagan, Ronald
  and astrology 35,36
  and Bitburg 36, 69
  and the *Challenger* 158–9
  and the crash 11
  and dogs 7–8
  failure to mount a coup d'etat 86
  fascist ideology 68–9
  and Fast, Howard 75
  at Fort Wacky 47
  and the homeless 43
  and Lenin 33
  as Leninist 28
  and liberation of Auschwitz 47
  and lying 198
  and 'recovery' 380
Reagan, Nancy 197–8
  benign effects of 39–40
  and North, Oliver 48
  and oral sex 46–7
  and Regan, Don 39
  and Weinberger, Cap 39
Redwood Summer 170–71
Reed, Julia 71
Reno, Janet 312–16, 323–4, 347
Reveille, Tom 151
Rich, Adrienne 319
Riconosciuto, Michael 266–7
Ridenhour, Ron 50–53
Ridgeway, James 422
Rio Summit 277–9
RJR-Nabisco 181–2
Robespierre, Maximilien 57, 58–9, 110–11
Robinson, Sidney K. 411
Rochester, N.Y. 201–2
Rohe, Mies van der 41
Romanoff, Czar Alexander III
  and dogs 94
  and founding of Hollywood 92
  and the Russian Revolution 92
Roosevelt, F.D. 193
Rose, Bleys 285
Ross, Jean 26–7
Rüdin, Ernst 328–9

Sachs, Jeffrey 127
Said, Edward 327, 417–18
Saint-Just 61–63
Sanders, Bernard 414–15
San Francisco Focus 174–6

Santa Cruz CA. 28
Scagliotti John 190, 233, 256, 318, 422, 424
Scheer, Robert 42–3
Scheper-Hughes Nancy 291
schizophrenia, in Ireland 290–91
Schmidt, Tom and Sue 15, 17
Schmitt, Carl 68
Schnaubelt, E.B. 171
Schwartz, Stephen 360
Scientology, International Church of 297–9, 393
sex, and nuclear war 386
sex survey 419
Shahak, Israel 129–30, 203–4
sharks, defense of 178–9
Shelden, Michael 114–16
Sherrill, Robert 422
Signorile, Michael 232–4
Silvers, Robert 361–2
Simpson, David, and Jane Lapiner 229, 272
Sloterdijk, Peter 81, 364–5
Smith, Gregory White 120
Smith, Liz 319
Smithsonian, 204
SNCC 355
Snepp, Frank 194
Somalia 303
Sonnenberg Ben, 87, 112, 118, 227, 268, 336, 373, 406
Sontag, Susan 336
Southern Air Transport 268
Soviet Union
  end of 225–8
  and Gang of Eight 223–4
  and Jews 240–41
  Moscow News poll 211
  reasons for collapse 241–4
  and the Third World 74–6, 226–7
Spanish Empire
  corrupted by silver 6–7
  wreck of the *Atocha* 6
Speck and Lady 7–8
spy network of US Army 324–5
St. Clair, Jeff 417
Stalin, Joseph 113, 156–7
Stein, Gertrude 319
Stein, Robert 219
sterilization 301–3, 404–6
stockmarket, crash of 1987 10–12
Stoltenberg and his penis 355–6
Stone, I.F. 10, 11
Stone, Norman 113

Stone, Oliver 253–5, 260, 263, 269–70, 353
strikes, difficulty of winning 211–12
Sufis, 395–6
Sweezy, Paul 103–4

Takiedinne, Diana 327
Taylor, Ellen 330
technology, liberal illusions about 356
teenager 'sex epidemic', bogus nature of 374–5
Temptations, The 422
Tessler, Gary 12
Thatcher, Margaret 212
Tienanmen Square 175
Time 298–9
Toklas, Alice B. 319
Tomlin, Lily 319
Tompkins, Stephen 325
Topanga Canyon 371, 385
Transition magazine 316
transvestism 37, 40
Trask, Mililani 341
Trotsky, Leon 7, 161–2, 242
Trump, Donald 147–8
Tukhachevsky 38, 75
TV and violence 362–3, 379

Ulagu the Mongol 203
unemployment
    and black workers 110
    in Los Angeles 37
Untrue 'Brit' 376
Utne Reader 247

Varga, Eugene 157
Velásquez 44
Venne, Sharon 342
Vesel, George 221
Victoria, Queen, love for John Brown 310
Victoria's Secret 183–4
Vien, Dr. Nguyen Khac 228, 231–2
Vietnam 184, 249
Vinci, Leonardo da 307
violence, in New York 179–81
Volcker, Paul 40

W.E.B. DuBois Club 358–9
Waco 322, 323, 346–7, 392–3
Wajda, Andrzej 92–3
Walesa, Lech 133
Walker, Dick 246
Wall Street Journal 109, 185, 192, 298, 307–8

Wanger, Shelley 289, 425
war crimes 99–101, 194–6
war and waste, necessity for, under capitalism 105–6
Ward, Skeeter 267–8
Washington Post 108–10
Washington, Harold 14, 15, 35
Wasson, R. Gordon 349
Watling's Island, as Columbus' landfall, 293
Watson, Tom 172–4
Watsonville 28 339–41
Waugh, Evelyn 142
Weaver, Dan 273
Wen Yi-Tuo 367
West, W.J. 134–5
West, Louis Jolyon ('Jolly') 328–9
'what if'
    and Eastern Europe 156
    and *Hamlet* 92–3
White, Lynn, Jr. 248
Wicker, Tom 108
Will, George 109
Williams, Honey 126
Windsor, House of 309–11
Winogrand, Gary 37–8
women
    and Chico 385
    and men in California 220
    and Newton, Helmut 89–92
    as Republicans 48
women's clothes 36, 37
Wood, Rich and Lisa 14
Woodward, C. Van 172–4
Worker, The 358–9
workers
    and accidents 202
    and Levi Strauss 295–6
    and NAFTA 295
    and strikes 133–4, 211–12
    and the 1,000-hour work year, 372
    and world unemployment 372, 386–8
Wren, Tally 273, 274
Wypijewski, JoAnn (J.) 36, 37, 40, 51, 104, 165, 179–81, 417, 425

Yeltsin, Boris 316–17, 343
Yoder, Ed 110
Youghal, Co. Cork, Ireland 291
Young, Andrew 42
Yurok 234–9

Zapatista rising 382–3, 387
Zhirinovsky, Vladimir 378